GW01458272

CHILD LABOUR IN A GLOBALIZED WORLD

To Agnes, Benedetta and Elena

Child Labour in a Globalized World
A Legal Analysis of ILO Action

Edited by

GIUSEPPE NESI, LUCA NOGLER and MARCO PERTILE
University of Trento, Italy

ASHGATE

© Giuseppe Nesi, Luca Nogler, and Marco Pertile 2008

All rights reserved. No part of this publication may be reproduced, stored in a retrieval system or transmitted in any form or by any means, electronic, mechanical, photocopying, recording or otherwise without the prior permission of the publisher.

Giuseppe Nesi, Luca Nogler, and Marco Pertile have asserted their moral right under the Copyright, Designs and Patents Act, 1988, to be identified as the editors of this work.

Published by
Ashgate Publishing Limited
Gower House
Croft Road
Aldershot
Hampshire GU11 3HR
England

Ashgate Publishing Company
Suite 420
101 Cherry Street
Burlington, VT 05401-4405
USA

www.ashgate.com

British Library Cataloguing in Publication Data
Child labour in a globalized world : a legal analysis of
    ILO action
    1. International Labour Organisation 2. Child labor - Law
    and legislation 3. Child labor - Law and legislation -
    Cases 4. Labor laws and legislation, International
    5. Industrial safety - Law and legislation
    I. Nesi, Giuseppe II. Nogler, Luca III. Pertile, Marco
    344'.0131

Library of Congress Cataloging-in-Publication Data
Child labour in a globalized world : a legal analysis of ILO action / edited by Giuseppe Nesi, Luca Nogler, and Marco Pertile.
    p. cm.
    Includes bibliographical references and index.
    ISBN 978-0-7546-7222-7 (alk. paper)
    1. Child labor--Law and legislation. 2. Child labor--Law and legislation--Cases.
3. International Labour Organization. 4. Labor laws and legislation, International. 5.
Industrial safety--Law and legislation. I. Nesi, Giuseppe. II. Nogler, Luca. III. Pertile,
Marco.

    K1821.C49 2008
    344.01'31--dc22

                                                                    2008011917

ISBN 978-0-7546-7222-7

Mixed Sources
Product group from well-managed
forests and other controlled sources
www.fsc.org Cert no. SA-COC-1565
© 1996 Forest Stewardship Council
FSC

Printed and bound in Great Britain by
MPG Books Ltd, Bodmin, Cornwall.

Contents

List of Contributors

Giovanna Adinolfi, Associate Professor of International Law, University of Milan

Julinda Beqiraj, PhD candidate in International Studies, University of Trento

Matteo Borzaga, Researcher in Labour Law, University of Trento

Alessandro Fodella, Associate Professor of International Law, University of Trento

Emanuela Fronza, Researcher in Criminal Law, University of Trento, Fellow of the Alexander von Humboldt Foundation, von Humboldt University, Berlin

Matthias Hartwig, Researcher in Public Law, Max Planck Institute for Comparative Public Law and International Law, Heidelberg

(Sir)Bob Hepple, QC, FBA, Emeritus Master of Clare College and Emeritus Professor of Law, University of Cambridge

Amadou Keita, Professor of Public Law, University of Bamako

Joost Kooijmans, Legal Officer, ILO

Giuseppe Nesi, Legal Advisor to the Permanent Mission of Italy to the UN, Professor of International Law, University of Trento

Luca Nogler, Professor of Labour Law, University of Trento

Yoshie Noguchi, Legal Officer, ILO

Fabio Pantano, Lecturer in Labour Law, University of Bologna

Marco Pertile, Researcher in International Law, University of Trento

Ravindra Pratap, Assistant Professor, Indraprastha University School of Law, Delhi

Guido Raimondi, Legal Advisor, ILO

Deepa Rishikesh, Coordinator, Child Labour Conventions, ILO

Riccardo Salomone, Associate Professor of Labour Law, University of Trento

Wilfredo Sanguineti Raymond, Professor of Labour Law, University of Salamanca

Silvia Sanna, Associate Professor of International Law, University of Sassari

Sabine Schlemmer-Schulte, Associate Professor of Law, McGeorge School of Law, University of the Pacific

Kolis Summerer, Lecturer in Criminal Law, University of Bologna

Lee Swepston, Former Senior Advisor on Human Rights, ILO

Anne Trebilcock, Former Legal Advisor, ILO (retired), currently associated with the Centre du Droit International, Paris X Nanterre

Preface

In times when even the most shocking events and sensitive moral issues only briefly command any public attention, the problem of child labour has maintained a singularly high profile and continues to be recognized as one of the major challenges for the international community. A number of initiatives to reduce its incidence have originated spontaneously within civil society and are now complemented by a wide range of measures adopted by public actors at the national and the international level. More than two decades after the problem was acknowledged at the global level, new international instruments have been adopted and ratified, and the existing legal framework has been revived through new ratifications and a more effective functioning of the supervisory systems. States are increasingly committed to adopt measures to prevent and eliminate the 'worst forms' of child labour. Mechanisms have been set up to assist States in the adoption of such measures. Much remains to be done, especially in developing coherent action to reduce poverty and increase education and human rights protection, which are essential to eradicating child labour. However, recently the view has been expressed that the eradication of child labour is not only a moral and legal imperative, but also a realistic objective to be achieved in the very near future.

It is against this backdrop that the Department of Law of the University of Trento initiated a research project on 'The Supervisory System of the ILO and Child Labour' in 2004. Indeed, in the last decade, the ILO has clearly assumed a leading role in the fight against child labour. In keeping with the Organization's traditional eclecticism, its activities in the field cover different types of measures ranging from standard-setting to supervision and technical cooperation. Within this framework, the purpose of the Project was to analyse the ILO's action in the fight against child labour and its 'worst forms' from a legal point of view. The research aimed to investigate the relevant legal instruments and their implementation through the ILO supervisory system and technical cooperation activities. Understanding the interaction of the ILO with other international agencies directly or indirectly dealing with child labour was a further objective.

The present book is the outcome of that project. Its 19 chapters are divided into three parts. Whereas the first part is mainly devoted to describing and analysing the ILO's activities in the fight against child labour, the second and the third parts focus on issues of implementation at the international and the domestic levels. A brief introduction addresses some cross-cutting issues such as the main features of the phenomenon, its legal definition and the general description of the legal framework. In the final chapter, Bob Hepple draws together the threads of the arguments that run through the book.

More specifically, the first part of the book describes the ILO's legal activities in the fight against child labour. Though combating child labour has been part of the ILO's core business since 1919, our focus here is on the most recent initiatives and the early steps are considered only to the extent necessary to understand the present legal framework. After an introductory chapter describing the range of the ILO's legal activities connected to child labour, Convention 138 of 1973 on the minimum age for admission to employment and the Declaration on Fundamental Rights and Principles at Work are the focus of individual chapters. Convention 182 of 1999 on the worst forms of child labour is subsequently analysed through five different contributions.

The second part of the book addresses issues of implementation, both at the international level and concerning selected problems of a substantive character. From the first perspective, we investigate how the interaction of the ILO with other international agencies may affect the implementation of ILO child labour standards. We devoted specific chapters to the United Nations, the European Union, the World Bank, and the World Trade Organization (WTO). Although we are fully aware that the number of international agencies having a say in the field is wider, we are persuaded that the four mentioned above critically influence the action of the ILO. From the second perspective, we aim at assessing the effectiveness of two general tools, which have been widely used (or perhaps even abused) in the implementation of child labour standards: social clauses and criminal law.

Finally, the third part presents three case studies. Three chapters analyse the problems connected to the implementation of ILO child labour standards in Africa, Asia, and South America. Although child labour is certainly also a relevant issue in the so-called Western world, we focus on those regions that, from a quantitative point of view, are mostly affected by the phenomenon.

As the reader will note from the outset, the book is not conceived as a 'textbook' on the ILO and child labour. As to the content of the chapters, we tried to make sure that the relevant points were covered and did not regard a slight overlapping as problematic. On the contrary, we believe that this quite possibly helps to depict a more complete picture and enrich the debate on the topic.

In choosing the contributors, we deliberately sought out authors from varied backgrounds. We wanted a polyphonic book able to bridge the gulf that all too often separates practitioners and academic scholars. The book itself is not aimed at reconciling different approaches and understandings. Rather, it is conceived as a survey of the work of the ILO in the field of child labour which also intends to highlight the achievements of the Organization and its relationship with other international bodies, as well as the problems and the prospects for change.

We had, of course, full confidence in the expertise of the authors and did not try to curb their 'freedom of expression and research'. From an editorial perspective we mainly tried to ensure that all of them shared the same method of analysis. That method can be roughly summarized as follows:

a. Detailed analysis of the practice of the Organization and of its supervisory system.
b. Reference to the *travaux préparatoires* and to the context of the adoption of the relevant instruments.

c. Awareness that child labour should be seen in a comparative perspective, with reference both to implementation in domestic systems and to the work of other international bodies operating in the field.

d. Awareness that the issue of child labour is to be placed in the wider context of the debate on the nature of labour standards, the transformation of the ILO and its role in addressing the problems connected with globalization.

Overall, this volume assumes that child labour is a complicated and multifaceted issue to which the law in itself cannot provide definitive solutions. Reasonable legal measures should be framed in the context of a combined effort of different instruments. In any case, we feel that the guiding question for the assessment of any intervention, in this as in other matters, should be: 'How will it impact on the life of the people?'. For jurists the answer is often disheartening. We hope this book will contribute to clarifying and improving the role of law in the fight against child labour.

This publication is up to date as of 31 August 2007.

Unless stated otherwise, the relevant ILO documents are available at <www.ilo.org/ilolex>. The dates of adoption and information on ratification of the relevant treaties are provided in the Table of Legal Instruments.

Giuseppe Nesi, Luca Nogler and Marco Pertile

Trento/New York
November 2007

Acknowledgements

The present book has been some time in the writing. The structure was largely decided through several discussions during a research visit to the International Labour Office in Geneva.

We gratefully acknowledge the support of the Italian Ministry for University and Research, which financed the project and the research visit in the framework of the 2004 PRIN project on 'The Monitoring System of the International Labour Organization and Child Labour'. We would, moreover, like to thank everyone at the ILO who provided us with 'a view from the inside'. Most of them are amongst the authors of the book, but we are glad to mention them here nevertheless. We are indebted to Guido Raimondi, Anne Trebilcock, Lee Swepston, Deepa Rishikesh, Yoshie Noguchi and Joost Kooijmans. Without their comments on the structure of the book and their help in accessing the relevant materials, it would not have been possible to realize this project.

Matteo Borzaga helped us greatly during the earlier phases and throughout the development of the project.

Particular thanks must go to Ton Notermans for his invaluable work on the manuscript and for his perceptive comments.

We are also very grateful to Julinda Beqiraj, who compiled the Bibliography and the Table of Legal Instruments.

During these years, we benefited, sometimes unwittingly, from several discussions and meetings that have contributed ideas to this project. Our deepest thanks go to Kaushik Basu, Silvana Sciarra, Jaap Doek, Norberto Liwski, Olga Beguin, Daniel Gomez and Cecilia Alberti. The usual disclaimers apply.

A substantial part of the project was researched at the Institut de Hautes Etudes Internationales and at the Library of the United Nations in Geneva. We are extremely grateful to the Institute and the Library staff for their hospitality and assistance. Cristina Giordano, at UNOG Library, tracked down unearthed documents before we even understood their worth.

The administrative staff of the Department of Law of the University of Trento have been consistently supportive. Our warmest thanks to Carla Boninsegna, Valentina Lucatti and Ornella Bernardi.

Table of Legal Instruments

ILO binding instruments

NIGHT WORK OF YOUNG PERSONS (INDUSTRY) CONVENTION, 1919 No. 6 (Date of adoption: 28/11/1919; Date of entry into force: 13/06/1921) 51 ratified, 8 denounced.

MINIMUM AGE (SEA) CONVENTION, 1920 No. 7 (Date of adoption: 09/07/1920; Date of entry into force: 27/09/1921) 5 ratified, 48 denounced.

MINIMUM AGE (AGRICULTURE) CONVENTION, 1921 No. 10 (Date of adoption 16/11/1921; Date of entry into force: 31/08/1923) 5 ratified, 50 denounced.

MINIMUM AGE (TRIMMERS AND STOKERS) CONVENTION (*Shelved*), 1921 No. 15 (Date of adoption: 11/11/1921; Date of entry into force: 20/11/1922) 10 ratified, 59 denounced.

MEDICAL EXAMINATION OF YOUNG PERSONS (SEA) CONVENTION, 1921 No. 16 (Date of adoption: 11/11/1921; Date of entry into force: 20/11/1922) 82 ratified, 0 denounced.

FORCED LABOUR CONVENTION, 1930 No. 29 (Date of adoption: 28/06/1930; Date of entry into force: 01/05/1932) 172 ratified, 0 denounced.

MINIMUM AGE (NON-INDUSTRIAL EMPLOYMENT) CONVENTION, 1932 No. 33 (Date of adoption: 30/04/1932; Date of entry into force: 06/06/1935) 3 ratified, 22 denounced.

MINIMUM AGE (SEA) CONVENTION (*Revised*), 1936 No. 58 (Date of adoption: 24/10/1936; Date of entry into force: 11/04/1939) 17 ratified, 34 denounced.

MINIMUM AGE (INDUSTRY) CONVENTION (*Revised*), 1937 No. 59 (Date of adoption: 22/06/1937; Date of entry into force: 21/02/1941) 11 ratified, 25 denounced.

MINIMUM AGE (NON-INDUSTRIAL EMPLOYMENT) CONVENTION (*Revised*) (*Shelved*), 1937 No. 60 (Date of adoption: 22/06/1937; Date of entry into force: 29/12/1950) 0 ratified, 11 denounced.

MEDICAL EXAMINATION FOR FITNESS FOR EMPLOYMENT IN INDUSTRY OF CHILDREN AND YOUNG PERSONS CONVENTION, 1946 No. 77 (Date of adoption: 09/10/1946; Date of entry into force: 29/12/1950) 43 ratified, 0 denounced.

MEDICAL EXAMINATION OF YOUNG PERSONS (NON-INDUSTRIAL OCCUPATIONS) CONVENTION, 1946 No. 78 (Date of adoption: 09/10/1946; Date of entry into force: 29/12/1950) 39 ratified, 0 denounced.

NIGHT WORK OF YOUNG PERSONS (NON-INDUSTRIAL OCCUPATIONS) CONVENTION, 1946 No. 79 (Date of adoption: 09/10/1946; Date of entry into force: 29/12/1950) 20 ratified, 0 denounced.

LABOUR INSPECTION CONVENTION, 1947 No. 81 (Date of adoption: 11/07/1947; Date of entry into force: 07/04/1950) 137 ratified, 0 denounced.

SOCIAL POLICY (NON-METROPOLITAN TERRITORIES) CONVENTION, 1947 No. 82 (Date of adoption: 11/07/1947; Date of entry into force: 19/06/1955) 4 ratified, 0 denounced.

LABOUR STANDARDS (NON-METROPOLITAN TERRITORIES) CONVENTION, 1947 No. 83 (Date of adoption: 11/07/1947; Date of entry into force: 15/06/1974) 1 ratified, 1 denounced.

FREEDOM OF ASSOCIATION AND PROTECTION OF THE RIGHT TO ORGANISE CONVENTION, 1948 No. 87 (Date of adoption: 09/07/1948; Date of entry into force: 04/07/1950) 148 ratified, 0 denounced.

NIGHT WORK OF YOUNG PERSONS (INDUSTRY) CONVENTION (*Revised*), 1948 No. 90 (Date of adoption: 10/07/1948; Date of entry into force: 12/06/1951) 51 ratified, 0 denounced.

THE MIGRANT WORKERS CONVENTION, 1949 No.97 (Date of adoption: 01/07/1949; Date of entry into force: 22/01/1952) 47 ratified, 0 denounced.

RIGHT TO ORGANISE AND COLLECTIVE BARGAINING CONVENTION, 1949 No. 98 (Date of adoption: 01/07/1949; Date of entry into force: 18/07/1951) 158 ratified, 0 denounced.

EQUAL REMUNERATION CONVENTION, 1951 No. 100 (Date of adoption: 29/06/1951; Date of entry into force: 23/05/1953) 164 ratified, 0 denounced.

SOCIAL SECURITY (MINIMUM PROVISIONS) CONVENTION, 1952 No. 102 (Date of adoption: 28/06/1952; Date of entry into force: 27/04/1955) 43 ratified, 0 denounced.

ABOLITION OF FORCED LABOUR CONVENTION, 1957 No. 105 (Date of adoption: 25/06/1957; Date of entry into force: 17/01/1959) 168 ratified, 2 denounced.

DISCRIMINATION (EMPLOYMENT AND OCCUPATION) CONVENTION, 1958 No. 111 (Date of adoption: 25/06/1958; Date of entry into force: 15/06/1960) 166 ratified, 0 denounced.

MINIMUM AGE (FISHERMEN) CONVENTION, 1959 No. 112 (Date of adoption: 19/06/1959; Date of entry into force: 07/11/1961) 8 ratified, 21 denounced.

RADIATION PROTECTION CONVENTION, 1960 No. 115 (Date of adoption: 22/06/1960; Date of entry into force: 17/06/1962), 47 ratified, 0 denounced.

SOCIAL POLICY (BASIC AIMS AND STANDARDS) CONVENTION, 1962 No. 117 (Date of adoption: 22/06/1962; Date of entry into force: 23/04/1964) 32 ratified, 0 denounced.

EMPLOYMENT POLICY CONVENTION, 1964 No. 122 (Date of adoption: 09/07/1964; Date of entry into force: 15/07/1966) 97 ratified, 0 denounced.

MINIMUM AGE (UNDERGROUND WORK) CONVENTION, 1965 No. 123 (Date of adoption: 22/06/1965; Date of entry into force: 10/11/1967) 22 ratified, 19 denounced.

MEDICAL EXAMINATION OF YOUNG PERSONS (UNDERGROUND WORK) CONVENTION, 1965 No. 124 (Date of adoption: 23/06/1965; Date of entry into force: 13/12/1967) 41 ratified, 0 denounced.

MAXIMUM WEIGHT CONVENTION, 1967 No. 127 (Date of adoption: 28/06/1967; Date of entry into force: 10/03/1970) 25 ratified, 0 denounced.

LABOUR INSPECTION (AGRICULTURE) CONVENTION, 1969 No. 129 (Date of adoption: 25/06/1969; Date of entry into force: 19/01/1972) 44 ratified, 0 denounced.

BENZENE CONVENTION, 1971 No. 136 (Date of adoption: 23/06/1971; Date of entry into force: 27/07/1973) 37 ratified, 0 denounced.

MINIMUM AGE CONVENTION, 1973 No. 138 (Date of adoption: 26/06/1973; Date of entry into force: 19/06/1976) 150 ratified, 0 denounced.

HUMAN RESOURCES DEVELOPMENT CONVENTION, 1975 No. 142 (Date of adoption: 23/06/1975; Date of entry into force: 19/07/1977) 65 ratified, 0 denounced.

MIGRANT WORKERS (SUPPLEMENTARY PROVISIONS) CONVENTION, 1975 No. 143 (Date of adoption: 24/06/1975; Date of entry into force: 09/12/1978) 23 ratified, 0 denounced.

TRIPARTITE CONSULTATION (INTERNATIONAL LABOUR STANDARDS) CONVENTION, 1976 No. 144 (Date of adoption: 21/06/1976; Date of entry into force: 16/05/1978) 121 ratified, 0 denounced.

OCCUPATIONAL SAFETY AND HEALTH (DOCK WORK) CONVENTION, 1979 No. 152 (Date of adoption: 25/06/1979; Date of entry into force: 05/12/1981) 26 ratified, 0 denounced.

WORKERS WITH FAMILY RESPONSIBILITIES CONVENTION, 1981 No.156 (Date of adoption: 23/06/1981; Date of entry into force: 11/08/1983) 38 ratified, 0 denounced.

INDIGENOUS AND TRIBAL PEOPLES' CONVENTION, 1989 No. 169 (Date of adoption: 27/06/1989; Date of entry into force: 05/09/1991) 18 ratified, 0 denounced.

PRIVATE EMPLOYMENT AGENCIES CONVENTION, 1997 No. 181 (Date of adoption: 19/06/1997; Date of entry into force: 10/05/2000) 20 ratified, 0 denounced.

WORST FORMS OF CHILD LABOUR CONVENTION, 1999 No. 182 (Date of adoption: 17/06/1999; Date of entry into force: 19/11/2000) 165 ratified, 0 denounced.

SAFETY AND HEALTH IN AGRICULTURE CONVENTION, 2001 No. 184 (Date of adoption: 21/06/2001; Date of entry into force: 20/09/2003) 8 ratified, 0 denounced.

MLC MARITIME LABOUR CONVENTION, 2006 (Date of adoption: 07/02/2006) 1 ratified, 0 denounced.

WORK IN FISHING CONVENTION, 2007 No. 188 (Date of adoption: 14/06/2007; Not yet into force).

ILO non-binding instruments

HOURS OF WORK (FISHING) RECOMMENDATION, 1920 No. 7 (Date of adoption: 30/06/1919).

MINIMUM AGE (NON-INDUSTRIAL EMPLOYMENT) RECOMMENDATION, 1932 No. 41 (Date of adoption: 30/04/1932).

MINIMUM AGE (FAMILY UNDERTAKINGS) RECOMMENDATION, 1937 No. 52 (Date of adoption: 22/06/1937).

SAFETY PROVISIONS (BUILDING) RECOMMENDATION, 1937 No. 53 (Date of adoption: 23/06/1937).

SOCIAL POLICY IN DEPENDENT TERRITORIES RECOMMENDATION (*Withdrawn*), 1944 No. 70 (Date of adoption: 12/05/1944).

MEDICAL EXAMINATION OF YOUNG PERSONS RECOMMENDATION, 1946 No. 79 (Date of adoption: 09/10/1946).

NIGHT WORK OF YOUNG PERSONS (NON-INDUSTRIAL OCCUPATIONS) RECOMMENDATION, 1946 No. 80 (Date of adoption: 09/10/1946).

MINIMUM AGE (COAL MINES) RECOMMENDATION (*Withdrawn*), 1953 No. 96 (Date of adoption: 19/06/1953).

WEEKLY REST (COMMERCE AND OFFICES) RECOMMENDATION, 1957 No. 103 (Date of adoption: 26/06/1957).

REDUCTION OF HOURS OF WORK RECOMMENDATION, 1962 No. 116 (Date of adoption: 26/06/1962).

VOCATIONAL TRAINING RECOMMENDATION, 1962 No. 117 (Date of adoption: 27/06/1962).

MINIMUM AGE (UNDERGROUND WORK) RECOMMENDATION, 1965 No. 124 (Date of adoption: 22/06/1965).

CONDITIONS OF EMPLOYMENT OF YOUNG PERSONS (UNDERGROUND WORK) RECOMMENDATION, 1965 No. 125 (Date of adoption: 23/06/1965).

MAXIMUM WEIGHT RECOMMENDATION, 1967 No. 128 (Date of adoption: 28/06/1967).

VOCATIONAL TRAINING (SEAFARERS) RECOMMENDATION, 1970 No. 137 (Date of adoption: 28/10/1970).

BENZENE RECOMMENDATION, 1971 No. 144 (Date of adoption: 23/06/1971).

MIGRANT WORKERS RECOMMENDATION, 1975 No. 151 (Date of adoption: 24/06/1975).

PROTECTION OF YOUNG SEAFARERS RECOMMENDATION, 1976 No. 153 (Date of adoption: 28/10/1976).

WORKERS WITH FAMILY RESPONSIBILITIES RECOMMENDATION, 1981 No. 165 (Date of adoption: 23/06/1981).

ASBESTOS RECOMMENDATION, 1986 No. 172 (Date of adoption: 24/06/1986).

NIGHT WORK RECOMMENDATION, 1990 No.178 (Date of adoption: 26/06/1990).

ILO DECLARATION ON FUNDAMENTAL PRINCIPLES AND RIGHTS AT WORK (Date of adoption: 18/06/1998).

HUMAN RESOURCES DEVELOPMENT RECOMMENDATION, 2004 No. 195 (Date of adoption: 17/06/2004).

WORK IN FISHING RECOMMENDATION, 2007 No. 199 (Date of adoption: 14/06/2007).

United Nations instruments

CONVENTION FOR THE SUPPRESSION OF THE TRAFFIC IN PERSONS AND OF THE EXPLOITATION OF THE PROSTITUTION OF OTHERS (Date of adoption: 02/12/1949; Date of entry into force: 25/07/1951) 14 Signatories, 74 Parties.

SUPPLEMENTARY CONVENTION ON THE ABOLITION OF SLAVERY, THE SLAVE TRADE, AND INSTITUTIONS AND PRACTICES SIMILAR TO SLAVERY (Date of adoption: 07/09/1956; Date of entry into force: 30/04/1957) 35 Signatories, 119 Parties.

INTERNATIONAL COVENANT ON CIVIL AND POLITICAL RIGHTS (Date of adoption: 16/12/1966; Date of entry into force: 23/03/1976) 67 Signatories, 160 Parties.

INTERNATIONAL COVENANT ON ECONOMIC, SOCIAL AND CULTURAL RIGHTS (Date of adoption: 16/12/1966; Date of entry into force: 03/01/1976) 66 Signatories, 156 Parties.

INTERNATIONAL CONVENTION ON THE ELIMINATION OF ALL FORMS OF RACIAL DISCRIMINATION (ICERD) (Date of adoption: 07/03/1966; Date of entry into force: 04/01/1969) 5 Signatories, 173 Parties.

VIENNA CONVENTION ON THE LAW OF TREATIES (Date of adoption: 23/05/1969; Date of entry into force: 27/01/1980) 45 Signatories, 108 Parties.

Other international instruments

List of Abbreviations

ACP	African, Caribbean and Pacific States
BGMEA	Bangladesh Garment Manufacturers' and Exporters' Association
CAAC	Working Group on Children and Armed Conflict
CCAS	Conference Committee on Application of Standards
CCT	conditional cash transfer
CEACR	Committee of Experts on the Application of Conventions and Recommendations
CEDAW	Convention on the Elimination of All Forms of Discrimination against Women
CEE	Central and Eastern Europe
CERD	Committee on the Elimination of Racial Discrimination
CESCR	Committee on Economic Social and Cultural Rights
CFA	Communauté Financière d'Afrique (African Financial Community)
ComEDAW	Committee on the Elimination of Discrimination Against Women
ComRC	Committee on the Rights of the Child
CONANDA	National Committee on the Rights of Children
CRC	UN Convention on the Rights of the Child
CSEC	commercial sexual exploitation of children
CSR	corporate social responsibility
CUBAC	children used by adults in committing crimes
DRC	Democratic Republic of Congo
DSU	Dispute Settlement Understanding
ECJ	European Court of Justice
FAO	Food and Agriculture Organization (of the UN)
FLSA	Fair Labor Standards Act
FTA	Free Trade Agreement
GATS	General Agreement on Trade and Services
GATT	General Agreement on Trade and Tariffs
GEF	Global Environment Facility
GSP	Generalized System of Preferences
HRC	Human Rights Committee
ICC	International Criminal Court
ICCPR	International Covenant on Civil and Political Rights
ICERD	International Convention on the Elimination of All Forms of Racial Discrimination
ICESCR	International Covenant on Economic Social and Cultural Rights
ICFTU	International Confederation of Free Trade Unions
ICTY	International Criminal Tribunal for the former Yugoslavia
IDA	International Development Association
ILC	International Labour Conference

ILO	International Labour Organization
IOE	International Organization of Employers
IPEC	International Programme for the Elimination of Child Labour
ITUC	International Trade Union Confederation
LILS	Legal Issues and Labour Standards
MDG	Millennium Development Goals
MIGA	Multilateral Investment Guarantee Agency
MLC	Maritime Labour Convention
NAALC	North American Agreement on Labor Cooperation
NGO	non-governmental organization
NHRC	National Human Rights Commission
OPC	Operations Policy Committee
PAOR	Participatory Action-Oriented Research
PETI	Programme for the Elimination of Child Labour
RAs	Rapid Assessments
SIMPOC	Statistical Information and Monitoring Programme on Child Labour
SIRTI	Regional Information System on Child Labour
TBP	Time-Bound Programmes
TRIPS	Agreement on Trade-Related Aspects of Intellectual Property Rights
UCEP	Underprivileged Children Education Programme
UCW	Understanding Children's Work
UN	United Nations
UNCTOC	United Nations Convention against Transnational Organized Crime
UNGA	UN General Assembly
UNICEF	United Nations Children's Fund
UNSC	United Nations Security Council
UN-SG	United Nations Secretary-General
USAID	US Agency for International Development
VAC	World Report on Violence against Children
WFCL	worst forms of child labour
WTO	World Trade Organization

Chapter 1

Introduction: The Fight Against Child Labour in a Globalized World

Marco Pertile

1.1 Child labour: the origin of the debate and the role of the ILO

Although deeply rooted in the history of humanity, child labour again became an issue for public debate quite recently, in the mid-1980s.[1] In that decade, thanks to extensive media coverage and increased circulation of information, the civil society of the so-called developed world became aware that the black and white pictures of children working during the Western Industrial Revolution might just as easily be taken in colour in other regions of the contemporary world.[2] Since then, few human rights issues have so constantly drawn the attention of public opinion as the one at hand, and the movement against child labour has continued to expand and gain support.

As often happens with problems that suddenly arouse the conscience of the general public, the initial reactions were rather instinctive and ill-coordinated. The effort involved (and still does) a range of participants, among them NGOs, trade unions, international corporations, international organizations and governments and private individuals. At the national and international levels, initiatives emerging from civil society generally paved the way for the intervention of governments and intergovernmental organizations. Private initiatives such as labelling schemes and corporates' codes of conduct mushroomed with little or only lukewarm support from the public sector. Only after some initial hesitation, spurred on by other international agencies and some of its constituents, the ILO developed a new approach to exploit its decades-long expertise and assumed a leadership role in the field.[3]

Indeed, the involvement of the ILO in the fight against child labour dates back to the early years of the Organization.[4] As testified to by the Preamble to the Constitution, the enhancement of the conditions of working children (and women) was in fact

---

1 See A. Fyfe, *The Worldwide Movement Against Child Labour – Progress and Future Directions*, Geneva, ILO, 2007, at 5–22. Note: for brevity the publisher for the International Labour Organization is shown throughout as 'ILO', although correctly this should be 'International Labour Office', which is the secretariat of the Organization.

2 Cf. K. Basu and Z. Tzannatos, *The Global Child Labor Problem: What Do We Know and What Can We Do?*, CAE Working Paper #03-06, at 1–2.

3 See Schlemmer-Schulte (this volume).

4 See Trebilcock, Raimondi (this volume).

one of the primary reasons justifying the adoption of the founding treaty.[5] In an initial phase, the activities of the Organization in the field almost entirely concerned standard-setting, and the approach mainly consisted of introducing a minimum age for admission to employment.[6] The first conventions, which dealt with specific sectors such as industry, agriculture, the work of trimmers and stokers, fishing and underground work, were revised by a comprehensive text in 1973: Convention 138 on the minimum age for admission to employment. Convention 138 introduced not only a general age-limit for admission to employment, but also a number of flexibility clauses aimed at favouring ratification by less-developed countries.[7] Nevertheless a substantial part of the membership of the Organization considered these measures unbalanced, reflecting the needs and the cultural tradition of the Western world.[8] The process of ratification was stuck for some years and the activity of the Organization in the fight against child labour seemed to have arrived at an impasse. The approach began to change in the 1990s as the interest in problems of child labour resurfaced within public opinion. At the UN World Summit of 1995, in Copenhagen, world leaders committed themselves to 'safeguard the basic rights and interests of workers and, to this end, freely promote respect for relevant International Labour Organization conventions'.[9] In the text of the Copenhagen Declaration on Social Development, the conventions on child labour were explicitly mentioned, alongside those on freedom of association, the right to organize and bargain collectively, and the principle of non-discrimination.[10]

Similarly, when the International Labour Conference adopted the much-discussed Declaration on Fundamental Principles and Rights at Work, in 1998, the effective abolition of child labour was included amongst the four fundamental principles of the Organization, together with the freedom of association and the right to collective bargaining; the elimination of forced or compulsory labour and the elimination of discrimination in respect of employment and occupation.[11] Merely by membership of the Organization, Member States were therefore bound to respect those principles, irrespective of their ratification of the relevant conventions.

The Declaration marked the emergence of a new approach centred upon the creation of priorities in the activity of the ILO. Such an approach was implemented in the field of child labour by the subsequent adoption of Convention 182 on the Worst Forms of Child Labour in 1999.[12] Convention 182 aimed to complement (not substitute for) Convention 138 on the minimum age by identifying the four worst forms of child labour to be targeted for immediate eradication.

---

5 See Trebilcock, Raimondi (this volume).

6 See Borzaga (this volume).

7 *Ibid.*

8 *Ibid.*

9 See *Report of the World Summit on Social Development*, 19 April 1995, A/CONF.166/9, available at <http://daccessdds.un.org/doc/UNDOC/GEN/N95/116/51/PDF/N9511651.pdf?OpenElement>.

10 *Ibid.*

11 See Swepston (this volume).

12 See Rishikesh (this volume).

In principle, the criticism of prioritization is as easy as effective. Creating priorities inevitably means ranking the rest as non-priorities. In this sense, it has been pointed out that the logic of the Declaration on Fundamental Principles and Rights at Work runs the risk of undermining the legal value of the obligations deriving from the ILO Conventions that do not fall under the scope of the four 'fundamental' principles.[13] However, concerning child labour in particular, it is to be underlined that the adoption of Convention 182 achieved a number of unprecedented results. Amongst them are the shaping of a consensus on a common core of child labour at the global level and the revitalization of the activities of the Organization in the field. Convention 182 was adopted unanimously and was very rapidly ratified by almost the entire membership of the ILO. The ratification process of Convention 182 generated a renewed interest in Convention 138, which received a substantial number of ratifications in its turn. At the time of writing, 165 and 150 States are party to Conventions 182 and 138 respectively. Most importantly, the whole process revived the interest of donor countries and the channelling of a substantial amount of funds to the fight against child labour.

On the operative side, apart from these developments in standard-setting, the year 1992 brought about the creation of IPEC, the International Programme for the Elimination of Child Labour. This probably was the most significant turning point in the involvement of the ILO in the fight against child labour. With its more than 450 staff and its annual budget of some 60 million US dollars, IPEC is not only the largest single programme within the ILO, but also the most important actor in the field of technical cooperation against child labour.[14] The Programme is mandated to assist Member States in fulfilling their obligations under the relevant treaties with a view to achieving the progressive elimination of child labour and the eradication of the worst forms as a priority.[15] Its activities range from advocacy and awareness-raising, to technical cooperation with governments and assistance to children in regional, sub-regional and national projects.[16] The focus is on favouring the adoption of national policies that remove children from hazardous work and provide alternatives for them. At present, IPEC operates in 88 countries and runs more than 250 projects.[17]

For a number of reasons, which will be explained below, it is argued that the ILO should continue to be the institution that coordinates the efforts of the international community against child labour in the years to come. Firstly, though, it is worth sketching the main features of the phenomenon of child labour and of the relevant legal issues.

---

13 See P. Alston, '"Core Labour Standards" and the Transformation of the International Labour Rights Regime', *European Journal of International Law*, Vol. 15, 2004, 457 ff.

14 *IPEC Action against Child Labour 2004–2005: Progress and Future Priorities*, Geneva, ILO, 2006; Fyfe, *The Worldwide Movement, supra* note 1, at v.

15 *IPEC at a Glance – Fact Sheet*, available at <www.ilo.org/childlabour>.

16 *Ibid.*

17 *Ibid.*

1.2 Child labour: a multidimensional issue

Articles and scholarly works on child labour routinely describe the problem as complex and difficult to solve. It seems fair to assume that that is not only due to the comprehensible difficulty of each and every scholar to admit that they have been entrusted with a menial task. One can easily share at least the characterization of child labour as 'multidimensional'.[18] Here, it is submitted that this is so under three, partially overlapping, perspectives: 1) subjective multidimensionality; 2) causal multidimensionality; and 3) multidimensionality on the grounds of solutions.

1.2.1 Subjective multidimensionality

Child labour reveals its multidimensional nature from a subjective point of view as several actors, different in nature and often having different agendas, may cause the problem or contribute to the quest for a solution. It follows that understanding the scope of child labour at the global level requires a careful analysis of the role of those actors. One usually thinks of developed countries, less-developed countries, trade unions, NGOs, transnational corporations, governmental authorities, intergovernmental organizations, and so on. Somewhat paradoxically, children are seldom mentioned. The main stakeholders are usually dealt with as the object of the problem rather than a subject capable of having their say and cooperating in the quest for a solution. This is legally sanctioned by municipal legal orders, which, at least up to a certain age, regard children as largely incapable of deciding for themselves.[19]

For its part, international law does not change the picture significantly. International legal obligations of a customary or conventional nature are generally framed as obligations resting on States. The latter ones are legally bound to adopt legislative or operational measures with a view to eradicating child labour, but the content of those obligations is scarcely connected to the need to learn the concerns of children from their voice, let alone to empowering children to decide for themselves in some respects. A notable exception to this is Convention 182 as complemented by Recommendation 190. In fact, article 6 of the Convention obliges States Parties to 'design and implement programmes of action to eliminate as a priority the worst forms of child labour' and to do so 'in consultation with relevant government institutions and employers' and workers' organizations, taking into consideration the views of other concerned groups as appropriate'. Article 2 of Recommendation 190 further specifies the meaning of 'other concerned groups', recommending that 'the programmes of action referred to in article 6 of the Convention should be designed and implemented ... taking into consideration the views of the children directly affected by the worst forms of child labour ...'. The approach is in line with the general principle laid down by article 12 of the Convention on the Rights of the Child, according to which 'States Parties shall assure to the child who is capable of

---

18 Cf. B.H. Weston and M.B. Teerink, 'Rethinking Child Labour: A Multidimensional Human Rights Problem', in B.H. Weston (ed.), *Child Labor and Human Rights: Making Children Matter*, London, Lynne Rienner, 2005, 3 ff.

19 Cf. Keita (this volume).

forming his or her own views the right to express those views freely in all matters affecting the child ...'. It appears, however, that these requirements have not been adequately implemented so far.

1.2.2 Causal multidimensionality

Child labour reveals its multidimensional nature also with respect to the causes lying at the basis of the problem and the factors impeding its solution; amongst them, poverty is universally recognized as a major cause for child labour. Recognition of its role as a determinant of the problem is so widespread that affirming that child labour is inextricably connected to the economic situation of a given region has become a truism. Indeed, poverty is often employed as a catch-all concept that includes reference to several factors such as, for instance, parents' illiteracy, insufficient adult wages, lack of schooling, natural disasters and endemic armed conflicts.[20] Somewhat inevitably, reference to 'poverty' often involves the assumption that child labour is not a deliberate choice of the children and the families, but the outcome of necessity.[21]

However, empirical studies demonstrate that child labour is not exclusively determined by market forces and economic factors: the overall picture is rather more complicated.[22] Child labour reveals its intricacies also in cultural terms. In every society, self-respect and social recognition are strictly related to the position of the individual in terms of occupation and social function. In traditional societies, some forms of child labour, far from being considered a scourge, often play a fundamental role in education, socialization and rites of passage.[23] In this perspective, it goes without saying that the role of children in a society cannot be conceived of as an independent factor, as it usually reflects the structure of a social organization that has developed over the centuries. It is therefore fundamental that the cultural and moral implications of the fight against child labour be carefully assessed and discussed.[24] Without such a debate, the fight against child labour runs the risk of bringing about the uncritical imposition of dominant values alien to the societies on which they are imposed.

Amongst the causes of child labour, and of virtually every issue connected to the condition of workers and social rights in general, the word 'globalization' crops up *ad nauseam*. It has been pronounced so often by scholars, politicians, and journalists that its meaning, provided that it ever had a precise one, seems to have

---

20 SIMPOC/IPEC, *Investigating the Worst Forms of Child Labour: A Synthesis Report of Selected Rapid Assessments and National Reports*, Geneva, ILO, 2005, at 7–10, 13, 17–18, 22.

21 K. Basu, *Child Labor and the Law: Notes on Possible Pathologies*, Harvard Institute of Economic Research, Discussion Paper No. 2052, at 3, available at <http://post.economics.harvard.edu/hier/2004papers/2004list.html>.

22 IPEC, *Les déterminants du travail et de la scolarisation des enfants: les enseignements des enquêtes biographiques du Burkina Faso et du Mali*, Geneva, ILO, 2007.

23 Cf. Keita (this volume).

24 V.A. Zelizer, *Pricing the Priceless Child: The Changing Social Value of Children*, Princeton NJ, Princeton University Press, 1994.

dissolved.[25] It has been rightly observed that the word is now commonly used as a generic description of present times.[26] It is not the purpose of this chapter to come up with a conceptualization of globalization,[27] but one has to recognize that some of the features of the phenomenon are directly relevant to child labour. Perhaps, a safe assumption to start with is that, whether good or bad, globalization is widely perceived as inevitable and has dramatically improved the ability of capital and finance to cross borders. By contrast, such is not the case for the large majority of workers. Whereas the world is a village for capital and a globalized multilingual elite, the opposite is true for a localized multitude of people.[28] For them, crossing the borders to improve their working conditions is often not an option. It is clear that there are winners and losers in a globalized world and that working children, probably the most fragile part of a society, tend to be amongst the latter category.

It is commonplace to count amongst the effects of globalization, and of the widespread use of new technologies, our changing perception of space and time. In a globalized world distances are eroded and that may generate paradoxical results. If, on the one hand, globalization and, in particular, the increased mobility of capital seem to aggravate the problem of child labour or at least to complicate the quest for a solution to it, on the other hand the very existence of a worldwide movement against child labour is in itself a product of globalization.

1.2.3 Multidimensional solutions

In such a framework it seems inevitable to conclude that, as far as the dimension of solutions is concerned, the fight against child labour must be conducted also at the international level. Whereas the adoption of concrete measures to eradicate the phenomenon often falls under the domain of state jurisdiction, the coordinating function of international actors and of international law is essential.

In any case, it should also be noted that the quest for a solution to a problem that has different determinants requires recourse to different tools. Simply put, a multidimensional issue requires multidimensional answers.

As mentioned above, child labour is to a large extent determined by economic factors. Solutions to the problem are therefore inevitably connected to the enhancement of the economic development of a given region and to the elimination of poverty. Legally speaking, that leads to the threadbare and fundamental issues connected to economic development and the nature of the obligations deriving from socio-economic rights. One might even wonder what the role of legal measures could be when the priority is simply to initiate a favourable economic cycle. In this regard neoclassical economists may take the view that the legal regulation of child

---

25 Z. Bauman, *Globalization: The Human Consequences*, New York, Columbia University Press, 2000, at 1–3.

26 J. Osterhammel and N.P. Petersson, *Geschichte der Globalisierung. Dimensionen, Prozesse, Epochen*, Munich, C.H. Beck, 2003, at 7.

27 On the definition of globalization, see D. Zolo, *Globalization: An Overview*, Essex, ECPR Press, 2007, at 1–5.

28 Bauman, *Globalization*, *supra* note 25, at 1–3.

labour is merely an obstacle to the efficient functioning of the market. Indeed, the proposition that in a situation of despair and severe economic crisis, everyone might be better off, including children, without any form of legal regulation seems to have some merits. One should take into account that the elimination of child labour does not necessarily imply the enhancement of child welfare.[29]

Should one conclude that legal regulation, with its inevitable rigidities and rhetorical features, is useless and may even be counterproductive, and that the adoption of the appropriate economic policies is in itself sufficient?

In fact, from a theoretical point of view, child labour has mainly attracted the attention of economists, social scientists, and historians whereas jurists, with a few notable exceptions, have stood on the sidelines. One might perhaps think that the latter ones are persuaded that the matter is to be confined to the political arena or left to wishful thinkers. It is quite clear that a prohibition on child labour will never be sufficient in itself to eliminate a problem rooted in economic and cultural factors and that the aim of legal measures cannot be to transform a child worker into a starving child. A blanket prohibition, when not combined with measures aimed at addressing the very roots of the problem and assisting children who leave child labour, is frequently useless. In many circumstances, concrete steps such as the supply of free meals to school pupils or incidental factors such as the adoption of new technologies and the reduction of fertility rates might be more significant than the adoption of a new legal instrument. Empirical experiences, in particular, demonstrate that the raising of the age of compulsory schooling within the context of a system that provides free education of good quality is one of the most effective strategies to reduce the incidence of child labour.[30]

Yet carefully drafted legal provisions, when part of a wider plan of action, are an essential component of that wide array of measures that might contribute to the elimination of child labour. Legal regulation can perform different functions in the fight against child labour. Some legal measures solemnly declare priorities and objectives, others sanction unacceptable behaviours, and yet others channel resources into some typologies of endeavours. Moreover, law might play an essential ancillary role to the adoption of economic policies when the economy is trapped in self-perpetuating

---

29 See Basu, *Child Labor and the Law*, *supra* note 20, at 7. One might think of the children working in bonded labour. When interviewed by the ILO, they revealed that they considered themselves better off in such exploitative working situations than when they lived with their families and they lacked food. See SIMPOC/IPEC, *Investigating the Worst Forms of Child Labour*, *supra* note 20, 2005, at 14.

Along the same lines, one might recall the so-called 'export processing zones'; that is, specific districts in developing countries in which the protective legislation for workers might be temporarily suspended or reduced so as to attract foreign investment. The empirical evidence demonstrates that workers are generally willing to move to those areas in order to find jobs and working conditions that are not available anywhere else in the country. On this latter point, see K. Basu, *Global Labor Standards and Local Freedoms*, WIDER Annual Lecture 7, UNU-WIDER, 2003, at 6–8.

30 See IPEC, 'Education as an Intervention Strategy to Eliminate and Prevent Child Labour', available at <www.ilo.org/public/english/region/asro/bangkok/apec/download/edu_strat.pdf>.

situations of extensive use of child labour.[31] In this context, international law may function as a coordinating tool ensuring that the objectives and the strategies of the fight against child labour are shared at the global level. It is common knowledge that in a globalized world decisions are often taken at the global level and that the room for manoeuvre of national authorities is increasingly reduced. That clearly poses the problem of the democratic legitimacy of international actors and the mechanisms of international law might not seem flawless in this respect. As has been repeatedly noted, the renewed interest in the elimination of child labour might be read in the context of the pursuit of a protectionist agenda by Western countries to the detriment of developing ones: The whole issue of child labour would constantly run the risk of falling prey to the interests of powerful lobbies.[32]

It is, however, submitted that in sensitive issues such as child labour, which concerns the most vulnerable sector of society and, at the same time, a sector that is crucial for its future development, the task of governing globalization must not be abandoned. Difficult as it may be, we are persuaded that the challenge of defining new mechanisms and a more democratic international order should be taken up. Through an incremental process, it seems feasible to identify a common ground even at the global level. The widespread rejection of the worst forms of child labour by the constituents of the ILO, that is, governments, workers and employers of the world, testifies to this.

1.3 Child labour: the quest for a definition

International law does not provide a clear definition of child labour. That comes as no surprise in view of the heterogeneity of the international community and the different political agendas of its members, which are often difficult to reconcile. For those same political, economic and cultural reasons that have long impeded the adoption of effective measures against child labour, the agreement on a comprehensive definition has not been an option even in recent times.

As is often the case with highly controversial issues, identifying common ground can only be possible through an incremental approach. In a very down-to-earth perspective, international law often crystallizes international consensus on a specific aspect of the matter when the time is ripe to do so, step by step through the adoption of instruments that are limited in scope.[33] In line with the decentralized nature of the international community, different forums and organizations are involved in the

---

31 The concept of multiple equilibria has been applied to child labour to demonstrate not only that market forces will not always reduce the incidence of the phenomenon but that they sometimes even may aggravate its scope. A vicious cycle might be interrupted by the adoption of adequately drafted legal sanctions, altering the ratio of adults' wages and childrens' wages. See K. Basu and P.H. Van, 'The Economics of Child Labour', *American Economic Review*, 1998, 412 ff.

32 Cf. Basu, *Global Labor Standards*, *supra* note 29, at 2.

33 As has happened, for instance, in the case of international terrorism. See A. Gioia, *The UN Conventions on the Prevention and Suppression of International Terrorism*, in G. Nesi (ed.), *International Cooperation in Counterterrorism*, Aldershot, Ashgate, 2006, 1 ff.

effort. Eventually customary law may emerge, but the assessment must be made very carefully, as the ratification of conventional instruments cannot be easily considered evidence of States' *opinio juris*.[34]

Along these lines, the international definition of child labour has emerged through the stratification of different legal instruments having different scope and object. Together with the ILO, different organizations at the global and the regional level took part in standard-setting: the UN, the OCDE, the European Union, the MERCOSUR and the Council of Europe are amongst them.[35] For a long time the approach of the ILO centred on the question of what forms of economic activity are to be precluded to children below a certain age. Later, four categories of worst forms of child labour to be eradicated immediately were singled out. But the issue of child labour is touched upon in different perspectives in other international legal instruments. Under specific conditions, some of the worst forms of child labour, for instance, can be qualified as international crimes *inter alia* under the Statute of the International Criminal Court.[36] Other worst forms of child labour, such as slavery and practices similar to slavery, are the objects of widely ratified specific conventions and of long-standing peremptory customary norms.[37] The sale of children, child prostitution and child pornography as well as the involvement of children in armed conflict are the object of two recently adopted and widely ratified additional protocols to the UN Convention on the Rights of the Child.[38] Moreover, several international instruments sanction a number of obligations of States Parties (and the corresponding rights of the children), which are more or less strictly related to child labour.[39] Article 32 of the Convention on the rights of the child is directly relevant as it obliges States Parties to 'recognize the right of the child to be protected from economic exploitation and from performing any work that is likely to be hazardous or to interfere with the child's education, or to be harmful to the child's health or physical, mental, spiritual, moral or social development'. Other international rights of the individual are indirectly but clearly relevant to child labour. One might think of social rights such as the right to education, the right to health, the right to an adequate standard of living, and the right to private and family life. Those are rights pertaining to each individual that assume a special meaning with regard to the situation of children and to child labour. They can be seen as preconditions for addressing the roots of the phenomenon and giving the fight against it a genuine anti-rhetorical dimension.[40]

---

34 See R.R. Baxter, 'Treaties and Custom', *Recueil des cours de l'Académie de droit international de la Haye*, 1970, 57–74.

35 See Fodella (this volume); Hartwig (this volume); Sanguineti-Raymond (this volume).

36 Rome Statute of the International Criminal Court, art. 8(2)(b), xxii, xxvi; art. 8(2)(d), vi, vii. The Statute is available at <www.icc-cpi.int/legaltools>.

37 See Sanna (this volume).

38 See Table of Legal Instruments this volume.

39 See Fodella (this volume).

40 Amongst the international treaties sanctioning those rights at the global and regional level one might quote the International Covenant on Social and Cultural Rights, the European Social Charter, and the African Charter on Human and Peoples' Rights.

Against this backdrop, it seems safe to assume that the core of child labour revolves around some form of exploitation of children or activities that are likely to impinge negatively on the child's education or development.

A more specific definition emerges adopting the point of view of ILO Conventions 138, on the minimum age for admission to employment, and 182, on the worst forms of child labour. The ILO instruments are certainly the more specific ones, are widely ratified nowadays, and represent the legal and policy framework for the most active international actor operating in the field. In this perspective, it should be pointed out that a dichotomy arises, as the legal framework does not exclude the fact that children legally carry out some forms of economic activity. A fundamental distinction can therefore be drawn between 'child work' and 'child labour'. The first concept identifies those economic activities carried out by children that are compatible with the provisions of the relevant treaties – in a nutshell, those activities that are not detrimental to the children's health, personal development, education, growth and so on. 'Child labour', in contrast, identifies any kind of employment or work carried out by children without complying with the requirements of Conventions 138 and 182.

Other chapters in this book will examine the content of those instruments. For the time being, suffice it to say that Convention 138 prohibits economic activity performed by children below the age of 13 (12 in developing countries) and sets the minimum age for admission to employment at 15 (14 in developing countries) or in any case the age corresponding to the end of compulsory schooling. A number of flexibility clauses are provided concerning the economic sector, the type of work and the level of economic development of the country concerned. Light work is permitted for those reaching 13 and 14 (12 and 13 in developing countries). As has been mentioned, Convention 182 prohibits four worst forms of child labour and calls for urgent elimination of them. They are defined as follows:

- All forms of slavery or practices similar to slavery, such as the sale and trafficking of children, debt bondage and serfdom and forced or compulsory labour, including forced or compulsory recruitment of children for use in armed conflict;
- The use, procuring or offering of a child for prostitution, for the production of pornography or for pornographic performances;
- The use, procuring or offering of a child for illicit activities, in particular for the production and trafficking of drugs as defined in the relevant international treaties;
- Work which, by its nature or the circumstances in which it is carried out, is likely to harm the health, safety or morals of children.

Within such worst forms, a distinction is usually drawn, in the practice of the ILO, between two sub-categories. The first three worst forms are termed 'unconditional' worst forms of child labour, whereas the last one is defined as 'conditional'.[41] Such

---

41 See, for instance, ILO, *A Future Without Child Labour – Global Report under the Follow-Up to the ILO Declaration on Fundamental Principles and Rights at Work*, Geneva, ILO, 2002, 9.

a distinction is essentially descriptive and does not reflect any difference in the legal regime regulating the four worst forms. It refers to the fact that, while the unconditional forms are always unacceptable as they are *per se* incompatible with the health and the development of children, hazardous work – the conditional form – identifies a category that is strictly dependent on the situation and the environment in which the work to be prohibited is carried out.[42] In other words, the category of hazardous work admits the possibility that the causes of the hazard could be removed. In such a case, a worst form of child labour might turn into a legitimate form of work, provided that the minimum age requirements are complied with.[43]

It might be argued that in this, as in many other sectors, the international legal framework is affected by an overproduction of standards. As mentioned, other instruments at the international level already addressed some of the problems lying at the basis of the worst forms of child labour. From different perspectives, they might qualify as violations of human rights or even as international crimes of the individual. It is however submitted that in the present case the inclusion in the ILO legal framework of legal concepts that were, at least in part, already regulated elsewhere, has some positive side effects.

Firstly, from a conceptual point of view, qualifying international crimes or violations of human rights as forms of work implies the full recognition of the economic dimension of those phenomena. Labelling the conduct and the facts that lie at the basis of slavery, forced prostitution and forced recruitment in armed conflict as worst forms of child labour means a step forward in the understanding of the problem. Criticizing this approach on the grounds that it could have a legitimizing effect for those conducts seems moot.[44] It is clear in the whole text of Convention 182 that the worst forms of child labour are illegal and must be eradicated immediately. Recognition of a painful reality in a legal text does not imply legalization.

Secondly, from an operational point of view, classifying such behaviour in terms of employment relationships prompts the involvement of the ILO and of its programmes in the fight against the phenomenon and in the assistance to its victims. For all the criticism of the action of the ILO and of its possible missteps, on the whole that would seem a positive result.

1.4 Child labour: the extension of the problem

An essential precondition for the adoption of effective policies against multifaceted problems is a thorough investigation of their factual dimension. Having provided a legal definition of child labour, the incidence of the problem and of its main features should be analysed so as to better evaluate the strategies to be adopted. As Recommendation 190 makes clear: 'Detailed information and statistical data on the nature and extent of child labour should be compiled and kept up to date to serve

---

42 See Beqiraj (this volume).

43 That explains the ample discretion left to national authorities in identifying typologies of work that fall under this last category. See Beqiraj (this volume).

44 See Kooijmans (this volume); Noguchi (this volume).

as a basis for determining priorities for national action for the abolition of child labour ...'.

To this end, the ILO established SIMPOC in 1998, the statistical unit of IPEC. The ILO Bureau of Statistics had first carried out experimental child labour surveys in 1992–93.[45] Obviously, estimating child labour at the global level may prove very difficult as different regions and contexts are involved and data of different institutions and sources must be taken into account and compared. Collecting data on domestic work performed by children and on the worst forms of child labour is even more difficult, given their hidden nature and/or their inevitable contiguity with the black market and the world of organized crime. Nevertheless, SIMPOC statistics, often compiled in cooperation with UNICEF, are generally recognized as a point of reference in the field. Subsequent information papers on global estimates on child labour were adopted in 2000 and 2004 and became the factual basis for the two global reports adopted by the International Labour Conference in 2002 and 2006. The method employed by SIMPOC for estimating child labour may obviously be debated and put into question.[46] However, the fact remains that that method has not changed significantly over the years and that the global estimates are fully comparable.[47] Therefore, irrespective of the uncertainties surrounding the figures, the global estimates are crucial in assessing emerging trends in the field.

SIMPOC estimates reveal a considerable decrease of child labour at the global level during the period 2000–04.[48] According to SIMPOC, in 2004 there were 190.7 million economically active children in the age group 5 to 14,[49] 165.8 million of which could be classified as child labourers and 74.4 million of those latter were engaged in forms of hazardous work. Four years earlier the number of economically active children was estimated to be 211 million, of which 186.3 million were child labourers, of whom 111.3 million engaged in hazardous work. The decrease for the three groups amounted to 9.6 per cent, 11 per cent and 33.2 per cent respectively. The analysis by economic sector and by regional trends reveals clear inequalities. Child labour is to be found for the most part – 69 per cent – in agriculture, whereas industry and services account for 9 per cent and 22 per cent respectively. Most importantly, the analysis of the global trends by region underlines that the 11 per cent decrease in the number of child labourers finds its main explanation in the decline in the rate in

---

45 ILO, *Child Labour Surveys: Results of Methodological Experiments in Four Countries 1992–1993*, ILO/IPEC Bureau of Statistics, 1996.

46 Cf. Basu and Tzannatos, *The Global Child Labor Problem*, *supra* note 2, at 13–15.

47 Cf. ILO, *The End of Child Labour: Within Reach – Global Report under the Follow-Up to the ILO Declaration on Fundamental Principles and Rights at Work*, Geneva, ILO, 2006, at 5.

48 The following data are taken from ILO, *The End of Child Labour*, *supra* note 47, at 5–9.

49 The concept of economic activity 'is a statistical rather than legal notion' and 'encompasses most productive activities undertaken by children, whether for the market or not, paid or unpaid, for a few hours or full time, on a casual or regular basis, legal or illegal; it excludes chores undertaken in the child's own household and schooling. To be counted as economically active, a child must have worked for at least one hour on any day during a seven-day reference period'. See ILO, *The End of Child Labour*, *supra* note 47, at 6.

South America. Here the number of working children decreased from 17.4 million in 2000 to 5.7 million four years later, and the activity rate declined from 16.1 per cent to 5.1 per cent. Progress in other regions is by far less significant. In Asia and the Pacific, the activity rate went from 19.4 to 18.8 per cent; in sub-Saharan Africa the rate fell from 28.8 to 26.4 per cent.

These figures clearly demonstrate that there has been a decline in child labour in the period examined. It should however be noted that there are no available data for the so-called 'unconditional worst forms of child labour'. Moreover, one might wonder what the actual impact of the strategies against child labour was in achieving such results or whether the economic trends are to be credited with the success. In this regard it is however worth mentioning that those countries of South America that have adopted national plans against child labour have achieved very significant results.[50] On the whole, the data do not seem to allow any assessment on whether the objective proposed by the 2006 Global Report on Child Labour – the total elimination of child labour by 2016 – is realistic.[51] In any case, the achievement of this objective will only be possible by addressing effectively the problem in sub-Saharan Africa, currently the region with the highest incidence of child labour and with a huge population growth rate.[52]

1.5 Why the ILO?

At the outset of this chapter, we maintained that, amongst the international actors operating in the fight against child labour, the ILO is the one best equipped to coordinate the efforts of the international community. Some of the following chapters will provide further elements to substantiate this statement. For the time being, suffice it to note four features of the Organization that testify to its uniqueness in the international arena and its potential in the fight against child labour. In such a field, the action of the ILO may profit by the existence of:

- a comprehensive standard-setting process
- a reliable supervisory system
- substantial expertise in technical cooperation; and
- a unique decision-making process inspired by the principle of tripartitism.

Of course, one might criticize each and every feature and identify a number of significant shortcomings. The action of the ILO against child labour is far from perfect. The legal framework reveals significant overlap, as the relevant conventions are not always coordinated with other international legal instruments. The supervisory system does not envisage an individual complaint procedure and, as is the rule with international monitoring systems, might leave the impression that it is to a large extent a paper tiger, lacking real powers of enforcement. The activities of technical cooperation are somehow patchy and clearly underdeveloped in some regions of

---

50 See Sanguineti-Raymond (this volume).

51 ILO, *The End of Child Labour*, *supra* note 47, at xiii.

52 See Keita (this volume).

the world. Again, the representativeness of the constituents of the ILO might be questioned, in a world where governments are being progressively expropriated of their jurisdiction, and the organizations of the employers and workers are in deep waters when it comes to keeping contact with rapidly changing grassroots movements.

That being said, the fact remains that the action of the ILO against child labour reveals many strong points. Legal instruments are detailed and specific. They emphasize the economic dimension of the exploitation of children, thus favouring the adoption of counterstrategies. The supervisory system is polycentric and employs a variety of methods, combining political and authoritative technical bodies.[53] It is amongst the most effective ones at the international level. As it is comprehensible, in a field that is deeply connected to economic rights and development strategies, it mainly aims at favouring the adoption of result-oriented national policies rather than imposing sanctions bluntly in case of non-compliance. That is all the more important as the Organization combines the activities of supervision with a significant effort on the side of technical cooperation. Over the years IPEC has gained an amount of project experience in the field which is unparalleled by other international bodies. Although the amount of funding devoted to those projects is totally inadequate when compared to the magnitude of the problem, it is nonetheless considerable. Finally, for all the criticism of the way the ILO constituents deal with the 'real world' of children, it is to be underlined that the principle of tripartitism constitutes a unique attempt to introduce democratic elements in a world that needs to find new approaches to centralization. For all its shortcomings, it favours openness and the creation of linkages between public opinion, civil society and the Organization in a way that is unknown to other international organizations operating at the global level. That is essential in the fight against child labour.

---

53 See Trebilcock and Raimondi (this volume). See also E. Gravel, *Les mécanismes de contrôle de l'OIT: bilan de leur efficacité et perspectives d'avenir*, in J.-C. Javillier and B. Gernigon, *Les normes internationales du travail: un patrimoine pour l'avenir – Mélanges en l'honneur de Nicolas Valticos*, Geneva, ILO, 2004, 3 ff.

PART I
The ILO's Action in the Fight Against Child Labour

Chapter 2

The ILO's Legal Activities Towards the Eradication of Child Labour: An Overview

Anne Trebilcock and Guido Raimondi[1]

2.1 Introduction

Since its inception, the International Labour Organization (ILO) has grappled with the situation of children and young persons in relation to the world of work. The Preamble to its Constitution addresses them both directly (with protection of children and young persons cited as an example of conditions of labour requiring urgent improvement) and indirectly (as part of the regulation of labour supply, and as beneficiaries of vocational and technical education).[2] Relevant International Labour Conventions and Recommendations – the main, but not the sole, means of the ILO's legal activity – have reflected various concerns over time. The most important contemporary instruments for the elimination of child labour, the Worst Forms of Child Labour Convention, 1999 (No. 182), and the Minimum Age Convention, 1973 (No. 138), mirror a modern blend of rights and protections for children and young persons, and serve as an essential bridge to economic and social development.

Alongside Conventions and Recommendations, the ILO has other legal means at its disposal in the fight to end child labour. Firstly, the International Labour Conference has adopted two Declarations that have created new legal frameworks for tackling child labour while also serving as vehicles to draw attention to the issue: the Declaration of Philadelphia (1944), which forms part of the ILO Constitution, and the Declaration on Fundamental Principles and Rights at Work (1998). As with the adoption of ILO standards, these Declarations reflect the power of consensus among representatives of governments, employers and workers (tripartism) in the organization's main policy-making organ, the International Labour Conference. The International Labour Conference also serves as a platform from which to call for the elimination of child labour (especially in its worst forms) and to share good practices. Secondly, the International Labour Office, the secretariat of the Organization, has used the functions attributed to it under article 10 of the ILO Constitution to collect and distribute information, prepare reports and publications, conduct special

---

1 The views expressed are those of the authors alone.
2 Constitution of the ILO, Preamble, para. 2.

investigations and 'accord to governments at their request all appropriate assistance ... in connection with the framing of laws and regulations on the basis of the decisions of the Conference and the improvement of administrative practices and systems of inspection'.[3] In addition, the ILO Governing Body adopted the Tripartite Declaration of Principles on Multinational Enterprises and Social Policy (1977), which was amended in 2000 to embrace the elimination of child labour as one of the guiding principles for such companies. Thirdly, the ILO has used its power to conclude various types of agreements (with other public international organizations, with governments, with employers and workers' organizations) as a means of tackling child labour. A blending of legal activity with practical action through technical cooperation in ILO Member States and advocacy has been the hallmark of the ILO's efforts to enable every child in the world to have the opportunity to realize his or her potential.

2.2 The International Labour Organization

Currently a specialized agency of the United Nations, the ILO was created at the end of World War I, by the 1919 Paris Peace Conference (Part XIII of the Treaty of Versailles), in the framework of the League of Nations.[4] As of July 2007, the ILO had 181 Member States.

The establishment of the ILO – the sole *tripartite* international organization (that is, an organization whose decision-making power is not reserved to Member States, but is shared with the representative organizations of employers and workers) – was the result of a strong movement of opinion aiming to improve the condition of workers. This movement was fuelled by interventions of scholars, political scientists and artists, which had accompanied, throughout the 19th and the beginning of the 20th century, the consolidation of the industrial revolution and its sometimes catastrophic impact on social structures and the ordinary lives of human beings, including children.[5]

---

3 *Ibid.*, art. 10, para. 2 (b).

4 On the history of the ILO: C.W. Jenks, 'Les origines de L'Organisation Internationale du Travail', in *Revue internationale du travail*, 1934, 575 ff; E. Haas, *Beyond the Nation State. Functionalism and International Organisation*, Stanford, 1964; D.A. Morse, *The Origin and Evolution of the I.L.O. and Its Role in the World Community*, New York, 1969; G.A. Johnston, *The International Labour Organisation. Its Work for Social and Economic Progress*, London, 1970; A.E. Alcock, *History of the International Labour Organisation*, London/Basingstoke, 1971.

5 On the ILO from a legal point of view, see: G. Scelle, *L'Organisation Internationale du Travail et le BIT*, Paris, 1930; C.W. Jenks, *Social Justice and the Law of Nations*, New York, 1970; G. Gaja, 'Organizzazione Internazionale del Lavoro', *Enciclopedia del diritto*, Vol. XXXI, Milan, 1981, 345; N. Valticos, *Droit international du travail*, Paris, 1987; V.Y. Ghebali, *The International Labour Organisation. A Case Study on the Evolution of United Nations Specialised Agencies*, Dordrecht/Boston/London, 1989; M. Imber, *The USA, ILO, UNESCO and IAEA*, New York, 1989; R. Adam, *Attività normative e di controllo dell'O. I.L. e evoluzione della comunità internazionale*, Milan, 1993; R. Adam, 'ILO (International Labour Organization)', *Digesto delle discipline pubblicistiche*, Vol. VIII, Turin, 1993, 97 ff;

The idea was to establish at the international level some authoritative source of minimum standards aimed at regulating the world of work, including social protection for workers, in order to effectively reply to the usual objection against initiatives taken at national level in order to improve the condition of workers: international competition. This objection assumes that any improvement granted to the workers in a given country raises the cost of that country's products, thus making them less competitive on the international market and undermining, at the end of the day, the country's prosperity.

Historically, the creation of this Organization was made possible mainly because of two factors. On the one hand the Soviet Revolution in Russia (1917) had shown to the world the risks to peace – at the domestic and the international level – of ill-managed social conflicts, thus calling for an effective response by the international community. On the other hand, organizations of workers and to a certain extent those of employers, had by the end of the 19th century reached a high level of effectiveness and gained a high number of members. Furthermore, these organizations had played an important role in the industrial effort of the winning powers in World War I and were thus well placed to press claims.

This short historical résumé shows the three main roots of the Organization, which we find in the Preamble of its Constitution, namely: the defence of peace, and its link to the promotion of social justice and the response to the international competition argument.

Firstly, the goal of the defence of peace can be found in the first sentence of the Preamble: 'Whereas universal and lasting peace can be established only if it is based upon social justice ...'. The idea is that effective labour legislation, whose floor is agreed by the international community, favours social peace within States, thus contributing to attenuate conflicts and tensions that may, if left un-addressed, spill over to the international level, thus endangering peace. The ILO's role in contributing to peace was recognized, in particular, with the attribution to the Organization, of the 1969 Nobel Prize for Peace.

Secondly, the promotion of social justice, which mirrors the humanitarian ideal of the defence of the rights of the worker as a human being, is expressed, in particular, by the second sentence of the Preamble, which refers to the workers' condition and to the urgency to improve it. It says:

> And whereas conditions of labour exist involving such injustice hardship and privation to large numbers of people as to produce unrest so great that the peace and harmony of the world are imperilled; and an improvement of those conditions is urgently required; as, for example, by the regulation of the hours of work including the establishment of a maximum working day and week, the regulation of the labour supply, the prevention of unemployment, the provision of an adequate living wage, the protection of the worker against sickness, disease and injury arising out of his employment, the protection of

---

H.G. Bartolomei de la Cruz and A. Euzéby, *L'Organisation Internationale du Travail*, Parigi, 1997; G. Raimondi, 'ILO (International Labour Organization)', in S. Cassese, *Dizionario di diritto pubblico*, Milan, 2006, Vol. IV, 2871 ff; F. Maupain, 'L'OIT, la justice sociale et la mondialisation', *Recueil des cours de l'Académie de droit international de la Haye*, Vol. 278, 1999, 201–396.

children, young persons and women, provision for old age and injury, protection of the interests of workers when employed in countries other than their own, recognition of the principle of equal remuneration for work of equal value, recognition of the principle of freedom of association, the organization of vocational and technical education and other measures; ...

To a large degree this is, in practice, the global programme of the ILO, still valid after almost 90 years. The protection of 'children' and 'young persons' was already enshrined in the first and most important instrument of the Organization.

Third, the question of international competition is addressed by the third sentence of the Preamble, which states: 'whereas also the failure of any nation to adopt humane conditions of labour is an obstacle in the way of other nations which desire to improve the conditions in their own countries'.[6]

No doubt, the tool created in 1919 is far from perfect from this point of view, because such a programme could be put into practice only by a body having universal powers to enact automatically binding legislation, which is not the case of the ILO. The main legal instruments at the disposal of the Organization are basically Conventions, which enter into force only between those States accepting to ratify them, and Recommendations, which are by definition non-binding instruments. As explored below, they are not its only legal tools, however.

The objectives of the Organization were redefined by the Philadelphia Declaration, adopted in 1944, which is now annexed to the Constitution, forming an integral part of it. This document extended the scope of the ILO beyond the narrow field of the world of work, proclaiming, *inter alia*, the right of all human beings, irrespective of race, creed or sex, to pursue both their material well-being and their spiritual development in conditions of freedom and dignity, of economic security and equal opportunity. Importantly, it also set out the ILO's responsibility 'to examine and consider all international economic and financial policies and measures'[7] in the light of the objective of social justice as a basis for lasting peace. This provision has provided an entry point for the Organization to bring its legal tools on child labour to bear in a development context.

2.3 Organs of the ILO

The institutional structure of the ILO relies on three main organs: the International Labour Conference, the Governing Body and the Secretariat, or International Labour Office.

The International Labour Conference, or General Conference of the ILO, is the most important organ, which decides, in particular, on the adoption of international

---

6 B. Langille, 'Re-Reading the 1919 ILO Constitution in Light of Recent Evidence on Foreign Direct Investment and Workers Rights', Vol. 42, 2003, *Columbia Journal of Transnational Law*, 101; B. Langille, 'What Is International Labour Law For?', The ILO Governing Body Public Lecture, Geneva, ILO, March 2005, available at <http://www.ilo.org/public/english/bureau/inst/download/langille.pdf>.

7 Declaration of Philadelphia, para. II (d).

labour standards – Conventions and Recommendations – and on instruments of amendment to the Constitution. Meeting annually, normally in Geneva, the Conference has also adopted several Declarations and numerous resolutions. It is composed of national tripartite delegations. Each Member State appoints four delegates, two from the government, one from the employers and one from the workers. This ratio reflects the sharing of the voting power within the Conference: 50 per cent to governments, 25 per cent to employers and 25 per cent to workers. Employer and worker delegates are to be appointed 'in agreement with the industrial organizations ... which are most representative of employers or workpeople, as the case may be, in their respective countries' (article 3, paragraph 5, of the ILO Constitution). Advisers may assist delegates.

The Governing Body is the executive organ of the ILO, responsible for directing the International Labour Office and setting the International Labour Conference's agenda. It is composed of 56 members, 28 from governments, 14 from employers and 14 from workers. Ten government seats are reserved to the States of chief industrial importance (currently Brazil, China, France, Germany, India, Italy, Japan, Russian Federation, the UK and the US). The remaining seats are attributed by election by the General Conference, which splits into three electoral colleges (Governments, Employers, and Workers) to do so.

The International Labour Office, led by its Director-General, who is elected by the Governing Body for a five-year renewable mandate, is responsible for the daily life of the Organization, including the preparation of appropriate normative proposals, the providing of technical cooperation and the production of information, including statistics, and publications on labour issues.

2.4 International labour standards

As far as the adoption of international labour standards is concerned, the ILO Governing Body selects, based on suggestions drawn up by the Office, questions deserving of proposals for normative action, and puts them on the agenda of the General Conference, which discusses them on the basis of drafts prepared by the Office. Instruments may be adopted after a single or a double discussion, but normally discussions are required at two different sessions of the Conference for the adoption of a Convention.[8] Up to June 2007, 188 Conventions and 199 Recommendations have

---

8 On the International Labour Standards and the ILO supervisory mechanism, see: C.W. Jenks, *Human Rights and International Labour Standards*, New York, 1960; J.F. McMahon, 'The Legislative Techniques of the International Labour Organization', in *British Yearbook of International Law*, 1965/66, 25 ff; N. Valticos and F. Wolf, 'L'O.I.T. et les pays en voie de développement: techniques et mise en oeuvre des normes universelles', in Société française de droit international, *Pays en voie de développement et transformation du droit international*, Paris, 1974, 127 ff; L. Cox, 'The International Labour Organisation and Fundamental Rights at Work', *European Human Rights Law Review*, Vol. 4, 1999, 451–8. E.A. Landy, *The Effectiveness of International Supervision – Thirty Years of I.L.O. Experience*, London/ New York, 1966; N. Valticos, 'Un système de contrôle international: La mise en oeuvre des conventions internationales du travail', *Recueil des cours de l'Académie de droit international*

been adopted; however, this number includes instruments that have been revised or superseded, so the number of up-to-date instruments is less than half of the totals.[9]

Once adopted, international labour standards give rise to reporting obligations on the part of ILO Member States under articles 19 and 22 of the ILO Constitution. All Member States are in any event obliged to submit instruments adopted by the Conference to the national authorities within whose competence the matter lies for the enactment of legislation or other action and to report on the extent to which effect has been given or is proposed to be given to the provisions of Conventions and Recommendations. Concerning Conventions, Member States also have to report on possible difficulties preventing or delaying ratification. As far as ratified Conventions are concerned, ratifying countries are obliged to apply them in national law and practice and to report on their application at regular intervals. The regular supervisory system includes an independent body, the Committee of Experts on the Application of Conventions and Recommendations (CEACR, composed of 20 distinguished lawyers/judges serving in their individual capacity) and the General Conference itself, which examines the CEACR's report through its Committee on the Application of Standards. In addition, representation and complaint procedures can be initiated against countries for alleged violations of a Convention they have ratified (see articles 24 and 26 of the ILO Constitution). The latter may ultimately come before the International Court of Justice.

Furthermore, the International Labour Conference offers constituents the opportunity to adopt resolutions and conclusions that, while not binding in the sense of an international Convention (which is a treaty in international law) or subject to the supervisory procedures as in the case of Conventions and Recommendations, can provide guidance for the implementation of those instruments. Recent examples relevant to the abolition of child labour include the conclusions reached at the Conference in relation to ILO technical cooperation (in 2006) and to decent work and the informal economy (in 2002), an area in which much child labour is found.

---

de la Haye, 1968-I, Vol. 123, 311–407; A.J. Pouyat, 'Les normes et les procédures de l'O.I.T. en matière de liberté syndicale. Un bilan', *Revue internationale du travail*, 1982, 309 ff; ILO, *Rules of the Game: A Brief Introduction to International Labour Standards*, Geneva, 2005.

9 Employers and workers play a very important role in the international labour standards system. As a component of the Governing Body of the ILO, they contribute to choosing subjects for new standards and decide, with governments, whether a standard is to be adopted or not by the General Conference. Government reports requested during the preparatory phase must be submitted to representative employers' and workers' organizations, which may comment on them. States having ratified the Tripartite Consultation (International Labour Standards) Convention, 1976 (No. 144) are obliged to hold tripartite consultations on proposed new instruments to be discussed at the Conference, on submissions of instruments to the competent authorities, on reports concerning ratified conventions, on measures related to unratified conventions and recommendations, and on proposals regarding the denunciation of conventions. See ILO, *Rules of the Game: A Brief Introduction to International Labor Standards*, Geneva, 2005, 22.

2.5 The core conventions and the ILO Declaration on Fundamental Principles and Rights at Work

Eight ILO Conventions relating to four areas (namely freedom of association and effective recognition of the right to collective bargaining, the abolition of forced labour and child labour, and the elimination of discrimination in employment and occupation) have been identified by the ILO as being fundamental to the rights of people at work, irrespective of the level of development of individual Member States. The eight fundamental Conventions are:

- Freedom of Association and Protection of the Right to Organise Convention, 1948 (No. 87)
- Right to Organise and Collective Bargaining Convention, 1949 (No. 98)
- Forced Labour Convention, 1930 (No. 29)
- Abolition of Forced Labour Convention, 1957 (No. 105)
- Equal Remuneration Convention, 1951 (No. 100)
- Discrimination (Employment and Occupation) Convention, 1958 (No. 111)
- Minimum Age Convention, 1973 (No. 138)
- Worst Forms of Child Labour Convention, 1999 (No. 182).

In adopting the ILO Declaration on Fundamental Principles and Rights at Work and its Follow-Up at its 86th Session (Geneva, June 1998),[10] the Conference solemnly stated that the principles and rights set out in its Constitution and in the Declaration of Philadelphia have been expressed and developed in the form of specific rights and obligations in Conventions recognized as fundamental both inside and outside the Organization.[11] All Members, therefore, even if they have not ratified the Conventions in question, have an obligation arising from the very fact of membership in the Organization to respect, to promote and to realize, in good faith and in accordance with the Constitution, the principles concerning the fundamental rights which are the subject of those Conventions, namely:

- freedom of association and the effective recognition of the right to collective bargaining;
- the elimination of all forms of forced or compulsory labour;
- the effective abolition of child labour; and
- the elimination of discrimination in respect of employment and occupation.

---

10 *ILO Declaration on Fundamental Principles and Rights at Work,* available at <http://www.ilo.org/dyn/declaris/DECLARATIONWEB.static_jump?var_language=EN&var_page name=DECLARATIONTEXT>.

11 On the Declaration, see Swepston (this volume). See also: H. Kellerson, 'La Déclaration de 1998 de l'OIT sur les principes et les droits fondamentaux: un défi pour l'avenir?', *Revue internationale du travail,* 1999, 244; C. Di Turi, 'Globalizzazione dell'economia e diritti fondamentali in materia di lavoro', *Rivista di diritto internazionale,* 2000, 113 ff; A. Trebilcock, 'The ILO Declaration on Fundamental Principles and Rights at Work: A New Tool', in R. Blanpain and C. Engels (eds), *The ILO and the Social Challenges of the 21st Century: The Geneva Lectures,* The Hague, 2001.

Under the follow-up procedure, Member States that have not ratified one or more of the core conventions are asked to report each year on the status of the relevant rights and principles within their borders, noting impediments to ratification, and areas where assistance may be required. This reporting process, legally grounded in article 19 of the ILO Constitution, provides governments with an opportunity to state what measures they have taken towards achieving respect for the Declaration. It constitutes the 'Annual Review' foreseen by the Follow-Up to the Declaration.

Furthermore, each year the Office prepares a 'Global Report' on one of the four areas concerned. The Global Report, which is discussed during the General Conference, provides a 'dynamic global picture' of the current situation of the principles and rights expressed in the Declaration. The Global Report is an objective view of the global and regional trends of the issues relevant to the Declaration and serves to highlight those areas that require greater attention. Discussion of the Global Report serves as a basis for the Governing Body to determine priorities for technical cooperation. Global reports have also explored the interdependence of the four sets of fundamental principles and rights.

Global Reports on child labour remain one of the major sources of knowledge, including statistics, in this area. The worldwide trends in child labour from 2000 to 2004, published in the second *Global Report on Child Labour*,[12] are quite encouraging. According to the new estimates, the number of child labourers – in this period – fell by 11 per cent and the number of children involved in hazardous work declined by 26 per cent. Yet, there are still some 218 million child labourers. The situation definitely improved in Latin America and the Caribbean, but did so only slightly in Asia and the Pacific, while in Africa the number of child labourers actually increased.[13]

Finally, while not a standard, the ILO Tripartite Declaration of Principles on Multinational Enterprises and Social Policy, adopted by the ILO Governing Body, acts as a touchstone for such companies in relation to the elimination of child labour. Regular review of activities under that Declaration by a Governing Body Subcommittee provides a forum for, *inter alia*, exchange of good practices and other relevant information. This link to such enterprises is all the more important with the development of supply chains[14] that can end in micro-enterprises where the risk of child labour is particularly high.

2.6 Relevant conventions and recommendations

The main ILO instruments on child labour are the two fundamental Conventions cited above, namely the Minimum Age Convention, 1973 (No. 138), accompanied by Recommendation No. 146, and the Worst Forms of Child Labour Convention,

---

12 ILO, *The End of Child Labour: Within Reach – Global Report under the Follow-Up to the ILO Declaration on Fundamental Principles and Rights at Work*, Geneva, 2006.

13 ILO-IPEC, *IPEC Action Against Child Labour, Highlights 2006*, Geneva, 2007, at ix.

14 See S. Hayter, *The Social Dimension of Global Production Systems: A Review of the Issues*, Working Paper No. 25 (Policy Integration Department), Geneva, 2004.

1999 (No. 182), accompanied by Recommendation No. 190. These instruments are treated in depth elsewhere in this volume.

The 1973 Convention on Minimum Age, which is of general application in all fields of economic activity, followed a series of Conventions on Minimum Age in various industrial sectors that had started already in 1919, at the first International Labour Conference, which adopted the Minimum Age (Industry) Convention, 1919 (No. 5). The concept of minimum age for admission to employment was subsequently extended to various economic sectors,[15] until it was felt that a general approach was more appropriate and Convention No. 138 and Recommendation No. 146 were adopted in 1973.

Apart from instruments on minimum age, a number of Conventions and Recommendations on night work by children and young persons, as well as five Conventions and one Recommendation concerning the medical examination of young persons, were adopted between 1919 and 2007.[16]

While the Conventions on minimum age stress delaying the entry of children into the labour market in a phased manner, the Worst Forms of Child Labour Convention picks up and expands upon Convention 138's ban on any type of employment or work which, by its nature or the circumstances in which it is carried out, is likely to jeopardize the health, safety or morals of any person below the age of 18. Together, the instruments provide specificity to the general prohibition against exploitation in the United Nations Convention on the Rights of the Child (1989).

---

15 The Minimum Age (Sea) Convention, 1920 (No. 7); the Minimum Age (Agriculture) Convention, 1921 (No. 10); the Minimum Age (Trimmers and Stokers) Convention, 1921 (No. 15); the Minimum Age (Non-Industrial Employment) Convention, 1932 (No. 33); the Minimum Age (Sea) Convention (Revised), 1936 (No. 58); the Minimum Age (Industry) Convention (Revised), 1937 (No. 59); the Minimum Age (Non-Industrial Employment) Convention (Revised), 1937 (No. 60); the Minimum Age (Fishermen) Convention, 1959 (No. 112); the Minimum Age (Underground Work) Convention, 1965 (No. 123); and the Minimum Age (Non-Industrial Employment) Recommendation, 1932 (No. 41); the Minimum Age (Family Undertakings) Recommendation, 1937 (No. 52); the Minimum Age (Coal Mines) Recommendation, 1953 (No. 96); and the Minimum Age (Underground Work) Recommendation, 1965 (No. 124).

16 The Night Work of Young Persons (Industry) Convention, 1919 (No. 6); the Medical Examination of Young Persons (Sea) Convention, 1921(No. 16); the Night Work of Young Persons (Non-Industrial Occupations) Convention, 1946 (No. 79); the Medical Examination for Fitness for Employment in Industry of Children and Young Persons Convention, 1946 (No. 77); the Medical Examination of Young Persons (Non-Industrial Occupations) Convention, 1946 (No. 78); the Medical Examination of Young Persons Recommendation, 1946 (No. 79); the Night Work of Young Persons (Industry) Convention (Revised), 1948 (No. 90); the Night Work of Young Persons (Non-Industrial Occupations) Recommendation, 1946 (No. 80); Medical Examination of Young Persons (Underground Work) Convention, 1965 (No. 124), Conditions of Employment of Young Persons (Underground Work) Recommendation, 1965 (No. 125) and the Night Work Recommendation, 1990 (No.178).

The relevant Conventions in the area of fishing will be revised once the Work in Fishing Convention, 2007 (No. 188) enters into force; the related Recommendation, 2007 (No. 199) has already superseded the Work in Fishing Recommendation, 2005 (No. 196), which revised the Hours of Work (Fishing) Recommendation, 1920 (No. 7).

Furthermore, there are references in other instruments to those under 18 and to phenomena of key importance to them, such as apprenticeship, vocational training, social protection, child benefit, etc., as explored further below. A number of provisions in other Conventions thus deserve mention.

The Forced Labour Convention, 1930 (No. 29), which admitted in some cases regulated forced labour in an early epoch, did so only for 'adult able-bodied males who are of an apparent age of not less than 18 … years' (article 11 (1)).

The Labour Inspection Convention, 1947 (No. 81) mentions amongst the functions of the Labour Inspection the task to secure the enforcement of the legal provisions relating to conditions of work and the protection of workers, including '… the employment of children and young persons …' (article 3(1)(a)).[17] This instrument and its counterpart, the Labour Inspection (Agriculture) Convention, 1969 (No. 129), are key tools in the fight against child labour.

The Private Employment Agencies Convention, 1997 (No. 181) states that the States' Parties 'shall take measures to ensure that child labour is not used or supplied by private employment agencies' (article 9). In an era of increasing reliance on such agencies, this too is an important protection against resort to child labour.

The Social Policy (Non-Metropolitan Territories) Convention, 1947 (No. 82) provides that the employment of persons below the school-leaving age during the hours when schools are in session shall be prohibited in areas where educational facilities are provided on a scale adequate for the majority of the children (article 19 (3)).[18]

The Labour Standards (Non-Metropolitan Territories) Convention, 1947 (No. 83) stipulates as a general rule (with some exceptions) that children under the age of 15 years shall not be employed or work in any 'public or private industrial undertaking, or in any branch thereof' (article 2).

Several instruments dealing with occupational safety and health contain age-specific provisions. The Radiation Protection Convention, 1960 (No. 115) stipulates that no worker under the age of 16 shall be engaged in work involving ionising radiations (article 7 (2)) and differentiates the position of workers under 18 as to the appropriate protection from ionising radiations (article 7 (1) (b)).

The Maximum Weight Convention, 1967 (No. 127), which deals with regular manual transport of loads, provides for a special protection for 'young workers', whose assignment 'to manual transport of loads other than light loads shall be limited' (article 7 (1)). Article 1 (c) defines 'young workers' as workers 'under 18 years of age'.

The Benzene Convention, 1971 (No. 136) stipulates that: 'Young persons under 18 years of age shall not be employed in work processes involving exposure to benzene or products containing benzene: Provided that this prohibition need not apply to young persons undergoing education or training who are under adequate technical and medical supervision' (article 11 (2)).

---

17 The same is done by the Plantations Convention, 1958 (No. 110), art. 74(1)(a) and the Labour Inspection (Agriculture) Convention, 1969 (No. 129), art. 6(a).

18 The same is done by the Social Policy (Basic Aims and Standards) Convention, 1962 (No. 117) (art. 15).

The Occupational Safety and Health (Dock Work) Convention, 1979 (No. 152) stipulates that a lifting appliance or other cargo-handling appliance shall be operated only by a person who possesses the necessary aptitudes and experience or a person under training who is properly supervised and 'who is at least 18 years of age' (article 38 (2)).

The Safety and Health in Agriculture Convention, 2001 (No. 184) stipulates that the minimum age for assignment to work in agriculture which, by its nature or the circumstances in which it is carried out, is likely to harm the safety and health of young persons shall not be less than 18 years (article 16(1)). The types of employment or work to which this provision applies shall be determined by national laws and regulations or by the competent authority, after consultation with the representative organizations of employers and workers concerned (article 16(2)). However, national laws or regulations or the competent authority may, after consultation with the representative organizations of employers and workers concerned, authorize the performance of work referred to in that paragraph as from 16 years of age, on condition that appropriate prior training is given and the safety and health of the young workers are fully protected (article 16(3)).

The recently adopted Maritime Labour Convention, 2006 (MLC) contains a number of provisions aimed to protect young seafarers (often deriving from earlier instruments), as follows.

Standard A1.1, like Convention 180, which it revises, stipulates that 'Night work of seafarers under the age of 18 shall be prohibited' (Paragraph 2). The same Standard provides that:

> The employment, engagement or work of seafarers under the age of 18 shall be prohibited where the work is likely to jeopardize their health or safety. The types of such work shall be determined by national laws or regulations or by the competent authority, after consultation with the shipowners' and seafarers' organizations concerned, in accordance with relevant international standards (Paragraph 4).

Guideline B1.1 of the MLC states that, 'when regulating working and living conditions, Members should give special attention to the needs of young persons under the age of 18' (Paragraph 1).

Standard A1.2.7, dealing with seafarers' medical certificates, stipulates that 'a medical certificate shall be valid for a maximum period of two years *unless the seafarer is under the age of 18, in which case the maximum period of validity shall be one year* [emphasis added]' (Sub-paragraph (a)).

Guideline B2.4.4.1 provides for a number of special provisions that should apply, in principle, to all young seafarers under the age of 18, at sea and in port:

> (a) working hours should not exceed eight hours per day and 40 hours per week and overtime should be worked only where unavoidable for safety reasons;
> (b) sufficient time should be allowed for all meals, and a break of at least one hour for the main meal of the day should be assured; and
> (c) a 15-minute rest period as soon as possible following each two hours of continuous work should be allowed.

Guideline B2.4.4.1, dealing with young seafarers, provides that special measures should be considered with respect to young seafarers under the age of 18 who have served six months or any other shorter period of time under a collective agreement or seafarers' employment agreement without leave on a foreign-going ship which has not returned to their country of residence in that time, and will not return in the subsequent three months of the voyage. Such measures could consist of their repatriation at no expense to themselves to the place of original engagement in their country of residence for the purpose of taking any leave earned during the voyage.

Guideline B2.5.2.3, addressing implementation by Members, states that if, after young seafarers under the age of 18 have served on a ship for at least four months during their first foreign-going voyage, it becomes apparent that they are unsuited to life at sea, they should be given the opportunity of being repatriated at no expense to themselves from the first suitable port of call in which there are consular services of the flag State, or the State of nationality or residence of the young seafarer. Notification of any such repatriation, with the reasons therefor, should be given to the authority which issued the papers enabling the young seafarers concerned to take up seagoing employment.

Standard A.3.2 stipulates that no seafarer under the age of 18 shall be employed or engaged or work as a ship's cook.

Standard A4.3.2 (b), dealing with occupational safety and health, stipulates an obligation to pay 'special attention' to the safety and health of seafarers under the age of 18.[19]

The Protection of Young Seafarers Recommendation, 1976 (No. 153) calls for their effective protection, including the safeguarding of their health, morals and safety, and the promotion of their general welfare, as well as vocational guidance, education and training.

Furthermore, ILO instruments of general application that address vocational and other forms of initial training are of particular relevance to persons under the age of 18. These are most notably the Human Resources Development Convention, 1975 (No. 142) and the Human Resources Development Recommendation, 2004 (No. 195). The Convention, which foresees comprehensive and coordinated policies and programmes of vocational guidance and vocational training, refers to children and young persons explicitly (article 3). The more recent Recommendation – aimed in particular to enhance lifelong learning – refers to young persons who were denied education and training opportunities (Paragraph 8 (b)).

---

19 A number of relevant provisions are to be found in several Recommendations. For instance: Safety Provisions (Building) Recommendation, 1937 (No. 53), Regulation 26, paragraph 10; Social Policy in Dependent Territories Recommendation, 1944 (No. 70, withdrawn), arts 18 and 19 and Annex; Weekly Rest (Commerce and Offices) Recommendation, 1957 (No. 103), Provision 4 (1 and 2); Reduction of Hours of Work Recommendation, 1962 (No. 116), Provision 18; Vocational Training Recommendation, 1962 (No. 117), Provision 21 (1); Maximum Weight Recommendation, 1967 (No. 128), Provisions 1 (c) and 22; Vocational Training (Seafarers) Recommendation, 1970 (No. 137), Provision 12 (g); Benzene Recommendation, 1971 (No. 144), Provision 20; Protection of Young Seafarers Recommendation, 1976 (No. 153), *passim*; Asbestos Recommendation, 1986 (No. 172), Provision 1(3).

In addition, the Indigenous and Tribal Peoples' Convention, 1989 (No. 169) calls for education of children belonging to the peoples concerned in their own language as well as fluency in the national language or an official language (article 28). Such measures focus on what children's work should be: gaining an education and skills to equip them for the labour market once they have reached the minimum age for admission to employment.

Furthermore, ILO Conventions that deal with workers' families are of course especially pertinent to children, and contribute indirectly to combating child labour. The Conventions on minimum wage-fixing take as their point of departure the needs of workers and their families (Convention 26 and article 5(a) of Convention 131). With economic deprivation driving much child labour, minimum wages fixed at appropriate levels for adults can be strong deterrents to the exploitation of children. In a similar vein, ILO Conventions on collective bargaining – in particular the fundamental Convention 87 – act as an indirect deterrent to child labour.

A number of instruments in the field of social security contemplate support for children, in particular the Social Security (Minimum Provisions) Convention, 1952 (No. 102), part VII of which covers family benefit (specifically mentioning children). And of course combined with this is the Workers with Family Responsibilities Convention, 1981 (No.156) and accompanying Recommendation (No. 165) that are aimed at enabling working parents to have the time to care for their children and steer them away from exploitative practices.

The Migrant Workers Convention, 1949 (No.97) refers to members of such workers' families in articles 5 and 8, and the Migrant Workers (Supplementary Provisions) Convention, 1975 (No. 143) embraces family members under the general principle of equality of opportunity and treatment (article 10). The latter is expanded upon in the Migrant Workers Recommendation, 1975 (No. 151).

The body of up-to-date ILO Standards thus contains a range of provisions of direct and indirect relevance to children and young persons.

2.7 The ILO supervisory system

The ILO supervisory system is an essential element of the normative action of the Organization. It is commonly recognized that the mechanisms set out already in 1919 by the ILO Constitution in order to ensure proper supervision of the implementation of international labour standards, played a pioneering role in the international protection of human rights. They represented a model for post-World War II systems, including for the European human rights mechanism, based on the 1950 European Convention for the Protection of Human Rights and Fundamental Freedoms, as well as later UN initiatives.

Apart from a regular supervisory system, the ILO Constitution provides for *representations*, which may be filed by industrial associations (article 24), and *complaints*, open to Member States, to the Governing Body and even to individual delegates to the General Conference (article 26). In addition, special procedures exist in the domain of the protection of freedom of association.

The regular supervisory system is based on the obligation of Member States (under article 22 of the ILO Constitution) to report regularly on measures they have taken to give effect to the provisions of the ILO Conventions they have ratified. For practical reasons, the constitutional provision calling for reports on an annual basis is invoked by the Office with a lesser frequency: reports are requested every two years for the eight 'fundamental' conventions referred to above, including the Minimum Age and the Worst Forms of Child Labour Convention, and for four other Conventions that are classified as 'priority Conventions'.[20] As far as other ratified Conventions are concerned, reports are requested every five years, except for Conventions considered obsolete that are no longer supervised on a regular basis (these are the so-called 'shelved' Conventions).

The pillar of the regular supervisory system is the Committee of Experts on the Application of Conventions and Recommendations (CEACR). This body, which is not referred to in the ILO Constitution, was set up in 1926 by the Governing Body of the ILO. It is composed of 20 prominent 'jurisconsults' appointed by the Governing Body for a renewable term of office of three years (by the CEACR's own decision, this for up to a maximum of five terms). Its role is to provide an impartial and technical evaluation of the status of application of international labour standards.

The CEACR's annual report is submitted to the General Conference of the ILO, where it is examined by the Conference Committee on the Application of Standards. While the analysis of the Committee is technical, the consideration of the same issues by the Conference is obviously of a political nature, but based on a solid legal basis.

Two main tools are used by the CEACR when considering the implementation of a given international labour convention by a State having ratified it: the *direct request* and the *observation*.

When noting a possible problem, the Committee normally addresses to the concerned State a *direct request*, containing technical questions or requests of further information. Direct requests are not published in the Committee's report, although they are available on the Web.[21]

In most cases, the reply of the concerned State to the direct request meets the Committee's concerns. Where that is not the case, and notwithstanding the government's explanations the Committee still sees a fundamental question raised on the application of a particular Convention, then the Committee adopts an *observation*; that is, a published comment on such a question. The observation is included in the annual report, and thus submitted to the General Conference for its consideration.

Returning to the specific supervisory procedures mentioned above, article 24 of the ILO Constitution gives an industrial association of employers or workers the right to present to the ILO Governing Body a *representation* against any Member

---

20 The four 'priority conventions' are: the Labour Inspection Convention, 1947 (No. 81); the Labour Inspection (Agriculture) Convention, 1969 (No. 129); the Tripartite Consultation (International Labour Standards) Convention, 1976 (No. 144); and the Employment Policy Convention, 1964 (No. 122).

21 Direct requests are available at <http://www.ilo.org/ilolex>.

State which, in its view, has failed to properly implement a convention it has ratified. If it considers the representation receivable, the Governing Body appoints a three-member tripartite committee that submits to it a report setting out the legal and practical aspects of the case, examines the information and the considerations presented by the government concerned, and concludes with recommendations. The tripartite committee's report may be published along with the representation and the response, when the latter is not considered satisfactory.

The *complaint* referred to in article 26 of the ILO Constitution, again on the non-compliance with a ratified convention, may result, if the Governing Body so decides, in the appointment of a Commission of Inquiry, consisting of three independent members. The Commission of Inquiry investigates the complaint and adopts a report which normally includes recommendations. Its report is published. The concerned government may either accept the recommendations or appeal to the International Court of Justice (article 29(2) of the ILO Constitution), a step not yet taken by any ILO Member State. In case of non-compliance of the concerned government with the recommendations of the Commission of Inquiry, the Governing Body of the ILO may take action recommending to the General Conference any appropriate measure to secure compliance (article 33 of the ILO Constitution).

2.8 The ILO supervisory system and child labour

The extensive comments made by the CEACR in relation to Conventions 138 and 182 are explored in specific chapters of this volume. To date, no representation or complaint has been filed concerning either of these Conventions. However, a number of representations filed in relation to other Conventions concern child labour. As far as complaints are concerned, the case involving the failure by the Government of Myanmar to give effect to the Forced Labour Convention, 1930 (No. 29) is relevant in this context, as explored further below.

With regard to representations, for instance, the allegations made by the Latin American Central of Workers (Central latinoamericana de trabajadores – CLAT) under article 24 of the ILO Constitution concerning non-observance by Brazil of the Forced Labour Convention, 1930 (No. 29), and of the Abolition of Forced Labour Convention, 1957 (No. 105), regarding alleged forced labour by children, can as well be mentioned. The case concerned, in particular, charcoal production in Maciso Florestal de Ribas do Río Pardo, Aguas Claras, Tres Lagoas and Navirai. It was found, *inter alia*, that children were not going to school but working at the site to help their parents; the children removed the charcoal from the ovens, where they were exposed to considerable risk, and there were countless accidents using the shovels. Furthermore, a report submitted by the government referred to a system of slave labour imposed on more than 1,500 rural workers, including about 150 children and adolescents in haciendas (*barreiras*) involved in the production of soy and tomatoes. The government likewise communicated the report of the Secretary of State of Justice and Citizenship of the State of Espíritu Santo (1993) concerning the complaint lodged by SINTRAL (Trade Union of Forestry and Firewood Workers from the North of the State of Espíritu Santo), which alleged the existence of slave labour involving 12,000 workers in the northern part of the state. The official government investigation revealed the existence of a situation of actual slave labour involving over 1,200 workers, including children between 9 and 11 years of age, who were being used by the '*empreteiras*' (service enterprises) working for large enterprises in the wood sector. The officials' report stated that the phenomenon known in Brazil as '*tercerizaçao*' (intermediate enterprises providing services for large enterprises or economic groups), which is aimed at getting more out of the manpower employed, encourages the exploitation of workers in conditions of slavery as well as impunity for large enterprises that benefit from such practices. A number of remedial actions were recommended by the tripartite committee appointed under article 24 of the ILO Constitution.[22]

Another representation lodged under article 24 of the ILO Constitution, by the Union of Workers of the Autonomous University of Mexico (STUNAM) and the Independent Union of Workers of La Jornada (SITRAJOR), on the alleged non-observance by Mexico of the Indigenous and Tribal Peoples Convention, 1989 (No. 169), raised issues concerning child labour. In particular, the tripartite committee noted that with regard to the situation of indigenous children, the complainants stated that the presence of soldiers and military operations had led to substantial displacements in indigenous areas, and that indigenous children who had migrated to the cities encountered enormous difficulties in continuing their schooling. The committee referred to the results of an investigation carried out in Sinaloa in 1994. It stated that visits carried out in 1999 and 2000 showed that the information from the first investigation continued to be relevant. In Sinaloa, 25 per cent of agricultural day labourers were younger than 14, 30 per cent were not registered or had no documents, 95 per cent did not have holidays, 80 per cent did not have a rest day, 50 per cent had been working for three years or longer and 100 per cent were not paid when off sick. The committee stated that, according to the Miguel Agustín Projuárez Human Rights Centre, in 1999 there were even children of 5 years of age working in family groups. These allegations were not substantially challenged by the government. A number of remedial actions were recommended by the tripartite committee.[23]

With regard to the complaint involving Myanmar,[24] it was initiated by 25 workers' delegates to the 83rd Session of the International Labour Conference (June 1996). It referred to the non-observance by Myanmar of the Forced Labour Convention, 1930

---

22 Governing Body, *Report of the Committee set up to examine the representation made by the Latin American Central of Workers (CLAT) under article 24 of the ILO Constitution alleging non-observance by Brazil of the Forced Labour Convention, 1930 (No. 29), and the Abolition of Forced Labour Convention, 1957 (No. 105)*, doc. (GB.264/16/7), Doc. No. (ilolex): 161995BRA029.

23 Governing Body, *Report of the Committee set up to examine the representation alleging non-observance by Mexico of the Indigenous and Tribal Peoples Convention, 1989 (No. 169), made under article 24 of the ILO Constitution by the Union of Workers of the Autonomous University of Mexico (STUNAM) and the Independent Union of Workers of La Jornada (SITRAJOR)*, doc. GB.282/15/3, GB.289/17/3, Doc. No. (ilolex): 162004MEX169A.

24 See the *Report of the Commission of Inquiry appointed under article 26 of the Constitution of the International Labour Organization to examine the observance by Myanmar of the Forced Labour Convention, 1930 (No. 29)*, 1996, Doc. GB.267/16/2, GB.268/14/8, GB.268/15/1), Doc. No. (ilolex): 151998BUR029.

(No. 29). The Governing Body of the ILO established a Commission of Inquiry, which finalized its report on 2 July 1998. The government's continued failure to implement the recommendations of this Commission of Inquiry has led the ILO to take unprecedented action under article 33 of its Constitution, and the matter is under regular review by its Governing Body and the International Labour Conference. The situation in Myanmar had already been brought to the attention of ILO[25] and UN[26] bodies at earlier dates.

The Commission of Inquiry found that children were fully involved in the forced labour practices widespread in Myanmar. Its conclusions state that, 'Forced labour in Myanmar is widely performed by women, *children* [emphasis added] and elderly persons as well as persons otherwise unfit for work'.[27] The Commission also found that the exaction of forced labour *inter alia* was preventing 'children from attending school'[28] and noted in its findings that there was 'regular forced recruitment throughout Myanmar, *including that of minors* [emphasis added], into the Tatmadaw and various militia groups, and that this did not occur pursuant to any compulsory military service laws, but arbitrarily'.[29]

Moreover, in its comments over the years, the CEACR has identified links between the prevention of child labour and certain ILO Conventions that, on the face of it, deal with a quite different subject matter. A clear example are its comments under the Discrimination (Employment and Occupation) Convention, 1958 (No. 111), where the Experts have seen the connection between measures to provide equality of opportunity in education and training for girls with the prevention of child labour among this particularly vulnerable group. Such comments buttress

---

See also *Concluding observations of the Committee on the Rights of the Child: Myanmar*, UN doc. CRC/C/15/Add.69 of 24 January 1997.

25 Myanmar's violations of the Convention (No. 29) had been criticized by the ILO's supervisory bodies for 30 years. In 1995, and again in 1996, they have been the subject of special paragraphs in the reports of the Committee on the Application of Conventions and Recommendations, and in 1996, the government was also singled out by the Committee for its 'continued failure to implement' the Convention. In addition, in November 1994, the Governing Body adopted the report of the tripartite Committee it had established to examine the representation under Article 24 of the ILO Constitution, filed by the International Confederation of Free Trade Unions (ICFTU) against the Government of Myanmar for its failure to ensure effective observance of Convention No. 29 (doc. GB.261/13/7).

26 The human rights situation in Myanmar was first examined by a United Nations body when the Commission on Human Rights considered the question in 1990 under the procedure established by Economic and Social Council resolution 1503. At the time of the complaint, the General Assembly, the Commission on Human Rights and certain of its subsidiary bodies, the Secretary-General and the Committee on the Rights of the Child were following closely the question of forced labour in the country.

27 § 531 of the cited *Report*. See also §§ 291, 302, 314, 323, 343, 368, 375, 384, 416, 430, 437, 456 and 511 of the same *Report*.

28 § 533 of the cited *Report*.

29 See § 489 of the cited *Report*. See also § 477.

efforts by the ILO's International Programme for the Elimination of Child Labour (IPEC) to strengthen the gender dimension of its work.[30]

2.9 Other ILO legal action buttressing international labour standards

In addition to adopting Conventions, Recommendations and Declarations, and monitoring their implementation through (respectively) the ILO supervisory machinery and the Follow-Up to the 1998 Declaration, the ILO has drawn on other legal tools to push for the elimination of child labour.

Under article 10 of the Constitution, the International Labour Office is charged with collecting and distributing information 'on all subjects relating to the international adjustment of conditions of industrial life and labour' and conducting 'special investigations as may be ordered by the Conference or by the Governing Body' (article 10(1)). A corollary is its task of editing and issuing 'publications dealing with problems of industry and employment of international interest' (article 10(2)(d)).

The Office has turned its attention to child labour chiefly in three periods: the early years of the organization, when the first instruments on minimum age were adopted; the period of intense activity related to employment in the 1970s with the World Employment Programme, when the focus was on the role of children in labour markets,[31] and more recently, beginning with the creation of an interdepartmental programme on child labour within the Office in the early 1990s, which led to the establishment of a special unit, the International Programme on the Elimination of Child Labour (IPEC), in 1992.[32] This latter period has coincided with the growing acceptance of the rights-based approach to development, of which the elimination of child labour is a prime example, and with increasing attention of the world community to poverty eradication.

In relation to poverty, the adoption of the Millennium Development Goals (MDGs) and targets following the Millennium Summit of 2000 has stimulated considerable thinking about improving measurement of progress towards goals such as the eradication of extreme poverty and hunger (MDG 1) and the achievement of universal primary education (MDG 3). In arguing that attainment of the Decent Work Agenda is an essential element for reaching the MDGs,[33] the ILO has drawn upon its normative instruments in terms of both substance and measurement.

The International Conference of Labour Statisticians, which is convened periodically under the auspices of the ILO, will have before it a background

---

30 ILO, *Gender Equality and Child Labour: A Tool for Facilitators*, Geneva, various dates in various languages.

31 See, for example, G. Rodgers and G. Standing (eds), *Child Work, Poverty and Underdevelopment*, Geneva, 1981.

32 See ILO-IPEC, *IPEC Action Against Child Labour: Achievements, Lessons Learned and Indications for the Future (1998–1999)*, Geneva, 1999.

33 ILO, *Decent Work and the Millennium Development Goals: An Information Folder*, Geneva, 2005; ILO, *Working Out of Poverty*, Report of the Director-General, International Labour Conference, 20th Session, Geneva, 2003.

document and proposals on child labour statistics for examination at its 18th session (24 November–5 December 2008). 'A set of agreed international statistical standards on child labour for its measurement, as foreseen, will be a critical element in the work towards a world without child labour.'[34] The area of gender-disaggregated statistics provides an additional example of how the ILO's legal framework serves as a basis for the development of practical tools for use by countries, in this case giving them internationally comparable methods of measuring child labour through a series of indicators. In one reflection of the role of the Office under article 10 of the Constitution, considerable thinking has gone into the means of measurement of child labour and building the evidence-base linking its reduction to development. A wider and deeper evidence-base in turn reinforces the degree to which international development institutions are willing to support country efforts to eliminate child labour and to recognize the value of relevant labour standards. Using other constitutional provisions (§ IV(c) and (e) of the Declaration of Philadelphia), the ILO also looks at the economic and financial policies being recommended by others to see if they are in fact contributing to social justice. The recent analysis by the ILO's IPEC Programme of conditional cash transfers in relation to reducing child labour is a case in point.[35]

It can be argued that the greatest impact has been through the assistance provided to Member States under article 10(2)(b) of the Constitution, whereby the Office draws on its normative instruments, the strengths of tripartism, and good practices derived from experience about what works and what does not at the national level. The classic area of technical assistance of the Office in the 'framing of laws and regulations' and the elimination of child labour is a central part of the ILO's Labour Legislation Guidelines.[36] It is also common for technical cooperation programmes focusing on the elimination of child labour to contain a legal component.[37] This assistance involves work relating to the formal and the informal economies.[38]

Such initiatives exist on a much larger scale than would otherwise be possible through reliance on another legal tool of the ILO: the agreements it has concluded. These include cooperation agreements with its Member States, both those committing to participate in activities with the ILO's IPEC programme, and those providing

---

34 ILO-IPEC, *IPEC Action Against Child Labour 2004–2005: Progress and Future Priorities*, Geneva, 2006, 62.

35 ILO-IPEC, *IPEC Action Against Child Labour: Highlights 2006*, Geneva, 2007, 60–61, and sources cited therein.

36 The Labour Legislation Guidelines are available at <http://www.ilo.org/public/english/dialogue/ifpdial/llg/main.htm>.

37 M. Vega Ruiz, *Libertad de asociación, libertad sindical y el reconocimiento efectivo del derecho denegociación colectiva en América Latina: el desarollo práctico de un principio fundamental*, Working Paper No. 28 of the InFocus Programme on Promoting the Declaration, Geneva, 2004.

38 For a discussion of the issues confronted, see A. Trebilcock, 'Using Development Approaches to Address the Challenge of the Informal Economy for Labour Law', in G. Davidov and B. Langille (eds), *Boundaries and Frontiers of Labour Law*, Oxford, 2006, and J.L. Daza, *Informal Economy, Undeclared Work and Labour Administration*, DIALOGUE Working Paper No. 9, Geneva, 2005.

technical cooperation funds to make it possible for the ILO to assist them to do so. Child labour by far attracts the most bilateral and multilateral support to the ILO.

ILO agreements with other public international organizations,[39] development banks,[40] institutions such as the Inter-Parliamentary Union,[41] and regional institutions have also played an important role in addressing child labour, along with other issues.[42] The ILO cooperates with the Global Compact (of which one of the four labour principles is the abolition of child labour), and draws on the ILO Declaration on Multinationals in doing so. The ILO has also entered into partnerships to combat child labour; the best known of these are those concluded in the garment sector in Bangladesh and in soccer ball production in Pakistan. Moreover, while not directly involving the Office, agreements reached between the peak bodies of employers and workers (the International Organization of Employers and the International Trade Union Confederation, which provide the secretariats for the Employers' and Workers' groups within the ILO) have lent critical political support to the fight against child labour. Working with the Office, the social partners draw on ILO instruments as a basis for their advocacy work – as illustrated in the most recent highlights of IPEC's work.[43]

The effective abolition of child labour thus remains, as it was at the time the ILO was founded in 1919, one of the most important priorities of the Organization.

2.10 Issues in debate

In a sense, the issues in debate around child labour are those painted on the larger canvases of controversy in public international law and in development policy: the degree of effectiveness of international labour standards and how their impact is measured;[44] the various paths to development in different cultural, social and economic circumstances, and the quest for greater coherence between policies at the global and national levels.

---

39 See, for example, the agreement concluded between the ILO and FAO, which refers to respect for fundamental principles and rights at work, 7 September 2004, available at <http://www.ilo.org/public/english/bureau/leg/agreements/fao3.htm>.

40 See, for example, the standards toolkit developed together by the Asian Development Bank and the ILO, later followed by conclusion of a framework agreement between the two institutions, available at <http://www.ilo.org/public/english/bureau/leg/agreements/asdb.htm>.

41 The Agreement, concluded in 1999, makes explicit reference to the Fundamental Principles and Rights at Work contained in the 1998 Declaration. See <http://www.ilo.org/public/english/bureau/leg/agreements/ipu.htm>.

42 See, for example, the agreements with the OAS, the African Union, the Arab League, and the exchange of letters with the European Commission. The text is available at <http://www.ilo.org/public/english/bureau/leg/rel_org.htm>.

43 ILO-IPEC, *IPEC Action Against Child Labour: Highlights 2006*, Geneva, 2007, 53–7.

44 G. Politakis (ed.), *Protecting Labour Rights as Human Rights*, Proceedings of International Colloquium on the 80th Anniversary of the ILO Committee of Experts on the Application of Conventions and Recommendations (Geneva 24–25 November 2006), Geneva, 2007.

Child labour is both a cause and a symptom of poverty. In its worst forms, it robs children of their health, their education and even their lives. As long as poverty pushes some families to send their children to work, the next generation is condemned to the same fate.[45]

As the second Global Report on child labour under the Declaration Follow-Up highlighted:

> … the most pressing challenge ahead is strengthening the worldwide movement as the principal catalyst for more effective mainstreaming of child labour concerns at the national level, where the battle against child labour is waged and must be won.[46]

The ILO's legal activities and tools are critical means for reaching that goal.

---

45 ILO, *Working Out of Poverty*, Report of the Director-General, International Labour Conference, 91st session, 2003, 10.

46 ILO, *The End of Child Labour Within Reach*, *supra* note 12, 84.

Chapter 3

Limiting the Minimum Age: Convention 138 and the Origin of the ILO's Action in the Field of Child Labour

Matteo Borzaga

3.1 Introduction

The efforts of the International Labour Organization (ILO) to limit the minimum age for admission to employment or work have a remote origin: the first Convention on this issue was adopted in 1919, the year when the organization was founded.[1]

The reason why the ILO's activities in this field began so early is straightforward: starting from the second part of the 19th century and the industrial revolution, children (and women) were considered in need of legal protection because of their particular vulnerability compared to adult male workers. Actually, this need of protection of children (and women) from abuse by their employers at the beginning of the industrial era was the most important reason for the creation of labour law in general, first at the national and subsequently at the international level.[2]

One of the first national regulations about child labour, for example, was the French law of 1841 that fixed the minimum age for admission to employment or work at 8 years of age and certainly represented an important model, together with other similar domestic regulations, for the first international rules on this issue.[3]

Concerning the international level, it is important to point out that the fight against child labour was not only the subject of one of the first ILO Conventions, but was also considered a core task of the Organization: in fact, in the first version of the Preamble to the ILO Constitution of 1919[4] the protection of children and

---

1 Minimum Age (Industry) Convention, 1919, <www.ilo.org/ilolex/english/index.htm>.

2 See N. Valticos, *Droit international du travail*, Paris: Dalloz, 1983, at 458.

3 N. Valticos and G. von Potobsky, *International Labour Law*, Deventer, Boston: Kluwer, 1995, at 216.

4 Preamble to the ILO Constitution; B. Creighton, 'Combating Child Labour: The Role of International Labour Standards', *Comparative Labour Law & Policy Journal*, Vol. 18, Spring 1997, 362 ff, at 364. See also art. 427 of the Treaty of Versailles of 1919 that established the special and urgent importance of some labour matters. In particular, point 6 of this provision affirmed the necessity of the '"abolition" of child labour and the imposition of such limitations on the labour of young persons as shall permit the continuation of their education and assure their proper physical development'. On this norm, see B. Hepple, *Labour Laws and Global Trade*, Oxford and Portland OR: Hart, 2005, at 30 and 31.

young persons was regarded, among other matters, as fundamental to improving the working and living conditions of employees.

Therefore, in 1919 the ILO started a very wide activity against child labour, with particular regard to three different fields of intervention: the fixing of a minimum age for the admission to employment or work; the prohibition (with exceptions) of night work for children, and the establishment of compulsory medical examination for working persons under 18 years of age.[5]

Among these three fields of intervention, the most important efforts of the ILO in combating child labour, at least in the first fifty years of the Organization, concentrated on the limitation of the minimum age for the admission to employment or work, as demonstrated by the Conventions adopted on this issue; 10 in all between 1919 and 1965. As will be explained in the next section, these various Conventions concerned different economic sectors and had diverse contents. In 1973, the International Labour Conference (ILC) decided to adopt a general consolidated convention, fixing a minimum age valid for all economic sectors and thus having a very broad scope.

This convention – the C138 Minimum Age Convention of 1973[6] – is characterized by a certain degree of flexibility, but has been accused, in the last decades, of reflecting a rigid Western or Eurocentric approach to the fight against child labour. The reason for this seemingly inconsistent view is that Convention 138, as the previous ones, was certainly based on a Western view of the problem of child labour, because of the Western countries' predominance amongst the ILO membership of those years. In that context, the flexibility clauses included in Convention 138 were considered by the ILO and its earliest Member States flexible enough to foster the ratification of the Convention and its subsequent implementation not only in developed countries, but also in the new developing Member States. This belief rapidly collided with the difficulties of the new Member States, which resulted from decolonization, in ratifying the Conventions on minimum age for admission to employment or work, both the previous ones and Convention 138, in spite of the flexibility clauses provided for by the latter. The difficulties of the new Member States in ratifying especially Convention 138 were due to legal and economic as well as cultural reasons. For those States it was very hard, if not impossible, to ratify and implement a Convention including substantive provisions that 'are highly prescriptive in character'.[7] This is clearly confirmed by the number of ratifications of Convention 138, which, until 1998, was very low (only 46), especially when compared to the number of ratifications of the other Conventions constituting the so-called 'core labour standards'.[8]

---

5 Valticos and von Potobsky, *International Labour Law*, *supra* note 3, at 216.

6 Convention concerning Minimum Age for Admission to Employment, adopted at the 58th Session of the International Labour Conference (26 June 1973) and entered into force 19 June 1976. This Convention has been ratified by 150 Member States (31 July 2007) and is available at <www.ilo.org/ilolex/english/index.htm>.

7 Creighton, 'Combating Child Labour', *supra* note 4, at 372.

8 About the core labour standards, see *infra*, section 3.4. As mentioned, in 1998 the Minimum Age Convention 138 of 1973 had been ratified by only 46 countries, whereas, for example, the C29 Forced Labour Convention of 1930 had been ratified by 146 countries, the C87 Freedom of Association and Protection of the Right to Organize Convention of 1948

This lack of ratifications of Convention 138 provoked a crisis of the standard-setting process in the field of child labour that persisted until 1996, when the Governing Body decided to place the adoption of a new Convention on the agenda of the ILC of 1998.[9]

Meanwhile, however, the approach of the ILO to the problem of child labour changed considerably: the development of globalization[10] and delocalization processes caused Western public opinion to become increasingly aware of the abuses perpetrated against child workers by employers from developed countries with production sites in the developing world. That situation, and the consequent reactions and protests of public opinion in Western countries, induced the ILO to adopt new strategies. First, the Organization started a public information campaign about child labour, characterized, in particular, by the dissemination of data and studies. Secondly, in 1991 the ILO launched the International Program for the Elimination of Child Labour (IPEC), in order to provide technical cooperation to the developing countries that wanted to eliminate the hateful forms of child labour.[11] In other words, the attention of the Organization shifted from the original idea that the fixing of a minimum age could be sufficient to guarantee the real elimination of child labour, to the belief that this problem was (and is) so widespread that it could be solved only gradually, providing for different tools.

Hence, the ILO decided to supplement the Minimum Age Convention 138 with a new one that embodied the new approach of the Organization to the problem of child labour. In 1999 the ILC approved the C182 Worst Forms of Child Labour

---

by 121 countries and the C111 Discrimination (Employment and Occupation) Convention of 1958 by 129 countries. For more details see F. Maupain, 'Revitalisation Not Retreat: The Real Potential of the 1998 ILO Declaration for the Universal Protection of Workers' Rights', *European Journal of International Law*, Vol. 16, No. 3, 2005, 439 ff, at 455. See also D. M. Smolin, 'Conflict and Ideology in the International Campaign against Child Labour', *Hofstra Labor & Employment Law Journal*, Vol. 16, Spring, 1999, 383 ff, at 420 and 421.

9 Creighton, 'Combating Child Labour', *supra* note 4, at 367 and 368.

10 B. Creighton, 'The Future of Labour Law: Is There a Role for International Labour Standards?', in C. Barnard, S. Deakin and G.S. Morris (eds), *The Future of Labour Law. Liber Amicorum Sir Bob Hepple QC*, Oxford and Portland OR: Hart, 2004, 253 ff, at 262 ff; L.R. Helfer, 'Understanding Change in International Organisations: Globalisation and Innovation at the ILO', *Vanderbilt Law Review*, Vol. 59, April, 2006, 651 ff., at 704 ff.; B. Hepple, 'New Approaches to International Labour Regulation', *Industrial Law Journal*, Vol. 26, No. 4, December 1997, 353 ff, at 353, 354 and 355.

11 See S. Hoffman and H. J. Maaßen, 'Der Kampf gegen die Kinderarbeit – Eine entwicklungspolitische Aufgabe der Internationalen Arbeitsorganisation', in Bundesministerium für Arbeit und Sozialordnung, Bundesvereinigung der Deutschen Arbeitgeberverbände and Deutscher Gewerkschaftsbund (eds), *Weltfriede durch soziale Gerechtigkeit. 75 Jahre Internationale Arbeitsorganisation*, Baden-Baden: Nomos Verlagsgesellschaft, 1994, 225 ff, at 234 ff; M.G. Davidson, 'The International Labour Organisation's Latest Campaign to End Child Labor: Will it Succeed Where Others Have Failed?', *Transnational Law & Contemporary Problems*, Vol. 11, Spring, 2001, 203 ff, at 210 and 211; B.M. Celek, 'The International Response to Child Labor in the Developing World: Why are we Ineffective', *Georgetown Journal on Poverty Law & Policy*, Vol. 11, Winter, 2004, 88 ff, at 101 and 102.

Convention,[12] addressing, as the title of the Convention shows, only some particularly grave kinds of child labour, in order to progressively eliminate at least those. In this context, the preamble of Convention 182 confirms that Convention 138 remains a fundamental instrument on child labour.[13] However, as mentioned above, the approaches underlying these two tools are very different, thus posing the problem of their coordination.

It is particularly interesting to assess what role the prescriptive regulations provided for by Convention 138 can play in the more programmatic perspective of Convention 182. This evaluation necessarily has to take into account that both Conventions are included among the four fundamental principles and rights at work, established by the so-called ILO Declaration of Geneva of 1998 and have, for this reason, the same fundamental status.[14]

In the following pages the ILO minimum age Conventions and the main contents of Convention 138 will be examined in this perspective, trying in particular to answer the question, if the latter really is a Western-centric tool. In this context, I will try to assess if Convention 138 has a programmatic or a prescriptive character, analysing its flexibility clauses and exceptions. This analysis will allow us to understand if these clauses and exceptions make Convention 138 flexible enough to favour its implementation not only in the developed, but also in the developing countries. Concerning this last point, the role of the Committee of Experts on the Application of Conventions and Recommendations (CEACR) in interpreting Convention 138 will be examined, because of the importance of the ILO's 'jurisprudence' for the national implementation of the ILO standards. Finally, the impact of the new ILO approach to the fight against child labour and Convention 182 of 1999 on the traditional minimum age instruments will be assessed, taking into account the fundamental status recognized to both tools on child labour by the Declaration of Geneva of 1998.

3.2 A historical overview of the first ILO activities in limiting the minimum age

As mentioned above, between 1919 and 1965 the ILC adopted 10 conventions concerning the minimum age for admission to employment or work and subsequently decided to consolidate all of these in the general C138 Minimum Age Convention of 1973.[15]

---

12 See, in general, M.J. Dennis, 'The ILO Convention on the Worst Forms of Child Labour', *American Journal of International Law*, Vol. 93, No. 4, 1999, 943 ff.

13 See Preamble of C182 Worst Forms of Child Labour Convention, 1999.

14 Regarding the Declaration of Geneva of 1998, see *infra*, section 3.4 and more particularly Swepston (this volume). See also H. Kellerson, 'The ILO Declaration of 1998 on Fundamental Principles and Rights: A Challenge for the Future', *International Labour Review*, Vol. 137, No. 2, 1998, 223 ff; P. Alston, '"Core Labour Standards" and the Transformation of the International Labour Rights Regime', *European Journal of International Law*, Vol. 15, No. 3, 2004, 457 ff; Maupain, 'Revitalization Not Retreat', *supra* note 8, at 439 ff.

15 About the earliest ILO conventions regarding the minimum age for admission to employment or work, see, in general, Smolin, 'Conflict and Ideology', *supra* note 8, at 408

The conventions can be divided into two groups: the earlier ones, adopted between 1919 and 1932, and the later ones, approved between 1936 and 1965.

The first group of conventions – consisting of the C5 Minimum Age (Industry) Convention of 1919, the C7 Minimum Age (Sea) Convention of 1920, the C10 Minimum Age (Agriculture) Convention of 1921, the C15 Minimum Age (Trimmers and Stokers) Convention of 1921 and the C33 Minimum Age (Non-Industrial Employment) Convention of 1932 – establishes a minimum age for admission to employment or work of 14 years, each one with regard to a particular economic sector.[16]

These early conventions also contained some exceptions and rudimentary flexibility clauses.[17] More particularly, Convention 5 of 1919 provided for an exception to the general rule of the minimum age of 14 years regarding children employed in family undertakings[18] and attending technical schools,[19] plus a flexibility clause that, in accordance with article 19(3) of the ILO Constitution, provided for a particular regulation for Japan (article 5) and excluded India from its scope (article 6).[20] Convention 7 established similar rules and exceptions for the sea sector, but contained no flexibility clauses. Regarding agriculture, Convention 10 of 1921 envisaged a less rigid regulation by stipulating that children under the age of 14 should not be employed in this sector, save outside school hours and that, in any case, their employment should not jeopardize their school attendance (article 1).[21]

With the two last Conventions of this period, the ILO, in addition to the establishment of a minimum age for admission to employment or work, also began to differentiate between work, light work and dangerous work.[22] The first step in this direction was taken by Convention 15 of 1921, with regard to the minimum age for people working as trimmers and stokers on ships and boats. In view of the hazards connected with these jobs, the ILC established a higher minimum age of 18 years (article 1), with some exceptions,[23] and flexibility clauses, again concerning Japan

---

and ff; Valticos, *Droit international du travail*, *supra* note 2, at 460 ff; Valticos and von Potobsky, *International Labour Law*, *supra* note 3, at 217 ff.

16 See art. 2 of Convention 5 of 1919, art. 2 of Convention 7 of 1920, art. 1 of Convention 10 of 1921, art. 2 of Convention 22 of 1932. The different sectors covered by each Convention were defined by the Convention itself, usually in its first article. On this point see also Committee of Experts on the Application of Conventions and Recommendations (CEACR), *General Survey of the Reports relating to Convention No. 138 and Recommendation No. 146 Concerning Minimum Age*, Geneva: ILO, 1981, 1 ff, at 5 and 6.

17 Regarding flexibility clauses, see, in general, Valticos and von Potobsky, *International Labour Law*, *supra* note 3, at 57 ff.

18 Article 2 of Convention 5 of 1919 defines these as undertakings 'in which only members of the same family are employed'.

19 As established by art. 3 of Convention 5 of 1919.

20 See, on this point, Smolin, 'Conflict and Ideology', *supra* note 8, at 410; CEACR, *General Survey*, *supra* note 16, at 8 and 9.

21 Valticos, *Droit International du travail*, *supra* note 2, at 461.

22 CEACR, *General Survey*, *supra* note 16, at 7 and 8.

23 Provided by art. 3(a) and (b) of the Convention 15 of 1921.

and India.[24] The idea of differentiating among work typologies was confirmed by Convention 33 of 1932, concerning non-industrial work in general. This instrument reaffirmed the minimum age of 14 years (article 2), but also established that children over 12 years of age could be employed in light work (article 4), and that ratifying States could fix a higher minimum age than the one of 14 years for 'any employment which, by its nature, or the circumstances in which it is to be carried on, is dangerous to the life, health or morals of the persons employed in it' (article 5).[25] It is also important to note that Convention 33 of 1932 for the first time established a connection between minimum age and school attendance, affirming that children over 14 years of age could not be employed if they had not finished primary school, in accordance with the relevant national laws and regulations (article 2).[26]

The second group of Conventions – consisting of the C58 Minimum Age (Sea) Convention (Revised) of 1936, the C59 Minimum Age (Industry) Convention (Revised) of 1937, the C60 Minimum Age (Non-Industrial Employment) Convention (Revised) of 1937, the C112 Minimum Age (Fishermen) Convention of 1959 and the C123 Minimum Age (Underground Work) Convention of 1965 – was characterized (except for Convention 123 of 1965[27]) by the establishment of a minimum age of 15 years.[28] In particular, Conventions 58, 59 and 60 formally constituted revisions of the previous conventions, in order to increase the minimum age.[29]

Regarding the specific contents of these Conventions, the most comprehensive ones certainly were Conventions 59 and 60 of 1937. The first applied to the industry sector and, besides setting the minimum age of 15 years, provided for some other regulations, in particular exceptions and (still rudimentary) flexibility clauses. Concerning the exceptions, Convention 59 affirmed that children under the age of 15 years could be employed in family undertakings, if such employments were not dangerous to their life, health or morals and, in any case, only if this possibility were admitted by national laws (article 2(2)). In comparison with the revised Convention 5 of 1919, Convention 59 of 1937 surely provided for stricter regulation on this point. Furthermore, the latter established another exception with regard to children attending technical schools, who were excluded from the personal scope of the Convention. Concerning flexibility clauses, special provisions were adopted, in 1919, for some explicitly mentioned Member States; that is, Japan (article 6), India (article 7) and China (article 8). Finally, it is important to point out that Convention 59 of 1937 introduced – for the first time in the industry sector – the possibility for Member States to adopt national laws establishing a minimum age higher than 15 years for dangerous employments. Instead, it said nothing about the possibility of relating the minimum age to school attendance.

---

24 See art. 3(c) of the Convention 15 of 1921.

25 Smolin, 'Conflict and Ideology', *supra* note 8, at 411 and 412.

26 Valticos and von Potobsky, *International Labour Law*, *supra* note 3, at 217 and 218.

27 In this case the minimum age for admission to underground work had to be decided by the ratifying member state: however, it could not be less than 16 years. See art. 2 of Convention 123 of 1965.

28 CEACR, *General Survey*, *supra* note 16, at 6 and 7.

29 See Valticos, *Droit international du travail*, *supra* note 2, at 462 and 463.

Convention 60 of 1937, which revised Convention 33 of 1932, concerns non-industrial employment and appears to have been the most advanced minimum age tool before the approval of the consolidated Convention 138 of 1973. In addition to establishing a minimum age of 15 years and containing provisions similar to the ones of Convention 59, Convention 60 also reasserted the distinction between work, light work and dangerous work which was introduced in 1932, and accordingly provided for a differentiated minimum age. The Convention established that children over the age of 13 could perform light activities while allowing (not obliging) the national legislation of the ratifying Member States to increase the general standard of 15 years with regard to dangerous employments.[30] Finally, Convention 60 confirmed the importance of the link between minimum age and school attendance, asserting that children who had not finished primary school could not be employed, even if older than 15 years.[31]

In sum, the first 10 ILO Conventions concerning minimum age for admission to employment or work were characterized not only by a progressive increase of the minimum age itself, but also by the development of normative techniques that took into account the flexibility needs of some Member States. However, this technique was still very elementary: in fact, the exceptions provided for by the first Conventions were less selective, because they related to developing Member States and not to sectors of the economy or work typologies.[32]

For this and many other reasons – including a general need to overcome the uncertainty created by the contemporary existence of 10 conventions on the same matter – in the early 1970s the ILC decided to adopt a general minimum age Convention that consolidated the contents of the previous ones and tried to award more flexibility to the ratifying Member States.[33]

3.3 The consolidated Minimum Age Convention 138 of 1973: a Western-centric instrument?

3.3.1 General remarks: a programmatic or a prescriptive legal instrument?

The C138 Minimum Age Convention of 1973, alongside the R146 Minimum Age Recommendation of the same year, represents the latest and most advanced ILO tool for the limitation of the minimum age for the admission to employment or work.

By approving Convention 138, the ILC consolidated the previous 10 Conventions – technically revising them – and tried to create a comprehensive legal instrument

---

30 Valticos and von Potobsky, *International Labour Law, supra* note 3, at 218 and 219.

31 See Smolin, 'Conflict and Ideology', *supra* note 8, at 413.

32 See the comments of the CEACR, *General Survey, supra* note 16, at 8 and 9, § 31.

33 On the aims pursued by Convention 138 of 1973, see, in general, E. Rubin (ed., in consultation with E. Kalula and B. Hepple), *Code of International Labour Law: Law, Practice and Jurisprudence,* Cambridge: Cambridge University Press, 2005, Vol. 1, Book, 1, 639 ff; Creighton, 'Combating Child Labour', *supra* note 4, at 371 ff; K. Cox, 'The Inevitability of Nimble Fingers? Law, Development, and Child Labor', *Vanderbilt Journal of Transnational Law*, Vol. 32, January, 1999, 115 ff, at 135 ff.

so as to considerably increase the number of ratifications. This idea of the broad applicability of a Convention regarding minimum age also convinced the ILC to provide, within the Convention itself, for several possible exceptions and flexibility clauses.

In this context, article 1 of the Convention for the first time binds ratifying Member States to pursuing a national policy intended to ensure the effective abolition of child labour and 'to raise progressively the minimum age for admission to employment or work to a level consistent with the fullest physical and mental development of young persons'.[34] According to this provision, it might seem correct to place Convention 138 among the programmatic ones adopted by the ILC since the late 1940s,[35] and to think that the ILO adopted a less rigid approach to minimum age than in the past.[36] This conclusion would appear confirmed also by the preliminary works to the Convention, affirming that the latter 'is not intended simply as a static instrument prescribing a fixed minimum standard but as a dynamic one aimed at encouraging the progressive improvement of standards and of promoting sustained action to attain the objectives'.[37]

However, as pointed out in the Introduction, this supposedly programmatic approach provided for by article 1 of Convention 138 contrasts with the prescriptive character of its other provisions. In order to enforce the Convention, ratifying States must set a minimum age for admission to employment or work, although they have the option to introduce exceptions or invoke flexibility clauses.

The rigidity of this instrument is then compounded by the fact that neither article 1, nor any other provisions of the Convention explain how the mentioned national policy has to be implemented.[38] The difficulties regarding the concrete implementation of this national policy are confirmed by another document, which also is part of the preliminary works, pointing out that 'article 1 does not impose an obligation to take any specific measures beyond those described in the subsequent

---

34 On art. 1 of the mentioned Convention, see, in general, Creighton, 'Combating Child Labour', *supra* note 4, at 371 and 372; Rubin, *Code of International Labour Law*, *supra* note 33, at 641 ff; Smolin, 'Conflict and Ideology', *supra* note 8, at 414; A.R. Ritualo, C.L. Castro and S. Gormly, 'Measuring Child Labour: Implications for Policy and Program Design', *Comparative Labor Law & Policy Journal*, Vol. 24, Winter, 2003, 401 ff, at 403 and 404.

35 For example, Convention 87 Freedom of Association and Protection of the Right to Organise of 1948 or C111 Discrimination (Employment and Occupation) Convention of 1958. Concerning the difference between programmatic and prescriptive Conventions, see M. Borzaga, 'Accommodating Differences: Discrimination and Equality at Work in International Labor Law', *Vermont Law Review*, Vol. 30, No. 3, Spring, 2006, 749 ff, at 774 ff.

36 Creighton, 'Combating Child Labour', *supra* note 4, at 371.

37 ILO, *Minimum Age for Admission to Employment, Report IV(1)*, International Labour Conference, 57th Session, Geneva, 1972, 31; also quoted in CEACR, *General Survey, supra* note 16, at 18.

38 See Creighton, 'Combating Child Labour', *supra* note 4, at 371. See also *infra*, sub-section 3.3.6.

provisions'.[39] According to Creighton,[40] this means that, in order to comply with the obligations established by the Convention, it would be sufficient to establish the required minimum age without engaging in other activities aimed at abolishing child labour. According to this narrow approach, the danger of the spread of pro forma ratifications was, and remains, very high.

The described inconsistencies, characterizing Convention 138, demonstrate the difficulties faced by the ILO in drafting a general tool for the fight against child labour, able to raise the minimum age for the admission to employment or work while simultaneously taking into account the needs of flexibility of the developing countries, which in those years had begun to join the Organization. The rigidities, contrasting with the supposed programmatic character of Convention 138, derive not only from the obligation to set a minimum age for admission to employment or work, but also from the other contents of the Convention and the way they were interpreted by the supervising bodies and in particular by the CEACR.

3.3.2 Contents and scope of Convention 138 of 1973

The most important provision of Convention 138 is certainly article 2, which obliges ratifying Member States to set a minimum age for admission to employment or work, specifying it in a declaration appended to the ratification (para. 1). According to paragraph 3 of article 2, the specified minimum age cannot be lower than that for completion of compulsory schooling, and, in any case, may not be lower than 15 years. Furthermore, article 2 establishes that ratifying Member States may notify the Director-General of the ILO of the increase of the minimum age set by the original ratification (para. 2).[41]

Convention 138 thus reaffirms the importance of the link between minimum age and school attendance, with a significant innovation, as it no longer makes reference to primary school, but to compulsory schooling in general. This link, which was introduced in the text of the Convention during the first discussion at the ILC in 1972,[42] should be interpreted in a strict sense; as the CEACR pointed out, those countries that did not establish a minimum age but only regulations forbidding employment of young persons during school hours, cannot be considered to have implemented the Convention correctly.[43] Hence, it is necessary that ratifying States set

---

39 ILO, *Minimum Age for Admission to Employment, Report IV(2)*, International Labour Conference, 58th Session, Geneva, 1973, 7; also quoted in CEACR, *General Survey, supra* note 16, at 18.

40 Creighton, 'Combating Child Labour', *supra* note 4, at 371.

41 On this provision, see, in general, Rubin, *Code of International Labour Law, supra* note 33, at 645 ff; Valticos and von Potobsky, *International Labour Law, supra* note 3, at 219 and 220; Valticos, *Droit international du travail, supra* note 2, at 464 and 465. The opportunity to progressively increase the originally fixed minimum age to 16 years is pointed out by Recommendation R146 of 1973, affirming that this should be a goal for all Member States. Regarding this point, see CEACR, *General Survey, supra* note 16, at 38.

42 Rubin, *Code of International Labour Law, supra* note 33 at 646.

43 See CEACR, *General Survey, supra* note 16, at 38. Creighton, 'Combating Child Labour', *supra* note 4, at 371.

a specific minimum age or completely prohibit children who have not accomplished the compulsory schooling from being employed, even if over 15 years of age.

Having established the necessity of setting the minimum age in the described way, paragraphs 4 and 5 of the same article 2 introduce a flexibility clause that permits ratifying States 'whose economy and educational facilities are insufficiently developed', to reduce the minimum age to 14 years.[44] This last provision clearly constitutes a compromise between the different minimum ages provided for by the two groups of Conventions described in section 3.2, in order to encourage the largest possible number of Member States to implement the Convention. At the same time, this provision testifies to the progressive approach of the Organization to the subject of minimum age. In fact, it is evident that the ILO pursues at least two goals in this field; in other words, obliging the ratifying States to set a minimum age for admission to employment or work, and promoting an increase of that minimum age from 14 to 15 or hopefully 16 years, as pointed out by Recommendation R146 of 1973.[45] Not surprisingly, therefore, article 2(5) requests Member States specifying a minimum age of 14 years to report to the Organization under article 22 of the ILO Constitution, explaining the reasons for doing so or agreeing to renounce the lower minimum age from a certain date onward.[46] With this provision, the ILO provides for a specific control of the reasons that induce some ratifying States not to apply the general standard of a minimum age of 15 years.

Having illustrated the main substance of article 2 of Convention 138, it is interesting to concentrate on the scope of the Convention itself, which can be deduced from the same provision and from article 1. As mentioned, Convention 138 revises the 10 previous Conventions on minimum age and applies to all economic sectors, thus having evidently a very broad scope.[47] Moreover, the Convention's nature is comprehensive also with regard to its personal scope; both article 1 and article 2 affirm that the established minimum age concerns the 'admission to employment or work'. This expression means, both according to the interpretation of the CEACR[48] and the literature,[49] that not only employees, but also self-employed people are covered by the Convention. Furthermore, the CEACR affirmed that also children working in family undertakings and at home are included in the personal scope of Convention 138,[50] unless ratifying States decided to invoke one of the exceptions provided for in articles 4 and 5 of the Convention.[51]

---

44 See Rubin, *Code of International Labour Law*, *supra* note 33, at 648 ff.

45 Regarding this point see *supra* note 41.

46 Rubin, *Code of International Labour Law*, *supra* note 33, at 650; CEACR, *General Survey*, *supra* note 16, at 10.

47 Smolin, 'Conflict and Ideology', *supra* note 8, at 413 and 414.

48 CEACR, *General Survey*, *supra* note 16, at 10 and at 19 ff.

49 Creighton, 'Combating Child Labour', *supra* note 4, at 372 and 373; Smolin, 'Conflict and Ideology', *supra* note 8, at 414; Rubin, *Code of International Labour Law*, *supra* note 33, at 643 ff.

50 See CEACR, *General Survey*, *supra* note 16, at 2 and 23; Creighton, 'Combating Child Labour', *supra* note 4, at 372 and 373; Rubin, *Code of International Labour Law*, *supra* note 33, at 644 and 645.

51 On these norms see, below, in this same sub-section and in the following one.

3.3.3 Exceptions to the application of minimum age provisions

The substantive contents of Convention 138, plus its very wide material and personal scope, seem to confirm that it has to be considered strictly prescriptive rather than programmatic. Actually, this opinion is contradicted by the possibility, provided by articles 4 and 5, of limiting the application of the minimum age provisions. As will be shown below, this possibility is in theory so wide that one scholar affirmed that such limitations could also be severe.[52]

First of all, article 4 of Convention 138 of 1973 affirms that the competent national authority can exclude some typologies of employment or work (like domestic work or home work) from the material scope of the Convention.[53] This exception is conceived very broadly, as article 4 does not contain a list of such typologies. The CEACR asserted that article 4 aims 'to leave the competent authorities in each country a wide measure of discretion to adapt the application of the Convention to the national situation'.[54]

This does not mean, however, that the exception provided for by article 4 can be utilized without any limitation: on the contrary, the same article establishes that employment or work considered dangerous for the health, safety and morals of young persons by article 3 of the Convention cannot be excluded from its material scope. In addition, article 4 affirms that exceptions may be permissible only if they are necessary, limited, connected to special and substantial problems of application, adopted after consultation with the organizations of employers and workers concerned and, finally, listed in the first report on the application of the Convention submitted to the Organization according to article 22 of the Constitution.[55]

This last precondition brings to light an important inconsistency within the article itself, that might considerably reduce its supposedly flexible character or even nullify it completely. As pointed out correctly, the requirement of listing the exclusions only in the first national report on the application of Convention 138 introduces a paradoxical element of rigidity into the flexibility clause of article 4.[56] In particular, Member States can test the practical impact of the Convention in the national context only in the first year after ratification – that is, until the deadline for the submission of the first national report – and thus must decide upon the possible exception in a very short period of time. After the submission of the first national report Member States can no longer modify the list of exceptions or provide one if no exceptions were included in the first report. This means also that the Member States having ratified the Convention cannot adapt their regulations to social and economic changes that might occur over the years.[57]

---

52 Cox, 'The Inevitability of Nimble Fingers?', *supra* note 33, at 136.

53 Creighton, 'Combating Child Labour', *supra* note 4, at 374; Rubin, *Code of International Labour Law, supra* note 33, at 658 ff.

54 CEACR, *General Survey, supra* note 16, at 24.

55 See Creighton, 'Combating Child Labour', *supra* note 4, at 374 and 375; CEACR, *General Survey, supra* note 16, at 24 and 25.

56 Creighton, 'Combating Child Labour', *supra* note 4, at 375.

57 See Creighton, 'Combating Child Labour', *supra* note 4, at 375.

As pointed out, at first sight article 4 appears to be a flexible provision, able to foster the progressive implementation of the whole Convention, but in truth it is rather rigid. The inconsistencies characterizing this norm, together with its interpretation provided by the CEACR, had important consequences on its real use by the Member States, as will be explained in detail in subsection 3.3.6.

Secondly, with regard to article 5 of Convention 138, it has to be pointed out that this norm only applies to developing countries or, as established by the provision itself, to the States 'whose economy and administrative facilities are insufficiently developed'. Article 5 affirms that the described countries can initially limit the scope of the Convention, excluding from it specified sectors of the economy. In this sense, the exception provided for by article 5 is wider than the one of article 4, which only concerns work or employment typologies.[58] Furthermore, the exception included in article 5 of Convention 138 can be used only if some conditions are met. The norm lists a range of economic activities that cannot be excluded from the material scope of the Convention.[59] The list is not always very precise in specifying the activities concerned and this may generate misunderstandings in the States that intend to make use of the exception provided for in article 5.[60] Moreover, article 5 affirms that economic sectors can only be excluded from the material scope of the Convention in consultation with the organizations of workers and employers concerned, and must be contained in a specific declaration appended to the ratification.

The flexibility clause established by article 5 substitutes the rudimentary ones contained in the previous conventions, which introduced specific regulations for particular countries such as Japan, China and India.[61] When compared to article 4, this flexibility clause seems really able to encourage the progressive ratification of Convention 138 in the developing countries, thus giving an important role to all the national reports submitted to the Organization according to article 22 of the Constitution and not only to the first one. In particular, Member States who have excluded one or more sectors of the economy from the material scope of Convention 138 must indicate their general position with regard to the employment or work of young persons in those sectors, also pointing out the progresses made towards a broader application of the Convention.[62] Furthermore, by addressing an appropriate declaration to the Director-General of the ILO, Member States can, at any time, formally extend the material scope of Convention 138 to one or more of the economic activities previously excluded.

---

58 CEACR, *General Survey, supra* note 16, at 31.

59 The list comprises, as established by art. 5(3): 'mining and quarrying; manufacturing; construction; electricity, gas and water; sanitary services; transport, storage and communication; and plantations and other agricultural undertakings mainly producing for commercial purposes, but excluding family and small-scale holdings producing for local consumption and not regularly employing hired workers'. See, CEACR, *General Survey, supra* note 16, at 30 ff.

60 Creighton, 'Combating Child Labour', *supra* note 4, at 376.

61 See *supra* section 3.2 and also Smolin, 'Conflict and Ideology', *supra* note 8, at 417.

62 CEACR, *General Survey, supra* note 16, at 32. Rubin, *Code of International Labour Law, supra* note 33, at 664 ff.

Before concluding on this point, it is important to mention that article 6 of Convention 138 provides for another exception to the application of the minimum age regulations, stipulating that they do not apply to work done by children and young persons in schools for general vocational or technical education or in other training institutions. The Convention is also inapplicable to young persons of at least 14 years of age, engaged in an apprenticeship.[63] Like the others, this exception can be utilized only if some conditions are met. In particular, the work performed by apprentices has to be carried out in accordance with the regulations approved by the competent authorities, after consultation with the organizations of employers and workers concerned. In addition, some other conditions concerning the management of the apprenticeship programmes have to be complied with.[64] It is clear that this exception follows, in a more detailed form, the similar ones concerning children attending technical schools and provided by many previous Minimum Age Conventions.[65]

3.3.4 Work, light work, dangerous work

With regard to the flexible application of Convention 138 it has to be pointed out that the latter maintains and develops the distinction between work, light work and dangerous work, which can be found in some of the most advanced Minimum Age Conventions approved by the ILO in the period 1919–65. This distinction cannot be considered a flexibility clause in the strict sense,[66] but it plays an important role in making as flexible as possible the national implementation processes of Convention 138, connecting diverse minimum ages to different work or employment typologies.

First of all, articles 7 and 8 of Convention 138 establish particular provisions concerning light work and artistic performances. Article 7 affirms that national laws or regulations may allow young people between the ages of 13 and 15 – or between 12 and 14 in the developing countries – to be employed or work only if the activity is a light one. According to the same provision, light work cannot be work harmful to the health or the development of the young persons concerned. Moreover, this kind of employment or work may not prejudice their school attendance, their participation in vocational orientation or training programmes approved by the national competent authority, or their capacity to benefit from the instruction received.[67] The same

---

63 See Creighton, 'Combating Child Labour', *supra* note 4, at 377.

64 See art. 6 of Convention 138, affirming that the apprenticeship carried out by young persons of at least 14 years of age have to be a part of: 'a) a course of education or training for which a school or training institution is primarily responsible; (b) a programme of training mainly or entirely in an undertaking, which programme has been approved by the competent authority; or (c) a programme of guidance or orientation designed to facilitate the choice of an occupation or of a line of training'.

65 See *supra* section 3.2.

66 Concerning the flexibility clauses provided for in the diverse international labour law Conventions, see Valticos and von Potobsky, *International Labour Law*, *supra* note 3, at 57 ff.

67 See art. (7)(1)(a) and (b) of Convention 138 of 1973. See also Creighton, 'Combating Child Labour', *supra* note 4, at 378; Rubin, *Code of International Labour Law*, *supra* note 33, at 672 ff; CEACR, *General Survey*, *supra* note 16, at 72 ff.

possibility of performing light activities is permissible for young persons of at least 15 years of age who have not yet completed their compulsory schooling.[68] Convention 138 grants the competent authorities the right to determine which activities can be considered light, and which employment and work accordingly can be permitted. Furthermore, the competent authorities also have to determine the number of working hours during which such employment or work can be performed and in which conditions.[69]

Article 8 adds another specific case in which children are permitted to work even if below the general minimum age of 15 years established by Convention 138: this case concerns such activities as participation in artistic performances.[70] Article 8 does not establish any minimum age in this respect, allowing every child to perform artistic activities, but only if some strict conditions are met. In fact, the competent authority, after having first consulted the organizations of employers and workers, has to create an authorization system based on individual applications, granting the permission of performing artistic activities to children of any age on a case-by-case basis. Moreover, the permits issued also must limit the number of hours and prescribe the conditions under which employment or work is allowed.[71]

Convention 138 also considers dangerous work, regulating it in article 3. Here, the ILC decided to provide for an increase of the general minimum age to at least 18 years 'for admission to any type of employment or work which by its nature or the circumstances in which it is carried out is likely to jeopardise the health, safety or morals of young persons.'[72] Furthermore, article 3 of Convention 138 establishes that the identification of dangerous types of employment or work has to be provided by national laws or regulations, or by the competent authority, after having consulted the employers' and workers' organizations.[73] Nevertheless, young persons from the age of 16 may be authorized to perform these dangerous activities, but only if their health, safety and morals are fully protected and if they have received adequate specific instruction or vocational training in the relevant branch of activity.[74]

---

68 Rubin, *Code of International Labour Law, supra* note 33, at 677 and 678.

69 See Rubin, *Code of International Labour Law, supra* note 33, at 674 and 675. CEACR, *General Survey, supra* note 16, at 80 ff.

70 Creighton, 'Combating Child Labour', *supra* note 4, at 379; Rubin, *Code of International Labour Law, supra* note 33, at 680 ff.

71 As pointed out in the preparatory work to the Convention, 'the requirement of individual permits ... is intended to ensure strict control over the circumstances and conditions in which such participation takes place.' See ILO, *Minimum Age for Admission to Employment, Report IV(2), supra* note 39, at 21; see also CEACR, *General Survey, supra* note 16, at 83 ff.

72 See art. 3(1) of Convention 138. See also Creighton, 'Combating Child Labour', *supra* note 4, at 379 ff; CEACR, *General Survey, supra* note 16, at 89 ff.

73 See Rubin, *Code of International Labour Law, supra* note 33, at 653 and 654; CEACR, *General Survey, supra* note 16, at 90.

74 The reason why the ILC decided to insert the provision reducing the minimum age in case of dangerous works into the text of art. 3 is related to the fact that 'the minimum age of 18 would apply to types of employment or work which are determined ... as being truly ... hazardous. ... There are, however, other occupations which may not be hazardous in this sense but which may require a certain maturity and for which a minimum age higher than the general

In the opinion of the CEACR, article 3 introduced a higher minimum age for hazardous works with the aim of protecting young persons from handling dangerous materials and substances 'before they have formed the judgement necessary to do so safely',[75] believing that the age at which this judgement can be considered to have been acquired is 18 years.

As pointed out, Convention 138 establishes a general minimum age of 15 years, but then provides for many flexibility clauses, exceptions and other tools – like the distinction among work, light work and dangerous work – in order to make the necessary fixing of a minimum age as flexible as possible.

Nevertheless, as is demonstrated by the low number of ratifications (at least until 1998), this flexible approach to the question of limiting minimum age did not produce the hoped-for results.[76] The next sub-section will analyse the reasons thereof, starting from the assumption that Convention 138 is prescriptive rather than programmatic, even though article 1 requires a national policy intended to progressively abolish child labour. Furthermore, the implementation problems of Convention 138 will be evaluated taking into account the argument that such problems, particularly in developing countries, are connected to the Western-centric approach followed by the ILO in drafting the minimum age provisions.

3.3.5 Assessing the nature of Convention 138: a Western-centric approach?

The implementation problems that characterized Convention 138 can probably be linked to two different but related phenomena. First, these problems may derive from the supposedly Western-centric approach of the Convention itself. Second, these problems are probably also connected with the ratification practices of the Member States, and with the interpretation provided by the CEACR regarding these same provisions.[77]

Starting from the first point, it is certainly correct that ILO minimum age provisions initially were based on a Western child-labour idea. As was mentioned in the Introduction, both national and international labour law was created to solve some important questions regarding the employment of persons (particularly children and women) considered weak and thus in need of special legal protection. Between the end of the 19th and the beginning of the 20th century, these questions essentially concerned Western European societies.[78]

In accordance with the values shared, at that time, by those societies, the problem of child workers was addressed by the establishing of a prescriptive minimum age for their admission to employment or work, founding this decision on the belief that

minimum would therefore be justified'. See ILO, *Minimum Age for Admission to Employment, Report IV(1)*, International Labour Conference, 58th Session, Geneva, 1973, 32.

75 See CEACR, *General Survey*, *supra* note 16, at 167. See also Creighton, 'Combating Child Labour', *supra* note 4, at 380.

76 Hepple, *Labour Laws and Global Trade*, *supra* note 4, at 43 ff.

77 On the implementation problems of the ILO minimum age provisions see Valticos and von Potobsky, *International Labour Law*, *supra* note 3, at 220 and 221; Valticos, *Droit international du travail*, *supra* note 2 at 465 and 466.

78 See Hepple, *Labour Laws and Global Trade*, *supra* note 4, at 27.

children should have a natural right not to work.[79] Consequently, the presence of children in the workplace was considered as the most important feature of the child labour problem.[80] Finally, the decision to provide prescriptive regulations setting a minimum age for admission to employment or work was also determined by the conviction that limiting the participation of children in the labour market could reduce the unemployment rates of adult workers.[81]

Subsequently, this Western-centric approach was confirmed by the consolidated Convention 138 of 1973, even if the decolonization processes had already begun to significantly modify the character of the Organization's membership.[82] After many decades characterized by the supremacy of the Western Member States, the admission of an increasing number of developing countries changed the internal balance of the ILO and, in particular, of its most important organ, the ILC.

In that context, conflicts emerged between new and old Member States about some of the values that until then had been considered the common basis of international labour law, in particular with regard to child labour. At least two different concepts of childhood and its role in society emerged, the first typically associated with Northern countries and the second with Southern ones.

According to the Northern view, childhood and adulthood have to be kept strictly separate, with the consequence that children remain dependent on their family also during adolescence. More particularly, they cannot work, not even in order to contribute to the family maintenance.

In the Southern societies, on the contrary, this strict separation does not fit with the conception of the family. There, children are considered mature starting with adolescence and thus are asked to play a frequently important role in order to increase their family's well-being. This is so because in these societies the value of family unity and solidarity definitely prevails over a presumed right of children not to work.[83] These differences between Northern and Southern countries led the latter to consider many of the international labour standards as inadequate to solve their labour and social problems and to frequently reject their domestic implementation.[84]

This development had the important consequences that, amongst the enlarged ILO membership, the conviction of the necessity of legal instruments providing for limitations of the minimum age for admission to employment or work no longer

---

79 On this issue see, in general, H. Cunningham, *The Children of the Poor: Representations of Childhood Since the Seventeenth Century*, Oxford: Blackwell, 1991; H. Cunningham, *Children and Childhood in Western Society since 1500*, London: Longman, 1995; H. Cunningham and P.P. Viazzo (eds), *Child Labour in Historical Perspective: 1800–1985. Case Studies from Europe, Japan and Colombia*, Florence: UNICEF, 1996.

80 W.E. Myers, 'The Right Rights? Child Labor in a Globalizing World', *Annals of the American Academy of Political and Social Science*, Vol. 575, 2001, May, 38 ff, at 46.

81 Myers, 'The Right Rights?', *supra* note 80, at 46.

82 See Hepple, *Labour Laws and Global Trade*, *supra* note 4, at 33 ff.

83 See Myers, 'The Right Rights?', *supra* note 80, at 40.

84 See B. White, 'Children, Work and Child Labour: Changing Responses to the Employment of Children', *Development and Change*, Vol. 25, 1994, No. 4, 849 ff; B. White, 'Globalisation and the Child Labour Problem', *Journal of International Development*, Vol. 8, 1996, No. 6, 829 ff.

constituted a shared value.[85] Therefore, the question of protecting children from abuse, and in particular abuse connected to their working activities, had to be tackled from a different point of view. As has been pointed out recently, international standards concerning childhood, including labour matters, must be constructed so as to accommodate the diverse views in different parts of the world.[86] The problem thus consists of devising regulations broad enough to create a common legal basis between both Northern and Southern societies concerning children's rights. This kind of approach definitely is hard to implement, because of the necessity for striking a balance between universalism and cultural relativism.[87]

During the last two decades, the international community has tried to overcome the relativistic – or Western-centric – concept of child labour, providing new instruments, which, however, did not abrogate the old one of Convention 138. These new instruments are the UN Convention on the Rights of the Child of 1989 and the more recent ILO Worst Forms of Child Labour Convention No. 182 of 1999. Both Conventions not only symbolize the difficulties of the international institutions in finding a more global approach to the issue of child labour, but also show that this new approach is irreversible and progressively makes minimum age tools anachronistic.[88]

This question will be analysed in depth in section 3.4, where the minimum age tools will be assessed within the new context of the core labour standards.

3.3.6 The national implementation of Convention 138 in developed and developing countries and the role of supervision bodies

As argued, the implementation problems of Convention 138 stem both from cultural and juridical differences amongst the ILO Member States. In this subsection these problems will be analysed from the juridical point of view, in order to assess how the numerous exceptions and flexibility clauses of Convention 138 have actually been used by the ratifying States; to describe other implementations problems that have emerged over the years; and to evaluate the role of the CEACR and its interpretations in favouring or hampering a flexible implementation of the Convention.

At first reading, Convention 138 seems to be a promotional tool, but a more thorough analysis reveals it to be a rather prescriptive tool instead. After having established a minimum age for admission to employment or work of 15 years, Convention 138 provides for many exceptions and flexibility clauses. The question here is to understand if these clauses, over the years, have favoured the domestic implementation of international minimum age provisions, or if they have had the paradoxical effect of deterring ratification by many developed and developing countries.

---

85 See Myers, 'The Right Rights?', supra note 80, at 43.

86 Myers, 'The Right Rights?', *supra* note 80, at 43.

87 This difficulty is clearly pointed out by P. Alston (ed.), *The Best Interests of the Child: Reconciling Culture and Human Rights*, Oxford: Clarendon, 1994.

88 See Myers, 'The Right Rights?', *supra* note 80, at 49.

First of all, the flexibility clause provided by article 4, as has to be recalled, allows the competent authorities of the ratifying States to exclude some categories of employment or work from the scope of the Convention. This seems to be an important source of flexibility, especially for particular situations like employment in family undertakings or home work.[89] The exclusions are subject to one condition in particular – that is, they have to be listed in the first report prepared by the member state in accordance with article 22 of the ILO Constitution. Accordingly it is not possible to modify the list of categories subsequently. As a result the flexibility clause of article 4 in actual fact displays a high level of rigidity. According to scholars, these inconsistencies have played an important role in discouraging the use of article 4.[90] In fact, the clause was invoked very rarely, as confirmed by the CEACR in the General Survey of 1981 and subsequent documents.[91]

Likewise, also article 5 was hardly ever used.[92] According to scholars, in this case the reasons are not related to the inconsistencies of the norm, but to the possible misunderstandings it might have generated in ratifying States, because the sectors that cannot be excluded from the scope of the Convention are not described clearly enough.[93] This problem mainly concerns the agricultural sector for which article 5 distinguishes between 'plantations and other agricultural undertakings mainly producing for commercial purposes' that cannot be excluded from the scope of the Convention, and 'family and small-scale holdings producing for local consumption and not regularly employing hired workers', that instead can be excluded. It is sufficient to read this part of the norm in order to understand that the distinction seems to be very difficult to apply. The bad drafting of the provision has particularly important consequences for developing countries, which in general are the addressees of the provision. For these States, agriculture is the most important economic activity and also the one in which child labour is principally employed. Exceptions concerning this sector should be fundamental for developing countries in order to guarantee the progressive implementation of Convention 138 and it is hence paradoxical that the

---

89 These are some of the examples made during the preparatory work for the adoption of Convention 183. See CEACR, *General Survey, supra* note 16, at 24.

90 See Creighton, 'Combating Child Labour', *supra* note 4, at 374 ff.

91 See CEACR, *General Survey, supra* note 16, at 25. Analysing in particular the CEACR individual observations to the ratifying Member States with regard to art. 4 of C138, it emerges that one of the few countries which utilized the norm was Sweden (observation published in 1997): in fact, that country had excluded domestic work in an employer's household from the application of the Convention, but afterwards it decided to eliminate this exclusion and not to use the possibility of exceptions anymore. Other countries to which the CEACR addressed direct requests about the utilization of art. 4 only were Antigua and Barbuda (observations published in 2003, 2005, 2006 and 2007) and Turkey (2004 and 2006).

92 See CEACR, *General Survey, supra* note 16, at 32. In order to update the old data contained in this General Survey, the CEACR individual observations to the ratifying Member States can be taken into account. They show that, starting from 1973, there were only two of such observations concerning art. 5 of Convention 138, both addressed to Turkey (published in 2004 and 2006).

93 Creighton, 'Combating Child Labour', *supra* note 4, at 376.

misunderstandings generated by article 5 have discouraged ratifying countries from employing exceptions and article 5 in general.

In conclusion, the two most important exceptions provided by Convention 138 have gone almost unutilized. On the contrary, the flexibility tool contained in article 2, which gives States the possibility to establish a minimum age of 14 instead of 15 years, has been widely used. Nevertheless, it is clear that ratifying processes of Convention 138 have been characterized by a serious lack of flexibility, in spite of the numerous exceptions and flexibility tools contained in the Convention itself.

The problems affecting the implementation processes of Convention 138 do not concern only exceptions and flexibility clauses, but also regard other provisions. Starting with the developed countries, the most important implementation problem they encountered concerned light work. Article 7 of Convention 138 affirms that Member States can allow young people between 13 and 15 years of age to work only if the performed activity can be considered light. The provision indirectly implies that children under 13 years of age are never permitted to work.

It was this last indirect prohibition that caused compliance problems in some developed countries, because of its lack of flexibility.[94] Although a compulsory schooling system up to the age of 15 years or more is in place in those countries, children below the age of 13 are often allowed to perform light activities outside of school hours or during vacations, within the protection provided for by the norms concerning occupational health and safety. These light activities cannot really be deemed possible abuses of child labour but, on the contrary, must be regarded as opportunities to gain experience. Accordingly this kind of child labour should be approached pragmatically, providing elastic norms allowing for a distinction between abuses and acceptable or even positive forms of child labour.[95]

However, such a pragmatic approach is incompatible with article 7 and also with the interpretation provided by the CEACR. The latter adopted a very strict approach on this point, affirming that employment or work of children below the age of 13 is never permissible.[96] These legislative and interpretative restrictions are probably responsible for the failure of some important developed States – Australia, Canada and New Zealand – to ratify Convention 138 also after the adoption of the Declaration of Geneva.[97]

Concerning developing countries, the implementation problems related to Convention 138 obviously are very different ones. In this case, the Convention in general, rather than any particular provision, caused compliance problems. One should recall that Convention 138 starts from the presumption that every form of child labour has to be eliminated, and this stands in strong contrast to the perception

---

94 See Creighton, 'Combating Child Labour', *supra* note 4, at 378 ff.

95 Creighton, 'Combating Child Labour', *supra* note 4, at 386.

96 See CEACR, *General Survey, supra* note 16, at 72 ff.

97 In fact, these three Member States are the only developed ones, with the US, that did not already ratify Convention 138. For an overview, see the table of ratifications of fundamental Conventions, at <http://www.ilo.org/ilolex/english/docs/declworld.htm>. Concerning the case of Australia see also CEACR, *General Survey, supra* note 16, at 75; and B. Creighton, 'ILO Convention No. 138 and Australian Law and Practice Relating to Child Labour', *Australian Journal of Human Rights*, Vol. 2, Issue 2, 1996, 293 ff.

of child labour in developing countries. In other words, it is principally a cultural and economic problem, although not exclusively so; compliance problems also derive from the lack of an adequate legal infrastructure, able to correctly implement and apply Convention 138.[98] The absence of an adequate legal infrastructure in those countries is strictly related to poverty and corruption.[99] Moreover, even if such an infrastructure existed, in many cases it might not be possible to control the generally rather diffused informal sector.

One should recall that Convention 138 provides for norms that try to accommodate the needs of developing States, as the flexibility options in article 2(4), article 4 and article 5 show. The problem was, and is, that this flexibility was not sufficient to foster the implementation of the Convention and was not used by the developing countries, for the reasons explained above. In general, the implementation problems of the developing countries stem from the real nature of Convention 138, which is indeed prescriptive.

It seems likely that the failure of many developing countries to ratify the Convention (almost until 1998 and the adoption of the Declaration of Geneva) depended on the fact that the latter does not give priorities to national action, simply stating, in article 1, that ratifying Member States have to adopt a policy able to ensure the effective abolition of child labour. Yet, for a developing country with widespread child labour, the need for priorities is particularly high. Simultaneously, developing countries with weak legal infrastructures may experience difficulties in determining national policy priorities.[100] These were some of the reasons why the ILO decided to modify its approach to the issue of child labour and to adopt a new convention.

Before describing these developments in the next section, the influence of CEACR interpretations on the national implementation processes of Convention 138 needs to be considered. First, it has to be pointed out that the interpretation approach of the CEACR to Convention 138 is quite similar to the one adopted by the Committee in general: the personal and material scopes of the Convention are interpreted in the broadest way whereas exceptions are interpreted in a strict way, so as to cover as many people and sectors as possible.[101] In fact, this method of interpretation tends to further restrict the few flexibility options of Convention 138, thus making it more rigid. Apparently the CEACR, in interpreting Convention 138, did not take into account the flexibility needs of developing countries, preferring

---

98 Hepple, *Labour Laws and Global Trade*, *supra* note 4, at 47.

99 See K. Basu, 'Global Labor Standards and Local Freedoms', Wider Annual Lecture 7, UNU World Institute for Development Economics Research: Helsinki, 2003, 1 ff, at 8 ff; K. Basu and Z. Tzannatos, 'The Global Child Labor Problem: What Do We Know and What Can We Do?', CAE Working Paper #03-06, June 2003, 1 ff; Cox, 'The Inevitability of Nimble Fingers?', *supra* note 33, at 145 ff.

100 Creighton, 'Combating Child Labour', *supra* note 4, at 390.

101 Regarding the interpretation activity of the CEACR, see, in general, I. Boivin and A. Odero, 'The Committee of Experts on the Application of Conventions and Recommendations: Progress Achieved in National Labour Legislation', *International Labour Review*, Vol. 45, No. 3, 2006, 207 ff; A. Wissenkirchen, 'The Standard-Setting and Monitoring Activity of the ILO: Legal Questions and Practical Experience', *International Labour Review*, Vol. 144, No. 3, 2005, 253 ff.

instead to provide a formal interpretation and thus compounding the compliance problems these countries face. In most cases, the consequences of this approach are apparent to the Committee itself, which has often pointed out the implementation problems deriving from its interpretations.[102]

Some examples may serve to better explain the role played by the CEACR. The first one concerns the interpretation of article 2(3) of Convention 138. The CEACR maintained that the existence and enforcement of a compulsory schooling system does not constitute adequate compliance with the Convention itself and that therefore it is necessary to provide appropriate restriction with regard to employment or work outside school hours and during holidays.[103] Moreover, countries not establishing a general minimum age for admission to employment or work but only a compulsory school system, forbidding children to work during school hours, fail to properly enforce Convention 138.[104] Actually, in such countries children are permitted to work outside school hours and during the holidays, with the consequence that their schooling 'may easily be prejudiced'.[105] On the same issue, the CEACR also rejected approaches aiming to permit children to work outside school hours or during the holidays in order to give them the opportunity to make a first contact with working life.[106]

The CEACR also provided strict interpretations concerning light and dangerous work. With regard to light work, the Committee did not accept the approach of many developed countries, believing that children under the minimum age of 13 years might profitably familiarize themselves with light working activities outside of school hours.[107] Relating to dangerous work, the CEACR affirmed that some countries adopted provisions forbidding young people to perform hazardous activities, or at least ones which regulated such activities in order to protect young people.[108] At the same time, however, the Committee strongly criticized the majority of ratifying States, asserting that they did not take proper measures or did so in a too generic way, thus not complying with the requirements of Convention 138.[109]

Finally, it might be interesting to give an example of a CEACR interpretation of exceptions. Concerning article 4 of Convention 138, the Committee interpreted the provision that ratifying Member States have to list the excluded categories of employment or work in the first report according to article 22 of the ILO Constitution strictly. In particular, it recalled that the exclusions, to be valid, have to be included

---

102 CEACR, *General Survey, supra* note 16, at 19 ff. Rubin, *Code of International Labour Law, supra* note 33, at 643.

103 CEACR, *General Survey, supra* note 16, at 164 ff. Rubin, *Code of International Labour Law, supra* note 33, at 646 ff.

104 CEACR, *General Survey, supra* note 16, at 165.

105 See CEACR, *General Survey, supra* note 16; Rubin, *Code of International Labour Law, supra* note 33.

106 CEACR, *General Survey, supra* note 16, at 57.

107 CEACR, *General Survey, supra* note 16, at 75.

108 CEACR, *General Survey, supra* note 16, at 167.

109 See CEACR, *General Survey, supra* note 16; Rubin, *Code of International Labour Law, supra* note 33.

in the first report,[110] must be very precise and limited, and are admissible only in case of special and substantial problems of application.[111]

As has been explained, the compliance problems of ILO Member States regarding Convention 138 were – and still partly are – very numerous. They depend upon various factors, including the paradoxical rigidity of Convention 138, in particular of its flexibility clauses, the non-utilization of such exceptions by the Member States, and the strict interpretations of the CEACR. Moreover, concerning developing countries, Convention 138 displays another problem, as it fails to identify priorities for national legislation.

For all of these reasons, the ILO changed its strategy on child labour from the 1990s onward. This approach will be analysed briefly in the next section, in order to evaluate the role played by Convention 138 after the adoption of the Declaration of Geneva of 1998.

3.4 The fight against child labour: assessing the real potential of minimum age regulations within the new context of core labour standards

The numerous application problems related to Convention 138 and the globalization processes affecting child labour convinced the ILO that the time had come to update the international minimum age tools.

In 1996, the Governing Body proposed to adopt a new instrument.[112] This proposal emerged from a progressive strategy change at the ILO[113] and the international organizations in general, starting with the approval of the UN Convention on the Rights of the Child of 1989.[114] Even this Convention can be considered to display a Western approach due to its conception of the childhood.[115] Yet it also presents some interesting innovations that are of particular importance in order to understand the new approach of the international organizations.

First of all, the UN Convention on the Rights of the Child (CRC) contains more than prescriptions, 'objectives and principles, thus leaving more room than does the Minimum Age Convention to implement it in a way appropriate to the member's situation'.[116] More particularly, the provision of the Convention regarding child labour (article 32) affirms that children have to be protected 'from economic exploitation and from performing any work that is likely to be hazardous or to interfere with the child's education, or to be harmful to the child's health or physical, mental, spiritual,

---

110 See, for example, the individual observation of the CEACR to Dominica (2004).

111 This is the interpretation provided by the CEACR in the individual observation addressed to Turkey (published in 2004).

112 Creighton, 'Combating Child Labour', *supra* note 4, at 392.

113 Smolin, 'Conflict and Ideology', *supra* note 8, at 419 ff.

114 On this Convention see Cox, 'The Inevitability of Nimble Fingers?', *supra* note 33, at 136 ff and Myers, 'The Right Rights?', *supra* note 80, at 48 ff.

115 See Myers, 'The Right Rights?', *supra* note 80, at 48.

116 So Myers, 'The Right Rights?', *supra* note 80, at 48.

moral or social development'[117] but does not categorically prohibit children from working.[118] Thus, the norm does not establish a minimum age for the admission to employment or work, assigning such a task to the ratifying States.[119]

With article 32 of the CRC, the UN concentrated on the elimination of some particularly intolerable forms of child labour, overcoming the original Western-centric idea that children should have a right not to work.[120]

In any case, this Convention certainly constitutes the first step towards a new approach regarding child labour. It appears that the international organizations gradually became aware of the inefficiency of a Western-centric tool like Convention 138. The UN (first) and the ILO (afterwards) probably came to believe that minimum age tools alone were no longer able to ensure the abolition of child labour, due to the many implementation problems of Convention 138 and the cultural disparities characterizing the international community. Starting from the Convention on the Rights of the Child, the UN and the ILO tried to discern shared values in order to combat child labour more effectively. These shared values produced a focus on the elimination of the worst forms of child labour.[121]

This new approach might be successful for at least two different reasons: because it provides for a progressive implementation of its norms and because it concentrates only on the most intolerable aspects of child labour, giving priorities to the Member States, in particular to the developing ones. It has to be said though, that the idea of singling out the worst forms of child labour also derives from the practical experience of the IPEC programme, launched by the ILO in 1992 and aimed at offering technical assistance to developing Member States on this question.[122] Not surprisingly, the initiative of the ILO Governing Body of 1996 concerned exactly the most intolerable forms of child labour. A new Convention on this issue was proposed and placed on the agenda of the ILC for 1998.[123]

In the same year, another important event regarding child labour occurred at the ILO level. In 1998 the ILC adopted the so-called Declaration of Geneva, a soft law instrument providing fundamental principles and rights at work.[124] Approving

---

117 Art. 32(1) of the UN Convention of the Rights of the Child, http://www.unhchr.ch/html/menu3/b/k2crc.htm.

118 Myers, 'The Right Rights?', *supra* note 80, at 48.

119 Art. 32(2)(a) of the UN Convention of the Rights of the Child, available at <http://www.unhchr.ch/html/menu3/b/k2crc.htm>.

120 According to one scholar, this is a positive choice, because it seeks to adopt a pragmatic approach to child labour, in order to provide for more effectiveness, particularly in developing countries: see Myers, 'The Right Rights?', *supra* note 80, at 48 and 49. However, others maintain that the absence of a general minimum age in art. 32 is the major weakness of the Convention: this is the opinion of Cox, 'The Inevitability of Nimble Fingers?', *supra* note 33, at 138 and 139.

121 Creighton, 'Combating Child Labour', *supra* note 4, at 392 ff.

122 Myers, 'The Right Rights?', *supra* note 80, at 51; Smolin, 'Conflict and Ideology', *supra* note 8, at 419.

123 Creighton, 'Combating Child Labour', *supra* note 4, at 392.

124 On this declaration see, in general, Maupain, 'Revitalization Not Retreat', *supra* note 8, at 439 ff; Alston, 'Core Labour Standards', *supra* note 14, at 457 ff; P. Alston, 'Facing

this Declaration, the ILC decided to give priority to some of the existing standards, choosing issues such as discrimination, forced labour and freedom of association, that were already considered fundamental, and adding to them child labour. This addition testifies to the new attention of the Organization towards this problem; an attention confirmed by the approval, in 1999, of ILO Convention 182 on the Worst Forms of Child Labour, deriving from the Governing Body's proposal of 1996.

According to the Declaration of Geneva,[125] the core labour standards presently consist of eight fundamental conventions: two of these, Convention 138 and 182, concern child labour. The Declaration of Geneva and Convention 182 will be thoroughly analysed in other chapters of this book.[126] Here it suffices to explain which are the effects of the new core labour standards approach on Convention 138 and what could be the role of this Convention in the future ILO strategy against child labour.

Concerning the first point, the simple recognition that Convention 138 is one of the eight fundamental ILO conventions obviously did not remove all the implementation problems that had characterized it. However, the Declaration of Geneva had the important effect of strongly increasing the number of ratifications after 1998. Until 1998, 46 States had ratified the Convention. According to the latest data, 150 States have done so now.[127] This extraordinary increase is very difficult to explain. On the one hand, recent ILO efforts to make the Member States conscious of the problem of child labour – including the IPEC programme and the dissemination of data – certainly played an important role. Also, the inclusion of Convention 138 amongst the fundamental ones may have had a significant impact, considering that ratifications have significantly increased for all fundamental Conventions.[128] On the other hand, the increase in ratifications may at least partially be due to the ILO's insistence that developing countries participate in the IPEC programme, and implement C138 when doing so. Actually, it may be that some Member States decided to ratify the Convention only in order to partake in the financial and technical

---

up to the Complexity of the ILO's Core Labour Standards Agenda', *European Journal of International Law*, Vol. 16, No. 3, 2005, 467 ff; B.A. Langille, 'Core Labour Rights – The True Story (Reply to Alston)', *European Journal of International Law*, Vol. 16, No. 3, 2005, 409 ff; Hepple, *Labour Laws and Global Trade*, *supra* note 4, at 56 ff.

125 ILO Declaration on Fundamental Principles and Rights at Work, 86th Session, Geneva, June 1998.

126 See Swepston (this volume) and Rishikesh (this volume) and the other chapters of the first part.

127 See the table of ratifications at <http://www.ilo.org/ilolex/english/docs/declworld.htm>.

128 At present, Conventions C87 and C98 concerning freedom of association and collective bargaining have been ratified first by 148 and 157 Member States respectively; Conventions C29 and C105 regarding the elimination of forced and compulsory labour have been ratified by 172 and 169 Member States respectively; Conventions C 100 and C111 on elimination of discrimination in respect of employment and occupation have been ratified by 164 and 166 countries respectively; Conventions C138 and C182 regarding the abolition of child labour have been ratified by 150 and 165 Member States respectively. Source: <http://www.ilo.org/ilolex/english/docs/declworld.htm>.

assistance of the Organization, particularly in the case of developing countries.[129] This tendency of pro forma ratifications seems to be confirmed by the high number of individual CEACR observations addressed to developing countries.[130] In any case, it clearly shows that those countries have various compliance problems with regard to Convention 138. Furthermore, even if 150 ratifications out of 180 Member States certainly are significant, many important developing Member States, particularly in Asia and Africa, did not ratify the Convention.[131]

With regard to the second question, it must be pointed out that the possible role of Convention 138 after the adoption of the Declaration of Geneva in 1998 is hotly debated. In fact, it is certainly true that the ILO decided to adopt the new instrument of Convention 182, instead of radically revising the existing one, also because of the deep crisis of the ILO standard-setting system[132] and of the lack of consensus about even an amended minimum age tool. Furthermore, the same ILO authorities, Governing Body and ILC in particular, insist on considering Convention 138 an essential tool for the eradication of child labour. This idea was laid out both in documents of the Governing Body[133] and in the Preamble of Convention 182. With regard to the latter, the ILC affirmed

> ... the need to adopt new instruments for the prohibition and elimination of the worst forms of child labour, as the main priority for national and international action, including international cooperation and assistance, to complement the Convention and the Recommendation concerning Minimum Age for Admission to Employment, 1973, which remain fundamental instruments on child labour.[134]

Scholars instead seem to be convinced that Convention 138 is anachronistic and obsolete, in particular because of the rigidities that have generated many implementation problems, its Western-centric approach, and its lack of priorities for national policy.[135]

The question is whether these two apparently contradictory positions can somehow be accommodated. The only way of doing so, it seems, consists of reasoning about priorities. At present, the most important question regards the need to combat the

---

129 Myers, 'The Right Rights?', *supra* note 80, at 47.

130 See the General Observation of the CEACR about Convention 138 of 1973 published in 2004 and the other 121 individual observations published between 1998 and 2007, concerning in the major part developing countries. It has to be recalled that, regarding Convention 138, the individual observations of the CEACR between 1973 and 1997 were only 25. Source: <http://www.ilo.org/ilolex/english/index.htm>.

131 The African countries that did not ratify the Convention are: Cape Verde, Gabon, Ghana, Guinea-Bissau, Liberia, Sierra Leone and Somalia. In Asia, Afghanistan, Bahrain, Bangladesh, Brunei Darussalam, India, Iran, Kiribati, Myanmar, Samoa, Saudi Arabia, Solomon Islands, Timor-Leste and Vanuatu have not ratified it. Source: http://www.ilo.org/ilolex/english/docs/declworld.htm.

132 See Creighton, 'Combating Child Labour', *supra* note 4, at 393 ff.

133 See ILO, *Child Labour: What Is To Be Done?*, Geneva: ILO, 1996.

134 Preamble to Convention 182 of 1999, first considerandum: Convention 182.

135 Myers, 'The Right Rights?', *supra* note 80, at 49; Creighton, 'Combating Child Labour', *supra* note 4, at 393.

worst forms of child labour, in particular in developing countries. It is therefore clear that Convention 138 presently remains in the shadows, even if ratified. Also the ILO authorities, although consistently recalling the fundamental importance of Convention 138, seem to concentrate on this priority, as demonstrated by the performance of the IPEC programme and of technical cooperation. Consequently, one might think that Convention 138 is important from a historical point of view, but will hardly become a priority again in the international fight against child labour. The most important obstacles to this still seem to be, on the one hand, the Western-centric approach of this tool and the ensuing difficulties of developing countries in implementing it. On the other hand, among the eight fundamental ILO conventions, Convention 138 is the only strictly prescriptive one. This characteristic is difficult to square with the core labour standards reasoning, which aims to progressively apply principles nowadays considered human rights.

3.5 Conclusion

During the last 10 years the fight against child labour has been characterized by the emergence of a new approach, focusing on the necessity to combat its worst forms. In that context, the ILO minimum age tools, and in particular Convention 138, have been subjected to a harsh discussion, particularly with regard to their lack of flexibility and of priorities for national policy, and their difficulty to apply in the developing countries.

Hence, the international community decided to approve a new Convention, the ILO Convention on the Worst Forms of Child Labour, partially anticipated by the UN Convention on the Rights of the Child. As this evolution demonstrates, the UN and, more particularly, the ILO tried to upgrade the instruments for the fight against child labour in order to establish international standards that could also be culturally and not just legally recognized by all Member States. For this purpose, the ILO partnered Convention 138 with Convention 182, including both in the core labour standards of the Declaration of Geneva of 1998. This means that both Conventions are still regarded as having the same importance by the ILO authorities for the fight against child labour. Nevertheless – and despite the strong increase of the ratifications of Convention 138 in recent years – it is clear that at the moment the priority of the Organization is represented by the worst forms of child labour: accordingly ILO activities concentrate on this issue and Convention 138 has lost a significant part of its importance. This Convention remains important from a historical point of view, because it represents the earliest international tool on this matter. However, it seems that this instrument should be deemed outdated from a cultural point of view, in particular because it is based on values that are shared only by Western countries, and in particular by the European ones, but not by the developing States, in which the problem of child labour currently is very severe.

Chapter 4

The Contribution of the ILO Declaration on Fundamental Principles and Rights at Work to the Elimination of Child Labour

Lee Swepston

4.1 Introduction

As other pieces in this book demonstrate amply, the ILO uses many tools for the elimination of child labour, all of which work together. The ILO has traditionally relied on international labour standards as the basic tool to frame consensus among States and to promote the implementation of the rights within its mandate, and has supplemented this with technical assistance whenever necessary. More recent developments have added analytical and assistance capacity that was missing earlier. This has resulted in significant advances in the realization of human rights in Member States, at the international level, and within and beyond the ILO itself.

There can be no doubt that the International Programme for the Elimination of Child Labour (IPEC) has done more than any other single programme to help the world move towards the elimination of the scourge of child labour. Yet it is also true that technical work alone cannot solve the problem altogether – additional conceptual and promotional work is needed, and this has been provided in part by the Declaration on Fundamental Principles and Rights at Work and its follow-up, to supplement the ILO's traditional supervisory efforts focusing on ratified Conventions.

In the years following the end of the Cold War, the framework within which the ILO was working underwent a major change, and the results of this change are only now becoming fully absorbed. The ILO was looking at a different world from that which had shaped its history since 1919, and to whose development it had made real contributions. Among them, the major political and economic blocs had broken down, and the respective roles of ILO constituents had begun to change. The ILO was called upon to emerge from the relatively restricted and comfortable role it had played, and to get more involved in the larger world of rights and development. In some areas it has done well, in some less well, but in respect of taking practical steps to develop the relation between rights, development and policy it has been making real strides – including in the elimination of child labour.

As the Director-General of the ILO said in a seminal report to the ILC in 1994:

> The International Labour Organization came into being at a time when communism was being set up in Russia. This means that part at least of the Organization's history can only

be understood by reference to the influence of that ideology in the world. It goes without saying that the recent disappearance of the communist bloc has sweeping implications for the life of our Organization, just as it has for all the agencies in the United Nations system, and indeed for the future of the whole world.[1]

Another factor in the changing landscape was economic globalization, and accompanying phenomena. By the mid-1990s, the ILO was beginning to realize that international labour standards by themselves were being overtaken by competing 'products' in the international development and policy markets. In the business community, companies were feeling the pressure for 'corporate social responsibility' (CSR), and various responses were being generated to fill that gap in a way that international law could not do directly. The CSR phenomenon was sometimes a necessary measure to fill gaps in national capacity to conceive and implement protection of workers, especially when multinational companies began to invest in countries that lacked the ability to adopt or enforce labour law. The ILO began to find that its labour standards were a rather distant reference to some of these efforts – and that sometimes they were being cited in ways that did not correspond to the way the ILO itself understood them. The UN Secretary-General established the Global Compact to influence the conduct of companies in developing countries, and in doing so established a relationship with the business community that is so important a part of the ILO's own constituency. The US and the EU continued to develop their Generalized System of Preferences (GSP),[2] and the US was successful in negotiating labour standards provisions into the North American Free Trade Agreement and later into various bilateral trade agreements. Private firms and some non-governmental organizations (NGOs) began to carry out 'social audits' to assess companies' performance on treatment of workers. All this began to challenge the ILO's monopoly of its labour standards mandate.

This labour standards 'monopoly' has resulted in part from a lack of interest by others in labour standards as a discipline. For instance, there are significant overlaps between the labour standards and human rights agendas, even if this relationship has been largely ignored by all concerned. In intergovernmental organizations, labour rights had long been peripheral to international discussions of human rights and development policy. In the rights arena, discussions had tended to focus exclusively on the UN's definitions of human rights, and until the mid-1990s the ILO described itself only incidentally as a 'rights' organization. The fruitless debate in human rights circles about whether economic, social and cultural rights were 'real' rights compared to civil and political rights had favoured the pre-eminence of civil and political rights until the 1993 International Conference on Human Rights in Vienna, with its affirmation that these two categories of rights were co-equal and indivisible.[3]

---

1 ILO, *Defending Values, Promoting Change: Social Justice in a Global Economy: An ILO Agenda*, Report of the Director-General, Report to the International Labour Conference, 81st Session, 1994, 3.

2 GSP provisions in both cases make trading privileges dependent on performance by exporting countries on labour standards, *inter alia*.

3 Vienna Declaration and Plan of Action, 1993, Part I, para. 5: 'All human rights are universal, indivisible and interdependent and interrelated.'

While this had an impact on the thinking inside the ILO secretariat, it only began to have an impact on the Organization as a whole when the World Summit on Social Development – the next in the monumental post-Cold War series of international conferences – was convened in Copenhagen in 1995.

In 1995, the Social Summit reaffirmed and amplified the role of what was called 'social' rights in development and in policy. In its concluding declaration, it called on States to ratify and apply core ILO standards on four subjects: freedom of association and collective bargaining, and the elimination of forced labour, child labour and discrimination at work.[4] This provided an impetus for three major initiatives in the ILO – the identification of certain Conventions as 'core' or 'fundamental' Conventions; the launching of a ratification campaign for them; and the beginning of the effort to adopt a new kind of instrument to supplement international labour standards, which five years later was to become the Declaration on Fundamental Principles and Rights at Work. This also began the ILO's movement towards identifying itself more consistently as a rights-based organization.

This is not to say that human rights had not played a significant role inside the ILO before then. Even while the ILO wisely held itself aloof from the discussions in the UN that divided human rights into two distinct categories, based on the spurious analysis that recognition of civil and political rights were merely a matter of political will whereas economic, social and cultural rights were dependent on economic development, it had taken an active part in the adoption in 1966 of the two international covenants on human rights that defined this split. The ILO's mandate fit most naturally into the International Covenant on Economic, Social and Cultural Rights, and articles 6 to 10 of that instrument were simply condensations of ILO instruments on a range of subjects that had been adopted up to that time.[5] Yet, one core ILO Convention had also succeeded in crossing the line between the two Covenants, with the inclusion in *both* instruments of a provision that recognized the rights to freedom of association and collective bargaining,[6] and of a savings clause in both instruments giving ILO Convention 87 supremacy over related provisions

---

4 Copenhagen Declaration on Social Development, 1995, Commitment 3(i): 'Pursue the goal of ensuring quality jobs, and safeguard the basic rights and interests of workers and to this end, freely promote respect for relevant International Labour Organization conventions, including those on the prohibition of forced and child labour, the freedom of association, the right to organize and bargain collectively, and the principle of non-discrimination.'

5 These articles list the various work-related rights, with little or no development of the concepts in the text of the Covenant. To declare a right to work, for example, without going into the content and the implications of such a right was not only inconsistent with the ILO position on the subject but left doubt and uncertainty about what the 'right' implied. For both this Covenant and that on civil and political rights the definition of the content and implications is left to the 'treaty bodies' to an extent that far surpasses the much more interpretative approach of the ILO. The Committee on Economic, Social and Cultural Rights, for instance, has recently elaborated its understanding of the meaning of the right to work in its General Comment No. 18, doc. E/C.12/GC/18, 6 February 2006.

6 Art. 22 of the International Covenant on Civil and Political Rights, and art. 8 of the International Covenant on Economic, Social and Cultural Rights.

of the Covenants. And several other parts of the CPR Covenant also touch on ILO concerns, for instance prohibitions on discrimination and on forced labour.[7]

On the core subject of this chapter, it is a historical curiosity that until the last two decades of the 20th century, child labour had not been developed, either in the ILO or elsewhere, as a core human rights subject, or even as a subject of great concern, in spite of the attention given to it early in the century.[8] The ILO's best-developed Convention on the subject, the Minimum Age Convention, No. 138 (1973), is a very technical instrument consolidating 10 earlier ILO Conventions on the same subject, which took the same approach for different economic sectors. It defines the acceptable conditions for gradual entry into the workforce of children and adolescents, and is not conceived as a rights instrument in spite of the obvious rights implications of its requirements.[9] As the first report submitted in 1998 to the ILO Conference for what was to become the Worst Forms of Child Labour Convention said:

> There were few institutions active in child labour, say, before the mid-1980s. For all practical purposes, the ILO was one of the few international organizations and ILO Conventions the only international instruments directly focused on and committed to the elimination of child labour. Until a few years ago, child labour was viewed with a mixture of indifference, apathy and even cynicism. It was so widely practised that it was accepted by many as part of the natural order of things. For others, child labour was equated with child work, excused with the argument that work is good for children and a means of helping families.[10]

Among operational agencies, the United Nations Children's Fund (UNICEF) had concentrated on child welfare rather than on the elimination of child labour, and neither the ILO itself nor any other international development agency had significant operational programmes focusing directly on child labour.

In the UN rights arena, the 1966 International Covenant on Economic, Social and Cultural Rights does include a paragraph in article 10 on family rights that picked up concepts adopted earlier in the long series of ILO minimum age Conventions, and reads as follows:

> 3. Special measures of protection and assistance should be taken on behalf of all children and young persons without any discrimination for reasons of parentage or other conditions.

---

7 See, respectively, articles 2 and 8 of the International Covenant on Civil and Political Rights.

8 One of the few books to consider the ILO and its relations to human rights was in fact co-authored by the author of this article: H. Bartolomei, G. von Potobsky and L. Swepston: *The International Labor Organization: The International Standards System and Basic Human Rights*, Boulder, Co.: Westview Press, 1996. It did not include child labour among the subjects covered.

9 It may be noted here that one of the striking characteristics of ILO standards compared to UN standards is that the former rarely refer to 'the right to ...', but concentrate instead on 'governments' obligation to ...'. Many of them are nevertheless detailed and effective rights instruments.

10 International Labour Conference, 86th Session of the ILO, Geneva, 1998, Report VI (1) – Child Labour: Targeting the Intolerable.

Children and young persons should be protected from economic and social exploitation. Their employment in work harmful to their morals or health or dangerous to life or likely to hamper their normal development should be punishable by law. States should also set age limits below which the paid employment of child labour should be prohibited and punishable by law.

This does not, of course, state what these special measures shall be, nor set an international minimum age, nor does it cover aspects of work beyond paid employment. This provision has not been developed significantly by the Covenant's treaty body, or in other UN human rights instruments. In 1989 the UN adopted the phenomenally successful Convention on the Rights of the Child. Even this convention, however, barely goes beyond the provisions of the Covenant – or of ILO Convention 138 – in respect of child labour, except to qualify protection from economic exploitation as a human right. This is dealt with in its minimalist article 32, which reads as follows:

1. States Parties recognize the right of the child to be protected from economic exploitation and from performing any work that is likely to be hazardous or to interfere with the child's education, or to be harmful to the child's health or physical, mental, spiritual, moral or social development.

2. States Parties shall take legislative, administrative, social and educational measures to ensure the implementation of the present article. To this end, and having regard to the relevant provisions of other international instruments, States Parties shall in particular:
(a) Provide for a minimum age or minimum ages for admission to employment;
(b) Provide for appropriate regulation of the hours and conditions of employment;
(c) Provide for appropriate penalties or other sanctions to ensure the effective enforcement of the present article.

This suffers from many of the same weaknesses as the earlier UN instruments. The requirements are very general, and paragraph 2 of this article deals only with employment and not with the far wider question of work. It calls for a minimum age to be set, but does not give guidance on what it should be.

4.2 The approach begins to change

By the mid-1990s, the climate had changed. As the 1998 Conference report also stated:

Today, child labour is one of the dominant issues of our time:
• There is an explosion in the literature on child labour and in the coverage of child labour abuses and violations in the international print and electronic media.
• Today, there is a large number of distinguished institutions at the forefront of the struggle against child labour. In 1986 UNICEF gave impetus to the cause through its programme on children in especially difficult circumstances. The body of international law and ILO instruments was given added momentum with the adoption, in 1989, of the United Nations Convention on the Rights of the Child. Perhaps less well known, but important too, was the increasingly central place that child labour was given in the

deliberations of the subcommittees of the Geneva-based United Nations Commission on Human Rights.

- Thanks to the commitment of thousands of concerned individuals and groups, the cause of child rights has been given a further boost by the emergence of numerous non-governmental organizations (NGOs) which have carried the torch and transformed what was at best a fledgling local concern into a formidable worldwide movement.[11]

By this time, also, the discussion of the 'social clause' was in full swing in the General Agreement on Trade and Tariffs (GATT), the predecessor of the World Trade Organization (WTO), and echoes were being felt in the ILO as well. A favourite target of the proposed social clause was child labour: the question posed by its proponents was why trade privileges should be allowed to countries that undercut decent conditions of work by exploiting children and other vulnerable groups. The US was the most prominent among the countries that had been promoting the inclusion of a social clause in the GATT, though it had received little support from other sources. The Uruguay Round of trade talks, which eventually led to the creation of the WTO, included a flurry of activity designed to get the new organization to deal with labour standards and their relation to trade. However, the ministerial declaration adopted in Singapore in 1996 put a halt to this endeavour, by declaring that labour standards were the exclusive mandate of the ILO.[12]

In 1998, the ILC agenda included two very exciting items. One was the first of two discussions on the adoption of what was to become the Worst Forms of Child Labour Convention, 1999 (No. 182). This was one of the rare international labour standards that had not emerged from a technical needs analysis of gaps in standards carried out by the International Labour Office, or an agreement based on competing political priorities. Instead it had been proposed and adopted for the Conference agenda in a rare spontaneous acceptance of the idea in 1996 across all lines of the Governing Body. The new Convention was to give concrete form to the idea that certain forms of child labour could actually be eliminated, through the adoption of policies specifically targeted to do so, and through 'time-bound programmes'. This gave a new emphasis to IPEC, which had been established in 1992 (see below), and helped create excitement around the subject in the ILO and elsewhere. The Convention would be adopted in 1999 after its second discussion, following the usual course of the ILO's standard-setting.

The second subject on the 1998 Conference was the adoption of the Declaration on Fundamental Principles and Rights at Work. This Declaration's adoption was

---

11 ILO, *Targeting the Intolerable, supra* note 10, 6.

12 In their declaration, the ministers of trade of the WTO said in Singapore that, while agreeing that the comparative advantage of countries, particularly low-wage developing countries, should in no way be called into question, they renewed their 'commitment to the observance of internationally recognised core labour standards'; they also recognized that the ILO was 'the competent body to set and deal with these standards': WTO: Singapore Ministerial Declaration (doc. WT/MIN (96)/DEC, 18 December 1996, § 4).

difficult and controversial, linked in part to the originality of the approach it took.[13] It has made a profound change in the way the ILO deals with human rights.

4.3 Towards the adoption of the Declaration[14]

The question of the ILO's future activities with regard to fundamental rights was raised in the Report of the Director-General to the 81st Session of the ILC (June 1994),[15] on the occasion of the ILO's 75th anniversary. This report proposed promoting the ILO's basic principles through means additional to its standards, and in particular through a more promotional approach in 'soft law' instruments. This principle of promotion of basic values was then taken up in the adoption by the World Summit for Social Development (Copenhagen, March 1995), of specific commitments and a Programme of Action on fundamental workers' rights, namely those relating to the prohibition of forced labour and child labour; freedom of association, freedom to form trade unions and carry out collective bargaining; equality of pay between men and women for work of equal value; and the elimination of discrimination in employment.

In May 1995, the ILO Director-General, referring to the need to follow up the World Summit for Social Development, sent the first of an annual series of letters inviting all those countries that had not ratified all the Conventions concerning fundamental rights to indicate whether they planned to do so and, if so, what timetable was envisaged and, if not, what substantive or technical difficulties delayed or prevented ratification. In the letters, he included the elimination of child labour among these subjects, following the example of the Social Summit – at the time this referred only to Convention 138.

Since then, each year the ILO Governing Body has examined the results of this ratification campaign on the basis of replies received to successive letters from the Director-General.[16] The results of the campaign are encouraging. In 1995, 21 States had ratified the seven fundamental Conventions; by the time this article was completed in early 2007, 123 States had ratified all the fundamental Conventions, now numbering eight with the addition of Convention 182 after its adoption; 20 States had ratified seven of them, etc.

---

13 The author of this chapter was closely involved in the Declaration's drafting and adoption, and served as the Deputy Representative of the Secretary-General (as the Director-General of the ILO is known in the Conference) when it was adopted.

14 This section draws heavily on the report submitted to the Conference as the basis for the discussion of the draft Declaration: Report VII, Consideration of a possible Declaration of Principles of the International Labour Organization concerning Fundamental Rights and its Appropriate Follow-Up Mechanism, International Labour Conference, 86th Session, Geneva, June 1998.

15 ILO, *Defending Values, Promoting Change, supra* note 1.

16 See, for example, document GB.297/LILS/6, Ratification and Promotion of Fundamental ILO Conventions, 297th Session of the ILO Governing Body (November 2006).

At its 262nd Session in June 1995, the Governing Body endorsed the proposal of its Chairperson to request the Director-General to submit a paper on the strengthening of the ILO's standards supervisory system. In November 1995, the Governing Body took another measure that prefigured the follow-up to the Declaration that would be adopted less than three years later. It decided[17] to extend the system of four-yearly reports hitherto required under article 19 of the Constitution[18] from countries that had not ratified the Discrimination (Employment and Occupation) Convention, 1958 (No. 111), to the six other Conventions concerning fundamental rights, including child labour (Convention 138). This decision was first implemented in 1997 with regard to the forced labour Conventions, and examined in the report of the CEACR, but shortly thereafter was replaced by the Declaration follow-up. [19]

At the same session in November 1995, the Governing Body considered the possibility of putting in place a new procedure for dealing with complaints regarding non-compliance with the principles of elimination of discrimination and forced and child labour. Such complaints would be examined by one or two ad hoc committees, in a procedure that would parallel complaints to the Committee on Freedom of Association. In the end this procedure was not adopted, but its discussion formed part of the basis for the eventual adoption of the Declaration.

During the November 1996 (267th) Session of the ILO Governing Body the employers' group outlined for the first time the principles that were to become the Declaration. While rejecting the idea of new complaints procedures, they did suggest that additional promotional measures should be taken. As they indicated during the discussion:

> To supplement the constitutional system of binding Conventions and supervisory machinery, the ILO should develop a parallel means of encouraging observance of the fundamental principles underlying the core Conventions. This should take the form of a statement of principles, which should be promoted, in a variety of ways, including:
>
> • through actions by Member States and by employers' and workers' organizations;
> • through the ILO's own technical cooperation programmes;
> • through country examinations related to employment policy;
> • through action in specific areas of the fundamental principles, such as by intensifying and publicizing ILO work on exploitative child labour and supporting an IOE (International Organization of Employers) programme of work in this important area.[20]

This was clearly the conceptual outline for what became the Declaration, and it was picked up as of the next Session of the Governing Body. At the 268th Session of

---

17 GB.264/9/2 (November 1995).

18 Art. 19 of the ILO Constitution is a unique and versatile provision, allowing the Governing Body to request reports from its Members on measures taken to implement Conventions they have not ratified, and on Recommendations.

19 Report of the Committee of Experts on the Application of Conventions and Recommendations, Report III (Part 1A), International Labour Conference, 86th Session (1998), §§ 94 et seq.

20 Report of the LILS discussion, November 1996. GB.267/9/2, § 38.

the Governing Body (March 1997), the Legal Issues and Labour Standards (LILS) Committee had welcomed the recognition given to the strengthened role of the ILO with regard to the fundamental human rights by the Copenhagen World Summit for Social Development and by the WTO Ministerial Conference in Singapore in December 1996.[21] In this context, the Committee stressed the great importance to the Organization's credibility of the promotion of basic principles and rights and the strengthening of the supervisory machinery. As a result, the Committee had endorsed a proposal by the employers' group, supported by a number of government representatives and also supported, after initial hesitation, by the workers' group, to make the mandate of the ILO more explicit 'by means of a document, which might take the form of a Declaration, which could be adopted by the Conference. This document would not modify the Constitution, but would clarify its meaning in relation to the fundamental principles.'[22]

Thus, by the time of the March 1997 Governing Body session, opinion was sufficiently clarified that in a discussion of the proposed Declaration the Office paper (GB.268/LILS/6) was able to state:

> The Governing Body has come to agreement in recent sessions that these instruments (i.e., those on freedom of association, forced labour and discrimination), together with the subject of child labour (at present represented by Convention No. 138) are the core standards of the Organization, and this should therefore be taken into consideration if a list of fundamental principles is drawn up.

Thus, the elimination of child labour was added to the list of fundamental principles of the ILO as that recognition was formalized for the first time in the process leading up to the adoption of the Declaration.

This proposal would also figure in the Report presented by the Director-General to the ILC at its 85th Session in June 1997.[23] The discussions on this question were very lively and revealed a number of misunderstandings.[24] This prompted the Director-General in his reply to the Conference discussions to make it clear that

> ... it is in no way a question of imposing, through such a Declaration, new obligations on Member States against their will. The Declaration is a means of reaffirming the logic of the commitments and the values to which States have already freely subscribed in joining the ILO [...] nobody could reproach the Organization for inviting its Members to take seriously such commitments by making them more explicit.

---

21 See section 4.1 above.

22 GB.268/8/2, § 54. As regards the origin of these proposals see also GB.268/ PV(Rev.).

23 The ILO, *Standard Setting and Globalization*, International Labour Conference, 85th Session, 1997, Report of the Director-General, 16–19 and 69, available at <http://www-old. itcilo.org/actrav/actrav-english/telearn/global/ilo/law/ilodg.htm>.

24 See GB.270/3/1(Add.) for extracts of statements made at the 85th Session of the International Labour Conference during the discussion of the Director-General's Report, concerning means of ensuring a universal guarantee of workers' fundamental rights and the possible adoption of a solemn Declaration.

Many delegates emphasized that at its June 1998 session the Conference should examine and adopt such a Declaration.

Immediately after the 1997 Conference, the Governing Body added an item to the agenda of its 270th Session (November 1997) concerning follow-up on the discussions of the Report of the Director-General 'in particular as regards the possibility of including on the agenda of the 86th Session (1998) of the ILC an additional item concerning a Declaration on workers' fundamental rights and follow-up arrangements.'[25]

Following in-depth discussions, the Governing Body decided to place on the agenda of the 86th (1998) Session of the ILC an additional item concerning the examination of a possible Declaration of principles concerning fundamental rights and its appropriate follow-up mechanism. The Office was asked to prepare the relevant documents, taking into account all the views expressed during the discussions and close consultation with the constituents.

Following the consultation process which took place in January and February 1998, a paper containing a preliminary draft was communicated by the Director-General to the Governing Body.[26] In general, this document was well received. Following the discussions, the Governing Body authorized the Director-General to prepare a draft of a possible Declaration of principles concerning fundamental rights and its follow-up mechanism for the 86th Session (1998) of the ILC, taking into account all the views presented in the debate in the Governing Body. In order to arrive at the most acceptable solutions, these proposals were to be prepared in close consultation with the tripartite constituents.

A working paper was prepared to facilitate informal tripartite consultations on the draft Declaration and follow-up mechanism. These consultations proved to be a very useful means of narrowing the range of differences that remained and helping the Office to prepare the report that was submitted to the Conference in June 1998. The Declaration was adopted, after difficult discussions, and came into force immediately. Even in the most animated discussions there was no serious suggestion that the elimination of child labour should not figure among the fundamental rights and principles embodied in the Declaration.

4.4 The Declaration and its follow-up

The Declaration on Fundamental Rights and Principles at Work is an unusual instrument, taking a promotional rather than a supervisory approach to the realization of certain fundamental rights. Its core provision, article 2, States that

> ... all Members, even if they have not ratified the Conventions in question, have an obligation arising from the very fact of membership in the Organization, to respect, to promote and to realize, in good faith and in accordance with the Constitution, the principles concerning the fundamental rights which are the subject of those Conventions, namely:

---

25 GB.269/205, § 2.
26 GB.271/3/1.

a. freedom of association and the effective recognition of the right to collective bargaining;
b. the elimination of all forms of forced or compulsory labour;
c. the effective abolition of child labour; and
d. the elimination of discrimination in respect of employment and occupation.

The Declaration has made three distinctive contributions to the elimination of child labour. The first is that the Declaration's adoption, and the discussions leading up to it, brought child labour squarely within the ambit of human rights in the ILO, and beyond, as has been described above. The second contribution lies in the follow-up to the Declaration, which consists of two parts: *Global Report*s and the *Annual Follow-Up*. As for the third, while for other basic human rights subjects the Declaration has also provided a framework for new technical assistance procedures, this is not the case with child labour, as IPEC already existed when the Declaration was adopted. However, the Declaration's technical assistance framework has helped to link the elimination of child labour to assistance on other human rights violations, in particular forced labour and discrimination.

4.5 Follow-up to the Declaration

Part of the Declaration's originality lies in its two principal follow-up mechanisms, both of which have made their own contribution to the elimination of child labour. As the Annex to the Declaration indicates:

OVERALL PURPOSE

1. The aim of the follow-up described below is to encourage the efforts made by the Members of the Organization to promote the fundamental principles and rights enshrined in the Constitution of the ILO and the Declaration of Philadelphia and reaffirmed in this Declaration.
2. In line with this objective, which is of a strictly promotional nature, this follow-up will allow the identification of areas in which the assistance of the Organization through its technical cooperation activities may prove useful to its Members to help them implement these fundamental principles and rights. It is not a substitute for the established supervisory mechanisms, nor shall it impede their functioning; consequently, specific situations within the purview of those mechanisms shall not be examined or re-examined within the framework of this follow-up.

4.6 Annual follow-up

The first of the Declaration's follow-up mechanisms provides for annual reports to the ILO by each State that has not ratified all the relevant Conventions. Unlike the procedure requiring regular reports on ratified Conventions,[27] this requirement was elaborated under the provisions of article 19 of the ILO Constitution, which allows

---

27 Required by art. 22 of the ILO Constitution.

the Governing Body to request reports, at appropriate intervals, on non-ratified Conventions and on Recommendations. The Declaration adapted this provision to its own characteristics, and provides that reporting is not to be on the non-ratified Conventions themselves, but rather on the *principles underlying* each Convention.[28] The procedure was described as follows:

II. ANNUAL FOLLOW-UP CONCERNING NON-RATIFIED FUNDAMENTAL CONVENTIONS

A. Purpose and scope

1. The purpose is to provide an opportunity to review each year, by means of simplified procedures to replace the four-year review introduced by the Governing Body in 1995, the efforts made in accordance with the Declaration by Members which have not yet ratified all the fundamental Conventions.
2. The follow-up will cover each year the four areas of fundamental principles and rights specified in the Declaration.

B. Modalities

1. The follow-up will be based on reports requested from Members under article 19, paragraph 5(e), of the Constitution. The report forms will be drawn up so as to obtain information from governments which have not ratified one or more of the fundamental Conventions, on any changes which may have taken place in their law and practice, taking due account of article 23 of the Constitution and established practice.[29]
2. These reports, as compiled by the Office, will be reviewed by the Governing Body.
3. With a view to presenting an introduction to the reports thus compiled, drawing attention to any aspects which might call for a more in-depth discussion, the Office may call upon a group of experts appointed for this purpose by the Governing Body.
4. Adjustments to the Governing Body's existing procedures should be examined to allow Members which are not represented on the Governing Body to provide, in the most appropriate way, clarifications which might prove necessary or useful during Governing Body discussions to supplement the information contained in their reports.

---

28 Art. II.B.1 of the Follow-Up to the Declaration provides: 'The follow-up will be based on reports requested from Members under article 19, paragraph 5(e), of the Constitution. The report forms will be drawn up so as to obtain information from governments which have not ratified one or more of the fundamental Conventions, on any changes which may have taken place in their law and practice, taking due account of article 23 of the Constitution and established practice.'

29 'Article 23 of the Constitution and the established practice' mean that governments' reports are sent to employers' and workers' organizations, which may make their own comments on them, supplement, or even contradict them. In addition, international organizations of employers and workers may comment. These comments may also be received when the government concerned has failed to report. This facility has been taken up very actively by workers' and employers' organizations at the national level, and by the International Confederation of Trade Unions (ICFTU), which in late 2006 merged with other international workers' organizations to form the International Trade Union Confederation (ITUC). The International Organization of Employers (IOE) has used this possibility to submit a general statement to the ILO each year.

As the follow-up mechanism was being established in the Governing Body following the Declaration's adoption, the Office took advantage of paragraph 3 of the provision reproduced above, and a committee was established under the name of the Independent Declaration Expert-Advisers, composed originally of seven persons, to compile an introduction to governments' reports for presentation to the Governing Body.[30]

At the time the Declaration was adopted Convention 138 was the least ratified of the fundamental Conventions, and the adoption of Convention 182 was still a year away. This meant that in the beginning reporting on the child labour principle was the most prolific. The large number of ratifications of all the Conventions since the Declaration's adoption – but especially of Conventions 138 and 182 – has resulted in a steady diminution of reporting on this principle since then.

How did this reporting advance the elimination of child labour? It did so in two ways. First, the fact that countries had to draft reports even if they had not ratified the Conventions meant that at least some consideration was being given at the national level to this principle. The need for countries to gather information, together with the involvement of the social partners of the ILO in the process of reporting, has always served as an incentive to reflection – leading eventually to action in many cases. And in a number of those cases, which have been detailed in the annual reports of the Expert-Advisers, governments have taken the occasion to request and receive assistance from the Office toward the ratification of the Conventions and towards the actual elimination of child labour.

Second, it has allowed the Governing Body to be informed in a more systematic way of the progress being made towards the achievement of the principle through the submission at each March session of the compilation of reports received, together with the introduction to these reports by the Expert-Advisers. This was an excellent complement to the reports submitted under the ratification campaign, which was launched in 1995. These two reports have different purposes. The report under the Declaration asks for progress in achieving the principle, while the report under the ratification campaign asks more specifically about the ratification prospects for the specific Conventions concerned. Even when governments report under the Declaration they regularly indicate whether they have made progress towards the ratification of the Conventions, but to this are added other reflections.

For instance, among the conclusions and observations stated by the Expert-Advisers in their January 2002 report were the following comments:

142. To the Expert-Advisers, the greater awareness of the undesirability of having children start work too early in their lives, or to carry out activities that harm them, seems reflected in the more intensive involvement of governments and the social partners in the fight to combat child labour throughout the world. The reports received mirror the growing attention given to the principle of abolishing child labour as a priority for human development.

---

30 See the Declaration web page for copies of the reports filed by governments, comments by employers' and workers' organizations, and the introduction provided by the Expert-Advisers each year: <http://www.ilo.org/dyn/declaris/DECLARATIONWEB. INDEXPAGE>.

143. It was disturbing to see the reports confirm that modernization and high per capita incomes do not, by themselves, lead to the disappearance of all forms of child labour. Rich countries are not immune to what is dubbed today the worst forms of child labour – hazardous work, prostitution, trafficking, etc. International trafficking, in particular, needs to be tackled more effectively by countries that would appear to have the resources to do so.

144. Several of the reports received from developing or transition countries point to poverty, particularly in agriculture and the informal sector, as being at the origin of various forms of child labour. Other factors include lack of education, legislation that is not adequate or not forcefully applied. The fact that the reports mention the adoption of national action plans and refer to ILO-IPEC's integrated approach and time-bound programmes holds promise that the tide can be turned against child labour. We appeal to the international organizations that need to contribute to good governance, schooling and the reduction of poverty, notably the international financial institutions, UNDP, UNICEF and UNESCO, to orient their work in consultation with governments, the social partners and the ILO in such a way that ILO-IPEC's time-bound programmes can achieve their goals.[31]

This procedure thus allows a broadly based view of the experience of countries that have not ratified Conventions and that therefore have not brought themselves under the ILO reporting procedure for these instruments. It also allows a review of the practical problems of implementation from a country viewpoint, without the need to take a defensive stance as sometimes happens when countries that have ratified Conventions try to justify their failure to meet their obligations. Under the Declaration the obligation is to make an effort, and not to apply the legal requirements of a normative instrument. Reporting in this way has been seen to foster a more self-critical evaluation and reporting from countries because they will not be held accountable for failure to implement.[32]

4.7 Global Reports

The second element of follow-up to the Declaration is the Global Reports which are published each year, in rotation among the four subjects. The year 2006 saw the publication of the second Global Report on the elimination of child labour.[33] The Declaration follow-up provides in this respect:

GLOBAL REPORT
A. Purpose and scope
1. The purpose of this report is to provide a dynamic global picture relating to each category of fundamental principles and rights noted during the preceding four-year

---

31 ILO, document GB.283/3/1, Governing Body, 283rd Session, March 2002.

32 It is therefore somewhat surprising that there has been such a wholesale movement towards ratification of the eight ILO's 'core' Conventions, and the consequent obligation to implement.

33 The author of this chapter oversaw the drafting and publication of the child labour report in 2006. Global Reports are available at the same Internet address as the annual reports.

period, and to serve as a basis for assessing the effectiveness of the assistance provided by the Organization, and for determining priorities for the following period, in the form of action plans for technical cooperation designed in particular to mobilize the internal and external resources necessary to carry them out.

2. The report will cover, each year, one of the four categories of fundamental principles and rights in turn.

B. *Modalities*

1. The report will be drawn up under the responsibility of the Director-General on the basis of official information, or information gathered and assessed in accordance with established procedures. In the case of States which have not ratified the fundamental Conventions, it will be based in particular on the findings of the aforementioned annual follow-up. In the case of Members which have ratified the Conventions concerned, the report will be based in particular on reports as dealt with pursuant to article 22 of the Constitution.

2. This report will be submitted to the Conference for tripartite discussion as a report of the Director-General. The Conference may deal with this report separately from reports under article 12 of its Standing Orders, and may discuss it during a sitting devoted entirely to this report, or in any other appropriate way. It will then be for the Governing Body, at an early session, to draw conclusions from this discussion concerning the priorities and plans of action for technical cooperation to be implemented for the following four-year period.

The Global Reports make an altogether different contribution. They are designed to present a 'dynamic global picture', and not a review of individual action at the country level. They focus on demonstrating the tendencies around the world in respect of a given right, proposing an action plan for the ILO to tackle these problems, and evaluating the effect of an action plan once it has been concluded. In addition, they cover both ratifying and non-ratifying countries.[34]

In respect of child labour one enormous contribution of the Global Reports has been to provide a basis for statistical analysis that might otherwise not have been carried out. In addition, it gives the basis for analysing trends in the data, and a prominent platform for presenting them. For instance, in its 2002 report the ILO issued a detailed estimate of child labour around the world, with different categories of child labour according to age and the severity of the problem. These figures were remarkable for the number of children they revealed to be engaged in work, and for the innovative statistical methods that had to be developed to measure this activity, which often is illegal. The statistics also helped to provide a focus for ILO action in the four years that followed.

The second Global Report on this subject four years later, in 2006, produced a very different effect when it revealed that efforts around the world to reduce child labour had been unexpectedly successful. It showed that there had been an 11 per

---

34 The Global Reports also serve a different function from the General Surveys carried out by the Committee of Experts on the Application of Conventions and Recommendations. The latter are intended specifically to examine the meaning and implementation of the Conventions they cover, and obstacles to their ratification. The Global Reports, on the other hand, examine global trends, and specifically avoid legal analysis of the implementation of ILO standards.

cent decrease in child labour; that the successes had been greatest in Latin America and the Caribbean and least so in sub-Saharan Africa; and provided a basis for the ILO to set the goal of eliminating the worst forms of child labour over the following decade. If the trends that emerged during the preceding four years are continued, it is mathematically possible that the worst forms of child labour can in fact be eliminated by 2016.

Another thing that the global reports have contributed to the elimination of child labour is to bring wider attention to the subject by presenting the concept in a more easily readable and understandable form than do the more technical reports issued by the ILO. An exact understanding of what child labour is can be elusive, especially as not all work by children is child labour of the kind that needs to be eliminated. By providing examples and clear explanations, the global reports have contributed to allowing more focused action to be taken on the actual abuses, and not be dissipated on tackling problems that do not exist.

Finally, the global reports allow successful action to be highlighted, and present the best practices in a way that is more easily accessible to those who are not specialists. The discussion of these reports in the annual ILC, often attended by ministers of state as well as by employers' and workers' organizations, allows the forging of alliances and a greater understanding on all sides of the difficulties that must be faced. And finally, these discussions lead to the presentation to the ILO Governing Body the following November of a plan of action for the Office and for the ILO's constituents for the coming four years to continue to fight child labour. The fact that it is discussed both in the Conference and in the Governing Body allows tripartite input into what could otherwise be an entirely technical exercise. The sense of ownership that this helps create is in itself a positive contribution to the elimination of child labour.

One other aspect that needs to be brought out is the contribution that the Declaration has made to viewing child labour in the wider context of human rights, and the interaction among these rights. For instance, the Global Report of 2006 drew attention to the interaction of discrimination and child labour:

> 108. However, poverty in itself is not a sufficient explanation of child labour, and it certainly fails to explain some of the unconditional worst forms of child labour. A human rights perspective is necessary for a fuller understanding of child labour, as it focuses on discrimination and exclusion as contributing factors. The most vulnerable groups when it comes to child labour are often those subject to discrimination and exclusion: girls, ethnic minorities and indigenous and tribal peoples, those of low class or caste, people with disabilities, displaced persons and those living in remote areas.

4.8 Concluding remarks

This article illustrates that the adoption of the Declaration of Fundamental Principles and Rights at Work, and the pursuit of its follow-up, have made a positive contribution to the elimination of child labour. The detailed supervision of Conventions takes place by the ILO's Committee of Experts on the Application of Conventions and Recommendations. The bulk of the technical work is carried out by the IPEC. There remains a place in this panoply of actions for the promotional work of the Declaration, and the focused discussions on the questions that arise, and the Declaration and its follow-up provide such a basis.

What is more, as has been shown above, the process leading to the adoption of the Declaration also helped to define the human rights character of the fight against child labour, and was essential in bringing this problem into high relief for the human rights and development communities.

But these different contributions illustrate in turn the complexity of tackling problems that have elements of both human rights and development, and the contribution that the integrated discussion of them can make to resolve the problems. The Declaration is a unique instrument of international law, drawing as it does on the Constitution of the ILO, expressing the requirement of pursuing principles as an obligation of Member States, and creating a reciprocal obligation on the Organization itself. The Declaration has made a difference, and will continue to do so.

Update

Just before this book went to press, in its June 2008 session the ILO Conference adopted an 'ILO Declaration on Social Justice for a Fair Globalization', which took the 1998 Declaration as one of its inspirations. The accompanying Resolution provides for an implementation plan to be submitted to the ILO Governing Body in November 2008, and adopted at the March 2009 session of the Governing Body. In addition, a review of the functioning of the 1998 Declaration is under way, but not yet completed in mid-2008. Some of the details of the follow-up to the 1998 Declaration may be modified as a result of these examinations, and readers will wish to consult the ILO website at www.ilo.org for an update.

Chapter 5

The Worst Forms of Child Labour: A Guide to ILO Convention 182 and Recommendation 190

Deepa Rishikesh[1]

5.1 Introduction

The adoption of international labour standards was for a long time the principal means used by the ILO to combat child labour. The ILO's standard-setting activities on child labour, which began with the creation of the ILO in 1919, reflect the conviction of ILO Member States that childhood is a period of life, which should not be devoted to work, but to the physical and mental development of children and their education. Action to combat the economic exploitation of children began at the international level with the adoption of the Minimum Age (Industry) Convention, 1919 (No. 5) by representatives of governments and of employers' and workers' organizations at the very first session of the ILC in 1919. In the years that followed, the concept of minimum age for admission to employment was extended to different economic sectors. Between 1919 and 1972, the Conference adopted or revised ten Conventions and four Recommendations on the minimum age for admission to employment or work in various sectors.[2] Moreover, three Conventions and two Recommendations on the night work of young persons, as well as four Conventions and one Recommendation concerning the medical examination of young persons,[3] and the conditions of work of children and young persons were also adopted by the Conference.

While the above instruments targeted specific sectors, namely industry, maritime work, non-industrial work and underground work, ILO constituents subsequently found that this sectoral approach was no longer sufficient to promote the well-being of children. A new instrument was needed that could be applied to all sectors and be

---

1 The views expressed here are the author's and do not necessarily represent those of the ILO.

2 See Borzaga (this volume). For a general overview of ILO Action in the field, see Trebilcock, Raimondi (this volume).

3 The Night Work of Young Persons (Industry) Convention, 1919 (No. 6); the Night Work of Young Persons (Non-Industrial Occupations) Convention, 1946 (No. 79); the Night Work of Young Persons (Industry) Convention (Revised), 1948 (No. 90); the Night Work of Young Persons (Non-Industrial Occupations) Recommendation, 1946 (No. 80); and the Night Work Recommendation, 1990 (No.178).

adapted to national situations. It was in this spirit that the Minimum Age Convention (No. 138) and Recommendation (No. 146) were adopted by the Conference in 1973.

However, child labour remained an important feature of the labour market and indeed appeared to grow in intensity in the 1980s. Child labour remained a matter of concern, particularly in view of the numbers of children involved, which remained very high. In 1996, the ILO Governing Body approved the development of a new ILO instrument on the subject. The aim of such an instrument was to consolidate the consensus, fuelled in part by the ILO's own increasing work under its IPEC programme,[4] that certain forms of child labour demanded urgent, immediate action for their prohibition and elimination. In terms of standard-setting on child labour, 1999 marked yet another milestone in the struggle to combat child labour with the unanimous adoption of the Worst Forms of Child Labour Convention (No. 182) and Recommendation (No. 190). The Convention entered into force 15 months after its adoption and has received 165 ratifications as of today.[5] It should be noted that, throughout the process leading to the adoption of Convention 182, discussions have been guided by a desire for consensus and by the objective of universal applicability. The inclusion of Convention 182 on the agenda of the ILC in 1998 was preceded, in particular, by an informal tripartite meeting at ministerial level at the 1996 session of the Conference.[6] Hence, the in-depth examination and numerous consultations, which preceded the adoption of Convention 182, are the guarantee of its relevance. The speed of ratification of Convention 182, which is unparalleled in the history of the ILO, has also been beneficial to Convention 138, for which the number of ratifications now stands at 148. There can be no doubt that this reflects a major political will to eradicate child labour, especially its worst forms.

5.2 Content of the standards on the worst forms of child labour

5.2.1 The prohibition and elimination of the worst forms of child labour

While Convention 182 is similar to Convention 138 in that both are fundamental Conventions that seek, in the final analysis, to attain the abolition of child labour, the immediate goal of Convention 182 and the means used to attain this goal are substantially different from those pursued under Convention 138. Unlike Convention 182, Convention 138 does not require that measures be taken to abolish child labour within a certain time frame. The primary objective of Convention 138 is the pursuit of a 'national policy designed to ensure the effective abolition of child labour and to raise *progressively* the minimum age for admission to employment or work (article 1 of Convention No. 138). Convention 182, on the other hand, focuses on certain forms of child labour that cannot be tolerated by Member States, whatever their

---

4 Established in 1992, IPEC is the ILO's biggest technical cooperation programme, with 30 funders. It operates in 88 countries, of which 60 have signed a Memorandum of Understanding with the ILO. It also has set up time-bound programmes (TBPs) in 23 countries.

5 27 August 2007.

6 See ITM/1/1996 and ITM/3/1996.

level of development or national circumstances, and therefore cannot be subject to progressive elimination.[7] Under article 1 of the Convention, 'Each Member which ratifies this Convention shall take *immediate* and effective measures to secure the prohibition and elimination of the worst forms of child labour as a *matter of urgency*'. Hence, the measures taken must ensure not only the prohibition, but also the elimination of the worst forms of child labour. For the effective elimination of child labour, both immediate action and time-bound measures would therefore seem to be necessary.[8]

5.2.2 Definition of 'child'

As mentioned in Chapter 3, Convention 138 sets out different minimum ages for admission to employment or work depending on the work involved. Convention 182, in contrast, in article 2 sets out a single age limit of 18 years below which it is forbidden to engage children in the worst forms of child labour as defined in article 3.

5.2.3 Definition of the worst forms of child labour

Article 3 of Convention 182 enumerates in detail the types of work that are prohibited for children under the age of 18. The worst forms of child labour include all forms of slavery or practices similar to slavery (clause a), prostitution and the production of pornography or pornographic performances (clause b), illicit activities (clause c) and hazardous work (clause d). A distinction can be drawn between two categories of the worst forms of child labour: (i) those that are termed the *unconditional* worst forms of child labour, as enumerated in clauses (a) to (c) of article 3, that are so fundamentally at odds with children's basic human rights that they are absolutely prohibited for all persons under the age of 18: and (ii) hazardous work, as defined in clause (d) of article 3, which is a *conditional* worst form of child labour. [9] If the nature of this type of work or the circumstances in which it is carried out is likely to harm the health, safety or morals of children, then it constitutes hazardous work that must be prohibited for persons under 18.

5.2.3.1 All forms of slavery or practices similar to slavery Under article 3(a) of Convention 182, 'the term "the worst forms of child labour" comprises all forms of slavery or practices similar to slavery, such as the sale and trafficking of children, debt bondage and serfdom and forced or compulsory labour, including forced or compulsory recruitment of children for use in armed conflict'. The expression 'the sale and trafficking of children' is not meant to cover issues unrelated to the worst forms of child labour, such as adoption or child victims of organ transplants. The

---

7 ILO, *Child Labour, Report IV (2A)*, ILC, 87th Session, 1999, Geneva, Office commentary, 34.

8 *Ibid.*

9 ILO, *A Future Without Child Labour – Global Report under the Follow-Up to the ILO Declaration on Fundamental Principles and Rights at Work*, Geneva: ILO, 2002, 9.

Office, at the request of the Government of Canada, confirmed this approach.[10] In view of the absence of a definition of slavery or practices similar to slavery, including forced or compulsory labour, reference must be made to the definition contained in article 2 of the Forced Labour Convention, 1930 (No. 29) which defines 'forced or compulsory labour' as 'all work or service which is exacted from any person under the menace of any penalty and for which the said person has not offered himself voluntarily'.[11] However, the forced or compulsory recruitment of children under 18 for use in armed conflict does not cover the situation of countries that allow voluntary enrolment of persons in the military service from the age of 16 or 17.[12]

5.2.3.2 Prostitution, pornography or pornographic performances Under article 3(b) of Convention 182, the term 'the worst forms of child labour' comprises 'the use, procuring or offering of a child for prostitution, for the production of pornography or for pornographic performances'. Clause (b) of article 3 of Convention 182 does not contain a definition in this regard since relevant international instruments exist in this domain. Hence, article 2 to the Optional Protocol to the Convention on the Rights of the Child on the sale of children, child prostitution and child pornography[13] provides that, for the purposes of the Protocol: (b) child prostitution means the use of a child in sexual activities for remuneration or any other consideration; (c) child pornography means any representation, by whatever means, of a child engaged in real or simulated explicit sexual activities or any representation of the sexual parts of a child for primarily sexual purposes. Another international instrument to which recourse may be had for definitional purposes is the Convention for the Suppression of the Traffic in Persons and of the Exploitation of the Prostitution of Others, 1949. It goes without saying that this provision of the Convention is also meant to regulate the relatively recent, yet ever-increasing phenomenon of using children for Internet pornography.[14]

5.2.3.3 Illicit activities Under article 3(c) of Convention 182, the term 'the worst forms of child labour' comprises 'the use, procuring or offering of a child for illicit activities, in particular for the production and trafficking of drugs...'. Clause (c) further mentions 'the relevant international treaties' in order to define the drugs to which this provision refers. The following treaties have been considered relevant: the Single Convention on Narcotic Drugs, 1961; the Convention on Psychotropic Substances, 1971; the Protocol amending the Single Convention on Narcotic Drugs, 1972; and the United Nations Convention against Illicit Traffic in Narcotic Drugs and Psychotropic Substances, 1988.[15]

---

10 See ILO, *Child Labour, supra* note 7, 60.

11 ILO, Record of Proceedings, Report of the Committee on Child Labour, ILC, 87th Session, 1999, Geneva, § 136, 19/31.

12 *Ibid*, §§ 141 and 143, 19/32 and 33.

13 Adopted by the General Assembly of the UN on 25 May 2000.

14 ILO, *Child Labour, supra* note 7, 60 and 61.

15 *Ibid.*

5.2.3.4 Hazardous work Under article 3(d) of Convention 182, the term 'the worst forms of child labour' comprises 'work which, by its nature or the circumstances in which it is carried out, is likely to harm the health, safety or morals of children'. Article 4(1) of Convention 182 further provides that, when determining the types of work referred to under article 3(d), national laws or regulations or the competent authority must give consideration to 'relevant international standards, in particular Paragraphs 3 and 4 … ' of Recommendation 190. This determination can only be made after consultation with the organizations of employers and workers concerned. Hence, in the absence of a specific definition of what activities or occupations constitute hazardous work in articles 3(d) and 4(1), the determination of types of work considered to be particularly hazardous – and therefore a worst form of child labour – should be left to the discretion of the Member States subject to two procedural requirements, namely consultation with employers' and workers' organizations concerned and the need to take into consideration relevant international standards. The latter would not imply any obligation to ratify or respect the relevant standards. Additionally, there is the requirement to make the determination in good faith consistent with the obligation on ratifying States under the international law of treaties to implement in good faith the Conventions that they ratify.[16]

Paragraph 3 of Recommendation 190 establishes the following list of activities or types of work to which consideration should be given when categories of hazardous work are being determined:

- work, which exposes children to physical, psychological or sexual abuse [clause a];
- work underground, under water, at dangerous heights or in confined spaces; [clause b];
- work with dangerous machinery, equipment and tools, or which involves the manual handling or transport of heavy loads [clause c];
- work in an unhealthy environment, which may, for example, expose children to hazardous substances, agents or processes, or to temperatures, noise levels, or vibrations damaging to their health [clause d];
- work under particularly difficult conditions such as work for long hours or during the night or work where the child is unreasonably confined to the premises of the employer [clause e].

Finally, reference should be made to the differences in the wording of hazardous work in Conventions 138 and 182. As mentioned in Chapter 3, article 3 of Convention 138 refers to 'any type of employment or work which by its nature or the circumstances in which it is carried out is likely to jeopardise the health, safety or morals of young persons', while article 3(d) of Convention 182 refers to 'work which, by its nature or the circumstances in which it is carried out, is likely to harm the health, safety or morals of children'. The principal difference is that the wording of Convention 138 covers a larger number of situations than Convention 182. Since the types of hazardous work covered by articles 3(d) and 4, paragraph 1 constitute the worst forms of child labour, the types of hazardous work covered by Convention 182 are more restrictive and less numerous than those referred to by Convention 138. The list envisaged by article 4, paragraph 1 of Convention 182 should therefore

---

16 *Ibid.*, 65 and 66.

contain the types of work considered to be particularly hazardous and which must thus be prohibited and eliminated in all sectors, in accordance with the objective of Convention 182 to prohibit types of work which are intolerable in all countries, irrespective of their level of development.[17] Accordingly, the types of hazardous work covered by Convention 182 are those which are likely to 'harm', and not only 'jeopardize', the health, safety or morals of children.

5.2.4 Standards relating to the effective implementation of Convention 182

5.2.4.1 Monitoring mechanisms Under article 5 of Convention 182, each Member State that ratifies the Convention shall establish or designate appropriate mechanisms to monitor the implementation of its provisions. These mechanisms must be determined after consultation with employers' and workers' organizations.

Paragraph 8 of Recommendation No. 190 indicates that 'Members should establish or designate appropriate national mechanisms to monitor the implementation of national provisions for the prohibition and elimination of the worst forms of child labour, after consultation with employers' and workers' organizations.'

Referring to a request for clarification from a government member on the meaning of the term 'appropriate mechanisms', in particular whether these would be national or international in scope, the Legal Adviser stated that the 'draft instruments did not define the nature of the mechanisms but required the establishment or designation of a national mechanism'.[18] With regard to the term 'monitoring', the Office pointed out that this expression meant 'overseeing implementation, and the monitoring body could involve representation from civil society'. The committees set up under the UN Convention on the Rights of the Child or national committees or advisory bodies on child labour were mentioned as examples by certain countries. 'The United Nations Committee on the Rights of the Child suggests that the reference be to a multidisciplinary mechanism.'[19]

5.2.4.2 Action programmes Under article 6(1) of Convention 182, governments shall 'design and implement programmes of action to eliminate as a priority the worst forms of child labour.' Moreover, article 6(2) stipulates that such 'programmes of action shall be designed and implemented in consultation with relevant government institutions and employers' and workers' organizations, taking into consideration the views of other concerned groups as appropriate'.

Paragraph 2 of Recommendation No. 190 indicates that the programmes of action referred to in article 6 of the Convention should be designed and implemented as a matter of urgency. The relevant government institutions and employers' and workers' organizations should be consulted, and the views of the children directly affected by the worst forms of child labour, their families and, as appropriate, other concerned groups committed to the aims of the Convention and the Recommendation, should be taken into consideration. The programmes should aim at, *inter alia*: (a) identifying

---

17 *Ibid.*, 62.

18 ILO, Record of Proceedings, *supra* note 11, § 194, 19/42.

19 ILO, *Child Labour*, *supra* note 7, 80.

and denouncing the worst forms of child labour; (b) preventing the engagement of children in or removing them from the worst forms of child labour; (c) giving special attention to younger children, the girl child and other groups of children with special vulnerabilities or needs; (d) identifying, reaching out to and working with communities where children are at special risk; and (e) informing, sensitizing and mobilizing public opinion and concerned groups, including children and their families.

5.2.4.3 Penalties Article 7(1) of Convention 182 provides that Member States which ratify the Convention shall 'take all necessary measures to ensure the effective implementation and enforcement of the provisions giving effect to this Convention including the provision and application of penal sanctions or, as appropriate, other sanctions'. The Convention does not enumerate the types of sanctions to be imposed. The objective is for sanctions to be imposed, which may be penal, or of any other nature as appropriate.[20] The necessary measures, which may be taken by a Member State, may take several forms including fines, sentences of imprisonment, a temporary or permanent prohibition from exercising a specific activity, or damages with interest.

Paragraph 12 of Recommendation No. 190 states that Members should provide that certain worst forms of child labour – referred to earlier on in this chapter as the unconditional worst forms of child labour – such as all forms of slavery or practices similar to slavery, as well as the use, procuring or offering of a child for prostitution, the production of pornography or pornographic performances, and for illicit activities, are criminal offences. Paragraph 14 of the Recommendation indicates that Member States could have recourse to other criminal, civil or administrative remedies, such as special supervision of enterprises which have used the worst forms of child labour, and, in cases of persistent violation, consideration of temporary or permanent revoking of permits to operate.

5.2.4.4 Effective and time-bound measures Under article 7(2), of Convention 182, each Member 'shall, taking into account the importance of education in eliminating child labour, take effective and time-bound measures to:'

- prevent the engagement of children in the worst forms of child labour [clause a];
- provide the necessary and appropriate direct assistance for the removal of children from the worst forms of child labour and for their rehabilitation and social integration [clause b];
- ensure access to free basic education, and, wherever possible, appropriate vocational training, for all children removed from the worst forms of child labour [clause c];
- identify and reach out to children at special risk [clause d]; and
- take account of the special situation of girls [clause e].

It is important to specify what is meant by the phrase 'take effective and time-bound measures'. Effective elimination would seem to require both immediate *and* time-bound measures. Immediate measures could include removal from intolerable

---

20 *Ibid.*, Office commentary, 98.

situations. For example, as soon as children are found in bondage, in a brothel or deep in a mine, it is necessary to take action, and emergency measures are required until assistance and rehabilitation can be provided for them. Other measures could then be taken, for example with a view to prevention, which could require a certain time frame for implementation and should be time-bound. Prevention, rehabilitation and social reintegration, as called for in clauses (a) and (b) of article 7(2) could give rise to immediate and time-bound action.[21]

It is worth noting that these time-bound measures, which are linked to the ILO/IPEC programme, have had a demonstrable impact in terms of the implementation of the Convention. Time-bound programmes (TBPs), which represent the latest step in IPEC's evolution, aim to eliminate the worst forms of child labour in a country within a specified, and relatively short, period of time. TBPs are designed as a comprehensive framework that governments can use to chart a course of action with well-defined targets. These are ambitious undertakings; in the first three countries to implement such programmes in 2001 – El Salvador, Nepal and the United Republic of Tanzania – nearly 100,000 children were targeted. There are currently 23 countries implementing or starting up IPEC's national time-bound support projects to TBPs.

5.2.4.5 International cooperation Under article 8 of the Convention, Member States that ratify it 'shall take appropriate steps to assist one another in giving effect to the provisions of the Convention through enhanced international cooperation and/or assistance including support for social and economic development, poverty eradication programmes and universal education.' With regard to the obligation for Member States 'to assist one another', the Legal Adviser of the ILO, in response to a question raised by a government member of the Conference Committee 'stressed the idea of partnership contained in the spirit of the Article'. He emphasized that 'no obligation would arise from either proposal for ratifying Member States in relation to a particular level or form of cooperation or assistance. There was only an obligation to take appropriate steps towards enhanced international partnerships, and it was up to individual States to decide on those appropriate steps.'[22] A government member of the Conference Committee, referring to the comments of the Legal Adviser, indicated that the term 'partnerships' used by the Legal Adviser meant 'working together' and that article 8 encouraged Member States to work together to meet the goals of the Convention. However, he further understood that in no way did article 8 require any member to provide any specific form or amount of cooperation or assistance. No legal obligation was created as to the nature of such cooperation or assistance and therefore the matter was left entirely to the discretion of individual Member States.[23]

Paragraph 11 of Recommendation No. 190 provides suggestions on the manner in which Member States could cooperate and/or assist in international efforts to prohibit and eliminate the worst forms of child labour. This could be done by: (a) gathering and exchanging information concerning criminal offences, including those involving

---

21 *Ibid.*, 34 and 35.

22 ILO, Record of Proceedings, *supra* note 11, § 242, 19/49.

23 *Ibid.*

international networks; (b) detecting and prosecuting those involved in the sale and trafficking of children, or in the use, procuring or offering of children for illicit activities, for prostitution, for the production of pornography or for pornographic performances; and (c) registering perpetrators of such offences. Paragraph 16 provides that such international cooperation and/or assistance should include: (a) mobilizing resources for national and international programmes; (b) mutual legal assistance; (c) technical assistance including the exchange of information; and (d) support for social and economic development, poverty eradication programmes and universal education.

5.3 Overview of recent trends and issues as noted by the CEACR, arising from the application of Convention 182

A reliable, if incomplete, picture of the concrete action taken by Member States and the social partners, often with the assistance of ILO/IPEC, to combat child labour and its worst forms after having ratified Convention 182, can be obtained through the comments made by the CEACR.[24] The CEACR's comments have been made on the basis of an analysis carried out by it on over 200 first reports submitted by States in recent years on the application of both Conventions 138 and 182.

The picture emerging from the comments provides an overview of action taken by governments on the legislative, policy and operational fronts as well as areas where more action is required. Hence, a large number of States have adopted legislation to prohibit trafficking in children, the use or procuring of children in prostitution and the production of pornography, and hazardous work for children under 18. An equally significant number of countries have adopted Plans of Action or time-bound measures to combat one or more categories of the worst forms of child labour. However, fewer countries have adopted measures, legislative or otherwise, to combat the forced labour of children or the use or procuring of children for illicit activities, in particular for the production and trafficking of drugs.

5.3.1 Legislative measures taken to apply the Convention

5.3.1.1 Trafficking and commercial sexual exploitation A positive trend emerging from the CEACR's comments is that a large majority of countries have adopted or amended legislation, slightly prior to, or soon after ratifying Convention 182, to prohibit trafficking in persons or children under 18[25] or, more specifically, children

---

24 On the role of the CEACR, see Trebilcock, Raimondi (this volume).

25 CEACR, Individual Observations concerning Convention No. 182: Albania 2005, Pakistan 2005, Thailand 2005, United States 2004; and Individual Direct Requests concerning Convention No. 182: Austria 2004, Belgium 2006, Bulgaria 2004, China 2005, Denmark 2004, Germany 2005, France 2004, Ghana 2005, Greece 2004, Hungary 2005, Iceland 2006, Islamic Republic of Iran 2005, Italy 2004, Malaysia 2003, Mauritania 2004, Mauritius 2003, Netherlands 2005, New Zealand 2004, Nigeria 2005, Norway 2004, Philippines 2004, Romania 2003, Slovenia 2005, United Kingdom 2004 and Yemen 2005.

for labour[26] or sexual exploitation.[27] The CEACR has also noted that such legislative measures were almost invariably accompanied by the inclusion of increased penalties in the Penal Code for trafficking in persons under 18 years.[28] This high level of activity in the adoption of legislation to prohibit the trafficking in children by a substantial number of countries from all parts of the world reflects a real commitment to combat a problem that appears to be steadily on the increase in some parts of the world.

Similar measures have been taken by a large number of countries to prohibit the use, procuring or offering of children under 18 for prostitution, pornography or pornographic performances. In certain cases, the CEACR has asked countries to extend the prohibition on the commercial sexual exploitation of children to boys where the legislation only applies to girls.[29] It has also asked some countries to adopt provisions to incriminate the client of a child prostitute where the applicable legislation only carries offences for the *procuring or offering* of a child for prostitution, but not for the *use* of a child for such a purpose.[30] On other occasions, countries have been requested to treat female prostitutes under 18 as victims rather than offenders when the legislation in question holds them liable to a criminal offence.[31] Overall, however, the ratification of Convention 182 has yielded positive legislative results with regard to government action in these two areas of unconditional worst forms of child labour.

5.3.1.2 Hazardous work As mentioned earlier, under article 3(d) of Convention 182, the term 'the worst forms of child labour' comprises 'work which, by its nature or the circumstances in which it is carried out, is likely to harm the health, safety or morals of children.' Hence, in the absence of a specific definition of what activities or occupations constitute hazardous work, the CEACR deems that this determination of types of work considered to be particularly hazardous – and therefore a worst form of child labour – should be left to the discretion of Member States subject

---

26 CEACR, Individual Observations concerning Convention No. 182: Bangladesh 2004, Burkina Faso 2004, Gabon 2005, Qatar 2006 and United Arab Emirates 2005; and Individual Direct Requests concerning Convention No. 182: Benin 2004, Mali 2003.

27 CEACR, Individual Observations concerning Convention No. 182: Bangladesh 2004, Czech Republic 2006, Dominican Republic 2004, El Salvador 2004, Indonesia 2004, Japan 2004, Mexico 2004, Morocco 2004, Sri Lanka 2006, Turkey 2004; and Individual Direct Requests concerning Convention No. 182: Canada 2004, Cyprus 2004, Luxembourg 2004, Sweden 2004, United Republic of Tanzania 2004, Vietnam 2004.

28 For example, CEACR, Individual Observation concerning Convention No. 182: Russian Federation 2005; and Individual Direct Requests concerning Convention No. 182: Bolivia 2006, Poland 2005, Republic of Serbia 2005.

29 For example, CEACR, Individual Direct Requests concerning Convention No. 182: Albania 2005, Bangladesh 2004, Fiji 2005, Jamaica 2006, Republic of Korea 2004, Lesotho 2004, Mali 2005.

30 For example, CEACR, Individual Direct Requests concerning Convention No. 182: Chad 2005, Congo 2005, Slovenia 2005, Vietnam 2004.

31 For example, CEACR, Individual Direct Request concerning Convention No. 182: Egypt 2006; Individual Observation concerning Convention No. 182: United Arab Emirates 2005.

to two procedural requirements, namely consultation with employers' and workers' organizations concerned and the need to take into consideration relevant international standards, in line with the requirements of article 4(1).

Another positive trend emerging from the CEACR's comments is that a substantial number of countries – either immediately prior to or pursuant to ratification of Convention 182 – have not only adopted legislation to prohibit children under 18 from carrying out hazardous work, but have also determined what activities or occupations constitute such hazardous work.[32] The CEACR has noted that not all countries prohibit the same types of hazardous work for children under 18 since the definition may vary from country to country depending on national circumstances and the conditions in which such work is undertaken. Moreover, the CEACR has noted that in some countries, the lists of the types of hazardous work to be prohibited for children under 18 are extremely detailed[33] whilst in others the lists are less extensive.[34]

In some instances, the CEACR has noted that the countries concerned have adopted a general prohibition on hazardous work for children under 18 but have yet to adopt a list containing such activities or occupations; it has accordingly suggested that these governments take due account of Paragraph 3 of Recommendation No. 190 when finalizing a list of types of hazardous work.[35] In other instances, however, the CEACR has noted with interest that the determination of hazardous work has been made or is in the process of being elaborated taking into consideration the types of work referred to in Paragraph 3 of Recommendation No.190.[36] Finally, there have also been instances where, although the types of hazardous work have already been determined in the national legislation, the CEACR has requested the country

---

32 CEACR, Individual Direct Requests concerning Convention No. 182: Albania 2005, Belgium 2005, Benin 2004, Brazil 2004, Cambodia 2003, Chile 2006, Costa Rica 2004, Côte d'Ivoire 2006, Croatia 2004, Cyprus 2004, Denmark 2005, Dominican Republic 2004, Ecuador 2003, Egypt 2005, Estonia 2004, Finland 2004, France 2004, Germany 2005, Ghana 2004, Guatemala 2006, Honduras 2004, Hungary 2005, Iceland 2004, Indonesia 2004, Islamic Republic of Iran 2005, Japan 2004, Jordan 2004, Republic of Korea 2004, Lithuania 2005, Luxembourg 2004, Malawi 2004, Malta 2004, Mongolia 2004, Nicaragua 2005, Nigeria 2005, Philippines 2004, Poland 2005, Portugal 2005, Russian Federation 2005, Rwanda 2003, San Marino 2005, Saudi Arabia 2005, Senegal 2003, Slovakia 2003, Slovenia 2005, Sri Lanka, 2005, Syrian Arab Republic 2006, Thailand 2005, Turkey 2004, Vietnam 2004, and Zimbabwe 2003.

33 For example, CEACR, Individual Direct Request concerning Convention No. 182: Cyprus 2004, where 115 types of works and processes are prohibited for children under 18 in Schedule to Law No. 48(I) of 2001 on the Protection of Young Persons at Work.

34 For example, CEACR, Individual Direct Requests concerning Convention No. 182: Estonia 2004 and Indonesia 2004, where relevant legislation contains respectively 24 and 13 types of hazardous work prohibited for children under 18.

35 For example, CEACR, Individual Direct Requests concerning Convention No. 182: Argentina 2004, Barbados 2005, Ecuador 2006, Fiji 2005, Jamaica 2005, Kenya 2004, Lesotho 2004, Moldova 2005.

36 For example, CEACR, Individual Direct Requests concerning Convention No. 182: China/Macau Special Administrative Region 2006, Finland 2004, Guyana 2006, Luxembourg 2004, Malaysia 2005, Mali 2005, United Kingdom (Guernsey) 2006.

concerned to adopt measures to prohibit children under 18 from engaging in types of work which the CEACR clearly considers to constitute hazardous work, be it the use of children under 18 in night work, work in mines, power line construction and maintenance and meat processing,[37] or the use of children under 18 in certain agricultural activities where there are found to be a high number of injuries and fatalities,[38] or the use of children as camel[39] or horse jockeys.[40]

5.3.2 Programmatic measures to implement the convention

5.3.2.1 Trafficking An encouraging development is that the CEACR has noted that a significant number of countries have adopted Programmes or Plans of Action to tackle one or more of the worst forms of child labour. These can consist of sub-regional projects to combat trafficking in children for sexual exploitation,[41] or labour exploitation.[42] National Plans of Action for combating trafficking in children have also been developed in various countries[43] where they aim to protect children who are victims of trafficking, to prevent future trafficking and to detect and prosecute the traffickers.

The CEACR has noted that such measures taken by governments to combat the trafficking of children for labour or sexual exploitation have yielded notable results, especially in terms of removing and rehabilitating child victims of trafficking through the establishment of specific medical and social assistance for these children as well as the establishment of reception centres for child victims of trafficking before their

---

37 CEACR, Individual Direct Request concerning Convention No. 182: Canada 2006.

38 CEACR, Individual Observation concerning Convention No. 182: United States 2006.

39 CEACR, Individual Observations concerning Convention No. 182: Qatar 2004 and United Arab Emirates 2004.

40 CEACR, Individual Direct Request concerning Convention No. 182: Mongolia 2005.

41 CEACR, Individual Direct Request concerning Convention No. 182: China 2005, where the CEACR noted that ILO/IPEC launched the second phase of the Mekong Sub-Regional Project to Combat Trafficking in Children and Women (TICW) in Cambodia, Yunnan Province of China, Lao PDR, Thailand and Vietnam in 2003 for a period of five years; Individual Observation concerning No. 182: Pakistan 2005, where the CEACR noted that ILO/IPEC launched in 2000 the sub-regional project to combat child trafficking (TICSA) in Bangladesh, Nepal and Sri Lanka; the project was extended to Pakistan, Indonesia and Thailand in 2003.

42 CEACR, Individual Direct Requests concerning Convention No. 182: Benin 2004, Burkina Faso 2004, Ghana 2004 and Togo 2004, where the CEACR noted that the Sub-Regional Project to combat the trafficking of children for the exploitation of their labour in West and Central Africa (IPEC/LUTRENA), which had commenced in July 2001, covered nine countries: Benin, Burkina Faso, Cameroon, Côte d'Ivoire, Gabon, Ghana, Mali, Nigeria and Togo.

43 CEACR, Individual Direct Requests concerning Convention No. 182: Norway 2004, Ghana 2004, Estonia 2004 and Vietnam 2004; and Individual Observations concerning Convention No. 182: Czech Republic 2004 and Indonesia 2004.

repatriation to their families in their country of origin.[44] Measures taken by countries have also included prosecuting perpetrators of the crime of trafficking in children.[45]

Finally, National Plans of Action have resulted in the establishment of Interdepartmental Units or Task Forces which are responsible for determining an integrated policy composed of an administrative component, as well as taking into account social and penal legislation and assistance for victims. These bodies, which invariably are composed of representatives of the Ministries of Justice and of the Interior, the police, the public prosecutors, the Social Inspectorate and the Immigration Service, aim to ensure a better cooperation and exchange of information between the various actors dealing with the sale and trafficking of children at international, national and local levels.[46]

The CEACR has noted with interest that pursuant to such National Plans of Action, and with regard to child victims of trafficking, much help is given to the activation of the assistance system, such as tracing the guardians of the child victims, organizing housing for those without a guardian, providing education on the same preconditions as citizens, and placing them in foster care, if necessary. Some countries go a step further by granting permits of residence to victims of trafficking as well as a discretionary period during which the victims can recover from their experiences and make a decision on cooperating with the authorities, in order not only to enable the protection of victims but also to help them against re-victimization.[47]

5.3.2.2 Commercial sexual exploitation Another area where an abundant number of programmatic measures have been taken by countries to tackle an unconditional worst form of child labour is the use and procuring of children in prostitution and pornography. As in the case of trafficking, a substantial number of countries have established sub-regional programmes[48] with the assistance of ILO/IPEC, which aim to withdraw children from commercial sexual exploitation and integrate them into school-life while providing economic alternatives to the families concerned. Other countries have adopted National Plans of Action,[49] which include a series of actions

---

44 CEACR, Individual Observations concerning Convention No. 182: Gabon 2006 and Qatar 2006.

45 CEACR, Individual Observation concerning Convention No. 182: China 2006.

46 CEACR, Individual Direct Requests concerning Convention No. 182: Belgium 2006, Croatia 2006.

47 CEACR, Individual Direct Request concerning Convention No. 182: Finland 2006.

48 CEACR, Individual Direct Requests concerning Convention No. 182: Argentina 2006, where the CEACR noted that ILO/IPEC set up a programme on the prevention and elimination of the commercial sexual exploitation of children at the border areas between Argentina, Brazil and Paraguay; Kenya 2004, where the CEACR noted that an ILO/IPEC project to combat child sexual exploitation in Anglophone countries covered Kenya, Ghana, Nigeria, Uganda and the United Republic of Tanzania.

49 CEACR, Individual Direct Requests concerning Convention No. 182: Angola 2004, Austria 2004, Bulgaria 2004, Finland 2004, Germany 2005, Indonesia 2004, Mexico 2004, Netherlands 2005, New Zealand 2004, Nicaragua 2004, Norway 2004, Philippines 2004, Sweden 2004, United Kingdom 2005; and Individual Observations concerning Convention No. 182: Czech Republic 2004, Mauritius 2005, Thailand 2005.

to prevent, protect and rehabilitate young victims as well as to punish perpetrators of such crimes. Still other countries have identified the commercial sexual exploitation of children as a worst form of child labour in respect of which they have undertaken to prevent, remove and rehabilitate child victims of commercial sexual exploitation within a certain time frame in the context of ILO/IPEC-supported Time-Bound Programmes.[50] The CEACR has noted that such measures have had a tangible impact, either through a decrease over the years in the number of victims of commercial sexual exploitation pursuant to measures taken within the framework of an Action Plan[51] or the removal of a certain number of children from commercial sexual exploitation pursuant to the implementation of a TBP, as well as vocational training, psychological counselling, health and nutrition services, refresher and literacy courses and school equipment for such children.[52]

In light of the explosive growth of the sex industry and the use of new information technologies, some countries have adopted specific measures to combat child pornography on the Internet. These measures include Action Plans to criminalize the sale, production and possession of child pornography,[53] and to provide for the organization of training seminars for parents, teachers, school psychiatrists, police officers and magistrates about Internet-related risks for sexual exploitation.[54] They also include the dissemination of information to citizens concerning hotlines against child pornography on the Internet,[55] computer programmes to identify child pornographic pictures and films on the Internet as well as the development, within the Federal Office for Criminal Investigations, of a comparative database that centralizes information about already-known victims and perpetrators of child pornography.[56] Finally, the CEACR has also noted measures taken by countries to combat the growing and relatively recent phenomenon of child sex tourism.[57]

5.3.2.3 Hazardous work An area where countries have taken considerable and concrete action to combat a worst form of child labour, and where they have made significant progress, is hazardous work. Hence, the CEACR has noted that a substantial number of countries have adopted various measures, including time-bound measures, to prevent the employment of children under 18 in hazardous work, as well as to provide for the removal and rehabilitation of those already engaged

---

50 CEACR, Individual Direct Requests concerning Convention No. 182: Brazil 2004, Costa Rica 2004, Dominican Republic 2006, Ecuador 2004, Indonesia 2004, Madagascar 2005, Philippines 2004, United Republic of Tanzania 2004.

51 See for example, CEACR, Individual Observation concerning Convention No. 182: Czech Republic 2004.

52 See for example, CEACR, Individual Observation concerning Convention No. 182: El Salvador 2006.

53 CEACR, Individual Direct Request concerning Convention No. 182: Austria 2004.

54 CEACR, Individual Direct Request concerning Convention No. 182: Bulgaria 2004.

55 CEACR, Individual Direct Requests concerning Convention No. 182: Finland 2004, Iceland 2004, Norway 2004.

56 CEACR, Individual Direct Request concerning Convention No. 182: Germany 2005.

57 CEACR, Individual Direct Requests concerning Convention No. 182: Brazil 2004, Finland 2004, Germany 2005, New Zealand 2005.

therein.[58] In this regard, the CEACR has noted that ILO/IPEC assists countries with Time-Bound Programmes (TBPs) to prioritize certain worst forms of child labour, including certain types of hazardous work, in consultation with the social partners. In some instances, the TBP prioritizes certain forms of hazardous work such as hazardous agricultural activities and hazardous work in the urban informal economy.[59] In other instances, the TBP targets children engaged in hazardous work in specific sectors such as construction, banana and flower-growing, small-scale mining, refuse dumps, the firework industry and sugar cane plantations.[60] In yet other instances, other priority groups for intervention within the TBP have been identified, such as child domestic labour, child labour in mining and quarrying, and in hazardous and unhealthy environments in the rural and urban sectors.[61] Other areas of hazardous work targeted by the TPB include the footwear industry, mining, deep-sea fishing,[62] rag-picking, portering, carpet-weaving, domestic service,[63] glass bangle-making, surgical instrument manufacturing, tanneries, coal mining, scavenging, ship-breaking and seafood processing.[64]

Pursuant to these TBPs, children under 18 in the sectors concerned are targeted for withdrawal and prevention from exploitative and hazardous work through the provision of educational and training services following direct action from the project. In addition, families whose children are involved in hazardous work benefit from socio-economic opportunities provided by the project, as do many communities in the target area. Strategies adopted under the TBPS include awareness-raising and community mobilization as well as capacity-building of poor families whose children are working or at risk of entering into the worst forms of child labour.

It must be emphasized that the CEACR has noted on several occasions that these time-bound measures have demonstrated rapid and tangible results in terms of the prevention, withdrawal and rehabilitation of children involved in hazardous work. In El Salvador, for example, in one instance, the CEACR has been able to note with interest that more than 29,600 children were prevented from being engaged in hazardous work in the following sectors: sugar plantations, the fishing industry, public refuse dumps, domestic work, the fireworks industry, coffee plantations and street markets; and that more than 12,000 children have been withdrawn and

---

58 CEACR, Individual Direct Requests concerning Convention No. 182: Bangladesh 2004, Benin 2004, Brazil 2004, Burkina Faso 2004, Costa Rica 2004, Dominican Republic 2004, Ecuador 2006, El Salvador 2006, Honduras 2004, Indonesia 2004, Kenya 2005, Malawi 2006, Lebanon 2005, Madagascar 2005, Mali 2005, Nepal 2005, Philippines 2005, United Republic of Tanzania 2005, Thailand 2005 and Turkey 2004.

59 CEACR, Individual Direct Requests concerning Convention No. 182: Brazil 2004 and Dominican Republic 2004.

60 CEACR, Individual Direct Requests concerning Convention No. 182: Ecuador 2006 and El Salvador 2006.

61 CEACR, Individual Direct Request concerning Convention No. 182: Madagascar 2005.

62 CEACR, Individual Direct Request concerning Convention No. 182: Indonesia 2004.

63 CEACR, Individual Direct Request concerning Convention No. 182: Nepal 2005.

64 CEACR, Individual Direct Request concerning Convention No. 182: Pakistan 2005.

rehabilitated in the same sectors.[65] In Mali, another instance, the CEACR has noted with interest that some 2,807 children (2,407 boys and 400 girls) have been removed from exploitative work since the launching of the IPEC programme (adopted in 2001), and that, between January 2001 and June 2005, some 1,307 children were removed from the worst forms of child labour in the agricultural and mining sectors and the informal economy. Over the same period, some 3,050 families and children benefited from vocational recycling measures and 1,500 children benefited from improved legal protection.[66] These are but a few examples of the progress noted by the CEACR on the effective implementation of the programmatic provisions of Convention 182.

5.4 Concluding remarks

There can be no doubt that Convention 182, which is linked to a major technical cooperation programme, has had a demonstrable impact. It was widely ratified within a very short time frame, which is unprecedented in the history of ILO's standard-setting activities. The action taken by Member States to ratify and apply this fundamental Convention is all the more remarkable given that it is a complex instrument encompassing penal law, labour law and technical cooperation components, thereby requiring ratifying Member States to take action on all these fronts.

Yet considerable action has been taken both on the legislative and technical cooperation fronts, especially in the areas of two unconditional worst forms of child labour – trafficking and commercial sexual exploitation of children – as well as in the domain of hazardous work. It is especially in these areas that developing and developed Member States have taken concrete measures, not only in the form of legislative amendments to their criminal codes and labour laws, but also through projects, programmes, action plans and time-bound measures to implement the Convention, more often than not with the assistance of ILO/IPEC.

It therefore comes as no surprise that since Convention 182 was adopted, efforts to prohibit and eliminate the worst forms of child labour have yielded positive results. As mentioned in the second Global Report under the Follow-Up to the ILO Declaration on Fundamental Principles and Rights at Work, the number of child labourers has declined by 11 per cent over the past four years.[67] It is of particular significance that the decline was greater in the area of hazardous work where the number of children decreased overall by 26 per cent.

These figures, together with what the CEACR has noted over the past few years in terms of action taken to implement Convention 182, reflect a major political consensus on the need for urgent and concrete action against the worst forms of child labour. Convention 182, with its multi-pronged approach, provides a good example

---

65 CEACR, Individual Direct Request concerning Convention No. 182: El Salvador 2006.

66 CEACR, Individual Direct Request concerning Convention No. 182: Mali 2005.

67 ILO, *The End of Child Labour: Within Reach – Global Report under the Follow-Up to the ILO Declaration on Fundamental Principles and Rights at Work*, Geneva: ILO, 2006, 7.

of the actions that should be taken to ensure that ratification is followed by constant and notable progress in implementation. There can be no doubt that the CEACR will continue to note the remarkable strides made in implementing this fundamental and innovative ILO Convention in the years to ahead.

Chapter 6

Slavery and Practices Similar to Slavery as Worst Forms of Child Labour: A Comment on Article 3(a) of ILO Convention 182

Silvia Sanna

6.1 Introduction

The definition of the worst forms of child labour (WFCL) by ILO Convention 182 comprises, under article 3(a): 'all forms of slavery or practices similar to slavery, such as the sale and trafficking of children, debt bondage and serfdom and forced or compulsory labour, including forced or compulsory recruitment of children for use in armed conflict'. This category is followed by three further broad groups of activities concerning the involvement of children in prostitution, production of pornography or pornographic performances (article 3(b)), illicit activities, in particular for the production and trafficking of drugs (article 3(c)) and work which, by its nature or the circumstances in which it is carried out, is likely to harm the health, safety or morals of children, usually referred to as 'hazardous work' (article 3(d)). These practices constitute intolerable forms of exploitation that irretrievably impair the education, the health and the physical, mental, spiritual, moral or social development of a child. Moreover they correspond to serious violations of children's basic human rights condemned by the relevant international norms. For this reason, Convention 182 establishes that no person under the age of 18 shall be subjected to any of the WFCL (article 2)[1] and every ILO Member State which ratifies the Convention shall take immediate and effective measures to secure the prohibition and elimination of those practices as a matter of urgency (article 1).

Before examining in more details the specific activities mentioned in article 3(a) of Convention 182, it is worth clarifying some general questions relating to

---

1 The definition of 'child' is in line with art. 1 of the Convention on the Rights of the Child (CRC). Furthermore, Convention 182 does not even include the exception allowed by the CRC in the event that 'under the law applicable to the child, majority is attained earlier'. See Y. Noguchi, 'ILO Convention No. 182 on the Worst Forms of Child Labour and the Convention on the Rights of the Child', *International Journal of Children's Rights*, Vol. 10, 2002, 355 ff, at 357.

the definition of WFCL and the inclusion of slavery and slave-like practices[2] in the provision.

6.2 The problem of defining 'child labour' in the framework of Convention 182

The major interpretative difficulty with the notion of WFCL is created by the lack of a clear definition of 'child labour'. International standards dealing with the matter and aiming to abolish the practice do not give a uniform and set definition of 'child labour' nor any illustrative list of specific activities covered by the notion.[3] Actually, the phenomenon comprises a great variety of situations which differ from country to country and among economic sectors. Furthermore, the qualification of a particular activity as 'child labour' may depend on the child's age and the type of work, as well as the conditions under which it is performed. This is why the term 'child labour' cannot be interpreted as encompassing all economic activities of children, and why international instruments usually allow national authorities some discretion in setting the boundaries for children's work.

Yet there can be no doubt that the constitutive element of child labour consists of the performance of a working activity by a child.[4] Even when particularly hazardous and dangerous, that activity usually corresponds to a form of employment or work that would be legitimate if carried out by a person above the minimum age set for that job.

Looking at the definition of WFCL adopted by Convention 182, however, it is evident that the notion has a broader scope. In addition to hazardous work, which in effect may be assimilated to the concept of 'child labour', article 3 covers acts that are not at all regular forms of employment, but serious violations of human rights, constituting criminal offences in most legal systems. With the adoption of Convention 182, the concept of 'child labour' hence extends to practices of exploitation that do not necessarily involve the carrying out of work by children. Despite this ostensible incoherence, the inclusion of those issues in the scope of Convention 182 was generally supported by the ILO constituents, though it was not beyond criticism.

---

2 The issues addressed might equally affect all or some of the other categories of WFCL. See also the chapters by Kooijmans, Noguchi and Beqiraj (this volume).

3 The ILO usually defines child labour as any kind of employment or work carried out by children that does not conform to the standards enshrined in the ILO Child Labour Conventions 138 and 182. Art. 32 of the Convention on the Rights of the Child 'recognize(s) the right of the child to be protected from economic exploitation and from performing any work that is likely to be hazardous or to interfere with the child's education, or to be harmful to the child's health or physical, mental, spiritual, moral or social development.' For a critique of the lack of an unambiguous notion of 'child labour' and the resulting shortcomings of the action against it, see K. Hanson and A. Vandaele, 'Working Children and International Labour Law: A Critical Analysis', *International Journal of Children's Rights*, Vol. 11, 2003, 73 ff; D.M. Smolin, 'Strategic Choices in the International Campaign Against Child Labor', *Human Rights Quarterly*, Vol. 22, 2000, 942 ff.

4 It is worth noting that the notion of 'child labour' usually covers both employment and work not within a formal employment relationship (such as domestic labour, self-employment or any form of unpaid work). See Noguchi, 'ILO Convention No. 182', *supra* note 1, at 360.

6.3 Some critical issues concerning the definition of WFCL

During the *travaux préparatoires* (1998–99) for Convention 182, some ILO constituents objected to the inclusion of these issues in clauses (a) to (c), because those activities do not constitute real kinds of work. They are forms of exploitation of children which entail criminal violations of human rights and are in no way legitimate forms of employment. Some of them do not even involve the performance of an economic activity by children (such as in the case of the sale and trafficking of children). It was thus proposed to include only those activities strictly considered exploitation of children's labour, such as forced labour, debt bondage and serfdom.[5] Otherwise the Convention might be seen to go beyond the sphere of labour and the scope of the ILO. Another matter of concern to ILO constituents related to the risk of devaluing the criminal nature of some practices by including them in a labour Convention.[6]

Despite the previous criticisms, the ILO survey of the constituents revealed a general agreement that all the items concerned are intolerable situations for children and should not be taken lightly by any new international standard on the most extreme forms of child labour.[7] This general consensus may be better understood in the light of Convention 182's aim to fight any form of child abuse in the sphere of labour, and any circumstance in which a child is exploited. In fact, even prior to the adoption of Convention 182 the same issues had been qualified both as forms of economic exploitation of children and as modern forms of slavery, subjecting children to irretrievable impairment and to full control by their exploiters.

Some reflections on the analogies between the WFCL and children's economic exploitation, on the one hand, and contemporary forms of slavery, on the other hand, might help to better understand the choice of the items included in article 3 of Convention 182 and, at the same time, may give valid answers to some of the critical questions raised in the *travaux préparatoires*.

6.3.1 WFCL as forms of 'economic exploitation'

The qualification of the practices banned by Convention 182 as economic exploitation is particularly useful to clarify why certain activities may be comprised among the WFCL, even if they do not consist of work carried out by a child. In this regard, it is worth noting that the WFCL coincide substantially with most categories of economic exploitation prohibited under article 32 of the UN Convention on the Rights of the

---

5 ILC, *Report IV(2A), Child Labour*, presented at the 87th Session of the Conference (1999), Mexico's general observations; General Confederation of Portuguese Workers' general observations.

6 See, for instance: *Ibid.*, Bolivia's and Spain's observations on art. 3, respectively.

7 The Convention's drafting was based on the replies received from Member States, employers' and workers' organizations to a questionnaire on the main issues to be dealt with in the proposed instrument. More than 100 governments and almost an equal number of employers' and workers' organizations responded. The information is summarized in ILC, *Report VI(2) – Summary of Replies*; Office Commentaries, presented at the 86th Session of the Conference (1998).

Child (CRC). The meaning of that expression was tackled by the Committee on the Rights of the Child at a 'General Discussion Day' held on 4 October 1993. During the opening statements, one of the Committee's members gave the following interpretation:

> This expression combines two distinct elements: economic and exploitation. Economic implies the idea of a certain gain or profit through the production, distribution and consumption of goods and services. This material interest has an impact on the economy of a certain unit, be it the State, the community or the family. Exploitation means taking unjust advantage of another person. It covers situations of manipulation, misuse, abuse, victimization, oppression or ill-treatment. Taking the Convention as the framework, one may recognize the existence of a material interest in activities such as child labour, child pornography or the use of children for criminal activities. On the other hand, we are confronted with a situation of exploitation when the human dignity of the child or the harmonious development of the child's personality is not respected – e.g. the sale of children, child bondage or child prostitution.[8]

In the light of this statement, it is evident that the WFCL included in article 3 of Convention 182 correspond to forms of children's exploitation in the perpetrator's material interest.[9] In consequence, none of the practices covered by the provision could have been reasonably ruled outside the scope of the Convention, even if they do not always involve a specific working activity performed by the victim. In fact, the sale and trafficking of children often occur for purposes of economic exploitation of children, such as forced labour, debt bondage or serfdom. For this reason, there is a narrow linkage between the various types of WFCL, so that the latter practices cannot be efficiently rooted out without eradicating the former and vice versa.

---

8 See: CRC/C/20, 4th Session, 4 October 1993, at 51. For a comment, see Hanson and Vandaele, 'Working Children', *supra* note 3, at 108. Actually, the CRC deals with some of the practices mentioned as forms of economic exploitation in two further provisions: art. 34 on sexual exploitation and art. 35 on sale and trafficking. The CRC's *travaux préparatoires* reveal that the issues were handled together in the first draft, but they were split up in the following version in order to better target their specificity. With regard to sale and trafficking, for example, it was acknowledged that they could aim not only at economic or sexual exploitation, but even at commercial adoption or organ transplantation. On the *travaux préparatoires*, see Office of the United Nations High Commissioner for Human Rights, *Legislative History of the Convention on the Rights of the Child*, Vol. II, New York and Geneva, 2007, available at <www.ohchr.org>. For a detailed analysis of the mentioned provisions, see S. Detrick, *A Commentary on the United Nations Convention on the Rights of the Child*, The Hague/Boston/London, 1999, at 558 ff.

9 In this regard, the Swedish tripartite ILO committee's general observation during the *travaux préparatoires* on the relationship between the prospective Convention and the CRC is revealing: 'The United Nations Convention on the Rights of the Child should be the starting-point for continuing work by the ILO, and a stronger link could be made to it in the proposed Convention. It would be logical if the proposed Convention came to be regarded as a refinement of Article 32(1) of the Convention on the Rights of the Child, in the same way that Convention No. 138 is in relation to Article 32(2)', ILC, *Report IV(2A)*, *supra* note 5. See also T. Hammarberg, 'Children', in A. Eide et al. (eds), *Economic, Social and Cultural Rights*, 2nd edn, The Hague, 2001, at 361.

6.3.2 WFCL as 'contemporary forms of slavery'

The activities included in article 3 of Convention 182 are not only forms of economic exploitation as defined by the CRC, but they also amount to practices similar to slavery, like those addressed by the UN Working Group on Contemporary Forms of Slavery (WGCS).[10] In fact, in addition to traditional slavery and slave trade, modern forms of slavery include, among others, sale of children, traffic in persons, sexual exploitation, and forcible recruitment of children into military service, as well as child labour in its strict sense.[11] In order to better understand the analogy between WFCL and contemporary forms of slavery, it is useful to briefly outline the scope of the relevant international norms.

6.3.2.1 The evolution of the notion of 'slavery' under international law The prohibition of slavery and slave trade is not only a long-standing rule included in many human rights treaties and domestic bills of rights, but it is also a well-known norm of customary international law.[12] The 1926 Slavery Convention was the first international agreement providing a definition of those practices.[13] Under article 1(1) 'slavery' was defined as: 'the status or condition of a person over whom any or all of the powers attaching to the right of ownership are exercised'. In addition, the Convention defined 'slave trade' as 'all acts involved in the capture, acquisition or disposal of a person with intent to reduce him to slavery' (article 1(2)). The 1926 Slavery Convention was originally conceived to address narrow circumstances where people involved in coercive labour practices did not possess, to some degree, a juridical personality under domestic law: 'Traditional slavery was referred to as "chattel slavery" on the ground that the owners of such slaves were able to treat them

---

10 This body, originally named Working Group on Slavery, was established in 1974 by the Sub-Commission on Prevention of Discrimination and Protection of Minorities of the UN Commission on Human Rights, in order to review developments in the field of slavery and slave trade. See <www.ohchr.org/english/issues/slavery/group.htm>.

11 See Fact Sheet No. 14, Contemporary Forms of Slavery, June 1991.

12 On the prohibition of slavery, see: J. Allain, 'The Definition of "Slavery" in General International Law and the Crime of Enslavement within the Rome Statute', ICC Guest Lecture Series of the Office of the Prosecutor, 2007, available at <www.icc-cpi.int/otp/otp_guest_lectures.html>; J. Quirk, 'The Anti-Slavery Project: Linking the Historical and Contemporary', *Human Rights Quarterly*, Vol. 28, 2006, 565 ff; M. Nowak, *UN Covenant on Civil and Political Rights – CCPR Commentary*, 2nd edn, 2005, 193 ff; N. Boschiero, 'Art. 4 - Proibizione della schiavitù e del lavoro forzato', in S. Bartole, B. Conforti and G. Raimondi, Commentario alla Convenzione europea per la tutela dei diritti dell'uomo e delle libertà fondamentali, Padua, 2001, 77 ff; F. Lenzerini, 'L'evoluzione contemporanea del concetto di schiavitù nel diritto internazionale consuetudinario', *Studi Senesi*, 2000, 470 ff; A.Y. Rassam, 'Contemporary Forms of Slavery and the Evolution of the Prohibition of Slavery and the Slave Trade Under Customary International Law', *Virginia Journal of International Law*, 1999, 303 ff.

13 League of Nations' Slavery Convention (date of adoption: 25 September 1926; date of entry into force: 9 March 1927), art. 1(1), available at <www.ohchr.org>. The Convention has been amended by the 1953 Protocol which transferred to the UN the duties and functions which the original Slavery Convention had invested in the League of Nations.

as if they were possessions, like livestock or furniture, and to sell or transfer them to others.'[14] Thus, the notion's defining feature was the relationship of ownership between the victim and their 'master', which deprived the former of their juridical capacity. The wording of the 1926 Convention, however, allows an even more expansive interpretation, since the expression 'any or all of the powers attaching to the right of ownership'[15] might be read as covering other situations of exploitation and personal dependence that do not necessarily entail the loss of the victim's legal capacity.[16]

Subsequently, some of those conditions were expressly addressed by the 1956 Supplementary Slavery Convention,[17] which, in addition to slavery, provided for the abolition of some institutions and practices, identified collectively as 'servile status', such as debt bondage, serfdom and certain forms of women's and children's exploitation. Article 1(d) of the Convention, in particular, prohibited delivering a child to another person, with a view to the exploitation of the child itself or its labour.

The 1956 Supplementary Convention thus introduced the concept of 'servitude', comprising some slave-like practices to be completely abolished 'whether or not they are covered by the definition of slavery contained in article 1 of the Slavery Convention' (article 1), since those situations bring about the same effects of slavery in its strict sense, *de facto* depriving the victims of their capacity of self-determination, even when retaining their *de jure* legal personality.[18]

A prohibition of slavery and servitude, nowadays, may be found in all comprehensive international and regional human rights instruments,[19] though none of them give a precise definition of the terms. From the drafting process of article 8 of the ICCPR, however, it emerged that 'slavery' was understood in its narrow sense of deprivation of the juridical personality, whereas 'servitude' was conceived as a broader concept covering all possible forms of degradation and dominance of one

---

14 E/CN.4/Sub.2/2000/3, § 18, at 7.

15 For a detailed discussion of the scope of the notion of slavery on the basis of the various 'powers attached to the right of ownership', see Allain, 'The Definition of "Slavery"', *supra* note 12, at 8.

16 It emerges from the drafting process that, according to the wording of art. 2(a), referring to 'the abolition of slavery in all its forms', the Convention might subsequently have covered other practices, such as serfdom, debt bondage or forced marriages. See Allain, 'The Definition of "Slavery"', *supra* note 12, at 3; E/CN.4/Sub.2/2000/3, *supra* note 14, at 5.

17 Supplementary Convention on the Abolition of Slavery, the Slave Trade, and Institutions and Practices Similar to Slavery, available at <www.ohchr.org>.

18 From a legal standpoint, thus, the terms 'servitude' and 'practices similar to slavery' should be deemed synonymous, both referring comprehensively to serfdom, debt bondage or any other slave-like circumstance, except for slavery in its narrow, traditional sense.

19 See, among others: Universal Declaration of Human Rights (UDHR), art. 4; International Covenant on Civil and Political Rights (ICCPR), art. 8; European Convention for the Protection of Human Rights and Fundamental Freedoms (ECHR), art. 4(1), American Convention on Human Rights (ACHR), art. 6(1) and African Charter on Human and Peoples' Rights (ACHPR), art. 5 (which refers only to slavery).

person over another.[20] Likewise, in a recent decision[21] concerning the application of article 4 of the European Court of Human Rights (ECHR), which prohibits slavery, servitude and forced labour, the ECHR has reasserted the distinction between these three practices and has identified the defining feature of slavery as the exercise of legal ownership over the victim.[22]

Although the position of the Court is no doubt consistent with the traditional meaning of the term 'slavery', it should be recalled that, in view of its absolute, universal character and its deeply rooted acceptance by the international community, the prohibition of slavery by now has attained the status of a fundamental norm of general international law, whose content covers a broader range of practices, including those listed by the UN Working Group of Contemporary Slavery (WGCS).[23] Furthermore, it is widely recognized that the customary international norm prohibiting slavery in its broader meaning is a peremptory norm under international law, thus ranked as *jus cogens*, permitting no derogation by treaty.[24]

Thanks to the evolution of the notion of slavery, other forms of child exploitation, such as sexual exploitation or child labour in its strict sense, are now considered modern forms of slavery.[25] Each of them has its specificity and does not necessarily meet the requirements of the classical definition in all circumstances. However, slave-like practices may produce analogous effects because the victims are subjected

---

20 On the scope of art. 8 of the ICCPR, see Nowak, U.N. Covenant, *supra* note 12, at 196.

21 *Siliadin v France*, (2006) 43 EHRR 16.

22 'Although the applicant was, in the instant case, clearly deprived of her personal autonomy, the evidence does not suggest that she was held in slavery in the proper sense, in other words that Mr and Mrs B. exercised a genuine right of legal ownership over her, thus reducing her to the status of an "object"', *Siliadin v France,* § 122. On the Court's judgement, see: H. Cullen, '*Siliadin v France*: Positive Obligations under Article 4 of the European Convention on Human Rights', *Human Rights Law Review*, Vol. 6, No. 3, 2006, 585 ff.

23 On the prohibition of slavery as a norm of customary international law and the evolution of its scope, see, in particular: Lenzerini, 'L'evoluzione contemporanea', *supra* note 12, at 514; Rassam, 'Contemporary Forms of Slavery', *supra* note 12, at 316.

24 See: Nowak, *UN Covenant*, *supra* note 12, at 197; Boschiero, 'Art. 4', *supra* note 12, at 87; Lenzerini, 'L'evoluzione contemporanea', *supra* note 12, at 479; J.M. Diller and D.A. Levy, 'Child Labor, Trade and Investment: Toward the Harmonization of International Law', *American Journal of International Law*, Vol. 91, 1997, 663 ff, at 669. The distinction between slavery and servitude made by some international human rights treaties should thus be read in the light of the status and the content's evolution of the general international norm prohibiting slavery. It follows that, while the word 'slavery' in human rights treaties is still interpreted as referring strictly to its classical meaning, the concept of servitude encompasses all other slave-like practices. In this way, both terms taken together would correspond to the broader notion of slavery under general international law. In this perspective, the decision of the ECHR mentioned above would be fully consistent with the customary international norm prohibiting slavery. On this point, see Allain, 'The Definition of "Slavery"', *supra* note 12, at 18.

25 On this issue, though with particular reference to minors' sexual exploitation, see: F. Lenzerini, 'Sfruttamento sessuale dei minori e norme internazionali sulla schiavitù', *La Comunità internazionale*, Vol. LIV, 1999, 474 ff, at 497.

to forms of physical and/or psychological coercion, depriving them of their freedom and exposing them to their exploiters' full or partial control.

A comprehensive notion of slavery, more consistent with the broader scope of the 1926 Convention and with the evolution of the concept under general international law, is now codified in the Statute of the International Criminal Court, which condemns 'enslavement' as a crime against humanity falling within the jurisdiction of the Court (article 7(1)(c)) and defines the term as 'the exercise of any or all of the powers attaching to the right of ownership over a person [including] the exercise of such power in the course of trafficking in persons, in particular women and children' (article 7(2)(c)).[26] In the Elements of the Crimes, it is further specified that the crime of enslavement may occur when '1. The perpetrator exercised any or all of the powers attaching to the right of ownership over one or more persons, such as purchasing, selling, lending or bartering such a person or persons, or by imposing on them a similar deprivation of liberty' (article 7(1)(c)).[27] According to a footnote to article 7(1)(c),

> It is understood that such deprivation of liberty may, in some circumstances, include exacting forced labour or otherwise reducing a person to a servile status as defined in the Supplementary Convention on the Abolition of Slavery [...] It is also understood that the conduct described in this element includes trafficking in persons, in particular women and children.[28]

A broader approach to the concept of slavery has been applied by the International Criminal Tribunal for the former Yugoslavia (ICTY) in the *Kunarac* case,[29] where it maintained that, under international customary law, enslavement, as a crime against humanity, may occur not only when the victims are deprived of their juridical personality, but also when they are *de facto* subjected to their exploiters' complete or partial control.[30]

Significant elements thus confirm that under general international law the norm which prohibits slavery encompasses both classical slavery and practices similar

---

26 Rome Statute of the International Criminal Court.

27 Art. 7(1)(c) of the Elements of the Crimes requires further that: '2.The conduct was committed as part of a widespread or systematic attack directed against a civilian population. 3. The perpetrator knew that the conduct was part of or intended the conduct to be part of a widespread or systematic attack directed against a civilian population.'

28 On the crime of 'enslavement' within the Rome Statute, see Allain, 'The Definition of "Slavery"', *supra* note 12, at 16. On the individual responsibility for 'enslavement' as an international crime, see: Boschiero, 'Art. 4', *supra* note 12, at 91; Diller and Levy, 'Child Labor', *supra* note 24, at 668.

29 *Kunarac* and others, Judgement, ICTY Trial Chamber III, IT-96-23 and IT-96-23/1-T (2001).

30 For a detailed analysis of the Trial and Appeal Chambers' rulings on this issue, see: Allain, 'The Definition of "Slavery"', *supra* note 12, at 19; and Lenzerini, 'La definizione internazionale di schiavitù secondo il Tribunale per la ex-Iugoslavia: un caso di osmosi tra consuetudine e norme convenzionali', *Rivista di Diritto internazionale*, Vol. LXXXIV, 2001, 1026 ff.

to slavery, like those banned by the 1956 Supplementary Convention, as well as modern forms of slavery identified by the UN's WGCS.[31]

Since all WFCL mentioned in article 3 of Convention 182 clearly are forms of exploitation that, due to the particular vulnerability of the victims, may subject them to the same effects brought about by any slavery-like practice, they had been legitimately assimilated in the concept of modern forms of slavery long before their condemnation in a specific Convention. The exclusion of some of the WFCL on the basis that they do not constitute real forms of work would thus have been inconsistent with the purpose of Convention 182, especially because the notion of WFCL, has been certainly conceived with a broader scope.

6.3.3 Convention 182's focus on children as 'victims', rather than 'workers'

The qualification of WFCL as types of economic exploitation and modern forms of slavery helps shed light on the reasons why Convention 182 does not make reference only to labour in the strict meaning of the term, nor considers specific working activities performed by children. The notion of WFCL is rather focused on the exploitative conditions children are subjected to, whenever they are engaged in licit or illicit activities akin to work. In other words, the WFCL are not banned because they consist of work carried out by children, but primarily because children are victims of those activities. Children are considered exploited victims in need of protection, and not as workers or authors of illegal activities. In fact, Convention 182 does not condemn the conduct of the child, but rather that of the exploiter.[32] Of course, the possible illegal behaviour of a child, involved in activities prohibited under national criminal legislation, would not at all be condoned by Convention 182. The Convention's approach in those circumstances, however, is to pay particular attention to children's vulnerability owed to their age and living conditions, in order to implement the necessary measures to strike at the economic and social root causes, and to ensure the children's rehabilitation and social reintegration. According to article 7(2) of Convention 182 States Parties

> ... shall, taking into account the importance of education in eliminating child labour, take effective and time-bound measures to: ... (b) provide the necessary and appropriate direct assistance for the removal of children from the worst forms of child labour and for their rehabilitation and social integration; (c) ensure access to free basic education, and, wherever possible and appropriate, vocational training, for all children removed from the worst forms of child labour.

---

31 In this light, terms like 'servitude', 'slave-like practices', and 'modern or contemporary forms of slavery' may be considered synonyms and will be used interchangeably in this chapter.

32 In responding to some constituents' requests, during the *travaux préparatoires*, the ILO Deputy Legal Adviser stated: 'Children making bricks in conditions of debt bondage were engaged in a worst form of child labour and were victims of it; whereas the adult who put them to such work was a criminal profiting from such work', ILC, *Report of the Committee on Child Labour*, presented at the Conference at its 87th Session (1999).

It is worth noting that the measures applied to rehabilitate marginalized children, possibly involved in illicit activities, should in no way amount to practices that could push them into another form of exploitation. For example, the 'rehabilitation through labour' systems, widespread in China as a compulsory measure for education and reform, must be deemed inconsistent with the prohibition of forced or compulsory labour, as defined by ILO Convention 29.[33] Under similar programmes, children guilty of minor public disorders or sexually related offences are detained, on the basis of mere administrative decisions, in 'work study' schools or in re-education through labour camps, where they are forced to work in harsh conditions.[34] Furthermore, the prohibition of children's forced labour is infringed in China, not only in the framework of re-educational and reformative measures, but also in regular work programmes at school![35]

6.3.4 ILO competence on regulating WFCL

The analogy between the WFCL and practices similar to slavery adds clarity, not only to the scope of the definition adopted by the Convention, but also to the ILO mandate on the subject. As noted, one of the critical issues raised in the drafting of Convention 182 concerned the ILO competence with regard to practices that are not genuine forms of work or do not even entail the performance of working activities by children. A few constituents held that the standard's scope should have been limited to forced labour, debt bondage, serfdom and hazardous work, or even only to the latter phenomenon. However this criticism does not appear consistent with the wide sphere of ILO action that, from the outset of the Organization's activities, has covered situations of exploitation akin to slavery and forced labour. In fact, even before the adoption of Convention 182, the ILO supervisory bodies had examined numerous slave-like cases, including child sale and trafficking or forced recruitment of child soldiers, in the context of the application of Convention 29, on the basis that these kinds of child exploitation as well as other slavery-like practices are considered types of forced labour.[36] Besides, ILO bodies continue to examine similar

---

33 Convention concerning Forced or Compulsory Labour (No. 29). Though China is not a party to Convention 29, reference to that instrument needs to be made, since Convention 182 does not give a precise definition of forced or compulsory labour.

34 The incompatibility with the principle of the elimination of forced or compulsory labour is not only due to harsh working conditions, but mainly because the labour is imposed by administrative or other non-judicial bodies. Art. 2(2)(c) of C29, in effect, provides that labour may be imposed on a person under detention only 'as a consequence of a conviction in a court of law', clearly in order to guarantee the respect of due process's rights and to avoid arbitrary detentions and punishments.

35 See CEACR, Individual Observation concerning Convention No. 182: China, 2007, Doc. No. 062007CHN182, where CEACR urges the government to take measures to ensure that people under 18 are not forced to work in the context of any of the mentioned systems or in any other situation. Those measures should include effective and dissuasive criminal penalties for persons who force minors to work.

36 See, for some examples, CEACR, Individual Observation concerning Convention No. 29: Bangladesh 1998, Doc. No. 061998BGD029; and ILCCR, Examination of Individual

cases in the framework of Convention 29 when they occur in States party to the latter Convention, but not to Convention 182.[37]

6.3.5 The criminal nature of WFCL

The *travaux préparatoires* of Convention 182 revealed a nearly unanimous consensus on the criminal nature of all kinds of exploitation of children and their labour, especially those currently included in article 3(a) to (c). The adoption of an international convention addressing issues like child enslavement and the use of children for pornographic performances or for trafficking of drugs, by an Organization playing a specific role in the field of work and setting labour standards, raised some concerns because of the risk of devaluing their criminal nature.

Nevertheless, this argument was not considered a valid justification for not including those abuses in a convention whose main purpose is to combat and eradicate the most extreme forms of child exploitation.[38] Besides, the inclusion of such criminal activities in an international labour convention in no way entails their legitimization. On the contrary, it aims to strengthen their condemnation and to broaden the tools for immediately and efficiently eliminating them. In this regard, it is worth recalling an Office observation on the assessment of the Convention's beneficiaries:

> It might also be useful to note that setting the age at 18 does not automatically imply that any work or activity mentioned in the instruments is suitable or should be allowed for those over 18, or indeed for any person, but rather reflects the focus of these instruments on children.[39]

Case concerning Convention No. 29: Bangladesh 1998, Doc. No. 131998BGD029 on various situations of children's exploitation in Bangladesh, including bonded labour and trafficking; ILCCR, Examination of Individual Case concerning Convention No. 29: Thailand 1995, Doc. No. 131995THA029; CEACR, Individual Observation concerning Convention No. 29, Sudan 1998, Doc. No. 061998SDN029. After a State ratifies C182, however, all kinds of children's exploitation amounting to WFCL are examined more specifically under that Convention, even if they may still be covered by C29.

37 For India, see ILCCR, Examination of Individual Case concerning Convention No. 29: India, 2003, Doc. No. 132003IND029.

38 See the ILO Office's observation in ILO, *Child Labour: Targeting the Intolerable, Report VI(1)*, presented at the 86th Session of the Conference (1998): 'Child prostitution, child pornography and the sale and trafficking of children are crimes of violence against children. They must be treated as crimes and attacked as the most serious crimes are attacked. Such repellent abuses are so far removed from any normal notion of work or labour that it seems strange to focus on them in an ILO report. Yet while they are crimes they are also forms of economic exploitation akin to forced labour and slavery. Any new international standards on the most extreme forms of child labour must therefore specifically aim at abolishing the commercial sexual exploitation of children.' Although focused on sexual exploitation, the sentence may, by analogy, refer to other WFCL. See ILC, Report VI(2), *supra* note 7, Office's observations on question 7, subparagraphs (a) and (b).

39 The sentence also refers to the freedom of any Member to adopt measures which ensure more favourable conditions to the beneficiaries concerned than those provided for in

At the same time, one should remember that when people commit any of the acts banned by Convention 182, their conduct should be condemned, whether or not the victims are engaged in illicit activities. It follows that even the exploitation of a child in a form of hazardous work incompatible with article 3(d) should be regarded as a crime *per se*, though the job would be absolutely legitimate when performed by an adult.

6.3.5.1 The provision of penal sanctions The criminal nature of the WFCL is not devalued either by article 7(1) which provides that 'each Member shall take all necessary measures to ensure the effective implementation and enforcement of the provisions giving effect to this Convention including the provision and application of penal sanctions or, as appropriate, other sanctions'. According to the rule's wording, the provision of criminal penalties looks more like an option left to States than a binding obligation. Recommendation 190,[40] however, affirms that all practices covered by article 3(a) to (c) should be considered criminal offences by national legislations (para. 12). During the *travaux préparatoires* this provision received the support of the vast majority of governments and organizations that replied to the ILO questionnaire.[41] Furthermore, when monitoring Convention 182's correct application, ILO bodies usually request States to provide adequate penal sanctions against these practices.[42] It follows that, notwithstanding its literal meaning, article 7(1) should be read as entailing a binding obligation on States to adopt penal sanctions, at least for practices similar to slavery, sexual exploitation or illicit activities. In these circumstances, in fact, penal sanctions would undoubtedly correspond to some of the necessary measures requested by article 7(1) to ensure the effective enforcement of the Convention.

With reference to hazardous work, Recommendation 190 suggests that penalties, including (where appropriate) criminal penalties, should be imposed for violations

---

the ILO standards, in compliance with art. 19(8) of the ILO Constitution.

40 Recommendation concerning the Prohibition and Immediate Action for the Elimination of the Worst Forms of Child Labour, date of adoption 17 June 1999. Despite its non-binding nature, the Recommendation is an important tool which specifies the contents of C182 obligations and guides States Parties to their correct implementation, whereas it suggests to States that have not ratified the Convention how to conform their legal systems and their action to the purposes of the international standards on the matter.

41 ILC, Report VI(2), *supra* note 7, States' and Office's observations on question 20.

42 Even before the adoption of the Convention, most of the practices mentioned in art. 3(a) to (c) were already condemned as criminal offences in every Member State. Afterwards, a significant trend towards the inclusion of new or increased penalties has been recorded, especially for child trafficking and sexual exploitation (see Rishikesh, this volume). Nevertheless, there are still some States where similar crimes may be punished with fines only (see the case of forced labour in China, *supra* note 40) or where punishments are not deemed sufficiently dissuasive (see for instance: CEACR, Individual Observation concerning Convention No. 182: Pakistan 2006, Doc. No. 062006PAK182; CEACR, Individual Direct Request concerning Convention No. 182: Cape Verde 2007, Doc. No. 092007CPV182; CEACR, Individual Direct Request concerning Convention No. 182: Democratic Republic of the Congo 2007, Doc. No. 092007COD182).

of the national provisions concerning the prohibition and elimination of any type of work referred to in article 3(d) of Convention 182 (para. 13). In this case, even more discretion is likely to be accorded to States concerning sanctions to be taken against violations of article 3(d), maybe because the banned activities do not usually constitute illicit work when performed by people over 18. However, when children engaged in working activities are exposed to dangerous and harmful conditions constituting direct violations of article 3(d), they would be subjected to forms of exploitation of the same severity as those covered by subparagraphs (a) to (c).[43] In other words, although the activity does not constitute a crime *per se*, its performance by a person under 18 in hazardous circumstances impairing its full development does constitute a violation of children's basic right not to be exposed to either WFCL or economic exploitation. Hence, the line of reasoning adopted above should extend to article 3(d) as well, primarily in order to avoid giving the impression that some WFCL are more serious and intolerable than others. In fact, during the elaboration of Convention 182, most ILO constituents agreed on the appropriateness of criminal penalties also for the infringement of prohibitions referring to hazardous work.[44] Moreover, ILO monitoring bodies request States to introduce penal sanctions even for breaches of article 3(d).[45] It follows that criminal penalties amount to necessary measures under article 7(1) so as to ensure the effective enforcement of every subparagraph of article 3.[46] Their provision, as well as the adoption of any other measure that may be appropriate to implement the Convention, would thus constitute a binding obligation for States.

Finally, it must be recalled that the infliction of criminal penalties for the illegal exaction of forced or compulsory labour is an explicit requirement under article 25 of Convention 29. So, whenever the involvement of a child in one of the practices banned by article 3 corresponds to forms of forced labour or other practices covered by Convention 29, it should be punished as a criminal offence. Hence, Convention 182 does not at all devalue the criminal nature of WFCL. On the contrary, it bolsters the ban on the activities concerned for those States that have ratified both Conventions. Furthermore, Convention 182's scope is even broader because it requires the provision of penal sanctions with reference to any WFCL, regardless of its exact correspondence to forced labour under Convention 29.

---

43 See ILC, *Report IV(2A)*, *supra* note 5, USA's observations on art. 3.

44 *Ibid.*, States' and Office's observations on question 21.

45 The CEACR does not leave any choice to States as regards the provision of penal sanctions for WFCL: 'The Committee recalls that, under Article 7, paragraph 1, of the Convention, the Government has to take all necessary measures to ensure the effective implementation and enforcement of the provisions giving effect to the Convention, including the provision and application of penal sanctions. The Committee therefore requests the Government to indicate the penal provisions relating to: the sale or trafficking of children for sexual exploitation; the forced or compulsory recruitment of children for use in armed conflict; the engagement of children in hazardous work in mines', CEACR, Individual Direct Request concerning Convention No. 182, Democratic Republic of the Congo, *supra* note 42.

46 In practice, the provision of penal sanctions for the crime of exploiting children in hazardous work is not as widespread as for breaches of subparagraph (a) to (c) of art. 3.

6.4 The relationship between different categories of WFCL

As noted, though not always amounting to slavery in its traditional meaning, all WFCL correspond to modern forms of slavery, like those outlined by the UN's WGCS. Yet article 3 of Convention 182 classifies WFCL in four distinct groups and, at first sight, only the issues in clause (a) are likely to be considered practices similar to slavery.

The most common explanation of the distinction between the activities covered by article 3(a) and other WFCL is that the former constitute forms of child exploitation perpetrated under circumstances of coercion. That does not necessarily imply the existence of generic compelling factors depending on the victims' living conditions, but requires effective control by a third party without the victim's consent. According to this approach, certain situations might fall outside the ban imposed by article 3, because it cannot be excluded that the children offered themselves voluntarily.[47] The choice of dealing with sexual exploitation, engagement in illicit activities or hazardous work in separate clauses would hence aim to clearly establish a prohibition covering any circumstance, irrespective of the consent of the children involved. This line of reasoning confirms the impression that, in the framework of Convention 182, only the situations listed in article 3(a) should be considered practices similar to slavery, because they are involuntary by definition.

Another view of the relationship between the different categories of WFCL, however, may be based on a broader interpretation of the coercive element required by the concept of 'practices similar to slavery'. Due to the lack of a definition of those situations, reference is often made to the concept of forced or compulsory labour outlined by article 2(1) of Convention 29: 'The term "forced or compulsory labour" shall mean all work or service which is exacted from any person under the menace of any penalty and for which the said person has not offered himself voluntarily.' The lack of voluntariness clearly is a constitutive requirement of the notion of forced labour and it is certainly true that the ILO has usually interpreted this element as calling for the exercise of a direct form of coercion on the victim by an active third party. Generic compelling factors related to the worker's poor conditions of life *per se* are not usually considered forms of coercion proving the absence of consent.[48]

---

47 Especially young adolescents may frequently and deliberately engage in illicit activities, like prostitution or pornography. Likewise, not all trafficked children enter the process against their will. What would then be the difference between situations of sexual exploitation under letter (b) and sale and trafficking under clause (a)?

48 'An external constraint or indirect coercion interfering with a worker's freedom to "offer himself voluntarily" may result not only from an act of the authorities, such as a statutory instrument, but also from an employer's practice, e.g. where migrant workers are induced by deceit, false promises and retention of identity documents or forced to remain at the disposal of an employer; such practices represent a clear violation of the Convention. However, the employer or the State are not accountable for all external constraints or indirect coercion existing in practice: for example, the need to work in order to earn one's living could become relevant only in conjunction with other factors for which they are answerable.' ILC, Report III (Part 1B) – General Survey concerning the Forced Labour Convention, 1930 (No.

The assessment of the coercive element, however, may depend on the subjective conditions of the victim and its particular vulnerability. Especially with reference to children, the ILO itself has recognized greater difficulty in establishing 'whether, and under what circumstances, a minor can be considered to have offered himself or herself "voluntarily" for work or service and whether the consent of the parents is required and may be considered sufficient'.[49]

In fact, it is usually argued that children, by virtue of their immaturity, can never engage in those practices on an authentically voluntary basis, whereas they are compelled by circumstances, such as the conditions of poverty and marginalization of their life, the exposure to violence and abuses and the lack of schooling. Hence, these factors would deprive the victims of any possibility of choice and would correspond to conditions of submission and loss of any chance of self-determination which are usually the hallmarks of slavery-like practices, even when the involvement in the practices concerned is ostensibly consensual given the absence of an active third party exercising direct coercion. In this regard CEACR's observation about forced child labour is significant: 'employment that is likely to jeopardize health, safety or morals is generally prohibited for persons below 18 years of age, in conformity with the relevant ILO Conventions, so that neither the children nor those having parental authority over them may give valid consent to their admission to such employment'.[50]

Though it does not amount exactly to forced labour or to any specific circumstance mentioned in subparagraph (a), any activity falling within the definition of WFCL, even in the context of Convention 182, corresponds to a practice similar to slavery that might actually be covered by the scope of article 3(a) and should then be merely considered a further specification of the issues banned by that provision.[51]

In consequence, the grouping of WFCL in four distinct categories is likely to be rather aimed at pinpointing and better targeting the specificity of each group, especially in order to outline, in the phase of Convention 182's implementation, the most appropriate policies. Clause (b) includes practices whose main feature is children's exploitation for sexual purposes, regardless of their licit or illicit nature in national legal systems. Clause (c) addresses, in general, children's involvement in any activity prohibited by international or national norms (different from those of a sexual kind), while clause (d) refers to any form of hazardous work that should be outlawed for people under 18, although they are in principle legitimate employment when performed by adults. Clause (a), finally, comprises practices whose peculiarity resides in the relationship between the victims and their exploiters, and not the type of the activity performed. Hence, they can not be defined as occupations in themselves, whereas they amount to conditions of complete or partial submission

---

29), and the Abolition of Forced Labour Convention, 1957 (No. 105), presented at the 96th Session of the Conference (2007), § 39.

49 *Ibid.*, § 41.

50 *Ibid.*

51 See also Boschiero, 'Art. 4', *supra* note 12, at 106; Lenzerini, 'L'evoluzione contemporanea', *supra* note 12, at 496; Lenzerini, 'Sfruttamento sessuale', *supra* note 25, at 506, Diller and Levy, 'Child Labor', *supra* note 24, at 668.

of a person to another. For this reason they may cut across various occupations in different economic sectors.

Although the purpose of C182 is to address each category of WFCL or even each phenomenon *per se*, in order to work out the best measures to efficiently combat them, in the majority of cases there might be a substantial overlap between the different practices concerned. Child sale and trafficking may occur with the intention of exploiting the victims in any other type of activity mentioned in article 3, while every situation falling within sexual exploitation, involvement in illicit activities or hazardous work may, under certain circumstances, amount to one of the practices banned by article 3(a).

The expression 'all forms of slavery or practices similar to slavery', in article 3(a), may be read as referring, in general, to any kind of activity impairing children's full development and for which the child has not offered voluntarily, but rather as a consequence of its situation of vulnerability or a third party's direct coercion. In this light, it is worth noting that the list included in subparagraph (a), as well as the situations covered by the following clauses, are not exhaustive, whereas other circumstances, though not explicitly envisaged by the provision, might come under the notion of WFCL,[52] unless they had been unequivocally left out from Convention 182's scope.[53]

6.5 WFCL prohibited under article 3(a)

As argued, by virtue of the analogy between the WFCL and the notion of slavery in its contemporary meaning, the first part of clause (a) of article 3 of Convention 182 may be read as a comprehensive provision potentially encompassing not only all practices expressly listed in the following subparagraphs, but also any other phenomenon of economic exploitation of children having similar effects.

Yet in its second part, the provision illustratively enumerates certain specific practices on which States Parties, in conjunction with the ILO, should focus their action. According to the 2002 ILO global estimates, at least 8.4 million children were involved in unconditional WFCL and two-thirds of them were trapped in

---

52 'A number of replies referred to the scope of the Convention and felt that the instruments should apply to (or in some cases exempt) home work by children, work in family enterprises or farms, street children, self-employed children in the informal sector, cross-border employment of children, minors who migrate to work, and compulsory labour of children in penitentiary institutions. Because the instruments have a broad application to all persons under age 18 (Point 7) none of these are excluded. The issue of apprenticeship was also raised to ensure that the problem of apprenticeships disguising child labour would be dealt with explicitly by the Convention. Again there is no exception for apprentices since the proposed instruments apply to extreme forms of child labour regardless of the employment status of the child.' ILC, *Report VI(2)*, *supra* note 7, Office's observations on question 28.

53 The prohibition of child sale and trafficking, for instance, does not cover cases of trafficking of children for adoption or for organ transplantation. ILC, *Report IV(2A)*, *supra* note 5, Office commentary on subparagraph (a).

various kinds of exploitation corresponding to those listed in article 3(a).[54] Although, in practice, there might be a substantial overlap between the various situations listed by article 3(a), from a legal standpoint, each one may be dealt with separately because of certain differences pertaining to the link between the victims and their exploiters or to the particular activities concerned. Hence, a given form of child exploitation may be qualified as one of the practices listed in article 3(a), when the specific conditions required are met. Since Convention 182 does not give a detailed definition of the categories expressly banned, reference should be made to other relevant international instruments addressing the phenomena.

The following paragraphs will briefly examine the typologies of WFCL mentioned in article 3(a), recalling their defining features under international law and considering some concrete cases which were dealt with by ILO monitoring bodies in the context of the application of Convention 182.

6.5.1 Serfdom and debt bondage

Since the adoption of the 1926 Convention, traditional slavery, characterized by the deprivation of the victims' juridical capacity to the point of objectifying them, has been progressively abolished in all domestic legal systems. Nevertheless, a few contemporary cases have been detected, particularly in certain African countries, where serious conditions of poverty and underdevelopment, political instability and endless internal armed conflicts, as well as conniving regimes, wipe out any efforts to eradicate long-standing practices rooted in the domestic social order.[55] As regards children, one should mention the persistence of traditional practices of ritual servitude, based on religious or spiritual reasons and particularly affecting girls, such as the *trokosi* system in some regions of Ghana, where young girls of about 10 years are pledged into perpetual bondage to serve fetish shrines in atonement of offences allegedly committed by their relatives.[56] In other West African countries, including Niger and Mauritania, many families entrust their children from the age of 5 or 6

---

54 ILO, *A Future Without Child Labour – Global Report under the Follow-Up to the ILO Declaration on Fundamental Principles and Rights at Work*, Geneva: ILO, 2002, at 18.

55 Vestiges of slavery have survived, such as in Mauritania, despite its formal abolition in 1981. Archaic forms of slavery have been detected even among nomadic communities in Niger. Similar practices involving not only children but also considerable parts of the adult population have been repeatedly addressed in the context of ILO action towards the abolition of forced labour, together with cases of massive abductions for slavery and forced labour closely linked to situations of armed conflicts in Sudan, Liberia, Sierra Leone and Uganda. See ILO, *Stopping Forced Labour – Global Report under the Follow-Up to the ILO Declaration on Fundamental Principles and Rights at Work, Geneva: ILO, 2001*, 61 ff; ILC, *Report III (Part 1B), supra* note 48, 35 ff. On the situation in Mauritania and Sudan, see also Quirk, 'The Anti-Slavery Project', *supra* note 12, at 571.

56 The practice has been the object of an absolute ban under the domestic Criminal Code since 1998, and some specific projects of sensitization and liberation have been undertaken: CEACR, Individual Direct Request concerning Convention No. 182: Ghana 2005, Doc. No. 092005GHA182; CEACR, Individual Direct Request concerning Convention No. 182: Ghana 2007, Doc. No. 092007GHA182.

until adolescence to spiritual guides (*marabouts*) or teachers of the Koran, who teach them religion in return for certain services, including begging. This is justified as a cultural and educational practice aimed at developing humility and compassion in adults. Those children, commonly known as *talibés*, are entirely at their teachers' mercy. As a consequence, they are often forced to hand over the daily proceeds of their begging and are used mainly as a source of income. Often *marabouts* and teachers are involved in child trafficking, too.[57]

Besides similar circumstances, article 3(a) covers other long-standing slave-like practices, such as serfdom and debt bondage, especially widespread in less-developed countries. According to the 1956 Slavery Supplementary Convention, 'serfdom' is defined as 'the condition or status of a tenant who is by law, custom or agreement bound to live and labour on land belonging to another person and to render some determinate service to such other person, whether for reward or not, and is not free to change his status' (article 1(b)). At that time, the notion strictly referred to ancient land tenure systems and to practices, widespread in Latin America, known as 'peonage'.[58] However, similar rural serfdom regimes still occur today not only in Latin America, where especially indigenous people are affected, but also in some African or Asian countries.[59] Often the phenomenon is linked to forms of 'debt bondage', too.

Debt bondage is defined in the 1956 Convention as 'the status or condition arising from a pledge by a debtor of his personal services or of those of a person under his control as security for a debt, if the value of those services as reasonably assessed is not applied towards the liquidation of the debt or the length and nature of those services are not respectively limited and defined' (article 1(a)). In the agricultural sector, bonded labourers are obliged to continue working for their landowner on account of debts they supposedly owe, as well as on account of their tenant status. Nowadays, moreover, the phenomenon is not limited to agriculture; it has also emerged in industrial and manufacturing sectors, such as mines, brick kilns, leather, fish processing and carpet factories.[60]

---

57 See CEACR, Individual Observation concerning Convention No. 182: Niger 2007, Doc. No. 062007NER182, where the government is encouraged to take the necessary steps to enforce the national legislation on begging and to punish *marabouts* who use children for purely economic ends. See also CEACR, Individual Direct Request concerning Convention No. 182: Mauritania 2005, Doc. No. 092005MRT182.

58 'Those practices, which had developed in a context of conquest, subjugation of indigenous peoples and seizure of their lands, involved a landowner granting a piece of land to an individual "serf" or "peon" in return for specific services, including (i) providing the landowner with a proportion of the crop at harvest ("share cropping"), (ii) working for the landowner; or (iii) doing other work, for example domestic chores, for the landowner's household. In each case, it is not the provision of labour in return for access to land which is in itself considered a form of servitude, but the inability of the person of serf status to leave that status.' E/CN.4/Sub.2/2000/3/Add.1, § 5.

59 ILO, *Stopping Forced Labour*, *supra* note 55, 21 ff.

60 For a detailed account of the phenomenon, with particular reference to Asian countries, see *Ibid.*, 32 ff.

Debt bondage particularly affects children who are usually pledged by their parents to repay a hereditary or other debt. Children are then bonded into agricultural labour, domestic work or sweatshops, at the mercy of the 'lender', suffering economic hardship, without knowing the amount of the debt they are working to pay off or the terms of repayment. Due to the high interest rates charged by the 'lender', the servitude engendered by the debt can be passed from one generation to the next.

Besides the staggering situation of Pakistan, where several million child labourers are reported, a large part of whom are engaged in debt bondage,[61] in the context of the application of Convention 182 the CEACR has noted the existence of the practice in a few other countries, such as Bolivia, where minors, especially from indigenous communities, are exploited in agricultural work.[62]

6.5.2 Forced or compulsory labour

Despite their specificity from a legal point of view, ILO organs often deal with these practices without distinguishing them from forced or compulsory labour, due to the unavoidable overlap between these forms of workers' exploitation in practice. Besides, all of them undoubtedly fall under the current prohibition of slavery. The international norm imposing a ban on forced labour, however, has had an autonomous evolution.[63] As pointed out, the 1930 ILO Convention 29 is still the relevant international instrument prohibiting and defining forced or compulsory labour,[64] whose principles have now attained the status of peremptory norms of international general law.[65]

---

61 See CEACR, Individual Observation concerning Convention No. 182: Pakistan 2006, Doc. No. 062006PAK182, where the Committee notes that, despite specific actions tackling the phenomenon, through information campaigns and projects aiming at removing children from debt bondage, providing for their rehabilitation and social integration, the existing legislation against bonded labour remains largely ineffective, people found guilty of violating child labour legislation are rarely prosecuted and when they are, the fines imposed are usually insignificant: in case of violation of the provision prohibiting forced or bonded labour, the Penal Code still admits the possibility of imposing a fine only!

62 See CEACR, Individual Direct Request concerning Convention No. 182: Bolivia 2007, Doc. No. 092007BOL182, which notes, in particular, the government's commitment to address the issue in a National Plan of Action for the Elimination of Forced Labour.

63 The 1926 Slavery Convention did not prohibit forced labour, since at that time it was a practice widely relied on for public works by colonial powers, however its art. 5 required to 'take all necessary measures to prevent compulsory or forced labour from developing into conditions analogous to slavery'.

64 See, for example. the reference made to Convention 29 by the ECHR, in order to interpret the notion of forced labour under art. 4 of the ECHR, in *Siliadin v France, supra* note 21, §§ 115–116. Convention 29 is usually referred to even when interpreting art. 8(3)(a) of ICCPR prohibiting forced labour with the exception of certain circumstances, which in substance correspond to those allowed for by C29. See Nowak, UN Covenant, *supra* note 12, at 201.

65 ILO, 'Forced Labour in Myanmar (Burma), Report of the Commission of Inquiry Appointed under Article 26 of the Constitution of the International Labour Organization to

According to Convention 29, the prohibition of forced or compulsory labour, referring to any work or service exacted under the menace of any penalty and for which a person has not volunteered,[66] allows of a few exceptions, specifically regulated by article 2(2) of the Convention, concerning, in substance, labour imposed as a consequence of a conviction in a court of law[67] and other forms of work or service constituting normal civic obligations, such as compulsory military service, work provided during emergencies and minor communal service.[68] Hence, a provision, like the one of the Labour Code of Belize, allowing the recruitment for light employment of young persons who have attained the age of 16 years, without their spontaneous consent but rather with the permission of the Labour Commissioner and the consent of their parents, would not appear a legitimate exception.[69]

Though not many governments have reported to the ILO supervisory body on measures to combat the forced labour of children, some particularly harmful circumstances have been addressed in light of the risk of their developing into authentic forms of forced labour; for example, the situation of street children engaged in various activities, including portering, ragpicking or begging,[70] exposing them to hazards both from the work itself and even more from the living environment, such as traffic, exhaust fumes, exposure to the elements, insecurity, harassment and violence. Most of the time children working or even living in the streets are at the mercy of adults, but they also may be self-employed. In both cases they are not registered and work under dangerous conditions without protection.

Examine the Observance by Myanmar of the Forced Labour Convention, 1930 (No. 29)', in Official Bulletin, 1998, 72.

66 On the meaning of the lack of voluntariness, see *supra* section 6.4. It is worth noting that the ban on forced labour has been reasserted and further specified by another fundamental ILO Convention on the matter – the Convention concerning the Abolition of Forced Labour, No. 105, which expressly prohibits the use of forced labour for political purposes, for purposes of economic development, as a means of labour discipline, as a punishment for strike action and as a means of discrimination (art. 1). See also H. Bartolomei de La Cruz, G. von Potobsky and L. Swepston, *The International Labor Organization: The International Standards System and Basic Human Rights*, Oxford, 1996, 131 ff.

67 See *supra* note 34.

68 Unless they are banned by other relevant norms, these exceptions apply equally to adults and to people under 18, despite art. 11 of C29 providing for the imposition of forced or compulsory labour only on 'males who are of an apparent age of not less than 18'. This provision has to be read in the light of art. 1(1) where the obligation to 'suppress the use of forced or compulsory labour within the shortest possible time' allowed States Parties to gradually apply the Convention. In that event, the recourse to forced or compulsory labour had to be regulated in accordance with arts 7–19 and with arts 22–24, which now should be regarded as outdated, since the prohibition of forced or compulsory labour has acquired an absolute character. On this point see ILO, Forced Labour in Myanmar, *supra* note 65, at 62.

69 CEACR, Individual Direct Request concerning Convention No. 182: Belize 2007, Doc. No. 092007BLZ182.

70 According to certain countries' legislation, begging is prohibited as an illicit activity falling under art. 3(c) of Convention 182; however, this does not prevent its qualification as forced labour when child beggars are submitted to their exploiters' coercion.

Domestic work, though legitimate as such, is another activity potentially ending up in forms of forced labour or debt bondage, since children, usually hidden from view in private households and isolated from their families,[71] are under the total control of their employers, often deprived of emotional support, good nutrition and education. The victims, mostly girls, may be subjected to long hours and harsh conditions of work, as well as to physical, psychological or even sexual abuse. Furthermore, in the majority of cases they are denied legal protection, because their situation is not covered by labour legislation. Though it is not expressly mentioned by Convention 182, the practice, affecting both rich and poor countries and often associated with other forms of exploitation like child sale and trafficking, has been specifically addressed by the CEACR in a few cases. For instance, a situation of particular concern has been detected in Morocco, where domestic work of children under conditions of servitude and sexual abuse is reported as a common practice.[72] Analogous circumstances have been pinpointed in Bangladesh[73] and the Philippines.[74]

6.5.2.1 Forced recruitment of child soldiers Among the WFCL, article 3(a) expressly includes 'forced or compulsory recruitment of children for use in armed conflict'. The practice falls within the sphere of the overall prohibition of forced labour, thus it is to be interpreted firstly in the light of that notion, though other specific international norms on the matter can not be ignored.[75]

The main implication of the express inclusion of the recruitment of child soldiers in Convention 182 is that every ratifying State has the obligation to adapt its legal

---

71 In truth, analogous situations of children being exploited often exist even in their parents' home, where they are kept to undertake long hours of domestic work, deprived of any form of education and legal protection.

72 See CEACR, Individual Observation concerning Convention No. 182: Morocco 2006, Doc. No. 062006MAR182, where it is reported the government's intention of enacting special legislation on the matter, while information and awareness-raising campaigns concerning the work of 'petites bonnes' are organized in conjunction with competent international organizations and NGOs. The Committee, however, observed the limits of the domestic Penal Code, banning forced labour only when exacted from people under 15 years.

73 CEACR, Individual Observation concerning Convention No. 182: Bangladesh 2005, Doc. No. 062005BGD182. According to official estimates, at least 300,000 child domestic workers are exploited in the country, although the government denies their conditions amount to forced or bonded labour, whereas only in exceptional cases they would be sexually or physically abused. Even if child domestic workers rarely have access to education, the government asserts that domestic work has the merits of preventing children's engagement in more hazardous work, from being trafficked or sexually exploited.

74 CEACR, Individual Observation concerning Convention No. 182, Philippines 2006, Doc. No. 062006PHL182, where the Committee notes the government's indication of efforts in order to enact a special legislation on the issue.

75 For the regulation of the phenomenon of child soldiers under international law, see G. Gioffredi, La condizione internazionale del minore nei conflitti armati, Milan, 2006, 177 ff. See also Y. Dinstein, *The Conduct of Hostilities under the Law of International Armed Conflict*, Cambridge, 2004, 141 ff; F. Lenzerini, 'La tutela del minore nei conflitti armati', *Rivista internazionale dei diritti dell'uomo*, 2000, 781 ff.

system, establishing a ban on the involuntary enrolment of any person under 18 years either by the regular armed forces or by any other entity.

Prior to the adoption of Convention 182 various international instruments imposed a ban on the recruitment and the direct participation in hostilities of children under the age of 15 years: besides article 38 of the CRC,[76] one might quote some of the most relevant treaties in the field of international humanitarian law, namely Additional Protocols I and II to the 1949 Geneva Conventions.[77] Moreover, in view of its widespread acceptance by the international community, the rule has long been regarded as part of customary international law.[78] Finally, it should be pointed out that the Statutes of the International Criminal Court[79] and the Special Court for Sierra Leone provide for the criminalization of the individual conduct contrary to the ban.[80]

Convention 182, however, is one of the first binding agreements[81] adopted in the wake of the growing international support for raising the age-limit for recruitment and participation in hostilities to 18 years.[82] One year later, the Optional Protocol to the Convention on the Rights of the Child on the Involvement of Children in Armed Conflict provided for the prohibition of compulsory recruitment of children under 18 years into the armed forces of States Parties (article 2), whereas the same ban extended to any forced or voluntary enrolment for armed groups distinct from the regular army (article 4). Since the recruitment into state armed forces of children

---

76 For an overview of the UN's action concerning the recruitment of child soldiers, see Fodella (this volume). For a specific comment on art. 38 of CRC, see Detrick, *A Commentary*, *supra* note 8, at 644 ff.

77 Additional Protocol to Geneva Conventions of 12 August 1949 and Relating to the Protection of Victims of International Armed Conflicts of 8 June 1977, art. 77(2); Additional Protocol to Geneva Conventions of 12 August 1949 and Relating to the Protection of Victims of Non-International Armed Conflicts of 8 June 1977, art. 4(3)(c).

78 International Committee of the Red Cross (ICRC), *Customary International Humanitarian Law*, ed. by J.-M. Henckaerts and L. Doswald Beck, Vol. I, Cambridge, 2005, 482 ff.

79 According to art. 8(2)(b)(xxvi) and art. 8(2)(e)(vii) of the Statute (see *supra* note 26), conscripting or enlisting children under 15 into armed forces or groups constitutes a war crime in both international and non-international armed conflicts, entailing the penal responsibility of individuals.

80 Statute of the Special Court for Sierra Leone, art. 4(c). It is worth noting that the Court has recently released a remarkable judgment condemning three former members of the Armed Forces' Revolutionary Council found responsible of several international crimes, committed during the conflict in Sierra Leone, since November 1996, including enslavement, sexual slavery and recruitment of child soldiers under 15. The Court's ruling is not only a significant step for the strengthening of the international community's action towards the condemnation and eradication of stubborn practices, but, from a legal standpoint, it also constitutes a further element for the consolidation of the peremptory nature of the international rules prohibiting similar crimes. See *Prosecutor* against *Brima, Kamara, Kanu*, SCSL-04-16-T, 20 June 2007.

81 See also art. 22(2) of the African Charter on the Rights and Welfare of the Child (date of adoption 27 June 1981; date of coming into force 21 October 1986).

82 ICRC, *Customary International Humanitarian Law*, *supra* note 78, at 484.

from 15 to 18 years remained allowed, provided it was genuinely voluntary,[83] the Protocol further requested State Parties to take all feasible measures to ensure that members of their armed forces below the age of 18 years do not take a direct part in hostilities (article 1).[84]

The detailed regulation provided for by the Optional Protocol might constitute the essential point of reference for ascertaining the scope of the prohibition of child soldiers' recruitment in Convention 182, since there is a substantial correspondence between the two agreements, notwithstanding a few ostensible inconsistencies. In particular, the wording of article 3(a) makes reference only to 'forced or compulsory recruitment', and thus might be seen to allow voluntary enlistment not only in the regular armed forces, but even in armed groups distinct from state armies. Such an interpretation, however, is denied by Convention 182's *travaux préparatoires* where the sole exception expressly mentioned was the voluntary enrolment of persons under 18, but not younger than 15 years of age, into the state armed forces.[85] It follows that Convention 182's provision is in line with the Optional Protocol on this point. A more significant difference between the two instruments may be found in the sentence of article 3(a), concerning the objective of children's forced or compulsory recruitment, namely 'for use in armed conflict'.

Because of this wording and the inclusion of the practice concerned in the notion of forced labour, it follows that the situations covered by article 3(a) are broader than those addressed by other international instruments, limiting their scope to the prohibition of children's direct participation in hostilities. Although the latter notion might be regarded as rather extensive, at least as far as children are concerned,[86]

---

83 Art. 3 establishes detailed criteria in order to verify the authentic voluntariness of the choice.

84 This provision is certainly more severe than those of Additional Protocol I and of the CRC, which ask State Parties, when recruiting children under 18, to give priority to the oldest ones.

85 The comment of the US government's representative may be revealing. He pointed out that art. 3(a) 'addressed effectively an essential concern: the abduction, coercion, and forced or involuntary recruitment of children for use as participants in armed conflict. The adoption of the above text would make the Convention stronger and would significantly strengthen current international standards concerning forced or compulsory enlistment. It would in no way undermine other international standards on the subject'. He stated that the US and some other countries permitted the lawful recruitment of 17-year-olds to volunteer – with parental consent – to serve in the armed forces, including when armed conflict was regrettably necessary. He did not believe that such voluntary enlistment in lawful national military service was the basis of the concern which had resulted in this text. ILC, *Report of the Committee on Child Labour, supra* note 32.

86 'The words "using" and "participate" have been adopted in order to cover both direct participation in combat and also active participation in military activities linked to combat such as scouting, spying, sabotage and the use of children as decoys, couriers or at military checkpoints. It would not cover activities clearly unrelated to the hostilities, such as food deliveries to an airbase for the use of domestic staff in an officer's married accommodation. However, use of children in a direct support function such as acting as bearers to take supplies to the front line, or activities at the front line itself, would be included within the terminology.' Draft Statute of the International Criminal Court, Report of the Preparatory Committee on

the exercise of certain military as well as civil activities not directly related to the conduct of hostilities would be left out, whereas the same acts would be certainly covered by Convention 182, had they been imposed on a child under coercion, in the context of an armed conflict. The thousands of abductions of young boys and girls destined to be exploited as servants, forced labourers in mines or sex slaves for soldiers have been reported in various situations of internal armed conflicts.[87] Some specific cases of forced recruitment of child soldiers, like those of Democratic Republic of Congo, Philippines, Sri Lanka or Sudan, have demonstrated the massive dimensions of the phenomenon, as well as the difficulties in addressing it effectively, despite the increasing commitment of the international community.[88]

In the end, it should be pointed out that, because of its qualification of the forced recruitment of children for armed conflict as a slave-like practice, Convention 182 makes a considerable contribution to strengthening international customary rules banning the forced recruitment of children and their participation in hostilities, by raising the age-limit to 18 years. Since the prohibition of slavery in all its forms is a non-derogable norm of *jus cogens*, conventional rules concerning the forced recruitment of child soldiers shall now be interpreted and applied in conformity with this innovative development of general international law.

6.5.3 Sale and trafficking of children

The sale and trafficking of human beings is an increasingly widespread phenomenon, affecting poorer and richer countries alike. While the present-day trafficking in persons is a dynamic, multifaceted practice, continuously assuming new forms and dimensions, its original form dates back to the slave trade, which has been the object of a specific prohibition under international law.[89] Further international norms dealing with trafficking were adopted from the beginning of the 20th century, though they mainly focused on the situation of women and children traded for purposes of prostitution or sexual exploitation in general.[90]

---

the Establishment of an International Criminal Court, UN Doc. A/CONF.183/2/Add.1, p. 21. For the debate on the notion of active or direct participation in hostilities under international humanitarian law, see ICRC, *Customary International Humanitarian Law*, *supra* note 78, 22 ff; J-F. Quéguiner, 'Direct Participation in Hostilities Under International Humanitarian Law', 2003, available at <www.ihlresearch.org/ihl/pdfs/briefing3297.pdf>.

87   See CEACR, Individual Direct Request concerning Convention No. 182: Democratic Republic of the Congo, *supra* note 47; CEACR, Individual Observation concerning Convention No. 182: Philippines, *supra* note 74; CEACR, Individual Observation concerning Convention No. 182: Sudan 2007, Doc. No. 062007SDN182.

88   *Ibid.* Sometimes domestic legislation is not even in compliance with the requirements of C182 (Sudan for example allows, under certain conditions, the recruitment and use of people of 16 years old) or is not effectively applied due to conflict-related instability.

89   See the 1926 Slavery Convention and art. 3 of the 1956 Supplementary Convention.

90   The most relevant instrument was the 1949 Convention on the Suppression of the Traffic in Persons and of the Exploitation of the Prostitution of Others. For an overview of the earlier instruments, see E/CN.4/Sub.2/2000/3/Add.1, *supra* note 58, §§ 25 ff.

With particular reference to children,[91] a general provision requesting States to prevent their abduction, sale or traffic 'for any purpose or in any form' was included in article 35 of the CRC, whose scope has been clarified by the Optional Protocol (2000) on the sale of children, child prostitution and child pornography. Here the sale of children is defined as 'any act or transaction whereby a child is transferred by any person or group of persons to another for remuneration or any other consideration' (article 2(a)), in particular for sexual exploitation, transfer of organs for profit, engagement in forced labour or illegal adoption (article 3(1)(a)).[92]

A comprehensive notion of 'trafficking in persons' may be found in article 3 of the Trafficking Protocol of 2000,[93] which is considered the main legal instrument addressing the phenomenon in all its aspects. In the framework of the Protocol, child trafficking refers to any act of recruitment, transportation, transfer, harbouring or receipt of children (defined as persons under 18 years of age) for the purpose of subjecting them to any form of exploitation, including prostitution or sexual exploitation in general, forced labour or services, slavery and practices similar to slavery and servitude or the removal of organs. In such circumstances, the crime of child trafficking may be established irrespective of the use of coercion or deceit, usually required as elements of the crime when the victims are adults.[94]

Regarding the ban on child sale and trafficking under article 3(a) of Convention 182, it was pointed out above that its scope is limited to circumstances in which children are trafficked for purposes of sexual or labour exploitation, excluding other aims, like adoption or organs transplantation.[95] Convention 182 addresses the trafficking of children whenever it is associated with forms of child labour, like those covered by the Convention itself. This choice, however, does not seem fully understandable given the broad scope of the notion of WFCL, amounting not only to forms of children's economic exploitation, but also to slave-like abuse perpetrated against a child. Regardless of the particular aim it pursues, since the trafficking of children is considered a form of economic exploitation and a practice similar to

---

91 According to ILO estimates, about 1.2 million children are trafficked to and from all regions of the world each year: see ILO, *A Future Without Child Labour*, *supra* note 54, at 18. See also V. Garrard, 'Sad Stories: Trafficking in Children – Unique Situations Requiring New Solutions', *Georgia Journal of International & Comparative Law*, Vol. 35, 2006, 145 ff; S. Scarpa, 'Child Trafficking: International Instruments to Protect the Most Vulnerable Victims', *Family Court Review*, Vol. 44, 2006, 429 ff.

92 Optional Protocol to the Convention on the Rights of the Child on the sale of children, child prostitution and child pornography. See Detrick, *A Commentary*, *supra* note 8, at 598 ff.

93 Protocol to Prevent, Suppress and Punish Trafficking in Persons Especially Women and Children, supplementing the United Nations Convention against Transnational Organized Crime.

94 '... the threat or use of force or other forms of coercion, of abduction, of fraud, of deception, of the abuse of power or of a position of vulnerability or of the giving or receiving of payments or benefits to achieve the consent of a person having control over another person ...', art. 3(a). None of these elements are required in case of trafficking of children, in accordance with art. 3(c).

95 See *supra* note 53.

slavery, it should be covered by Convention 182. Despite the position taken by ILO constituents during the *travaux préparatoires*, a less restrictive interpretation of article 3(a) on this matter would certainly be more consistent with the overall aim of the Convention. Apart from this, reference should be made to those international norms specifically addressing the sale and trafficking of children, in order to assess the scope of the provision.

Among the issues falling under article 3(a), the sale and trafficking of children is the area where most initiatives have been undertaken by States since the adoption of Convention 182. Nearly all state reports submitted to the CEACR address the issue and testify to the genuine commitment to bring domestic legislation in line with the international rules, and to adopt effective programmes of action at the national or international level to tackle some or all of the problematic aspects of the phenomenon. Yet continuous efforts are needed worldwide to achieve its complete eradication.[96]

6.6 Concluding remarks

As pointed out, all practices mentioned in article 3(a) have been regulated for a long time by international norms of a customary or conventional nature, aiming to abolish those forms of exploitation. ILO Convention 182, however, is a unique instrument addressing similar issues in a comprehensive manner, focusing solely on children as a particular category of victims. With a view to attaining the overall objective of the Convention, namely the prohibition and elimination of the WFCL as a matter of urgency, State Parties are required to enact or amend national legislations, imposing at least bans on each practice covered by the Convention, properly defined in light of the relevant international instruments, and providing for appropriate penalties.

Beyond the legal prohibition of the WFCL, Convention 182 requires States to fulfil substantive obligations on establishing appropriate mechanisms for monitoring the national situation and the implementation of the Convention's provisions (article 5); for designing plans of action to address the most problematic issues at the national level (article 6); and for taking effective, time-bound measures in order to prevent children's involvement in the WFCL and to provide for their removal from those forms of exploitation, their rehabilitation and their education, paying particular attention to girls and other categories at special risk (article 7(2)). In other words, governments are requested to elaborate comprehensive policies targeted on the conditions of children's exploitation in their country. When needed they may request the assistance of other States Parties and international agencies, in order to better tackle transnational phenomena (for example, sale and trafficking) or to support 'social and economic development, poverty eradication programmes and universal education' (article 8).

---

96 Even the US – considered the world's leader in the fight against trafficking in persons – has been invited by the competent ILC Committee 'to redouble its efforts to eliminate the trafficking of children under 18 years of age for labour and sexual exploitation'. ILCCR: Examination of Individual Case concerning Convention No. 182, United States 2006, Doc. No. 132006USA182.

Moreover, a distinctive feature of ILO conventions is the significant involvement of workers' and employers' organizations in their drafting, implementation and monitoring. In addition, Convention 182 calls for the participation, at least in the drafting of national plans of action, of other actors concerned, such as NGOs or competent community-based groups (article 6(2)).

Eventually, the governments' action is guided in detail not only by the specific provisions of the Convention, but also by the supervisory mechanisms of ILO, whose main task is to verify the correct application of the Convention and to pinpoint the progress made, in order to put pressure on governments, but above all to better target the technical cooperation provided by the ILO itself.

Thanks to the inclusion of article 3(a) in Convention 182, the international action against the forms of children's exploitation it addresses has profited from a new, strongly action-oriented instrument. While considerable improvements have been reported for the sale and trafficking of children, forced labour and other practices falling under the same subparagraph have not received comparable attention, so far. Yet the continuous monitoring by ILO bodies as well as the pressures for increased efforts will help achieve greater progress.

Chapter 7

Prostitution, Pornography and Pornographic Performances as Worst Forms of Child Labour: A Comment on Article 3(b) of ILO Convention 182

Joost Kooijmans[1]

7.1 Introduction

The commercial sexual exploitation of persons as an issue related to labour rights is a relatively new topic within the work of the ILO. Only in the early 1990s did the ILO's supervisory machinery start to systematically address such exploitation in a forced labour context under the Forced Labour Convention, 1930 (No. 29), recognizing that sexual exploitation often involves elements of coercion and involuntariness on the part of the exploited person.[2]

The Worst Forms of Child Labour Convention, 1999 (No. 182) is the first ILO standard to *explicitly* recognize sexual exploitation as a labour rights matter. The Convention recognizes the 'use, procuring or offering of a child for prostitution, for the production of pornography or for pornographic performances' as a worst form of child labour which requires immediate prohibition and elimination as a matter of urgency.[3] The Convention defines a child as any person under the age of 18 years.[4]

The present chapter provides a broad analysis of the commercial sexual exploitation of children, as defined by article 3(b) of Convention 182. It will address the preparatory history of this provision, its relationship with other international standards, as well as the meaning given to it by ILO Member States and supervisory bodies. First, some conceptual issues will be clarified, and a brief overview of the actual situation worldwide will be presented.

---

1 The views expressed here are the author's and do not necessarily represent those of the ILO.

2 For an overview of comments by ILO supervisory bodies relating to sexual exploitation under ILO Conventions, see the ILOLEX Database, available at <http://www.ilo.org/ilolex>.

3 Articles 1 and 3(b), Convention 182.

4 *Ibid.*, art. 2.

7.2 Some conceptual issues

As has been seen in Chapter 5 above, article 3 of Convention 182 defines four broad categories of worst forms of child labour which require immediate action by governments:

   a. all forms of slavery or practices similar to slavery, such as the sale and trafficking of children, debt bondage and serfdom and forced or compulsory labour, including forced or compulsory recruitment of children for use in armed conflict;
   b. the use, procuring or offering of a child for prostitution, for the production of pornography or for pornographic performances;
   c. the use, procuring or offering of a child for illicit activities, in particular for the production and trafficking of drugs as defined in the relevant international treaties;
   d. work which, by its nature or the circumstances in which it is carried out, is likely to harm the health, safety or morals of children.

A close look at this provision raises a number of questions that require clarification for a good understanding of the concept of sexual exploitation under Convention 182. These questions mainly relate to the relationship between sexual exploitation as a worst form of child labour and the other categories of 'unconditional' worst forms of child labour.[5] First some reflections are made regarding the meaning of the terms 'work' and 'labour' in the context of sexual exploitation of children.

7.2.1 Is prostitution or sexual exploitation 'work'?

Since the Convention defines prostitution as a worst form of child 'labour', the question arises whether this means that the ILO recognizes prostitution as work. This has indeed been the concern of a number of ILO constituents during the *travaux préparatoires* (1998–99) of the Convention. For example, in its comments on the proposed convention in 1999, Venezuela opposed

> … the reference to prostitution, the production of pornography and pornographic performances as forms of work because this degrades the very concept of labour and the use of children for such activities is a crime against childhood and a violation of the human rights of children that merits universal condemnation and repudiation. Considering prostitution as a form of labour legitimizes an activity that is supposed to be eliminated, and fundamentally contradicts the very spirit of the proposed Convention.[6]

A similar view was expressed by the General Confederation of Portuguese Workers (CGTP-IN):

---

5 The term 'worst forms of child labour' encompasses both hazardous work (art. 3(d)) and the 'unconditional' forms (art. 3(a) – (c)). The difference is that while hazardous work, through changes in the work environment and the work itself, can sometimes be modified to remove the hazardous aspects, the unconditional forms can under no circumstance be considered acceptable. On the point see also: Pertile (this volume); Rishikesh (this volume).

6 ILC, Report IV(2A), 87th Session (1999), 58.

The main shortcoming in the proposed instruments is their scope, which is too restricted and, moreover, liable to give the idea that the other forms of child labour not mentioned could, in some way, be acceptable. However, even taking as inevitable the need to restrict the scope of the proposed Convention to the 'worst forms of child labour', it is imperative that the definition of what constitutes these forms of work be absolutely clear and objective, on the one hand corresponding strictly to situations considered to be work in the true sense and, on the other, to as broad a range as possible of situations involving child labour. Therefore, it is necessary first of all not to lose sight of the fact that the Conference is defining 'forms of labour', which means that other forms of child exploitation, however disgusting and intolerable they may be (such as prostitution or the use of children in illicit activities such as drug trafficking), do not fall within this sphere, because they do not correspond to the concept of work. In spite of the proposed Convention, and other international instruments condemning these forms of child exploitation, it does not seem appropriate to define them as 'forms of labour'.[7]

Similar concerns were also expressed during the first Conference discussion on the draft convention in 1998, by the governments of Peru, India, Venezuela and Uruguay.[8] In reaction, the Secretariat of the Conference[9] stated that:

Some of the replies had hesitated to include such practices as slavery, child prostitution, child pornography and the sale and trafficking of children in the new instruments. While these were crimes which should be treated and attacked as such, they were also forms of economic exploitation akin to forced labour.[10]

This statement directly echoed the position taken in the first report submitted by the ILO to the Conference in 1998, entitled *Child Labour: Targeting the Intolerable*:[11]

Child prostitution, child pornography and the sale and trafficking of children are crimes of violence against children. They must be treated as crimes and attacked as the most serious crimes are attacked. Such repellent abuses are so far removed from any normal notion of work or labour that it seems strange to focus on them in an ILO report. Yet while they are crimes they are also forms of economic exploitation akin to forced labour and slavery. Any new international standards on the most extreme forms of child labour must therefore specifically aim at abolishing the commercial sexual exploitation of children.[12]

In conclusion, it is clear that neither the Convention nor the ILO at large take a position on the question whether prostitution could potentially be a legitimate form of work.

Nevertheless, the Convention does have consequences for those countries that have legalized or condone prostitution: the Convention very clearly requires that

---

7 *Ibid.*, 14 and 54.

8 ILC, Provisional Record No. 19, 86th Session (1998), §§ 45, 118, 132 and 134.

9 Whenever reference is made to the Secretariat, this means the representative of the Secretary-General of the Conference, who also represents the ILO.

10 ILC, Provisional Record No. 19, *supra* note 8, § 11.

11 ILC, Report VI(1), 86th Session (1998).

12 *Ibid.*, 31.

even in these countries, it must be effectively prohibited for any person below the age of 18 years to engage in such activities. This was made clear already in 1998:

> Some countries pointed out that there might be a problem where prostitution was legal below the age of 18 or the age of sexual consent less than 18 years. This provision would still prohibit the use, engagement or offering of a person under 18 for prostitution. A child's consent to a sexual act would not exclude it from the prohibition. It is not unusual in national law for the age of sexual consent to be less than 18, but for it still to be a crime to entice persons under 18 into sexual acts, to procure them for prostitution or to draw economic benefit from sexual activities involving them.[13]

7.2.2 The right terminology: seeing children as victims, not perpetrators?

A number of terms are currently used within the ILO and UN system to denote 'sexual exploitation'. An often-used term is 'commercial sexual exploitation' or 'sex work', whereas, as noted, the Convention speaks of 'prostitution', the 'production of pornography' or 'pornographic performances'. In the foregoing section, it was already established that, whatever the terminology used in the context of the ILO, it does not imply that such work is recognized as legitimate. That remains for the Member States to decide.

In Convention 182, the terms 'prostitution' and 'pornography' were retained, because the Convention calls for penal sanctions[14] and there was thus considered to be a need to mention the specific activities and actions that would be penalized.[15]

Yet the choice of words may also carry significance for other questions. This is mostly connected to the need to see children as 'victims' of sexual exploitation, and

---

13 ILC, Report VI(2), 86th Session (1998), 52–3. In this respect, an interesting case can be found regarding Switzerland by studying the Direct Requests of the CEACR of 2004 and 2006 under Convention 182. The Swiss Federal Council stated that, 'under Swiss penal law, the age of sexual consent is 16 years (section 187 of the Penal Code) and that children between 16 and 18 years of age may prostitute themselves provided they do so of their own free will ... in the view of the Federal Council, in so far as persons of 16 to 18 years of age who prostitute themselves are not used or procured for the purpose of prostitution, their conduct does not fall within the scope of Convention No. 182.' At first glance, it seems a bit puzzling that the CEACR in its 2004 Direct Request requested the Swiss Government to 'specify the criteria for ascertaining whether persons from 16 to 18 years of age who prostitute themselves do so of their own free will', as if it accepted the Swiss argument. In its Direct Request of 2006, the CEACR did not add anything new, probably because the indications supplied by the Swiss Government – as noted in the Direct Request of 2006 – did not really address the issue. Clearly, the CEACR was merely still trying to establish the exact facts regarding the regime governing 16–18 year olds. In a 2008 Observation, however, the CEACR unequivocally urged 'the Government to take the necessary measures to also prohibit and criminalize the use of a child aged between 16 and 18 years for prostitution, thereby specifying that the sexual freedom granted to children as from 16 years of age by the penal legislation does not include the freedom to prostitute themselves'. Individual Direct Requests (2004 and 2006) and Observation (2008) concerning Convention No. 182: Switzerland, Doc. Nos. 092004CHE182, 092006CHE182 and 062008CHE182.

14 Art. 7(1), Convention 182.

15 ILC, Provisional Record No. 19, *supra* note 8, § 131.

not as 'perpetrators' of prostitution. For that reason, sometimes the term 'commercial sexual exploitation' or 'sexual exploitation' is preferred, because 'prostitution' is often associated with criminalization, whereas – according to prevalent views – children involved in prostitution should not be criminalized but seen as victims in need of protection. Likewise, the term 'sex work' is often used in the context of UNAIDS, where it was felt necessary to focus particularly on the category of activities involving sex for commercial purposes.[16] The 2007 UNAIDS Terminology Guidelines illustrates this outlook as follows:

> The term 'sex worker' is intended to be non-judgmental, focusing on the conditions under which sexual services are sold. Alternate formulations are: 'women/men/people who sell sex'. Clients of sex workers may then also be called 'men/women/people who buy sex'. The term 'commercial sex worker' is no longer used, primarily because it is considered to be saying something twice over in different words (i.e. a tautology).[17]

Interestingly, the Guidelines also note in respect of the sexual exploitation of children: 'PROSTITUTION – Use this term in respect to juvenile prostitution. Otherwise for people of older ages use "commercial sex" or "the sale of sexual services".' Clearly, here the term 'prostitution' is preferred when referring to children in order to distinguish it from sex work by adults that may according to some views be regarded as legitimate or at least condonable, whereas the sexual exploitation of children is never acceptable.

The Optional Protocol to the CRC on the sale of children, child prostitution and child pornography provides that 'Child prostitution means the use of a child in sexual activities for remuneration or any other form of consideration'.[18] The United Nations Special Rapporteur on the sale of children, child prostitution and child pornography notes: 'The working definition adopted under this mandate for the term "child prostitution" is "the sexual exploitation of a child for remuneration in cash or in kind, usually but not always organized by an intermediary (parent, family member, procurer, teacher, etc.)".'[19]

The foregoing illustrates that there are various views on what should be the appropriate term to refer to the sexual exploitation of children, and these views depend on the perspective of the organization involved.

7.2.3 Is prostitution or sexual exploitation 'slavery' or 'forced labour'?

In many cases, the involvement of children in sexual exploitation involves situations that can be clearly qualified as forced labour, or other slavery-like practices such as

---

16 The UNAIDS Terminology Guidelines suggest not using the term 'commercial sex work', but rather one of the terms 'sex work or commercial sex or the sale of sexual services'. They are available at <http://data.unaids.org/pub/Manual/2007/20070328_unaids_terminology_guide_en.pdf>.

17 *Ibid.*

18 Optional Protocol to the Convention on the Rights of the Child on the Sale of Children, Child Prostitution and Child Pornography, UNGA Res. A/RES/54/263 of 25 May 2000, art. 2.

19 UN DOC A/49/478 of 5 October 1994, § 117.

child trafficking. In fact, some argue that the sexual exploitation of children should always be regarded as a situation in which the child is compelled, since even where the involvement is consensual, this is the result of the vulnerability of a child's situation. This vulnerability is caused by a variety of factors identified *inter alia* by ILO research through its IPEC programme. Amongst others, these factors concern poverty, the failure of education, exposure to sexual abuse within the family, poor parenting, marginalization as a result of HIV/AIDS, etc.

Yet, even though such circumstances can doubtlessly be recognized as compelling, they do not fulfil the criterion of 'coercion' inherent in the 'slavery and practices similar to slavery' of article 3(a) of the Convention. That is so because the definition of slavery and forced labour, from the ILO perspective, is based on the Forced Labour Convention, 1930 (No. 29), which defines forced or compulsory labour as 'all work or service which is exacted from any person under the menace of any penalty and for which the said person has not offered himself voluntarily.'[20] Compelling circumstances – as tragic as they may be – cannot be equated with the coercion envisaged in Convention 29, which presupposes an active third party exercising the coercion. Thus, prostitution and the production of child pornography were not included in article 3(a) of Convention 182, but classified separately under letter (b) of the same article. It should nonetheless be clear that the sexual exploitation of children can – and often does – take place in conditions of forced labour, and that a significant number of trafficked children end up in commercial sexual exploitation. Likewise, the fact that the drafters of the Convention decided that prostitution merited its own 'worst form of child labour' category in Convention 182 indicates that it is irrelevant whether or not the involvement in prostitution had the consent of the child and/or its parents or guardians: any type of sexual exploitation of persons under 18 years of age is to be prohibited.

7.2.4 What is the distinction from 'illicit activities'?

In the early drafting process of Convention 182, the sexual exploitation of children was lumped together with the use of children in illicit activities.[21] In 1998, the proposed version of article 3 contained as clause (b) 'the use, engagement or offering of a child in illegal activities, for prostitution, production of pornography or pornographic performances'.[22] During the Conference discussions in 1998, it was proposed that, 'for the purpose of clarity, mention of sexual exploitation should be separated from mention of illegal activities'.[23]

It is not entirely clear from the Conference proceedings what the precise reasons were for separating the two issues, other than the reference to 'clarity'. One view was that putting these two worst forms into separate categories would prevent any wrong impression that prostitution and pornography were the illicit activities to be

---

20 ILO, Forced Labour Convention, 1930 (No. 29), art. 2.
21 For a detailed discussion on illicit activities, see Noguchi (this volume).
22 See ILC, Report VI(2), *supra* note 13 174.
23 See ILC, Provisional Record No. 19, *supra* note 7, § 131.

prohibited, to the exclusion of other illicit acts.[24] More importantly though, separating the two issues would clarify that whereas prostitution, production of pornography and pornographic performances were intended to be prohibited regardless of whether they were illegal under national legislation, illicit activities would be subject to national legislative determination.[25]

7.3 The situation worldwide: the phenomenon and available data

What do we know about the scope of the sexual exploitation of children worldwide? There are almost no data that give a reliable idea as to how widespread the phenomenon really is. In its global estimates from 2002, the ILO noted:

> The commercial sexual exploitation of children is a global issue. About 1.8 million children are affected. It is prevalent in all major world regions, particularly so in Latin America & the Caribbean, the Asian-Pacific region and developed economies. Patterns are complex and tend to differ between countries and regions. For instance, whereas in some cases the commercial sexual exploitation of children seems clearly related to tourism, in others it mainly serves a domestic market. Most affected children are reported to be in the 15–17 age range.[26]

The figure of 1.8 million children may not be precise: in presenting its global estimates on the 'unconditional' worst forms of child labour, the ILO pointed to the severe lack of sound statistics. The collection of reliable data is further hampered by the hidden nature of child prostitution. Despite the lack of figures, there is plenty of anecdotal evidence from many different sources that makes it safe to assume that commercial sexual exploitation of children below 18 years is widespread. A few facts coming from Rapid Assessments conducted by ILO/IPEC may illustrate this.

In Sri Lanka, children often become the prey of sexual exploiters through friends and relatives. The prevalence of boys in prostitution is strongly related to foreign tourism.[27] An estimated 12,000 Nepalese children, mainly girls, are trafficked for sexual commercial exploitation each year within Nepal or to brothels in India and other countries.[28] Some 84 per cent of girls in prostitution interviewed in Tanzania reported having been battered, raped or tortured by police officers and *sungu sungu* (local community guards). At least 60 per cent had no permanent place to live.

---

24 *Ibid.*, § 135.

25 *Ibid.*, § 134. In fact, it is therefore a legitimate question whether 'illicit activities' should be qualified as an 'unconditional worst form of child labour' (see note 5), since just like hazardous work, it appears – at least to an extent – subject to national determination.

26 ILO, *Every Child Counts – New Global Estimates on Child Labour*, Geneva, April 2002, 26. The recently released new ILO global estimates of 2006 did not provide new data on the sexual exploitation of children.

27 See ILO, Rapid Assessment No. 18, Sri Lanka: The Commercial Sexual Exploitation of Children: A rapid assessment, Geneva, 2002, 79 et seq.

28 See ILO, Rapid Assessment No. 2, Nepal: Trafficking in Girls with Special Reference to Prostitution: A rapid assessment, Geneva, 2001, 17 et seq.

Some of these girls started out as child domestic workers.[29] In Dar es Salaam alone, some 1,500 children were estimated to be in commercial sexual exploitation.[30] In El Salvador, one-third of the sexually exploited children between 14 and 17 years of age are boys. The median age for entering into prostitution among all children interviewed was 13 years. They worked on average five days per week, although nearly 10 per cent reported that they worked seven days a week.[31] In Madagascar, 80 per cent of the children interviewed no longer attended school, and some 65 per cent were engaged exclusively in commercial sexual exploitation.[32] In Viet Nam, family poverty, low family education and family dysfunction were found to be primary causes for CSEC. Sixteen per cent of the children interviewed were illiterate, 38 per cent had only primary-level schooling. Sixty-six per cent said that tuition and school fees were beyond the means of their families.[33]

This type of evidence does not give direct pointers towards the extent of child sexual exploitation. But it does illustrate that factors that are commonly known to be prevalent in many regions, such as poverty, failing education, social marginalization, and a high demand for commercial sex, are all contributing to the phenomenon.

7.4 International standards covering the sexual exploitation of children

7.4.1 The Worst Forms of Child Labour Convention No. 182 and Recommendation No. 190

Convention 182, accompanied by Recommendation 190, reflects the widespread recognition over the past years and a global consensus that there should be an immediate end to the worst forms of child labour. Convention 182 covers all girls and boys under the age of 18[34] in line with the definition of the child under the CRC.[35] It calls for 'immediate and effective measures to secure the prohibition and elimination of the worst forms of child labour as a matter of urgency.'[36]

------

29 See ILO, Rapid Assessment No. 12, Tanzania: Children in Prostitution: A rapid assessment, Geneva, 2001, 29.

30 *Ibid.*, 26.

31 See ILO, Rapid Assessment No. 30, El Salvador: La exploitación sexual comercial infantil y adolescente: Una evaluacion rapida, Geneva, 2002, 42.

32 See ILO, Rapid Assessment No. 25, Madagascar: Les enfants victimes de l'exploitation sexuelle à Antsirana, Toliary et Antananarivo: Une évaluation rapide, Geneva, 2002, xiii.

33 See ILO, Rapid Assessment No. 16, Viet Nam: Children in Prostitution in Hanoi, Hai Phong, Ho Chi Minh City and Can Tho: A rapid assessment, Geneva, 2002, 26 et seq.

34 Convention 182, art. 2.

35 A slight difference between the Convention and the definition of a child in art. 1 of the CRC is that whereas the latter defines a child as 'every human being below the age of eighteen years unless under the law applicable to the child, majority is attained earlier', the Convention requires that every person below the age of 18 is protected from each and every worst form of child labour (as defined in art. 3), irrespective of whether according to law they attain majority at an earlier age.

36 *Ibid.*, art. 1.

The Convention, as noted above, defines the worst forms of child labour as follows: (a) slavery and forced labour, including child trafficking and forced recruitment for armed conflict; (b) the use of children in prostitution and the production of pornography; (c) the use of children in illicit activities such as the production and trafficking of drugs; and (d) work likely to harm the health, safety or morals of children. It provides significant detail concerning the policy and operational aspects of the fight against child sexual exploitation and the other worst forms. It requires ratifying States to design and implement programmes of action[37] to eliminate the worst forms as a priority and establish or designate appropriate mechanisms for monitoring[38] the implementation of the Convention. It also calls for time-bound measures[39] for prevention; for providing support for the removal of children from sexual exploitation and their rehabilitation; for ensuring access to free basic education or vocational training for all children removed; for identifying children at special risk; whereby such measures should take account of the special situation of girls.

The Convention also calls for international cooperation or assistance in efforts to ensure the effective implementation of its provisions, including support for social and economic development, poverty eradication and education.[40] International cooperation is of particular significance to worst forms of child labour of a transnational nature, such as the trafficking of children for the purpose of sexual exploitation.

In keeping with the ILO's tripartite principles, the Convention also provides for broad consultation among governments, workers and employers – the 'social partners' in the ILO's tripartite structure. However, the Convention further requires that programmes of action should be designed and implemented, taking also 'into consideration the views of other concerned groups'.[41] Thus, the Convention recognizes the importance of the contributions of other actors, such as non-governmental organizations, community-based groups, and – importantly – of children and their parents.

Convention 182 is very much an action-oriented instrument, containing not only obligations in the field of law, but also policy obligations. Such requirements for action are spelled out as substantive provisions. Not only does this provide more guidance for governments in taking action, it also makes it easier to point to the inaction of governments, and to place pressure on them through the supervisory machinery of the ILO. But importantly, the specific requirements also shape the nature of the policies of governments and the international agencies that support them.

In addition to the Convention, its accompanying – not legally binding – Worst Forms of Child Labour Recommendation, 1999 (No.190) offers a wide range of guidelines for action, from international efforts in gathering and exchanging

---

37 *Ibid.*, art. 6.
38 *Ibid.*, art. 5.
39 *Ibid.*, art. 7.
40 *Ibid.*, art. 8.
41 *Ibid.*, art. 6(2).

information and the extraterritorial pursuit of offences by nationals even when the offences are committed in another country, to a broad social mobilization. Even though not binding, Recommendation 190 is a unanimously adopted international instrument – reflecting a global consensus on its contents – and should be referred to as a guideline for action in any country, irrespective of the ratification of Convention 182, and also for action at local or international level. Thus, the principles of the Convention and the Recommendation go much beyond a simple prohibition of the sexual exploitation of children and other worst forms of child labour.

7.4.2 The UN Convention on the Rights of the Child and its Optional Protocol on the sale of children, child prostitution and child pornography

Convention 182 has a clear link with the CRC.[42] A number of common features deserve mention here.[43] Convention 182 covers all persons under the age of 18, in line with the definition of the child under the CRC. How 'child' is defined in national law varies per country. From the perspective of the Convention, it does not matter whether someone under the age of 18 is called 'child', 'adolescent' or 'young person' under national laws, as long as all such persons are covered by the measures of protection against sexual exploitation. In fact, even if the law defines a 'child' as a person under 18, if prohibitions of sexual exploitation in a particular situation apply only up to a lower age, this will have to be extended to cover all girls and boys under 18. For example, in respect of Mexico, the CEACR noted in a Direct Request in 2005:

> The Committee draws the Government's attention to the fact that, under the terms of Article 1 of the Convention, each Member which ratifies the Convention shall take immediate and effective measures to secure the prohibition and elimination of the worst forms of child labour in respect of persons under the age of 18 years. The Committee notes that section 366III of the Federal Penal Code covers young persons under 16 years of age. It also notes the Government's indication that, with regard to section 366-*ter* of the Federal Penal Code, the term 'young person' means a person under 16 years of age. The Committee notes that, although the Government has adopted several measures to combat the sale and trafficking of children, particularly for sexual exploitation, the problem persists. Indeed, there is abundant information reporting the trafficking of persons, including persons under 18 years of age, for sexual exploitation. The Committee therefore requests the Government to increase its efforts to secure the protection of children against sale and trafficking for sexual exploitation, including prostitution. It also asks the Government to take the necessary measures to extend the prohibition of the sale and trafficking of young persons to all girls and boys under 18 years of age. It further requests the Government to provide information on the imposition of penalties in practice, by providing, among other information, reports on the number of convictions.[44]

---

42 UNGA Res. 44/25 of 20 November 1989.

43 See also Y. Noguchi, 'ILO Convention No. 182 on the Worst Forms of Child Labour and the Convention on the Rights of the Child', *International Journal of Children's Rights*, No. 10, 2002, 355–69.

44 CEACR, Individual Direct Request concerning Convention No. 182: Mexico, 2005, Doc. No. 062005MEX182.

The forms of sexual exploitation addressed by Convention 182 to an important extent are expressly linked to the CRC: children in sexual exploitation (article 34), trafficking in children – which includes trafficking for sexual exploitation (article 35), and children in armed conflict – where sexual exploitation is also a common form of exploitation (article 38).

The period of negotiation and elaboration of Convention 182 and the Optional Protocol to the CRC on the sale of children, child prostitution and child pornography overlapped.[45] Thus, the Optional Protocol refers to Convention 182 in its preamble. While it covers topics also covered by Convention 182, as a separate international legal instrument it has its own scope of application and requirements. For example, the Protocol provides more detail on measures concerning protection of and assistance to victims,[46] and provides for certain principles regarding the extradition of suspects.[47] Beyond doubt, the Protocol therefore is a useful guideline for understanding and implementing Convention 182. The system of reporting on the implementation of the Optional Protocol further adds to the possibilities of international supervision over this worst form of child labour.

7.4.3 Other international instruments relevant to sexual exploitation of children

In addition, some other international instruments are relevant to child sexual exploitation. ILO bodies supervising the application of international labour standards have already dealt with the issue of the commercial sexual exploitation, trafficking and forced labour of children in several countries under the Forced Labour Convention, 1930 (No. 29). The United Nations Convention against Transnational Organized Crime and in particular its additional Protocol to Prevent, Suppress and Punish Trafficking in Persons, Especially Women and Children (known as the 'Palermo Protocol' and adopted in 2000[48]), are important instruments for shaping legislative and policy action against the trafficking of adults and children – *inter alia* for the purpose of sexual exploitation – and are having their impact on both national legislation and international instruments against human trafficking.

7.5 The sexual exploitation of children – the requirements of Convention 182

As noted above, one of the primary obligations under the Convention is to immediately *prohibit* sexual exploitation in all its forms, which requires proper definitions and prohibitions in criminal law, and the setting of appropriate penalties. Secondly, the Convention requires countries to *monitor* the national situation and to take appropriate *action* to eliminate sexual exploitation, through plans of actions and effective and time-bound measures. Lastly, countries are required to pursue international efforts to strengthen the fight against the sexual exploitation of children. In order to get a full

---

45 Convention 182 was adopted in June 1999, and the Protocol in May 2000.
46 Optional Protocol, art. 8.
47 *Ibid*, articles 5 and 6.
48 UNGA Res. 55/25 of 15 November 2000.

TYPES
• Paid sexual intercourse and sexual/erotic activities
• Production of pornographic material
• Public or private sex or erotic shows

METHODS*			
Local exploitation	**Sex tourism**	**Trafficking of children**	**Circulating pornography**
Nationals or residents in the country who use girls or boys in any form of sexual exploitation.	National and foreign tourists who visit certain places or areas of the country with the purpose of satisfying their sexual desires with underage persons.	Luring and transporting underage persons to places in or outside the country, with or without their consent or that of their relatives, in order to sexually exploit them.	Pornographic material circulated on the internet or via other channels, meaning there is no direct contact between the person who 'consumes' the pornography and the victims. However, both national and foreign intermediary exploiters are involved in the process.

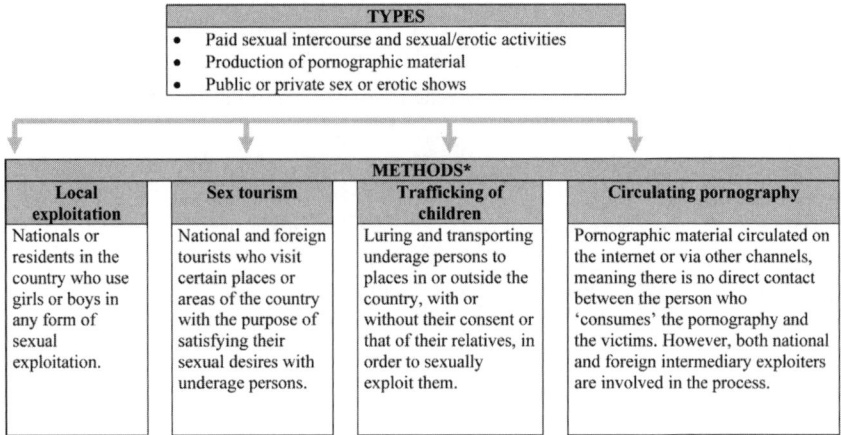

Figure 7.1 ILO's typology of child sexual exploitation
*The different methods of exploitation depend on the place of origin of both the exploiter and the underage person.

grasp of the extent of the issues involved, it is worth looking at a typology of child sexual exploitation recently developed by the ILO.[49]

7.5.1 Defining and prohibiting the sexual exploitation of children

Action against child sexual exploitation firstly involves properly defining it, and then prohibiting it and establishing appropriate sanctions. As was stated above, while prostitution in many countries is illegal, no matter what the age of the persons involved, children in prostitution are often seen as victims. This distinction is important, as it differentiates between responses to child sexual exploitation and to prostitution more generally. In the following section, examples will be given from national legislation involving responses to the sexual exploitation of children.[50]

7.5.1.1 Prostitution As noted above, countries that have ratified Convention 182 are required to effectively prohibit in their legislation 'the use, procuring or offering of a child for prostitution'. Legislation prohibiting children's involvement in prostitution should thus establish crimes committed by those who pimp, procure or otherwise induce children into prostitution; by clients of prostitution involving children; and by those who derive a profit from children engaged in prostitution.

Penalizing pimping, procuring or inducing children into prostitution. Often, legal provisions make a connection to trafficking in children, or to pornography

---

49 ILO, *A Shared Responsibility: Workers' Organizations in the Fight Against the Commercial Sexual Exploitation of Children* (forthcoming); available in Spanish: *Una responsabilidad compartida: las organizaciones de trabajadores en la lucha contra la explotación sexual comercial de niños, niñas y adolescentes* (OIT, 2007), 2.

50 This information is in part derived from a new ILO/IPEC publication: *ILO Modern Policy and Legislative Responses to Child Labour* (main author: D. Tajgman), Geneva, 2007.

involving children or both.[51] In light of the dependent nature of children, legislation in many countries places the lion's share of blame on the procurers of children in prostitution and their customers rather than on the children themselves. In Denmark, for example, the penalty for pimping may be higher where the sexual exploitation concerns a person below 21 years of age.[52] Anti-pimping provisions focusing on children may be very simple, as in New Zealand, stating that no person may cause, assist, facilitate or encourage persons below 18 years of age to provide commercial sexual services to any person.[53]

Anti-pimping/facilitation laws could include standards concerning the knowledge or intent of the persons involved. The standard might be set very high (that is, intending or actually knowing that the person concerned would be involved in prostitution), with corresponding high penal sanctions. The same law may also foresee a second lower standard, such as 'having reason to believe' that the person will be so employed or used. The element of deceit may also be included within provisions governing trafficking, where deception is a constituent element of the crime of bringing in or taking out from the national territory a person in order to subject that person to sexual exploitation.[54] In Chile, for example, the law criminalizes the promotion or facilitation of travel of persons to become prostitutes, whether inside *or outside* the country.[55]

Unfortunately, a number of countries still make gender distinctions, where it is specified as unlawful only to induce a *female* to become involved in prostitution.[56] Gender-based distinctions are inappropriate since the harm caused by exploitation in the context of prostitution is not gender-dependent, and boys must be equally protected from this kind of exploitation. The CEACR has, on a number of occasions, urged countries to extend coverage of legislation against sexual exploitation to all children (girls and boys) under the age of 18 years.[57]

---

51 See, for example, Japan, Law for Punishing Acts Related to Child Prostitution and Child Pornography, and for Protecting Children (No. 52, 1999) of 26 May 1999 (revised 2004); Honduras, Acuerdo Ejecutivo No. STSS-211-01 por el que se aprueba el Reglamento sobre Trabajo Infantil en Honduras, Art. 2; Ecuador, Codigo de la Niñez y Adolescencia, codificación no. 2002-100, Registro Oficial 737, art. 69.

52 Denmark, Criminal Code 1930, art. 228(2). See also, for example, Argentina, Codigo Penal, art. 125bis, where two levels of increased prison terms are set as penalties depending on the age of the prostitute – younger than 18 and younger than 13 – and a third level is introduced where deceit, violence or abuse of authority, among other things, are used to commit the crime, or where the procurer/exploiter is a relative, spouse, brother, teacher or other person responsible for the child prostitute's upbringing or education.

53 New Zealand, Prostitution Reform Act 2003, art. 20.

54 See, for example, Malaysia, Penal Code (Act 574) 2002, art. 372.

55 Chile, Código Penal (revised 1995), art. 367bis(1).

56 See, for example, Jordan, Penal Code Act No. 16 1960, art. 310; Seychelles, Penal Code, Penal Code (Amendment) Act 1996, art. 138.

57 See, for example, CEACR, Individual Direct Request concerning Convention No. 182: Seychelles, 2006, Doc. No. 092006SYC182; CEACR, Individual Direct Request concerning Convention No. 182: Ireland, 2006, Doc. No. 092007IRL182.

Penalizing clients of prostitution involving children. Legislation dealing with clients of children in prostitution is usually very straightforward. In New Zealand, for example, no person may enter into a contract or other arrangement for commercial sexual services from a person under 18 years of age and no person may receive commercial sexual services from a person under 18 years of age.[58] In Japan, the promise to give remuneration is sufficient to constitute child prostitution.[59] In the UK, the user's knowledge or reasonable belief as to the child's age is taken into account, along with a list of acts or contacts that give the basis in law for prosecution.[60]

In Greece, the penalty for engaging in a lecherous act with a minor is fixed as a function of the age of the minor. The highest penalty is for a crime involving a victim under 10 years of age, a lesser penalty involving a minor between 10 and 15 years, and the lowest level of penalty involving minors older than 15 years.[61]

It should of course be noted that sexual relations between an adult and a person below a specified age are commonly held to be a criminal offence, whether or not money or things of value are exchanged, and often whether or not there is evidence of some form of consent (children are often considered not capable of giving consent recognizable in law to such relations). With such a prohibition in place, some countries find it unnecessary to establish further specific policies or laws directly aimed at the customers of child *prostitution*; they are in any case guilty of a criminal sexual offence. However, the specified age of consent is often lower than 18 years and thus does not provide for the protection called for by international standards.

Penalizing those who derive a profit from children engaged in prostitution. With respect to penalizing the making of a profit from the use of children in prostitution, experience shows that few countries deal specifically with child prostitution in their legislation; the prohibition of profiting from prostitution generally would also cover child prostitution. However, in the Philippines, profiting from child prostitution is expressly forbidden, including profiting from the operation of a bar, disco or other place of entertainment or establishment serving as a cover or engaging in prostitution in addition to the activity for which it is licensed.[62] In New Zealand, a degree of knowledge is required in order to establish a crime; that is, 'no person may receive payment or other reward that he or she knows, or ought reasonably to know, is derived, directly or indirectly from commercial sexual services provided by a person under 18 years of age'.[63]

7.5.1.2 The production of pornography and pornographic performances The Optional Protocol to the CRC on the sale of children, child prostitution and child pornography defines 'child pornography' as 'any representation, by whatever means,

---

58 New Zealand, Prostitution Reform Act 2003, art. 22.

59 Japan, Law for Punishing Acts Related to Child Prostitution and Child Pornography, and for Protecting Children (No. 52, 1999) of 26 May 1999 (revised in 2004), art. 2(2).

60 United Kingdom, Sexual Offences Act 2003, art. 47.

61 Greece, Penal Code, articles 349 and 351A.

62 Philippines, Republic Act No. 9231 (Act on the Special Protection of Children Against Child Abuse, Exploitation and Discrimination of 2003), art. 5.

63 New Zealand, Prostitution Reform Act 2003, art. 21.

of a child engaged in real or simulated explicit sexual activities or any representation of the sexual parts of a child for primarily sexual purposes'.[64] This implicitly covers all recorded media. Legislation should foresee prohibitions and sanctions for *luring children* into the production of pornography, *engaging children and work with them in* producing pornography; *selling or otherwise distributing* child pornography; and *buying or otherwise possessing* child pornography. An example of such a broad prohibition can be found in Barbados, where anyone who takes, permits to be taken, distributes, shows, has in his or her possession, publishes or causes to be published 'indecent photographs' of a child is guilty of an offence. 'Indecent photograph' can be taken to mean any kind of pictorial representation.[65]

A number of countries have expressly prohibited the obtaining by *electronic means* (such as the Internet) of pornography depicting children.[66] In defining child pornography, Greece uses the phrase 'any description or real or virtual representation, on any device, of the body aiming at sexual arousal'.[67] An interesting question concerns the case where no real children have been used in producing the pornographic material (such as when photographs have been manipulated) or where no real children are depicted (by using virtual information technology). Quite a few countries have opted to penalize the production, distribution and possession of such materials – despite the fact that no children were involved in its production – because these materials nevertheless promote child pornography. For example, New Zealand targets as 'objectionable' publications that 'promote or support', or 'tend to promote or support', the exploitation of children or young persons for sexual purposes.[68] In Ireland, the definition of 'child pornography' includes 'any representation, description or information produced by or from computer-graphics or by any other electronic or mechanical means' and representations that give the impression of children being sexually engaged, even if in reality the persons concerned were not children.[69]

As regards the other element in article 3(b), concerning child pornographic performances, prohibitions and sanctions for the use of children in pornography often also cover using children in pornographic performances. For example, in Slovakia, 'pornographic work involving a child' is defined by the Criminal Code as 'the display of sexual intercourse or other methods of sexual contact with a child or between children, or the display of naked parts of the body of a child in order to provoke sexual arousal or sexual satisfaction'.[70] This definition, using the term 'display', would appear to cover both recorded pornography and pornographic performances. However, in other cases legislative prohibitions specifically refer to performances. For instance, in Ecuador, the Code of Children and Adolescents specifically

---

64 Optional Protocol on the sale of children, art. 2(c).

65 Barbados, Protection of Children Act 1990, art. 3(1).

66 See, for example, Switzerland, Code Pénal Suisse (CP; RS 311.0) 1937, art. 197(3bis)(1); San Marino, Act No. 61 of 30 April 2002 Act for the Repression of the Sexual Exploitation of Minors, art. 177 ter; South Africa, Films and Publications Amendment Act. No 34 of 1999, art. 2.

67 Greece, Penal Code, art. 348A (as reported to the ILO by the government).

68 New Zealand, Films, Videos and Publications Classification Act 1993, art. 3(2)(a).

69 Ireland, Child Trafficking and Pornography Act 1998, art. 2(1).

70 Slovakia, Criminal Code, art. 89(25).

prohibits the participation of minors in programmes, advertising programmes and pornographic productions or performances not adapted to their age.[71]

7.5.1.3 Practical action against the sexual exploitation of children As was outlined above, Convention 182 is an action-oriented instrument, requiring – in addition to the prohibition of the worst forms of child labour – the adoption of policy measures aimed at prevention, elimination, and rehabilitation of victims. To what extent have these policy requirements already been translated into action? In contrast to information on legislative action – which, in the case of sexual exploitation of children, appears to indicate that many countries are making efforts to shore up legislation – there is precious little information available on what policy measures have been implemented by countries. This appears consistent with the findings of the ILO's second Global Report on Child Labour, entitled *The End of Child Labour: Within Reach,*[72] which indicates that overall legislative activity had been higher than in the field of policy during the period 1999–2006.

The Global Report notes that, while it is inherently difficult to obtain a complete picture of all actions and measures taken by countries to combat child labour, a reliable way of measuring the impact of the Conventions on action since 1999 can be obtained through the supervisory work of the CEACR.[73] The comments adopted by the Committee in respect of the application by countries of the Conventions reflect the steps that ratifying countries have taken to implement these instruments and eliminate child labour. Taking 1999 as a starting point, the cases of action registered by the Committee provide a reasonably accurate picture of the extent to which countries' commitments under the Conventions have given rise to positive measures. The picture emerging provides an interesting overview regarding areas of high activity and areas where more action is required.

---

71 Ecuador, Codigo de la Ninez y Adolescencia, no. 2002-100, art. 52(1).

72 ILO, *The End of Child Labour: Within Reach – Global Report under the Follow-Up to the ILO Declaration on Fundamental Principles and Rights at Work*, Report to the International Labour Conference, 95th Session, 2006, Report I(B).

73 *Ibid.*, 17.

	%
Plans of Action	51.2%
Prohibition of hazardous work	37.8%
Legislative prohibitions on trafficking	35.4%
Legislative prohibitions on prostitution	29.3%
Determination of hazardous work	29.3%
Withdrawal and rehabilitation	23.2%
Legislative prohibitions on pornography	20.7%
Monitoring mechanisms	20.7%
National policy formulated	19.5%
Prevention	19.5%
Measures to ensure universal basic education	17.1%
IPEC-supported time-bound measures	15.9%
Adoption/amendment of legislation on minimum age	15.9%
Any other penal and other sanctions	17.1%
Special attention to children most at risk	17.1%
Legislative prohibitions on slavery	14.6%
Legislative prohibitions on illicit activities	13.4%
Legislative prohibitions on forced labour, bondage	12.2%
Legislative prohibitions on child soldiers	11.0%
Definition and regulation of light work	9.8%
Special attention to girls	4.9%

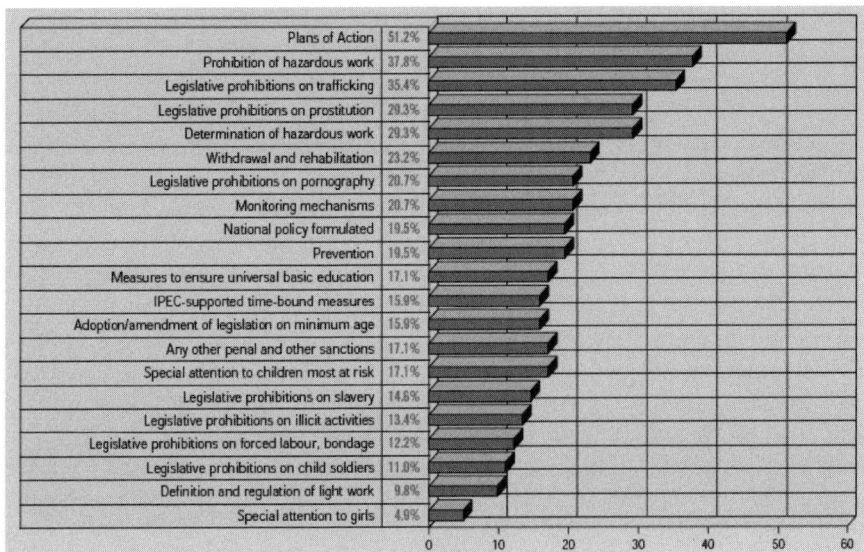

Figure 7.2 Action reported under Conventions Nos. 138 and 182 since 1999 (percentage of reports submitted)
Source: ILO, *The End of Child Labour Within Reach – Global Report*, 2006[74]

The picture presented here is, of course, by no means complete. Yet the significant levels of activity that can be distinguished are as follows: the adoption of legislation against the trafficking of human beings, particularly children; the involvement of children in prostitution and the production of pornography; and the prohibition of hazardous work for all children under 18 years. Another significant development can be seen in the adoption of Plans of Action to tackle one or more categories of child labour and its worst forms. However, the assessment in the Global Report does not differentiate between policy measures against sexual exploitation and other worst forms. The fact that within those policies and plans of action there is only limited attention to the most vulnerable children, and even more modest attention for the special situation of girls, seems to suggest that the focus in these policy measures on child prostitution and child pornography may be limited. In fact, analytical work done by ILO/IPEC suggests that specific action by countries against the sexual exploitation of children is, for the moment, quite modest. This is disappointing, also in view of the 1996 Stockholm Declaration and Agenda for Action[75] – a document adopted at the World Congress against Commercial Sexual Exploitation of Children

---

74 *Ibid.*

75 Declaration and Agenda for Action from the World Congress Against the Commercial Exploitation of Children (Stockholm, 27–31 August, 1996), Section 2(i)(a) of the Agenda for Action, at <http://www.ilo.org/public/english/comp/child/standards/resolution/stockholm.htm>.

– which requires all participating countries to draw up a national agenda for action to address this problem by the year 2000.[76]

A number of countries are cooperating with ILO/IPEC in devising policy initiatives. Sometimes these technical cooperation activities specifically target commercial sexual exploitation.[77] More often, targeting sexual exploitation is part of a larger cooperation framework, such as country programmes or time-bound programmes (TBPs).[78] Other countries have taken initiatives independently. For example, Switzerland has established a centralized office to coordinate the fight against criminality on the Internet, including distribution of child pornography.[79] France has established an Internet site that collates useful information about the laws and regulations on the protection of minors in the country and offers Internet users a form they can use to report child pornography activities.[80] Denmark has authorized enforcement authorities to use special investigative procedures in cases of child pornography.[81] In Brazil, in June 2000, the National Committee on the Rights of Children (CONANDA) approved the National Plan to Confront Sexual Violence against Children and Adolescents, called the Sentinel Programme. The Sentinel Programme encompasses a set of combined actions involving specialized social assistance for child and adolescent victims of sexual violence through the payment of grants to the exploited victims.[82]

Concerning international cooperation and extraterritorial jurisdiction, some countries explicitly allow for legal proceedings to be brought for acts committed outside their own territory, if those acts are prohibited both in the country where they occurred and in the prosecuting country. Such laws can be used against nationals who commit offences abroad such as sex tourism. The UK, for example, provides in its Sexual Offences Act:

> … any act done by a person in a country or territory outside the United Kingdom which (a) constituted an offence under the law in force in that country or territory, and (b) would constitute a sexual offence to which this section applies if it had been done in England and

---

76 Participating countries undertake to 'urgently strengthen comprehensive, cross-sectoral and integrated strategies and measures, so that by the year 2000 there are national agenda(s) for action and indicators of progress, with set goals and time frames for implementation, targeted at reducing the number of children vulnerable to commercial sexual exploitation and nurturing an environment, attitudes and practices responsive to child rights'.

77 Such as Bangladesh, Indonesia, Kenya, Mexico, Nicaragua, Pakistan, Tanzania, Thailand, Uganda, Zambia.

78 A TBP is essentially a set of tightly integrated and coordinated policies and programmes to prevent and eliminate a country's worst forms of child labour within a defined period of time. It is a comprehensive approach that operates at many levels, including international, national, provincial, community, and individual or family. For more information on the various forms of technical cooperation provided by ILO/IPEC, see <www.ilo.org/childlabour>.

79 Information provided by the government to the ILO.

80 Second Periodic Report by France to the Committee on the Rights of the Child, UN Doc. CRC/C/65/Add.26, 9 October 2003.

81 Information provided by the government to the ILO.

82 Combined Report (initial, second and third) of Brazil to the UN Committee on the Rights of the Child, UN Doc. CRC/C/3/Add.65, 17 December 2003.

Wales or in Northern Ireland, constitutes that sexual offence under the law of that part of the United Kingdom.[83]

7.6 The way forward: combining law and policy

How can the fight against commercial sexual exploitation of children be won? Convention 182 clearly spells out three tracks that require action. First, there is a necessity to repress demand for the sexual services of children. Second, children in sexual exploitation need to be detected, withdrawn and rehabilitated. Lastly, children at risk of falling victim to sexual exploitation need to benefit from preventive action.

7.6.1 Targeting the demand side

As pointed out above, there is a high demand for children in sexual exploitation in all its aspects, ranging from prostitution, to child pornography and pornographic performances. A first clear step to reduce demand is to provide a clear legal prohibition together with appropriate penalties and credible enforcement. This issue was addressed above, but credible enforcement also requires the empowerment of law enforcement authorities and the requisite institutional resources. This responsibility is implicit in the obligation of signatories to Convention 182, to 'take all necessary measures to ensure the effective implementation and enforcement of the provisions giving effect to this Convention including the provision and application of penal sanctions or, as appropriate, other sanctions.'[84]

In the fight against child labour, legislative and law enforcement measures are not the only way to address the demand side. Other action, including raising public awareness and working with employers' and workers' organizations, may lead to reduced demand for child labour. Yet, when targeting demand for commercial sex, we are up against a particularly complex task, because so much of its demand is interwoven with human nature and prevalent attitudes or indifference in society. Evidence for this is provided by studies conducted by ILO/IPEC in Latin America. For example, research in Costa Rica, El Salvador, Guatemala, Honduras, Nicaragua, Panama and the Dominican Republic among males from the general population found a high level of tolerance for engaging in sex with children and adolescents, despite the serious violation of human rights that such practices entail. Despite the existence of international conventions, national laws protecting children and adolescents and even criminal laws that prescribe heavy prison sentences for offences involving commercial sexual exploitation, the perceptions held by the study subjects lead them, in almost every instance and every country, to argue in favour of such practices.[85]

---

83 United Kingdom, Sexual Offences Act 2003, art. 72.

84 Art. 7(1) of Convention 182.

85 *Explotación sexual comerial y masculinidad* (ILO, 2004); for English summary, see ILO, *Commercial Sexual Exploitation and Masculinity: A Qualitative Regional Study of Males from the General Population*, Geneva, 2004.

In other words, traditional attitudes towards commercial sex in many societies are such that even effective law enforcement and credible sanctions are not sufficient to deter demand for it.

The above illustrates that policy and campaign work to change attitudes towards using children in sexual exploitation – an integral part of the policy requirements of Convention 182 – is perhaps even more pressing than in the struggle against other forms of exploitation of children. It touches after all upon a demand that is directly related to human nature. However, a combination of strong law enforcement and sustained public information campaigns is an essential instrument in fighting the sexual exploitation of children.

7.6.2 Withdrawal and prevention

Targeted interventions to withdraw children from sexual exploitation and action to rehabilitate them, as well as preventive action, require far-reaching efforts from countries in terms of policies and operational action. As illustrated above, these governmental responsibilities are firmly rooted in the policy requirements of Convention182.[86] A great variety of actions can be envisaged, which are beyond the scope of this article. Nevertheless, it is instructive to recall the Global Commitment adopted in 2001 in Yokohama, Japan, at the 2nd World Congress against Commercial Sexual Exploitation of Children. The Congress took stock of developments since the 1st World Congress held in Stockholm, Sweden, in 1996, and the text of its Global Commitment provides useful examples of effective action against the commercial sexual exploitation of children, such as:

> enhanced actions against child prostitution, child pornography and trafficking of children for sexual purposes, including national and international agendas, strategies or plans of action to protect children from sexual exploitation, and new laws to criminalize this phenomenon, including provisions with extra-territorial effect;

> the promotion of more effective implementation/enforcement of policies, laws and gender-sensitive programmes to prevent and address the phenomenon of sexual exploitation of children, including information campaigns to raise awareness, better educational access for children, social support measures for families and children to counter poverty, action against criminality and the demand for sexual exploitation of children, and prosecution of those who exploit children;

> the provision of child-sensitive facilities such as telephone helplines, shelters, and judicial and administrative procedures to prevent violations of the rights of the child and to provide effective remedies;

> the comprehensive, systematic and sustained involvement of the private sector, such as workers' and employers' organizations, members of the travel and tourism industry, including Internet Service Providers and other businesses, in enhancing child protection,

---

86 Articles 5, 6, 7 and 8 of Convention 182.

including their adoption and implementation of corporate policies and codes of conduct to protect children from sexual exploitation.[87]

Technical cooperation activities undertaken by the ILO, through IPEC, typically include several of these elements, and the ILO is working to document the practices it has developed. It is important that countries benefit from such information resources and exchange information among each other when giving shape to their national policies and programmes to combat the sexual exploitation of children.

7.7 Conclusion

The problem of sexual exploitation of children clearly poses many challenges, and some key causes of the phenomenon, particularly on the demand side, may never be entirely repressed. Yet international standards and a growing body of information and knowledge are providing more and more tools that can be used by countries. It is important that broad alliances of government agencies, employers' and workers' organizations, non-governmental organizations and other interested groups are formed at the international and national level to underpin and help shape policy and action. Effective legislation and credible sanctions, as well as committed law enforcement efforts, are indispensable components in this regard. Convention 182, and the subsequent efforts undertaken by ILO technical cooperation programmes such as IPEC, other UN agencies and governments to implement its requirements, are important contributions to achieving a world in which every child enjoys real protection from being subjected to sexual exploitation.

---

87 The 'Yokohama Global Commitment 2001' is available at <http://www. csecworldcongress.org>.

Chapter 8

The Use of Children in Illicit Activities as a Worst Form of Child Labour: A Comment on Article 3(c) of ILO Convention 182

Yoshie Noguchi[1]

8.1 What is the issue, and why an ILO convention?

8.1.1 Carrying out illicit activities – is it 'labour'?

Article 3(c) of the ILO Convention on the Worst Forms of Child Labour, 1999 (No. 182) is very explicit that the definition of the worst forms of child labour (WFCL) comprises, among other things: 'the use, procuring or offering of a child for illicit activities, in particular for the production and trafficking of drugs as defined in the relevant international treaties'. Some may argue that drug trafficking and other illicit activities should be treated as criminal rather than 'labour' issues to be regulated by international labour standards. The ILO has been facing a somewhat similar question when dealing with commercial sexual exploitation of children (CSEC), since some argue that sexual exploitation is not labour and therefore should not be dealt with by the ILO. However, the ILO and its supervisory mechanism was already examining situations of CSEC in the context of the application of the ILO Forced Labour Convention, 1930 (No. 29), prior to the adoption of C182 which explicitly included CSEC also in the definition of the worst forms of child labour.

It must be underlined that the inclusion of such 'criminal' or 'illicit' issues – also the case of slavery under forced labour Conventions – in the scope of international labour standards neither legitimizes such activities, nor signifies an obligation to regulate the relevant activities. The clear objective of C182, as shown in its full title, is the elimination of the involvement of children in such activities through 'prohibition and immediate action'.

---

1 The views expressed here are the author's and do not necessarily represent those of the ILO.

8.1.2 Brief history of the provision during the drafting of C182

As situations of CSEC had been examined by the ILO bodies under C29 before C182 came into existence, it could probably have been argued that, because children cannot possibly offer themselves voluntarily in a valid manner to engage in an illicit activity, their use is an instance of forced labour falling within the scope of C29. Even more generally, the CEACR once raised the following question on the scope of C29 regarding child labour:[2]

> For forms of child labour other than bonded labour, the question arises, with regard to article 2(1) of the Convention [that is, C29], whether, and if so, under what circumstances a minor can be considered to have offered himself 'voluntarily' for work or service, whether or when the consent of the parents is needed or even sufficient in this regard, and what are the sanctions for refusal.

The explicit inclusion of the issue in the definition under C182 has erased any doubt about the coverage. It also added clarity on the mandate of the ILO. This is particularly important for the technical cooperation activities of the ILO, which will be discussed later. As to the forced labour of children, which is now covered by both C29 and C182, the CEACR seems to deal with issues relating to forced labour of children under C182, where both C29 and C182 are ratified.

Returning to the provision of article 3(c) of C182; if we look at the process that led to the adoption of C182, article 3, items (b) and (c) of the final text at the beginning were proposed as a single item. The very first questionnaire sent to the ILO constituents sought opinions on a proposed item named 'the use, engagement or offering of a child for *prostitution, production of pornography or pornographic performances, production of or trafficking in drugs or other illegal activities*' (emphasis added).[3] This proposed item was clearly distinguished from the preceding item concerning forced labour in various subsets, which became article 3(a). It was during the Committee discussion at the 1998 ILC that the two items were, for the purpose of clarity, separated into two clauses covering CSEC, and the use of children in drug trafficking and other illicit activities.[4]

Simultaneously the Conference discussion considered a proposed amendment to replace the words 'the use, engagement,[5] or offering of a child in …' with the words '*exploitation* of a child for the purpose of …' (emphasis added). The decision to retain the original wording reflects an implicit understanding that there should be criminal penalties and that therefore the acts concerned should be enunciated as

---

2 CEACR Observation, 1996, on the application of C29 in Pakistan. It should be recalled that, in March 1996, the Governing Body of the ILO decided to place the issue of child labour on the agenda of 1998 ILC, with a view to adopting standards.

3 International Labour Conference (ILC), Report VI(1) Questionnaire: Child Labour, 86th Session (June 1998), see point 7(b) of the Questionnaire (P.4 in the English version).

4 ILC, Provisional Record 19, 86th Session (June 1998), at §§ 131–140.

5 This word 'engagement' was replaced by 'procuring' during the same discussion in 1998; see *Ibid.*, at § 135.

clearly as possible.[6] Thus, the term 'exploitation' – a word which probably conveys a stronger sense of criticism than 'the use ...' – was not used in the definition of the exact act to be covered by the Convention. The proposal to use that term '*exploitation*' nevertheless conveys the feeling behind the inclusion of this topic. It should be recalled that the inclusion of the use of a child in illicit activities in the scope of an ILO Convention by no means signifies the legitimization of related acts but, on the contrary, has the effect of urging action to prohibit and eliminate it, in a similar way that CSEC is dealt with only for the purpose of action against it and not for condoning or regulating the conditions.

8.1.3 '*Illicit*' versus '*illegal*' activities

The Office explanation for the adoption of two separate clauses included several reasons for the preference of the term 'illicit' over 'illegal': in other words, by using the word 'illegal', the coverage might become too narrow – an activity of drug trafficking not prohibited by the national law of the country might fall outside of the scope – or become too broad – a performance by a child in theatrical production breaching copyright might fall within the scope.[7] Therefore, the term 'illicit', which has a more moral connotation, was proposed by the Office, accepted by the ILC in 1999, and became the final term in C182.

8.1.4 What are the illicit activities to be covered?

It should perhaps be clarified that the definition provided under article 3(c) of C182 of 'the use, procuring or offering of a child for illicit activities' as one of the WFCL does not signify a requirement to criminalize or make 'illegal' the activity itself in which a child is used, or for which he/she is procured or offered. This is a question distinct from prohibiting and applying sanction on 'the use, etc.' of children in such activities. The issue of sanctions on those who use, procure or offer children will be discussed later. Certainly, there is a social desire to fight against illicit acts themselves, but it is not for an ILO Convention to incorporate an obligation to criminalize them.

What, then, are the illicit activities to be covered under this provision? Since the criterion cannot be a simple distinction between legal and illegal acts in terms of national legislation the answer is not straightforward. With reference to the wording of article 3(c), it is obviously not enough to consider the production and trafficking of drugs alone, which is only mentioned as one example. Even though the illegality of the activity is not a criterion used in the provision of the Convention, crimes as defined in national law would be a natural scope of illicit activities in which children must not be used.

---

6 See *Ibid.*, §§ 131–132; the discussion on 'exploitation' was made with reference to the use of a child in prostitution and pornography, but the newly separated item on the use of a child in illicit activities retained exactly the same wording.

7 ILC, Report IV(2A): Child Labour, 87th Session (June 1999), see Office commentary on Article 3, Subparagraph (c), at 61–2.

Recommendation 190, which supplements C182, in Paragraph 12, refers to another example: [the use, procuring or offering of a child for illicit activities, in particular for ...] 'or for *activities which involve the unlawful carrying or use of firearms or other weapons*' (emphasis added). This part of the provision was added to R190 during the second discussion at the 1999 Conference,[8] based on an amendment proposed by the worker members of the Child Labour Committee. Being a provision of a Recommendation, this reference to firearms and other weapons does not have binding force, but offers an insight as to the types of activities – namely activities involving armed violence – in which the use of a child should be stopped as a matter of urgency. In reality, some situations of drug production and trafficking may be closely related to the carrying and use of firearms, both being intrinsic parts of organized crime. For instance, some campaign activities in Brazil, while tackling the use and involvement of children in certain types of drug-related crime, sent out an alert that children are highly exposed to armed violence in the situation, making it even comparable to 'armed conflict'[9] – which is another explicit aspect of WFCL if a child is forcibly brought into it.

8.1.5 Children used in begging

There is another frequently asked question: should the use of a child in 'begging' be included in this category of worst form of child labour? As a matter of fact, CEACR has raised the question in the examination of a number of countries' application of article 3(c) of C182.[10] It must again be underlined that dealing with begging in the context of C182, article 3(c) does not imply a requirement to criminalize begging or to punish children used in begging. Therefore the issue here is not whether begging itself should be punished. Indeed, where a general obligation to work, or a prohibition of vagrancy, leading a 'parasitic way of life', or 'anti-social life', is defined in an unduly extensive manner and enforceable by penal sanctions, that would in itself fall within the scope of the Forced Labour Convention (No. 29) as forced or compulsory labour imposed by the State.[11]

However, there is a tendency in national legislation on human trafficking to include 'begging' among the types of exploitation that are the end results or the purposes of trafficking. Therefore, the situation of child trafficking leading to their use in begging at the destination is also a concern under C182.[12] Similarly, in some

---

8 ILC, Provisional Record 19, 87th Session (June 1999), at §§ 336–338.

9 L. *Dowdney, Children of the Drug Trade – A Case Study of Children in Organised Armed Violence in Rio de Janeiro*, Rio de Janeiro, 2003.

10 For instance, see Direct Requests (2007) on the application of C182 in Belgium, Belarus, Fiji, Kazakhstan and Trinidad and Tobago, in which the CEACR has noted legislative provisions of the respective country prohibiting the use of children in begging, with reference to art. 3(c) of C182.

11 CEACR, General Survey concerning the Forced Labour Convention, 1930 (No. 29), and the Abolition of Forced Labour Convention, 1957 (No. 105), ILC, 96th Session, 2007, Report III (Part 1B), at §§ 86–88.

12 For instance, the CEACR has noted the information concerning trafficking in children, including for the purpose of begging, as regards developing countries (Observation (2006)

cases the use of children in begging in itself has been examined as a situation of forced or compulsory labour of children, when it occurred in the context of traditional and 'religious' exercises. Perhaps in such cases the situation is even clearer; it is the act of 'using' children or 'trafficking' them for the purpose of begging that must be prohibited and punished, and the children involved should be treated as victims and not as offenders. Some examples of national legislation were referred to in the CEACR *General Survey* on forced labour of 2007.[13]

8.2 What is required as action under C182?

8.2.1 C182 requirements regarding the worst forms of child labour

The title of C182 tells us the intention of the instrument – that is, not only to prohibit the worst forms of child labour but also to take immediate action for the elimination of such forms. Thus, legislative prohibition of a worst form of child labour is, of course, a first step to express a willingness to tackle the problem, but it will not be sufficient as a full response to it. C182 is much more explicit than many international labour standards in specifically setting forth types of action that must be taken for the attainment of the ultimate objective: mechanisms to monitor (article 5); responsible authority or authorities for enforcement (article 7(3)): plans or programmes of action (article 6); prohibition and sanctions (article 7(1)); wide-ranging 'effective and time-bound' measures against it (article 7(2)) – including those for prevention, withdrawal and rehabilitation – and international cooperation and assistance (article 8). Each of these practical measures, when relating to the use of children in illicit activities, must take account of specific features of the situation – very often occurring as illegal and criminal acts – quite distinct, for instance, from measures of enforcement of the minimum age rules or improvement of working conditions in legitimate places of

---

on C182, Thailand), developed countries (Direct Requests (2006) on C182, Belgium and the Netherlands), and in transition (Direct Request (2006) on C182, Republic of Moldova). A number of other countries have their legislative prohibition of child trafficking for the purpose of their use in begging noted by the CEACR.

13 CEACR, General Survey, *supra* note 11, footnote 180: Italy, Act No. 228 of 23 August 2003 on measures against the trafficking in persons, which amended certain provisions of the Penal Code, giving a fuller definition of reducing or maintaining a person in slavery or servitude (section 600) and of trafficking in persons in a situation of slavery or servitude (section 601); these provisions are very broad in scope and cover the exploitation of persons in general, as well as, in particular, incitement to or exploitation of prostitution, begging, and the performance of work in conditions where the worker is exploited or subjugated by the employer. See also footnote 181: France, Penal Code, as amended in 2003, section 225-4-1, which stipulates: 'Human trafficking is the recruitment, transport, transfer, accommodation, or reception of a person in exchange for remuneration or any other benefit or for the promise of remuneration or any other benefit, in order to put him at the disposal of a third party, whether identified or not, so as to permit the commission against that person of offences of procuring, sexual assault or attack, exploitation for begging, or the imposition of living or working conditions inconsistent with human dignity, or to force this person to commit any felony or misdemeanour.'

work. It would, first of all, become necessary to make the commitment made under C182 known widely within the country, much beyond the usual tripartite constituents involved in labour issues, and especially among the government bodies such as the police, criminal justice authorities and the courts. It cannot be overemphasized that an international labour Convention is binding on the ILO member '*State*' which ratifies it and that the responsibility for its application is not limited to the ministry responsible for labour. Not only because of the diversity of measures required to tackle the worst forms of child labour (for example, educational and social measures) but also because of the nature of the issues involving WFCL, C182 by definition requires political commitment at the highest possible level so as to permit strong collaboration of different parts of the government in addition to the social partners and other concerned groups.

8.2.2 Legislative prohibition

Almost by definition, illicit activities covered by C182 article 3(c) are or should be illegal also in national law.[14] In particular, against illicit traffic in drugs and other substances, there exist several international treaties,[15] and that is why the C182 provision can refer the detailed definition of the scope of the coverage to other treaties. Thus, the legal prohibition of illicit activities themselves could be more or less taken for granted in many countries, or otherwise pursued as general legal action against common crimes. However, such criminalization of illicit activities is by no means sufficient legislative action to give effect to C182 article 3(c). It is not even enough to 'protect children from' drug abuse itself, although as in the UN Convention against Illicit Traffic in Narcotic Drugs and Psychotropic Substances of 1988, some legislative provisions[16] concerning drugs deal with the two issues at the same time: the protection of children from the consumption or abuse of drugs, and their protection from being used in drug production and trafficking. In terms of C182 article 3(c), what needs to be prohibited and subjected to the appropriate sanctions is '*the use, procuring or offering* of a child for' illicit activities, even where the illicit activities in question already constitute a crime. This purpose may be accomplished by providing for, for instance, aggravation of an offence when it is committed using a minor as accomplice. An IPEC publication concerning legislative action advises

---

14 See above discussion on illegal versus illicit, for the reason why this is 'almost' and not 'always' by definition.

15 ILC, Report IV(2A): Child Labour, 87th Session (June 1999), see Office commentary on Article 3, Subparagraph (c), footnote 9: 'The Office views the relevant treaties as the Single Convention on Narcotic Drugs, 1961; Convention on Psychotropic Substances, 1971; Protocol amending the Single Convention on Narcotic Drugs, 1972; and the United Nations Convention against Illicit Traffic in Narcotic Drugs and Psychotropic Substances, 1988.'

16 For example, in Ecuador, it is an offence under the Code of Children and Adolescents (2003) to sell narcotic drugs and addictive psycho-active substances, alcoholic beverages, firearms or explosives of any kind to minors (s. 27, at the end). Minors have a right to be protected against the consumption and undue use of alcoholic beverages, narcotic and psycho-active substances, as well as against their participation in the production, commercialization and advertising thereof, which is considered a form of abuse (*abuso*) (s. 78 (1) and (2)).

aggravating sanctions to be provided and applied on the involvement of minors in crimes.[17]

8.2.3 Penal or other sanctions

It is one thing to define an act as one of the prohibited worst forms of child labour, but it is quite another thing to provide for and enforce penal sanction for such an act. We should have a quick look at article 7(1) of C182, which calls for 'all necessary measures to ensure the effective implementation and enforcement ... including the provision and application of penal sanctions *or, as appropriate, other sanctions*' (emphasis added).

During the elaboration of C182, consideration was given to 'the provision and strict enforcement of adequate criminal penalties' in the prospective Convention.[18] Given the reactions from constituents, the Office emphasized the meaning of this current clause as intending 'that there have to be sanctions but that the types of sanctions could be, as appropriate, penal or other sanctions', underlining the need to provide and apply some form of sanctions against WFCL.[19] In other words, it is not an option to provide no sanction at all. However, this provision still gives a certain discretion to the ratifying State as to whether each WFCL should be subject to penal sanction or just other sanctions.

This might look rather weak compared to C29 on Forced Labour that explicitly requires under its article 25 the strict enforcement of adequate penalties to the illegal exaction of any forced or compulsory labour, especially because the issues under article 3(a) to (c) of C182 used to be regarded as possible forced labour issues under C29 even without explicit reference to each issue in the Convention. Thus, the application of penal sanction to the use of forced child labour is a clear obligation under C29, while it remains optional under C182. The difference could be attributed to the fact that article 7(1) of C182 is applicable also to the use of children in hazardous work (covered by articles 3(d) and 4) that might not always be suitable for penal sanctions. Nonetheless, if the use of children for such activities as begging could be considered a form of forced or compulsory labour, the obligation to apply penal sanction under C29 is relevant in the more than 160 countries in the world that have ratified the Forced Labour Convention. R190 also recommends States to provide that the use of children in illicit activities, together with other acts covered by article 3(a) and (b) of C182, should be a criminal offence.[20] This becomes an important recommendation if a country has ratified C182 but not yet C29.

---

17 IPEC, *Eliminating the Worst Forms of Child Labour under Time-Bound Programmes: Guidelines for Strengthening Legislation, Enforcement and Overall Legal Framework*, 21–2, available online at the IPEC Information Resource Centre <http://www.ilo.org/ipec/Informationresources/lang--en/index.htm>.

18 ILC, Report VI(2): Child Labour, 86th Session (June 1998), see Question 9, § (1) (p. 61) and especially the Office commentary on p. 71 in the English version.

19 ILC, Report IV(2A): Child Labour, 87th Session (June 1999), see Office commentary on Article 7, § (1), at p. 98.

20 See R190, § 12 (c).

8.2.4 Other international instruments

There exist several international instruments that require legislative measures to stop the use of minors in crimes, especially in drug trade. For instance, the UN Convention against Illicit Traffic in Narcotic Drugs and Psychotropic Substances of 1988 calls for the national authorities to take account of aggravating factors including victimization *and use of* minors, and also offences committed in educational institutions among other things.[21] Its article 3(5) reads:

> 5. The Parties shall ensure that their courts and other competent authorities having jurisdiction can take into account factual circumstances which make the commission of the offences established in accordance with paragraph 1 of this article particularly serious, such as:
>
> ...
>
> f) The victimization or *use of minors*;
> g) The fact that the offence is *committed in a penal institution or in an educational institution or social service facility or in their immediate vicinity or in other places to which school children and students resort for educational, sports and social activities*;
> ... [emphasis added]

The Convention on the Rights of the Child (CRC) also includes a provision specifically concerning drugs, including the use of children in the illicit production and trafficking:

> Article 33
> States Parties shall take all appropriate measures, including legislative, administrative, social and educational measures, to protect children from the illicit use of narcotic drugs and psychotropic substances as defined in the relevant international treaties, and *to prevent the use of children in the illicit production and trafficking of such substances* [emphasis added].

The CRC more generally protects children from all forms of 'exploitation,' which may be regarded as possibly including their use in crimes and illicit activities. The relevant provisions read:

> Article 36
> States Parties shall protect the child against all other forms of exploitation prejudicial to any aspects of the child's welfare.
>
> Article 39
> States Parties shall take all appropriate measures to promote physical and psychological recovery and social reintegration of a child victim of: any form of neglect, exploitation, or abuse; torture or any other form of cruel, inhuman or degrading treatment or punishment; or armed conflicts. Such recovery and reintegration shall take place in an environment which fosters the health, self-respect and dignity of the child.

---

21 UN Convention against Illicit Traffic in Narcotic Drugs and Psychotropic Substances, 1988, available at <http://www.unodc.org/pdf/convention_1988_en.pdf>.

However, when it comes to the reporting process under the CRC, the official guidance from the CRC Committee neither requires any specific data or information concerning article 36 of the Convention, nor does it mention exploitation of children by using them in crimes.[22] Article 39 of the CRC is more specifically referred to in connection with the rehabilitation and reintegration of children involved in armed conflict (article 38), for instance.[23] Therefore, even though these other international instruments touch upon the issue of using children in drug production and trade as well as in other crimes, the inclusion of the topic in C182 has an added value in explicitly widening the scope (not limited to drug-related crimes) and in requiring specific action by the States against the phenomenon – not only ensuring legal prohibition, but also including direct intervention such as rehabilitation and social reintegration, prevention, and measures to tackle the root causes of the problem.

8.2.5 Examples of national legislative provisions

Now, let us look at some examples of national legislative texts concerning the use of children in illicit activities.[24] There are different ways and different types of law that can address this issue, starting with criminal laws that directly provide for an offence of involving a minor in criminal activities, or more specifically in drug production or distribution. For example, the Criminal Code of the Ukraine, in section 304, stipulates an offence of engaging a minor in criminal activity (or in drinking alcohol, begging or gambling) with sanction of confinement or imprisonment up to five years; and in section 309(3), the involvement of minors into drug production, distribution, etc. with imprisonment from five to eight years.[25] In addition, section 149 of the same Code defines human trafficking as 'selling, other paid transfer of human beings ... for sexual exploitation, utilization in the production of pornography, or for pornographic performances, *involvement in criminal activity*, debt bondage...' (emphasis added). Such crimes are punishable by imprisonment for a term of three to eight years. Further, paragraph 2 enumerates aggravating factors (punishable by imprisonment of five to twelve years with or without the forfeiture of property), including when committed in respect of a *minor*, through abuse of office, or by a person on whom the victim was financially or otherwise dependent.

The Penal Code of France provides for an offence of directly provoking a minor to commit a felony or a misdemeanour, punishable with five years' imprisonment and

---

22 CRC, CRC/C/58/Rev.1, 29 November 2005: 'General Guidelines regarding the Form and Contents of Periodic Reports to be submitted by States Parties under Article 44, Paragraph 1 (b), of the Convention', available at <http://www.unhchr.ch/tbs/doc.nsf/898586b1dc7b4043c1256a450044f331/af20808817648df4c12570fa002ba893/$FILE/G0545289.pdf>, see 'ANNEX, VIII. Special protection measures'.

23 *Ibid.*, Annex.

24 A limited number of examples of national provisions are cited here in order to illustrate concrete ways of legislating on the issue. References to particular provisions do not imply any judgement of their value; and the absence of mention of a particular country is not to be construed as a sign of non-existence of relevant legislation.

25 Law on Criminal Code of Ukraine (CCU) # 2341-14, 5 April 2001, available at <http://www.legislationline.org/upload/legislations/2e/4b/e7cc32551f671cc10183dac480fe.htm>.

a fine of €150,000, with aggravation where involving a child under 15, provoking habitual acts, or where committed in or around educational establishments etc.[26] The Penal Code of Bulgaria (section 188(1)) stipulates that: 'A person who compels a minor or an underage person to commit a crime or to engage in prostitution, shall be punished by deprivation of liberty for up to 5 years ...'. The Penal Code of Vietnam stipulates an offence not only of enticing a minor into committing a crime, but also of harbouring a juvenile offender.[27] Since information on the actual enforcement of these provisions is not available to the author, it is not possible to ascertain exactly what act of '*using*' a child would constitute these offences. Because the terms cited here are translations (such as 'enticing', 'engaging', 'involving' or 'compelling'), it is hard to appreciate the degree of coercion or force involved. This would be an interesting topic for a comparative examination of law and practice.

The second type of legislation is the provision to prohibit the engagement of persons under the age of 18 in hazardous work (corresponding to article 3(d) of C182). It is possible that the specific list of prohibited hazardous work includes certain activities related to drug production, etc., because of the possible harm to their health or moral integrity. For instance, in the case of Moldova, the prohibition of hazardous work covers, among other things, manufacture, transportation and trade in alcoholic drinks, tobacco products, *narcotic and toxic products*.[28] In Jamaica, a provision of the child protection law even provides an offence of 'purchasing intoxicating liquor or tobacco products from a child' in addition to employing a child to sell such products.[29]

---

26 France, Code Pénal, art. 227-21: 'Le fait de provoquer directement un mineur à commettre un crime ou un délit est puni de cinq ans d'emprisonnement et de 150000 euros d'amende. Lorsqu'il s'agit d'un mineur de quinze ans, que le mineur est provoqué à commettre habituellement des crimes ou des délits ou que les faits sont commis dans les établissements d'enseignement ou d'éducation ou dans les locaux de l'administration, ainsi que, lors des entrées ou sorties des élèves ou du public ou dans un temps très voisin de celles-ci, aux abords de ces établissements ou locaux, l'infraction définie par le présent article est punie de sept ans d'emprisonnement et de 150000 euros d'amende.' Available at <http://www.legifrance.gouv.fr/>.

27 Vietnam, Penal Code, section 252 (Crimes of enticing/compelling juveniles to commit offences or harbouring juvenile offenders) states that 'those who entice or compel juveniles into criminal activities or a deprived life or harbour juvenile offenders shall be sentenced to between one and five years of imprisonment', and aggravated up to 12 years of imprisonment if such offences are committed against children under 13 years of age, among other things. The offenders may also be subjected to a fine of up to thirty million dong. For full text see <http://www.worldlii.org/vn/legis/pc66/s252.html>.

28 Moldova, Labour Code, no. 154-XV of 28.03.2003, section 255 (1), which reads: 'Persons under the age of eighteen are forbidden to perform heavy work and work in harmful and/or dangerous working conditions, underground work, and also work that can cause harm to their health and their moral integrity (gambling, work in night institutions, manufacture, transportation and trade in alcoholic drinks, tobacco products, narcotic and toxic products). ...' [emphasis added]; unofficial English translation available at <http://www.ilo.org/dyn/natlex/docs/SERIAL/64896/63849/F1780758090/MDA64896ENG.PDF>.

29 Jamaica, The Child Care and Protection Act of 2004, section 40 (excerpt) states that: '(1) An owner or operator of an establishment that sells or serves intoxicating liquor or tobacco

Some clarification might be due here on the relation between article 3(c) and article 3(d). As has been explained elsewhere in the present volume, the worst forms of child labour as defined under article 3(a) to (c) of C182 are sometimes referred to as 'unconditional' worst forms,[30] to distinguish them from the so-called 'hazardous' work covered by articles 3(d) and 4 – that is, '*work which, by its nature or the circumstances in which it is carried out, is likely to harm the health, safety or morals of children*'. Article 4 requires each country to determine the exact contents of hazardous work (covered by article 3(d)) by means of national legislation or in a similar way after tripartite consultation. In some cases of hazardous work (for example, a workplace that is too hot), the conditions could be improved and the young person, if above the minimum working age, may be permitted to continue after removing the hazards (for example, by introducing air-conditioning).

In contrast, for unconditional worst forms, in a sense there is no dependence on conditions; it is not a question of improving conditions of drug dealers to render it permissible for under-18's. Nevertheless, there is a certain overlap between the two issues because activities included in the unconditional worst forms most probably are also extremely bad for the young people's health, safety and morals. One point to bear in mind here is that, unlike hazardous work covered by article 3(d), the worst forms as defined under article 3(a) to (c) neither require nor depend on national determination. In other words, the countries do not have an option to say that, for example, the use of children in prostitution or in illicit activities is not a worst form under certain conditions. It should be emphasized that, even where illicit activities such as drug trafficking are not among the listed prohibition of hazardous work, there is an obligation to stop the use of children in it, by virtue of article 3(c) of C182.

The third type of legislative action against the use of children in illicit activities are provisions in the law on children's rights. In Mongolia, for instance, the Law on the Protection of the Rights of the Child,[31] prohibits '[the attraction of] the child into crimes, violence, gambling, conflict among adults, drinking, smoking, narcotics and other psychotropic substances and abuse and violence...'; and under the same law,[32] it is further prohibited for 'individuals, economic entities and organizations to employ the child ... to engage in begging and to conduct profit making activities on their behalf illegally'. The Tunisian Code on the Protection of the Child prohibits the exploitation of a child in different forms of organized crime.[33] Many other examples can be found on the prohibition of using a child specifically in *begging*. In Zimbabwe,

---

products shall ensure that ... (b) no child is employed by the establishment to sell or assist in the selling of intoxicating liquor or tobacco products. (2) A person commits an offence if that person ... (b) employs a child to sell or assist in selling intoxicating liquor or tobacco products; or (c) purchases intoxicating liquor or tobacco products from a child'.

30 See Rishikesh (this volume). This term was first used by the ILO in the 2002 Global Report on Child Labour. See ILO, *A Future Without Child Labour*. ILC 90th Session, 2002, Report I (B), § 26, available at <http://www.ilo.org/public/english/standards/relm/ilc/ilc95/pdf/rep-i-b.pdf>.

31 Mongolia, Law on the Protection of the Rights of the Child of 1996, section 7(4).

32 *Ibid.*, section 7(6).

33 Tunisia, Code de la protection de l'enfant, promulgué par la Loi no. 95-92 of 9 November 1995: '19. Il est interdit d'exploiter l'enfant dans les différentes formes de

for example, the Children's Protection and Adoption Act[34] provides that any parent or guardian of a child or young person who allows that child or young person or any person who causes any child or young person; (a) to beg; or (b) to accompany him or any other person while he begs; or (c) to induce or to endeavour to induce the giving of alms; or (d) to perform or be exhibited in any way for public entertainment in a manner likely to be detrimental to the child's or young person's health, morals, mind or body; shall be guilty of an offence. In Singapore, Section 6 of the Children and Young Persons Act (No. 1 of 1993) covers not only the use of a child in begging but also in illegal lotteries, gambling, and other activities.[35]

In some cases, the legislative provision is an extremely general one that prohibits all the worst forms of child labour by children under 18, virtually reproducing the text of article 3 of C182. For example, a labour code provision in the Democratic Republic of the Congo abolishes among other things 'the use, procurement or offering of a child for illicit activities, namely the production and trafficking of drugs'.[36] This may have the value of declaring the principle and setting the framework for further legislative and other action. However, especially where such a general provision is found in labour law, the effective enforcement of the blanket prohibition would seem rather difficult without further specifications or the creation of enforcement mechanisms, in particular in collaboration with the criminal justice system. In Indonesia, a legal provision provides for special protection of child victims in the context of substance abuse by stipulating:

(1) Special protection of the child being victim of abuse of narcotic, alcohol, psychotropic, and other additives as meant in article 59 and involved in production and distribution is executed through supervisory, preventive, curative and rehabilitating efforts by the government and society.[37]

---

criminalité organisée, y compris le fait de lui inculquer le fanatisme et la haine et de l'inciter à commettre des actes de violence et de terreur.'

34 Zimbabwe, Children's Protection and Adoption Act, 1971 (No. 22), as amended by Act No. 23 of 2001, section 10.

35 The provision reads: 'any person who causes or procures any child or young person or, having the custody charge or care of a child or young person, allows that child or young person to be in any street, premises or place for the purpose of –(a) begging or receiving alms, or of inducing the giving of alms, whether or not there is any pretence of singing, playing, performing or offering anything for sale; or (b) carrying out of illegal hawking, illegal lotteries, gambling or other illegal activities or activities detrimental to the health or welfare of the child, shall be guilty of an offence and shall be liable on conviction to a fine not exceeding $2000 [approximately 1,180 US$ at the time of writing] or to imprisonment for a term not exceeding 12 months or to both.'

36 See the Democratic Republic of the Congo, Labour Code (of October 2002), section 3. In other cases, a similar provision may be found in other levels of regulations, for instance, in Honduras, 'Acuerdo Ejecutivo No. STSS-211-01 por el que se aprueba el Reglamento sobre Trabajo Infantil en Honduras', section 10 prohibits the engagement of adolescents in the worst forms of child labour including their use, etc., in illicit activities.

37 Indonesia, Child Protection, Law No. 23/2002, 22 October 2002, section 67.

(2) Everyone is prohibited from placing, letting, involving and asking intentionally for involving the child in the abuse, production and distribution of the drugs as meant in paragraph (1).

It would be extremely useful and interesting if more information could be gathered on the actual application of these legislative provisions, not just for the sake of knowledge about the application of laws, but also for assessing and monitoring the progress against the use of children in illicit activities – something which is particularly difficult to monitor among the unconditional WFCL. Such information would also respond to the requirements under C182 of monitoring 'the implementation of the provisions giving effect to this Convention' (article 5) and of clearly designating the competent authority responsible for their implementation (article 7(3)).

8.2.6 Linkage with the juvenile justice issue

While there are provisions in the CRC concerning the rights of children in the context of their treatment or punishment including in situations of conflict with the law, as well as other international rules on the topic, the legal issue of juvenile justice *per se* is beyond the scope of the present chapter. Article 3(c) of C182 does not seem to provide specific requirements in this regard, except that the proper establishment and operation of the juvenile justice system is of crucial importance in relation with the practical measures – covered by article 7 of C182 – for withdrawal of children from this worst form of child labour, as well as their rehabilitation and social integration. A change of viewpoint is needed here: a child (or adolescent) would not appear in front of an authority as a victim of a WFCL (used in illicit activity), but instead is likely to be caught as a delinquent or suspect of an offence. C182 article 3(c) introduces another perspective: is there an adult who used that child in committing the offence? What was the background situation? How could other children be prevented from falling into that trap? What are the best ways to ensure that the child withdrawn from the activity is rehabilitated and socially integrated, which is also an effective way to prevent the same child from committing further illicit activities? Article 8 of C182 goes a step further and calls for international assistance or cooperation to tackle the root causes of WFCL, for instance by providing assistance in poverty reduction and universal education. In this sense, invoking C182 could offer an argument for widening the measures against illicit or criminal activities, especially where they are committed by children under the age of 18, from concentration on penal law enforcement to comprehensive action including much broader measures ranging from prevention to rehabilitation, and even aiming to tackle the economic and social root causes of the phenomenon.

Several texts of international guidance from the human rights perspective on the issue of juvenile justice already exist: for example, the UN Guidelines on the Prevention of Juvenile Delinquency (the 'Riyadh Guidelines' of 1990); the UN Minimum Rules for the Administration of Juvenile Justice (the 'Beijing Rules' of 1985); and the UN International Covenant on Economic, Social and Cultural Rights

(ICESCR 1966).[38] The CRC also contains detailed provisions on the subject.[39] Even

---

38 For international standards on juvenile justice, see for example, <http://www.juvenilejusticepanel.org/en/standardsoverview.html>.

39 CRC art. 37 reads: 'States Parties shall ensure that: (a) No child shall be subjected to torture or other cruel, inhuman or degrading treatment or punishment. Neither capital punishment nor life imprisonment without possibility of release shall be imposed for offences committed by persons below eighteen years of age; (b) No child shall be deprived of his or her liberty unlawfully or arbitrarily. The arrest, detention or imprisonment of a child shall be in conformity with the law and shall be used only as a measure of last resort and for the shortest appropriate period of time; (c) Every child deprived of liberty shall be treated with humanity and respect for the inherent dignity of the human person, and in a manner which takes into account the needs of persons of his or her age. In particular, every child deprived of liberty shall be separated from adults unless it is considered in the child's best interest not to do so and shall have the right to maintain contact with his or her family through correspondence and visits, save in exceptional circumstances; (d) Every child deprived of his or her liberty shall have the right to prompt access to legal and other appropriate assistance, as well as the right to challenge the legality of the deprivation of his or her liberty before a court or other competent, independent and impartial authority, and to a prompt decision on any such action.'

CRC art. 40 reads: '1. States Parties recognize the right of every child alleged as, accused of, or recognized as having infringed the penal law to be treated in a manner consistent with the promotion of the child's sense of dignity and worth, which reinforces the child's respect for the human rights and fundamental freedoms of others and which takes into account the child's age and the desirability of promoting the child's reintegration and the child's assuming a constructive role in society. 2. To this end, and having regard to the relevant provisions of international instruments, States Parties shall, in particular, ensure that: (a) No child shall be alleged as, be accused of, or recognized as having infringed the penal law by reason of acts or omissions that were not prohibited by national or international law at the time they were committed; (b) Every child alleged as or accused of having infringed the penal law has at least the following guarantees: (i) To be presumed innocent until proven guilty according to law; (ii) To be informed promptly and directly of the charges against him or her, and, if appropriate, through his or her parents or legal guardians, and to have legal or other appropriate assistance in the preparation and presentation of his or her defence; (iii) To have the matter determined without delay by a competent, independent and impartial authority or judicial body in a fair hearing according to law, in the presence of legal or other appropriate assistance and, unless it is considered not to be in the best interest of the child, in particular, taking into account his or her age or situation, his or her parents or legal guardians; (iv) Not to be compelled to give testimony or to confess guilt; to examine or have examined adverse witnesses and to obtain the participation and examination of witnesses on his or her behalf under conditions of equality; (v) If considered to have infringed the penal law, to have this decision and any measures imposed in consequence thereof reviewed by a higher competent, independent and impartial authority or judicial body according to law; (vi) To have the free assistance of an interpreter if the child cannot understand or speak the language used; (vii) To have his or her privacy fully respected at all stages of the proceedings. 3. States Parties shall seek to promote the establishment of laws, procedures, authorities and institutions specifically applicable to children alleged as, accused of, or recognized as having infringed the penal law, and, in particular: (a) The establishment of a minimum age below which children shall be presumed not to have the capacity to infringe the penal law; (b) Whenever appropriate and desirable, measures for dealing with such children without resorting to judicial proceedings, providing that human rights and legal safeguards are fully respected. 4. A variety of dispositions, such if C182 does not specifically impose obligations in terms of juvenile justice, it could be presumed that where the existing rules and related rights of children are not respected, one can strongly suspect also the insufficiency or absence of appropriate measures required under C182 to ensure rehabilitation and social integration of the children withdrawn from the use in illicit activities.

One last point of caution should be raised here about a linkage with another aspect of WFCL: when a child is found to be used in illicit activities, or at high risk of being so, the measures taken must not leave the child in another form of WFCL, namely forced or compulsory labour. The general definition of forced labour under C29 excludes from its scope compulsory labour 'as a consequence of a conviction in a court of law'.[40] In other words, the question of forced labour arises if work is imposed by other bodies than a court of law (such as administrative or other non-judicial bodies or authorities), or does not result from a conviction (for example, persons awaiting trial or detained without trial).[41] The mere fact of the person involved being a minor must not lead to an arbitrary imposition of compulsory labour or to an absence of due process in the examination of cases where children are allegedly used in illicit activities. This does not mean that children found, or suspected to be, in conflict with the law should be dealt with just like adults. On the contrary, those children need special attention and consideration because of their age. As already discussed, the important perspective offered by C182 is that of tackling the issue in a comprehensive manner including rehabilitation, social reintegration and the prevention of recurrence. Thus, the establishment and operation of an appropriate juvenile justice system becomes all the more important in order to guarantee the rights of children and at the same time to respond to their need to be rehabilitated in an appropriate manner, which may well involve their preparation for and introduction to decent work.

8.2.7 The minimum age for criminal responsibility

It should be noted that question of the age of criminal responsibility is not directly linked here. Article 3(c) of C182 is silent as to whether the child who has been used by an adult or an older child in committing illicit activities should be punished or not. However, it is obvious from other provisions (such as article 7) of the C182 that practical measures need to be taken for the prevention and withdrawal and rehabilitation of children involved in the worst forms of child labour. Thus, there could be possible themes for analytical examination, for instance, of why children are used in crimes such as drug trafficking, in relation to the age of criminal responsibility.

---

as care, guidance and supervision orders; counselling; probation; foster care; education and vocational training programmes and other alternatives to institutional care shall be available to ensure that children are dealt with in a manner appropriate to their well-being and proportionate both to their circumstances and the offence.'

40 ILO, C29, art. 2(2)(c).
41 See CEACR, General Survey 2007, § 48 et seq.

8.3 What do we already know about it?

8.3.1 General obligation to find out about a worst form of child labour

If you wish to tackle a problem, the first thing is to know about its existence and extent. This desire to obtain information about WFCL is implicit in the provision of C182 to take 'all necessary measures to ensure the effective implementation and enforcement'. Moreover, under article 7(1), the States that ratify it are requested, by means of the Report Form adopted by the Governing Body of the ILO, to supply, 'where such statistics exist, information on the nature, extent and trends of the worst forms of child labour' among other information on practice. R190 is much more explicit in recommending, in paragraph 5, that:

> Detailed information and statistical data on the nature and extent of child labour should be compiled and kept up to date to serve as a basis for determining priorities for national action for the abolition of child labour, in particular for the prohibition and elimination of its worst forms as a matter of urgency.

This is a huge challenge regarding the use of children in illicit activities, since such activities are normally outside of the scope of 'labour' statistics, and disaggregated data on children's involvement are rare. However, this issue is by no means limited to developing countries, as demonstrated for instance by the reference to child drug runners in the UK in the 2006 Global Report of the Director General of the ILO.[42]

8.3.2 A global estimate

It is extremely difficult to know the exact extent and the nature of the use of children in illicit activities. In the Global Report on Child Labour released in 2002, the ILO made its very first attempt to give an overview of child labour with a separate set of data on the worst forms of child labour, giving the estimate of 600,000 children in illicit activities.[43] Although this is a very small figure compared to the more than 200 million child labourers worldwide, it is double the estimate of children in armed conflict (300,000) and the issue could be relevant to any country in the world irrespective of the level of economic development. The 2002 Global Report remarked that 'countries facing serious problems with the drugs trade, from Colombia to Cambodia and the United States to the Russian Federation, know all too well that children, including very young children, can be swept up in such activity'.[44] It was clearly noted in the 2002 Global Estimate that the figure was a minimum

---

42 ILO, *The End of Child Labour: Within Reach – Global Report under the Follow-Up to the ILO Declaration on Fundamental Principles and Rights at Work*, Report to the ILC, 95th session, 2006, Report I (B). See Box 2.6, 44, available at <http://www.ilo.org/public/english/standards/relm/ilc/ilc95/pdf/rep-i-b.pdf>.

43 For details of the findings, definitions and methodology, see ILO, 'Every Child Counts – New Global Estimate on Child Labour', Geneva, 2002, available online at the IPEC Information Resource Centre <http://www.ilo.org/ipec/Informationresources/lang--en/index.htm>.

44 ILO, *A Future Without Child Labour*, *supra* note 30, § 118.

estimate, based on conservative calculations. Given the general paucity of reliable data on children's illicit activities (for example, petty crimes such as small thefts), this estimate followed the emphasis under C182 which refers as an example to the involvement of children in the production and trafficking of drugs, and concentrated on children in drug manufacture, including work in poppy plantations, and trafficking of illegal substances. The methodology used for this estimate – as well as other 'unconditional worst forms of child labour' – was completely different from the general child labour estimates basically derived from the statistics of economically active children. Activities such as stealing or begging would not appear as such in the statistical data on economic activities, although some children used in illicit activities may have been counted among general child labourers, such as street vendors, if they were engaged also in other activities. The ILO/IPEC is continuing its endeavour to investigate and develop methodologies for better collection of statistical data and other information of unconditional worst forms, at least to permit rough estimates of the extent of the problem in each country. Due to its hidden nature, estimates of the use of children in illicit activities may remain the most difficult.

8.3.3 Information on infringements

In the meantime, one possible source of information could be the adults or older children who have used children in illicit activities. The Report Form to be used by the governments to supply reports on ratified Conventions includes a part on C182 stating: '... please supply copies or extracts from official documents ... and, where such exists, information on ... the number and nature of infringements reported, penal sanctions applied, etc.'[45] Obviously, not all instances of the use of children in crimes will be detected and sanctioned. It is not at all easy to estimate the percentage of detected cases so as to calculate the number of persons actually committing the offence. Furthermore, any increase in the number of reported or sanctioned cases could be due either to the increase of the problem or to improved law enforcement.

In any case, this area would require close collaboration between the ministry responsible for labour, which reports to the ILO on ratified conventions, and the police or criminal justice authority, which is in a position to obtain information regarding the use of children in illicit activities. C182, article 7(3), explicitly mentions the need to designate 'the competent authority responsible for the implementation of the provisions' giving effect to the Convention, and this provision should be actively used to solicit collaboration of the relevant authorities. The Report Form asks the governments, concerning article 7(3), to 'indicate the authority or authorities designated', implying the likelihood that more than one authority need to work in collaboration concerning different worst forms. Similarly, article 5 of C182 requires ratifying States to 'establish or designate appropriate mechanisms to monitor the implementation': the term 'mechanisms' here is in plural. Therefore, it is expected that more than one mechanism will be necessary to monitor C182 nationally. While

---

45 Part V of the Report Form on C182. The Report Forms are adopted by the Governing Body for each Convention, and this one is available at <http://www.ilo.org/ilolex/english/reportforms/pdf/22e182.pdf>.

labour inspection generally oversees the application of national labour law provisions which give effect to international labour standards, that alone will not be sufficient to cover the issues such as the use of children in the drug trade, crimes generally and other illicit activities. It is an obligation for the government as a whole to report regularly on ratified Conventions.[46] Instead of considering it an administrative burden for the responsible ministry (usually of labour), this reporting process may also serve as an opportunity to call upon the involvement of other bodies or authorities (such as the police or criminal justice system) who monitor and collect information on such specific topics as the use of children in illicit activities.

8.3.4 Rapid assessment methodology

Another effort to find out more about the worst forms of child labour, including illicit activities, is the Rapid Assessments (RAs), a methodology jointly developed by the ILO and the UNICEF.[47] This is a method of gathering descriptive information on hidden or illicit forms of child labour quickly and in a limited geographical area. It is often used at the first stage of programme planning. The method has proved very useful for obtaining detailed knowledge of the conditions and life circumstances of children who are the victims of the worst forms of child labour. In general, the RA methodology is not designed to extrapolate figures or make generalizations outside the scope of the interviewed respondents. ILO/IPEC has carried out RAs concerning the involvement of children in illicit drug-related activities in four countries, namely: Brazil, Estonia, Philippines and Thailand. Given the nature of the drug trade, the researchers used a variety of techniques to access children and other informants, including semi-structured interviews with children and adults in the drug trade, focus groups and interviews with a variety of stakeholders, including community leaders, police and government officials.[48] All the related reports are available online from ILO/IPEC website.[49] These reports include valuable insights into the background of children and conditions in which they are found, as well as suggestions concerning

---

46 For the details of the reporting on child labour under C138 and C182, see ILO, Practical Guide to Child Labour Reporting, ILO Geneva and International Training Centre of the ILO, Turin, 2006, available online at the IPEC Information Resource Centre <http://www. ilo.org/ipec/Informationresources/lang--en/index.htm>. There is also a need to involve, apart from the various responsible authorities, the employers' and workers' organizations, in the preparation process of the report to the ILO, but it is beyond the scope of this chapter.

47 ILO/UNICEF, *Manual on Child Labour Rapid Assessment Methodology*, Geneva, 2005, available online at the IPEC Information Resource Centre <http://www.ilo.org/ipec/ Informationresources/lang--en/index.htm>.

48 See also ILO/IPEC, *Investigating the WFCL: A Synthesis Report of Selected Rapid Assessment and National Reports*, 2005, 21, available online at the IPEC Information Resource Centre <http://www.ilo.org/ipec/Informationresources/lang--en/index.htm>.

49 The RA reports concerning the use of children in illicit activities (namely drug trafficking) in Brazil, Estonia, Philippines and Thailand are available online at the country information page of the IPEC Statistical Information and Monitoring Programme on Child Labour (SIMPOC), following the link for each country, at <http://www.ilo.org/ipec/ ChildlabourstatisticsSIMPOC/lang--en/index.htm>.

strategies for successfully withdrawing those children from the drug trade. It should be learned from these specific studies that knowing more about the children involved and the circumstances they are found in is the very first step to take preventive measures and to withdraw them from the activities and rehabilitate and socially reintegrate them. These measures are indeed explicit requirements of C182, namely under article 7(2), and will also be discussed below in the framework of existing action by ILO/IPEC.

8.3.5 Rapid assessment findings

The RA Philippines notes that C182 'is unheard of at the local level. The idea of children in the drug trade is new and there are no programmes and policies relating to this subject matter'.[50] The same report points out that 'in Cebu City, adult drug traders are deliberately using children in the business, and hide behind them'.[51] These facts underline a huge need for awareness-raising and sensitization on the topic, using C182 as a tool, not only in identifying the problem, but also in analysing the situation and taking effective countermeasures.

The RA in Thailand examined four main factors that relate to the involvement of children in illicit drug activities, namely: economic factors, family behaviour, education and lifestyle. The report concluded that it will not be effective to use only law enforcement measures to eliminate children's involvement in the drug trade; and that preventive measures must also be taken to address the root and primary causes of the problem.[52] RAs examine not only the factors that draw children into drug trafficking, but also those that keep children from entering drug trafficking, or help them leave that activity (for example, the Brazil and Estonia RAs). Studies generate very useful information if the research also involves a group of children who are not involved in the drug trade, as did the Philippines RA.

There are also RAs targeting other categories of WFCL such as child trafficking or, more generally on WFCL, in which the findings include the involvement of children in illicit activities such as drug trafficking.[53] For instance, in a RA report on trafficking in children in Ukraine, it was noted:

- 'that both children and families are often reluctant to report coercion, for example into begging, to the authorities' (p. 11).
- 'that many of the children were engaged in begging and that official Ukrainian data on child trafficking does not include begging as a form of labour exploitation. Children exploited in this way therefore have even less recourse to legal redress' (p. 29).

---

50 RA Philippines report, xiv.

51 *Ibid.*, 78.

52 RA Thailand report, 33–4.

53 L. Dunn, *Investigating the Unconditional Worst Forms of Child Labour: A Synthesis Report on Selected Rapid Assessments, National and Institutional Reports*, forthcoming from ILO.

- 'and there is Case study 3: Oleg, 16 years, Kiev – a story of a boy – in search of earning opportunity – who was trafficked to be used in begging' (p. 31).[54]

8.3.6 UN Study on Violence against Children

The World Report on Violence against Children (VAC) was launched in 2006. Mandated by the General Assembly (UN GA Resolution 57/190), the United Nations Secretary-General (UN-SG) appointed an Independent Expert – Professor Paulo Sérgio Pinheiro – to lead a UN-wide study on violence against children.[55] The UN-SG's report based on this comprehensive and participatory study, including recommendations, was presented to the UN General Assembly and discussed in the Third Committee.[56] This Study was a UN-led collaboration, rooted in children's human right to protection from all forms of violence. It aims to promote action to prevent and eliminate violence against children (under 18 years) in different settings – including in places of work – at international, regional, national and local levels. The ILO, as a key partner of the Study, contributed to the process of distilling the key issues related to violence against children who are working. The VAC Study shed a new light on the situations and sufferings of working children – whether legally or illegally, including children used in illicit activities.

First of all, Chapter 6 (violence against children in places of work) of the VAC Report touches upon illicit activities and especially children involved in trading drugs among the 'high risk work settings' where they are particularly at risk of or exposed to violence. During the regional consultation processes of the VAC Study, concern was expressed in many parts of the world, from the Caribbean to Europe and Central Asia, over a growing number of children working on the streets and their involvement in illicit activities from petty theft, begging to drug trafficking. The VAC Report points out that:

> In many parts of the world, police assume that children trying to earn money on the street are necessarily involved in illegal activity, adding to the violence in these children's lives. In some countries, such children are legally defined as potentially deviant or criminalised as outcasts, and the police are entitled to arrest them.[57]

However, the VAC Report also covers other settings such as the community (Chapter 7) and care and justice institutions (Chapter 5) – which in fact are the settings where children are actually involved in illicit activities, or placed as a

---

54 RA 'A Rapid Assessment of Trafficking in Children for Labour and Sexual Exploitation in Ukraine', ILO, Geneva, 2003, available online at the IPEC Information Resource Centre <http://www.ilo.org/ipec/Informationresources/lang--en/index.htm>.

55 See for details and documents, including the World Report, <http://www.unviolencestudy.org/>. Chapter 6 covers violence in places of work.

56 The UN-SG Report is available at <http://www.unicef.org/violencestudy/reports/SG_violencestudy_en.pdf>.

57 P.S. Pinheiro, World Report on Violence Against Children, United Nations Secretary General's Study on Violence against Children, 2006, 250, available at <http://www.unviolencestudy.org>.

consequence of such activities. For instance: the Report notes in Chapter 7 that *gangs* 'are an important factor in violence among and against children in many parts of the world'. It goes on to analyse that the repressive law enforcement tactics used by many governments to deal with children in organized armed violence would be ineffective if the root causes of the problem are not tackled and the juvenile justice and penal systems are inadequate.[58] Chapter 5 examines in detail the situations of children in custody and detention and points out that: 'In too many countries, the criminal justice system is used as a substitute for adequate care and protection systems. The police are often the first and only agency to respond to children in need and lacking appropriate alternatives, place vulnerable children in police lock-ups or in detention.'[59] Further, children in detention or police custody are then exposed to experiences of violence in those situations.

These findings from the UN VAC Study raise a big concern from the viewpoint of ensuring the rehabilitation and social reintegration of children used in illicit activities – which is a clear obligation for more than 160 countries that have ratified C182 (article 3(c) and article 7(2) read together). The UN Study sends out an alert that: 'Children subjected to detention are more likely to commit offences in the future than children placed in diversion programmes', and quotes one juvenile justice expert as saying: 'incarcerating young offenders in large, congregate-care juvenile institutions does not effectively rehabilitate and may actually harm them'.[60]

8.3.7 Ethical considerations for researches

Many research reports on the use of children in drug trafficking or other illicit activities – be it an RA or other types of studies – point to the potential danger to the children involved, especially in organized crime, as well as to the researchers themselves, because of the illicit nature of the activities. There exist a whole range of ethical considerations to be kept in mind in researching the issues of child labour and especially its worst forms.[61] These issues spread throughout the research process: from pre-research consideration of research risks, and informed consent; through issues during research of language and logic, trust, and conditions of listening; to the post-research issues of the right to privacy and sharing the research results. It has been recognized that 'not telling the truth is but one of many coping strategies that girls and boys rely on for survival in precarious situations'.[62] However, extra caution and appropriate considerations must be kept in mind when researching the involvement of children in illicit activities – such as drug trafficking – because of the nature of the situation. It is understandable that children are hesitant, wary or reluctant to answer some of the questions. Special care must be taken during the

---

58 *Ibid.*, 304–6.

59 *Ibid.*, 195 et seq.

60 *Ibid*, 200, see Box: 'Does child detention "work"?'.

61 See for instance, ILO/IPEC, *Ethical Considerations When Conducting Research on Children in the Worst Forms of Child Labour*, 2003, available online at the IPEC Information Resource Centre <http://www.ilo.org/ipec/Informationresources/lang--en/index.htm>.

62 *Ibid.*, 9.

research activities, for example, to limit the sharing of certain information such as the location studied or the names of field researchers, even with the police.[63]

8.4 What has been done?

The main purpose of this chapter is to examine the legal implications of covering the use of children in illicit activities as a WFCL under C182, and not to examine what the ILO or, more specifically, the IPEC has done against it. Nevertheless, it is of interest to look into possible practical approaches to put these legal requirements and considerations in practice. Thus two distinct experiences will briefly be covered here: one on the research side (in South East Asia), and the other on the juvenile justice side (in South Africa).

8.4.1 Example 1: South East Asia – participatory action-oriented research

The first example relates the ILO/IPEC experience in Indonesia, the Philippines and Thailand tackling the use of children in the production, sale and trafficking of drugs through participatory action-oriented research (PAOR).[64] This approach started from the recognition that there is insufficient knowledge on the causal relationship between drug use and addiction and the involvement of children in drug sales and trafficking. It is a two-pronged process, consisting of research and documentation, plus an effort to build and enhance the capacity of partners and the community to deal with drug-related issues and to strengthen direct interventions. The PAOR process also intends to contribute to establishing networks among agencies tackling the issue of children in drug trafficking. Thus in PAOR, research does not stop at simply identifying the children involved in the production, sale and trafficking of drugs and obtaining information from them, but maintains contacts with them for the duration of the project and provides or strengthens alternative options to them, as well as following up on progress (or set-backs). It further allows the drawing of lessons for the prevention and withdrawal of children, as well as for developing guidelines for PAOR in assessing the situation of children in such activities. The PAOR also produced a document covering intervention models: school-based, community-based and street-based. Similar approaches are being developed in Brazil as well.

---

63 See also ILO/IPEC, *Investigating the WFCL, supra* note 48.

64 E. Porio and C.S. Crisol, *The Use of Children in the Production, Sales and Trafficking of Drugs, a Synthesis of Participatory Action Oriented Research Programmes in Indonesia, the Philippines and Thailand*, ILO/IPEC, 2004: available online at the IPEC Information Resource Centre <http://www.ilo.org/ipec/Informationresources/lang--en/index.htm>; L. Moeliono and N. Sunarno, *Guidelines for Participatory Action-Oriented Research in Assessing the Situation of Children in the Production, Sales and Trafficking of Drugs* (Based on Lessons Learned from Indonesia, the Philippines and Thailand), ILO/IPEC, 2005, available online at the IPEC Information Resource Centre <http://www.ilo.org/ipec/Informationresources/lang--en/index.htm>.

8.4.2 Example 2: South Africa – children used by adults in committing crimes (CUBAC)

The second example is a national project in South Africa on 'children used by adults in committing crimes' (CUBAC), concentrating more on focused interventions for children who have been involved in crimes, alongside action on investigating and prosecuting adults.[65] In 2005, the project undertook extensive research on children used by adults or older children to commit crimes. While being a part of a project tackling a wider range of WFCL in South Africa, the CUBAC project placed a strong emphasis on the integration of the issue into criminal justice policies and practice. The executing agency of the project has sought collaboration with a wide range of South African government departments, such as those responsible for justice, social development, labour, education, safety and security and local government. Even though there exists a general understanding that children accused of crimes are entitled to certain rights and procedural guarantees, little thought has been given to the fact that child offenders are also victims of the worst forms of child labour. Therefore, the objectives of the project included not only the direct provision of services to children who have been used (withdrawal) or are at risk (prevention) but also the strengthening of key institutions for delivering services for CUBAC, awareness raising among role-players in child justice and amongst the larger community, and increased knowledge about the nature, extent and cause of CUBAC.

8.4.3 Comments arising from the examples

These two examples are not the only regions where the problem exists, nor are they the only experience of ILO/IPEC. Many other programmes and projects supported by the ILO/IPEC are tackling the issue, either as such or as part of other issues.[66] These include projects for street children, in Central and Eastern Europe (CEE), where it has been pointed out that 'many of the children trafficked for labour exploitation typically end up in some form of street-based illicit activity including petty theft, begging and pimping'.[67] Even though the use of children in drug production and trafficking is one explicit example under article 3(c) of C182, it is not the exclusive scope of the provision. The use of children in other forms of illicit activities should not be lost from sight, although such activities might be even more complex and hard to tackle compared to the drug issue that may already be receiving specific attention, especially in the criminal justice field.

There are plenty of common elements in action against the use of children in illicit activities compared with action against the worst forms of child labour in

---

65 For information and the publication produced by the project on CUBAC, see <http://www.communitylawcentre.org.za/Childrens-Rights/03cubac>. This is a website of the executive agency – the Children's Rights Project, Community Law Centre, University of the Western Cape.

66 For up-to-date information on ILO/IPEC projects, visit <http://www.ilo.org/ipec/index.htm>.

67 ILO, *The End of Child Labour Within Reach*, Report I(B), § 200.

general (and especially what we call 'unconditional WFCL' because of the illegal or illicit nature of the situations), from action-oriented research to comprehensive measures of prevention, withdrawal and rehabilitation. Legal prohibition is not going to solve the problem on its own, if it is not accompanied by other measures of direct support, including 'the necessary and appropriate direct assistance for the removal of children from' their use in illicit activities and 'for their rehabilitation and social integration' as required under article 7(2)(b) of C182. In addition, such measures must be 'effective and time-bound' and should not stop at simply declaring the abstract objective far away in time and removed from reality. C182's requirements include measures to 'ensure access to free basic education, and, wherever possible and appropriate, vocational training, for all children removed from the worst forms of child labour' (article 7(2)(c)). It is by no means for the ILO/IPEC alone to assist in these practical measures. Effective collaboration with different government authorities and other bodies is indispensable to achieve such ambitious goals within a well defined time frame.

Finally, reference should be made to an explicit obligation for international cooperation or assistance under article 8 of C182 – which was an innovative feature in international labour standards that usually offer parameters for setting national labour standards of the ratifying State. The international collaboration of police, judiciary and any other concerned authorities is important in tackling crimes across borders, and the use of children in them. 'Support for social and economic development, poverty eradication programmes and universal education' – as explicitly required under article 8 – is also indispensable to help less-developed countries in addressing the root causes of WFCL, including the use of children in illicit activities.

8.5 Concluding remarks

The use of children in illicit activities is a new issue within the child labour concern. The explicit inclusion of this as a worst form of child labour under C182 creates an impetus to address the involvement of children in drug trade and other crimes and begging and other illicit activities from a new angle. C182 is strongly action-oriented and includes specific provisions requiring specific measures, from prohibition and the provision of sanctions to comprehensive time-bound measures for prevention, withdrawal and rehabilitation. Therefore, the use of children in illicit activities, as one of the WFCL, is not only an issue of criminal or juvenile justice, but must also be tackled from different approaches. The problem cannot be solved solely by strengthening law enforcement against offenders who use children in illicit activities, and even less so by only punishing those children for the act itself. Even though C182 does not require 'de-criminalization' of the children in the cases where they are used by adults or others, it places the use of children in crimes on the same level as other forms and situations of exploitation where children should be regarded as victims.

A fundamental question therefore might arise; that is, whether it is appropriate to treat children used by adults so distinctly from children who have committed crimes on their own accord, where the mechanisms that draw children into illicit activities are not that obvious. There might already have been a lot going on in the field of crime prevention to help children, irrespective of whether they were used by others. As noted in the case of the RA in the Philippines, there may be many situations where C182 is not heard-of among the communities, actors or authorities facing the increasing use of children in crimes. In turn, those who handle C182 and other ILO standards may not be aware of all the actions in the same country about children in conflict with the law, and information simply does not get reported to the ILO's supervisory mechanisms. While actual knowledge is generally limited for the time being to the involvement of children in drug trafficking, there seems to be a huge potential to use C182 in raising awareness about the issue and also to link the measures of criminal justice with a wider action to tackle the root causes, including educational, economic and social measures.

Immediate action against the worst forms of child labour is exactly what C182 requires the Member States to take, including the cases of using children in illicit activities. Such action must be wide-ranging, from withdrawal and rehabilitation to prevention. On this issue, the 2006 ILO Global Report on Child Labour underlines that there is 'considerable scope for collaboration' with different bodies or agencies interested in the protection of children, and the prevention of crimes. The reference to C182 would be a valuable entry point to raise awareness on the issue and to link various actors for the same cause: prohibiting and effectively eliminating the use of children in illicit activities.

Chapter 9

Hazardous Work as a Worst Form of Child Labour: A Comment on Article 3(d) of ILO Convention 182

Julinda Beqiraj

9.1 Introduction

The proclamation of the eradication of the worst forms of child labour as a major and urgent priority for national and international action that inspired the adoption in 1999 of ILO Convention 182 has shed light on the complex problem of hazardous work performed by children. Defining the worst forms of child labour, article 3 of the Convention includes under the letter (d): 'work which, by its nature or the circumstances in which it is carried out, is likely to harm the health, safety or morals of children'. This type of work is often referred to as 'hazardous work'. The Convention further states that, after determining the harmful types of work for children, national authorities shall take immediate and effective measures towards their prohibition and elimination.

Concern about child labour and the protection of children from its most intolerable forms is also expressed in other relevant international instruments. Foremost among these are article 10(3) of the International Covenant on Economic Social and Cultural Rights (ICESCR) and article 32(1) of the Convention on the Rights of the Child (CRC), which address the economic exploitation of children in hazardous work. However, a gap was perceived in international standards as concerns the setting of clear priorities for national and international action focused on children in hazardous work and in other intolerable situations. In this context, ILO C182 presents a focused and action-oriented response to growing concerns about the widespread phenomenon of child labour in its most intolerable forms.

ILO estimates suggest that in 2004, 126 million child labourers, that is more than 50 per cent of all economically active children, were engaged in hazardous work, and the problem does not concern developing countries only. A decline of the phenomenon of child labour was measured between 2000 and 2004, and this was even larger for children engaged in hazardous work. From a gender perspective, data show that boys are more exposed to work of a hazardous nature than girls, and this difference increases with age. Working children are mainly employed in agriculture (almost 70 per cent) and services (22 per cent), while only 9 per cent are employed in industry. Moreover, the 2002 ILO Global Report indicates that most child labour is found in the informal economy. This invisible part of the phenomenon not only cuts across all economic sectors, but is often closely linked to the formal sector of production through outsourcing to small-scale family production.

Considering the unsettled reasons[1] for the slight progress in the elimination of hazardous work shown by this brief global picture, it should be clear that the starting point of any strategy for action must be the deep understanding of the phenomenon – both of its substance and of the reasons why it is considered to be a worst form of child labour. The creation of a solid framework of child labour laws is particularly important in the context of hazardous work performed by children, given their particular vulnerability in the labour market. Along these lines, this chapter focuses on the analysis of the concept of hazardous work within the ILO system[2] and examines how the ILO supervisory system can mainstream at the national level legislative and pragmatic action against work that is detrimental to the health, safety or morals of children.

9.2 Hazardous work within the ILO framework: a systemic analysis

The unanimous adoption of C182 by the ILC and the very high rate of ratifications obtained in a relatively short period are signs of a broad recognition by the international community of the need to immediately eradicate the worst forms of child labour and, among these, hazardous child labour.[3] However, this was not an ILO success in one go in this domain. It can be submitted that the underlying assumptions to the fight against hazardous child labour as established in article 3(d) of C182 were already present in the existing ILO normative framework.[4] This consideration sheds light on a crucial aspect of hazardous child labour, namely that it is a cross-cutting concept, emerging from the regulation of different labour issues such as age, occupational safety and health, gender, etc. Therefore, in order to better understand the role of

---

1 The ILO acknowledges that 'it is premature to speculate on the reasons for this overall decline'. ILO, *The End of Child Labour: Within Reach*, ILC, 95th session, Report I (B) 2006, at 9.

2 For the link between the ILO and UN systems see Fodella (this volume).

3 See *supra* note 1.

4 This normative framework consists not only of traditional instruments, namely international labour conventions and recommendations, that are technically referred to as 'international labour standards' but also of other types of instruments such as the ILO Declaration on Fundamental Principles and Rights at Work and its Follow-Up (18 June 1998), which is a promotional instrument. The Declaration is nonetheless relevant in the hazardous child labour context, especially from a monitoring perspective. ILO Conventions No. 138 and No. 182 are recognized as the fundamental instruments that single out the right under letter (c) of the Declaration: 'the effective abolition of child labour'. For a critical appraisal of the concept of 'international labour standards' in relation to the Declaration, see P. Alston, '"Core Labour Standards" and the Transformation of the International Labour Rights Regime', *European Journal of International Law*, Vol. 15, 2004, 457–521; B.A. Langille, 'Core Labour Rights – The True Story (Reply to Alston)', *European Journal of International Law*, Vol. 16, 2005, 409–37; F. Maupain, 'Revitalization Not Retreat. The Real Potential of the 1998 ILO Declaration for the Universal Protection of Workers' Rights', *European Journal of International Law*, Vol. 16, 2005, 439–65. See also Swepston (this volume).

C182 in the prevention of hazardous child labour and the removal of children from hazardous work it is important to examine briefly the ILO normative framework in which the adoption of article 3(d) of the Convention on the Worst Forms of Child Labour took place. The analysis that follows will be limited to those instruments and provisions that are strictly related to the issue of hazardous child labour.

Outlining the normative itinerary that led to the adoption of article 3(d) of C182, it can be asserted that the contribution of previous ILO instruments to the articulation of the concept of hazardous child labour is twofold: relatively to the establishment and progressive refinement of the principle of minimum age for employment, which constitutes a necessary conceptual prerequisite in dealing with the problem of hazardous work performed by children,[5] and in relation to the identification and regulation of specific branches of industry or particular conditions of work that are predominantly detrimental to the health of children.

As concerns the first path, in 1919, the ILO adopted the Minimum Age (Industry) Convention No. 5 (C5), which prohibits children under the age of 14 years to be employed or work in industrial establishments. While C5 contains an important derogatory clause for two relevant ILO members, Japan and India, other subsequent conventions and recommendations adopted by the ILO have progressively contributed to raising the standard.[6] Despite frequent exceptions and limitations, these standards brought about progressive improvements by raising the minimum age for employment from 14 to 15 years,[7] by establishing a link between minimum age for work and compulsory education,[8] and by recognizing that certain categories of work and occupations are 'dangerous to the life, health or morals of the persons employed therein' and therefore require a higher minimum age for admission to employment.[9]

This last aspect involves an important distinction between 'hazardous work' in general, and the concept of 'hazardous child labour'. The latter category is included in the former and, in addition, takes account of the particularly detrimental effects

---

5 A. Bequele and W. Myers, *First Things First in Child Labour: Eliminating Work Detrimental to Children*, Geneva, ILO, 1995, at 89.

6 After 1919 the ILO has adopted several other instruments on the minimum age for employment applying to specific sectors such as industry (C5 and C59), agriculture (C10), trimmers and stokers (C15), maritime work (C7 and C58), non-industrial employment (C33, C60 and R41), fishing (C112), underground work (C123 and R124) and family undertakings (R52).

7 See Convention fixing the Minimum Age for the Admission of Children to Employment at Sea (Revised), No. 58; Convention fixing the Minimum Age for Admission of Children to Industrial Employment (Revised), No. 59; Convention concerning the Age for Admission of Children to Non-Industrial Employment (Revised), No. 60.

8 See Convention concerning the Age for Admission of Children to Non-Industrial Employment, No. 33; C60 Minimum Age (Non-Industrial Employment) Convention (Revised).

9 See C59 Minimum Age (Industry) Convention (Revised); C60 Minimum Age (Non-Industrial Employment) Convention (Revised); Convention concerning the Minimum Age for Admission to Employment as Fishermen, No. 112; Convention concerning the Minimum Age for Admission to Employment Underground in Mines, No. 123.

that certain types of work, activities, materials or instruments may have on children. The distinction introduces the second path through which existing ILO instruments have led to the adoption of article 3(d). As to this, while some ILO standards, without making explicit reference to younger people, nonetheless help to depict the panorama of activities and/or occupations which are inherently hazardous,[10] other ILO instruments or provisions set higher standards for various activities and conditions of work performed by children. Along these lines, the ILO conventions of 1919 and 1948 on the Night Work of Young Persons (Industry) establish 18 years as the minimum age for employment during the night.[11] Similarly, underground work, the use of white lead in painting, and employment as trimmers or stokers are regarded as particularly harmful to the health or morals of children and therefore require a higher minimum age for the employment of children and adolescents in such occupations.[12]

On the whole these instruments have played a basic role in setting a specific regulatory regime for the work of younger people employed in different sectors or in specific occupations that can be detrimental to their health and safety. The principles and ideas established therein were bolstered by the adoption of the ILO Minimum Age Convention (No. 138).[13] Indeed, during the 1970s, the fits-and-starts approach in the establishment of a minimum age for work was perceived as rather inadequate and the need for a system renovation was openly acknowledged in the Preamble of C138, stating that 'the time has come to establish a general instrument on the subject, which would gradually replace the existing ones applicable to limited economic sectors, with a view to achieving the total abolition of child labour'.

As concerns children engaged in 'employment or work which by its nature or the circumstances in which it is carried out is likely to jeopardize [their] health, safety or morals', C138 establishes a minimum age of 18 years (article 3), leaving it to national authorities to determine the content of these activities. The same convention further states (article 3(3)) that a lower age of 16 years may be authorized by national authorities after consultation with the employers' and workers' organizations and on condition that (a) the health, safety and morals of children are fully protected

---

10 This group includes the international labour Conventions and Recommendations concerning exposure of workers to radiation, the manual transport of heavy loads, exposure to benzene, anthrax, white phosphorus, asbestos, specific chemicals and to carcinogenic substances and agents, as well as exposure to working environment dangers due to air pollution, noise or vibration.

11 Convention concerning the Night Work of Young Persons Employed in Industry, No. 6; Convention concerning the Night Work of Young Persons Employed in Industry (Revised), No. 90. Nonetheless, the conventions contain multiple flexibility clauses that broadly reduce the strong impact of the provision; this establishes therefore a dynamic goal, to be progressively achieved.

12 Convention fixing the Minimum Age for the Admission of Young Persons to Employment as Trimmers or Stokers, No. 15, art. 2; Convention concerning the Minimum Age for Admission to Employment as Fishermen, No. 112, art. 3; Convention concerning the Use of White Lead in Painting, No. 13, art. 3.

13 Convention concerning Minimum Age for Admission to Employment, No. 138. See ILO, *Child Labour – Targeting the Intolerable*, Geneva, ILO, 1998, at 24.

and that (b) they receive adequate instruction or vocational training in the specific branch of activity. The accompanying Recommendation No. 146 offers support for national policies on these topics and establishes (§ 9) that where the minimum age for admission to hazardous work is below 18 years, immediate steps should be taken to remedy the situation.

Despite focusing mainly on the minimum age for employment, C138 and R146 can be considered to have paved the way for the identification and refining of the concept of 'hazardous work' performed by children as it is established in article 3(d) of C182. However, in comparison to the latter, C138 pursues broader aims and this is reflected in the language of the instrument as well as in its high level of built-in flexibility.[14]

9.3 Hazardous work in the *travaux préparatoires* of C182

In 1996, governments attending the ILC agreed to prepare a new convention on the 'most intolerable forms of child labour', aimed at preventing and eliminating, among other types, 'hazardous forms' of child labour.[15] The common denominator of the types of child labour that were considered consists in their absolute intolerability, irrespective of a country's level of development. While these issues were addressed also in other international instruments, the added value of the new ILO instrument was its entire focus on the extreme forms of child labour and their coverage by one specific instrument.

Hazardous work is one of the topics over which the most fervent discussion among the various actors within the ILO – governments, employers' organizations and trade unions – took place. The debate over what constitutes hazardous child labour and over what forms should be covered by the scope of the new instrument was intense. The adoption of C182 and R190 by June 1999 was possible also as a result of compromises on several points. The following brief account summarizes the major issues concerning hazardous work that were discussed during the negotiations.

9.3.1 Hazardous work as an independent concept

The replies to the questionnaire delivered to States in view of the discussions at the 86th session (1998) of the ILC[16] highlight that, although hazardous work was placed since the beginning among the 'most abusive and intolerable' forms of child labour, its identification as an autonomous category, relatively to the encompassing

---

14 See Borzaga (this volume).

15 ILC, Effect to be given to the resolution concerning the elimination of child labour, adopted by the Conference at its 83rd Session (June 1996), at §§ 4, 9.

16 A questionnaire tackling the main aspects of the future convention was submitted to States and received a record number of replies by Member States and employers' and workers' organizations. On the basis of these replies the Committee on Child Labour prepared a list of Proposed Conclusions that served as a basis for discussion at the 86th Session (1998) of the ILC.

concept of 'worst' or 'extreme' forms of child labour, was initially subject to some confusion.

This inconsistency was probably due to a certain level of ambiguity characterizing the questionnaire itself: it referred to 'any type of work which, by its nature or the circumstances in which it is carried out, is likely to jeopardize [the] health, safety, or morals' of children (question 7(c)) without specifying that this was the definition of hazardous work. Reference to this latter concept was made in the questionnaire only in the heading to questions 13 and 14, regarding the provisions that would have been included in a possible accompanying recommendation. Questions 13 and 14 concerned the concrete action to be taken by States in the determination of the types of work that are detrimental to the health, safety and morals of children, and the inclusion of a non-exhaustive list of examples of these types of work.

The direct link between the provision in question 7(c) and the reference to hazardous work in the heading to questions 13 and 14 does not emerge clearly in some replies. For instance, in their observations, Portugal, New Zealand and Canada indifferently refer to hazardous forms of child labour, 'most intolerable' or 'extreme' forms of child labour – concepts that according to them would include slavery, bonded and forced labour.[17] Although the Portuguese government recognized that 'children should also be protected from work that compromises their future; threatens their safety, health and welfare'[18] it is not clear whether this was considered to be hazardous work. In contrast, positions such as those of the Turkish and Mexican governments or of the Canadian Employers Council (CEC) set forth a clear distinction between the concepts of 'slavery, bonded, forced labour' and other intolerable forms which are generally considered illegal, and 'hazardous work' that, despite being a worst form of child labour, is not illegal and therefore requires a different approach.[19] The latter interpretation was finally adopted in the Proposed Conclusions, which specifically list hazardous work as one of the extreme forms of child labour.[20]

9.3.2 The debate on subparagraph (d)

Besides the issue of the autonomous standing of the category of hazardous work among the worst forms of child labour, a major focus of debate concerned the level of detail in the Convention and the amount of flexibility to be left to national authorities in the determination of hazardous work.[21] Within the group of governments and

---

17 ILC, Report VI(2): Child Labour, 86th Session (June 1998), at 44: Canada's observations under question 7; New Zealand's observations under question 1; Portugal's general observations.

18 ILC, Report VI(2), *supra* note 17, Portugal's general observations.

19 ILC, Report VI(2), *supra* note 17, at 45, 47, 49: Turkey's, Mexico's and Canadian CEC's observations under question 7.

20 The Proposed Conclusions discussed by the Conference Committee in 1998 had referred to 'extreme' forms of child labour, but the reference was later amended to read the 'worst' forms of child labour. ILC, Child Labour, Report IV(2A) presented at the Conference at its 87th Session (1998), at 19.

21 ILC, Report VI(2), *supra* note 17, at 53: Office commentary to question 7.

workers' organizations who wanted the text of the Convention to be more specific[22] – namely on the process for determining hazardous types of work, and on the adoption of a non-exhaustive list of forms of work and working conditions to be considered hazardous – proposals were also advanced to include such provisions in an annex to the Convention.[23] The *ratio* behind these proposals was to qualitatively improve the instrument by eliminating the possibility for governments to set weak criteria.[24] On the contrary, another group opted for abandoning the idea of a universal definition and argued that differences between States in the level of economic, social and technological development should have been taken into consideration.[25] In any case a list in the Convention providing a catalogue of different types of hazardous work was considered by some as 'limitative' and soon to be 'outdated'.[26] Ultimately, agreement was reached on the need for a 'short, clear and concise'[27] text that might quickly obtain universal ratification by ILO Member States. The achieved compromise text of the Convention defines only the contours and the limits within which the determination of what constitutes hazardous work can be established rather flexibly by Member States. More detailed guidelines for national action as well as a non-exhaustive list of hazardous types of work are provided for in the accompanying Recommendation, which is however non-binding.

9.3.3 The issue of education in the definition of hazardous work

Another controversial aspect of the negotiations concerned the establishment of a direct link between hazardous work and its adverse effects on education. More specifically, delegates discussed the proposal advanced by some governments and workers' organizations to include the detrimental effects of some types of work on education opportunities as a qualitative element of the concept of hazardous work.[28] This point was broadly raised in the replies to the questionnaire, and an amendment extending the scope of the Convention to include work that prevents children from taking advantage of compulsory education opportunities was submitted by a large group of governments, including the majority of European States, the US, Canada, New Zealand and Turkey.[29]

---

22 ILC, Report of the Committee on Child Labour, presented at the Conference at its 87th Session (1999), at §§ 10, 176.

23 In this sense see opinions expressed by Canada, Lebanon, Netherlands, Norway and Ukraine under question 7 of the ILC, Report VI(2), *supra* note 17, at 42 ff.

24 ILC, Report VI(2), *supra* note 17, at 50: UK Trade Union Confederation's observations under question 7.

25 US, Korea, Venezuela, New Zealand, India, Canada and Ukraine belong to this group. See ILC, Report VI(2), *supra* note 17, at 42 ff.

26 ILC, Report VI (2), *supra* note 17, at 53: Office commentary on question 7(c).

27 ILC, Report of the Committee on Child Labour, *supra* note 22, at § 24.

28 These detrimental effects can be produced through the number of hours worked, the time of work, or its location. See ILC, Report IV(2A), *supra* note 20: observations on the proposed Convention, Office commentary on article 3(d).

29 ILC, Report of the Committee on Child Labour, *supra* note 22, at § 178.

The inclusion of this element would have been an important junction in the elimination of hazardous forms of child labour. Creating a connection between the establishment of compulsory education in law and practice and the fact that hazardous forms of occupation and work often hinder these opportunities would have sectioned transversally the phenomenon of hazardous work, helping to combat it even in the informal sector or in invisible environments such as domestic occupations.[30] However, the proposal raised concerns among States that a reference to education would have turned out to be an obligation on governments to ensure universal basic education, and, as the Indian delegate noted, this would have raised a significant barrier to the implementation and ratification of the Convention.[31] Moreover, he stressed the fundamental difference between the immediate elimination of the abuses addressed by the Convention and education opportunities that are only achievable 'progressively and in a developmental context'.[32]

Although with some regret, the amendment was finally withdrawn, and the removal of the rehabilitation process for children from the worst forms of child labour served as a compromise issue.[33] Indeed, the education issue reappears in article 7(2)(c) of the Convention in the form of an obligation for States to 'ensure access to free basic education ... for all children removed from the worst forms of child labour'. With regard to the notion of 'basic education', in order to avoid misunderstandings between countries with more or less advanced educational systems,[34] the worker and employer members clarified that basic education includes eight or nine years of education (that is, primary education plus one year) based on curriculum and not on age.[35]

9.3.4 The different approach to hazardous work in relation to C138

Another concern that emerged during the discussions on the adoption of C182 was the similarity with the provisions in article 3 of Convention 138 on the higher minimum age for hazardous work and the implications for the scope of the proposed Convention.[36] On the one hand, the constituents expressed the need for consistency

---

30 See Y. Noguchi, 'ILO Convention No. 182 on the Worst Forms of Child Labour and the Convention on the Rights of the Child', *International Journal of Children's Rights*, Vol. 10, 2002, 355 ff, at 360.

31 ILC, Report of the Committee on Child Labour, *supra* note 22, at § 179.

32 The 'Convention had a more limited scope and was concerned with hazardous work which posed imminent danger or with work which should not be tolerated under any circumstances.' Moreover, mentioning the denial of access to basic education 'would have expanded the scope of the Convention to virtually all forms of child labour which were rooted in poverty' and 'would be tantamount to imposing sanctions on poverty'. See *ibid.*, at §§ 10, 179.

33 *Ibid.*, at §§ 178, 218.

34 The reference to 'basic education' may contrast with C138 which refers to 'the age of completion of compulsory schooling' and with other flexible definitions, such as that given by UNESCO. See ILC, Report IV(2A), *supra* note 20, at 66–7: Office commentary on article 3(d).

35 ILC, Report of the Committee on Child Labour, *supra* note 22, at §§ 218, 388.

36 ILC, Report IV(2A), *supra* note 20, at 62: Office commentary on article 3(d).

while, on the other, there was the desire for a new instrument that would have created immediate, concrete and action-oriented obligations. The final version was the result of a compromise between some governments and workers' organizations that insisted on the insertion of a reference to the complementarity link involving the two conventions,[37] and others, including a fair number of employers' organizations, who were concerned about de-linking the language of subparagraph (d) from that of Convention No. 138.[38]

Despite certain similarities with C138, different principles govern the two instruments. Therefore, while it is established that the new Convention does not replace or undermine Convention 138, and that it is consistent with it, the added value of the new instrument lies in the fact that it deals with certain forms of child labour that cannot be condoned.[39] Convention 138 remains the fundamental ILO Convention for the complete abolition of child labour, and the new instruments help to achieve this goal by considering the immediate elimination of the worst forms of child labour as a priority for action. This being so, the scope of C182 and R190 is more limited,[40] yet they set a higher standard than the one laid down in Convention 138, because States commit themselves more decisively to the prevention and elimination of hazardous work. This can be derived from, firstly, the lack of exceptions for certain branches of economic activity in C182 (as compared with article 5 of Convention 138) or for certain categories of employment or work, under article 4(1); secondly, from the absence of an automatic exclusion for training situations similar to that of article 6 of C138 or in special cases for activities like artistic performances, contemplated in article 8 of C138; and thirdly, from the removal from the Convention of the provision concerning the authorization of certain types of hazardous work from the age of 16 (article 3(3) C138) and its inclusion into the text of the Recommendation.

9.3.5 Hazardous work under article 3(d) of C182 and the accompanying R190

As has been mentioned, the ILO normative framework within which the adoption of article 3(d) took place already contained the principal elements of the concept of 'hazardous work' performed by children. According to this perspective, the added value of article 3(d) of C182 is twofold. On the one hand, article 3(d) provides a better synthesis and crystallization of a notion that was blurrily outlined in a series of previous instruments and provisions. On the other hand, being included in a binding

---

37 The preamble of C182 states: 'Considering the need to adopt new instruments for the prohibition and elimination of the worst forms of child labour, as the main priority for national and international action, including international cooperation and assistance, to complement the Convention and the Recommendation concerning Minimum Age for Admission to Employment, 1973, which remain fundamental instruments on child labour.'

38 ILC, Report IV(2A), *supra* note 20, at 65: Office commentary on article 3(d).

39 *Ibid.* at 10: general commentaries, Federation of Jordanian Chambers of Commerce.

40 At the 87th session of the ILC, the US government delegate commented: 'Rather, the new instrument should be viewed as applicable to a subset of the types of labour covered by Convention No. 138. Such a view does not compromise Convention No. 138. In fact, it permits consistency with Convention No. 138 where appropriate, and going beyond it where necessary.' *Ibid.*, at 17.

instrument that specifically focuses on the worst forms of child labour, article 3(d) strengthens the ILO commitment to the elimination of the most hazardous child labour and set it as a priority for national and international action.[41]

The compromise on the issue of hazardous work was to create a kind of 'empty box' which delineates the contours and limits of the phenomenon at the international level, and contextually leaves some flexibility for national determinations to take into account specific circumstances in different countries.[42] This effect was reached through the binomial definition-determination of the concept of hazardous work. C182 broadly *defines* as hazardous for children under 18 years the 'work which, by its nature or the circumstances in which it is carried out, is likely to harm [their] health, safety or morals' (article 3(d)) and sets an obligation for ratifying States to *determine* at the national level the specific types of hazardous child labour to be prohibited and eliminated (article 4). This should be done after consultation with workers' and employers' organizations; and by taking into consideration the relevant international standards, in particular paragraphs 3 and 4 of R190. Considering the advancing scientific and technological knowledge, the Convention further states that the list determined at the national level should be periodically reviewed in consultation with employers' and workers' organizations (article 4(3)).

In relation to article 3 of C138, the wording of C182 is more precise and targeted. By defining hazardous work only as 'work which by its nature …'[43] and not as 'any type of employment or work', and by using the expression 'likely to harm' instead of the broader 'likely to jeopardize', C182 covers only those types of hazardous work considered as 'worst forms'.[44] This would therefore result in a narrower range of situations to be included in the determinations by national authorities envisaged by article 4 of C182, in comparison to article 3(2) of C138.[45]

---

41 See Preamble of C182.

42 See ILC, Report of the Committee on Child Labour, *supra* note 22, at § 143; ILC, Report IV(2A), *supra* note 20, at 65: Office commentary on article 3(d).

43 In comparison to what was proposed during the drafting of C182, art. 3 now refers to 'work' rather than to 'work or activity'. The intent was to eliminate confusion between the different concepts of 'work', 'activity' and 'occupation', and clarify that 'the type of work determined under Article 4 to come within the definition of subparagraph (d) could be activities or occupations'. See ILC, Report of the Committee on Child Labour, *supra* note 22, at § 143; ILC, Report IV(2A), *supra* note 20, at 65–6: Office commentary on article 3(d).

44 This opinion is confirmed by the discussions during the *travaux préparatoires*. ILC, Report of the Committee on Child Labour, *supra* note 22, at § 10. However, with regard to art. 3(d), the representative of the government of Egypt declared that [his] Government did not interpret the substitution of "jeopardize" with "harm" as adding any new obligations or widening the scope of the proposed Convention as compared to Convention No. 138. This remark also applied equally to art. 4(1), where the phrase "taking into consideration relevant international standards" was added.' See ILC, Report of the Committee on Child Labour, *supra* note 22, at § 255.

45 R. Hernandez-Pulido and T. Caron, 'Protection of Children and Young Persons', in ILO, *Fundamental Rights at Work and International Labour Standards*, Geneva, ILO, 2003, 89 ff, at 109.

Differently from the other forms of child labour covered by C182 (the so-called 'unconditional' worst forms[46]), hazardous work is a concept related to the intolerability of the conditions of work and to the level of occupational safety and health, more than to the intolerability of the work itself. It is a borderline concept covering activities that, despite being performed in legitimate economic sectors, may nonetheless be detrimental to child workers and therefore subjected to penalties.[47] Under this line of reasoning, R190 draws a distinction between subparagraph (d) and subparagraphs (a) to (c), as regards national measures to be taken for the prohibition and elimination of the worst forms of child labour. While the activities in article 3 subparagraphs (a) to (c) should be proclaimed criminal offences by national authorities, for the activities related to article 3(d), R190 suggests that penalties – but not necessarily criminal penalties – be applied when violations occur. However, as has been noted by the International Labour Office, 'the subparagraphs of Article 3 are not mutually exclusive and any particular type of work could fall within one or more of these categories'.[48]

The underlying assumption of the approach of C182 on hazardous child labour is that children, by reason of their physical and psychological vulnerability, are susceptible to specific hazards in the work environment, additional to and different from those affecting adults, both from a quantitative and a qualitative perspective. Therefore, the concept of hazardous work under C182 can be doubly characterized by an objective element, which takes into account the chemical, physical, biological and psychological hazards related to the nature of work or to the conditions in which work is performed, and by a subjective element which takes into account the developmental aspects of childhood. The required causal link between the hazards and the harmful effects for the 'health, safety or morals of children' is more than 'possibility' and less than 'certainty'. This interpretation is confirmed by the negotiating history of article 3(d), which records that the amendment presented by employers' members to replace the words 'is likely to' with the words 'will', referring to the harmful effects produced by hazardous work, was ultimately withdrawn, and it was clarified that the expression 'likely to harm' indicates a link of probability between the work performed and the occurrence of harmful effects.[49] According to the definition, the harmful effects should affect 'the health, safety or morals of children', and the International Labour Office has clarified that 'health', incorporates broadly physical and psychological health.[50] The latter aspect introduces another dimension of the concept of hazardous work as defined in the Convention, one that highlights the importance of combating also those forms of hazardous child labour in which the harmful effects on children are not immediately obvious.

---

46 ILO, *A Future Without Child Labour – the Global Report under the Follow-Up to the ILO Declaration on Fundamental Principles and Rights at Work*, Report to the International Labour Conference, 90th session, 2002, Report I (B), at 11, § 31.

47 *Ibid.*

48 ILC, Report IV(2A), *supra* note 20, at 67: Office commentary on article 3(d).

49 It was also specified that this was different from 'may' which referred to possibility. ILC, Report of the Committee on Child Labour, *supra* note 22, at §§ 171, 174.

50 ILC, Report IV(2A), *supra* note 20, at 65: Office commentary on article 3(d).

The concept of hazardous work is complex and its boundaries cannot always be easily drawn. Hazards for the health, safety or morals of children may be inherent to the nature of work and the tasks to be accomplished, or linked to the circumstances in which work is carried out, such as the use of unsafe tools, exposure to hazardous substances, agents or processes, and the hours and conditions of work. These categories were mentioned in R190,[51] and serve as guidelines for States, workers' and employers' organizations in the determination of what constitutes hazardous work. The preliminary works of the Recommendation highlight that through the use of the formula 'consideration should be given, *inter alia*, to' instead of the original 'should include', the guidance to national legislation was rendered less categorical.[52] The letter of R190 (paragraph 4), as well as the drafting history of C182 suggest that another aspect to be considered is whether adequate training and full protection is provided.[53] Moreover, article 4(1) of C182 identifies the 'relevant international standards' and in particular paragraphs 3 and 4 of R190 as sources to which national authorities must give consideration when determining the types of work referred to under article 3(d).

The standards which can aid in the determination of what is likely to jeopardize the health, safety or morals of children are those referred to in section 9.2 above. However, it is debatable whether an obligatory minimum list could be configured under the Convention; that is, whether the provision of article 4 sets a formal obligation to include certain types or work of activities in the national lists of hazardous work prohibited to children.

There are two issues here. On the one hand, from the letter of article 4 it can be assumed that the obligation therein established is a procedural one, and consists in the examination in good faith by State authorities of the types of work included in these instruments and in the evaluation of the opportunity to include them in national lists. This interpretation is reinforced by the commentary of the International Labour Office, clarifying that the provision of article 4 does not create obligations

---

51 The list includes: (a) work which exposes children to physical, psychological or sexual abuse; (b) work underground, under water, at dangerous heights or in confined spaces; (c) work with dangerous machinery, equipment and tools, or which involves the manual handling or transport of heavy loads; (d) work in an unhealthy environment which may, for example, expose children to hazardous substances, agents or processes, or to temperatures, noise levels, or vibrations damaging to their health; (e) work under particularly difficult conditions such as work for long hours or during the night, or work where the child is unreasonably confined to the premises of the employer.

52 'Giving "consideration to" implies that the list is not necessarily determinative, but must be taken into account in making the determination. Yet it is envisaged that most of the work listed would necessarily be deemed a worst form of child labour.' ILC, Report IV(2A), *supra* note 20: Office commentary on §3 of R.190; ILC, Report VI (2), *supra* note 17: Office commentaries on question 14.

53 Referring to the interpretation of the phrase 'by its nature or the circumstances in which it is carried out', the representative of the Secretary-General suggested considering as a circumstance in which the work was carried out the provision of adequate training or full protection. ILC, Report IV(2A), *supra* note 20: Office commentary on article 3(d).

on Member States which have not ratified other standards to comply with them.[54] On the other hand, the International Labour Office clarified during the preliminary works of C182 that, apart from the necessity for a determination to be made, 'there is no obligatory minimum list under the Convention' and 'there are no grounds for the Committee of Experts[55] to request the inclusion of any particular types of work in the list'.[56] However, in its general observations and individual direct requests on C182 the Committee of Experts persistently calls on the governments to give due consideration to the types of work listed in paragraph 3 of R190, not only when there is no determination of dangerous work, but also if the lists contain very few items. Therefore, the types of work listed in paragraph 3 of R190 could be configured as the minimum content of the national lists of hazardous work prohibited to children. Indeed, it should be emphasized that in several cases the CEACR has asked the governments to indicate whether consideration was given to the types of hazardous work enumerated in paragraph 3 of Recommendation No. 190 that were not included in the national lists.[57]

Another important issue concerns the scope of coverage of the concept of hazardous child labour under C182. Differently from C138, the elimination of hazardous child labour in C182 cuts transversally all sectors, without exceptions. However, even though the issue is not mentioned in the text of C182, interpretatively the work of children employed in *bona fide* family farms or holdings is considered to fall outside the scope of the Convention. This point became the object of an understanding between the workers' and employers' groups, as it emerges from the negotiating history of article 3(d). Nevertheless it was specified that similar situations, in which parents had little or no control over working conditions and therefore could not protect their children from abuse and exploitation, or in which children employed within a family context were subject to abusive working conditions, would have been covered by the Convention.[58]

The last aspect that needs to be mentioned here concerns the supervision and guidance offered by the ILO in the process of national determination of the prohibited types of hazardous child labour. In the first place, the ILO monitors the efforts undertaken by States through its supervisory system, which is considered to be one of the most advanced. Contemporaneously, with the help of its IPEC Programme,[59] the ILO offers guidance and helps mainstreaming action against hazardous child labour at the national level, through technical assistance to Member States and

---

54 ILC, Report IV (2A), *supra* note 20, at 77: Office commentaries on article 4(1).

55 CEACR.

56 *Ibid.*, at 76.

57 CEACR, Individual Direct Request concerning Convention No. 182: Kuwait, 2004, Doc. No. 092004KWT182; CEACR, Individual Direct Requests concerning Convention No. 182: Panama, 2004, Doc. No. 092004PAN182 and 2006 Doc. No. 092006PAN182; CEACR, Individual Direct Request concerning Convention No. 182: Ireland, 2005, Doc. No. 092005IRL182.

58 ILC, Report of the Committee on Child Labour, *supra* note 22, at §§ 172–173.

59 Over the course of the biennium 2006–07, IPEC will be operational in 88 countries with approximately 250 projects. ILO-IPEC, *IPEC Action against Child Labour: Highlights 2006*, Geneva, ILO, 2007 at 29.

programmes involving more countries, aimed at determining hazardous child labour for the first time or at revising existing lists. Efforts are undertaken also at regional levels through workshops involving sharing of information and creation of networks for technical assistance.

9.4 Hazardous work in the light of the ILO supervisory system and of the subsequent practice of Member States

The issues discussed until now have highlighted that the identification and the definition of the concept of hazardous work as one of the worst forms of child labour turned out to be highly controversial. The debate that took place at the ILC on the topic of hazardous child labour epitomizes the different interests and positions of the ILO constituents. Accordingly, the tripartite structure of the International Labour Organization is reflected in the final version of C182 which – as explained above – was the result of compromises on the most contrasting points. ILO Convention 182 leaves broad discretion to individual countries in determining the specific content of what constitutes 'hazardous work'. However, States are not only required to determine hazardous child labour by drafting a list of hazardous types of work prohibited to children under 18, but must also translate the lists into concrete action to eliminate hazardous child labour.

In these regards, the national and international level of normative production, monitoring and implementation are strictly interconnected. Government policy expressed through the channel of the adoption and enforcement of laws is basic in preventing and eliminating the participation of children in hazardous work. This section will discuss some key aspects of this process, namely: the establishment of a minimum age for admission to hazardous employment; definition of hazardous work; the determination of hazardous types of work; useful criteria for the compilation of lists; the role of partnerships in the implementation of C182; main gaps and shortcomings; putting the lists into action and the challenges ahead.

9.4.1 The minimum age for admission to hazardous employment

The system of international supervision and national implementation documents a large variation in national law and practice. A number of countries report that the principle of prohibition and elimination of hazardous child labour is enshrined in their Constitution, while for the majority it is established in other normative acts and/or in judicial decisions and collective agreements.[60] The legislation of several countries is in line with C182, which prohibits the employment of persons under the

---

60 CEACR, Individual Direct Request concerning Convention No. 182: Namibia 2004, Doc. No. 092004NAM182; CEACR, Individual Direct Request concerning Convention No. 182: Brazil 2005, Doc. No. 092005BRA182; CEACR, Individual Direct Request concerning Convention No. 182: Ghana 2005, Doc. No. 092005GHA182; CEACR, Individual Direct Request concerning Convention No. 182: Lesotho 2005, Doc. No. 092005LSO182; CEACR, Individual Direct Request concerning Convention No. 182: Malawi 2005, Doc. No. 092005MWI182. See also Governing Body, Review of Annual Reports under the Follow-Up

age of 18 in hazardous types of work. However, in many other cases there is either a generic proclamation of the principle of prohibition of work that is hazardous for children, without any age specification, or the minimum age for admission to hazardous employment is set at the lower age of 16 or 17.[61] Some countries set a different minimum age for hazardous work for boys and girls. In other cases, and for specific hazardous activities, countries allow the employment of children of 14 and 15 years. Regarding these cases, the Committee of Experts has persistently recalled that Convention 138 only authorizes the employment in hazardous work of children between 16 and 18 years under strict conditions. A few other countries such as Chile, Brazil and Uruguay, fix a higher age, 21 years, for some specific activities, like stevedoring and underground work, or work in cabarets, presenting live performances and offering alcoholic beverages.[62] Similarly, New Zealand and Pakistan, despite having a lower limit of 15 and 14 years respectively for general admission to hazardous types of work, set different age-limits for specific activities. Pakistani's legislation requires a minimum age of 21 for admission to road service transport for occupations other than driver.[63] Armenia records the highest age for admission to some hazardous types of work, which is 23 years.[64]

9.4.2 National definitions of hazardous work

Additional variety in national law and practice derives from the definition of what constitutes hazardous work. Australian law, for instance, protects all workers against hazardous work indiscriminately,[65] while a considerable number of countries include in their legislation a general ban on the engagement of children in work that is dangerous for their safety and health, and many of them make a specific reference to work that is physically arduous. While health and safety of child workers are the two most cited and protected public goods, countries such as Algeria, Belgium, Chile, Iran, Republic of Korea, Burundi, Chad and others mention also the harmful effects on morals, in order to comply with what is required under article 3(d).[66] On several occasions, the CEACR has emphasized that this is an essential element of the definition.

While the general trend in State practice is to define hazardous work alongside the general terms of the C182, in a few cases national definitions of hazardous work

---

to the ILO Declaration on Fundamental Principles and Rights at Work, Part I, 2004, Doc. No. GB.292/4, at 24, § 122.

61 ILO, *Targeting the Intolerable, supra* note 13, at 48.

62 ILO, *Targeting the Intolerable, supra* note 13, at 41–2.

63 CEACR, Individual Direct Request concerning Convention No. 182: Pakistan 2006, Doc. No. 092006PAK182.

64 Governing Body, Review of Annual Reports, *supra* note 60, at 26, § 129.

65 *Ibid.*

66 CEACR, Individual Direct Request concerning Convention No. 182: Algeria 2005, Doc. No. 092005DZA182; ILO-IPEC, *Lists and Laws on Hazardous Child Labour: Eliminating Hazardous Child Labour Step by Step*, CD-Rom compiled by ILO-IPEC, June 2006; ILO, *Targeting the Intolerable, supra* note 13, at 52.

go beyond what is established in article 3(d). Legislation in Angola,[67] Ecuador, Greece and Poland, for example, refers to the detrimental effects on the normal physical and mental development of children.[68] Similarly, article 176 of the Mexican Federal Labour Act (*Ley Federal del Trabajo*) refers to work which on account of its nature or the physical, chemical or biological conditions of the environment in which it is performed, or the composition of the raw materials used, is liable to affect the life, development, and physical and mental health of young persons. Slovenia also prohibits 'work which can have a harmful influence on and seriously endanger children's health or development'.[69] Jamaica and Saint Kitts and Nevis add the notion of education and prohibit work that 'is likely to be hazardous or to interfere with the child's education or to be harmful to the child's health or physical, mental, spiritual or social development'[70] or occupations 'likely to be injurious to his [the child's] life, limb, health or education, regard being had to his physical condition'.[71] In some countries, the involvement of young people in situations in which their inexperience and immaturity could cause risks to their safety or to the safety of others is linked to the concept of hazardous work. Along the same lines, work which young persons might not be able to perform safely due to lack of experience or training or attention to safety is prohibited under the legislation of Lithuania, Malta, Slovenia and Iceland.[72] The Netherlands also proscribes the employment of children in such types of work unless supervision is provided.[73] Similar provisions can also be found in the German Youth Worker Protection Act of 1976 as amended in 2003, which establishes that children under the age of 18 shall not perform work involving risks of accidents that young workers could not avoid due to their lack of awareness or experience.[74] In Finland hazardous work is defined also as work which involves considerable responsibility for personal safety or the safety of others, or which involves accident risks that young persons are unable to identify or avoid because they may not be able to take sufficient account of safety factors or do not have enough training or experience.[75]

---

67 Decree No. 58/82 on Measures for Protection of Children, art. 2. Source: ILO-IPEC, *Lists and Laws*, *supra* note 66.

68 See International Labour Office, *Targeting the Intolerable*, *supra* note 13, at 52.

69 *Ibid.*, at 50.

70 CEACR, Individual Direct Request concerning Convention No. 182: Jamaica 2006, Doc. No. 092006JAM182.

71 CEACR, Individual Direct Request concerning Convention No. 182: Saint Kitts and Nevis, 2006, Doc. No. 092006KNA182.

72 CEACR, Individual Direct Requests concerning Convention No. 182: Malta 2006, Doc. No. 092006MLT182; Lithuania 2006, Doc. No. 092006LTU182; Slovenia 2006 Doc. No. 092006SVN182; Iceland 2005, Doc. No. 092005ISL182.

73 CEACR, Individual Direct Request concerning Convention No. 182: Netherlands 2006, Doc. No. 092006NLD182.

74 CEACR, Individual Direct Request concerning Convention No. 182: Germany 2006, Doc. No. 092006DEU182.

75 CEACR, Individual Direct Request concerning Convention No. 182: Finland 2006, Doc. No. 092005FIN182.

9.4.3 National efforts in the determination of hazardous types of work

As a substitute for, or in addition to a general definition of hazardous work, which focuses mainly on the harm produced or likely to be produced (health, safety, morals or education), countries also include in their legislation more-or-less detailed lists determining the specific hazards in industries, occupations, activities or agents, in relation to which employment of young persons is prohibited. The latter constitutes a precise obligation under article 4(1) of C182 which, as noted by the CEACR, is not accomplished merely through the establishment of a general ban on the employment of children under the age of 18 years in 'any work that is likely to be hazardous or to interfere with the child's education or to be harmful to the child's health or physical, mental, spiritual or social development; or in night work or an industrial undertaking'.[76]

As to the formal features of the lists, article 4(1) establishes that these types of work shall be determined by national laws or regulations or by the competent authority. In State practice, lists are included either as articles of provisions of law or attached as a schedule. Sometimes hazardous work is defined directly, and in a single document (law, code, act), while in other cases the determination of hazardous child labour must be deduced indirectly from provisions scattered in various laws and regulations such as occupational health and safety laws, minimum age legislation, child rights and welfare regulations, and more generally national labour law. In these cases a specific and clear list needs to be put in place or existing ones need to be revised.

As far as the substantial content of the lists is concerned, national practice varies both quantitatively and qualitatively. In 2003, with IPEC's support, the government of Egypt adopted a detailed list of 44 types of hazardous work that are prohibited for children below 18 years. In addition to these, a specific ban is established for the occupation of children who have not reached 16 years in 'types of work where children are exposed to physical, chemical, biological, mechanical hazards or all of them'.[77] In Iran, a law passed by the Council of Ministers provides for a list of 36 types of hazardous work forbidden for persons below 18 years, including work in mines or underground work, work with flammable or explosive materials, work that implies exposure to radioactivity, construction work, work with dangerous machinery, and the production of chemical and toxic substances.

Among the examples of legislative prohibitions one can also find more specific determinations designated by administrative authorities. The US State Department of Labour, for instance, has issued 28 Hazardous Occupations Orders under the Federal Fair Labor Standards Act (FLSA): 17 for young persons under the age of 18 employed in non-agricultural sectors, and 11 orders for children under the age of 16 employed

---

76 CEACR, Individual Direct Request concerning Convention No. 182: Jamaica, 2006, *supra* note 70.

77 CEACR, Individual Direct Request concerning Convention No. 182: Egypt 2006, Doc. No. 092006EGY182.

in agricultural activities.[78] The Mongolian legislation on this topic highlights the complexity that some of these listings may imply. An order of the Minister of Health and Social Welfare issued in 1999 establishes a list of jobs prohibited to children which, without addressing the psycho-social effects of hazardous work, includes 16 sections reflecting different sectors of employment, each one split into specific occupations, materials and processes to be prohibited.[79]

The adoption of lists becomes more significant when different actors, such as the workers' and employers' organizations, are involved in the process. Between 2003 and 2004, Morocco and Nicaragua adopted lists containing the types of hazardous work for children and in both cases the CEACR noted with interest that these lists had been prepared in consultation with the social partners, and in Nicaragua also with the involvement of governmental institutions, NGOs, employers' and workers' organizations and universities.[80] A similar multilateral involvement, bringing together representatives of workers and employers, experts in the field, representatives of academia, and the government, led to the determination of a catalogue of prohibited occupations for minors in the Republic of Korea.

In addition to observations concerning the determination of prohibited hazardous work for children, on several occasions the CEACR has requested that governments take measures to plan periodic reviews and revisions of the adopted lists, because technological and industrial development and changes in work processes may engender or remove risks. In Sri Lanka, for example, the introduction of new machineries in the diamond industry induced new hazards of exposure to solvents and laser rays.[81] The EU members generally complement listings of harmful agents and occupations with references to relevant EU Directives.[82]

---

78 ILO, *Targeting the Intolerable, supra* note 13, at 51; CEACR, Individual Observation concerning Convention No. 182: United States 2003, Doc. No. 062003USA182.

79 ILO-IPEC, *Resources and Processes for Implementing the Hazardous Child Labour Provisions of ILO Conventions Nos 138 and No. 182*, Report of the ILO Asian Regional Tripartite Workshop held in Phuket, Thailand, 11–13 July 2005, at 138–145.

80 CEACR, Individual Direct Requests concerning Convention No. 182: Morocco 2006, Doc. No. 092006MAR182; Nicaragua 2006, Doc. No. 092006NIC182.

81 ILO-IPEC, *Resources and Processes, supra* note 79, at 79.

82 See Council Directive 83/477/EEC of 19 September 1983 on the Protection of Workers from the Risks Related to Exposure to Asbestos at Work, Official Journal, L 263, 24 September 1983, at 25–32; Commission Directive 91/322/EEC of 29 May 1991 on Establishing Indicative Limit Values by Implementing Council Directive 80/1107/EEC on the Protection of Workers from the Risks Related to Exposure to Chemical, Physical and Biological Agents at Work, Official Journal, L 177, 5 July 1991, at 22–4; Council Directive 96/82/EC of 9 December 1996 on the Control of Major-Accident Hazards Involving Dangerous Substances, Official Journal, L 10, 14 January 1997, at 13–33; Directive 2000/54/EC of the European Parliament and of the Council of 18 September 2000 on the Protection of Workers from Risks Related to Exposure to Biological Agents at Work, Official Journal, L 262, 17 October 2000, at 21–45; Directive 2003/10/EC of the European Parliament and of the Council of 6 February 2003 on the Minimum Health and Safety Requirements Regarding the Exposure of Workers to the Risks Arising from Physical Agents (Noise), Official Journal, L 42, 15 February 2003, at 38–44.

In general, underground work, work with dangerous machinery, equipment and moving tools, and work involving the manual carrying of heavy weights are among the examples that most frequently appear in the listings.[83] As regards the last category, several countries regulate in detail the maximum amounts of weight allowed for specific ages and differentiated by gender (for example, Niger, Congo, Benin, Mali and Egypt).[84] Other categories of hazardous work are linked to the geographical position of a country, the characteristics of its economy or its cultural tradition. This explains why certain types of hazardous work appear more frequently in the listings in certain areas of the world. Mineral-producing countries like Colombia, for example, include in the list of prohibited work for children underground employment in mines; the Philippines' and other island economies' legislations incorporate underwater work and deep-sea fishing; poor countries like Bangladesh, Sri Lanka or Togo comprise domestic labour, and tourist destination countries like Thailand or Mexico include the entertainment industry or specific activities like 'camel jockeys' in the case of United Arab Emirates.[85]

9.4.4 The criteria for the compilation of lists

The identification of objective criteria for the compilation of lists has been an important difficulty encountered by States in the implementation of the provision of article 4(1) of C182. As to this, the Sri Lankan experience sheds light on some useful standards for the compilation of a list of hazardous occupations and for prioritization among these. The Sri Lankan National Labour Advisory Council, a tripartite body chaired by the Minister of Employment and Labour, extended an initial list of 25 occupations likely to harm the health, safety or morals of children to 49 occupations, following criteria such as: the potential for occupational accidents, biological, chemical, ergonomic, physical and psycho-social hazards; overall negative working conditions; gender issues; seriousness of the impact on health and development; visibility of the specific hazardous work; and concentration and quantity of exposure to the hazard.[86] The criteria used were a more elaborated version of a simple tool developed initially in the Philippines for assessing hazards involved in the work environment. The Hazard Rating Matrix considers several degrees of safety of working conditions (work environment, materials and equipment) and the different work intensity (frequency and duration of work, body position, movements involved in the task).[87]

---

83 ILO, *Targeting the Intolerable, supra* note 13, at 49.

84 ILO-IPEC, *Lists and Laws, supra* note 66.

85 ILO, *Targeting the Intolerable, supra* note 13, at 48; CEACR, Individual Observation concerning Convention No. 182: United Arab Emirates 2005, Doc. No. 062005ARE182.

86 By July 2005 the list was in the process of being approved and incorporated in a revised version of the Employment of Women, Young Persons and Children Act. See ILO-IPEC, *Resources and Processes, supra* note 79, at 79.

87 In that specific case the matrix was used to identify work hazards that might not appear as harmful for children. ILO, *A Future Without Child Labour, supra* note 46, at 64.

9.4.5 The role of partnerships in the implementation of Convention 182

Article 8 of the Convention sets an obligation of 'mutual assistance' for States ratifying the Convention. As to this, the Legal Adviser of the ILO 'stressed the idea of partnership contained in the spirit of the Article', while emphasizing that 'it was up to individual States to decide on those appropriate steps'.[88] As concerns the specific topic of this chapter, insofar as country experiences with hazardous child labour are similar, dialogue and sharing of information on the resources and processes for implementing the hazardous child labour provisions of C182 and C138 at the regional level may become a significant strategy.

A networking effort of this kind was organized under the sponsorship of ILO-IPEC during a regional tripartite workshop in July 2005, with the participation of delegations from 13 States of South, South East and East Asia, along with ILO specialists on health and safety issues, employers' and workers' organizations. The workshop was a successful experiment presenting an important opportunity to clarify the obligations of ratifying States under C182, broadening information and knowledge about the determination of lists of hazardous work prohibited to children, and linking with resources for the needed technical expertise.[89] Among EU member countries, a process of harmonization of national legislations on the issue of protection of young people at work has taken place along the institutionalized track of EU directives. The Council Directive 94/33EC on the protection of young people at work, which anticipates many of the principles established by C182 on hazardous child labour, requires Member States to conform their legislation to the system of protection laid down by the directive.[90] Its scope of application covers any work that is likely to harm the 'safety, health or physical, mental, moral or social development' of young people or to 'jeopardize their education', but is limited only to employment relationships or contracts.[91]

The exploitation of regional synergies has been highlighted by IPEC also as a relevant strategy for concrete action towards the removal of children from hazardous work and their rehabilitation.[92] Along these lines IPEC is involved in different regional projects, such as the cocoa/commercial agriculture project in West and Central Africa; the commercial and agriculture project in Eastern and Southern Africa; the child domestic labour project involving Kenya, Tanzania, Uganda and Zambia in Africa and Cambodia, Indonesia, Pakistan and Sri Lanka in Asia; the project on the prevention and elimination of child labour in mining in West Africa; several regional projects on skills, training, and vocational education in Africa; and many others.[93]

---

88 ILC, Report of the Committee on Child Labour, *supra* note 22, at §§ 242, 243.

89 ILO-IPEC, *Resources and Processes, supra* note 79.

90 Council Directive 94/33/EC of 22 June 1994 on the Protection of Young People at Work, Official Journal L 216, 20 August 1994, 12–20.

91 A peculiar aspect of the directive is that it sets obligations on States as well as on employers.

92 ILO-IPEC, *IPEC Action against Child Labour 2004–2005: Progress and Future Priorities*, Geneva, ILO, February 2006, at 26–33.

93 *Ibid.*

9.4.6 Principal gaps and shortcomings in the adoption of lists

Through individual observations and direct requests, the CEARC offers guidance to States in the process of adaptation of their legislation to the standard set by C182, also by highlighting specific gaps in the national normative regime due to peculiar circumstances in that country. In the case of Benin, for example, besides recognizing the efforts undertaken for the adoption of detailed provisions on the activities prohibited to children, the CEACR noted that the list did not mention any type of work that would harm the morals of children. Being concerned about the situation of 100,000 '*vidomégons*'[94] children in Benin, the Committee of Experts invited the government to report on the measures taken to include in the list of hazardous types of work, also work which exposes children to physical, psychological or sexual abuse, in line with paragraph 3 of R190.[95] Referring to the situation in Madagascar, the CEACR underlined the need for revision of the existing legislation on the prohibition of hazardous work for children and welcomed the incorporation of such revisions in the national Labour Code. In other cases like Suriname, the major obstacle rests with the lengthy procedure for the amendment and adoption of legislation.[96]

Besides reporting on specific shortcomings, the CEACR has often highlighted also more serious gaps in the implementation of the hazardous child labour provisions of C182. Quite often, the hidden side of the adoption of detailed and comprehensive lists of forbidden hazardous activities for minors is their limited applicability to certain sectors, an aspect that drastically narrows the scope of such efforts. Self-employed work occurring in hazardous conditions, for example, is frequently left uncovered by legislation prohibiting hazardous work.[97] The Committee of Experts has raised the point several times in 2005 and 2006, asking States to take the necessary measures to secure the protection of self-employed child workers. Other

---

94 The CEACR report explains that '*vidomégons*' are 'children placed in the home of a third party by their parents or by an intermediary in order to provide them with education and work. Once considered a sign of traditional solidarity between parents and family members, the practice has become open to abuse. Some of the children involved in the system are subjected to ill-treatment, or even physical and psychological violence.' See CEACR, Individual Direct Request concerning Convention No. 182: Benin 2005, Doc. No. 092005BEN182.

95 *Ibid*. This reflects a broader problem illustrated during the ILO-Asian regional tripartite workshop on hazardous child labour. Among the results was the recognition of a tendency to focus principally on the physical hazards and less on psycho-social effects of hazardous child labour. Out of 13 States reviewed only two include psycho-social effects in their lists. See *supra* note 79.

96 Governing Body, Review of Annual Reports, 2004, *supra* note 60, at 30, § 142.

97 CEACR, Individual Direct Requests concerning Convention No. 182: Mongolia 2005, Doc. No. 092005MNG182; Iran 2006, Doc. No. 092006IRN182; Benin 2005, Doc. No. 092005BEN182; Ethiopia 2006, Doc. No. 092006ETH182; Cameroon 2006, Doc. No. 092006CMR182; Algeria 2005, Doc. No. 092005DZA182; Chad 2006, Doc. No. 092006TCD182; Switzerland 2006, Doc. No. 092006CHE182. Differently, in the case of Hungary the Committee of Experts noted with interest that the provisions of the code regarding work performed by persons under 18 years were extended to work performed by way other than an employment contract. CEACR, Individual Observation concerning Convention No. 182: Hungary 2006, Doc. No. 092006HUN182.

common exclusions from coverage concern employment in small agricultural farms; family undertakings defined more or less rigorously; small undertakings employing less than a certain number of workers; domestic service, apprentices or traineeship; and temporary and casual workers.[98] Exclusions may be of little importance and less visible in a certain economy or attract the attention of different actors at the national and international levels, as occurred with children employed in agriculture in the US. The issue became the object of a constructive 'dialogue' – consisting of comments from the CEACR, observations made by employers' and workers' organizations, subsequent replies from States, and an individual observation by the Conference Committee in 2006 – intended to gradually address the loopholes in legislation and enforcement.[99]

9.4.7 Putting the lists into action: the challenges ahead

Besides drawing up a national list of hazardous work prohibited to children, States ratifying C182 must accomplish two additional obligations: one concerning the identification of where the types of hazardous work determined in the lists exist (article 4(2)), and the other requiring the designation and implementation of programmes of action for the elimination of the hazardous forms of child labour (article 6(1)). Therefore, putting the lists into action becomes the next challenge in the implementation at the national level of the hazardous child labour provisions of C182. This process, however, is far from easy.

A first obstacle consists in the above-mentioned gaps in the existing laws. Secondly, there is an issue of enforcement of existing legislation.[100] Indeed, weak enforcement mechanisms seriously impair effective legal protection. Thirdly, while legislation is necessary in the fight against hazardous child labour, law by itself is insufficient for its elimination, because it cannot protect children in places where the law does not reach, such as the informal economy.[101] It follows that in those areas where the law does not function well, legal prohibition must be combined with concrete action for combating hazardous child labour. As noticed above, IPEC has played and continues to play a crucial role in supporting national responses in this regard.

As to these challenges, the number of labour inspectors enforcing national measures plays a crucial role in the protection of the health, safety and welfare of

---

98 CEACR, Individual Direct Requests concerning Convention No. 182: Iran 2006, Doc. No. 092006IRN182; Bahrain 2005, Doc. No. 092005BHR182; Morocco 2006, Doc. No. 092006MAR182.

99 The process that continues since 1999 can be traced through the periodical individual observations and individual direct requests of the Committee of Experts as well as from the Individual Observation of the Conference Committee in 2006.

100 The Committee of Experts has raised this problem with regard to the situation in the Democratic Republic of the Congo. CEACR, Individual Observation concerning Convention No. 182: Democratic Republic of the Congo 2006, Doc. No. 062006COD182.

101 See note by the ILO Director-General Juan Somavia in ILO, Combating Child Labour: Building Alliances Against Hazardous Work, Conference held in the Hague, Netherlands, 25–27 February 2002.

children. In the informal sector the importance of labour inspectors may captured by extending their monitoring and investigating powers to the conditions of all children involved in hazardous work, whether in the formal or in the informal sector. Progress, however is not straightforward because of the multiple difficulties encountered by labour inspectors, such as the lack of material and economic resources, or the lack of appropriate training on the special vulnerability of children and the special hazards to which they are exposed.[102] Therefore, progress in enforcement requires the involvement and cooperation of different actors, such as governments, labour inspectorates, social partners, international organizations, and NGOs, operating at different levels – prevention, removal, rehabilitation, social assistance, health and education.

9.5 Concluding remarks

As reported at the beginning of this chapter, the majority of all working children are engaged in hazardous types of work. Therefore, understanding, determining and combating hazardous child labour is crucial for the abolition of child labour. In this context, the implementation of the hazardous child labour provisions of C182 provides the international community with the challenge of translating the contours of the discipline thereby established into pragmatic norms and targeted action.

The analysis of this chapter has highlighted that C182 was conceived to allow States to tailor their fight against hazardous child labour to the specific form the phenomenon takes in each national context. In other words, it sets an obligation of result and not an obligation of means. However, States are not left alone in their efforts to combat hazardous child labour. The ILO's contribution in this respect is both multi-faceted and multi-level. Through conciliatory instruments such as technical assistance and legal advice to governments, and through its unique supervisory system, the ILO guides the process of implementation of the obligations on hazardous child labour contained in C182.

However, it has become clear that while national and international standards are necessary to tackle hazardous child labour, law by itself is insufficient for its elimination because the phenomenon often occurs between the folds of the system, where law does not exist or is inappropriate. In this regard the increased focus of national policies on pragmatic action – both preventive and rehabilitative – against hazardous child labour represents an important tool in the fight against hazardous child labour on a lasting basis.

---

102 ILO, *Targeting the Intolerable, supra* note 13, at 91.

PART II
The Implementation of Child Labour Standards: Selected Instruments and ILO's Interaction with Other International Organizations

Chapter 10

Freedom from Child Labour as a Human Right: The Role of the UN System in Implementing ILO Child Labour Standards

Alessandro Fodella

10.1 Introduction: the role of the UN system in the fight against child labour

The role of the United Nations in the fight against child labour, and especially the worst forms of it, is certainly a crucial one in many respects.

Historically, the action of the UN in this area of law has almost paralleled that of the ILO, following the course marked out by the latter in some cases, but also leading the way in others. The first steps taken by the UN in this area of international law date back more than fifty years ago, with the adoption of treaties indirectly dealing with specific aspects of what will later be defined as the 'worst forms' of child labour.[1] A first attempt to deal with the issue from a general perspective was made in 1966, with the adoption by the UN General Assembly of the International Covenant on Economic, Social and Cultural Rights,[2] which already enshrined some general key principles in this field some years before the ILO adopted one of its main general instruments on the matter: the Convention concerning Minimum Age for Admission to Employment.[3] The most significant UN instrument in this regard, however, is certainly the Convention on the Rights of the Child, adopted 23 years later in 1989.[4] The CRC not only embodied some fundamental general provisions on the protection of the child related to work as such; it tackled also some specific issues relating to the exploitation of children, that the ILO built upon for the development of its fight against the worst forms of child labour, in particular with the adoption of the Convention concerning the Prohibition and Immediate Action for the Elimination of

---

1 See the Convention for the Suppression of the Traffic in Persons and of the Exploitation of the Prostitution of Others (hereafter: UN Convention on Traffic in Persons and Prostitution) and the United Nations Supplementary Convention on the Abolition of Slavery, the Slave Trade, and Institutions and Practices Similar to Slavery (hereafter: UN Supplementary Convention on Slavery). Both treaties are available at <www.ohchr.org/english/law>.

2 Hereafter: ICESCR, available at <www.ohchr.org/english/law>.

3 Hereafter: C138 Minimum Age Convention.

4 Hereafter: CRC, available at <www.ohchr.org/english/law>.

the Worst Forms of Child Labour[5] ten years after the CRC. In this regard, the UN was arguably the trigger for subsequent intense development of the international agenda in this sector, explicitly inspiring the evolution of the normative framework on the matter. Even when the ILO took the leadership in this sector of international law, the UN did not step out of the process. On the contrary, its role was enhanced through the adoption of several other crucial initiatives, at the institutional and normative level. More and more UN agencies and UN-related organizations started to deal with this issue,[6] but, more significantly, important ad hoc normative instruments on the so-called 'worst forms' of child labour were adopted within the UN.[7]

While it is thus clear that the UN has significantly integrated, expanded and even inspired ILO standards on the matter, its role has arguably gone beyond this. In fact, apart from its quantitative contribution to the international legal and institutional framework in this field, the UN has been decisive also from the qualitative point of view, by shifting the overall perspective on child labour at the international level. Within the UN system, the issue has been taken beyond the conceptual construction or the mere implementation of labour standards, and has been addressed in terms of fundamental rights of the individual. From the normative point of view, the inclusion of the fight against child labour in UN human rights instruments has transformed the issue, from a 'simple' question of standard-setting to a real human rights issue: in other words, the fight against child labour has eventually developed, as the title of the present contribution suggests, into *freedom from child labour as a human right*.[8]

Such a change of perspective has not only affected the substantial, normative framework, but has also improved the implementation machinery on child labour. In

---

5 Hereafter: C182 Worst Forms of Child Labour Convention.

6 See, for example, the activities of UNICEF (<www.unicef.org/protection/index.html>), UNESCO especially as far as education is concerned (<www.unesco.org/education/index. shtml>), and more recently the FAO on child labour in agriculture (<www.fao.org/SARD/ en/init/964/2687/2875/index.html>). On the action of intergovernmental organizations on child labour, see B. White, 'Shifting Positions on Child Labor: the Views and Practice of Intergovernmental Organizations', in B.H. Weston (ed.), *Child Labor and Human Rights: Making Children Matter*, London, Lynne Rienner, 2005, 319 ff.

7 For example, the Optional Protocol to the Convention on the Rights of the Child on the sale of children, child prostitution and child pornography (hereafter: CRC Optional Protocol on Sale and Sexual Exploitation of Children); Optional Protocol to the Convention on the Rights of the Child on the involvement of children in armed conflict (hereafter: CRC Optional Protocol on Children in Armed Conflict); Protocol to Prevent, Suppress and Punish Trafficking in Persons, Especially Women and Children, Supplementing the United Nations Convention Against Transnational Organized Crime (hereafter: Transnational Organized Crime Convention Protocol on Trafficking in Persons). All treaties are available at <www. ohchr.org/english/law>.

8 On the issue of child labour from the point of view of the international protection of human rights see G. Van Bueren, *The International Law on the Rights of the Child*, Dordrecht, Martinus Nijhoff, 1995, at 262 ff; C. Campiglio, 'La tutela internazionale del fanciullo da nuove forme di violenza', *Rivista internazionale dei diritti dell'uomo*, 1996, 549 ff; Weston (ed.), Child Labor, *supra* note 6; M.C. Maffei, 'La tutela internazionale dei diritti del bambino', in L. Pineschi (ed.), *La tutela internazionale dei diritti umani*, Milan, Giuffrè, 2006, 251 ff.

this regard, as will be seen, the monitoring mechanisms of the ILO have generally been supplemented by the UN human rights ones.

The role of the UN system in this regard may be very important, also due to the very nature of the issue at stake. In fact, 'child labour' is not really a single issue, but rather a complex and a multi dimensional one, which is linked with, and touches upon, many others, especially in the area of human rights.[9] Fighting against child labour means also dealing with *inter alia* the right to education, the prohibition of slavery and non-discrimination, the regulation of armed conflicts, and poverty eradication and development. One should therefore take into account the overall institutional and normative framework in these related fields and for these linked issues. From this point of view, the UN system may be particularly significant, as the UN as a whole seems the only forum that might be capable of dealing with such a multifaceted issue in a comprehensive manner, addressing such a diversified matter with all its ramifications and implications for international law.

10.2 General principles and obligations on child labour in the UN system

Within the UN system, only a few general norms have been developed to address child labour as such, often only indirectly. A more substantial normative and implementation framework is devoted to the elimination of specific problems, which are defined as 'worst forms' of child labour in the context of the ILO. Whereas we will concentrate on the second set of issues in the next section, an account of the first norms will be provided in the present one. In this regard, general, broad provisions, directly or indirectly relevant for child labour, are contained in the two Covenants adopted in 1966, the International Covenant on Civil and Political Rights[10] and the ICESCR, as well as in the CRC.

10.2.1 The International Covenant on Civil and Political Rights

The ICCPR contains only a general provision on the protection of the child, which states that 'Every child shall have, without any discrimination ... the right to such measures of protection as are required by his status as a minor, on the part of his family, society and the State.'[11] While the norm does not address child labour as such, the Human Rights Committee (HRC, the treaty body in charge of monitoring the implementation of, and compliance with, the Covenant)[12] seems to suggest that the provision may be linked to the establishment of a minimum age for work (even if no specific standard is set),[13] and to a more general prohibition of child

---

9 See B.H. Weston and M.B. Teerink, 'Rethinking Child Labour: A Multidimensional Human Rights Problem', in Weston (ed.), *Child Labour, supra* note 6, 3 ff.

10 Hereafter: ICCPR, available at <www.ohchr.org/english/law>.

11 ICCPR, art. 24(1).

12 On the monitoring mechanism of the ICCPR, see *infra* section 10.3.1, in particular note 70.

13 'States should also indicate the age at which a child is legally entitled to work and the age at which he is treated as an adult under labour law' (HRC, General Comment No. 17:

exploitation for labour purposes.[14] The ICCPR, which provides also for a remarkable monitoring system, may be more relevant in addressing some of the worst forms of child labour.[15]

10.2.2 The International Covenant on Economic Social and Cultural Rights

The ICESCR is certainly more important from this point of view. Article 10(3) establishes that:

> ... Children and young persons should be protected from economic and social exploitation. Their employment in work harmful to their morals or health or dangerous to life or likely to hamper their normal development should be punishable by law. States should also set age limits below which the paid employment of child labour should be prohibited and punishable by law.

This provision is supplemented by other norms in the Covenant: article 12 recognizes the right to the highest attainable standard of health and requires Parties to adopt provisions 'for the healthy development of the child'. To this end,[16] article 13 includes obligations regarding the right to education, such as primary free and compulsory education for all children. Overall the ICESCR seems to embody the following fundamental general principles: children should be protected from exploitation,[17] *inter alia* by setting minimum age limits for their paid employment and by prohibiting those forms of work that may be harmful or dangerous for them, or that may hamper their normal development and their education. Given the nature of ICESCR's obligations, these should be considered as objectives that States would be required to achieve through a process of progressive implementation, taking concrete steps to the maximum of their available resources[18] (although article 10 §3

Rights of the Child (art. 24), 7/4/1989, § 4, available at <http://www.ohchr.org/english/bodies/hrc/comments.htm>).

14 See, for example, HRC, Concluding Observations on Uganda, ICCPR, A/59/40 vol. I (2004) 47 at § 70(20): 'The State party should adopt measures to avoid the exploitation of child labour and to ensure that children enjoy special protection, in accordance with article 24 ...'; Kyrgyzstan (ICCPR, A/55/40 vol. I (2000) 57 at § 413); Portugal (ICCPR, A/58/40 vol. I (2003) 56 at § 83(19)); Uzbekistan (ICCPR, A/60/40 vol. I (2005) 56 at § 89(25)); Brazil (*infra* note 150). All HRC Concluding Observations are available at <www.ohchr.org/english/bodies/hrc/sessions.htm>.

15 See *infra* section 10.3, in particular 10.3.1.

16 ICESCR, art. 12(2)(a).

17 On the concept of 'exploitation' see Van Bueren, *The International Law*, *supra* note 8, at 264 ff.

18 ICESCR, art. 2(1). See also Committee on Economic Social and Cultural Rights (hereafter: CESCR) (on the CESCR see *infra* note 22), General Comment n. 3: article 2(1): The Nature of States Parties Obligations, Fifth session, 1990, E/1991/23 available at <www.ohchr.org/english/bodies/cescr/comments.htm>; M.C.R. Craven, *The International Covenant on Economic, Social, and Cultural Rights*, Oxford, Clarendon Press, 1995, at 106 ff; L. Pineschi, 'Il Patto delle Nazioni Unite sui diritti economici sociali e culturali', in L. Pineschi (ed.), *La tutela internazionale*, *supra* note 8, 129 ff, at 131 ff.

has been mentioned as an example of a provision that is also 'capable of immediate application by judicial and other organs in many national legal systems'[19]).

These obligations reflect ILO standards, though with some differences. The ICESCR establishes a general prohibition of exploitation and of harmful work that is wider than the relevant ILO standards, and supplementary to them in this regard.[20] As far as minimum age requirements are concerned, the ICESCR establishes only a general obligation to set a minimum age, without providing an international standard, thus leaving much flexibility to the parties. On the other hand, minimum age, in the Covenant, refers only to 'paid employment', with the consequence that the ICESCR does not prohibit unpaid employment or work by children under a certain age.[21]

An important role in clarifying these provisions has been played by the monitoring mechanism of the treaty, managed by the CESCR.[22] The latter has given, through its Concluding Observations on States' reports as well as its General Comments, some interesting indications as to how the general obligations on child labour identified above should be interpreted and implemented, and in doing so it has very often made reference, directly and indirectly, to ILO standards. Based on the CESCR's Observations and Comments one may argue that a State may not be in compliance with the ICESCR *inter alia* when the incidence of child labour is too high;[23] when it is carried out at the expense of school attendance or hampers the right to education;[24]

---

19 CESCR, General Comment n. 3, *supra* note 18, at § 5.

20 The C138 Minimum Age Convention provides for exceptions to its application for some categories or types of work or economic sectors, and the C182 Worst Forms of Child Labour Convention applies only to certain categories of worst forms of child labour.

21 The ICESCR has thus a more restricted scope of application than the relevant ILO standards, as the ILO C138 Minimum Age Convention sets age-limits for 'employment or work'.

22 On the mechanism for the monitoring of ICESCR's implementation and compliance and the CESCR see P. Alston, 'The Committee on Economic, Social and Cultural Rights', in P. Alston (ed.), *The United Nations and Human Rights: A Critical Appraisal*, Oxford, Clarendon Press, 1992, 473 ff; Craven, *The International Covenant*, *supra* note 18, at 30 ff.

23 See, for example, CESCR Concluding Observations on Colombia, E/1996/22 (1995) 41 at § 189; Paraguay, E/1997/22 (1996) 22 at § 77; Russian Federation, E/1998/22 (1997) 27 at § 104. All CESCR Concluding Observations are available at <www.ohchr.org/english/bodies/cescr/sessions.htm>.

24 See, for example, CESCR Concluding Observations on Vietnam, E/1994/23 (1993) 34 at § 142; Morocco, E/1995/22 (1994) 28 at § 116; Egypt, E/2001/22 (2000) 38 at § 163. Some Observations can be very specific, such as that on Tunisia (E/2000/22 (1999) 36 at § 169) whereby 'The discrepancy between the age fixed in law for the completion of mandatory education, which is 16 years, and the minimum age for employment, which is 15 years for the manufacturing sector and 13 years for the agricultural sector, is of concern', or that on Mexico (E/2000/22 (1999) 62 at § 384), whereby 'The State party's lack of commitment to increasing the minimum working age of children from 14 to 16 years is regretted, since the age of 16 is when basic education is normally concluded'. Moreover, in a General Comment the inextricable link between the right to education and the fight against child labour is emphasized, *inter alia*, by establishing an obligation for States Parties 'to ensure that communities and families are not dependent on child labour' (CESCR, General Comment n. 13: Article 13: The Right to Education, Twenty-first session, 1999, E/2000/22 (1999) 111 at § 55).

when there is a lack of labour legislation or of its implementation;[25] or when no measures are taken to fight some of the worst forms of child labour.[26] Some of the above-mentioned observations are already in line, sometimes specifically, with ILO standards on the matter.[27] But elsewhere the CESCR has even taken ILO standards as the explicit reference for the assessment of the respect of the ICESCR: in some cases countries are simply encouraged to ratify the relevant ILO instruments, in some others they are explicitly[28] or implicitly[29] required to implement and respect them in order to comply with the CESCR, with particular reference to ILO Conventions 138 and 182. The CESCR seems to have taken ILO standards as the reference for ICESCR's implementation in general, sometimes even beyond the requirements of the Covenant as such,[30] and even if the countries concerned are not parties to the instruments

---

25 See, for example, Concluding Observations on Morocco, *supra* note 24, at § 116; Philippines E/1996/22 (1995) 30 at § 112; Peru, E/1998/22 (1997) 33 at § 161; Sri Lanka, E/1999/22 (1998) 22 at § 76.

26 See, for example, forced labour (Concluding Observations on Estonia, *infra* note 28 and Congo, *infra* note 58), traffic of children (*infra* note 87), child soldiers (*infra* note 116) and sexual exploitation (*infra* note 151).

27 The Concluding Observations on Tunisia and Mexico (*supra* note 24), for example, seem to recall the requirements of ILO C138 Minimum Age Convention on the relationship between minimum working age and age of completion of compulsory school (C138 Minimum Age Convention, art. 2 (3)).

28 See, for example, CESCR, Concluding Observations on Peru, E/1998/22 (1997) 33 at § 163: 'Other steps should be taken to prevent and combat the use of child labour, based on the full observance of international standards relating to the minimum age for the employment of children, as set forth in ILO Convention No. 138 ...'; Uruguay, E/1998/22 (1997) 67 at § 370: '... the minimum working age as provided for in ILO Convention No. 138 ... is not fully respected ...'; Germany, E/1999/22 (1998) 54 at § 332: 'Effective measures should be taken to regulate child labour, in compliance with the Covenant and the relevant ILO conventions'; Morocco, E/2001/22 (2000) 82: '... concern is expressed that certain issues contained in the draft Labour Code, such as the minimum age for labour and conditions of child labour, are not in conformity with the relevant ILO Conventions (Nos 138 and 182 respectively), which the State party has not yet ratified' (§ 528), 'The State party is urged to ... ensure that the provisions thereof are in conformity with ... the Covenant, as well as with the relevant ILO conventions to which Morocco is party' (§ 552), '... the State party is urged to raise the minimum working age from 12 to 15 years, in accordance with ILO standards (Convention No. 138)' (§555); Estonia, E/2003/22 (2002) 68 at § 518: 'The Committee recommends that the State party make work for convicted prisoners conditional on their consent, in conformity with ILO Convention No. 29 (1930) concerning forced or obligatory labour.'

29 See, for example, CESCR Concluding Observations on Guatemala, E/1997/22 (1996) 29 at § 144: 'Further measures should be taken to prevent and combat ... child labour, including through full respect for the international standards relating to the minimum age of employment for children.' See also Concluding Observations on Sri Lanka, E/1999/22 (1998) 22 at § 90.

30 See, for example, Concluding Observations on Uruguay (*supra* note 28) at § 370 and on Morocco (*supra* note 28) at § 555, where the CESCR insists on the parties' compliance with minimum working age requirements provided by ILO C138 Minimum Age Convention, while it should only be concerned with minimum age for paid employment, according to what it has been said above.

containing those standards.[31] Whether ILO standards may be 'incorporated' into the ICESCR itself through this process is a matter for discussion. Technically CESCR comments and observations are non-binding, although the weight that they carry in clarifying the precise scope of ICESCR obligations is undoubtedly a significant one,[32] and any interpretation of the ICESCR in light of another treaty should be applicable only to States Parties to both treaties.[33] In any case, the activity of the CESCR can be considered as a *de facto* critical contribution to the monitoring and implementation of ILO standards in this field and should not be underestimated.

10.2.3 The Convention on the Rights of the Child

One of the most important instruments in this field of international law is certainly the CRC, which was the first UN treaty to address child labour in a comprehensive manner, laying down not only general principles (article 32), but also dealing with critical issues that are also worst forms of child labour (articles 33–36 and 38).[34] Being nearly unanimously accepted,[35] the CRC provides for obligations that bind virtually the entire international community and has established itself as the normative reference for the regulation of the worst forms of child labour, subsequently developed through ad hoc Protocols to the CRC itself and by the ILO.

The general provision of the CRC dealing with child labour is article 32, which recognizes the right of the child to be protected 'from economic exploitation' and 'from performing any work that is likely to be hazardous or to interfere with the child's education, or to be harmful to the child's health or physical, mental, spiritual, moral or social development'.[36] In order to ensure the implementation of this provision, States are required to take 'legislative, administrative, social and educational measures'.[37] To this end, 'having regard to the relevant provisions of

---

31 See, for example, Concluding Observations on Morocco (*supra* note 28) at § 528.

32 See Craven, *The International Covenant*, at 91.

33 Vienna Convention on the Law of Treaties (date of adoption 23 May 1969; date of coming into force: 27 January 1980), available at <http://untreaty.un.org/ilc/texts/1_1.htm> (hereafter: VC), art. 31(3)(c). For a discussion of this complex issue see A. Haratsch, 'Overlapping Human Rights Guarantees and the "Pacta Tertiis" Rule', in E. Klein (ed.), *The Monitoring System of Human Rights Treaty Obligations*, Colloquium, Potsdam 22/23 November 1996, Berlin, Berlin Verlag A. Spitz, 1998, 167 ff.

34 On the CRC and child labour see L. Swepston, 'The Convention on the Rights of the Child and the ILO', *Nordic Journal of International Law*, Vol. 61, No. 1, 1992, 7 ff; A.G. Mower Jr, *The Convention on the Rights of the Child: International Law Support for Children*, London, Greenwood, 1997 at 43 ff; S. Detrick, *A Commentary on the United Nations Convention on the Rights of the Child*, The Hague, Martinus Nijhoff, 1999 at 558 ff; Y. Noguchi, 'ILO Convention No. 182 on the Worst Forms of Child Labour and the Convention on the Rights of the Child', *International Journal of Children's Rights*, Vol. 10, 2002, 355 ff.

35 The CRC has 193 States Parties (only Somalia and the US have not yet ratified it) (information updated as of 13 July 2007, from <http://www.ohchr.org/english/countries/ratification/11.htm>, last visited 1 August 2007).

36 CRC, art. 32(1).

37 *Ibid.*, § 2.

other international instruments', they are obliged to 'provide for a minimum age or minimum ages for admission to employment'[38] and to 'provide for appropriate regulation of the hours and conditions of employment'.[39]

The provision is similar to article 10(3) of the ICESCR,[40] and it may therefore catalyze few of the considerations made thereof. In particular, like the ICESCR, the CRC establishes a general right for the child to be free from economic exploitation[41] and from any harmful work (a human right that integrates ILO standards on the matter, having a wider scope of application),[42] but it does not prohibit child work below a certain age *per se*. In fact, minimum age-limits are required for 'admission to *employment*', which means that 'work' not under an employment relationship (such as within the family), by children of any age-limit, would not be prohibited *as such*.[43] Moreover, the CRC includes only an obligation to provide for a minimum age, without setting such a standard.[44] From this point of view, the CRC, like the ICESCR, may be considered to be more general and flexible,[45] and to take a narrower approach than relevant ILO instruments, in particular the C138 Minimum Age Convention. However, the text of the CRC itself is explicit in referring to 'other international instruments' as parameters to be taken into account by parties in their regulation of the minimum age for admission to employment and the hours and conditions of the same.[46] ILO standards in this sector certainly fall under this definition.[47]

---

38 *Ibid.*, § 2(a).

39 *Ibid.*, § 2(b).

40 The text of the CRC recalls this article in its Preamble, and some say that the CRC has 'reinforced the approach' of the ICESCR (Van Bueren, *The International Law*, *supra* note 8, at 264).

41 The ICESCR is slightly broader as it applies to economic and social exploitation.

42 *Supra* note 20.

43 This is confirmed by the *travaux préparatoires* of the Convention (see S. Detrick (ed.), *The United Nations Convention on the Rights of the Child: A Guide to the 'Travaux Préparatoires'*, Dordrecht, Martinus Nijhoff, 1992 at 422). See also ComRC (on the ComRC see *infra* note 48), General Comment No. 4 (2003), Adolescent Health and Development in the Context of the Convention on the Rights of the Child, 1 July 2003, CRC/GC/2003/4, at § 18. All General Comments of the ComRC are available at <www.ohchr.org/english/bodies/crc/comments.htm>.

44 The Basic Working text, as adopted by the 1980 Working Group (Doc E/CN/.4/1349, p. 6), provided for a prohibition on employment before the age of 15, but the option was immediately dropped (Detrick (ed.), *The United Nations Convention*, *supra* note 43, at 418).

45 This does not mean, however, that the CRC contains only general obligations requiring progressive implementation; the issue of the nature of CRC's obligation is a very complex one which cannot be dealt with here. In this regard see ComRC, General Comment No. 5 (2003), General Measures of Implementation for the Convention on the Rights of the Child, 3 October 2003, CRC/GC/2003/5. For comments on detailed obligations required by each article see Detrick, *A Commentary*, *supra* note 34, (at 562 ff on CRC, art. 32).

46 CRC, art. 32(2)(a) and (b).

47 See in this sense also Swepston, 'The Convention', *supra* note 34, at 10; Detrick, *A Commentary*, *supra* note 34, at 564 ff.

The ComRC, the body entrusted with the monitoring of the implementation of the CRC,[48] has further built upon the above explicit textual connection, by making constant reference to ILO standards in its General Comments[49] and Concluding Observations on parties' reports on their implementation of the CRC. The ComRC has in many occasions encouraged parties to ratify the relevant ILO instruments, to implement and respect them,[50] and to seek technical assistance from the ILO in order to solve specific child labour problems. The Committee has also assessed parties' lack of compliance with ILO standards, in isolation or in conjunction with the CRC, in such a way that the former appear to be 'imported' as substantial parameters in the latter.[51] The same perplexities expressed above, about the role of the CESCR in this

---

48 On the monitoring system of the CRC and the ComRC see Mower, *The Convention*, *supra* note 34, at 63 ff; G. Lansdown, 'The Reporting Process under the Convention on the Rights of the Child', in P. Alston and J. Crawford (eds), *The Future of UN Human Rights Treaty Monitoring*, Cambridge, Cambridge University Press, 2000, 113 ff.

49 See in this regard ComRC, General Comment No. 4, *supra* note 43, at § 18: '... The Committee urges States Parties to take all necessary measures to abolish all forms of child labour, starting with the worst forms, to continuously review national regulations on minimum ages for employment with a view to making them compatible with international standards, and to regulate the working environment and conditions for adolescents who are working (in accordance with article 32 of the Convention, as well as ILO Conventions Nos. 138 and 182), so as to ensure that they are fully protected and have access to legal redress mechanisms.'

50 'Specific attention should be given to monitoring the full implementation of ... ILO Convention No. 138 ...' (Concluding Observations on Togo, CRC/C/69 (1997) 39 at § 290); 'The Committee recommends that the State party, in accordance with article 32 of the Convention and ILO Conventions Nos. 138 ... and 182 ... which the State party has ratified: (a) Take immediate and effective steps to ensure the implementation of article 32 of the Convention and ILO Conventions Nos. 138 and 182, taking due account of the ILO Minimum Age Recommendation, 1973 (No. 146) and the Worst Forms of Child Labour Recommendation, 1999 (No. 190)' (Romania, CRC/124 (2003) 49 at § 255). All Concluding Observations of the ComRC are available at <www.ohchr.org/english/bodies/crc/sessions. htm>.

51 'The State party is encouraged to revise its labour legislation ... in light of the relevant international standards, especially ILO Convention No. 138 and ILO Recommendation No. 146' (Concluding Observations on Finland, CRC/C/50 (1996) 35 at § 239); '... notes with concern that there is no legal minimum age for employment in accordance with ILO Convention No. 138 ...' (Concluding Observations on Gambia, CRC/C/111 (2001) 89 at § 460); '... recommends that the State party ... Pursue its plans to erase the gap between the school-leaving age and the minimum age for employment by increasing both to 15, in conformity with ILO Convention No. 138' (Concluding Observations on Lebanon, CRC/C/114 (2002) 11 at § 51). See, in particular, Concluding Observations on Oman CRC/C/111 (2001) 36: 'The Committee is seriously concerned at the hazardous situation of children involved in camel racing ... It concurs with the ILO Committee of Experts ... which has previously indicated that the employment of children as camel jockeys constitutes dangerous work under article 3(1) of ILO Convention No. 138' (§ 199). 'In accordance with article 32 of the Convention and ILO Convention No. 182, which the State party has ratified, the Committee recommends that the State party: (a) Take immediate and effective steps to ensure the implementation of article 32 of the Convention and ILO Convention No. 182 ...' (*ibid.*, § 200). Similar Concluding Observations on the same problem have been issued for Qatar (CRC/C/111 (2001) 59 at

regard, may be recalled for the ComRC as well, although with some differences.[52] Such an activity, undertaken by the monitoring body of the most widely accepted human rights treaty of the UN system, has in any case a great potential for the improvement of the implementation of ILO instruments in international law.

10.3 The implementation of ILO standards on the worst forms of child labour within the UN system

Building upon the general principle, contained in the instruments illustrated so far, that exploitation and harmful work of children shall be prohibited, international law has concentrated on developing a more specific normative and implementation framework for the so-called 'worst forms of child labour': the use of children in illicit activities; their sexual exploitation; forced labour and slavery; their sale and trafficking or their recruitment as child soldiers. Despite the above definition, which has attracted some controversy,[53] these are in fact also violations of fundamental human rights, transnational crimes, war crimes, or even matters that may threaten international peace and security, and they have been addressed as such within the UN. The UN system thus plays a major role in this field. ILO standards were developed by taking the CRC as a reference. Thereafter, more ad hoc instruments were adopted within the UN system to develop further the normative framework in this regard. Finally, the issues at stake are very broad and complex, and they touch upon many other non ad hoc UN instruments and institutional activities. One may say that the 'centre of gravity' of the international legal and institutional framework in this regard may have moved from the ILO to the UN at large.

The key ILO instrument in this regard is the Convention 182 on the Worst Forms of Child Labour, which will be taken as the reference for the present analysis.[54] The Convention builds upon other ILO instruments (in particular the Minimum Age Convention C138) and on the CRC,[55] in particular upon the general prohibition of child economic exploitation and hazardous or harmful work contained therein, and it requires States to take 'immediate and effective measures to secure the prohibition

---

§§ 320–321) and United Arab Emirates (CRC/C/118 (2002) 90 at §§ 406–407). See also Concluding Observations on France CRC/C/140 (2004) 124 at § 632: 'The Committee recommends that the State party, in accordance with article 32 of the Convention and ILO Conventions No. 138 ... and No. 182 ... vigorously pursue measures ... to dismantle trafficking and exploitation networks, in particular of foreign children ...'; Albania, CRC/C/146 (2005) 19 at § 144; Nicaragua, CRC/C/150 (2005) 132 at § 653 ('The Committee recommends that the State party ... Ensure the implementation of legislation fully covering article 32 of the Convention, and ILO Conventions No. 138 (1973) and No. 182 (1999)').

52 *Supra* section 10.2.2. While the output of the ComRC's activities, like that of the CESCR (*supra* note 32), technically is non-binding (even though it may be important to clarify the obligations of the treaty), the textual reference in the CRC to 'other international instruments' may support the view that ILO standards may be applicable also to CRC's Parties that are not parties to the former (see *supra* note 33).

53 For a short account of the debate see Maffei, 'La tutela', *supra* note 8, at 261–3.

54 On the Convention in general see Rishikesh (this volume).

55 C182 Worst Forms of Child Labour Convention, Preamble.

and elimination of the worst forms of child labour as a matter of urgency'.[56] Worst forms of child[57] labour comprise, according to article 3 of Convention 182: all forms of slavery or practices similar to slavery, including the sale and trafficking of children, and forced or compulsory labour, including forced or compulsory recruitment for use in armed conflict (subpara. a); the sexual exploitation of children (subpara. b); the use of children in illicit activities, in particular for the production and trafficking of drugs (subpara. c); any work which 'by its nature or the circumstances in which it is carried out, is likely to harm the health, safety or morals of children' (subpara. d).

General prohibitions of exploitation and harmful work of children, contained in the UN instruments mentioned above, already provide for some protection and are used to address some of these matters. Moreover, many other normative instruments and institutional mechanisms concur to establish a composite framework to tackle these problems.

10.3.1 Slavery, practices similar to slavery, and forced or compulsory labour of children

Many treaties in the UN system contribute to the fight against slavery, practices similar to slavery and forced labour contained in article 3 subpara. (a) of ILO Convention 182.

First of all, slavery and forced labour of children are addressed under the relevant general provisions of the ICESCR[58] and the CRC[59] on child labour analysed above.

Moreover, an ad hoc instrument, the UN Supplementary Convention on Slavery, recalled by the Preamble of Convention 182 itself, requires States to criminalize slavery and enslavement[60] and to 'bring about progressively' the abolition of 'practices similar to slavery', such as debt bondage and serfdom and specifically the delivery of children to others with a view to exploitation of their labour.[61] This, however, is a rather weak treaty in terms of the scope of its obligations (criminalization and progressive abolition of targeted practices are narrower duties than what is provided for in other instruments), and it does not have any ad hoc monitoring mechanism.

A much greater contribution is made by the ICCPR. The HRC has made reference to forced labour of children as being addressed by article 24 on the rights of the child[62] and by article 8 which establishes that: '1. No one shall be held in slavery; slavery and the slave-trade in all their forms shall be prohibited. 2. No one shall be

---

56 *Ibid.*, art. 1.

57 A child is defined as any person under the age of 18 (*ibid.*, art. 2).

58 See, for example, ICESCR, Concluding Observations on Congo, E/2001/22 (2000) 43 at §§ 204, 210. See also Concluding Observations on Estonia, *supra* note 28.

59 See, for example, ComRC Concluding Observations on Sudan, CRC/C/20 (1993) 22 at § 108 and CRC/C/121 (2002) 53 at §§ 280–281; Pakistan, CRC/C/29 (1994) 10 at § 46; Georgia, CRC/C/97 (2000) 18 at § 131; Cameroon, CRC/C/111 (2001) 71 at § 383; Niger, CRC/C/118 (2002) 37 at §§ 189–190; Ukraine, CRC/C/121 (2002) 70 at § 357.

60 UN Supplementary Convention on Slavery, articles 5–6.

61 *Ibid.*, art. 1.

62 'Every possible economic and social measure should be taken to ... prevent [children] from being subjected to acts of violence and cruel and inhuman treatment or from being exploited

held in servitude. 3. (a) No one shall be required to perform forced or compulsory labour ...'.[63] The HRC has issued also several Concluding Observations on countries' reports, highlighting the necessity to prohibit and eliminate these practices involving children.[64] While the prohibition on slavery and servitude in the ICCPR is absolute,[65] article 8 provides for some exceptions to the prohibition on forced labour.[66] It is unclear whether these apply to forced labour of children as well. Reference may be made to article 11 of ILO Convention 29 concerning Forced or Compulsory Labour,[67] which establishes that forced labour may be imposed only on 'males who are of an apparent age of not less than 18' (at least for Parties to both treaties).[68] The same conclusion (for all Parties) could probably be reached by interpreting the norm in light of other provisions of the Covenant (including article 24), and of the object and purpose of the Covenant.[69] The added value of the inclusion of slavery and forced labour of children within the ICCPR lies with its monitoring mechanism: unlike other human rights instruments considered so far, the ICCPR provides also for an optional mechanism of inter-State complaints and individual redress, in addition to Concluding Observations and General Comments.[70] The former would enable child victims to present individual petitions to the HRC in order to obtain its 'views' on

---

by means of forced labour or prostitution, or by their use in the illicit trafficking of narcotic drugs, or by any other means' (HRC, General Comment No. 17, *supra* note 13, at § 3).

63 The HRC has suggested that, in order to implement art. 8, States should take measures to protect children from slavery (including that 'disguised, inter alia, as domestic or other kinds of personal service') and to eliminate trafficking of children and forced prostitution (HRC, General Comment No. 28: Equality of Rights between Men and Women (article 3), 29 March 2000, CCPR/C/21/Rev.1/Add.10, at § 12).

64 See, for example, HRC, Concluding Observations on Dominican Republic, A/48/40 vol. I (1993) 95 at § 464; Haiti, A/50/40 vol. I (1995) 46 at § 234; Mali, A/58/40 vol. I (2003) 47 at § 81(17): '... the Committee remains concerned about the trafficking of Malian children to other countries ... and their subjection to slavery and forced labour'; on Uganda (*supra* note 14): 'The Committee has observed with concern the forced employment of children in activities harmful to their health and well-being, as well as the ineffectiveness of the measures adopted to deal with this problem (articles 8 and 24).'

65 The right to be free from these practices is also a non-derogable one (ICCPR, art. 4(2)).

66 Forced or compulsory labour may be permitted as a punishment for a crime (ICCPR, art. 8(3)(b)); moreover, the definition does not include work normally required under detention (*ibid.*, subpara. (c) (i)), any military or similar service (*ibid.*, subpara. (c) (ii)), service exacted in cases of emergency (*ibid.*, subpara. (c) (iii)) or which form part of normal civil obligations (*ibid.*, subpara. (c) (iv)).

67 Hereafter: C29 Forced Labour Convention. The Convention is also recalled in the Preamble of ILO Convention 182.

68 VC, art. 31(3)(c) (*supra* note 33).

69 VC, art. 31(1).

70 On the monitoring system of the ICCPR and the HRC see T. Opsahl, 'The Human Rights Committee', in Alston (ed.), *The United Nations, supra* note 22, at 369 ff; M. Nowak, *UN Covenant on Civil and Political Rights: CCPR Commentary*, Kehl am Rhein, Engel, 1993, 506 ff; D. McGoldrick, *The Human Rights Committee: Its Role in the Development of the International Covenant on Civil and Political Rights*, Oxford, Clarendon Press, 1994; P.R.

their individual cases. This 'quasi-judicial' mechanism gives also evidence of the nature of the ICCPR's obligations in this field: the Covenant requires States to adopt positive measures to ensure the rights included therein, but it contains also subjective rights, which are capable of being immediately implemented, and which are directly applicable, enforceable and justiciable.[71]

An almost verbatim provision reflecting article 8 of the ICCPR is also contained in article 11 of the International Convention on the Protection of the Rights of All Migrant Workers and Members of Their Families,[72] and the issue has been dealt with also by the UN Security Council as far as children in armed conflicts are concerned.[73] Finally, problems linked to the worst forms of child labour, including slavery, servitude and forced labour, may also raise discrimination issues.[74]

Within the UN system, these practices have thus been clearly prohibited through a comprehensive normative framework which establishes a right to be free from slavery, servitude and forced labour that is sometimes also couched as a justiciable individual right.

10.3.2 The sale and trafficking of children

Article 3(a) of ILO Convention 182 places 'sale or trafficking of children' under slavery or practices similar to slavery. While the sale and trafficking in human beings is certainly connected with slavery (the slave trade having historically been one of the first human rights issues to be addressed by the international community), the phenomenon is in fact a much broader and cross-cutting one, which is also related to other worst forms of child labour, such as sexual exploitation. There is a plethora of general and ad hoc international instruments on the matter which deal with traffic of

---

Ghandhi, *The Human Rights Committee and the Right of Individual Communication: Law and Practice*, Aldershot, Ashgate, 1998.

71 On the nature of ICCPR's obligations see Nowak, *UN Covenant*, *supra* note 70, at 26 ff; McGoldrick, *The Human Rights Committee*, *supra* note 70, at 269 ff.

72 Available at <www.ohchr.org/english/law>.

73 See *infra* section 10.3.3 (in particular note 130).

74 See, for example, the Concluding Observations by the Committee on the Elimination of Racial Discrimination (CERD) on Venezuela's compliance with the International Convention on the Elimination of All Forms of Racial Discrimination (ICERD, date of adoption 21 December 1965; date of coming into force 4 January 1969, available at <www.ohchr.org/english/law>): 'The Committee notes with concern that ... there is evidence that indigenous children and adolescents are subjected to labour exploitation and the worst forms of child labour, including servitude and slavery, child prostitution, trafficking and sale' (A/60/18 (2005) 71 at § 381). All CERD Concluding Observations are available at <www.ohchr.org/english/bodies/cerd/sessions.htm>. The monitoring system of the ICERD, like that of the ICCPR, provides also for inter-State complaints and individual petitions (see R. Wolfrum, 'International Convention on the Elimination of all Forms of Racial Discrimination', in Klein (ed.), *The Monitoring System, supra* note 33, 49 ff). The ComRC has suggested that the same considerations, from the point of view of discrimination, may be made under the CRC: 'The Committee is also concerned at practices of forced labour among children belonging to certain groups of the population, such as the Pygmies and the Kirdi' (Concluding Observations on Cameroon, CRC/C/111 (2001) 71, at § 383).

human beings as such, as well as with traffic for one or more specific purposes, thus giving rise to a considerable amount of overlaps. Within the UN system the sale and trafficking of children must be prohibited and prevented, and detailed provisions are established, especially in ad hoc instruments, on substantial as well as procedural requirements for its criminalization and the protection of the victims.

Traffic in persons for specific sexual exploitation purposes was targeted already in 1949 by the UN Convention on Traffic in Persons and Prostitution.[75] The Convention requires States to punish *inter alia* persons who procure, entice or lead away, for purposes of prostitution, or exploit the prostitution of, another person (even with the consent of that person)[76] and to regard these as extraditable offences.[77] Parties also undertake to adopt measures to 'check the traffic in persons ... for the purpose of prostitution', in particular by making regulations to protect 'immigrants or emigrants, and in particular women and children, both at the place of arrival and departure and while en route'.[78] Parties shall also take 'measures for the supervision of employment agencies in order to prevent persons seeking employment, in particular women and children, from being exposed to the danger of prostitution'.[79] The Convention contains some interesting monitoring provisions: the Parties must communicate (annually) to the Secretary-General of the UN the measures that they have taken to implement the Convention, and such information is published periodically and circulated by the UN-SG to all other Member States of the UN.[80]

The UN Supplementary Convention on Slavery, apart from slavery and forced labour itself,[81] also addresses the trade in slaves. The treaty requires States to criminalize any 'act of conveying or attempting to convey slaves from one country to another by whatever means of transport, or of being accessory thereto' and to provide for 'severe penalties' for such offences,[82] as well as to take measures to prevent them.[83]

---

75 The Convention is considered as the 'consolidating treaty' of previous instruments on the suppression of the traffic in women and children (UN Convention on Traffic in Persons and Prostitution, Preamble).

76 *Ibid.*, art. 1. Art. 2 integrates the list of persons to be punished (by referring to the keeping, managing or financing of brothels or other places used for prostitution).

77 *Ibid.*, art. 8. Art. 9 adds that States shall prosecute and punish their nationals who have committed these offences abroad, if their extradition is not permitted by law.

78 *Ibid.*, art. 17(1).

79 *Ibid.*, art. 20.

80 *Ibid.*, art. 21. The treaty also contains a binding dispute settlement clause, which entails the possibility of bringing a case before the International Court of Justice at the request of one of the Parties to the dispute (*ibid.*, art. 22).

81 See *supra* section 10.3.1.

82 UN Supplementary Convention on Slavery, art. 3(1).

83 States are required to take all effective measures to prevent their ships and aircrafts to be used for such practices and to punish persons guilty of such acts, as well as to ensure that their ports and territory are not used for that purpose (*ibid.*, art. 3(2)). Slaves that take refuge on board a vessel of a State party are ipso facto free (*ibid.*, art. 4).

The ICCPR also contains obligations relating to slave-trading in article 8, and they are specifically applicable to children.[84] The HRC has also clarified that trafficking of children may be addressed under article 24 (the rights of the child), but it may also violate other provisions of the Covenant,[85] and it is considered among the 'most serious violations of human rights'.[86]

The CESCR has interpreted the ICESCR as including obligations to prevent traffic of children as such, for forced labour purposes or sexual exploitation.[87]

A general provision on the sale and traffic of children is contained also in the CRC, which provides that States shall take all appropriate measures 'to prevent the abduction of, the sale of or traffic in children for any purpose or in any form'.[88] The CRC has been supplemented by the Optional Protocol on Sale and Sexual Exploitation of Children, which is designed to fight these phenomena through general obligations of prevention, as well as detailed substantial and procedural criminal law obligations. The Protocol requires States to prohibit and criminalize the sale of children under their criminal or penal law, whether the offence is committed domestically or transnationally, by individuals or on an organized basis.[89] States are required to cover 'as a minimum' the 'offering, delivering or accepting, by whatever means' of a child for the purpose of *inter alia* sexual exploitation or forced labour.[90] Parties also have obligations to establish jurisdiction over these offences.[91] Other procedural duties

---

84 *Supra* note 64. See also Concluding Observations on Philippines, ICCPR, A/59/40 vol. I (2003) 15 at § 63(13); Sri Lanka, ICCPR, A/59/40 vol. I (2003) 30 at § 66(14).

85 On traffic for sexual exploitation purposes see, for example, Concluding Observations on Venezuela, ICCPR, A/56/40 vol. I (2001) 49 at § 77(24); Guatemala, ICCPR, A/56/40 vol. I (2001) 93 at § 85(26). Sale and traffic of children as such (regardless of its purpose) may fall also under articles 3 (equality of rights), 6 (the right to life), 8 and 7 (prohibition of torture and inhuman or degrading treatment) of the ICCPR. See Concluding Observations on Guatemala, ICCPR, A/56/40 vol. I (2001) 93 at § 85(15); Lithuania, ICCPR, A/59/40 vol. I (2004) 52 at § 71(14); Serbia and Montenegro, ICCPR, A/59/40 vol. I (2004) 68 at § 75(16).

86 Concluding Observations on Argentina, ICCPR, A/56/40 vol. I (2001) 38 at § 74(5).

87 See, for example, Concluding Observations on Venezuela, E/2002/22 (2001) 29 at § 89; Bolivia, E/2002/22 (2001) 52 at § 297; Togo, E/2002/22 (2001) 57 at § 317; Ukraine, E/2002/22 (2001) 78 at §§ 492 and 510; Greece, ICESCR, E/2005/22 (2004) 23 at §§ 138 and 159; Serbia and Montenegro, E/2006/22 (2005) 41 at § 285.

88 CRC, art. 35. The ComRC has explicitly stated that 'It is the obligation of States Parties to enact and enforce laws to prohibit all forms of sexual exploitation and related trafficking' (General Comment No. 4, *supra* note 43, at § 37).

89 CRC Optional Protocol on Sale and Sexual Exploitation of Children, articles 1 and 3(1). The sale of children is defined as 'any act or transaction whereby a child is transferred by any person or group of persons to another for remuneration or any other consideration' (*ibid.*, art. 2 (a)).

90 *Ibid.*, art. 3(1)(a)(i). The Protocol also covers the sale aimed at the transfer of organs for profit (*ibid.*) as well as the intermediation in an adoption which is carried out in violation of international instruments on the matter (*ibid.*, art. 3(1)(a)(ii)). Under certain conditions, States are also required to establish criminal, civil or administrative liability for legal persons for these offences (*ibid.*, art. 3(4)).

91 A party must establish its jurisdiction when the offences are committed in its territory or on board a ship or aircraft registered therein (*ibid.*, art. 4 (1)), or when the alleged offender,

regard extradition,[92] cooperation between the Parties in investigations or criminal proceedings,[93] the adoption of specific executive measures (for example, seizure and confiscation of goods)[94] and the protection of the child in criminal procedures.[95] States shall also adopt laws, measures, policies and programmes to prevent the offences dealt with in the Protocol, including measures to protect children who are vulnerable to such practices,[96] and the strengthening of international cooperation in addressing the root causes of the latter.[97] Measures must be taken also to protect child victims, including by social reintegration, physical and psychological recovery[98] and by ensuring that they have access to adequate procedures to seek compensation.[99] The Protocol is subject to the monitoring mechanism of the CRC before the ComRC.[100]

In the same year as the adoption of the CRC Optional Protocol, another ad hoc treaty on the traffic of human beings with a particular focus on children was adopted by the UNGA: the Protocol to Prevent, Suppress and Punish Trafficking in Persons Especially Women and Children, supplementing the United Nations Convention against Transnational Organized Crime.[101] The Protocol is framed to be the universal instrument that addresses all aspects of trafficking in persons (especially women and children), based on the assumption that 'a comprehensive international approach in the countries of origin, transit and destination that includes measures to prevent such trafficking, to punish the traffickers and to protect the victims' is required to this end.[102] The Protocol defines 'trafficking in persons', as far as the child is concerned,[103] as 'the recruitment, transportation, transfer, harbouring or receipt of persons' for the purpose of exploitation, with the latter including 'at a minimum' prostitution and sexual exploitation in general, slavery, practices similar to slavery, servitude or forced labour and the removal of organs.[104] States are required to establish as criminal offences such conducts, when committed intentionally,[105] and the Protocol will apply to them when they are 'transnational in nature and involve an

---

which is one of its nationals, is present in its territory and the State does not extradite him or her to another State Party (*ibid.*, art. 4 (3)). A party may also establish its jurisdiction when the alleged offender or the victim is its national, or when the former has his habitual residence in its territory (*ibid.*, art. 4(2)).

92 *Ibid.*, art. 5.

93 *Ibid.*, art. 6.

94 *Ibid.*, art. 7.

95 *Ibid.*, art. 8.

96 *Ibid.*, art. 9(1).

97 *Ibid.*, art. 10(3).

98 *Ibid.*, art. 9(3).

99 *Ibid.*, art. 9(4).

100 *Ibid.*, art. 12.

101 Hereafter: UNCTOC, available at <www.unodc.org/unodc/en/crime_cicp_convention.html>.

102 Transnational Organized Crime Convention Protocol on Trafficking in Persons, Preamble; *ibid.*, art. 2.

103 The definition of trafficking is different if a child is involved (*ibid.*, art. 3 (a) and (c)). A child is any person under 18 years of age (*ibid.*, art. 3 (d)).

104 *Ibid.*, art. 3.

105 *Ibid.*, art. 5.

organized criminal group'.[106] Apart from such obligations of criminalization, States are required to adopt measures for the prevention,[107] investigation and prosecution of such offences, as well as for the protection of the victims thereof.[108] Finally, the Protocol is integrated by the obligations contained in the UNCTOC,[109] *inter alia* on jurisdiction and extradition.[110] As a positive remark, the Protocol establishes a very broad framework to address trafficking of children in a comprehensive manner, with indications of very detailed measures that States *should* adopt in this regard (beyond criminalization, the specific measures are often optional). However, the monitoring mechanism does not seem very extensive, as it provides only for the examination of countries' reports by the Conference of the Parties to the UNCTOC which has the task 'to promote and review the implementation of the Convention'.[111]

Finally, the trafficking of children has been addressed also under the ICERD[112] and the Convention on the Elimination of All Forms of Discrimination against Women.[113]

---

106 *Ibid.*, art. 4.

107 States are required to establish 'comprehensive policies, programmes and other measures' to this end, including, for example, educational, social and economic initiatives and measures, also tackling factors that make children vulnerable to trafficking (such as poverty) and addressing the demand that fosters traffic (*ibid.*, art. 9). They are also expected to cooperate for the improvement and strengthening of law enforcement across borders, specially as far as borders' control and immigration are concerned (*ibid.*, articles 10–12).

108 The Protocol mentions *inter alia* measures to protect their privacy and identity, to provide for their physical, psychological and social recovery or their physical safety, to ensure their possibility to obtain compensation (*ibid.*, art. 6), as well as those to permit victims to remain in the receiving State's territory (*ibid.*, art. 7) and to facilitate their repatriation (*ibid.*, art. 8).

109 The Protocol should be interpreted together with the Convention (*ibid.*, art. 1(1)), the provisions of the Convention apply *mutatis mutandis* to the Protocol (*ibid.*, art. 1(2)) and the offences established in accordance with the Protocol are regarded as offences also in accordance with the Convention (*ibid.*, art. 1(3)).

110 UNCTOC, articles 15–16.

111 *Ibid.*, art. 32(1). For relevant Decisions of the Conference of the Parties in this regard see <www.unodc.org/unodc/en/crime_cicp_convention.html#conference>.

112 *Supra* note 74. See also Concluding Observations on Kazakhstan, CERD, A/59/18 (2004) 54 at § 293; Azerbaijan, CERD, A/60/18 (2005) 18 at § 59; Nigeria, CERD, A/60/18 (2005) 54 at § 297.

113 Hereafter: CEDAW, available at <www.ohchr.org/english/law>. Art. 6 of the CEDAW provides that 'States Parties shall take all appropriate measures, including legislation, to suppress all forms of traffic in women and exploitation of prostitution of women'. The provision is clearly applicable also to girls: see, for example, the Committee on the Elimination of Discrimination Against Women (hereafter: ComEDAW) Concluding Comments on India, A/55/38 part I (2000) 7 at § 62; Russian Federation, A/57/38 part I (2002) 40 at §§ 393–396; Mexico, A/57/38 part III (2002) 205 at § 435; El Salvador, A/58/38 part I (2003) 41 at §§ 271–272; Norway, A/58/38 part I (2003) 61 § 421; Brazil, A/58/38 part II (2003) 93 at §§ 116–117; Ecuador, A/58/38 part II (2003) 122 at §§ 309–314. All Concluding Comments are available at <www.un.org/womenwatch/daw/cedaw/sessions.htm>. On the monitoring system of the CEDAW, which provides also for an individual petition mechanism, see M.C.

From the institutional point of view, it is also worth noting that a *Special Rapporteur on the sale of children, child prostitution and child pornography* has been appointed by the Commission on Human Rights,[114] and that the trafficking of children has been considered also by the UNSC.[115]

10.3.3 The recruitment of child soldiers

ILO Convention 182 also addresses the 'forced or compulsory recruitment of children for use in armed conflict' under article 3 subpara. (a). The contribution by the UN in this field is extremely relevant, as the connection of the worst forms of child labour with broader international law issues is particularly evident here. From the substantial as well as from the institutional point of view, the action within the UN system goes well beyond ILO standards.

While the problem of child soldiers may be relevant under the ICESCR,[116] the ICCPR[117] and the CEDAW,[118] it is within the CRC that the issue has been fully considered. Article 38 of the CRC already dealt with the matter, but with a rather weak approach from the point of view of the protection of the child. In fact, alongside general principles of respect for rules of international humanitarian law that are relevant to the child,[119] the CRC prohibited recruitment in armed forces and direct participation in hostilities by children below *fifteen* years of age.[120] Such protection was later seen as insufficient, in light especially of the widespread expansion of the phenomenon of child soldiers and of the reaction by the international community, in other contexts including within the ILO.[121]

In order to strengthen the rights embodied in the CRC in this field, an Optional Protocol on Children in Armed Conflict was eventually adopted. This treaty, in line with ILO standards, obliges States to ensure that children under *eighteen* years of

---

Maffei, 'La condizione della donna tra protezione e divieto di discriminazione', in Pineschi (ed.), *La tutela internazionale, supra* note 8, 173 ff at 191 ff.

114 The Special Rapporteur has *inter alia* the capacity to receive individual complaints (see <www.ohchr.org/english/issues/children/rapporteur/index.htm>). The ComRC, in its Concluding Observations, often refers to it, and asks that States take into consideration its recommendations.

115 *Infra* section 10.3.3. See in particular *infra* note 130.

116 Concluding Observations on Colombia, ICESCR, E/2002/22 (2001) 110 at § 790: 'The Committee calls upon the State party urgently to undertake measures to ... prevent and discourage children from taking up arms'.

117 ICCPR, Concluding Observation on Philippines, A/59/40 vol. I (2003) 15 at § 63(17): 'children as young as 13 allegedly being used by armed groups without adequate measures of protection by the State (art. 24); The State party should: ... Take all appropriate measures to ensure protection of children who have been involved in armed conflict'.

118 CEDAW, Concluding Comments on Democratic Republic of the Congo, A/55/38 part I (2000) 21 at § 218: 'The Government should ensure that children are not recruited as soldiers'.

119 CRC, art. 38 §§ 1, 4.

120 *Ibid.*, art. 38 §§ 2–3.

121 ILO Convention 182 applies to children below 18 years of age.

age are not compulsory recruited.[122] Beyond the ILO Convention, however, the Optional Protocol establishes also obligations in other related matters, as far as age limits for participation in armed conflicts in general[123] and voluntary recruitment[124] are concerned. The Protocol addresses also 'armed groups that are distinct from the armed forces of a State', which 'should not, under any circumstances, recruit or use in hostilities persons under the age of 18 years', and requires States to take all feasible measures to prevent such recruitment and use.[125] Parties are finally obliged to take all necessary measures for the implementation of the Protocol and 'all feasible measures' to ensure that child victims are released from services and properly assisted for their physical and psychological recovery and social reintegration.[126] The Protocol is subject to the same monitoring mechanisms of the CRC.

The issue of child soldiers has been tackled within the UN system also through the involvement of its institutional framework at the highest level. In this regard, a *Special Representative of the Secretary-General for children and armed conflict* has been established since 1997,[127] but the most notable action in this field has been taken by the UNSC. Since 1999, the UNSC has adopted a number of resolutions on children and armed conflict that are extremely important from the point of view of the development of international law in this area.[128] Through such resolutions, the UNSC has clarified that the impact of armed conflict on children falls under its responsibility for the maintenance of international peace and security;[129] it has condemned the recruitment and use of children in armed conflict in violation of international law;[130] it has urged States to end this practice[131] and it has called upon them to comply with international law and standards on the matter, mentioning *inter alia* in this regard the CRC, its Optional Protocol on Children in Armed Conflict and

---

122 CRC Optional Protocol on Children in Armed Conflict, art. 2.

123 States must take 'all feasible measures' to ensure that children under the age of 18 years do not take a direct part in hostilities (*ibid.*, art. 1).

124 In this regard no precise age-limits are set: parties must simply raise the minimum age for voluntary recruitment that is set out in art. 38(3) of the CRC (*ibid.*, art. 1) and they are required to adopt safeguards, *inter alia*, to ensure that the recruitment is 'genuinely voluntary' (*ibid.*, art. 3).

125 *Ibid.*, art. 4.

126 *Ibid.*, art. 6.

127 See the official website of the Special Representative for all documents and references (<www.un.org/children/conflict/english/home6.html>).

128 UNSC res. 1261 (1999) of 25 August 1999; UNSC res. 1379 (2001) of 20 November 2001; UNSC res. 1460 (2003) of 30 January 2003; UNSC res. 1539 (2004) of 22 April 2004; UNSC res. 1612 (2005) of 26 July 2005. All UNSC resolutions are available at <www.un.org/Docs/sc/>.

129 UNSC res. 1379 (2001), Preamble; UNSC res. 1460 (2003), Preamble; UNSC res. 1612 (2005), Preamble.

130 UNSC res. 1261 (1999), § 2; UNSC res. 1612 (2005), § 1. The UNSC has also condemned, in addition to the acts above, 'trafficking, forced labour and all forms of slavery and all other violations and abuses committed against children affected by armed conflict' (UNSC res. 1539 (2004), § 1).

131 UNSC res. 1261 (1999), § 12; UNSC res. 1460 (2003), § 3; UNSC res. 1539 (2004), § 6.

ILO Convention 182.[132] The relevant resolutions were accompanied by requests to the UN-SG to monitor their implementation and review parties' compliance with them. The UN-SG was requested specifically to provide a list of parties (State and non-State actors) that recruited or used children in armed conflicts in violation of their international obligations,[133] to monitor the progress made by such parties towards the ending of recruitment of child soldiers and to assess violations thereof.[134] Parties themselves were called upon to prepare 'concrete time-bound action plans' to halt the recruitment of child soldiers.[135] The UNSC repeatedly suggested that it would take appropriate steps in accordance with the UN Charter to further address the issue if insufficient progress were made.[136] Eventually, this process was institutionalized: the UN-SG was required to prepare and implement a comprehensive monitoring, reporting and compliance system to address violations of international standards *inter alia* on the recruitment or use of children as soldiers and a *Working Group on Children and Armed Conflict* of the UNSC (hereafter: CAAC) was established to address the matter.[137] The CAAC, which consists of all members of the UNSC, reviews the reports resulting from the mechanism devised by the UN-SG, the progress made by the parties in the development and implementation of their action plans to stop recruitment of child soldiers,[138] as well as any other relevant information; it may then make recommendations to the UNSC and requests to other UN bodies for supporting action.[139] The UNSC may thereafter '... consider imposing, through country-specific resolutions, targeted and graduated measures ... against parties to situations of armed conflict which are on the Security Council's agenda and are

---

132 UNSC res. 1261 (1999), § 3; UNSC res. 1314 (2000), § 3; UNSC res. 1379 (2001), § 8. See also UN-SG, Report of the Secretary-General on Children and Armed Conflict, *infra* note 137.

133 UNSC res. 1379 (2001), § 16; UN-SG, Report of the Secretary-General on Children and Armed Conflict of 26 November 2002. Doc. S/2002/1299 (all Reports of the UN-SG to the UNSC on Children and Armed Conflict are available at <www.un.org/children/conflict/ english/reports89.html>). The list concerned both situations on the UNSC agenda as well as those that could be brought to the attention of the UNSC by the UN-SG according to art. 99 of the UN Charter.

134 UNSC res. 1460 (2003), § 16.

135 UNSC res. 1539 (2004), § 5(a).

136 UNSC res. 1460 (2003), § 6. The UNSC specified that it may impose 'targeted and graduated measures, through country-specific resolutions, such as, inter alia, a ban on the export or supply of small arms and light weapons and of other military equipment and on military assistance, against these parties' (UNSC res. 1539 (2004), § 5 (c); see also *ibid.*, § 6).

137 See UNSC res. 1539 (2004), § 2; UNSC res. 1612 (2005), §§ 3, 8. The monitoring mechanism is contained in UN-SG, Report of the Secretary-General on Children and Armed Conflict, Doc. A/59/695-S/2005/72 of 9 February 2005, at §§ 58 ff. Among 'the standards that constitute the basis for monitoring' for the protection of children in armed conflicts, the UN-SG includes the CRC, its Optional Protocol on Children in Armed Conflict and the ILO C182 Convention (*ibid.*, paras 69–70). The complex mechanism implies the collection of information using all relevant UN sources and their mainstreaming, through the Special Representative of the UN-SG, to the UN-SG, which prepares a report on the matter.

138 *Supra* note 135.

139 UNSC res. 1612 (2005), § 8.

in violation of applicable international law relating to the rights and protection of children in armed conflict'.[140]

The CAAC has so far issued conclusions on six countries[141] and Reports by the UN-SG on four more countries are still awaiting consideration.[142] It is worth underlining that the CAAC may recommend to the UNSC to impose targeted sanctions on individuals or groups who are responsible for the recruitment of children.[143] The UNSC has in fact decided to adopt such sanctions in the case of the Democratic Republic of Congo: travel bans and assets freezes have been imposed on 'political and military leaders recruiting or using children in armed conflict in violation of applicable international law', operating in the DRC, and designated by the Sanctions Committee on the DRC.[144]

Finally, it should also be noted that conscripting or enlisting of children under the age of 15 into national armed forces or using them to participate actively in hostilities is a crime under the Statute of the International Criminal Court (hereafter: ICC)[145] and that the UNSC may refer cases relating to such crimes to the ICC for its consideration.[146]

The implementation, monitoring, and enforcement system for the recruitment of child soldiers clearly may be the strongest one for any of the worst forms of child labour considered here.

10.3.4 Sexual exploitation of children

Article 3 subpara. (b) of ILO Convention 182 targets the sexual exploitation of children, or 'the use, procuring or offering of a child for prostitution, for the

---

140 *Ibid.*, § 9. In its action plan for the monitoring, reporting and compliance mechanism, the UN-SG mentioned, among the measures that the UNSC may take in cases of grave and persistent violations, 'the imposition of travel restrictions on leaders, their exclusion from any governance structures and amnesty provisions ... a ban on military assistance, restrictions on the flow of financial resources to offending parties ...' (Report of the Secretary-General on Children and Armed Conflict, *supra* note 137, at § 115).

141 On Democratic Republic of the Congo (DRC) (Doc. S/2006/724, 11 September 2006), Sudan (Doc. S/2006/971, 13 December 2006), Burundi (Doc. S/2007/92, 15 February 2007) and Côte d'Ivoire (Doc. S/2007/93, 15 February 2007), Sri Lanka (Doc. S/AC.51/2007/9, 15 June 2007) and Nepal (S/AC.51/2007/8, 15 June 2007). All documents are available at <www.un.org/children/conflict/english/securitycouncilw182.html>.

142 On Somalia (Doc. S/2007/259, 7 May 2007), Uganda (Doc. S/2007/260), Democratic Republic of the Congo (Doc. S/2007/391, 28 June 2007) (second report), Chad (Doc. S/2007/400, 3 July 2007). All documents are available on the website indicated *supra* note 141.

143 The CAAC has done so, for example, in the case of the DRC (Doc. S/2006/724, *supra* note 141) and Sri Lanka (Doc. S/AC.51/2007/9, *supra* note 141).

144 UNSC res. 1698 (2006) of 31 July 2006, § 13. Interestingly, the UNSC has requested the CAAC to assist the Sanctions Committee on the DRC in the designation of the individuals referred to above (*ibid.*, § 17).

145 ICC Statute, available at <www.un.org/law/icc/statute/romefra.htm>, art. 8(2)(b)(xxvi).

146 *Ibid.*, art. 13(b).

production of pornography or for pornographic performances'. This issue is strongly linked to others, such as slavery and traffic of human beings (or even degrading treatment),[147] and thus entails many normative overlaps.

The UN Convention on Traffic in Persons and Prostitution, as seen above,[148] requires States to punish persons engaged in sexual exploitation of others, and to take or encourage measures for the prevention of prostitution and for the rehabilitation of the victims thereof.[149]

Sexual exploitation, child prostitution and pornography are also prohibited by the ICCPR[150] and the ICESCR.[151] These practices may also be relevant under other treaties in terms of discrimination in general[152] and in particular with regards to girls.[153]

However, it is within the CRC that the protection for the child in this regard has been expanded. Article 34 of the CRC already required States to protect the child from 'all forms of sexual exploitation' and to take, in particular, all appropriate measures to prevent: '(a) The inducement or coercion of a child to engage in any unlawful sexual activity; (b) The exploitative use of children in prostitution or other unlawful sexual practices; (c) The exploitative use of children in pornographic performances and materials'. Such general obligations have been reinforced through the CRC Optional Protocol on Sale and Sexual Exploitation of Children, which prohibits child prostitution and child pornography[154] and which requires States to prevent and criminalize, following the detailed obligations and principles illustrated above,[155]

---

147 Van Bueren, *The International Law*, *supra* note 8, at 278-279.

148 *Supra* section 10.3(2).

149 UN Convention on Traffic in Persons and Prostitution, art. 16.

150 'The State party should enforce laws prohibiting ... child labour and child prostitution and should implement programmes to prevent and combat such human rights abuses' (HRC Concluding Observations on Brazil, ICCPR, A/51/40 vol. I (1996) 44 at § 336). See also Concluding Observations on Mexico ICCPR, A/54/40 vol. I (1999) 61 at § 327; Venezuela, ICCPR, A/56/40 vol. I (2001) 49 at § 77(24); Thailand, ICCPR, A/60/40 vol. I (2005) 83 at §§ 95(20) and 95(23), where reference to articles 8 and 24 of the ICCPR is explicit. According to the HRC, apart from art. 24, the issue of child prostitution and pornography may also raise violations under articles 9 (right to liberty of the person) and 17 (right to privacy and family life) of the Covenant (Concluding Observations on Japan, ICCPR, A/54/40 vol. I (1999) 36 at § 171).

151 Concluding Observations on Philippines and Sri Lanka (*supra* note 25); Venezuela and Bolivia (*supra* note 87); Sweden, E/1996/22 (1995) 35 at § 146; Italy, E/2001/22 (2000) 34 at §§ 121, 134; Portugal, E/2001/22 (2000) 70 at § 424; Ukraine, E/2002/22 (2001) 78 at §§ 492 and 510.

152 See CERD, Concluding Observations on Venezuela, *supra* note 74.

153 See ComEDAW Concluding Comments, *supra* note 113 (which addresses trafficking and prostitution of girl children) and specifically on prostitution: ComEDAW, Concluding Comments on Democratic Republic of the Congo, CEDAW, A/55/38 part I (2000) 21 at § 219; Suriname, A/57/38 part II (2002) 82 at §§ 49–50; Guatemala, A/57/38 part III (2002) 171 at §§ 184–185.

154 CRC Optional Protocol on Sale and Sexual Exploitation of Children, art. 1.

155 See *supra* section 10.3.2.

the 'offering, obtaining, procuring or providing a child for child prostitution'[156] and the 'producing, distributing, disseminating, importing, exporting, offering, selling or possessing for the above purposes child pornography'.[157]

10.3.5 The use of children in illicit activities and hazardous work

ILO Convention 182 prohibits 'the use, procuring or offering of a child for illicit activities, in particular for the production and trafficking of drugs as defined in the relevant international treaties'.[158] UN instruments do not deal with participation of the child in illicit activities as such, but rather concentrate on the aspect related to drugs production and trade. Article 33 of the CRC requires Parties to take all appropriate measures to protect children from the illicit use of narcotic drugs and psychotropic substances and, in particular, to prevent the use of children in the illicit production and trafficking of such substances. The HRC has also clarified that this may fall under the ICCPR as well.[159] Finally, a UN Convention against Illicit Traffic in Narcotic Drugs and Psychotropic Substances may also be relevant on the matter.[160]

Article 3 subpara. (d) of ILO Convention 182 contains a broad, residual provision, which prohibits work which 'by its nature or the circumstances in which it is carried out, is likely to harm the health, safety or morals of children'.[161] There is no ad hoc corresponding provision in UN treaties. General norms on the protection of the child in human rights conventions, such as article 24 of the ICCPR,[162] article 10(3) of the ICESCR[163] and article 32 of the CRC,[164] may fill this gap. The latter is further supplemented by CRC article 36, whereby Parties must protect the child 'against all other forms of exploitation prejudicial to any aspects of the child's welfare'. All these provisions may also be used to address the participation of the child in illicit activities beyond the production and trade in drugs mentioned above.

10.4 General reflections and concluding remarks

As the present analysis clearly shows, the UN has certainly made a decisive contribution to the implementation of ILO standards on child labour. From the

---

156 CRC Optional Protocol on Sale and Sexual Exploitation of Children, art. 3(1)(b). Child prostitution is defined as 'the use of a child in sexual activities for remuneration or any other form of consideration' (*ibid.*, art. 2(b)).

157 *Ibid.*, art. 3(1)(c). Child pornography is defined as 'any representation, by whatever means, of a child engaged in real or simulated explicit sexual activities or any representation of the sexual parts of a child for primarily sexual purposes' (*ibid.*, art. 2(c)).

158 ILO Convention 182 , art. 3 (c).

159 HRC, General Comment No. 17, *supra* note 62.

160 See Noguchi (this volume).

161 For an analysis of the provision, see Beqiraj (this volume).

162 *Supra* section 10.2.1.

163 *Supra* section 10.2.2.

164 *Supra* section 10.2.3.

substantial point of view, there are many UN treaties that either deal with child labour as such, or that address more specific issues that are considered worst forms of child labour, or are connected to them. Such an 'extra normative layer' of substantial obligations is in itself a positive factor which enhances the protection for the child, but the positive impact of the UN involvement in this sector may be relevant also from the point of view of implementation, monitoring and compliance mechanisms.

UN instruments containing general obligations on child labour embody the basic features of freedom from child labour as a human right: a prohibition of economic exploitation of the child, and of work that may be harmful to the same, as well as general obligations to set minimum age limits for their employment. This broad human right has been interpreted, due to the activity of the UN treaty monitoring bodies (and to explicit linking provisions in the treaty texts themselves, such as in the CRC), with constant reference to ILO standards, in such a way that these latter in some cases seem to have been integrated into the UN instruments, providing for the greatest protection for the individual. This has a considerable impact also from the point of view of the monitoring process, as UN bodies address also the implementation and compliance of Parties with ILO standards as well. In this sense, the latter benefit from a double monitoring level from the quantitative, but also from the qualitative point of view: whereas for some UN treaties the monitoring mechanisms may be similar to those of the ILO, in other cases they may be truly additional to the ILO ones, such as with the ICCPR, which provides for a system of individual redress for treaty violations, highlighting the dimension of freedom from child labour also as a justiciable subjective human right.

The role of the UN is even more relevant as far as the worst forms of child labour are concerned. In this regard, the UN system has developed an ad hoc and very detailed and comprehensive normative framework that develops general obligations established under the ILO. Moreover, given the nature of the issues at stake, namely practices that may violate several fundamental human rights, or that may even qualify as international crimes, also many non-ad hoc UN instruments or non-ad hoc provisions become applicable. The monitoring, implementation, and compliance verification machinery of the UN is particularly strong in this regard. In addition to specific *treaty-bodies*, the UN is equipped also with a broad system of *charter-based* bodies (such as the Human Rights Council, Special Rapporteurs on thematic issues, Special Representatives of the UN-SG and so on) which are capable of making a significant contribution to the monitoring of human rights implementation and violations. The most significant mechanism, however, is the one related to the recruitment of child soldiers, which benefits from an outstanding enforcement system created under the UNSC's responsibility that entails the possibility of imposing individual sanctions for those who violate international standards in this regard, including ILO Convention 182.

This wealth of normative solutions and institutional monitoring implementation and compliance mechanisms, from both the ILO and the UN, is certainly a positive factor *per se*, but in order to ensure the best protection for the child, coordination and integration between the activities and the normative frameworks of the two organizations (as well as within either of them) is a priority, in order not to interpret the two fields as self-contained regimes. Within the UN system it seems that this opening towards ILO instruments has been attempted. The same 'bridge' towards the relevant developments of the UN system at large should be built within the ILO.

Finally, the potential of UN action in this field of international law may be even more important. The UN as such, with its comprehensive normative and institutional framework, is probably the only organization that may be capable of addressing a complex issue such as that of child labour, with all its implications, touching not only upon labour standards and rights as such, but also upon all the human rights and international security issues involved, as well as upon the root causes of child labour, such as poverty or underdevelopment.

Chapter 11

The Contribution of the World Bank in Fostering Respect for ILO Child Labour Standards

Sabine Schlemmer-Schulte[1]

11.1 Introduction

The 20th century saw great progress in reducing poverty and improving well-being. During its last four decades life expectancy in the developing world increased 20 years on average, the infant mortality rate fell by more than half, and fertility rates declined by almost half.[2] During its last two decades net primary school enrolment in developing countries increased by 13 per cent. Between 1965 and 1998 average income more than doubled in developing countries, and from 1990 to 1998 alone the number of people in extreme poverty fell by 78 million.

However, as the world moved into the 21st century, poverty remained a global problem of huge proportions. Of the world's 6 billion people, 2.8 billion live on less than US\$2 a day, and 1.2 billion on less than US\$1 a day. Six infants out of every 100 do not see their first birthday, and 8 do not survive to their fifth. Of those who reach school age, 9 boys in 100 and 14 girls in 100 do not go to primary school. While in rich countries fewer than 5 per cent of all children under five are malnourished, in poor countries as many as 50 per cent are.

Despite continuous attempts to address the issue of poverty in the Third World, the divide between the North and the South (that is, the 'haves' and the 'have-nots') keeps growing. Average income in the richest 20 countries is 37 times the average in the poorest 20 countries – a gap that has doubled over the past 50 years. The phenomenon of globalization has not been able to reverse this trend. The earlier optimism that growth and globalization would automatically trickle down to the benefit of all has faded in light of data on poverty.

Child labour is a prime example of the increasing North–South divide. Though its incidence has somewhat declined, children in developing countries continue to work in large numbers and for long hours, more so than should be tolerable in this age of globalization and prosperity. The world has an estimated 186 million child

---

1 The author thanks Mohamed Sawani, JD cand., for valuable research assistance.

2 Figures and data referred to in the introduction of this chapter are taken from the *World Development Report 2000/2001 – Attacking Poverty*, Washington DC, World Bank, 2001, unless otherwise indicated.

labourers – 5.7 million in forced and bonded labour, 1.8 million in prostitution and 0.3 million in armed conflict – a failure of stunning proportions.[3]

Despite its persistence in the developing countries, until a decade ago, child labour had only been a concern for UNICEF and the ILO. Global development institutions such as the World Bank[4] largely ignored the issue until the mid-1990s when it began occupying centre stage in international policy settings. While children's concerns in general had, since the end of the 1960s, been on the agenda of the World Bank's financing of social programmes on health, education and population, as a second prong added to its traditional prong of financing bricks-and-mortar projects, child labour had received little attention within the Bank until NGOs, labour unions and the ILO began, in the wave of growing international awareness, pressuring the Bank into action.

The purpose of this chapter is to trace the history of the World Bank's increasing involvement in the global fight against child labour; analyse the substance of the Bank's take on child labour from both the legal and development policy perspective; identify the similarities and differences between the Bank's approach and the one taken by other agencies advocating the cause; record the dynamics of the inter-agency debate on child labour between the World Bank and the ILO, eventually resulting in the ILO's adoption of an approach similar to the Bank with the 1999 Convention on the Elimination of the Worst Forms of Child Labour (No. 182);[5] and conclude with a critical note on the Bank's recent introduction of child labour benchmarks in the assessment of its borrowers from its soft-lending arm, the International Development Agency (IDA).[6]

---

3 In the mid-1990s, the ILO estimated that approximately 250 million children between the ages of 5 and 14 were employed worldwide – 120 million full-time workers and 130 million working part-time, 61 per cent of which are found in Asia, 32 per cent in Africa and 7 per cent in Latin America. These figures may, however, have underestimated the problem of child labour. Because statistical surveys did not cover children employed under the age of 12, there was often only inadequate documentation and, frequently, monitoring of child labour in countries was not allowed. These figures are taken from estimates by the ILO. See ILO, *Child Labour: Targeting the Intolerable*, Geneva, ILO, 1996.

4 Unless indicated otherwise, the term World Bank (or Bank) covers both the International Bank for Reconstruction and Development (IBRD) and the International Development Association (IDA). See <www.worldbank.org>.

5 This convention will hereinafter be referred to as 1999 Convention on Worst Forms of Child Labour or 1999 Convention.

6 The International Development Agency (IDA) was created in 1960 as the third financial arm of the World Bank Group. With (today) 166 members, IDA extends credit to countries that because of their poverty level require lending on more concessional terms than IBRD can provide. IDA credits typically carry a service charge of 0.75 per cent and generally have 35- or 40-year final maturities and a 10-year grace period for principal repayments. IDA's capital is, as a consequence of its soft lending conditions, subject to fast depletion. IDA's capital is therefore on a regular basis 'replenished', based on voluntary capital contributions by rich IDA members.

11.2 A historical account of the World Bank's engagement in the global fight against child labour

11.2.1 Child labour: a dormant issue within the Bank until the mid-1990s

Until the mid-1990s, the Bank had not addressed the issue of child labour as a prominent and/or free-standing concern in its operations.[7] With the international community's growing awareness of the issue and recognition of its pressing nature, the Bank's attitude changed. The change in attitude can be traced back in particular, though not exclusively, to the correspondence of several NGOs with the Bank's President as well as the ILO's effort to call on the Bank to use its financial muscle to urge its borrowing members to ratify its 1973 Minimum Age Convention (No. 138), which set general age standards for admission of children to employment along with several sectoral ILO conventions, and to improve implementation and compliance of these conventions by Bank borrowers that were parties to these ILO conventions.

Before the above-mentioned NGO and ILO pressure, the Bank had addressed the issue of child labour under some other titles, for example in the policy papers on women in development and labour migration. The 1995 World Development Report (WDR), a major World Bank research and vision publication, was also devoted to labour issues. One of its findings was:

> National legislation and international conventions banning child labor have symbolic value as an expression of society's desire to eradicate this practice. But they cannot deliver results unless accompanied by measures to shift the balance of incentives away from child labor and toward education. The most important ways in which governments can shift this balance are by providing a safety net to protect the poor, expanding opportunities for quality education, and gradually increasing institutional capacity to enforce legislated bans. Programs that provide income security for poor households, such as food-for-work or other public works programs, will have beneficial effects on child labor. Measures to reduce the cost of school attendance (subsidies, construction of schools closer to children's homes) and improve the quality of education (changes in curricula, more and better teachers) could also help. As the incidence of poverty falls and education improves, child labor will decline. That in turn will make enforcement of legislated bans easier, starting with such universally abhorred forms of child labor as prostitution and hazardous work.

Bank economists had further studied the question of child labour.[8] Despite the absence of an operational policy on child labour, the Bank contributed to child labour reduction through its financing of projects for education, health, nutrition,

---

7 See Ibrahim F.I. Shihata, 'The World Bank's Protection and Promotion of Children's Rights', *International Journal of Children's Rights*, Vol. 4, 1996, 383–405 (noting that the Bank started considering child labour as an issue to be specially addressed in its development assistance to borrowers in 1996).

8 Papers which were the result of such studies include F. Siddiqui and H. Patrinos, 'Child Labour – Issues, Causes and Interventions', World Bank Human Resources Development and Operations Policy Working Paper No. 56, 1995; C. Grootaert and R. Kanbur, 'Child Labour – A Review', Washington DC, World Bank Research Working Paper No. 1454, 1995.

population and social safety nets.[9] The Bank had thus long recognized its linkage to poverty and to the poor quality or availability of education.

11.2.2 External criticism fuelling the Bank's internal debate

In the mid-1990s, child labour became a central focus of the international debate on the positive and negative effects of globalization. Several NGOs skilfully made the case before Bank management to address child labour issues in a more focused way, while the ILO called for World Bank child labour lending conditionalities. Bank management felt that the time was ripe for the Bank to develop a more explicit position on the issue of child labour.

At consecutive meetings of the Bank's Operations Policy Committee (OPC), World Bank senior management took stock of the economists' studies on child labour as well as the question of the Bank's direct involvement in child labour issues from a legal perspective.[10] Consensus among senior management was soon arrived at, holding that child labour in terms of development economics – the science and its evolving teachings have ever since the creation of the Bank in 1944 contributed to changes in Bank policies – was a complex subject. While often harmful, part-time work in many countries was a fact of life for many children and neither exploitative nor detrimental to the child's development. If not exceeding certain proportions in terms of the types of work given to children, the conditions in which they perform it, the duration per day and week, etc., it can, in contrast, help young children acquire skills and build confidence. However, if it amounts to exploitation, as in the most obvious and outrageous cases of bonded labour, prostitution, military groups, the drug trade and highly hazardous occupations, it endangers children's health and development and often also their survival.

From a legal perspective, World Bank senior management was briefed about existing legal frameworks to combat child labour at the national and international level.[11] Management was in particular advised that the 1989 United Nations Convention on the Rights of the Child, while addressing all of children's rights, included a provision highlighting the right of children under the age of 18 to be protected from exploitative labour,[12] and made the elimination of such labour a public policy objective to the extent that state parties to the CRC had resources available to eradicate child labour, rather than according it the status of an absolute right for the

---

9 The Bank spent on average about 20 to 25 per cent of its lending on education, health, population and nutrition programmes. See consecutive World Bank Annual Reports (1995–99), Section Overview of World Bank Activities in respective fiscal year.

10 For a detailed analysis of the legal issues, see *infra* section 11.3.

11 See Background Note on International Approaches to Child Labour prepared by the Bank's Office of the Senior Vice President and General Counsel for the OPC Meeting on September 23, 1996.

12 See the general provision of art. 32 of the UNCRC on the 'right of the child to be protected from economic exploitation and performing any work that is likely to be hazardous … or to be harmful to the child's health' plus the special provisions of articles 33, 34, 35 and 38 of the UNCRC singling out as unacceptable forms of work trafficking in substances, prostitution, abduction and sale of children, and work in the armed forces.

individual child enforceable against the State Party to the CRC. Bank management was further made aware of the fact that, at the time of the OPC's meetings, the CRC had been ratified by more than 185 countries.

On the contrary, Convention 138, as well as its sectoral conventions, which introduce strict minimum age standards prohibiting any type of employment below a certain age or before completion of compulsory education and set a further age standard prohibiting any type of employment likely to jeopardize the health, safety, or morals of young persons below that age, had, at the time, a very poor ratification record with barely some 50 countries having accepted the ILO conventions as legally binding.

Senior management was finally advised that the Bank's mandate set limits for the structure and substance of Bank lending conditionalities as a result of the Bank, unlike ILO, not being an international agency with a purpose of setting standards nor having the role of a world police officer 'enforcing' national or international standards by conditioning lending upon a borrowing country's compliance with such standards. Nothing, however, would legally prevent the Bank from financing programmes that extended incentives to families who withdrew their children from the streets and labour in order to send them to school.

In light of the economists' assessment of child labour in the development context, as well as the possible ways of Bank involvement in the fight against child labour under its legal mandate, Bank senior management decided that, for a development institution like the Bank, solutions such as the imposition of a minimum age for employment or the requirement of having completed compulsory education prior to beginning working, while possibly justified for other organizations, economically ran the risk of worsening the situation of children because they ignored economic, social and cultural factors underlying child labour. Legally, these solutions would risk turning the Bank into a standard-setting agency or police force.

Hence, in order to remain truthful to its legal mandate and avoid making mistakes from the development economics perspective, the Bank would assist its developing members by financing special child labour eradication programmes, but would not condition its overall lending on the members' record in terms of child labour eradication. In other words, the Bank was to provide an alternative for the children and their families in order to prevent the situation where children dismissed from work in accordance with employment laws would be left to fend for themselves in the streets or be forced into taking up even more hazardous employment on the black market.

11.2.3 Adoption of the World Bank Child Labour Paper

Based on the conviction that exploitative child labour has a negative impact on the economic and social development of countries, the Bank's management, in 1997, prepared a position paper on child labour ('The World Bank's Child Labour Paper'). This paper was submitted to the Bank's Board of Executive Directors for their consideration in May 1997. In their discussion of this paper in July 1997, the Executive Directors agreed with the new approach by the Bank to child labour issues, as proposed by management. They also agreed to the publication of the position paper with some revisions.[13]

According to the position paper, the Bank's new approach to child labour issues includes: (a) giving more focus to child labour issues in the policy dialogue with borrowing countries; (b) improving partnership on these issues with other relevant international organizations and NGOs; (c) raising the awareness and sensitivity of Bank staff regarding the issues involved; (d) giving more emphasis to child labour issues in existing lending activities; (e) requiring compliance with applicable child labour laws and regulations in specific projects where exploitative child labour is otherwise likely to occur; and (f) designing specific projects or components of projects to target the most harmful forms of child labour, possibly starting with pilot projects in countries where child labour is seen as a serious problem.

11.3 Pioneering a developmental approach to child labour

11.3.1 The World Bank's constructive move in the fight against child labour

Legally, the World Bank faced some constraints in dealing with the matter of child labour as a result of its special mandate. Unlike the UN or the ILO, it could not act out of a general concern for human rights or labour rights. The World Bank's perspective on child labour had to be the development perspective.

Under its Articles of Agreement, the Bank's express purposes are primarily to 'facilitate the investment of capital for productive purposes', 'promote private foreign investment ... for productive purposes', and 'encourage international investment for the development of the productive resources of members, thereby assisting in raising productivity, the standard of living and conditions of labour in their territories'.[14] In other words, the Bank's objective is to promote reconstruction and economic growth and development of its borrowing members.

To effectively carry out its function of economic development assistance, the Bank is authorized to make loans and guarantees on loans for the financing of specific programmes and projects.[15]

The Bank is explicitly prohibited from taking non-economic considerations into account in its decisions. According to its Articles of Agreement, 'the Bank and its officers shall not interfere in the political affairs of any member; nor shall they be influenced by the political character of the member or members concerned'.[16]

---

13 See P. Fallon and Z. Tzannatos, *Child Labour – Issues and Directions for the World Bank*, Washington DC, World Bank, Human Development Network Social Protection, 1998.

14 See art. I (i), (ii) and (iii) of IBRD's Articles of Agreement. Compare also with art. I of IDA's Articles of Agreement, which, to a certain degree, uses similar language. It should be noted that 'conditions of labour' in art. I of the IBRD's Articles of Agreement is meant as a reference to the realization of the Bank's objectives, not as an objective in and by itself.

15 See art. III, section 4 of IBRD's Articles of Agreement. Compare with art. V, section 2 of IDA's Articles of Agreement (limiting the Association's form of financing to loans).

16 See art. IV, section 10 of IBRD's Articles of Agreement and article V, section 6 of IDA's Articles of Agreement.

The Articles of Agreement require furthermore that 'only economic considerations shall be relevant to [the Bank's] decisions'.[17] Consequently, the Bank, as a basically financial, economic development institution, is prohibited from getting involved in the political affairs of its members.

Over time, the Bank's financial assistance to its members, which under the Bank's charter related literally only to the financing of assistance to promote economic growth and development, evolved in practice,[18] with the Bank's Executive Directors, when endorsing this evolving practice, exercising their power to interpret the Bank's Articles of Agreement.[19] As a result of that evolution, social development (for example, health, education and population concerns) became a second main goal of the World Bank in the 1970s, in addition to infrastructure, industry and agriculture, in other words the Bank's original bricks-and-mortar business.[20] In the 1980s, the social prong of the World Bank's development assistance broadened further and began to include the environment, women and gender issues, and social security issues which were neither expressly referred to in the Bank's Articles of Agreement nor of purely economic nature.

When the extent of public spending was questioned in the 1980s, in the context of the global recession and the debt crisis particularly affecting Latin-America and sub-Saharan Africa, another shift in emphasis was adopted by the Bank.[21] The third prong consisted of the promotion of policies that would achieve macro-economic stability,

---

17 *Ibid.*

18 For an account of the Bank's evolution from a mere bricks-and-mortar financier to a supporter of social programmes in the 1970s as well as ultimately a major policy-maker in the Third World since the 1980s, see E.S. Mason and R.E. Asher, *The World Bank Since Bretton Woods*, Washington DC, Brookings Institution, 1973; and D. Kapur, J. Lewis and R. Webb, *The World Bank – Its First Half Century*, Washington DC, Brookings Institution, 1997.

19 Under the Bank's Articles of Agreement, the Board of Executive Directors has the power to interpret these Articles subject only to possible review by the Board of Governors upon request of a Bank member. See art. IX of the IBRD Articles of Agreement and art. X of the IDA Articles of Agreement. For most of the time since IBRD's and IDA's creation, the Board of Executive Directors did not issue formal interpretations of the Articles but discussed issues of interpretation alongside their decisions on policy matters or their approval of loans and guarantees. Frequently, these discussions took place in the light of a legal opinion by the Bank's General Counsel. The General Counsel's legal opinions clarify the meaning of the Bank's Articles and suggest to the Board an interpretation that is both legally sound and suits the purposes and interests of the Bank and its members as a whole. For details regarding the role of the Board of Executive Directors and the General Counsel in interpreting the Bank's Articles, see Ibrahim F.I. Shihata, 'Interpretation and Amendment of the IBRD Articles of Agreement', Chapter 1 in Shihata, *The World Bank in a Changing World*, Vol. III, The Hague, Martinus Nijhoff, 2000.

20 For a more detailed description of the evolution of the Bank's development assistance, see *ibid.*, Chapter 3.

21 During the 1980s, many developing countries had to cope with severe macro-economic crises. From the financial constraints resulting from these crises, the need arose to formulate adjustment policies which paid attention to both the needs of the economy in general as well as the needs of the poor. Bank experience with adjustment loans and credits to developing countries for the restructuring of the economy in general showed that it was possible to shift

open the economies, integrate them into world markets, promote investment and cut public spending.[22] Another refinement of the Bank's financing of macro-economic, sectoral and structural adjustment programmes of its borrowing members consisted of its assistance to developing countries under the rubric of 'good governance'[23] and in the promotion of the 'rule of law'[24] in a number of areas with relevance to their economic development, such as efforts to improve public sector management, address weaknesses in the civil service, strengthen legal, regulatory and judicial frameworks, and reduce corruption.[25]

These literal provisions of the Bank's charter, as well as their authoritative interpretation by virtue of practice, had implications for the question of how the Bank could address the issue of child labour.

---

public spending in favour of the poor, even within an overall framework of increased fiscal discipline. See *World Development Report – Poverty*, Washington DC, World Bank, 1990, 3.

22　See *ibid.*, 3 and 56–73. For these above-noted adjustment measures plus several further measures, including privatization and tax reforms, John Williamson of the Institute for International Economics in Washington DC coined the term 'Washington Consensus' measures because these measures became the favourite prescription of several major players in development finance headquartered in Washington DC, who recommended them to developing countries. See John Williamson, 'What Washington means by Policy Reform?', in John Williamson (ed.), *Latin-American Adjustment: How Much Has Happened?*, Boulder CO, Westview, 1986. Among the DC-headquartered institutions adhering to the 'Washington Consensus' are the International Monetary Fund (IMF), the World Bank, the US Agency for International Development, and US think tanks. The 'Washington Consensus' prescription is still prevalent in adjustment programmes financed by the IMF and the World Bank. For details, see S. Schlemmer-Schulte, 'Die Rolle der Internationalen Finanzinstitutionen im Nord-Süd-Konflikt', in W. Meng, U. Magnus, S. Schlemmer-Schulte, T. Cottier, P-T. Stoll and A. Epiney (eds), *Das Internationale Recht im Nord-Süd-Verhältnis* – Berichte der Deutschen Gesellschaft für Völkerrecht, Vol. 41, Heidelberg, Müller, 2005, 149–221, at 158 et seq.

23　For its purposes, the Bank has defined governance as 'the manner in which power is exercised in the management of a country's economic and social resources for development', thus limiting its concern for good governance to issues which have undisputed economic implications. For details of the definition of the term 'governance' in the Bank's work and the legal rationale of extending the Bank's work to governance issues on the basis of the Articles of Agreement, see Shihata, 'The World Bank and "Governance" Issues in Its Borrowing Members', in *The World Bank*, Vol. I, 1991. See also Shihata, *Governance: The World Bank's Experience*, Washington DC, World Bank, 1994.

24　For the special meaning of the term 'rule of law' within the context of World Bank finance, see Ibrahim F.I. Shihata, *The World Bank Legal Papers*, Springer, 2000, 245–82; and S. Schlemmer-Schulte, 'The World Bank's Promotion of the Rule of Law in Developing Countries', in S. Schlemmer-Schulte and K-Y. Tung (eds), *Liber Amicorum Ibrahim F.I. Shihata – International Finance and Development Law*, The Hague, Kluwer, 2001, 677–725.

25　For an overview of the Bank's work in the field of governance, see World Bank, *World Development Report – The State in a Changing World*, Washington DC, World Bank, 1997, in particular at 79–98 on institution building, and at 99–109 on efforts to reduce corruption. For a comprehensive description and legal analysis of the Bank's governance work, see Ibrahim F.I. Shihata, *Complementary Reform – Essays on Legal, Judicial and Other Institutional Reforms supported by the World Bank*, The Hague, Kluwer, 1997.

Child labour had often been described as an enforcement issue. The Bank's range of action in addressing enforcement of measures against child labour was, however, limited. As an international development finance institution and not a world government, the Bank did not have a general mandate to act as an enforcement agency for international or national law.[26] Thus it could not require its member countries, as a general proposition, to enforce child labour standards regardless of their relevance to the Bank's operations.[27]

In terms of its lending policies, this meant that the Bank could impose conditionalities regarding child labour standards on its financial assistance, but only to the extent that lack of compliance with such standards undermined the execution or the developmental objective of its programmes or projects.[28] Consequently, the Bank could include a provision in the loan agreements of specific projects where there are good reasons to believe that exploitative child labour (such as in an infrastructure project it finances) may occur. According to such a provision, the borrower would undertake to enforce its laws with respect to child labour, including the treaties to which it is a party, in the implementation of such Bank-financed projects. Failure to observe such covenants would be an act of default, which allows the Bank to suspend in whole or in part the right of the borrowing country to make withdrawals from the loan account. In the context of project-lending there therefore exists a limitation on the Bank in terms of the geographical scope of child labour conditionalities.[29]

The above-described geographical limitation in the scope of conditionalities does not apply to Bank conditionalities in the context of non-project-lending.[30] Policy changes which the borrower is required to make in the context of an adjustment

---

26 For details on how the limitations of the Bank's charter impact on the Bank's approach to human rights in general, see S. Schlemmer-Schulte, 'The World Bank and Human Rights', *Austrian Review of International and European Law*, Vol. 4, 1999, 230–268.

27 Thus, if the idea had been to finance the appointment of an inspectorate in projects where it is felt that there is a clear danger of child labour being employed, it needs again to be emphasized that: firstly, the borrower is responsible for the enforcement of labour laws in the implementation of its projects; and, secondly, that inspectors would need to be recruited by the borrower himself since the Bank has to respect the borrower's jurisdiction on its own territory.

28 The special situation of financing projects out of funds of the Global Environment Facility (GEF) is an exception to this general rule. Ratification of a number of international environmental conventions by the recipient country of GEF funds is a pre-condition for eligibility to receive GEF funds. It must be emphasized that the GEF is a special financing mechanism, in other words a trust fund in respect of which the Bank serves as trustee. Together with the Bank, two other organizations, UNDP and UNEP, are engaged in this enterprise. The GEF needs, however, to be distinguished from the main Bank business in connection with which the Bank does not require borrowing countries to ratify international treaties.

29 A limitation of a temporal nature ensues as well once the project financed by the Bank has been completed and conditionalities 'expire.'

30 Non-project-lending within the Bank's terminology refers to the financing of structural and sectoral adjustment programmes under the then-applicable World Bank policy on adjustment lending. The latter, reflecting many of the 'Washington Consensus' prescriptions of the bank and the IMF for Third World countries, has recently been replaced by a new policy which now calls adjustment lending 'development policy lending'.

programme financed by the Bank (that is, the major form of non-project-lending) typically entail changes in the country's legislation covering the entire territory of the borrowing country. However, these conditionalities, while normally unlimited in their national geographical scope, are subject to limitations in temporal terms. The conditionalities' 'life' time does not extend beyond the time of the programme. Recommended changes, therefore, should in principle not include the request to ratify international treaties potentially incorporating in their substance some of the Bank recommended standards because such ratification would bind the borrower beyond the execution of the programme financed by the Bank.[31] The borrower is supposed to maintain control over its own standards after the execution of an adjustment programme which would not be the case were the ratification of international treaties requested. It is in this sense that conditionalities, even in conjunction with adjustment lending, did not ask for the adoption or enforcement of non-national child labour standards.[32]

Child labour, as a phenomenon whose prevalence is linked to economic poverty and poor quality or availability of education, did not raise the issue of the Bank's violating the prohibition of political activities.[33]

11.3.2 Spill-over effects on ILO: from strict minimum age approach to worst forms of child labour

The ILO's long-standing approach to child labour is part-and-parcel of its objective of raising labour standards in its Member States. To that end, the ILO has for decades been active in adopting conventions on the minimum working age.[34] Before the ILO adopted its latest child labour convention focusing on the worst forms of child labour in June 1999, its most important convention was the 1973 Minimum Age Convention (No. 138), setting general age standards for admission to employment (along with the accompanying Recommendation No. 146). Convention 138 entered into force in

---

31 Moreover, adjustment loans are legally structured in a way to allow for the borrower to decide to step away from them at any time he so wishes without such a decision amounting to a breach of contract. See S. Schlemmer-Schulte, 'Die Rolle der Internationalen Finanzinstitutionen im Nord-Süd-Konflikt', in Meng et al. (eds), *supra* note 22, 149–221, at 163–5.

32 It may be noted that the Bank follows the route outlined above with respect to human rights treaties. With respect to members' accession to the WTO, the lines are more blurred. While the Bank did not directly require ratification of WTO agreements, it however supported indirectly such ratification and ultimately accession to WTO in parallel or even prior to members' negotiations on accession by conditioning its adjustment lending, among others, on trade liberalization, liberalization of financial and capital markets, and deregulation.

33 Protection of children against exploitative child labour in Bank-financed projects could hardly be seen as interference in the political affairs of the countries concerned. For details of the prohibition of political activities for the Bank, see Shihata, *The World Bank Legal Papers*, *supra* note 23, 245–82 and 799–810.

34 There are, in addition to the umbrella Convention 138, a number of sectoral conventions regulating admission to employment in specific sectors (industry, sea, agriculture, trimmers and stokers, non-industrial employment, fishing and underground work).

1976. It served as ILO's general instrument on the subject of child labour and was meant to gradually replace earlier conventions setting age standards for employment in a number of specific economic sectors.

Convention 138 explicitly stated as its objective 'the effective abolition of child labour'.[35] It further set the general minimum age for admission to employment at the age of 15 (or, if compulsory schooling is completed later than that, at that later age).[36] However, exceptions are possible down to the lower age of 14 in countries with insufficiently developed economies and educational facilities.[37] Some forms of work by children 12 or 13 years old are also allowed under the Convention, on the condition that they do not impede education. The minimum age for admission to work that is likely to jeopardize the health, safety or morals of young persons is set at the age of 18.[38] Nevertheless, in exceptional cases such work may be authorized from the age of 16 years.[39]

As Convention 138 was not ratified as widely as other ILO Conventions,[40] the problem of child labour persisted, both on the ground as well as in the eyes of the very agency created for dealing with labour issues. When the World Bank, in tandem with the international debate, took the lead in addressing the issue focusing on the most harmful forms of child labour from a developmental perspective, ILO began rethinking its approach to child labour partly as a result of the dynamics of the inter-agency debate with the Bank as well as based on its own experience with its IPEC programme.[41] Intrigued by the World Bank's focus on harmful child labour (that is, forms of child labour that were unacceptable no matter what level of poverty), ILO decided to place child labour anew on its agenda with a view to adopting new international labour standards to stop the exploitation of children in harmful work and activities. The Convention Concerning the Prohibition and Immediate Elimination of the Worst Forms of Child Labour (No. 182) was drafted and negotiated under ILO's auspices within three years and finally adopted in June 1999.

The new ILO Convention makes it mandatory for States becoming parties to it to prohibit the 'worst forms of child labour'.[42] Such harmful child labour consists of certain types of labour undertaken by 'all persons under the age of 18'.[43] The definition of the notion of 'worst forms of child labour' rests on two pillars. One pillar is expressly determined by the Convention itself. This pillar comprises three types of child labour: (a) slavery (including forced or compulsory recruitment of children for use in armed conflict); (b) prostitution and pornography; and (c) illicit

---

35 See art. 1 of Convention 138.

36 See art. 2(3) of Convention 138.

37 See art. 2(4) of Convention 138.

38 See art. 3(1) of Convention 138.

39 See art. 3(3) of Convention 138.

40 It may be noted that by the end of 1996, 1997 and 1998, only 52, 59 and 69 countries, respectively, had ratified the ILO Minimum Age Convention.

41 With IPEC, ILO is assisting countries in elaborating and implementing comprehensive policies and targeted programmes and projects, launched in 1992 with financial support from several governments.

42 See art. 1 of Convention 182.

43 See art. 2 of Convention 182.

activities, in particular drug trafficking.[44] In substance, this part of the definition of 'worst forms of child labour' rests on a consensus on these types of labour as certainly being detrimental to children.

The second pillar refers to 'work which, by its nature or the circumstances in which it is carried out, is likely to jeopardize the health, safety or morals of children'.[45] The concrete types of work that will fall under this rather vague description of the notion of worst forms of child labour shall be determined by 'national laws or regulations or by the competent authority, after consultation with the organizations of employers and workers concerned, taking into account relevant international standards'.[46]

The Convention's notion of worst forms of child labour consists thus of two parts, the first including expressly defined and universally applicable standards, the second allowing for a flexible country-by-country approach in the definition of harmful child labour other than slavery, prostitution/pornography, and illicit activities such as drug trafficking. A Recommendation accompanying the Convention provides (non-mandatory) guidance for the purposes of determining further the types of work which are likely to harm children. The Recommendation refers to a number of types of work to which consideration in the determination of further harmful child labour by contracting parties should be given (that is, work exposing children to physical, emotional or sexual abuse; work underground, under water, at dangerous heights or in confined spaces; work with dangerous machines or equipment; work in an unhealthy environment exposing children to hazardous substances, agents or processes etc. dangerous to their health; or work under difficult conditions such as for extensive hours or during the night etc.).

The crucial link of a successful elimination of the worst forms of child labour through the assurance of children's education is acknowledged by the Convention in its express statement that parties to it shall, among others, 'take into account the importance of education in eliminating child labour [when taking measures in this respect]' and 'rehabilitate and socially reintegrate children who have worked through access to free basic education'.[47]

Although Convention 182, from the perspective of the ILO, is meant to complement the earlier Convention 138,[48] and countries thus ideally are supposed to ratify both conventions, there is no requirement for countries to actually do so. Becoming a party to only the more recent Convention 182, for example, makes it possible for countries to tolerate non-harmful child labour undertaken by children not only between the ages of 18 and 14 but even below the age of 14.[49]

Even when countries are subjecting themselves to both ILO child labour conventions, the overall regime by which they are bound after Convention 182 entered

---

44 See art. 3(a) to (c) of Convention 182.

45 See art. 3(d) of Convention 182.

46 See art. 4(1) of Convention 182.

47 See 4th paragraph of the preamble of Convention 182.

48 See 3rd paragraph of the preamble of Convention 182.

49 This may, among others, be the reason why Convention 182 has, as of the date of writing, been ratified by significantly more countries than Convention 138. By August 2007, 165 states had ratified Convention 182 and 150 had ratified Convention 138.

into force may arguably be less harsh than the one introduced by the Convention 138, a feature making it more attractive for developing countries to sign off on the latter than it used to be. Convention 138 prohibited '*any* type of employment or work which by its nature or the circumstances in which it is carried out is likely to jeopardize the health, safety or morals of young persons [below the age of 18 years]' with the determination of these prohibited types of employment to be made by the national governments.[50] Whereas the 1999 Convention equally prohibits 'work, which by its nature or the circumstances in which it is carried out, is likely to harm the health, safety or morals of children' with governments determining the details of this category of work, the provisions, despite similar wording, may be construed differently as a result of the different overall objectives of the two conventions. Convention 138's desire to prohibit children below certain ages from working calls potentially for a broader meaning of the prohibition of any type of employment detrimental to children's health, safety or morals undertaken between the ages of 18 and 15/14 years respectively. By contrast, Convention 182 focuses on the prohibition and elimination of the worst forms of child labour and explicitly list examples of such forms of child labour. The further forms to be determined to constitute prohibited forms of child labour may potentially be construed more narrowly in order for these forms of child labour to match the explicitly referred to forms.

11.4 Mainstreaming child labour concerns into the Bank's work

11.4.1 Living up to the Child Labour Paper's promise

Following the Board of Executive Directors' approval of the Child Labour Paper, Bank management immediately set to work on the efforts listed in the Paper.

While the Bank, to date, has refrained from adopting a mandatory formal policy on child labour, its practice has certainly followed the directions of its Child Labour Paper.[51] Clauses requiring the borrowing country, in connection with industry and similar projects, to make sure no child labour is employed while the project is implemented, have become common in Bank investment loans. For example, the Bank's credit agreement for the Silk Development Project in Bangladesh, which was approved in late 1997, comprised covenants requiring Bangladesh to make sure that contractors hired by the Silk Foundation (the agency responsible for the implementation of the project in Bangladesh) undertake to abide by the applicable laws of Bangladesh, including child labour laws, in their carrying out of the project.

Many special child labour-related projects have been undertaken by the World Bank. Some examples include: (a) the Ceará Water Management and Urban Development Project in Ceará, Brazil (the 'ABC' programme);[52] (b) the Child

---

50 Emphasis added. Compare art. 3(1) of Convention 138.

51 For legal details of formal Bank policies, see S. Schlemmer-Schulte, 'The World Bank's Promotion of the Rule of Law in Developing Countries', in Schlemmer-Schulte and Tung (eds), *Liber Amicorum Ibrahim F.I. Shihata*, *supra* note 23, 677–725, at 713–716.

52 This project addresses the issue of street children.

Development Project in Yemen;[53] (c) the Back-to-School Programme in Indonesia;[54] (d) the Child Welfare Reform Project in Romania[55] and (e) the District Primary Education Project in India.[56]

Needless to say that, as a result of the convergence in their approach to child labour, cooperation between the Bank and ILO in connection with concrete projects in developing countries has considerably increased.

Reducing child labour is a difficult task, involving a broad range of general and more specific measures, from poverty alleviation to programmes which encourage greater school attendance. In order to incorporate the concern with child labour into the Bank's work, it established a Child Labour Programme in May 1998.[57] The Child Labour Programme promotes a range of practical initiatives to combat child labour and builds up knowledge on the topic. The programme is housed in the Human Development Network and is the focal point for Bank-wide child labour activities, projects and policy. The programme supports various child labour and child labour-related projects, including research and analyses, pilot studies, child labour reduction evaluations, and internal and external dissemination through training, seminars and via the child labour website.[58] Policy implications derived from these projects feed into Bank dialogue with clients and donors, Bank country assistance strategies and lending activities.[59]

Last but not the least, child labour concerns have also been incorporated into the work of the Multilateral Investment Guarantee Agency (MIGA),[60] the Bank's private sector arm created in 1985 to extend political risk insurance to private investors investing in developing countries. In connection with MIGA's general capital increase in 1998, MIGA adopted a policy requiring from the investors covered by

---

53 This project is executed jointly with UNICEF. It provides targeted interventions in the areas of health, nutrition and education – especially for girls. The project includes rigorous evaluations, which can guide the development of policies that can reduce child labour and its harmful effects.

54 This programme consists of scholarships for poor students and block-grants to schools in deprived areas.

55 This project aims at reforming the childcare and child protection systems. It focuses on institutionalized and street children.

56 The project focuses on increasing access to primary education (particularly for working children, girls and other disadvantaged groups) and on building institutional capacity, improving the quality of education, increasing the completion of the primary education and reducing drop-out rates. For detailed figures on the Bank's spending on children and child labour programmes, see I. Kaur and Z. Tzannatos, *The World Bank and Children: A Review of Activities*, Washington DC, World Bank, 2002.

57 For details, see The Child Labour Program, Washington DC, World Bank, Human Development Network Social Protection, 1999.

58 See <http://www.worldbank.org/sp/>.

59 For Bank research as a basis of the Bank's actual dialogue with its borrowers, see A. Cigno, F.C. Rosati and Z. Tzannatos, *Child Labour Handbook*, Washington DC, World Bank, Social Protection Paper Series No. 0206, May 2002; and S. Bhatlotra and Z. Tzannatos, 'Child Labour: What Have We Learned?', Washington DC, World Bank, Social Protection Discussion Paper Series No. 0317, September 2004.

60 See <www.miga.org>.

its risk insurance to respect certain labour standards. MIGA's standard contracts of guarantee provide that it may cancel contracts if the project enterprise in the host country hires, among others, harmful child labour. MIGA's definition of harmful child labour recites the definition used in the CRC and on which the spirit of the Bank's Child Labour Paper had rested.[61]

11.4.2 The pitfalls of child labour performance criteria for allocation of IDA credits

As a result of recent 'replenishments' for IDA, the Bank's soft-lending arm,[62] which extends credit of highly concessional nature to its poorer members, the list of performance criteria which primarily determine the allocation of future IDA resources amongst its members has been expanded and now includes country performance in the area of labour standards. Among the latter standards with which compliance by the borrowing IDA country is measured, both Convention 138 and 182 feature.[63]

Evaluating a borrowing country's performance in a certain area, or measuring its compliance with ILO child labour conventions, means moving away from the usual approach of the Bank's development assistance in general, and with respect to child labour in particular, at least as originally laid out in the 1998 Child Labour Paper. That position paper had opted to extend extra financial assistance to borrowing countries following a 'carrot' approach in order to assist members to address the issue of child labour. Making a country's performance with respect to ILO conventions' 'do' and 'don't' provisions a prerequisite for any IDA financial assistance seems turning in the opposite direction and applying a big 'stick' before extending any credit.

From a policy perspective, this may not necessarily be the best approach, in particular because it singles out the poorer IDA members; that is, those who have already been more marginalized by the negative effects of globalization than their relatively well-off IBRD borrowing neighbours. In light of the fact that, aside from child labour performance criteria, there are a host of many more performance criteria based on which IDA members are evaluated before finance will be extended to them, the burdens on certain developing countries multiply before they get what they need to actually address poverty in its diverse facets on the ground.[64]

11.5 Conclusion

This chapter has shown how outsiders, including the ILO, successfully pushed the World Bank to adopt a child labour policy in the mid-1990s. However, instead of

---

61 See L. Dodero, 'MIGA: the Vision of Ibrahim Shihata', in Schlemmer-Schulte and Tung (eds), *Liber Amicorum Ibrahim F.I. Shihata, supra* note 23, 109–39 at 121–2.

62 See *supra* note 5, for a brief description of IDA.

63 See World Bank, Country Policy and Institutional Assessments – 2005 Assessment Questionnaire, Washington DC, World Bank, Operations Policy and Country Services, 20 December 2005, at 27.

64 For a discussion of a potentially Bank-made vicious cycle for IDA borrowers, see S. Schlemmer-Schulte, 'Internationales Währungs- und Finanzrecht', in C. Tietje (ed.), *Internationales Wirtschaftsrecht*, 2007, section on IDA.

basing its child labour policy on existing ILO minimum age conventions strictly prohibiting children from engaging in any work prior to reaching a certain age, as suggested by the outsiders, the World Bank's child labour policy introduced the concept of harmful and unacceptable forms of child labour. Under the World Bank policy, children in developing countries may engage in work that does not interfere in an extreme way with their education or harm their physical, mental, spiritual, moral, or social development, and may, thereby, contribute to the family income. The World Bank's pragmatic move ultimately triggered the ILO's abandonment of its old minimum age approach to child labour and its adoption of a new Convention on worst forms of child labour. Unlike the previous minimum age conventions, the new ILO Convention has been rapidly ratified by the majority of countries in the world, including many developing countries. The 'legislative' history of both the World Bank policy and the ILO Convention showcases cross-fertilization between two international agencies with a different substantive mandate. In principle, the differences provide for division of labour among international organizations and make cooperation on a number of subject-matters impossible. The case of child labour, though, illustrates how standard-setting international organizations, like the ILO, and action-oriented organizations, such as the World Bank, may team up in promoting human rights standards globally.

To what extent the focus on child labour in particular, or the focus on human rights in general, may be able to stop the North–South divide from growing remains, aside from the success story of World Bank–ILO collaboration, a big question.

Chapter 12

The Elimination of Child Labour and the EU

Matthias Hartwig

12.1 The EU and labour law

12.1.1 The development of the treaty provisions in the field of labour law

In contrast with the US, which is not subject to restrictions with respect to the range of its competences, the European Union[1] disposes only of those competences which have been transferred to it by the Member States through the constituent treaties. The principle of the *'competences attribuées'* is fundamental to communitarian law. To what extent the EU can be involved in the elimination of child labour will depend on the competences of the EU in the field of labour law.

At the beginning of its existence the European Community had very scarce competences in the field of labour law. Labour law aspects played a minor role in the context of the freedom of movement, ruled by secondary communitarian law; that is, by directives and regulations often based on article 100, in the old version of the EEC treaty, which allowed for the harmonization of norms but exclusively for the functioning of the internal market. The main provisions concerning this topic were articles 117 and 118, in the old version of the treaty. But these articles laid down a political programme in the field of labour law instead of fixing obligations of the Member States, or even transferring specific competences to the Union's organs to empower them to adopt binding norms. The norms affirmed the consensus of the Member States on the necessity to improve living and working conditions, and the Commission had the task to promote collaboration between the Member States in these fields. In 1987, the Single European Act inserted article 118(a) into the Treaty of the European Community, which authorized the European organs for the first time to regulate labour safety by means of directives; that is, to adopt norms in this field independently of its links with the internal market. However, the Council of the European Community was restricted to the adoption of directives which set up the minimum standards of labour protection.

In 1989, the Community Charter on the fundamental social rights of the workers was signed by 11 of the 12 Member States – the UK refused.[2] This Charter contains a number of social rights, among them a chapter on the protection of youth and

---

1 The term 'European Union' or 'EU' will be used as it is commonly understood, also for the European Community in a stricter sense.

2 Office of Official Publication of the European Communities, 1990; for an analysis of this Charter see B. Bercusson, *European Labour Law*, London, 1996, 575 ff.

the prohibition of child labour. (points 20 to 23). However, in contrast with the expectations of the European Parliament, the Charter was reduced to a mere solemn proclamation of fundamental social rights without any directly binding legal force.[3] However, it gained importance by the reference made to it by the preamble of the Treaty on the European Union, in the consolidated version by the Amsterdam Treaty, and especially by it being mentioned in article 136 of the Treaty on the European Community[4] in the version after the Amsterdam Treaty.[5] Today it forms part of the *acquis communautaire*, which has to be accepted by all new members of the EU without acquiring binding force.[6] Through the reference in article 136 of the ECT it defines the goals to be pursued by the EC and its Member States.

The Treaty of Maastricht of 1993 restricted itself to a protocol on social policies that, due to UK reservations, was not directly integrated in the text of the treaty. A breakthrough came with the Treaty of Amsterdam, which not only partly incorporated the goals of the Community Charter on Fundamental Social Rights into the Treaty, as mentioned above, but it vested the Community organs with far-reaching legislative competences. The former article 118(a) of the ECT was reformulated and became article 136 ECT. With reference to the Social Charter of 1961[7] and to the Charter on Fundamental Social Rights, it fixed the goals to be pursued by the Member States and the Community, among them the improvement of living and working conditions. Article 137 ECT specifies the goals, enumerating them in a list. Of particular importance are those listed in para. (a), which fixes the improvement of the working environment to protect the worker's health and safety as a main goal. This notion is interpreted in a broad sense, including all measures aiming at the prevention of accidents and protection of the worker's health in a concrete as well as in a general sense. The improvement of the working environment includes the protection of youth and the prohibition of child labour.[8]

Article 137 ECT conveys competences to the Community organs to pursue the goals mentioned in article 136 ECT. The Community is required to support and complement the activities of the Member States. With respect to the improvement of the working environment the Council of the European Community can adopt directives which set minimum standards.[9]

---

3 See Advocate General Jacobs in Case C-67/96, Albany International BV v. Stichting Bedrijfspensioenenfonds Textielindustrie, judgment of 21 September 1999, § 137.

4 Hereafter: ECT.

5 The UK meanwhile ended its resistance to the Community Charter on Fundamental Social Rights, therefore it could be referred to by the provisions of the treaty on the European Community.

6 Langer, in H. von der Groeben and J. Schwarze, *Vertrag über die Europäische Union und Vertrag über die Gründung der Europäischen Gemeinschaft*, 6th edn, Baden-Baden, 2003, Vorbemerkung zu art. 136 and 137(23).

7 529 U.N.T.S. 89.

8 S. Krebber, in C. Calliess and M. Ruffert, *Kommentar zu EU und EG Vertrag*, Neuwied, 2002, art. 137(18).

9 Art. 137(2)(b) ECT.

12.2 Implementation of the primary norms: the EC directives and other measures in the field of the elimination of child labour

12.2.1 The example of the Recommendation of 1967

As early as 1967 the Commission of the European Communities adopted a Recommendation under the former articles 117 and 118 and 155 ECT, concerning the protection of young people in the working environment.[10] This document recommends the Member States to adopt comprehensive national legislation on this topic, extending it to all persons under 18 years irrespective of the type of employment. A few exceptions were admitted, such as work in the child's own household. The main provisions were wide-ranging: the minimum age for the admission to work was raised to 15 years; in a family enterprise a child could not be occupied at an age below 12; there was confirmation of restrictive conditions such as the ban on work at night (8 pm to 6 am); the daily working hours of persons under 18 years were limited to 8 hours, the weekly working hours to 40; there were minimum regulations on breaks, etc. This recommendation had no binding force, but it was in line with a general tendency of the members of the Community to restrict child labour; therefore enforcement, for which the EC at that time lacked competences, was not necessary.

12.2.2 The Directive of 1994

The most important instrument aiming at the protection of children and young people was the EC Council Directive 94/33 of 22 June 1994.[11] It was based on former article 118(a) of the ECT (actual article 136, 137 ECT). In its preamble the Directive refers to the Community Charter of the Fundamental Social Rights of Workers of the Council of Europe of 1989 and to the principles of the ILO regarding the protection of young people at work, including those relating to the minimum age for access to employment or work. In general, the content of the directive takes its orientation from Convention 138 concerning the minimum age for admission to employment. The overall objective of the directive – as of the cited convention – is the general prohibition of child labour.[12] This is précised towards the end – copying the relevant provision of the ILO Convention – that children must not be admitted to employment below the minimum age at which compulsory full-time schooling as imposed by national law ends, or 15 years in any event. However, the Directive allows for exceptions. The States may exclude the application for occasional or short-term domestic works or work for family undertakings regarded as not being harmful, damaging or dangerous. With respect to cultural and artistic activities, sports, and advertising activities, the States can grant individual exceptions for children under

---

10 Recommendation of the Commission 67/125/European Economic Community of 31 January 1967, Official Journal, 1967, 405.

11 Directive 94/33/EC of the Council of 22 June 1994, Official Journal, 1994. No. L 216, 12.

12 See art. 1 of the Directive.

13 years and in general exceptions for all older children, to the extent that these activities are neither harmful to the children's health nor to their attendance at school.[13] Likewise, according to article 4 of the Directive, children of at least 14 years may perform light work in the frame of a work/training scheme; however, in contrast to article 5 of the ILO Convention, the Directive does not provide for the right of the Member States to exclude the application of the Directive, when their economic or administrative facilities are insufficiently developed. The reason for the stricter approach of the European Community is that their Member States are more homogenous and therefore are expected to fulfil the requirements of the Directive.

Apart from the above-mentioned specific rules, the Directive applies to all persons under 18 years having an employment contract or an employment relationship. Young persons between 15 and 18 years may do any work not damaging their health and compatible with their vocational formation. Going beyond Convention 138, the Directive rules on working time, annual vacations, breaks during working hours, and restriction of night work.

The Directive did not intend to establish common standards to which all Member States would have to adhere. It expressly stated that the Member States could set higher standards: article 16 ruled that the Directive should not constitute valid grounds for reducing the general level of protection afforded to young people.

The directive had to be implemented by municipal legislation or by collective agreements concluded between the two sides of industry by 22 June 1996.[14] By that date three countries had not yet transposed the Directive into national law, two Member States – France and Luxembourg – were convicted for their omission to transpose the Directive.[15] Following these judgments both States fulfilled their obligations.

The Directive imposed an obligation on the Member States to report to the Commission every five years on the implementation of the provisions of the Directive.[16] The Commission had to periodically submit a report to the European Parliament, the Council and the Social Council.[17] The Member States fulfilled this obligation and the Commission published its report in 2004, based on the State reports.[18] It underlined that the Member States, to a large extent, did not need to change their legislation as it was already in line with the requirements of the Directive. Some countries claimed that their protection even went further than the requirements of the Directive. However, in almost all countries – with the exception of few countries such as Ireland[19] – only minor amendments were necessary, which mostly were accomplished within the time-limits set by the Directive.[20] According

---

13 See art. 5 of the Directive.

14 Art. 17(1) of the Directive.

15 *Community v. Luxembourg*, Court ruling of 16 December 1999, C-47/99; *Commission v. France*, Court ruling of 18 May 2000, C-45/99.

16 Art. 17(4).

17 Art. 17(5).

18 The Report is available at <http://eur-lex.europa.eu/LexUriServ/LexUriServ.do?uri=CELEX:52004DC0105:EN:HTML>.

19 See point 4.5 of the Report.

20 See the exceptions of France and Luxembourg, *supra* note 11.

to the report of the Commission the legislation of the Member States was not only in line with the directive, but furthermore, the countries in general respected their own legislation. The changes in some countries were so insignificant that it could not be stated if the new legislation had had any impact on the labour market and especially on the protection of children.[21] However, some countries pointed out that new restrictions in the labour legislation entailed the decrease of jobs for persons under 18 years. Moreover, in some countries there were fears of an increasing black market.[22]

In the end, the Commission concluded that:

> In most Member States, legislation provided for protection of young workers and prohibition of child labour already before the Directive was adopted. The transposition therefore seems to have been conducted without major difficulties. For some countries, the Directive has led to a considerably higher level of protection for young workers.

All Member States have entrusted organs with monitoring the extent to which the transposed principles of the directive are respected. The norms will not remain purely paper laws. In practice, especially Portugal encounters some difficulties in the strict application of the norms, particularly in rural areas where it is still common practice to use child labour.[23]

It should be mentioned that the Directive of 1994 did not implement all requirements of the Charter of the Fundamental Social Rights of Workers, which set the standards to be followed in 1989. Especially it did not deal with the question of the entitlement of young people to complementary vocational training of a sufficient duration. However, the Charter not being binding, as explained above, the legal basis of the Directive was article 118(a) ECT, and this provision did not refer to the Charter at that time. Even now it will be difficult to adopt such norms under article 137 because a respective competence is not provided and the general reference to the Charter on Fundamental Social Rights is not justified. Specific communitarian legislation on vocational training for young people has not yet been adopted.

12.3 The Charter of Fundamental Rights of the European Union

In 2000 the summit meeting at Nice solemnly proclaimed the Charter of Fundamental Rights of the EU. At that time, no binding force was attached to this document. It was to form part II of the treaty on the constitution of the EU and become applicable by the entering into force of this treaty. With the failure of the referenda in France and in the Netherlands the applicability was postponed. Only in June 2007 at the

---

21 See a respective remark by Finland at point 4.13 of the Directive.

22 This problem was mentioned expressly by Italy, see point 4.8. of the Report.

23 See point 4.12. of the Report; this corresponds to the report ISCECR E/2001/22 (2000) 70 at § 412, 416, 423 and 424, criticizing the existence of child labour in Portugal, likewise ICCPR, A/58/40 Vol. I (2003) 56 at § 83(19).

Brussels summit did the Member States decide to make the Charter binding, which at the time of writing still requires a ratification of the amendment of the treaties.[24]

Article 24 of the Charter guarantees the rights of the child: 'Children shall have the right to such protection and care as is necessary for their well-being'. An express prohibition of child labour is not incorporated in the Charter. However, the worst forms of child labour, as defined in Convention 182, constitute violations of the Charter. Slavery and debt bondage are prohibited (article 5). Prostitution and pornography are incompatible with human dignity (article 1) and with the right to the integrity of the person (article 3) – and it may even be qualified as torture or inhuman treatment, as prohibited by article 4. The use of child labour for illicit or damaging activities also would infringe upon the right to the integrity of the person. Even if the State itself is not exploiting the children it cannot live up to the obligations deriving from the fundamental rights by the pure abstention from the prohibited acts. It is well-established jurisprudence, as proven by the European Court of Human Rights, that human rights guarantees impose the obligation on the State to take active measures for the protection of the guaranteed rights.[25] Therefore, the EU will have to implement these obligations within its competences and take steps, if this has not already been done, to eliminate the worst forms of child labour. Furthermore, article 24 obliges the EU to adopt all acts indispensable for the protection of the children.

The European Parliament referred to the Charter when urging the Member States to ratify the relevant ILO Conventions. It argued that the non-ratification would run counter to the Charter.[26]

12.4 European law and the ILO

Apart from the treaties and the secondary law, international law is an additional source of Community law. As many international standards in labour law have been developed through international treaties, especially by the ILO, it is important to analyse the relationship between the EU and the ILO.

12.4.1 The participation of the EU in the elaboration of ILO Conventions under ILO law

The EU is neither a member of the ILO nor has it concluded any of the treaties drafted within this organization. Membership of the ILO is defined by article 1(2) of the ILO Constitution which reserves membership to State parties. According to article 19(5)(d) of the ILO Constitution, only Member States may ratify Conventions which have been drafted within the ILO. The EU as a supranational organization

---

24 See point 9 of the mandate of the Council of the European Union for the Intergovernmental Conference 2007, <http://register.consilium.europa.eu/pdf/en/07/st11/st11218.en07.pdf>.

25 C. Dröge, *Positive Verpflichtungen der Staaten in der Europäischen Menschenrechtskonvention*, Heidelberg, Berlin, 2003.

26 See below sub-section 12.5.1.

does not have the status of a State. One can conclude that, under the law of the ILO, the EU cannot be bound directly by the Conventions of the ILO.

However, this does not mean that the EU has no role to play at all. In the context of the elaboration of ILO Convention 153 on working hours and rest periods in road transport, a working document was drafted in order to facilitate the participation of the EU in the negotiations. Originally refused by the employers and workers who feared to lose influence in the ILO, the document was supplemented in 1989. In the outcome, the ILO allowed that the Community Members could authorize the Commission to propose amendments on their behalf in the negotiation process, and that the draft convention could be referred to the Council of the European Community – instead of the competent authorities of the Member States – and finally, that the ratification of the Member States could be declared by the Commission after prior notification of the Member States to accept this measure as ratification. However, it was underlined that the Member States of the EU, as the only members to the Convention, will be held liable for any breach of the Convention, even if it were attributable to the organs of the European Community.[27]

12.4.2 The treaty-making power of the European Community under EU law

12.4.2.1 General remarks Even if the ILO provides for the possibility to have the EC involved in the elaboration and ratification of ILO Conventions, that does not mean that the Community has the competence to participate in the conclusion of a convention under the perspective of communitarian law.

The EC treaty does not intensely deal with the question of the treaty-making power of the EC. Express competences to this end are transferred to the European Community in article 133 – concerning treaties on commerce – and in article 310 – concerning association treaties, as well as in article 111(3) – concerning treaties on currency matters.

The jurisprudence of the European Court of Justice became most important in the AETR case.[28] The Court held that the treaty-making competences of the European Community correspond to the internal competences. The EC may conclude international treaties on all matters in which it disposes of (internal) competences conveyed by the EC treaty. It has exclusive treaty-making power if it has the exclusive competences in the given field. This might be ruled in the treaty itself as, for example, with respect to commercial policies or the conclusion of association treaties. Furthermore, the European Court of Justice held that the EC may gain an exclusive competence in all fields in which it issued norms in order to implement a policy of the EC. The Member States are excluded from concluding a treaty in a field where the European organs ruled on the matter exhaustively, because the conclusion of a treaty, even if in line with the existing communitarian law, would hamper the future development of this legislation by the EC organs to the extent that the Member States are bound by the treaties entered into. On the other hand, if there

---

27 The whole proceeding is described in the opinion 2/91 of the ECJ, Reports of Cases 1993 I-1066 ff.

28 AETR 22/70 Collection of decisions 1971, 263, § 95.

is no exhaustive ruling of the EC organs, or even a regulation which is sufficiently intense to exclude any form of State obligations entered into by the conclusion of a treaty, the States are not deprived of their treaty-making power. In this sense the European Court of Justice refused an exclusive treaty-making power of the EC with respect to the General Agreement on Trade and Services (GATS) and the Agreement on Trade-related Aspects of Intellectual Property Rights (TRIPS).[29]

12.4.2.2 Treaty-making power with respect to ILO Conventions The competence of the EC to participate in ILO Conventions – from the viewpoint of communitarian law – was subject to some discussion within the EC. The central arguments were developed in opinion 2/91 of the European Court of Justice (ECJ). The ECJ stated that the exclusive or non-exclusive nature of the Community's competence may derive from the provisions of the Treaty as well as from the scope of the measures which have been adopted by the Community organs to implement those provisions. It held that, with respect to the improvement of the working environment regarding the health and safety of workers, the Council has the power to establish minimum requirements by means of directives under article 118(a) ECT. This, however, implies that the Member States are not prevented from introducing more stringent measures for the protection of working conditions. As the Community has internal competences in the field of working conditions it disposes likewise of external competences; in other words, under communitarian law the Community can conclude conventions on working conditions. However, the treaty-making power is not exclusive, for the Member States, which are entitled to adopt stricter municipal rules than the EC norms, likewise have the competence to conclude international treaties to this end. If the EC adopts rules less strict than the provisions of a respective ILO Convention concluded by the EC Member States, the latter will be in line with article 118(a) ECT, as this provision allows for stricter regulations.[30]

The necessity of the implementation of treaty provisions by national authorities does not deprive the EC of its treaty-making power, if it has a general competence in the field. With respect to the mixed competences in the field of the improvement of the working environment and the health and safety of workers, the ECJ points to the necessity of a close cooperation between the Member States and the EC.

The argumentation of Opinion 2/91 of the ECJ, which concerned an ILO Convention on the safety in the use of chemicals at work, can be transferred to the question of the elimination of child work, as this aspect likewise concerns the question of the improvement of working environment as regards health and safety, as defined by article 118(a) ECT. To the extent that the EC has not adopted specific rules in the field, the Member States can conclude ILO Conventions. If the legislative competence of the EC is concerned, they will have to find a manner to get the EC involved in the negotiations on the treaty. The way that was taken in the elaboration of ILO Convention 170 may serve as an example. As the international

---

29 Opinion 1/94 (WTO Agreement), Collection 1994 I-5264, § 25.

30 If, however, the EC rules will be stricter than the ILO Convention the former will prevail, as art. 19(8) of the ILO Constitution enables the Member States to adopt more stringent rules.

law stands at present, the treaty partners for the ILO Conventions will be exclusively the Member States, because the ILO Constitution does not allow the ratification of ILO Conventions by others than Member States. International organizations thus are not admitted to the ILO. However, as pointed out above, the ILO allows for the authorization of the EC by the Member States to participate in the negotiations, the implementation and the ratification of ILO Conventions. The Member States will be responsible vis-à-vis the other convention parties.

This does not mean that the convention is irrelevant for the EC. Under Community law, the EC Member States, when entering into ILO Conventions, are acting on behalf of the Community to the extent that it enjoys the exclusive treaty-making power and implementing competence.[31] The Member States are acting somehow as proxies of the EC, which at the same time, has to act under communitarian law and is prevented from acting under ILO law. Therefore, the obligations entered into by the Member States have to be treated under communitarian law as obligations of the EC, to the extent the EC has exclusive competences. From the perspective of ILO law, instead, they are in the last resort obligations of the Member States, because the EC cannot be a party to the treaties. Actually it is not possible to hold that the EC will succeed in the treaty obligations of the Member States with regard to the ILO Conventions as it was considered to have succeeded in the case of GATT obligations. Among the conditions for succession, as established by the ECJ, is the exclusive competence of the EC in the given field.[32] As has been pointed out above, the EC does not yet enjoy such a competence.

Another question will be who factually will fulfil the obligations deriving from the ILO Conventions, such as the duty to regularly deliver reports according to article 22 of the ILO Constitution. Here, the EC may claim the competence as far as it is responsible for the respective matter internally. It did so with respect to ILO Convention 170 in 1988, assuming that it had exclusive competence in the matter, which, however, was contested by the Member States. In general, under communitarian law the EC will be competent to deliver the reports to the extent that it is competent in the matter internally. This does not take away the responsibility of the Member States vis-à-vis the ILO.

As a matter of fact, neither Convention 138 nor Convention 182 have been ratified by the Member States through a declaration of the EU; indeed, all EU Member States have been parties to the two conventions for a long time,[33] and ratified them at different times. The annual reports on the implementation of the child labour norms to the International Labour Conference are delivered by the States, not by the

---

31 Opinion 2/92, Reports 1993 I, 1076, § 5: 'In any event, although, under the ILO Constitution the Community cannot itself conclude Convention No 170, its external competence may, if necessary, be exercised through the medium of the Member States acting jointly in the Community's interest.' See also E.-U. Petersmann and C. Spennemann, in von der Groeben and Schwarze (eds), *Vertrag über die Europäische Union*, *supra* note 6, Vol. 4, art. 307(23).

32 International Fruit Company, Reports 1972, 1219, 1228.

33 Therefore, the European Parliament has urged the Member States which have not yet ratified ILO Conventions 138 and 182 to do so because otherwise they would not be in line with the Charter of Fundamental Rights, see below sub-section 12.5.1.

European Community. Actually there is no claim by the EC to get involved in the reporting system vis-à-vis the ILO in the field of child labour. However, taking into consideration that the EU has been active in the field of child protection, it would be in line with above-mentioned opinion 2/91 if the EU were to deliver its own reports in the name of the Member States.

Concluding the foregoing, it can be stated that, in the field of the prohibition of child work, the European Community is inspired by Convention 138, but does not participate formally in the respective activities of the ILO. Here, the Member States still are engaged exclusively. The adoption of Convention 182 did not lead to new legislative initiatives by the EC, although the directive on child labour was issued before Convention 182 entered into force. The reason is that the Directive of 1994 had already responded to all the criteria of the ILO Convention by prohibiting all forms of labour which could endanger the health or the morals of young people. The worst forms of child labour, in the sense of Convention 182 are of such a type as to be a risk to these values, and thus are prohibited.

12.5 Activities of the EU in foreign relations

Beyond the normative measures most prominently reflected in the Directive of 1994, the European organs feel bound to promote the protection against child labour on an international level. In 2005 the Commission issued a Communication on the Strategic Objectives 2005–09 which states: 'A particular priority must be effective protection of the rights of children, both against economic exploitation and all forms of abuse with the Union acting as a beacon to the rest of the world.' This aimed to contribute to the protection against child labour not only within the EU but throughout the world.

12.5.1 The obligation of Member States to ratify the ILO Conventions

Where the EU does not exercise its own competences to act in the field of the elimination of child labour, its organs (the Commission and the Parliament) are urging the Member States to undertake international obligations. In this sense, the Commission called on the Member States to ratify Convention 182.[34] The Commission as well as the European Parliament have expressed an obligation to ratify both Convention 138 and 182.[35] The link to European law was established in the resolution of 5 July 2005 of the European Parliament. It stated that the non-ratification of the above-mentioned Conventions would run counter to the obligations deriving from the Charter of Fundamental Rights.[36]

---

34 Recommendation of 15 September 2000, C 2000/2674.

35 Resolution of the European Parliament of 5 July 2005, Official Journal, 2006, C 157 E/85 point 2; meanwhile Latvia ratified ILO Convention 182 in 2006 and the Czech Republic and Estonia ratified ILO Convention 138 in 2007, <http://www.ilo.org/ilolex/cgi-lex/ratifce>.

36 See above section 12.3.

The EU imposed obligations on candidate countries willing to adhere to the EU. For example, the Joint Memorandum on Social Inclusion between the EU and Bulgaria tackles the problem of the elimination of the worst forms of child labour. This goal will be subject to a monitoring and review process in the frame of the IPEC, and the process will benefit from resources from the Social Fund.[37] The respective Joint Memorandum between the EU and Romania does not address the problem of child labour.[38] However, the European Parliament recommends that the Commission make the ratification of Conventions 138 and 182 a prerequisite for the accession to the EU.[39]

12.5.2 The question of the elimination of child labour in relationships with non-Member States

However, the EU does not limit itself to call its own Members to adhere to international instruments aiming at the elimination of child labour. It also tries to make third States respect the international standards in this field. These measures are of utmost importance as, in practice, child labour plays a more important role in the economies of developing countries than in the Member States of the EU.

12.5.2.1 Cooperation with international organizations in the field of the eradication of child labour in developing countries: the EU and the ILO In July 2004 the Commission signed a Strategic Partnership Agreement with the ILO in the field of development; one of the priorities is the prevention of child labour.[40] This Partnership does not refer to the situation within the EU, but according to the Memorandum of Understanding, the geographical scope is exclusively on the so-called developing countries. A close cooperation between the ILO and the EU is established with regard to the promulgation of the core labour standards 'with a special focus on child labour and education'. The cooperation includes financial assistance by the EU for special activities undertaken by the ILO. In this context, the Commission is discussing with African, Caribbean and Pacific States (ACP) partners an action programme to fight child labour together with the ILO/IPEC. The action will focus on capacity-building, targeted interventions and legal frameworks to ensure that children removed from child labour will receive primary education. The overall budget is in the order of €15 million.

---

37 See 'Joint Memorandum on Social Inclusion of the Republic of Bulgaria', available at <http://ec.europa.eu/employment_social/social_inclusion/docs/jim_bg_en.pdf>, 36; ILC, *The End of Child Labour: Within Reach – Global Report under the Follow-Up to the ILO Declaration on Fundamental Principles and Rights at Work*, International Labour Conference, 95th Session, 2006, Report I B, 57.

38 <http://ec.europa.eu/employment_social/social_inclusion/docs/jim_ro_en.pdf>, 28.

39 Resolution of 5 July 2005, Official Journal, 2005, C 157 E/86 point 4; Romania and Bulgaria – at that moment still candidates for the accession to the EU – have ratified both Conventions before joining the EU, although a direct obligation to this end has not been established.

40 The text of the Agreement is available at <http://ec.europa.eu/employment_social/international_cooperation/docs/ilo_memorandum_en.pdf>.

12.5.2.2 The cooperation between the EU and developing countries in the elimination of child labour. The question of child labour within the Cotonou Treaty. Before the agreement with the ILO the EU laid down provisions on child labour in a treaty with the ACP States. The Treaty of Cotonou, concluded between the European Community and its Member States and the ACP States in 2001 guarantees in its article 26 basic rights to children.[41] Article 50 is more specifically dedicated to the establishment of trade and labour standards, referring to the relevant ILO Conventions, among them the Convention on the elimination of the worst forms of child labour. The parties to the treaty commit themselves to cooperate in the field of the exchange of information, the formulation of national legislation, educational programmes and enforcement of national legislation. They establish a system of cooperation for the future, but not a regime of sanctions in case of the violation of the standards. This approach is reflected in article 50(3): 'The Parties agree that labour standards should not be used for protectionist trade purposes.' This provision quite clearly states that the respective markets cannot be closed to the import of goods produced in a country not respecting the labour standards, among them the prohibition of the worst forms of child labour. This corresponds to a scheme strongly favoured especially by developing countries; that is, the clear division between the freedom of trade and the protection of minimum labour standards, reflected in the division between the WTO and the ILO.[42]

On the level of cooperation between the ACP and EU organs the ACP–EU Joint Parliamentary Assembly adopted a resolution that requires the ratification of the relevant ILO Conventions prohibiting child labour, and calls on the Commission and the Council of the EU to secure the universal ratification of these instruments in a dialogue with the ACP countries;[43] programmes are to be developed to support countries in securing the implementation of the instruments guaranteeing the children's rights.

Trade policy – the Generalized System of Preferences Scheme. Another way of inducing third States to introduce provisions on the protection against child labour is the Generalized System of Preferences (GSP) Scheme established by regulations. This practice was established in 1994[44] and it is renewed periodically.[45] The Scheme promotes the economies of developing countries by granting preferential customs tariffs in a differentiated manner. This type of preference is generally covered by the Enabling Clause of the WTO.[46] Special incentive preferences are included in the scheme. Additional reductions in the already reduced GSP tariff rate may be granted

---

41 The text of the Treaty of Cotonou is available at <http://ec.europa.eu/development/body/cotonou/pdf/agr01_en.pdf#zoom=100>.

42 See below, sub-section headed 'Trade policy – the General Scheme of Preferences'.

43 Official Journal of the European Union, 2004, C 26/19.

44 Council Regulation No. 3281/94 of 19 December 1994.

45 In 2001 Council Regulation 2501/2001 of 10 December 2001 on Applying a Scheme of Generalized Tariff Preferences for the Period from 1 January 2002 to 31 December 2004, art. 7, 2001, Official Journal (L 346) 1, 5–6; in 2005 Regulation (EC) No 980/2005, Official Journal, 2005 L 169, 1–43.

46 Differential and More Favourable Treatment, Reciprocity and Fuller Participation of Developing Countries, GATT Doc. L/4903 (Nov. 28, 1979).

if the privileged country respects standards in the combat against drugs, in the environmental protection or in the field of labour. The tariff reduction for industrial goods can double and for agricultural goods it can nearly double.[47] Originally the countries which wanted to take advantage of the additional reduction had to prove that they had adopted the relevant ILO Conventions, especially Conventions 138 and 182. After 2001, the criteria were lowered; and the EU considered it to be sufficient that the respective States incorporated the substance of the law. Actually, the Council Regulation on Applying a Scheme of Generalized Tariff Preferences again requires the ratification and implementation of international treaties, listed in an annex to the Regulation, as a precondition for the granting of special preferential tariffs.[48] In the first place it mentions the Core Human Labour Rights UN/ILO Conventions. According to article 9 of the Regulation, the listed Conventions must be ratified and effectively implemented. Furthermore, the beneficiary States must commit to maintain the ratification and accept regular monitoring with respect to the implementation of the Conventions. The benefits of the special incentives arrangements shall be granted upon the request of a country; which must provide all information necessary to verify that it fulfils all the requirements. It must accept the commitments regarding the monitoring and review mechanism envisaged in the relevant instruments. The Commission shall decide on the request, taking into account the findings of the relevant international organizations and agencies. Within the special incentive arrangement, the common customs tariffs *ad valorem* and specific duties shall be suspended.

According to article 16 of the Regulation, the preferential arrangements can be temporarily withdrawn if a beneficiary country seriously and systematically violates the Conventions which it had to ratify and implement in order to qualify for the preferences.

In 2002, a dispute arose between India and the EC. India claimed that incentives violated the principle of the most favoured nation.[49] Under the Enabling Clause, exceptions from this principle are allowed to promote the trade of developing countries. India claims that the incentives do not aim at India's trade capacities but at changing its internal legislation. However, the Enabling Clause states that the customs preferences shall be designed to respond positively to the developmental and the financial and trade needs of the developing countries. The traditional interpretation of this clause has been purely in economic terms; that is, only economic objectives could justify special preferences. However, the recent case law of the WTO bodies shows that the notions of the treaty shall be interpreted in harmony with the actual necessities. In this sense, the Appellate Body stated that the notion of exhaustible resources must be read in line with the contemporary understanding which includes

---

47 A.N. Cole, 'Labor Standards and the Generalized System of Preferences: the European Labor Incentives', *Michigan Journal of International Law*, Vol. 25, 2003, 179 ff, at 193.

48 Regulation (EC) No 980/2005, Official Journal, 2005, L 169, 1–43.

49 Request of India of 6 December 2002 for the Establishment of a Panel; the panel shall decide if the special incentive preferences are compatible with the Enabling Clause, available at <http://docsonline.wto.org>; Cole, *supra* note 47, 179.

living stocks.[50] In this line of reasoning, one could hold that the economic necessities today contain social aspects,[51] although the WTO Ministerial Conference stated in Singapore in 1996 that the ILO is the international organization competent for social standards, not the WTO.[52]

A further question which has been raised in this context is whether the Member States to the WTO may refer to article XX (b) of the WTO Agreement allowing trade restrictions in order to protect life and health. Even if there can be no doubt that the prohibition of child labour aims at these objectives, it is highly disputed if only persons within the State referring to this provision can be protected or if the provision extends to persons living in other States.

Bilateral cooperation agreements. In bilateral cooperation agreements the question of child labour, as a rule, is not expressly mentioned. Normally, a general provision is dedicated to the development of human resources.[53] Such formulas, however, are not always followed by concrete measures in the field. To stay with the example of India, in 2004 the Commission stated that the EU should engage India on such topics as child labour.[54] The problem of child labour is addressed, for example in article 10 of the EU–Bangladesh Cooperation Agreement, which states that the Parties acknowledge the necessity of safeguarding the basic rights of workers by taking account of the principles in the relevant ILO instruments, including those on forced and child labour.[55] The wording of this provision demonstrates great prudence. It does not directly establish reciprocal obligations, which in the end would have resulted in unilateral commitments of Bangladesh vis-à-vis the EU, but

---

50 WTO Appellate Body Report, United States – Import Prohibition of Certain Shrimp and Shrimp Products, WTO Doc. WT/DS58/AB/R, DSR 1998:VII 2755 (12 October 1998).

51 J. Diller and D. Levy, 'Child Labor, Trade and Investment: Toward the Harmonization of International Law', *American Journal of International Law*, Vol. 91, 1997, 663, 678 ff.

52 Singapore Ministerial Declaration of 13 December 1996; the statement of the ministers reads: 'We renew our commitment to the observance of internationally recognized core labour standards. The International Labour Organization (ILO) is the competent body to set and deal with these standards, and we affirm our support for its work in promoting them. We believe that economic growth and development fostered by increased trade and further trade liberalization contribute to the promotion of these standards. We reject the use of labour standards for protectionist purposes, and agree that the comparative advantage of countries, particularly low-wage developing countries, must in no way be put into question. In this regard, we note that the WTO and ILO Secretariats will continue their existing collaboration.' This was reaffirmed by the Doha Conference in 2001, see <http://www.wto.org/english/thewto_e/minist_e/min01_e/mindecl_e.htm#para8>.

53 See, for example, art. 18 of the Cooperation Agreement between the European Community and India on partnership and development of 20 December 1993, Official Journal, 1994, L 223/224, which reads: 'They [that is, the Contracting Parties] agree that human resource development shall constitute an integral part of both economic and development cooperation.' This clause could be interpreted to include measures aiming at the elimination of child labour.

54 Communication from the Commission to the Council, the European Parliament and the European Economic and Social Committee – An EU-India Partnership, COM (2004) 430 final of 16 June 2004, welcomed by the Council Conclusions of 11 October 2004.

55 Official Journal of the European Communities, 2001, L118/48.

each party admits the importance of the core labour standards. Here again, the text of the Agreement proves to be not very demanding: It does not require the Parties to strictly respect the principles of the ILO Conventions but only to take account of them. This contrasts with article 1, which declares the strict guarantee of general human rights to be an essential element of the Agreement. The special provision of article 10, dedicated to the social rights of workers, does not underline the particular importance of these rights but lowers the level of protection. This certainly is a concession to the situation in Bangladesh where the elimination of child labour will not take place by way of a spontaneous prohibition.

The Cooperation Agreement of 2001 between Pakistan and the EU may serve as a third example.[56] Article 1 guarantees the respect of human rights in the same wording as article 1 of the agreement with Bangladesh. Human resources development is dealt with by article 14. The core labour standards are mentioned in § 3 of this provision:

> The Parties recall the importance of the observance of internationally recognized core labour standards set in the relevant instruments of the International Labour Organisation, which is the competent body to set and deal with these standards, as a major factor of social and economic progress. They also recognize that economic growth and development fostered by increased trade and further trade liberalization contribute to the promotion of these standards.

The wording of this provision again is quite telling and reflects the prudence of addressing this topic. Recalling the importance of the observance of internationally recognized labour standards does not lay the ground for a very strong obligation. Even more interesting is the reference to the functions of the ILO. There is a long-standing dispute at the WTO if core labour standards can be incorporated into the WTO system, either by an amendment or by interpretation. As shown above, the Ministerial Conference of the WTO still pleads in favour of a strict separation between the tasks of the WTO and those of the ILO.

Unilateral EU acts aiming at the elimination of child labour. The European Parliament has adopted many resolutions that call on non-Member States to eliminate child labour.[57] Recently the European Commission issued a Communication in

---

56 The text of the Agreement is available at <http://ec.europa.eu/external_relations/pakistan/intro/coop_agree_11_01.pdf>.

57 See, for example, the Resolution of the European Parliament of 18 January 2001 and the Resolution of the Parliament of 11 April 2003, Official Journal, 2003, C 127 E/691 ff, in which it calls on the EU and its Member States to cooperate in supporting universal ratification of the treaties recently concluded to strengthen the position of children (among them ILO Convention 182), and that strong mechanisms to monitor government obligations are in place; the ratification of key instruments protecting the position of the children is be a priority of the Council in its dialogue with third parties. Likewise it welcomes the commitment of the Commission to integrate a children's rights perspective into the development cooperation instruments. Resolution of the European Parliament of 13 June 2002, Official Journal, 2003, 261 E/587E, dealing especially with child labour in the production of footballs, calling on the European Union to integrate provisions in agreements with the relevant countries – especially India and Pakistan – to eliminate child labour. Resolution of 5 July 2005, Official Journal, 2005, C 157 E/84.

which it proposed to establish a comprehensive strategy on the rights of the child.[58] Within this communication special emphasis has been put on the protection against economic exploitation. In its external relations, according to the Communication, the EU will urge the ratification of the relevant instruments on child protection such as the Convention on the Rights of the Child and the ILO Convention on the elimination of the worst forms of child labour; priorities shall be identified for future actions; the children's rights shall be respected in all internal and external policies of the EU (so-called mainstreaming); and efficient coordination and consultation mechanisms shall be established among the main stakeholders.

The introduction of a labelling system. The European Parliament has repeatedly raised the question of the introduction of a labelling system that would identify imported goods produced without the use of child labour.[59] The proposals do not go so far as to require an import prohibition, but the consumers should be made aware of how the good was produced. The European Parliament limits itself to propose – not to require – that such a system shall be introduced; it also calls on the Commission to check if it is possible to introduce mechanisms for the punishment of persons who import goods produced with the use of child labour. Here again, the Parliament proves to be very careful, leaving the decision with the Commission. This is due to previous experiences with social labelling.

In 1993/94 the US experience has shown that a labelling system is able to significantly influence consumer choice.[60] The Harkin bill, according to which goods produced with child labour shall be prohibited, did not enter into force, but it inspired the introduction of a system of social labelling, which led to reduced imports of garments from Bangladesh. Subsequent investigations showed that the children engaged in the garment production lost any form of material assistance or found other work on the black market under even worse conditions.[61] The ILO acknowledged that it made some mistakes in implementing actions against child labour without organizing social safety nets first.[62]

The conclusion drawn from this experience was that the unilateral imposition of a labelling system without collateral measures to compensate the consequences of the consumer boycott might have counterproductive effects. This might explain the great prudence the Parliament shows when touching upon the question of a labelling system.

12.6 Concluding remarks

The elimination of child labour has been on the agenda of the EU for a long time. By progressively enlarging its competences in the field of social politics, including

---

58 Communication of the European Commission of 4 July 2006, at <http://eur-lex. europa.eu/LexUriServ/site/en/com/2006/com2006_0367en01.doc>.

59 See, for instance, Resolution of the European Parliament of 5 July 2005, Official Journal, 2006, C 157E/84, Point 44.

60 Briefing, <http://www.cuts-international.org/Brf-3-2003.pdf>, 5.

61 *Ibid.*

62 Global Report (Bulgaria), p. 75.

labour law, it was able to adopt effective secondary norms, especially the Directive of 1994, which obliges the Member States to transpose the core labour standards into national law. The reports of the Member States and the EU show that the implementation of this Directive did not meet any difficulties. To a large extent, the Member States already had introduced legislation respecting the standards set by the Directive. Therefore, the Directive cannot be qualified as a turning point in the fight for the elimination of child labour in Europe.

The relation between the EU and the ILO, as the main international actor in the field of establishing and protecting the core labour standards including the elimination of child labour, suffers from the fact that the ILO admits only States as Members and as parties to the Conventions elaborated under its guidance. The competences of the EU have to be determined along the lines of communitarian law which leads to the conclusion that the EU may develop external activities in the field of the elimination of child labour. However, the EU has not been involved in the ratification of the relevant Conventions. This was done exclusively by the Member States, although there are good arguments in favour of a certain competence of the EU relating to the elimination of child labour as part of the core labour standards. The most important act up to date is the cooperation agreement with the ILO, which exclusively focuses on developing states; and does not aim to sanction States that do not respect the core labour standards, but to promote the knowledge about these principles and their implementation.

In its relations with developing countries, the EU does not make the respect of the core labour standards a precondition for economic relations. The importance of these standards – among them the prohibition of child labour – is underlined, in very prudent formulations. The parties to the respective treaties must acknowledge the importance of these principles, but a direct obligation to respect and implement them is not imposed. Accordingly the parties do not establish sanctions in case of the violation of the principles. The ACP–EU Cooperation Agreement even explicitly states that the question of the respect of the core labour standards shall not serve as a ground for protective measures. This approach is also reflected in the statement that the protection of the core labour standards is vested with the ILO – insofar as these treaties are following the line of keeping trade and social norms separated; an approach favoured by many developing countries and liberal circles.

The only field where trade-related provisions are directly linked to the respect of core labour standards is the General Scheme of Preferences; that is, the special preferences granted conditionally upon the respect of these standards. In spite of many discussions concerning the admissibility of this linkage under WTO law, the EU continues to implement this policy.

The failure to introduce a labelling system which might influence consumer behaviour is quite telling for the EU approach to the problem of child labour. It has not yet decided the basic question, namely what the most appropriate way is to deal with this still widespread phenomenon, the carrot or the stick. Where child labour has almost been eradicated – that is, in the EU itself – it imposes sanctions for the violation of the prohibition. However, where child labour is a mass phenomenon it prefers programmes in education, information, legislation, implementation and monitoring. This can be justified by the respect of the sovereignty of the States involved, but it might derive from the philosophy that the best way to overcome child labour is to elevate the standard of living in the respective countries, as has been expressly laid down in the treaty between the EU and Pakistan. Trade sanctions would be counterproductive, and they always raise doubts if behind noble ideas hide economic interest, as the developing countries are wont to assume.

The insecurity of the European institutions on the best way to guarantee the protection against child labour is documented in the Resolution of the European Parliament of 5 July 2005, where the Parliament admonishes the Commission to bring its trade policy into harmony with the EU's obligation to protect and promote children.[63] The Parliament did not specify how this harmony could best be reached. The goal is clear – and the EU does not leave any doubt about the necessity to eliminate child labour – however, with respect to the strategy many doubts remain.

---

63 Official Journal, 2006, C 157 E/84.

Chapter 13

ILO Child Labour Standards in International Trade Regulation: The Role of the WTO

Giovanna Adinolfi

13.1 The debate on establishing a link between labour and trade issues in international law

Since its beginnings, the ILO has promoted the adoption of national legislations designed to protect children against economic exploitation. The approval and entry into force of the 1999 Convention on the Worst Forms of Child Labour (No. 182), now counting 165 contracting parties, is one of the latest main achievements: ILO members have undertaken the obligation to take immediate and effective measures (including the provision and application of penal sanctions or, as appropriate, other sanctions) to secure the prohibition and elimination of worst forms of child labour. Practices coming under this definition comprise slavery or similar practices, use of children in sexual and illicit activities, and work which, by its nature or the circumstances under which it is carried out, is likely to harm the health, safety, or morals of children.

The normative standards, progressively developed by the ILO, integrate and are complementary to the international human rights regime, and in particular to all those regulations concerning the protection of children, whether they are involved in economic activities or not. Thus, they directly enter into the current and heated debate over the place of international human rights regulation within the international trading system; a system administered since 1995 by the World Trade Organization (WTO),[1] that succeeded to the General Agreement on Tariffs and Trade of 1947 and the regulation adopted under its aegis.

The WTO pursues aims of economic growth and welfare by means of trade instruments. Since its legal regime includes explicit reference neither to human rights nor to workers' rights, the issue is whether it constitutes a 'self-contained

---

1 The WTO Agreement and its annexes are published in *The Legal Texts. The Results of the Uruguay Round of Multilateral Trade Negotiations*, Cambridge, Cambridge University Press, 1999. They were concluded at the end of the Uruguay Round of multilateral trade negotiations, held under the aegis of GATT 1947.

regime' where other rules of international law can play no role,[2] or whether it is open to non-economic values guaranteed by general rules of public international law or by other international agreements.

In a report issued in April 1996, the WTO Appellate Body stated that the General Agreement on Tariffs and Trade of 1994, one of the WTO annexes, 'should not be read in clinical isolation from public international law'.[3] Since that assertion was made to justify the application by WTO organs of customary rules of international law on treaty interpretation, in the present chapter its wide purport needs to be specified in order to ascertain to what extent the WTO can take into consideration international rules concerning child labour. The debate, which involves many scholars, is about the contribution the WTO can make to the promotion of non-economic values, thus complementing the activities of other international organizations or legitimizing actions unilaterally taken by States. What is at stake is the legitimacy of trade policy instruments forbidding or limiting the sale in domestic markets of products obtained through the exploitation of child labour or imported from countries not complying with international rules on the matter.[4] The question to be settled is whether the enforcement of rules imposing the elimination of worst forms of child labour may justify the recourse to trade restrictions against offending States, thus derogating from WTO obligations.

Trade and labour issues have been analysed on the basis of different approaches.[5] Briefly, from a social perspective it is assumed that the violation of basic workers' rights entails lower costs of production and thus an unfair competitive advantage on the international markets. Thus, trade unions and national producers' lobbies in developed countries affirm the need to impose trade restrictions against those States (and in particular, developing States) where core labour standards are not respected. Similarly, trade unions are worried about a possible 'race to the bottom', as developed countries may be induced to lower workers' social guarantees in order to protect national markets against more competitive products from developing countries. Accordingly trade restrictions would be necessary to protect national workers' welfare. Finally, from a 'humanitarian' perspective, there is said to be an urgent need to prohibit the import of goods whose production process entails the violation of basic workers' rights or, more generally, of fundamental human rights.

The critics of those who advocate a link between trade and labour issues, underline the protectionist intents behind any legislation pursuing the protection of human rights by means of trade measures. The humanitarian arguments are rejected as well, on the grounds that they are based on a Western view of human rights and

2 For a critical appraisal of this view see P. Picone and A. Ligustro, *Diritto dell'Organizzazione mondiale del commercio*, Padua, CEDAM, 2002, at 624 ff.

3 See Unites States – Standards for Conventional and Reformulated Gasoline, WT/DS2/AB/R, 29 April 1996, 16.

4 The distinction between tailored, semi-tailored and general human rights trade countermeasures has been underlined by S. Cleveland, 'Human Rights Sanctions and International Trade: A Theory of Compatibility', *Journal of International Economic Law*, Vol. 5, No. 1, 2002, 133 ff, at 138 ff.

5 For an overview see M.J. Trebilcock and R. Howse, 'Trade Policy and Labor Standards', *Minnesota Journal of Global Trade*, Vol. 14, No. 1, 2005, 261 ff, at 266 ff.

are not equally voiced in the fight against violation of national workers' rights in developed countries.

In this opposition between developed and developing countries, usually a joint support is expressed for the protection of human and workers' rights and for the need to protect those who are more likely to become the victims of their violation – that is, children. The basic difference concerns the proposed strategies to reach this aim. Developing States oppose the adoption of trade sanctions, and instead propose a long-term approach, where intensified protection of human rights will only be possible in conjunction with an effective fight against poverty – a fight that can only be jeopardized by the imposition of import restrictions by developed States. Furthermore, the efficacy of trade sanctions is questioned by many economic studies on the ground that child labour is exploited mainly for the production of goods for internal consumption and not for foreign markets.[6] Those same economic studies, however, show that a better protection of workers' rights would not jeopardize the competitive advantage of developing countries, as the increase in production costs would be counterbalanced by higher productivity. It could be part of a long-term strategy aiming to improve national welfare.

13.2 The WTO and workers' rights: the road to and from Singapore

The current debate on the possible role of international trade law in the enforcement of workers' rights and child labour prohibitions is not a novelty in interstate relations. Proposals were put forward long before the establishment of the WTO, but no positive outcome has ever been obtained.

The analysis here will be limited to the last decades.[7] The idea that workers' rights should be dealt with within the multilateral trade discipline was examined during the diplomatic talks leading to the conclusion of the WTO Agreement. Firstly, in the consultations for the start of the Uruguay Round, the US government advanced specific proposals to this extent.[8] It upheld a double approach, making reference to the aim to 'ensure that expanded trade benefits all workers in all countries', recognizing simultaneously that 'denial of workers' rights can impede attainment of the objectives of the GATT and can lead to trade distortions'. However, it met with strong opposition. The issue was also raised during the negotiations that followed,[9] but the final texts agreed upon (that is, the WTO Agreement, its annexes and a

---

6 For an economic analysis of the child labour issues see A. Cigno and F.C. Rosati, *The Economics of Child Labour*, Oxford, Oxford University Press, 2005.

7 For a more comprehensive analysis see S. Charnovitz, 'The Influence of International Labour Standards on the World Trading Regime', *International Labour Review*, Vol. 126, 1987, reprinted in S. Charnovitz (ed.), *Trade Law and Global Governance*, London, 2002, 211 ff; C. McCrudden and A. Davies, 'A Perspective on Trade and Labour Rights', in F. Francioni (ed.), *Environment, Human Rights and International Trade*, Oxford-Portland OR, Hart Publishing 2001, 179 ff.

8 See GATT doc. PREP.COM(86)W/43 of 25 June 1986.

9 See GATT doc. L/6196 of 3 July 1987 and MTN.GNG/NG7/W/57 of 17 October 1989.

considerable number of ministerial decisions and declarations) make no reference to it.[10]

On the eve of the first WTO Ministerial Conference, scheduled for 1996 in Singapore, some members once more insisted on discussing the trade–labour linkage.[11] The text of the final declaration adopted in Singapore contains express reference to the matter, but a balance was struck between the different views expressed during the debate. Most WTO members completely rejected the idea of recognizing a WTO competence: the ILO was considered the forum best suited for discussion, and strong opposition was raised against the idea of allowing the use of trade restrictions to enforce labour standards, seen by Brazil simply as a means for developed countries to solve their structural problem of unemployment.[12] However, it was also argued that the WTO should not avoid discussing social issues, because of the *de facto* impact of trade-led globalization on national social patterns and labour markets. Proposals in this case ranged from the creation of an appropriate WTO working party to the establishment of closer cooperation with the ILO. All proposals were based on the idea that the WTO's role, as stated by the US, 'must reflect the needs of the various constituencies involved in world trade' and should be recognized.[13] It is worth noting that the debate was based on the unanimous commitment to respect core labour standards, and that some statements made express reference to child labour, strongly condemning it.

Paragraph 4 of the Singapore Ministerial Declaration deals expressly with the issue.[14] The ILO is defined as the competent body for setting and dealing with internationally recognized core labour standards and States commit themselves to cooperate in that framework to enhance their implementation. At the same time, the existence of a link between trade and labour issues is passingly recognized in the statement that 'economic growth and development fostered by increased trade and further trade liberalization contribute to the promotion of these standards'. However, the opposition of some States, in particular of those claiming that it would be unrealistic 'to link labour rights with trade liberalization programmes'[15] or that explicitly rejected 'any attempt to link labour standards and other social clauses to trade and trade action',[16] has led to a strong and open condemnation of any recourse to labour standards for protectionist purposes, and to the acknowledgement that efforts should simply be directed at fostering closer cooperation between the WTO and the ILO.

Successive attempts to reopen the debate all led to no concrete results. On the occasion of the 1999 Ministerial Conference, convened with the purpose to start a new round of multilateral trade negotiations, a working group was established to discuss

---

10 However, see the analysis in McCrudden and Davies, *A Perspective*, *supra* note 7, at 182.

11 See WTO doc. WT/GC/M/13 § 8 and the WTO Press brief 'Trade and Labour Standards', 1996.

12 See WTO doc. WT/MIN(96)/ST/8.

13 WTO doc. WT/MIN(96)/ST/5.

14 Singapore Ministerial Declaration, WT/MIN(96)/DEC, 13 December 1996.

15 Statement of Colombia in WTO doc. WT/MIN(96)/ST/23.

16 Statement of Malaysia in WTO doc. WT/MIN(96)/ST/64.

the matter. However, the meeting failed and no final declaration was adopted. Among the reasons for the failure was the declaration of the then US President, Bill Clinton, affirming that one day trade sanctions could become the proper weapon to retaliate against labour standards violations. Hostility by developing countries followed, out of the fear that the veil of workers' rights violations could cover protectionist intents. At the 2001 Ministerial Conference, the issue was discussed once more, but States simply agreed to reaffirm the previous 1996 Declaration and to take note of the ILO activities on the so-called 'social dimension of globalization',[17] which in the meantime had taken some important steps. Indeed, with the adoption of the 1998 Declaration on Fundamental Principles and Rights at Work, the International Labour Conference 'declared' that ILO members are under an obligation to respect, promote and realize four core labour standards (whether they have ratified the pertaining ILO conventions or not), conceived as 'common rules of the game'. One of these principles calls for the effective abolition of child labour.[18] Thereafter, negotiations have led to the conclusion and entry into force of Convention 182.

Does the 2001 WTO Ministerial Declaration mark the definitive end of the WTO debate on the social dimension of globalization? It is the purpose of the present contribution to answer this question, aiming to assess the compatibility of national and international regulations providing for the adoption of trade restrictions against States responsible for child labour exploitation, with WTO regulations. The analysis will focus on the US and EC practice, as they both sustain the establishment of a link between trade liberalization and protection of human rights, even though pursuing different approaches.

13.3 The use of trade measures under the ILO Constitution

ILO Convention 182 does not provide for ad hoc enforcement regulation. Disputes concerning its violations may be settled by having recourse to the ILO supervisory mechanisms. Besides the regular evaluation of the annual reports submitted by the Member States (article 22), a representation procedure (article 24) and a complaint procedure (article 26) are also envisaged. Notwithstanding their differences, both have a clearly conciliatory character and aim to persuade States to fully comply with their obligations. The complaint procedure expressly provides for the adoption of enforcement measures. Indeed, the failure to implement the recommendation of an ad hoc commission of inquiry or a decision of the International Court of Justice (competent to examine the commission's report if so requested) may lead the Governing Body to recommend the Conference to adopt any action deemed 'wise and expedient' to secure compliance (article 33).

---

17 Ministerial Declaration, WT/MIN(01)/DEC/1, 14 November 2001 § 8.

18 The others concern the freedom of association and the effective recognition of the right to collective bargaining; the elimination of all forms of forced or compulsory labour; and the elimination of discrimination in respect of employment and occupation.

Since 1919, these measures have been adopted only once, in 2000 against Myanmar, held responsible for the violation of the ILO forced labour convention.[19] In that case, the Conference resolution invited members to review their relations with Myanmar and to take 'appropriate measures' to ensure that it does not take advantage of them to perpetrate or extend the practice of forced or compulsory labour.[20] Nevertheless, on the basis of that determination, and in consideration of the strong and massive human rights violations occurring in that country, in 2003 the US Congress passed the Burmese Freedom and Democracy Act,[21] calling the President to impose a ban over the import of any product of Myanmar, until a democratically elected government requests its removal and certain fundamental human rights are appropriately respected. The Act conditions the extinction of the trade embargo upon a number of factors, among which the issuance of a report by the Secretary of State ascertaining, in consultation with the ILO, that Myanmar no longer systemically violates workers' rights, including the use of forced and child labour and conscription of child-soldiers.

The US practice shows that the violation of ILO regulations may induce States to resort to trade countermeasures, notwithstanding the fact that the ILO Constitution does not directly refer to them. Clearly, to the extent that all States concerned are both members of the ILO and the WTO (as the US and Myanmar), the exercise of the faculty granted under the former implies a wrongful act under the latter.[22]

13.4 US and EC normative instruments linking trade and labour issues

13.4.1 The US free trade agreements

National and international trade policy instruments adopted by the US administration often make reference to the concept of 'internationally recognized labour rights'. After having been included in internal legislative acts, it has been incorporated in successive free trade agreements (FTAs). Basically, it lists a catalogue of workers' rights whose guarantee is pursued in the relationships with foreign trade partners. The list does not mirror the content of ILO conventions and recommendations; furthermore, it does not always correspond to the 1998 Declaration, consistent

---

19 See F. Maupain, 'Is the ILO Effective in Upholding Workers' Rights?: Reflections on the Myanmar Experience', in P. Alston (ed.), *Labour Rights as Human Rights*, Oxford, Oxford University Press, 2005, 85 ff.

20 Resolution concerning the measures recommended by the Governing Body under article 33 of the ILO Constitution on the subject of Myanmar, adopted by a large majority on 14 June 2000.

21 Pub. L. 108-61 (whose renewal is scheduled in 2008). See the President's Executive Order 13,310 of 28 June 2003, giving effect to the embargo.

22 The Myanmar government has not brought the issue before the WTO adjudicating bodies. In this regard, it should be noted that in 2003 Thai imports from Myanmar have counterbalanced the negative trade effects of the US sanctions. See Key Indicators 2006: Measuring Policy Effectiveness in Health and Education, published by the Asian Development Bank, available at <www.adb.org>.

with the fact that the US has not ratified all conventions related to the principles affirmed there.[23] As regards child labour, it usually refers only to the introduction of a minimum age for employment.

The elapsed Bipartisan Trade Promotion Authority Act of 2002,[24] covering agreements concluded by 1 July 2007 under the so-called 'fast-track procedure', fixed the objectives to be pursued by the President in his negotiating authority. Specific provisions were included for labour matters, making express reference to child labour and to the pertinent ILO conventions. Indeed the promotion of respect for children's rights, consistent with ILO core labour standards, was included as an overall objective, although the introduction of a minimum age for employment (governed by ILO Convention 138) was mentioned, whereas the effective abolition of child labour (as recommended by the 1998 Declaration) was not.[25] The gap was filled by including as a principle objective the universal ratification of and full compliance with the Convention 182.[26]

The act was based on an 'enforce-your-own-laws' approach. While recognizing the discretion of States in the field of labour laws, it adopted as one of its objectives to arrange rules ensuring that their enforcement by the counterparts is not carried out in a manner affecting trade with the US. As a matter of fact, the purpose of the envisaged negotiations would be neither the complete harmonization of national labour laws nor the establishment of common minimum standards, but simply to avoid that their enforcement adversely influence US producers. Should this be the case, recourse to retaliatory measures should be allowed.

Under the 2002 statute, Congress has adopted the implementing legislation of a considerable number of FTAs[27] (to which should be added the 2000 agreement

---

23 For example, no reference is made to the elimination of discrimination in any form of employment and occupation, whereas 'acceptable conditions of work with respect to minimum wages, hours of work, occupational safety and health' is always included. It is worth noting that the US has not ratified all ILO conventions that correspond to the 1998 principles, but only the Forced Labour Convention (No. 105) and Convention 182.

24 Pub. L. 107-215; 19 U.S.C. §§ 3801 ff (2006).

25 In general, see E.E. Potter, 'The Growing Significance of International Labor Standards on the Global Economy', *Suffolk Transnational Law Review*, Vol. 28, No. 2, 2005, 243 ff, at 251. With the intent to obtain Congress approval of the highly opposed free trade agreements with Peru and South Korea, in May 2007 House Democrats and the Bush Administration have agreed on a Bipartisan Trade Promotion Template. The arrangement has revised the list of the internationally recognized labour principles, making it perfectly consistent with the ILO Declaration. See Cho, 'The Bush Administration and Democrats Reach a Bipartisan Deal on Trade Policy', *ASIL Insight*, Vol. 12, No. 3, 2007, and the documents there cited.

26 For the distinction between overall and principle objectives see T.J. Manley and L. Lauredo, 'International Labor Standards in the Free Trade Agreements of the Americas', *Emory International Law Review*, Vol. 18, No. 1, 2004, 85 ff, at 107.

27 FTAs have been concluded with Chile (Pub. L. 108-77), Singapore (Pub. L. 108-78), Australia (Pub. L. 108-296), Morocco (Pub. L. 108-286), the Dominican Republic and five Central American States (Pub. L. 109-53), Bahrain (Pub. L. 109-169), Oman (Pub. L. 109-283) and Peru (Pub. L. 110-138). Furthermore, trade agreements signed with Colombia (2006), South Korea (2007) and Panama (2007) are still under congressional consideration.

with Jordan[28]), including specific provisions concerning labour standards. Based on the 1993 North American Agreement on Labor Cooperation (NAALC), the labour side-agreement of NAFTA,[29] none of them excludes the adoption of trade countermeasures against the contracting party held not to be in full compliance with obligations assumed in labour matters.

All these agreements contain a list of labour rights, whose drafting has undergone considerable evolution over the years. Indeed, NAALC makes no reference to ILO standards or conventions, and simply sets a list of eleven general 'labour principles' to be incorporated in national labour laws. Concerning child labour, the adoption of 'labour protections for children and young persons' is required (article 49(e)), which implies, according to Annex 1, the introduction of 'restrictions on those employments that might jeopardize physical, mental, and moral development of the child'. The 2000 FTA with Jordan instead expressly recalls the obligations assumed by the contracting parties as members of the ILO; however, it makes reference to the internationally recognized labour rights concept (article 6 (1)), hence to the mere 'establishment of a minimum age for the employment of children'. Since the 2003 agreement with Chile, a more general provision has been incorporated, making reference to 'labour protections for children and young people', including 'the prohibition and elimination of worst forms of child labour' (consistent with the Convention 182, in the meantime entered into force) (article 18 (8)). The 2007 agreements with Peru and South Korea mark a further step ahead. Indeed, for the first time one of the first provisions of the labour chapter (named 'Fundamental labour rights') recalls the 1998 ILO Declaration, hence the 'effective abolition of child labour' envisaged there, together with the elimination of worst forms of child labour.[30]

Once having defined the content of 'internationally recognized' or 'fundamental' labour rights, all FTAs impose the obligation to 'strive to ensure' that they are protected and recognized by domestic labour laws, which should provide for labour standards consistent with them.[31] Since the agreement with the Dominican Republic and five Central American countries, the express obligation to 'improve' national standards in the light of the international ones has also been introduced.[32] The contents of the provision has been definitely reinforced in the 2007 agreements, whose contracting parties undertake to 'adopt and maintain' the rights of the 1998 ILO Declaration in their statutes, regulations and practices.

The core obligations of the labour chapters deal with the possible effects of national labour legislation on bilateral trade flows. Since the agreement with Jordan, the possibility that contracting parties may be induced to revise their labour laws

---

28 Pub. L. 107-43.

29 Pub. L. 103-182.

30 See, for example, art. 17.2 of the US–Peru FTA.

31 See, for example, art. 6 §§ 1 and 3 of the US–Jordan FTA.

32 See art. 16.1 § 2 of the US–Dominican Republic–Central America FTA. For the peculiarities of the negotiations with Central American countries see Potter, 'The Growing Significance', *supra* note 25, at 251 ff, and Manley and Lauredo, 'International Labor Standards', *supra* note 26, at 111.

in order to facilitate exports has been recognized: thus, the prohibition to waive or derogate from them 'as an encouragement for trade with the other party' (article 6 (2)).[33] Anyway, the main obligation is to prohibit the enforcement of domestic laws in a manner affecting trade.[34]

A final aspect of US FTAs concerns dispute settlement. According to the FTA with Jordan, failure to implement the obligations set out in the labour chapter entails activation of the general diplomatic dispute settlement procedure, which contemplates recourse to 'any appropriate and commensurate measure' by the complaining party in case a mutually agreed solution is not found with the party complained against (article 17 (2)(b)).[35] In contrast, most FTAs concluded under the 2002 statute contain specific provisions for the settlement of disputes in labour matters, derogating from the general procedure applicable to all other disputes, both in the ascertainment and in the enforcement phase.[36] Most agreements provide for ad hoc bilateral and multilateral consultations for every matter arising under the labour chapter in order to arrive at a mutually satisfactory solution.[37] Only in cases where the dispute concerns the enforcement of domestic labour laws in a manner affecting trade flows may recourse be had to the general procedure,[38] but only after the ad hoc mechanism has been exhausted. If the parties fail to reach a mutually agreed solution by means of a new phase of multilateral consultations, the complaining party may request that the matter be referred to a dispute settlement panel. If it determines that there has been a violation of the enforcement obligation, the parties shall find a resolution of the dispute, normally consistent with the panel determinations and recommendations, if there are any, and, whenever possible, providing for the elimination of the non-conformity.

A special discipline is envisaged in case the parties are unable to reach an agreement or disagree as to whether it is going to be fully implemented, with the

---

33 The agreement with Chile adds 'in a manner that weakens or reduces adherence to internationally recognized labor rights' (art. 18.2 § 2).

34 See, for example, art. 6 § 4.a of the US–Jordan FTA. NAALC contains a more general provision, stating the duty to enforce labour laws through appropriate actions, with no express reference to trade effects (art. 3).

35 In an exchange of letters between US and Jordan representatives, it was agreed that in any case compliance will be secured without recourse to traditional trade sanctions (US Congressional Record of 31 July 2001).

36 See note 38. The following analysis is based in the US–Chile FTA: most subsequent agreements provide for a similar procedure, with only some minor differences. Basically, it resembles the mechanism envisioned by NAALC, even if with certain important differences (see B. Hepple, *Labour Laws and Global Trade*, Oxford, Hart, 2005, at 108 ff).

37 See art. 18.6 §§ 1–6 of the US–Chile FTA.

38 With the 2007 FTAs with Peru and South Korea, recourse to the general dispute settlement procedure is once again envisaged for every dispute concerning the labour chapter, and not only for those involving a violation of the enforcement obligation (for example, see art. 17.7 § 6 of the US–Peru FTA). However, the purport of this provision, with respect to the extensive obligation to adopt and maintain statutes, regulations, and practices consistent with the 1998 ILO Declaration rights, has been limited to establishing that claims may only regard violations affecting trade between the Parties (for example, see note 1 of the US–Peru FTA labour chapter).

purpose to defer, if not avoid, the suspension of benefits that would otherwise occur under the general procedure. Indeed, it is established that the panel may be reconvened to impose on the defending party an annual monetary assessment, to be paid into a common fund used for appropriate labour initiatives including efforts to improve and enhance its labour law enforcement. Only if the responding party fails to pay the monetary assessment may the complainant secure compliance resorting to appropriate measures, including the suspension of trade benefits arising from the FTA.[39] When determining the economic value of the suspension, the agreement's objective of eliminating barriers to trade has to be kept in mind.[40] The recent FTAs with Peru and South Korea envisage the adoption of 'tailored' countermeasures (which shall not be manifestly excessive), directed to affect those sectors in which the unlawful act has occurred. In case this course of action is not practicable or effective, suspension of benefits in other sectors remains a viable alternative.[41] In any case, according to all FTAs, a compliance review panel may be convened, and if it determines that the non-conformity was eliminated, the suspended benefits must be reinstated.[42]

13.4.2 Workers' rights in EC external relations

The European Community has a long-standing practice of pure and mixed agreements with third countries including reference to human rights. Because of its less intrusive approach and softer enforcement strategy, this sharply contrasts with US practice.

The present practice was initiated in 1995 and resorts to the so-called 'essential element' and 'non-execution' clauses.[43]

According to the former, respect for democratic principles and fundamental human rights, as defined in some international instruments, informs the domestic and external policies of the EC and the country concerned, and constitutes an essential element of their bilateral relationship.[44] Usually, the documents referred to are non-binding instruments. However, according to the EC Commission, the clause

---

39 In the 2007 FTAs, instead the monetary assessment may be proposed by the defendant party in order to avoid recourse to suspension of benefits, to which the complaining party is entitled if there is no agreement over a compensation to be given after the panel has adopted a non-compliance determination (for example, see art. 21.16 § of the US–Peru FTA).

40 See art. 22.16 § 5 of the US–Chile FTA.

41 See art. 21.16 § 5 of the US–Peru FTA.

42 It is worth noting that, except for the 2007 FTAs with Peru and South Korea, other agreements do not provide for the possibility of the defendant party requesting and obtaining an independent assessment of the suspension of benefits proposed by the complaining party before its implementation. Only by resorting to the compliance review procedure may the reinstatement of the original trade concessions be obtained.

43 See L. Bartels, *Human Rights Conditionality in the EU's International Agreements*, Oxford, Oxford University Press, 2005, and Communication on the Inclusion of Respect for Democratic Principles and Human Rights in agreement between the Community and Third Countries, COM(95)216, May 23, 1995.

44 See, for example, art. 2 of the 1999 agreement concluded with South Africa, and entered into force in 2004 (Official Journal, L 311, 4 December 1999, 3 ff).

encompasses the core labour standards as set out in the ILO Conventions concerning the principles stated in the 1998 Declaration.[45]

Under the non-execution clause, the contracting parties commit themselves to take any measures required to fulfil their obligations under the agreement and to attain its objectives. More importantly, after a consultation procedure, they are entitled to take 'appropriate measures' against the contracting party considered not to have respected the provisions of the agreement, among which is the essential element clause.[46] Concerning the nature of these measures, it is usually established that priority should be given to those less disruptive to the functioning of the agreement. Furthermore, nearly all EC agreements provide that the 'appropriate measures' referred to are those taken in accordance with international law, thus opening the text to any provision of customary or conventional international law applicable to the relation between the EC and the contracting party in question.

The 2000 Cotonou Agreement with the ACP countries presents some peculiarities.[47] Firstly, the non-execution clause is specifically designed for the violation of the essential element clause set out in article 9 (2). The latter is somewhat more detailed than other essential elements clauses, since the parties refer to the international obligations already assumed and to commitments to respect human rights and undertake to promote and protect all fundamental freedoms and human rights. In addition, respect for social rights is considered an integral part of sustainable development, whose attainment is the purpose of the overall cooperation established between the contracting parties (article 9 (1)). In this context, the reference to international labour standards both in the preamble and in the text of the Agreement is remarkable. In particular, in article 50 (which does not come under the purport of the non-execution clause) the parties reaffirm their commitment to internationally recognized core labour standards as defined by ILO conventions, among which is the elimination of worst forms of child labour, and agree to enhance cooperation in this area. The closing paragraph states that 'labour standards should not be used for protectionist trade purposes'.

In practice, the EC has never invoked the essential element clause to justify the suspension of trade benefits. In line with the approach endorsed by the Council of Ministers in 1999,[48] it prefers to have recourse to political and diplomatic instruments and to positive measures in order to exert pressure for a more effective implementation of the human rights clauses.[49]

---

45 See Promoting Core Labour Standards and Improving Social Governance in the Context of Globalisation, COM(2001) 416 final, 18 July 2001, at 12. A European Parliament resolution adopted in February 2006 (in Official Journal, C 290, 29 November 2006, 107 ff, at 109) has called for a strengthening of the essential element clause, through an express reference to ILO conventions.

46 See for example art. 3 of the agreement concluded with South Africa, *supra* note 44.

47 See K. Arts, 'ACP–EU Relations in a New Era: the Cotonou Agreement', *Common Market Law Review*, Vol. 40, No. 1, 2003, 95 ff, at 102 ff.

48 See 'Council Conclusions of October 1999 on Trade and Labour', quoted in COM(2001) 416 final, annex 1, *supra* note 45. See also Bartels, *Human Rights Conditionality*, *supra* note 44.

49 See Bartels, *Human Rights Conditionality*, *supra* note 43, at 35 ff.

13.4.3 Unilateral legislation providing for recourse to trade measures against a State violating international prohibitions on child labour

The adoption of trade measures against States held responsible for the exploitation of child labour is also envisaged by some US statutes.[50] Section 307 of the Tariff Act of 1930,[51] and Section 301 of the Trade Act of 1974[52] are worth citing in this respect.

The former encompasses a ban on imports of goods made by convict, forced and/or indentured labour under penal sanctions.[53] The 2000 amendment added that the latter two terms include forced and indentured child labour as well.[54] As a consequence, the Act does not prohibit imports of any article made with child labour, but aims to avoid the entry into the US of goods manufactured in working conditions that are likely to jeopardize the health and well-being of children.[55] A mandatory exception is included, according to which the import prohibition does not apply to forced and indentured labour (but remains valid for convict labour) in case of goods not produced in the US in such quantities as to meet the national consumption needs. As a matter of fact, the market access limitations cannot prevent the satisfaction of consumers' demand, regardless of the labour exploitation occurring in the exporting country.

In practice, Section 307 has been invoked only rarely to halt importation of goods produced with child labour, and no action has ever been taken. Rather, the petition submitted in 2002 for prohibiting market access to cocoa produced by forced child labour in Côte d'Ivoire was dismissed on the ground of the domestic consumption exception.[56]

---

50 See S.H. Cleveland, 'Norm Internalization and U.S. Economic Sanctions', *Yale Journal of International Law,* Vol. 26, No. 1, 2001, 1 ff; and F.J. Garcia and S. Jun, 'Trade-Based Strategies for Combating Child Labor', Boston College Law School, Research Paper no. 59, 2005.

51 See 19 U.S.C. § 1307 (2007).

52 See 19 U.S.C. § 2411 (2007).

53 For an interpretation of the statute, in light of its legislative history, see R. Bhala, 'Clarifying the Trade–Labor Link', *Columbia Journal of Transnational Law*, Vol. 37, No. 1, 1998, 11 ff, at 45 ff.

54 See J.M. Diller and D.A. Levy, 'Child Labor, Trade and Investment: Toward the Harmonization of International Law', *American Journal of International Law*, Vol. 91, No. 4, 1997, 663 ff, at 687 ff; they hold that the term 'forced labour' included child labour already in 1930.

55 In the 1990s, the US Congress repeatedly examined, but never approved, proposals for the enactment of a Child Labor Deterrence Act, forbidding the importation of any product manufactured by children less than 15 years old. See T.P. McElduff and J. Veiga, 'The Child Labor Deterrence Act of 1995: A Choice between Hegemony and Hypocrisy', *St. John's Journal of Legal Commentary*, Vol. 11, No. 2, 1996, 581 ff; and A. Garg, 'A Child Labor Social Clause: Analysis and Proposal for Action', *NYU Journal of International Law and Policy*, Vol. 21, No. 2/3, 1999, 473 ff.

56 *International Labor Rights Fund, Global Exchange, and Fair Trade Federation v. United States and Chocolate Manufacturers Association*, 29 August 2005. In a previous case the Court had affirmed that with the adoption of section 307, 'Congress intended to

The other normative instruments that could be used to limit imports from countries permitting exploitation of child labour are contained in Section 301 of the Trade Act of 1974. The statute has always been considered one of the most controversial instruments of US trade policy, and its compatibility with the WTO regime has been questioned since 1995. Its text includes provisions granting the United States Trade Representative (USTR), *inter alia*, the discretion to restrict imports from foreign countries determined to adopt an unreasonable act, policy or practice burdening or restricting US commerce. With the 1988 amendment, Congress has expanded its purview, adding the possibility that a judgment of unreasonableness be delivered in case the affected country is considered to permit any form of forced and compulsory labour, or failing to provide a minimum age for the employment of children.[57]

These provisions have been invoked only in a few instances, and in no case have petitions been admitted. The very first petition was filed in 2004 by a US trade union, claiming that the Chinese government's persistent violation of workers' basic rights enabled local producers to take advantage of lower costs of production, thus burdening US commerce. A similar petition was presented in 2006 as well. However, in both cases the USTR decided not to conduct the requested investigations, on the ground that trade remedies would not be a proper instrument to secure improvements in the Chinese labour regime, and that appropriate pressure by political means should be applied instead.[58]

Finally, reference should also be made to the EC and US generalized systems of preferences (GSP),[59] granting developing countries a differentiated and more favourable treatment as regards market access.

In the EC scheme, all targeted developing countries benefit from a general regime of tariff suspension or reduction, whose temporary withdrawal is provided for in case the beneficiary is held responsible for serious and systematic violations of principles laid down in a number of human rights conventions and in the core labour standards ILO conventions. In addition, the ratification and effective implementation of those agreements allow some of the GSP beneficiaries to access a special regime, granting a further reduction of import duties. In the evaluation of the requests of eligible

---

protect domestic workers and producers from unfair competition. But this concern as well as any desire to improve foreign labor conditions were clearly subordinate … to concerns for the American consumer's access to merchandise not produced domestically in quantities sufficient to satisfy consumer demand' (*McKinney, et al. v. U.S. Department of the Treasury, et al*, 23 July 1985).

57 19 U.S.C. § 2411(d)(3)(B)(iii)(III) and (IV) (2007).

58 J.P. Hiatt and D. Greenfield, 'The Importance of Core Labor Rights in World Development', *Michigan Journal of International Law*, Vol. 26, No. 1, 2004, 39 ff, at 49 ff. The text of the 2006 petition may be found on the AFL-CIO website (<www.aflcio.org>); see also USTR press release 21 July 2006. In China a new labour law was entered into force in January 2008.

59 EC regulation 980/2005, in Official Journal, L 169, 30 June 2005, 1 ff; and 19 U.S.C. §§ 2461 ff (2007).

countries, the EC has to take into account the findings of the relevant international organizations, hence of the ILO as regards workers' rights and child labour.[60]

In the US scheme, in contrast, respect for workers' rights is one of the conditions that must be satisfied in order to become eligible for, and to continue to benefit from, the GSP. Indeed, the statute excludes that, lacking any prevalent national economic interest, the President may designate as beneficiary of the duty-free treatment countries that either have not taken or are not taking steps to grant internationally recognized workers' rights, or that have not implemented their commitment to eliminate the worst forms of child labour. Contrary to the EC approach, the US legislation does not specify the mentioned workers' rights and worst forms of child labour by expressly referring to the pertinent ILO conventions. Like the FTAs, it contains an autonomous list of internationally recognized workers' rights, which only partially corresponds to the principles of 1998 ILO Declaration. However, the practices considered worst forms of child labour mirror the scope of application of ILO Convention 182.

13.5 The compatibility of trade measures with WTO obligations

It is beyond the scope of the present chapter to draw conclusions on the effects of the described measures on working conditions in targeted countries. Rather, the analysis that follows aims to ascertain their compatibility with the WTO legal regime. Indeed, they all contravene at least the basic non-discrimination and market access obligations undertaken by WTO members on the basis of GATT 1994. The non-discrimination principle is embodied in articles I and III. According to the former, States are due to grant unconditional most-favoured-nation status (that is, to apply the best market access conditions) to like products imported from all WTO members, whereas article III imposes a prohibition of discrimination between a party's national products and like products of all other WTO members (so-called national treatment).[61] Finally, article XI forbids instituting or maintaining quantitative limitations on imports and exports, such as quotas and embargoes.

The WTO has not yet been asked to rule on the admissibility of trade limitations for workers' rights purposes under the WTO trade liberalization obligations and the exceptions codified in the agreements entered into force in 1995. Yet the core issue

---

60 See decision 2005/925/EC in *Official Journal*, L 337, 22 December 2005, 50, for the list of 15 countries benefiting from the incentive regime until the end of 2008.

61 Articles I and III impose non-discrimination between 'like' products: some authors question whether goods could be treated alike if they embody different production processes and some of them have been obtained through labour exploitation. The dichotomy between product-based and process-based measures under art. III has been extensively analysed by the legal literature: also for further references, see R.E. Hudec, 'GATT/WTO Constraints on National Regulation: Requiem for an "Aim and Effects" Test', *International Lawyer*, Vol. 32, No. 3, 1998, 619 ff; R. Howse and D. Regan, 'The Product/Process Distinction – An Illusory Basis for Disciplining "Unilateralism" in Trade Policy', *European Journal of International Law*, Vol. 11, No. 2, 2000, 249 ff. See also C. Dordi, *La discriminazione commerciale nel diritto internazionale*, Milan, Giuffrè, 2002, 119 ff.

remains to understand if and to what extent the multilateral trade regime can be interpreted and applied in such a way as to permit trade restrictions adopted on the basis of the normative instruments described above.

13.5.1 The relevance of jus cogens *norms within GATT 1994 article XXI on security exceptions*

As argued by the Appellate Body, the WTO regime cannot be read in 'clinical isolation' from other rules of public international law. The WTO Agreement and its annexes were concluded with the purpose, *inter alia*, to reinforce the previous multilateral trade regime, adopted under the aegis of the GATT 1947, with a dispute settlement discipline that would grant the right to have recourse to trade countermeasures against States not complying with the obligations undertaken. As pointed out by the doctrine, it can be considered a self-sufficient system to the extent that the wrongful conduct under one of the WTO annexes cannot but be remedied through the enforcement mechanism provided for by the Dispute Settlement Understanding (DSU), which bans recourse to unilateral countermeasures not authorized by the WTO itself.[62] But, it can not be considered a closed regime, where other rules of public international law can play no role.[63] This consideration implies that appropriate consideration has to be given to other customary and conventional international norms addressed to the WTO members, in the interpretation and application of the WTO rules. Among the customary norms, general peremptory rules imposing collective (*erga omnes*) obligations deserve particular attention.

Peremptory rules are defined by article 53 of the 1969 Vienna Convention on the Law of Treaties as accepted and recognized 'by the international community as a whole' as norms from which no derogation is permitted and which can be modified only by subsequent norms of general international law having the same character. Article 53 does not identify the material content of these norms. Since it is included in an agreement codifying general international law applicable to treaties, it focuses on the effects of peremptory rules over the latter. In this regard, it establishes that in no case *jus cogens* norms may be derogated by the contrary will of a group of States enshrined in a conflicting agreement. This treaty is null and void, and its nullity can be claimed by any of its contracting parties. In the present contribution, the incompatibility of the WTO regime with *jus cogens* norms is not an issue (since they are not about international trade cooperation),[64] but rather the issue is that the

---

62 See Picone and Ligustro, *Diritto, supra* note 2, at 625 and 657 ff. However, it is underlined that the customary regime of the responsibility of States for international unlawful acts might be revived in case of a failure by the DSU procedure to guarantee appropriate reactions to the violation of WTO annexes (at 667 ff).

63 For an extensive analysis of the openness of the WTO regime to customary and conventional public international law: Picone and Ligustro, *Diritto, supra* note 2, at 625 ff; and J. Pauwelyn, *Conflict of Norms in Public International Law. How WTO Law Relates to Other Rules of International Law*, Cambridge, Cambridge University Press, 2003.

64 However, some authors do not exclude the relevance of *jus cogens* norms in international economic cooperation, and assume the existence of a peremptory rule prohibiting States to

regime has to be interpreted and applied taking into consideration that those rules are in force in the relationships between WTO members.[65]

Though the boundaries of peremptory rules are not clearly defined and controversies exist as to their material scope of application, it is common opinion that they concern some fundamental values and interests and regard (not exclusively) the protection of individuals against serious and extensive violations of their fundamental human rights. Prohibition of practices such as slavery, apartheid, and genocide is widely accepted.

A further characteristic of the rules at issue is that they may impose upon States collective obligations.[66] As held by the International Court of Justice in its famous *obiter dictum* in the *Barcelona Traction* case, *erga omnes* obligations (which may derive *inter alia* 'from the principles and rules concerning the basic rights of the human person, including protection from slavery and racial discrimination') '[b]y their very nature ... are the concern of all States. In view of the importance of the rights involved, all States can be held to have a legal interest in their protection.'[67] Thus, according to the ICJ, they do not apply in the bilateral relationships within couples of States, but provide for obligations that any State is due to respect in its relationships with the international community as a whole. Hence, in case the relevant protected value and interest is jeopardized by the wrongful conduct of one State, all other States can be considered to have a 'legal interest' to react.[68]

---

adopt measures that could seriously jeopardize the economy of other States (see B. Conforti, *Diritto internazionale*, Naples, Editoriale Scientifica, 2006, 7th edn, at 167).

65 Specific circumstances where peremptory rules may be implemented by WTO dispute settlement organs are illustrated in Picone and Ligustro, *Diritto*, *supra* note 2, at 629 ff.

66 The interesting legal analysis criticizing the commonly accepted opinion that all peremptory norms impose erga omnes obligations is worth mentioning: P. Picone, 'La distinzione tra norme internazionali di jus cogens e norme che producono obblighi erga omnes', Rivista di Diritto internazionale, Vol. XCI, 2008, No. 1, 5 ff, and by the same author, 'Obblighi *erga omnes* e codificazione della responsabilità degli Stati', Rivista di diritto internazionale, Vol. 88, No. 4, 2005, 893 ff, at 921 ff and 932 ff and 'Obblighi reciproci ed obblighi erga omnes degli Stati nel campo della protezione internazionale dell'ambiente marino', in V. Starace (ed.), *Diritto internazionale e protezione dell'ambiente marino*, Milan, Giuffré, 1983, 15 ff, at 39 ff. See also M.I. Papa, *I rapporti tra la Corte internazionale di giustizia e il Consiglio di sicurezza*, Padua, CEDAM, 2006, at 280 ff.

67 Barcelona Traction, Light and Power Company Ltd (*Belgium v Spain*), ICJ Reports, 1970, 3 ff, §§ 33–34. For other relevant ICJ statements, see Papa, *I rapporti*, *supra* note 66, at 492 ff, note 14.

68 The legal literature has qualified the meaning of the ICJ finding that 'all States can be held to have a legal interest' in the protection of *erga omnes* obligations. One of the main contributions underlines that *erga omnes* obligations concern fundamental values and interest removed from the free determination of individual States and rather ascribable to the international community itself (Picone, 'Obblighi reciproci', *supra* note 66, at 26 ff and, by the same author, *Diritto internazionale dell'economia e costituzione economica dell'ordinamento internazionale*, in P. Picone and G. Sacerdoti (eds), *Diritto internazionale dell'economia*, Milan, 1982, 31 ff at 59). Therefore, these norms do not apply in the reciprocal relationships between States, but impose on each of them an obligation owed to the international community itself. Since the latter does not possess its own organs, and cannot be considered as an entity

To the extent that some of the prohibitions concerning child labour contained in Convention 182 also come under the scope of general international law peremptory rules imposing *erga omnes* obligations,[69] the possibility may arise that States adopt countermeasures consisting of the suspension of trade benefits under the WTO regime.[70] Those countermeasures may aim to affect the defaulting State (either

---

separate and materially autonomous from States, all States have a collective right (not an individual right, as laid down by some authors: see the references in Papa, *I rapporti, supra* note 66, at 517, note 68) to protect the values at issue and to invoke the responsibility of any defaulting State, acting *uti universi* on behalf of the international community. In this case, they would not intervene as third parties, but as holders of the said collective right (Picone, Obblighi reciproci, *supra* note 66, at 77 ff). For the peculiar concept of 'international community' adopted by the author see 'Diritto', at 45 ff, 'Obblighi reciproci', *supra* note 66, at 53 ff, and 'Obblighi erga omnes', *supra* note 66, at note 6.

69 Some authors do not exclude that the violation of core labour rights may fall under their purview (F. Francioni, 'WTO Law in Context: the Integration of International Human Rights and Environmental Law in the Dispute Settlement Process', in G. Sacerdoti, A. Yanovich and J. Bohanes (eds), *The WTO at Ten: The Contribution of the Dispute Settlement System*, Cambridge, 2006, 143 ff, at 146 ff). The possibility is admitted, with some reservations, in Picone and Ligustro, *Diritto, supra* note 2, at 628. See also S.H. Cleveland, 'Human Rights Sanctions and the World Trade Organization', in Francioni (ed.), *Environment, supra* note 7, 199 ff, at 205 ff. The child labour issue is discussed by S. Sanna, *Diritti dei lavoratori e disciplina del commercio nel diritto internazionale*, Milan, Giuffrè, 2002, at 115 ff, and by C. Blengino, *Il lavoro infantile e la disciplina del commercio internazionale*, Milan, Giuffré, 2003, at 60 ff, C. Di Turi, *Globalizzazione dell'economia e diritti umani fondamentali in materia di lavoro: il ruolo dell'OIL e dell'OMC*, Milan, Giuffré, 2007, at 108 ff. Some interesting remarks are made by F. Lenzerini, 'International Trade and Child Labour Standards', in Francioni (ed.), *Environment, supra* note 7, 287 ff, at 292 ff. For a contrary opinion, see T.A. Glut, 'Changing the Approach to Ending Child Labor: an International Solution to an International Problem', *Vanderbilt Journal of Transnational Law*, Vol. 28, No. 5, 1995, 1203 ff, at 1215. The existence of a *jus cogens* norm applying to child labour is mainly affirmed on the basis of the prohibition of slavery and practices similar to slavery, whose material scope of application has progressively widened to include also sexual exploitation: see A.Y. Rassam, 'Contemporary Forms of Slavery and the Evolution of the Prohibition of Slavery and Slave Trade Under Customary International Law', *Virginia Journal of International Law*, Vol. 39, No. 2, 1999, 303 ff and by the same author, 'International Law and Contemporary Forms of Slavery: An Economic and Social Rights-Based Approach', *Penn State International Law Review*, Vol. 23, No. 4, 2005, 809 ff.

70 According to the legal literature we are making reference to in these notes, in case an *erga omnes* obligation is not complied with, the claims that may be made by States acting *uti universi* depend upon the content of the rule at issue. A distinction is drawn between breaches that infringe the collective rights of all States and individual rights of one or more them (that is, armed aggression against the territory of a State) and breaches contravening only the collective rights of all States (Picone, 'Obblighi reciproci', *supra* note 66, at 77 ff and 82 ff). The latter circumstance may occur when a State is responsible for genocide or flagrant and systematic violations of human rights occurring within its borders: as no materially injured State exists, it is only the collective reaction by all other States acting *uti universi* that would guarantee the enforcement of the breached *erga omnes* obligation, otherwise void of any consequence (Picone, 'Obblighi erga omnes', *supra* note 68, at 934 ff). The author underlines

because it is directly responsible for serious and extensive violations or because it tolerates their occurrence within its jurisdiction) in the form of a total embargo on imports or market access restrictions for products whose production process embodies the wrongful conduct. In case countermeasures are objected to before the WTO, the adjudicating bodies would not be competent to pronounce on the violation of the peremptory rule and to determine the legitimate action that may be taken against the responsible State, but only to examine the consistency of the trade countermeasures already in force with the WTO regime. The Organization would intervene after the main dispute had arisen. Only evaluating the lawfulness of the suspension of trade benefits may it be requested to ascertain that the primary violation has occurred and to link up to it the consequences that may be legitimately adopted under general international law.[71]

---

the difficulties in identifying the different disciplines that may be applied to the protection of fundamental human rights, making illustrative reference to torture (note 118). He concludes that it may be considered as prohibited by a general international law rule imposing erga omnes obligations only when it corresponds to a systematic and extensive practice of a State (and not in case of single and autonomous violations) that determines the exercise of power by political authorities within their jurisdiction and in their interstate relations.

71 See Picone and Ligustro, *Diritto*, *supra* note 2, at 629. See also J. Pauwelyn, 'The Role of Public International Law in the WTO: How Far Can We Go?', *American Journal of International Law*, Vol. 95, No. 3, 2001, 535 ff, at 554 ff. One of the main references of the adjudicating bodies could be the Project of articles on State responsibility adopted by the UN International Law Commission in 2001 (Report of the International Law Commission on the Work of its Fifty-Third Session, 2001, UN doc. A/56/10, 43 ff). At the beginning of its work, the *Commission* had drawn a distinction between 'international delicts' and 'international crimes', the latter being defined as 'the breach by a State of an international obligation so essential for the protection of fundamental interests of the international community that its breach is recognized as a crime by that community as a whole', such as a serious breach, *inter alia*, 'on a widespread scale of an international obligation of essential importance for safeguarding the human being, such as those prohibiting slavery, genocide and apartheid' (see art. 19(2) of the 'Draft Articles of State Responsibility', Yearbook of the International Law Commission, 1976, II, 2, 95 ff). A more severe regime of responsibility would apply to crimes: according to the Commission commentary, in this case States other than the one directly injured could be entitled to invoke the responsibility of the guilty State and punitive measures could be applied (ibid., at 97 ff and 110 ff). The discipline has undergone a considerable re-examination, whose outcome has met a high criticism (see even, for further references, Picone, 'Obblighi erga omnes', *supra* note 66, passim). In the 2001 Project the concept of international crimes has been replaced by the notion of 'serious breaches of obligations under peremptory norms of general international law', defined as gross or systematic failures by a State to fulfil the said obligations (art. 40(2)). *Erga omnes* obligations are still mentioned, even if in a regulation not devoid of contradictions and inconsistencies. In its commentary, the Commission holds that they substantially overlap with the notion of serious breaches of peremptory rules (Report, at 277 ff, in particular at 281; for a relevant different approach see references *supra* note 66, and for a critique to the comment see Picone, 'Obblighi erga omnes', *supra* note 66, at 928 ff). As to the consequences of the mentioned serious violations, the Commission has agreed on a 'soft' regime of responsibility, as art. 41 refers only to an obligation upon States other than the injured one to cooperate to bring to an end the wrongful conduct through lawful means (§ 1) and not to recognize as lawful, nor render aid or assistance in maintaining, the

A similar circumstance is not outside the scope of the current WTO regime, on the basis of an appropriate interpretation of GATT article XXI(c), which allows WTO members to adopt any action in pursuance of the obligations under the UN Charter for the maintenance of international peace and security. This subordination clause of the WTO regime in favour of the obligations imposed by the UN Security Council concerns the adoption under article 41 of the UN Charter of measures not involving the use of armed force against States held responsible for a threat to peace, a breach of peace, or an act of aggression. In the light of the UN practice in the last decades, sanctions might be adopted when a violation of a peremptory rule imposing an *erga omnes* obligation occurs (particularly in case of serious violations of fundamental human rights), to the extent that it is considered to come under the purport of one of the circumstances mentioned in article 39 of the Charter, and in particular under the 'threat to the peace' concept. Indeed, its vagueness has sometimes allowed the Security Council to exercise its wide discretion and to decide the adoption of trade sanctions in response to human rights violations taking place within the boundaries of a State.[72]

---

situation created by the breach (§ 2). *Erga omnes* obligations are also mentioned in part II of the Project dealing with the invocation of responsibility: indeed, art. 48(1)(b) recognizes that any State other than the injured State is entitled to invoke the responsibility of another State if 'the obligation breached is owed to the international community as a whole'. It may claim the cessation of the wrongful act, assurances and guarantees of non-repetition, and performance of the obligation of reparation in the interest of the injured State or of the beneficiaries of the obligation breached (art. 48.2). To that end, according to art. 54 (included in part III of the Project dealing with countermeasures, which, according to art. 49, may be taken only by the injured State) all States have the right to take 'lawful measures' (leaving thus to the further development of international law the resolution of the matter concerning the entitlement of any State than an injured State to take countermeasures – Report, at 355). According to the legal literature to which we are making reference (Picone, Obblighi *erga omnes*, *supra* note 68, at 938 ff) this is just a minimum regulation on reactions to the violation of any *erga omnes* obligations, as it does not take into appropriate consideration that the latter do not constitute a homogeneous category. Indeed, they may vary considerably as to their material scope of application. In the light of this consideration, the application of different regimes of international responsibility may be justified, which nevertheless have not been codified by the Commission. However, a 'saving clause' is inferred from art. 41, where, once having defined the consequences of serious violation of *jus cogens* norms, it is provided that further consequences that may entail under international law are not prejudiced. In this way, the Project legitimates all ad hoc regulations concerning the serious violation of any *erga omnes* obligation provided for by general international law, and recognizes, even if by interpretation, the entitlement of any State to react for the protection of the various values concerned in the exercise of the collective rights, obligations or powers conferred to them.

72 Under this perspective, one may mention the attempt by the US to discuss the Myanmar situation within the Security Council. In the proposal put forward in January 2007 (UN doc. S/2007/14), supporting the good offices mission of the Secretary-General, the US underlined the need for tangible progress in the overall situation in Myanmar in order to minimize 'the risks to peace and security in the region'. The aim was not the adoption of measures under art. 41 of the UN Charter (which could eventually support the already adopted US trade ban), but a number of requests were nevertheless formulated towards the Myanmar authorities,

However, within the WTO the relevance of peremptory norms imposing *erga omnes* obligations cannot be limited to those cases where their enforcement is pursued by means of sanctions imposed by the UN Security Council, because any State may legitimately react against the violation of those rules. Secondary general international law rules concerning the consequences of serious unlawful conducts may allow the suspension of non-derogable norms (hence, also the obligations assumed within the WTO) in the relation with the defaulting State.[73]

In such circumstances it might be appropriate to have recourse to other article XXI clauses, and in particular those clauses that grant States a wide margin of discretion in taking action they consider necessary to protect their essential security interests (sub-paragraph b). Among the hypothetical circumstances, sub-paragraph b.iii) mentions 'emergency in international relations'.

The vagueness of the expression raises some interpretative difficulties, which cannot be overcome by reference to the practice as no adjudicatory body has ever been called to give its opinion on article XXI.[74] However, the expression has been construed to imply that 'emergencies in international relations' occur whenever peremptory norms imposing *erga omnes* obligations are seriously violated.[75] In principle, if the breach concerns provisions of ILO Convention 182 that also come under the scope of a *jus cogens* norm imposing *erga omnes* obligations, the existence of an ILC determination inviting States to adopt appropriate measure against a member could play a significant role. Indeed, it could help prove that a trade ban was not adopted on the basis of purely unilateral considerations, but that it satisfies a common concern of the international community. The main argument might be that it

---

in particular to put an end to human rights and humanitarian law violations associated with military actions against minorities, and to fully cooperate with the ILO and its representatives in order to eradicate forced labour. The proposal was not adopted because of the Chinese and Russian veto. In the course of the debate (in UN doc. S/PV.5619), the States, which then voted against or abstained, recognized the great challenges Myanmar is facing today, relating *inter alia* to child labour and human rights. But, as stated by the Chinese representative, 'no country is perfect' (at 2); the matter falls within the Myanmar domestic jurisdiction; and in no case could it be considered as a threat to peace and international security (in the light of the political dialogue carried out within ASEAN).

73 State practice records cases where unilateral trade countermeasures against States considered non-compliant with *jus cogens* rules concerning human rights have been adopted. The most well-known concern is the embargo imposed by the US in 1978 against Uganda (justified as a reaction against the serious human rights violations perpetrated by Idi Amin's brutal regime); the ban on trade with Poland and the USSR in consequence of the 1981 decision of the Polish authorities to introduce martial law and to suspend some fundamental freedoms; most recently, the 2003 US Burmese Freedom and Democracy Act.

74 In the WTO, no reports have been adopted concerning the application of GATT 1994 art. XXI. For an analysis of disputes under the GATT 1947, see A. Ligustro, *Le controversie tra Stati del diritto del commercio internazionale: dal GATT all'OMC*, Padua, CEDAM, 1996, at 429 ff; and Hahn, 'Vital Interests and the Law of GATT: An Analysis of the GATT's Security Exception', *Michigan Journal of International Law*, Vol. 12, No. 3, 1991, 558 ff.

75 Picone and Ligustro, *Diritto*, *supra* note 2, at 346 ff; Cleveland, 'Human Rights Sanctions', *supra* note 4, at 183 ff.

emerged in an international organization with a high number of Member States (181) where representatives of all actors involved in labour standards have a voice.[76]

13.5.2 The 'enabling clause' and the general exceptions clause

Other WTO exceptions may be invoked to justify recourse to trade measures against States responsible for the exploitation of child labour. The matter could be relevant also when trade restrictions are imposed to implement an ILO determination, under article 33, against a State not complying with Convention 182, and whose behaviour cannot be traced to any peremptory rule of general international law imposing *erga omnes* obligations.[77]

Firstly, it is worth mentioning the 'enabling clause', forming part of the GATT 1947 *acquis* that applies between WTO members as well. It authorizes WTO members to waive the most-favoured-nation obligation in order to grant 'generalized, non-reciprocal and non-discriminatory preferences' to developing members. The requirement of non-discrimination has been invoked in 2002 by India claiming the unlawfulness of the incentive special regime provided for in the EC GSP, in favour of beneficiary countries making considerable efforts to combat drug production and trafficking and to protect labour rights and the environment. In the request for consultations, the complaint referred to all three special schemes; afterwards, it was restricted to the drug scheme. In its judgment, the Appellate Body found that GSP schemes may differentiate among beneficiary countries without contravening the non-discrimination principle, but only if 'the tariff preferences are addressed to a particular development, financial or trade need and are available to all beneficiaries that share that need'.[78]

---

76 See Maupain, 'Is the ILO Effective?', *supra* note 19, at 118 ff.

77 In this case, an interference would exist between the WTO regime and the ILO regime, as the WTO prohibition to introduce restrictions on trade flows would be set against a mere entitlement, which does not correspond to a legal obligation, to adopt trade measures to implement the ILO recommendation (see Picone and Ligustro, *Diritto*, *supra* note 2, at 638 ff). To ascertain the legal meaning of such interference, both the WTO and the ILO agreements give no guidance, nor would the application of general international law on successive treaties, as codified in the 1969 Vienna Convention on the Law of Treaties, be appropriate. In fact, art. 30 of the Vienna Convention provides for the application of the *lex posterior* principle. Paragraph 3, concerning successive treaties concluded by the same States, would not come into play, as WTO and ILO memberships do not fully overlap. In this case, paragraph 4 could be applied, and at first sight it could be argued that the trade liberalization obligations under the WTO agreement and its annexes would prevail over the ILO norms in the relations between States that are both members of the WTO and the ILO. However, it is hard to define a clear temporal relationship between the two legal systems, as they both evolve continuously in their membership and scope of application (see Pauwelyn, 'The Role', *supra* note 71, at 545 ff).

78 WTO doc. WT/DS246/AB/R European Communities – Conditions for the Granting of Tariff Preferences to Developing Countries, 7 April 2004, § 165. See L. Bartels, 'The WTO Enabling Clause and Positive Conditionality in the European Community's GSP Program', *Journal of International Economic Law*, Vol. 6, No. 2, 2003, 507 ff; A. Ligustro, 'L'Organizzazione mondiale del commercio condanna lo Schema di preferenze generalizzate

Article XX on 'general exceptions' is a basic provision for our purposes. It confers upon WTO members a certain measure of discretion to adopt import and/or export restrictions for the pursuit of non-trade policy objectives. In fact, it is admitted that States may sacrifice trade liberalization to protect social values. In order to avoid that those same values are invoked with protectionist intents, some requirements have to be met.

First of all, the measure has to come under the purview of one of the national policy objectives included in article XX. In addition, the requirement imposed by the chapeau has to be satisfied; that is, the application of measure must not constitute 'a means of arbitrary or unjustifiable discrimination between countries where the same conditions prevail, or a disguised restriction on international trade'.

Before outlining some criteria for the interpretation of article XX, a preliminary issue to be ascertained is whether it may be invoked for the protection of established policy objectives outside the boundaries of the State imposing restrictions. The issue was first examined in two GATT 1947 disputes concerning article XX(g) on the conservation of exhaustible natural resources. In the first case, a GATT panel excluded any extra-territorial effect to measures authorized under article XX; otherwise, it was held, each contracting party might unilaterally determine the national policies from which their trading partners could not deviate without jeopardizing their rights under the GATT (*US-Tuna I*).[79] A successive unadopted panel report showed a change of mind, as it noted that the language of article XX(g) did not specify whether the resources to be conserved had to be located inside or outside the defendant party (*US-Tuna II*).[80] The issue has been definitely settled in one of the main WTO disputes (*US-Shrimp*), where the Appellate Body held that it is sufficient for a restrictive measure to be legitimate if it pursues one of the policy objectives included in article XX, and that it is not necessary to assume that requiring from exporting countries compliance with, or adoption of, certain policies prescribed by the importing country renders a measure *a priori* incapable of justification.[81]

On the basis of the evaluation of both panels, but mainly the Appellate Body, in a number of complaints, some criteria may be drawn to ascertain whether the general exceptions provision may be appropriate to justify import bans against States responsible for the exploitation of child labour.[82] The practice shows a certain

---

della Comunità europea per il carattere discriminatorio del "regime droga"', *Diritto pubblico e comparato europeo*, 2005, 432 ff.

79   United States – Restrictions on the Imports of Tuna, DS21/R, 3 September 1991. The report was not adopted by the GATT Contracting Parties.

80   United States – Restrictions on Imports of Tuna, DS29/R, 16 June 1994.

81   United States – Import Prohibition of Certain Shrimp and Shrimp Products, WT/DS58/AB/R, 15 June 2001 § 121. Moreover, the prison labour exception under sub-paragraph (e) shows that extraterritorial effects are not alien to art. XX (see Lenzerini, 'International Trade', *supra* note 70, at 301 ff. See also the comment by Diller and Levy, 'Child Labor', *supra* note 54, at 683 ff).

82   On the interpretative criteria applicable in the assessment of the conformity with art. XX of both unilateral trade measures and conflicting obligations imposed by non-WTO treaties, see Picone and Ligustro, *Diritto*, *supra* note 2, at 645 ff. The authors exclude an exclusive role of customary international rules on treaty interpretation, as codified in articles

deference to non-WTO agreements, whose provisions are used to interpret article XX.

Among the policies that may legitimately allow the adoption of trade restrictions, article XX includes the protection of public morals (sub-paragraph a) and human health (sub-paragraph b).[83] Concerning the latter, it is beyond any doubt that the worst forms of child labour jeopardize the physical and mental health of children.

The general and vague public moral exception, in contrast, cannot be easily interpreted. Yet recent practice may give us some guidance. Its meaning was elucidated for the first time in a dispute concerning the parallel provision of the WTO General Agreement on Trade in Services (*US-Gambling*). The panel considered public moral a concept variable over time and space, and depending upon a range of factors, including prevailing social, cultural, ethical and religious values. It has interpreted the concept to denote 'standards of right and wrong conduct maintained by or on behalf of a community or nation',[84] allowing each State a margin of appreciation to freely determine if a certain concern comes under the purport of the public moral concept. However, it cannot be excluded that the 'prevailing values' may attain to a common interest of States as well[85] (as the protection of children from the worst forms of economic exploitation),[86] also in the light of existing non-WTO international agreements on the issue.

This last consideration is supported by the findings of the Appellate Body in *US-Shrimp*. It maintained that nothing prevents an interpretation of article XX 'in the light of contemporary concerns of the community of nations'.[87] In that specific

---

31–33 of the 1969 Vienna Convention. In their opinion, a proper interpretation of art. XX requires considering both the interpretative criteria illustrated by the Appellate Body in the *US-Shrimp* case, and some general interpretative principles (as necessity, proportionality, and evolutionary interpretation) whose effects have to be determined case by case. In this regard, see Francioni, *Environment, supra* note 7, at 22 ff.

83 See Diller and Levy, 'Child Labor', *supra* note 54, at 681 ff.

84 United States – Measures Affecting the Cross-Border Supply of Gambling and Betting Services, WT/DS285/R, 10 December 2004, §§ 6.461 and 6.465.

85 C.T. Feddersen, 'Focusing on Substantive Law in International Economic Relations: The Public Morals of GATT's Article (a) and "Conventional" Rules of Interpretation', *Minnesota Journal of Global Trade*, Vol. 7, No. 1, 1998, 75 ff (stating that 'an interpretation … must be found which can be consistently shared among all GATT members', at 77). See also B.J. Stevenson, 'Pursuing an End to Foreign Child Labor through U.S. Trade Law: WTO Challenges and Doctrinal Solution', *UCLA Journal of International Law and Foreign Affairs*, Vol. 7, No. 1, 2002, 129 ff, at 159 ff; P. Mavroidis, *The General Agreement on Tariffs and Trade. A Commentary*, Oxford, Oxford University Press, 2005, at 208 ff; and A. Blackett, 'Whither Social Clause? Human Rights, Trade Theory and Treaty Interpretation', *Columbia Human Rights Law Review*, Vol. 31, No. 1, 1999, 1 ff, at 76 ff.

86 S. Charnovitz, 'The Moral Exception in Trade Policy', *Virginia Journal of International Law*, Vol. 38, No. 4, 1998, 689 ff, at 740 ff; and F. Francioni, 'Environment, Human Rights and the Limits of Free Trade', in Francioni (ed.), *Environment, supra* note 7, 1 ff, at 18 ff. See also R. Howse, 'The World Trade Organization and the Protection of Workers' Rights', *Journal of Small & Emerging Business Law*, Vol. 3, 1999, 131 ff.

87 *US-Shrimp, supra* note 81, § 129. For the application of an evolutionary interpretation of the concept of public morals incorporated in art. XX(a) see Trebilcock and Howse, 'Trade

circumstance the challenged measure was claimed by the responding State to pursue environmental protection, thus referring to article XX(g). The issue was whether this sub-paragraph applies only to the preservation of non-living natural resources or to living natural resources as well. The case was settled on the basis of an interpretative approach founded on article 31 of the 1969 Vienna Convention, which establishes that a treaty has to be interpreted in good faith in accordance with the ordinary meaning to be given to its terms in their context and in the light of its object and purposes. To settle the dispute, the Appellate Body has given particular importance to the preamble of the WTO agreement, which mentions the aim of sustainable development, stating that 'the generic term "natural resources" in Article XX(g) is not "static" in its content or reference but is rather "by definition, evolutionary"'.[88] In ascertaining its relevance in the case at hand and in finding that article XX(g) also applies to living resources, the Appellate Body has drawn considerable attention to some universal treaties.[89]

In practice, non-WTO agreements could come into play also from the perspective of the necessary requirement that must be met in order to lawfully introduce a trade ban in the context of sub-paragraphs (a) or (b). In the case concerning imports of beef in South Korea (*Korea-Beef*) the Appellate Body, on the basis of its previous jurisprudence, stated that 'whether a measure is necessary should be determined through a process of weighing and balancing a series of factors', and that this process is 'comprehended to the determination of whether a WTO-consistent alternative measure which the Member concerned could "reasonably be expected to employ" is available, or whether a less WTO-inconsistent measure is "reasonably available"'.[90] The meaning of this statement was clarified in the *US-Gambling* case. Here the Appellate Body held that the process begins with an assessment of the 'relative importance' of the interests or values furthered by the challenged measure; then other factors have to be considered, the contribution of the measure to the realization of its aims, its restrictive trade impact. As a final step, a comparison between the measure and possible alternatives should be undertaken

> the *results of the comparison should be considered in the light of the importance of the interests at stake* ... it is on the basis of this 'weighing and balancing' and comparison of measures, *taking into account the interests and values at stake*, that a panel determines whether a measure is 'necessary' or, alternatively, whether another, WTO-consistent measure is 'reasonably available'.[91]

In the *Korea-Beef* dispute the Appellate Body has maintained that 'the more vital or important the common interests or values pursued, the easier it would be to accept

---

Policy', *supra* note 5, at 289.

88 *US-Shrimp*, *supra* note 81, § 130.

89 See the remarks made by Cleveland, 'Human Rights Sanctions', *supra* note 4, at 161 ff.

90 Korea – Measures Affecting Imports of Fresh, Chilled and Frozen Beef, WT/DS/169/AB/R, 11 December 2000, respectively §§ 164 and 166.

91 United States – Measures Affecting the Cross-Border Supply of Gambling and Betting Services, WT/DS285/AB/R, 7 April 2005, §§ 306 and 307.

as "necessary" measures designed to achieve those ends'.[92] The existence of a non-WTO agreement, especially of an universal open treaty concluded under the aegis of a competent intergovernmental universal organization and ratified by a considerable number of States, as ILO Convention 182, is clear evidence that a common interest of States exists within the international community and it could be used to affirm the necessity of trade restrictions.

In ascertaining compliance with the necessity requirement, the dispute settlement organs have also considered that trade restrictions could have been avoided if parties had been able to reach an agreement over the disputed matter. From this perspective, in *US-Gambling*, the panel found that the US restriction could not be considered 'necessary', since no negotiations had taken place with the complaining party before its implementation, notwithstanding numerous requests by Antigua.[93] According to Antigua, negotiations and conclusion of an understanding constituted a reasonable alternative. The Appellate Body reversed the panel finding, unequivocally excluding that consultations are an appropriate alternative measure: they are 'by definition a process, the results of which are uncertain and therefore not capable of comparison with the measure at issue'.[94]

Once a finding of conformity with a particular policy objective has been reached, adjudicating bodies have to ascertain whether the measure under consideration is consistent with the article XX chapeau. This does not relate to the challenged measure itself, but to the manner in which it is applied, and it makes clear that in article XX a balance is struck between 'the right of a Member to invoke an exception ... and the duty of that same Member to respect the treaty rights of the other Members'.[95]

In particular, the measure must not be applied in a manner that would constitute 'a means of arbitrary or unjustifiable discrimination between countries where the same conditions prevail, or a disguised restriction on international trade'. The two effects (arbitrary or unjustifiable discrimination and disguised restriction on trade) have been interpreted as related concepts imparting meaning to one another.[96] Nevertheless it is worth recalling the interpretation of the term 'disguised' in the *EC-Asbestos* case, where the panel has opined that 'a restriction which formally meets the requirements of Article XX(b) will constitute an abuse if such compliance is in fact only a disguise to conceal the pursuit of trade-restrictive objectives'.[97] For some of the measures we have examined above it would be difficult to affirm in absolute terms that they do not constitute a 'disguised' restriction, as the protectionist intent in favour of national producers was invoked in the debates preceding their adoption and has been evidenced by national courts.[98]

---

92 *Korea-Beef*, *supra* note 90, § 162.

93 *US-Gambling*, *supra* note 84.

94 *US-Gambling*, *supra* note 93, § 317.

95 *US-Shrimp*, *supra* note 81, respectively §§ 156 and 151.

96 US-Gasoline, *supra* note 3, at 21 ff.

97 EC – Measures Affecting Asbestos and Asbestos-Containing Products, WT/DS135/R, 18 September 2000, § 8.236.

98 In particular we refer to section 307 of the US Trade Act of 1930, as interpreted by the Court of International Trade in 1985 (see *supra* note 56).

In any case, it would be even more difficult to sustain that those same measures do not amount to an arbitrary or unjustifiable discrimination. The *US-Shrimp* case is enlightening in this aspect. The dispute had arisen between the US and a group of developing countries, and the Appellate Body explicitly recognized that the conditions prevailing in the latter had to be taken into account before introducing a restriction on imports. On the assumption that the censured discriminatory effect could occur not only between exporting countries, but also between the exporting member and the importing member concerned,[99] it held that discrimination exists when the application of the restrictive measure and the procedure that has led to its adoption do not allow for any inquiry into the appropriateness of the regulatory programme behind the restriction on imports for the conditions prevailing in the exporting countries:

> It is not acceptable, in international trade relations, for one WTO Member to use an economic embargo to require other Members to adopt essentially the same comprehensive regulatory program, to achieve a certain policy goal, as that in force within that Member's territory, without taking into consideration different conditions which may occur in the territories of those other Members.[100]

A further consideration has led the Appellate Body to censure the US in the *Shrimp* case.[101] Namely, it was the circumstance that, before adopting and implementing the trade restrictions, the US had not started consultations with all interested exporting countries in order to reach an agreement that could serve the policy objective of environmental protection. Indeed, agreements had been concluded only with some interested States, and the US had not shown any serious intent to do so also with other exporters. This circumstance was considered to amount to an unjustifiable discrimination.

The statement introduces some ambiguity into the interpretation of the chapeau, since it is not clear if, to satisfy the non-discrimination requirement, it is sufficient to request consultations, or whether it is necessary that they be concluded, even without a positive outcome. In the compliance review complaint over the *US-Shrimp* case, the Appellate Body, upholding the panel findings, has given some useful indications in order to ascertain the lawfulness of States' behaviour, grounding its finding on the principle of good faith binding upon all States. In particular, it has been interpreted to mean that comparable efforts of negotiations should be made with all interested parties, and not just with some of them, and that comparable resources should be devoted to securing an international agreement.[102] However, it has also been pointed out that the conclusion of an international agreement is not

---

99　*US-Gasoline*, *supra* note 3, 21 ff.

100　*US-Shrimp*, *supra* note 81, §§ 164 and 165.

101　*Ibid.*, §§ 166 ff.

102　United States – Import Prohibition of Certain Shrimp and Shrimp Products, WT/DS58/AB/RW, 22 October 2001, § 122. It should also be considered that, if trade-related child labour matters are involved, the principle of good faith would impose to run consultations within the appropriate framework, the ILO, and to apply trade restrictions only as a remedy of last resort.

always possible notwithstanding all efforts, and that 'requiring that a multilateral agreement be concluded ... would mean that any country party to the negotiations ... whether a WTO Member or not, would have, in effect, a veto' over whether the responding party could fulfil its article XX chapeau obligations.[103]

13.5.3 Measures adopted consistently with FTAs

Bilateral and regional trade agreements concluded by the US and the EC fall under the purview of a WTO coordination clause. Indeed, GATT 1994 article XXIV allows WTO members to depart from the most-favoured-nation obligation to institute custom unions or free trade areas, where participating States exchange market access conditions more favourable than those undertaken in the WTO, such as exemptions on duties and the elimination of other restrictive regulations. The provision is based on the assumption that a higher degree of trade liberalization among some WTO members may generate a global increase in trade flows, if some substantive requirements are met. Obviously, they concern trade matters, in particular the extent to which trade flows are really liberalized inside the custom union or the free trade area (internal requirement), and the effect of the agreement on trade relations with non-participating countries (external requirement).[104] The aim is to hamper the creation of trade areas that could jeopardize the liberalization process pursued within the WTO.

Agreed on in 1947, the clause has survived the passage to the WTO. At present, it no longer seems appropriate to rule the trade integration phenomena, since in many cases the current practice goes well beyond the traditional custom unions or free trade areas.[105] However, it is obvious that the labour chapters incorporated in the US FTAs, or the essential element and non-execution clauses of the EC trade agreements, are not subject to the control of the WTO organs competent to examine the compatibility of the agreements with article XXIV, unless it is held that they jeopardize the trade liberalization process between contracting parties. In this regard, there is still uncertainty over the proper interpretation of article XXIV's internal requirement, as the debate is focused on the alternative between a quantitative and a qualitative threshold; that is, whether it would be more appropriate to fix a percentage of trade flows which should be liberalized or rather to consider article XXIV complied with if the abolition of duties and other trade regulations concerns most productive sectors. Whatever interpretation is preferred, the right to suspend the application of the trade rules of the FTA in case of labour rights violations is nothing but an exception to the liberalization regime whose application in specific

---

103 Ibid., § 123.

104 Art. XXIV lays down the obligation to eliminate 'with respect to substantially all the trade' duties and other restrictive regulations of commerce between the participating States (§ 8.a), and prescribes that the duties and other regulations of commerce imposed on products of non-participating parties after the conclusion of the agreement shall not be on the whole higher or more restrictive than 'the general incidence of the duties and regulations of commerce' previously applied (§ 5).

105 See Picone and Ligustro, *Diritto, supra* note 2, at 499 ff (in particular 526 ff).

circumstances cannot invalidate the overall compatibility of the agreement with article XXIV. Nothing in article XXIV seems to prevent members from agreeing to have recourse in their mutual relations to trade measures aiming to promote non-trade interests of common concern. Moreover, article XXIV itself states that the compatibility with the internal requirement would not be affected if the FTA allows parties to avail themselves of trade restrictions aiming to give effect to some GATT provisions, among which is article XX.

In any case, as already shown, most FTAs provide for specific dispute settlement procedures where claims alleging failure to implement labour provisions and unlawful application of trade-related countermeasures can be brought. WTO dispute settlement organs would not have any competence to examine either matter, since they concern the implementation of non-WTO rules.[106] Indeed, according to article 1 and article 3(2) of the DSU, the WTO dispute settlement procedure is limited to those complaints concerning the application and interpretation of WTO agreements and serves to preserve the rights and obligations of members. Furthermore, it is excluded that rulings and recommendations adopted in the framework of that procedure could add or diminish rights and obligations provided for in WTO agreements.

13.5.3.1 The opening of the WTO to the settlement of disputes arisen under non-WTO agreements The FTA concluded in 2004 between the US, five Central American countries and the Dominican Republic partially departs from the described practice. It includes a provision according to which, in case they agree that a matter arising under the labour chapter '*would be more appropriately addressed* through another agreement', the interested contracting parties shall refer it for appropriate action in accordance with that agreement (article 16.6 § 9). Also the dispute settlement chapter incorporates a forum shopping clause of general application (as in all other US FTAs), but it refers to cases *arising* under both the FTA and the WTO. The different meaning of the two provisions seems to imply that the decision to refer the matter to the WTO under the labour chapter could be based not only on substantive considerations (the WTO rules provide for a preferred discipline on the matter) but also, or exclusively, on procedural considerations (the WTO procedure is better suited to secure compliance).

The clause has a particular significance, since at the time of negotiations the agreement was strongly opposed in the US, exactly because of low workers' rights standards and ineffective enforcement procedures in the counterparts. It has been interpreted as opening the possibility that the WTO be called to settle a dispute in labour matters.[107]

At first sight, this would mean that through a successive agreement, the jurisdiction of the WTO dispute settlement organs is extended to include claims concerning non-WTO rules, as it is sufficient that a common understanding exist between the parties

---

106 *Ibid.* at 659. As the Appellate Body declared, 'We see no basis in the DSU for panels and the Appellate Body to adjudicate non-WTO disputes': Mexico – Tax Measures on Soft Drinks and Other Beverages, WT/DS308/AB/R, 6 March 2006, § 56.

107 R. Grynberg and V. Qalo, 'Labour Standards in US and EU Preferential Trading Agreements', *Journal of World Trade*, Vol. 40, No. 4, 2006, 619 ff, at 640.

concerned that the matter would be more appropriately addressed in that framework. Derogation from DSU article 1 and article 3(2) would thus occur. However, a proper evaluation of the issue has to take also into account the reasons for referring the matter to the WTO.

In case substantive considerations prevail, it is clear that the complaint could not concern violations of the obligation to strive to ensure that internationally recognized labour rights are recognized by national legislations, as it does not come under the scope of WTO agreements. On the contrary, it could concern the restrictive trade effects of the improper enforcement of national labour laws under the procedure for so-called 'non-violation complaints'.[108] Indeed, under GATT 1994 article XXIII § 1.b, WTO members may resort to the dispute settlement procedure also in cases where benefits accruing under the WTO agreements are being nullified or impaired, or the attainment of any one of their objectives is being impeded, as the result of the application by another contracting party of *any measure* not in conflict with the WTO obligations. However, the clause has never been applied and is considered by many to have fallen into disuse. Nevertheless, it is worth noting that, contrary to violation complaints, the withdrawal of the measure could not be ordered by the dispute settlement organs and no trade countermeasures might be authorized.

Hypothetically, WTO substantive provisions could come into play also to challenge trade restrictions adopted against the State violating the enforcement obligation. In this regard, it is interesting to note that the trade chapter of the FTA, besides prescribing the elimination of custom duties, incorporates the GATT national treatment clause, as well as the prohibition of import and export quotas. The implementation of restrictions obviously constitutes a violation of article XI, and may imply non-conformity with GATT article I to the extent that the most favoured nation treatment is suspended. The possibility to resort to WTO dispute settlement procedures could be of the utmost importance since, as we have seen, the labour chapter does not provide for the possibility for the defendant party to object to the countermeasures before their implementation.[109] However, we can exclude that the US has agreed on a similar limitation of the large measure of discretion it enjoys; in any case, it could claim the legitimacy of its action on the basis of GATT 1994 article XX.a or XX.b.[110]

---

108 See Pauwelyn, 'The Role', *supra* note 71, at 559.

109 *Supra* note 42.

110 In a recent dispute, both the panel and the Appellate Body (*supra* note 106) rejected the arguments of the defendant party (Mexico) that justified the challenged taxes on beverages under art. XX.d (allowing WTO members to adopt measures 'necessary to secure compliance with laws or regulations which are not inconsistent with the provisions' of GATT), arguing that they were countermeasures designed to induce the US to comply with its NAFTA obligations regarding market access. The findings have been interpreted to mean that 'WTO panels lack a mandate to adjudicate defences to WTO obligations based on other international law', in particular on human rights international law (J.P. Trachtman, 'The Constitutions of the WTO', *European Journal of International Law*, Vol. 17, No. 3, 2006, 623 ff, note 43). But appropriate consideration should be given to the fact that the case exclusively concerned trade matters, and the exception invoked, as pointed out by the adjudicating bodies, refers only to internal or domestic laws, and not to compliance with international agreements.

Procedural considerations may lead States to defer the matter to the WTO organs as well, particularly in view of the right to adopt countermeasures provided for in the DSU. But it is necessary to understand the outcome of a hypothetic application before the WTO over compliance exclusively with the FTA rules. Indeed, on the basis of the previous consideration, it is clear that, if the complaint may be referred to GATT norms as well, WTO panels and the Appellate Body would act within their competence. This, however, would not hold true if the FTA provisions under scrutiny do not refer to them, such as when claims challenge compliance with provisions of national labour laws or concern the effect on trade flows of an improper enforcement of the latter. As to the former obligation, resort to the DSU for labour matters would be contrary to the principle of good faith that would instead impose recourse to the ILO, insofar as the claim questions the implementation of 'internationally recognized labour rights' covered by an ILO convention. In any case, the programmatic character of the obligation could not be denied by the dispute settlement organs that would have to enforce a mere duty 'to strive to ensure'.

As to a dispute concerning the trade effects of the enforcement of national labour laws, WTO jurisdiction ought to be excluded on the ground of DSU articles 1 and 3(2). Yet, it remains to be seen if they can be waived by the conclusion of an *inter se* agreement. Even though the DSU acknowledges a specific role of conventional instruments in the settlement of disputes among WTO members,[111] it has to be ascertained to what extent they may be resorted to in order to agree on a derogation from articles 1 and 3(2).

Indeed, according to article 30(4) of the Vienna Convention on the Law of Treaties, the *lex posterior* principle would apply and efficacy ought to be recognized only to those WTO provisions that are compatible with the FTA. Nevertheless, appropriate consideration has to be given to two other provisions of the Vienna Convention. Firstly, article 41, establishing that a modification to a multilateral treaty may be agreed on by some of its contracting parties to the extent that (a) it is not prohibited, (b) the enjoyment by the other parties of their rights or the performance of their obligations are not affected, and (c) the modification does not relate to a provision, derogation from which is incompatible with the effective execution of the object and purpose of the treaty as a whole. Secondly, according to article 5, the *lex posterior* principle may be applied to the constituent instrument of an international organization without prejudice to any relevant rule of the organization. If a special discipline is applicable, it prevails over the general regulation of the Vienna Convention.

These elements call into play some relevant features of the WTO regime. Formally, it is worth noting that the DSU does not contain any provision opening the enforcement procedure to the settlement of disputes dealing with non-WTO rules, as for example, art. 239 of the EC Treaty of Rome.

Substantially, the WTO regime does not prohibit modifications to its texts, but in this regards it includes some provisions. First of all, article X of the WTO Agreement on amendments, stipulates that modifications to the DSU may be adopted by a

---

111 For an examination of the EC practice, see A. Tancredi, 'EC Practice in the WTO: How Wide is the "Scope for Manoeuvre"?', *European Journal of International Law*, Vol. 15, No. 5, 2004, 933 ff.

consensus decision of the Ministerial Conference, hence without the opposition of any WTO member. Similarly, the members that are contracting parties to a non-WTO trade treaty may propose to the Ministerial Conference its addition to the WTO Annexes, so that even if binding only upon members wishing to accept it, it would come under the scope of the WTO enforcement procedures. Also in this case, the Ministerial Conference is to decide by *consensus*. Finally, the outcome of multilateral negotiations held under the aegis of the WTO (hence those concerning the DSU as well), favouring progress in the trade liberalization process, enters into force only if accepted by all members. Even if these rules do not directly concern *inter se* modifications of the WTO discipline by the conclusion of successive treaties under the meaning of article 41 of the Vienna Convention, they demonstrate nevertheless that the multilateral trading system has been conceived as a regime whose modifications are effective only in the case all members agree.

Furthermore, it has to be considered that the WTO dispute settlement procedure is one of the main achievements of the Uruguay Round and may well be regarded as the core of the Organization. In this framework, DSU article 1 and article 3(2) are two of the main provisions, since they exclude that the WTO may exercise a normative activity through the enforcement procedure. This is consistent with one peculiarity of the WTO regime: no rule-making activity has been conferred upon any WTO organ, and rules in force between members are agreed on by the States themselves in the context of multilateral negotiations.

If trade rules are defined by the States, their enforcement procedure is designed to punish non-compliance with WTO discipline as it implies an alteration of the balance between the trade benefits States have mutually extended to each other. The final outcome of the procedure can only be the withdrawal of the wrongful measure, and even if compensatory measures and countermeasures are considered, they are only meant as provisional actions allowing a temporary re-establishment of the balance.

In case of a claim before the WTO over compliance with the enforcement obligation of the FTA under consideration, the WTO assessment would exclusively concern the observance of obligations included in the bilateral agreement and the effects over the trade flows determined by the discipline there provided for. This would not affect the enjoyment of rights or the performance of obligations of other WTO members. However, it would be contrary to the *ratio* that has led to the conclusion of the DSU, considered part of the balance of benefits WTO members have agreed to exchange with each other, and to the closed character of the WTO regime mentioned above. Furthermore, particular significance should be given to the fact that an explicit outcome of the Uruguay Round is that the multilateral regime, is not open to deal with the trade and labour issue. This position is strenuously adhered to by many WTO members and has received a formal recognition in 1996, when the Ministerial Conference acknowledged the ILO as the competent body for dealing with internationally recognized core labour standards.

Chapter 14

The Implementation of ILO Child Labour Standards in Domestic Legal Systems: The Role of Criminal Law

Emanuela Fronza and Kolis Summerer[1]

14.1 Introduction: the role of criminal law

The evolution of regulations in the area of child labour and exploitation features both a high level of internationalization and complex interaction of very different sources.

The criminal law scholar recognizes immediately that – as is the case for other areas regarding transnational crime – the almost always decisive role of criminal law on this matter is determined mainly by non-State, international and EU actors through binding and non-binding instruments of harmonization which force States to undertake adequate measures of protection, including penal action.[2] Though the UN and the EU are not directly responsible for matters of criminal law, they certainly have a profound influence on national laws.

Harmonization is subject to the margin of autonomy given to States in choosing how to comply with supranational guidelines. Domestic legislation need only be *compatible* with them and not necessarily *coincide*. In this particular area, individual Member States have not impeded the implementation process since child labour and exploitation are part of the so-called natural crimes, whose criminalization is widely approved of. The necessity of legal protection, or in some cases of punishing, concerns highly damaging conduct that are strongly disapproved of on a collective

---

1 Sections 14.2, 14.3 and 14.8 have been written by Emanuela Fronza. Kolis Summer is the author of sections 14.4, 14.5, 14.6 and 14.7. Sections 14.1 and 14.9 have been written jointly.

2 On the necessity of the harmonization of transnational crime and on criminal law as a driving force of the process of criminal harmonization, see M. Delmas-Marty, M. Pieth, U. Sieber (eds), *Les chemins de l'harmonisation pénale, Société de législation comparée, Collection: Unité mixte de recherche de droit comparé de Paris*, vol. 15, 2008. As stressed by Mireille Delmas Marty in the Introduction of this book, 'le droit penal se trouve paradoxalement en première ligne de l'harmonisation du droit'. On this subject see also G. Grasso, Comunità europee e diritto penale: i rapporti tra l'ordinamento *comunitario e i sistemi penali degli stati membri*, Milan, Giuffrè, 1989. See also S. Canestrari and L. Foffani (eds), *Il diritto penale nella prospettiva europea. Quali politiche criminali per quale Europa?, Atti del Convegno di Bologna (2002)*, Milan, Giuffrè, 2005.

level. This type of conduct is often punished independently by domestic legal systems.

Moreover, it clearly appears from examining supranational sources that criminal law plays a decisive role – rendered explicit in many EU legislative measures – and it is often identified as the primary instrument for challenging criminal phenomena connected to the economic and sexual exploitation of minors. We can also discern contemporary criminal law tendencies in this area: expansion, hypertrophy and, as we shall see, the symbolic use of criminal legislation.[3] We shall return to these issues after examining supranational and domestic regulations in order to demonstrate the importance of punishment as a tool in a larger campaign to challenge transnational crimes.

14.2 Child labour and child exploitation as modern forms of slavery

The issue of child exploitation and labour as new forms of slavery currently raises new and pressing requirements with regard to protection from crimes against the person. It also draws attention to the problem of the effectiveness and adequacy of the political choices in addressing phenomena perceived by the community as important and alarming.

The criminal phenomena related to child exploitation, slavery and the trafficking of children have increased remarkably over the last few decades, becoming increasingly larger and better organized, and revealing a marked transnational character. Forced labour, forced mendicancy, debt bondage, child exploitation, child prostitution, child pornography and sexual tourism are true forms of neo-slavery, characterized as such by the fact that human beings find themselves in the condition of slaves subjected to the power of a master. The traditional forms of slavery were founded primarily on the economic exploitation of the person, constituting thus a customary element of the social structure, even an integrated part of the productive and economic system. In the current context, however, it assumes various forms, sometimes regardless of the complete depersonalization of the person and implying the exploitation of his/her specific performances (not only as labour, but also sexual and other kinds).

The new forms of slavery include a variety of conducts that are often the result of a relationship of total domination over the victim and imply violating of various rights of the human person. Examples include currently widespread phenomena such as buying and selling minors for child pornography, prostitution and domestic labour; the sale of organs; the exploitation of child labour and mendicancy; the involvement of children in armed conflicts; forced labour and debt bondage. These are all illegal and clandestine practices that primarily affect poor and vulnerable social groups, and in particular children.

Moreover, neo-slavery is no longer a geographically confined criminal phenomenon. Rather, it generally is connected with the modern phenomenon of

---

3 J.M. Silva Sanchez, *L'expansión del derecho penal. Apectos de la política criminal en las sociedades postindustriales*, Madrid, Civitas Ediciones, 1999; M. Donini, 'Sussidiarietà penale e sussidiarietà comunitaria', *Rivista italiana di diritto e procedura penale*, Vol. 1–2, 2003, 141–83.

trafficking of persons and migrants. The involvement of many States make these criminal problems both dynamic and transnational. The international trafficking in persons for the purposes of sexual or economic exploitation implies the presence of a variety of criminal actors, associated with the various stages of moving persons from one State to another. The transnational nature of such activities implies the involvement of a number of different criminal organizations of various ethnic backgrounds operating in various States in order to plan and manage the complex network of contacts and the impressive flow of persons.

Children account for a large part of the victims of trafficking, destined to feed the market of sexual exploitation. In particular, children are highly prone to being enslaved or becoming the victims of trafficking. Among the various triggering factors are increasing poverty, sexual discrimination and the lack of job opportunities in the countries of origin.

Within the larger scheme of the new forms of slavery, child labour, as a particular way of exploiting minors, is a central and highly profitable sector of the criminal market. Nevertheless, it would be mistaken to associate every form of work performed by minors with the concept of child labour, given that the former does not always mean violation of a minor's dignity. We cannot overlook the fact that a vast grey area exists in which positive and negative factors are at play. In order to avoid the dangers of a blanket criminalization, the principle of *extrema ratio* in criminal matters must be held onto firmly, also the idea that recourse to criminal law should only be a form of support to other more effective and adequate instruments.[4] In light of these considerations, it would be more appropriate to speak of 'various form of child labour' as opposed to simply 'child labour'. The phenomenon varies enormously, thus requiring careful contextualization in order to understand the exact nature of the work performed by children.

As has been consistently argued in this volume, based on similar considerations, a distinction has recently emerged in the international debate between the concepts of 'child labour' and 'child work'. The former indicates exploitative work whereas the latter refers to non-detrimental labour, commonly done by children for their own family and usually not interfering with school attendance. This distinction can be seen also in different national legal systems: child labour is not prohibited across the board, but only the forms considered harmful. This division, however, can lead to oversimplification. When first examined, this differentiation would mirror, on the one hand, detrimental work connected to abuse, exploitation and slavery of children; and, on the other, the 'light' activities that do not necessarily deserve punishment and that are often a means for guaranteeing children better living conditions and a basic education. Therefore, we should identify the phenomenon's pathological aspects and set the limits of a narrower concept of child labour.

In this context, there has been an effort to identify the characteristics that undoubtedly lead to child exploitation (full-time work at an early age, long working hours, physical, psychological or social stress, bad living conditions, inadequate

---

4 Furthermore, we should not forget that this area always involves the danger of prosecuting persons who are not offenders and might become innocent victims of unfair trials.

pay, excessive number of duties, compromising the dignity or self-esteem of the child, impossibility of receiving an adequate education, damage to the physical, psychological and social development of the child). It appears impossible to provide a definition and a homogenous category of child labour, making it more advantageous to work with descriptions differentiated by context (within or outside the family, agricultural or industrial work, etc.).

We are dealing, therefore, with a new criminal law frontier, the result of the intersection of several phenomena and norms, distinct in matter and area of normative intervention: slavery; trafficking; child labour; sexual assault; prostitution; pornography; international cooperation, international crimes and organized crime. In this context, policies centred on only one aspect prove ineffective in practice since they neglect the phenomenon's complexity.

The issues identified will be analysed using a comparative method – vertically (comparing supranational norms with national laws) and horizontally (comparing the different supranational norms with national ones) – with special reference to the case of Italy.

14.3 Supranational law as the core standard of protection at the national level

14.3.1 Preliminary remarks

This section provides a brief summary of the norms contained in international and EU instruments related to the regulation of child labour and to the suppression of the sexual exploitation of children. A review of these norms is useful for examining the role assigned to law and criminal trial within the larger system of challenging criminal phenomena. It is also useful for verifying the influence of these sources on national law and, especially, on the normative options in terms of measures of protection, punishable conducts and punishments. This analysis seeks to identify the margin of autonomy given to national legislatures in determining this sector's criminalization.

By examining supranational regulations, we can see features typical of the sectors where harmonization has reached an advanced stage. First of all, in this particular area, as in all the areas related to protecting fundamental rights and the economy,[5] there are a high number of legislative measures (*hypertrophy*); second, these provisions are highly heterogeneous in terms of nature, content and binding power (*heterogeneity*).

In these documents, different supranational actors that have a harmonizing scope (the UN, ILO, EU, Council of Europe) only indicate minimum standards and the States maintain a margin of autonomy in order to adopt norms that are consistent with their specific national context; compatibility instead of uniformity. The vocabulary of harmonization, as opposed to unification, contains expressions for

---

5 Concerning the protection of fundamental rights see M. Delmas Marty, *Le relatif et l'universel*, Paris, Puf, 2004; concerning the crime of corruption see M. Pieth, 'Harmonising Criminal Law', in M. Delmas-Marty, M. Pieth, U. Sieber (eds), *Les chemins de l'harmonisation pénale*, *supra* note 2.

dealing with the domestic adoption of supranational guidelines, such as 'appropriate measures', 'adequate measures' and 'effective measures'. In some cases, however, the supranational lawmaker goes beyond claiming that protection is required by indicating the instrument to be used, namely criminal law.[6] This setup triggers the dynamics of harmonizing national laws, which see domestic lawmaking bodies either transposing supranational input word for word or nearly so.

The number and variety of sources, the lack of coordination between them and the potential overlap have an effect on how coherently child labour and exploitation are challenged. They also influence the predictability of the rule applicable to a specific case, regardless of whether a State chooses literal or partial implementation.

Within this interaction between supranational and national regulations, the role of criminal law should be subordinate to other means of intervention such as administrative and civil law. Similarly, parameters must be established for assessing whether the national measures adopted are adequate.

This section is divided in two parts. The first part deals with international instruments and the second with EU instruments.

14.3.2 International instruments

It would be impossible to analyse here all the current instruments for addressing the problems of child labour and exploitation. As mentioned above, this chapter focuses on those measures important to an evaluation of (a) to what extent supranational norms require national legislatures to provide protection; (b) when this requirement implicates criminal law protection; and (c) the possible specifications for penal measures, such as the type and scope of the punishment.

Fundamental works in this area include ILO Convention 138 of 1973 regarding the minimum age for admission to employment, the UN Convention on the Rights of the Child of 1989 plus the two optional protocols of 2000, and ILO Convention 182 of 1999 on the Worst Forms of Child Labour.

Conventions 138 and 182 are fundamental conventions. In fact, under the ILO Declaration on Fundamental Principles and Rights at Work, the Member States that have not yet ratified these conventions should nevertheless respect, promote and realize their principles. It should also be pointed out that these international measures do not prohibit child labour across the board but require States to establish a minimum age for employment and to eliminate some of the 'worst forms' of child labour.

The Minimum Age Convention of 1973[7] requires State Parties to guarantee the 'effective' elimination of child labour and to gradually raise the minimum age for entering employment, in order to protect the physical and mental development of young persons. Every State Party must establish a minimum age and no minor under

---

6 For several examples of the influence of European law on national criminal laws see C. Sotis, *Il diritto senza codice, Uno studio sul sistema penale europeo vigente*, Milan, Giuffrè, 2007.

7 The Convention must be read in conjunction with the Recommendation No. 146 of 1973 concerning Minimum Age for Admission to Employment.

that age may be employed (article 2(1)). Several flexibility clauses are provided for thus tempering the scope of the general obligation.[8] Article 9(1) states that for an effective *enforcement* of the convention the States must adopt 'all necessary measures', including 'appropriate penalties'.

The 1999 Worst Forms of Child Labour Convention supplements the preceding Minimum Age Convention. This convention, the ILO protection system, the conventions on forced labour and on the abolition of slavery, and the 1989 Convention on the Right of the Child are fundamental texts for opposing the worst forms of child labour.[9] Convention 182 requires that State Parties adopt '*immediate and effective* measures to secure the prohibition and elimination of the worst forms of child labour' (article 1). The term 'child' in this convention means a person under the age of 18 (article 2). Article 3 lists the *worst forms* of child labour.

Article 7 of the Convention establishes that every member shall adopt measures for the effective implementation and enforcement of these provisions, including *penal sanctions* or, when appropriate, other sanctions. Thus international guidelines in this case go beyond those of Convention 138 because they require the adoption of appropriate measures and explicitly include penal sanctions. Moreover, the Convention calls for a mechanism monitoring implementation (article 5) and action plans for eliminating the worst forms of child labour (article 6).

Similar measures can be found in Recommendation 190. Section 12 defines what types of conduct are to be treated as 'criminal offences' by the Member States[10] and the type of sanction to be applied, making explicit reference to criminal sanctions.[11]

The abolition of slavery and forms similar to slavery had already been the subject of the 1926 United Nations Slavery Convention and the 1956 Supplementary Convention on the Abolition of Slavery, the Slave Trade, and Institutions and Practices Similar to Slavery. These documents required States to adopt legislative measures for abolishing different forms of slavery. The 1956 Supplementary Convention specified practices that are similar to slavery, including:

> (a) Debt bondage, that is to say, the status or condition arising from a pledge by a debtor of his personal services or of those of a person under his control as security for a debt, if the value of those services as reasonably assessed is not applied towards the liquidation of

---

8 See Borzaga (this volume).

9 Also this Convention must be read jointly with Recommendation 190 of 1999.

10 '12. Members should provide that the following worst forms of child labour are criminal offences: (a) all forms of slavery or practices similar to slavery, such as the sale and trafficking of children, debt bondage and serfdom and forced or compulsory labor, including forced or compulsory recruitment of children for use in armed conflict; (b) the use, procuring or offering of a child for prostitution, for the production of pornography or for pornographic performances; and (c) the use, procuring or offering of a child for illicit activities, in particular for the production and trafficking of drugs as defined in the relevant international treaties, or for activities which involve the unlawful carrying or use of firearms or other weapons' (emphasis added).

11 '13. Members should ensure that penalties including, where appropriate, *criminal penalties*, are applied for violations of the national provisions for the prohibition and elimination of any type of work referred to in Article 3(d) of the Convention' (emphasis added).

the debt or the length and nature of those services are not respectively limited and defined; (b) Serfdom, that is to say, the condition or status of a tenant who is by law, custom or agreement bound to live and labour on land belonging to another person and to render some determinate service to such other person, whether for reward or not, and is not free to change his status; (c) Any institution or practice whereby: (i) A woman, without the right to refuse, is promised or given in marriage on payment of a consideration in money or in kind to her parents, guardian, family or any other person or group; or (ii) The husband of a woman, his family, or his clan, has the right to transfer her to another person for value received or otherwise; or (iii) A woman on the death of her husband is liable to be inherited by another person; (d) Any institution or practice whereby a child or young person under the age of 18 years is delivered by either or both of his natural parents or by his guardian to another person, whether for reward or not, with a view to the exploitation of the child or young person or of his labour.

Furthermore, article 6 of the Supplementary Convention adds that:

The act of enslaving another person or of inducing another person to give himself or a person dependent upon him into slavery, or of attempting these acts, or being accessory thereto, or being a Party to a conspiracy to accomplish any such acts, shall be a criminal offence under the laws of the States Parties to this Convention and persons convicted thereof shall be liable to punishment.

In the larger picture of regulations for protecting children's rights we can find similar norms containing specific instructions for the measures to be adopted by States in order to combat child labour and exploitation. Particular reference is made here to the 1989 UN Convention on the Rights of the Child, the Optional Protocols on the involvement of children in armed conflicts and on sale of children, child prostitution and child pornography of 25 May 2000.

The Convention on different occasions calls for the State Parties to adopt 'appropriate measures' (article 34 on sexual exploitation) or 'legislative, administrative or other measures' – including social and educational ones – to protect the rights established by the Convention (see articles 4, 19 and 22). In other cases, it requires the institution, if necessary, of a 'judicial mechanism' (article 19). Article 32(1) recognizes the need to protect children from work that can be harmful, interfere with their education or jeopardize their health or physical and mental development. This same article also requires that States Parties identify a minimum age for admission to employment, appropriate regulation of working hours, and that they provide penalties or other sanctions to ensure the article's effective implementation (article 32(2)). This sub-section therefore expressly contemplates the use of penal sanctions.

Moreover, article 38(2) requires State Parties to take every practical measure possible to ensure that children who have not yet reached the age of 15 do not participate actively in armed conflicts.

Article 3 of the Optional Protocol on the sale of children, child prostitution and pornography demands that States penalize the following conduct, regardless of whether committed on a national or transnational level, by an individual or by an organized operation: the sale of children, offering, delivering or accepting a child, regardless of the means, for sexual exploitation, for selling his organs or for engaging him in forced labour, offering, obtaining, procuring or providing a child for prostitution, producing, distributing, disseminating, importing, exporting, offering, selling or possessing child pornography. Moreover, it calls for penalties for attempting to commit such acts as well as complicity and participation. Each State Party should introduce adequate punishment considering the grave nature of these crimes and establish the liability of legal persons, which may be criminal, civil or administrative.

Both the UN Convention against Transnational Organized Crime (hereafter: Palermo Convention) and the Additional Protocol concerning the trafficking in women and children play a leading role. Both have thoroughly accepted and crystallized definitions long-standing in the international field, representing a clear and important point of reference for future national and international legislative interventions.[12] The Convention's primary goal is to prevent and fight against the international trafficking in persons managed by transnational criminal organizations. To this end, the Convention introduces a common legal framework for the various States and provides strategies of international cooperation with regard to investigation.[13]

Article 3, subparagraph (a) of the Protocol to prevent, suppress and punish trafficking in persons, especially women and children, supplementing the UN Convention against transnational organized crime, defines trafficking as:

> ... the recruitment, transportation, transfer, harbouring or receipt of persons, by means of the threat or use of force or other forms of coercion, of abduction, of fraud, of deception, of the abuse of power or of position of vulnerability or of the giving or receiving of payments or benefits to achieve the consent of a person having control over another person, for the purpose of exploitation. Exploitation shall include, at minimum, the exploitation of prostitution, of others or other form of sexual exploitation, forced labour or services, slavery or practices similar to slavery, servitude or the removal of organs.

With reference to children, the Protocol emphasizes the irrelevance of the possible consent given by the victim (article 3(b)) and the subsistence of the crime of trafficking to the prejudice of minors independently of the use of violent or fraudulent means (article 3(c)).[14]

The Convention endorses the clear differentiation, employed nowadays on an institutional and international level, between the trafficking in human beings and aiding

---

12	On transnational organized crime, see V. Militello, 'Partecipazione all'organizzazione criminale e standards internazionali di incriminazione', *Rivista italiana di diritto e procedura penale*, 2003, 184; and V. Militello, L. Paoli and J. Arnold (eds), *Il crimine organizzato come fenomeno transnazionale. Forme di manifestazione, prevenzione e repressione in Italia, Germania e Spagna*, Milan/Freiburg i.Br., Giuffrè, 2000.

13	More specifically, the goal of the Convention is to prevent and fight smuggling and trafficking, as well as to promote the cooperation between participating States. Moreover, the objective of the Protocol on trafficking is to protect and assist the victims, with the full respect of their human rights, whereas the Protocol on migrants aims primarily to protect the human rights of the migrants.

14	Art. 3(b), establishes that 'the recruitment, transportation, transfer, harbouring or receipt of a child for the purpose of exploitation shall be considered "trafficking in persons" even if this does not involve any of the means set forth'.

illegal immigration, also referred to as 'smuggling of migrants'.[15] These are, in truth, two aspects of the same phenomenon: the international trafficking in persons from one country to another. Trafficking in human beings is distinguished from the mere smuggling of clandestine immigrants in virtue of the type of relationship established between the migrant and the dealer. In this case the migrant is recruited in the country of origin by means of violence, threat or deceit, and becomes enslaved and subject to exploitation once arrived in the country of destination. The transfer from one State to another is generally made for the purpose of exploiting the victim sexually (and/or economically), or of inserting him/her into the criminal circuits active in the various countries and controlled by the affiliated criminal organizations. The transfer itself, however, may be either lawful or unlawful. Smuggling, by contrast, consists of the mere illegal transfer of the migrant to another country, and usually involves the termination of the migrant's relationship with the trip organizer upon entering the destination State or shortly afterwards. However, the line that separates smuggling from trafficking is a very thin one. No guarantee exists, even when the migrant disposes of the financial means to pay the criminal groups managing the transfer, of being shielded from becoming the object of exploitation and/or trafficking.

Article 3 of the Protocol establishes that a child is regarded as a victim of trafficking whenever he or she has been recruited or transported with a view to being exploited, even if there is no use of means such as coercion, fraud, deception or abuse of power. The child's consent is completely irrelevant. This aim would make the distinction between child trafficking and migration for employment of adolescents above the minimum working age extremely clear.

Considering that ILO Convention 182 had already explicitly defined trafficking in children as one of the worst forms of child labour (article 3), a distinction should be made between the two conventions' areas of application when the victim is a child: the Palermo Convention and Protocol tackle trafficking in children from the angle of a transnational crime, while ILO Convention 182 covers cases where trafficking in children occurs within a national boundary and does not involve organized criminal groups.[16]

In particular, article 5 of the Protocol on trafficking requires the criminalization of specific criminal offences:

1. Each State Party shall adopt such legislative and other measures as may be necessary to establish as criminal offences the conduct set forth in article 3 of this protocol, when committed intentionally.
2. Each State Party shall also adopt such legislative and other measures as may be necessary to establish as criminal offences: (a) subject to the basic concepts of its legal

---

15 Art. 3 of the 'Protocol against the smuggling of migrants by land, sea and air, supplementing the UN Convention against transnational organized crime', defines smuggling as 'the procurement, in order to obtain, directly or indirectly, a financial or other material benefit, of the illegal entry of a person into a State Party of which the person is not a national or a permanent resident'. In turn, illegal entry is defined as 'crossing borders without complying with the necessary requirements for legal entry into the receiving State'.

16 See the ILO, *Human Trafficking and Forced Labor Exploitation: Guidance for Legislation and Law Enforcement*, Geneva, ILO, 2005, at 24.

system, attempting to commit an offence established in accordance with paragraph 1 of this article; (b) participating as an accomplice in an offence established in accordance with paragraph 1 of this article; and (c) organizing or directing other persons to commit an offence established in accordance with paragraph 1 of this article.

Other provisions concern specific aspects such as border control, cooperation between customs authorities and exchange of information on the methods, means, documents and identities used by organized criminal groups. Finally, with regard to the protection of the victims, the Protocol calls for the confidentiality of personal data in judicial procedures, the concession of a residence permit in the destination State, and the right of the victim to return to his/her country of origin.

14.3.3 Instruments of the EU

EU instruments for combating child labour and exploitation also prove to be heterogeneous in nature as well as content. Significant first- and third-pillar provisions in force are presented here in chronological order to help identify the standards of protection required of the Member States.

Council Directive 33 of 22 June 1994 on the protection of young people at work, in line with the Community Charter of Fundamental Social Rights of Workers and ILO principles, requires that States adopt measures to prohibit child labour (definitions of 'young person', 'child' and 'adolescent' are found in article 3). According to this directive, children under the age of 15 may not be hired (article 1(1)). Similarly, States are to protect young persons from economic exploitation and from work that could be damaging to their safety, health, education and their physical, psychological, moral and social development (article 1(3)). The article entitled 'Measures', however, is the most relevant part for our purpose. Article 14 in Section IV stipulates that 'Each Member State shall lay down any necessary measures to be applied in the event of failure to comply with the provisions adopted in order to implement this Directive; such measures must be effective and proportionate'. Here, the directive uses a widespread Community formula which does not require States to implement penal measures but only adequate ones.

The significant international contribution of the Palermo Convention was followed by the European Council Framework Decision, approved on 19 July 2002 (2002/629/GAI). This decision lays down the standard parameters for national legislations when developing normative instruments in matters of trafficking.[17] Its preamble reiterates how the work of the EU in this field should complement the important work of the UN (§ 6). Trafficking in humans must be dealt with using a comprehensive approach, which should include the constituent elements of criminal law, such as effective, proportionate and dissuasive sanctions (§ 7). This particular

---

17 The time limit for adapting national legislation was set for 1 August 2004. Following the European Conference on prevention and punishment of trafficking held in Brussels in September 2002, a Declaration was adopted, containing the recommendation to institute a task force on trafficking. With its decision of 25 March 2003, the Commission has instituted the 'Task force on the trafficking of human beings'. It is composed of 20 members nominated by the Commission and has advisory and cooperative tasks.

framework decision seeks to introduce common measures for determining and regulating decisive issues like criminalization, sanctions, aggravating circumstances, competence and extradition. Its other main objective is to harmonize member State laws in order to facilitate judicial and investigative cooperation.

In line with the Additional Protocol to the Palermo Convention, the framework decision calls for penal action to be taken against the following acts when committed for the purposes of exploiting a person's labour or services, prostitution and other forms of sexual exploitation: recruitment, transportation, transfer, harbouring, reception of a person, including exchange or transfer of control over that person, where use is made of coercion, force or threat, including abduction, or use is made of deceit or fraud, or there is an abuse of authority or of a position of the victim's vulnerability, in which the victim has no real and acceptable alternative but to submit to the abuse involved, or payments or benefits are given or received to achieve the consent of a person having control over another person. The decision also reconfirms that any victim's consent is irrelevant and that such behaviour constitutes a criminal offence damaging children regardless of the use of violence, threats, fraud or abuse of authority.

In terms of the impact of EU measures on the Member States sovereignty in the area of criminal law, this framework decision, as opposed to previous instruments, explicitly asks for the adoption of penal sanctions that must be effective, proportionate and dissuasive. The obligation of 'adequate protection' is not opposed to the obligation to introduce 'criminal protection'. They may overlap.[18]

Article 2 directs States to make punishable the instigating of, aiding, abetting or attempting to commit the offences mentioned therein. Article 3 designates the penalties and even specifies that their maximum should not be less than eight years of imprisonment when the offence has been committed against a particularly vulnerable victim; for example, when the victim has not yet reached the age of consent, or if the offence has been committed for exploiting the prostitution of others or other forms of sexual exploitation, including pornography (sub-paragraph b).

Furthermore article 4 requires States to guarantee that also legal persons are held liable, sanctions for which are provided by article 5.

The Framework Decision of 22 December 2003 on combating the sexual exploitation of children and child pornography (2004/68/GAI) ranks among the EU instruments against trafficking in human beings and the sexual exploitation of children. After reiterating that EU instruments are to supplement those of international organizations, such as the UN (§ 6), the decision stipulates that Member States must address grave criminal offences by 'a comprehensive approach in which the constituent elements of criminal law, including *effective, proportionate and dissuasive sanctions*, form an integral part, together with the widest possible judicial cooperation' (§§ 7 and 10) and that these sanctions must be 'adjusted in line with the activity carried on by legal persons' (§ 10). 'In accordance with the principles of subsidiarity and proportionality, this framework Decision confines itself to the *minimum* required in order to achieve those objectives at European level' (§ 8).

After having defined a child as a person below the age of 18 (article 1), the decision describes in great detail the offences related to the sexual exploitation of

---

18 See Sotis, *Il diritto*, *supra* note 6.

children (article 2) and child pornography (article 3). Just like the 2002 framework decision on combating trafficking in human beings, it calls for the punishment of instigating, abetting, aiding, or attempting such offences (article 4). Article 5(1) is particularly interesting because it insists that criminal law is a required instrument for challenging these problems and, it does not hesitate to specify the penalty: '... each Member State shall take the necessary measures to ensure that the offences referred to in articles 2, 3 and 4 are punishable by criminal penalties of a maximum of at least between one and three years of imprisonment'. Paragraph 2 determines that for particularly grave offences the maximum penalty of imprisonment should be higher, at least between five and ten years.

According to the scheme adopted by the framework decision on combating trafficking in human beings, the subsequent articles provide for the liability of legal persons (article 6) and the sanctions on them (article 7), the rules for establishing jurisdiction (article 8) and the measures for assisting and protecting the victims (article 9), reiterating that in the context of sexual exploitation children are considered particularly vulnerable victims.

14.3.4 Final remarks

This brief examination suggests some general observations on supranational regulations, which should not be analysed separately but rather – as mentioned by the documents themselves – in a unified way. In fact, EU instruments 'complement' those of the UN.

As stated before, these texts assign an important role to criminal law in the effort to combat the problems analysed here. As we have seen, sometimes States are required to simply provide protection, and other times penal measures are explicitly called for. This pattern appears in instruments of hard law as well as soft law. Moreover, many of these documents, especially those of the EU, describe in detail what conduct is punishable. Furthermore, they influence the configuration of what is unlawful: requiring protection, making forms of participation punishable, obliging States to hold legal persons liable (as an ideal type of liability in EU law).

As for sanctions, supranational input can be summarized as follows: (a) adequate protection is required (and not necessarily penal measures); (b) criminal measures are required (which are not required to be adequate); (c) adequate criminal measures are required. Therefore, supranational obligations can combine two requirements – a sanction that is both penal and adequate – and not view them as alternatives. Supranational rules indicate the minimum when expressly calling for recourse to penal action – a practice peculiar to the EU.

The space given to criminal law as an instrument is quite significant and has consequences on a legal level (in terms of defining the scope of individual criminal responsibility) and for criminal policy (in terms of what message criminalization sends to public opinion).

Before further examining the role of criminal law and its internationalization, we should analyse how supranational measures have been translated nationally and, as a result, how States may use the margin of autonomy provided by harmonization instruments. This analysis will use Italian legislation as an example.

14.4 Child labour in domestic legal systems: the Italian legal framework

Current Italian legislation in this area is the result of a series of different legislative measures adopted over the last decade. As such, it is a clear example of how national legislation does not always resort to criminal law in a coherent and coordinated manner. Indeed, the domestic lawmaker is motivated, on the one hand, by the need to keep international commitments and, on the other, by the pressure from public opinion to adopt criminal measures. Thus the task of protecting children from work-related and sexual exploitation does not rely on a single law but is spread over different sectors depending on what aspects are considered prevalent (protecting the physical and psychological well-being of children workers, protecting individual personality and freedom, protecting physical and psychological development, or sexual self-determination, etc.).

In this framework, paradoxically, child protection from labour *strictly speaking* does not seem to receive the same amount of attention that has recently been given to the fight against sexual abuse and exploitation of children. In fact, protection of children from being illegally employed is limited to a law which is inadequate for dealing with the new forms of child exploitation and criminal phenomena.

The approach of national legislation is wide and complex, considering that it is no easy task to harmonize the different norms on child work and labour (law 977/1967 and subsequent changes), sexual assault (law 66/1996), prostitution and child pornography (law 75/1958, law 269/1998, law 38/2006), slavery and trafficking in persons (law 228/2003), and to identify the applicable norms.[19]

Child protection from labour is ensured by the Constitution: article 37 assigns lawmakers the task of establishing the minimum age for remunerated employment, and goes on to say that the Republic protects children from labour with special laws and ensures their right to equal pay for equal work.

The main act on child labour is law 977 of 17 October 1967, later modified by legislative decree 345 of 1999 and 262 of 2000. Decree 345/1999 introduced important changes and additions to the original law in order to tailor the regulation to the principles and limits of directive 94/33/CE issued by the Council of the European Union on 22 June 1994.[20] The Decree has reworded the 1967 law, in order to reinforce the centrality of education and the need to improve the work environment so as to

---

19 The same complexity in terms of overlapping of several legislative measures can be found in other national legal systems such as Germany and Spain. For an overview of German legislation see K.H. Gössel, *Das neue Sexualstrafrecht*, Berlin, De Gruyter, 2005; on Spain see J.P. Tamarit Sumalla, *La protección penal del menor frente al abuso y explotación sexual: analisis de las reformas penales en materia de abusos sexuales, prostitución y pornografia de menores, 2nd edn, Cizur Menor* (Navarra), Aranzadi, 2002.

20 Art. 1 of the European Directive establishes that '1. Member States shall take the necessary measures to prohibit work by children.

'They shall ensure, under the conditions laid down by this Directive, that the minimum working or employment age is not lower than the minimum age at which compulsory full-time schooling as imposed by national law ends or 15 years in any event.

'2. Member States ensure that work by adolescents is strictly regulated and protected under the conditions laid down in this Directive.

better protect the health of young workers. The reform also restructured the penalty system.[21]

Law 977/1967 sets the minimum work age for children (minors not yet 15 years old or still subject to mandatory education) and adolescents (minors between the ages of 15 and 18 or who no longer have scholastic requirements to fulfil) who have a contract or work relationship as the moment when a child has completed mandatory education and is not under the age of 15 (article 3).

The law, however, does not apply to adolescents employed part-time or temporarily in domestic services within the family or in a family-run business, as long as that work is not harmful, detrimental or dangerous (article 2). In the case of so-called light work[22] the law presumes that no exploitation exists, in light of the working environment in which the young person works. This solution raises some questions since it juxtaposes domestic work within the family against domestic work for third Parties, only the latter having a negative connotation. The law seems to overlook the fact that collaborating in family work can be a source of hardship and downgrading for the child, leading to the child's marginalization and degradation.

The law prohibits the use of children for work, with an exception for cultural, artistic, athletic or advertising activities, as long as the work in question does not compromise the child's physical and psychological well-being and development, school attendance or vocational training (article 4). As for adolescents, in appendix (a), the law lists series of activities in which they may not participate, such as work that includes exposure to physical, chemical and biological agents, and particularly unhealthy production processes. Adolescents, however, may perform these activities for educational or professional training purposes, as long as they are supervised by instructors trained in prevention and protection techniques and all the safety and health conditions required by law are respected.

Italian legislation also provides a series of rules for protecting minors in terms of safety, working hours, resting periods, night work, vacation work, qualifications and medical examinations.

The law also provides for different types of sanctions (criminal and administrative).[23]

The most serious acts that endanger the child's life and health are punished with up to six months' imprisonment. Applicable cases are when children (except in artistic and cultural sectors) and adolescents are employed in the dangerous work

---

'3. Member States shall ensure in general that employers guarantee that young people have working conditions which suit their age.

'They shall ensure that young people are protected against economic exploitation and against any work likely to harm their safety, health or physical, mental, moral or social development or to jeopardize their education.'

21 On the modifications concerning penalties in Italian criminal labour law introduced with the Decree of 1994, see T. Padovani, 'Il nuovo volto del diritto penale del lavoro', *Rivista italiana di diritto penale dell'economia*, 1996, 1157 ff; D. Pulitanò, 'Quale riforma del diritto penale del lavoro?', *Rivista italiana del diritto del lavoro*, 1994, 205 ff.

22 See art. 3(d) of the European Directive 94/33/CE.

23 For instance, in Germany and Spain: see the German Jugendarbeitsschutzgesetz of 12 April 1976 and the Real decreto legislativo 5/2000 of 4 August.

processes and jobs mentioned in the appendix. This punishment also applies when a medically unfit minor is employed.

The punishment for a different set of violations calls for imprisonment for less than six months or, as an alternative, a fine of up to approximately €5,000. These violations include failure to respect certain provisions such as the minimum age for employment or the conditions permitting adolescents to perform the dangerous work mentioned in the appendix. The same sanction also applies to when employers violate the legal requirements for preventing risks, night work, work hours, weekly rest and evaluation of the young person's ability.

For minor violations and violations regarding the administrative formalities of the work relationship (for example, assigning particular jobs to children or adolescents without asking for authorization), law 977/1967 provides only administrative fines of between €500 and €2,500.

At this point some critical remarks are in order. First, in article 1 the law limits its scope to minors employed with a contract or work relationship, including special ones, regulated by the laws in force.[24] What law applies when a minor works *without* a contract of employment? What work situation has been considered by the EU and, as a result, by individual national laws? What is the actual scope of the measures for protecting children from labour?

The law does not seem to consider the actual child labour situation and its heterogeneous nature as it ignores that child labour is predominantly undeclared, illegal and clandestine, and carried out by minors in places and circumstances beyond any form of regulation and control. The law's applicability is confined to situations in which the employer – in an *ab origine* context of the legal employment of minors – endangers their physical and psychological well-being or jeopardizes their education.[25] The worst forms of child labour, in contrast, are part of an *ab origine* unlawful context and fall outside the law's scope, because the employer's intention is the illegal exploitation of minors and their services. These acts are far more serious than the violations included in the 1967 law and overlap with the offences contemplated by laws regarding slavery, human traffic and sexual exploitation of children.

This brief description of the Italian legislation on child labour shows how lawmakers have complied with supranational guidelines by adopting fundamental principles and content through changes to legislation and reforms. Nevertheless, young workers' protection as provided by this law is limited in terms of *quantity* (because it is limited to improving work and safety conditions and ensuring basic education) and *quality* (because the sanction system is not at all appropriate for the gravity of certain acts and for the protected interest at stake). One of reasons for this is related to the law's date of issue. In 1967, systematic and organized exploitation of children was not yet widespread, neither in the form of child labour nor as sexual exploitation (the increase in organized crime related to prostitution, child

---

24 This norm literally reproduces art. 2(2) of the European Directive.

25 As demonstrated by the fact that criminal judgments on child labour law concern only similar situations (in particular the omission of compulsory medical control or the violation of the limitations of working hours).

pornography, including via the Internet, and sex tourism, is of a more recent date). At the time, protection limited to ensuring work conditions that did not jeopardize a minor's psychological and physical well-being or his/her education was deemed appropriate and sufficient.

The emergence of new grave forms of exploiting children has led lawmakers to intervene, though not specifically in the field of child labour (which is not included in the criminal code but in the so-called *complementary criminal law*) but in the field of sexual crimes and crimes of slavery and trafficking in persons (usually included in the *Kernstrafrecht*[26]). As we shall see in the next section, minors enjoy wide-ranging protection in these fields against any type of abuse or illegal exploitation (with a tendency to give progressively more attention to protective measures and to stipulate harsher penalties).

We are still left with some doubts when considering the enormous difference between the sanctions provided by law for child labour (imprisonment for up to six months is the maximum penalty) and those for child prostitution and pornography, slavery and human trafficking (the maximum penalty goes as far as 20 years' imprisonment, without including potential aggravating circumstances).

14.5 The need for reform and the legislator's intervention against sexual violence, child prostitution and pornography, and slavery and trafficking

14.5.1 The protected interest

Heading III of title XII of the criminal code, devoted to crimes against individual freedom, has undergone important modifications over the last couple of years. The first intervention led to a radical reform of the norms against sexual assault (law 66 of 15 February 1996); shortly afterwards the second one introduced new crimes concerning exploitation of prostitution, pornography and sex tourism to the detriment of minors (law 269 of 3 August 1998, recently reformed by law 38 of 6 February 2006); and the last one dealt with the offences of slavery and trafficking in human beings (law 228 of 11 August 2003).

The interest legally protected by the instruments under examination is freedom, the *status libertatis*, of the individual, understood as a human being's primary interest. The protection of the *status libertatis* is also recognized in the Constitution where, in addition to the explicit protection of physical and personal freedom (articles 13, 23, 32), the exercise of rights and the fulfilment of duties of solidarity presupposes the integrity of the individual's freedom and personality (articles 2, 3, 31).[27]

Only from this point of view is it possible to grasp the extreme gravity of such crimes. Reduction into slavery and trafficking depersonalize the individual

---

26 This concept, today widespread in the criminal law sector, defines the part of criminal law contained in the code; in other words, the core of criminal law as separate from the rules made outside the code.

27 See F. Mantovani, *Diritto penale, Parte speciale, Vol. I, Delitti contro la persona*, 2nd edn, Padua, CEDAM 2005, 255 ff; G.M. Flick, 'Libertà individuale (delitti contro la)', in *Enciclopedia del diritto*, 1974, at 535.

through subjugation to another and through the individual's physical and economic exploitation. The individual's depersonalization is an evident negation of the centrality allocated to human beings within the Italian legal framework.

What follows is an analysis of the legislative measures in various areas relating to the worst forms of child labour.

14.5.2 Sexual violence

The reform reworded the provisions on sexual assault, re-classified them as offences against the person (article 609-*bis* – 609-*decies* criminal code) and introduced specific aggravating circumstances for sexual assault of minors between the ages of 10 and 14 (16 when the accused is a relative, including an adoptive parent or guardian) (article 609-*ter* criminal code).

Moreover, the reform (article 609-*ter*) draws the line between legality and illegality for sexual acts with consenting minors at the age of 14. The consent of a minor below 14 years of age is deemed irrelevant (legal presumption). When committed by a parent, including an adoptive parent, guardian, or any other person to whom the child is entrusted for care, education, instruction, surveillance or guardianship, the relevant age is 16 years.

The legally protected interest is the sexual freedom and intangibility of the minor (the proper development of their sexuality) which needs to be protected from conduct that could take advantage of the immaturity of the minor and condition their behaviour (kinship relationships, subjection, age, etc.).[28]

14.5.3 Prostitution and child pornography

The subsequent reform introduced by law 269/1998 follows the principles mentioned in the UN CRC and during the World Global Forum against the Sexual Exploitation of Children held in Stockholm in August of 1996. The new law's title refers to the criminal conduct cited as 'new forms of reduction into slavery'. The same Stockholm Declaration considers sexual exploitation of children for commercial purposes a type of coercion and violence equal to forced labour and other forms modern slavery.

The criminal concept of 'slavery', used in article 600 of the criminal code, includes defining elements that have no counterpart in the offences introduced by law 269/1998, which actually do not 'technically' constitute special situations of slavery. They are criminal offences regarding acts that do not have the same capacity of harming protected interests (the individual freedom and personality of the minor) as the reduction into slavery. They aim for a preventive protection of the child's personality from damage to their psycho-physical development by sexual conduct.

Undoubtedly, sexual exploitation of minors as a lucrative activity justifies its comparison with crimes of slavery as well as the more rigorous sanctions as compared to the exploitation for the purpose of satisfying sexual libido (sexual assault). They are violations of the child's still-developing sexuality which lead to

---

28 On the Italian legislation on sexual violence, see A. Cadoppi (ed.), *Commentario delle norme contro la violenza sessuale e contro la pedofilia*, 4th edn, Padua, 2006, CEDAM 415 ff.

the total denial of freedom by eliminating individual personality. Commercializing humans, reducing them to mere objects of pleasure and economic exploitation, is nothing less than a form of depersonalization, the basis for slavery crimes.

In comparison with the law on sexual assault (which sets 14 as the age of consent), Italian lawmakers have introduced a stricter discipline with more severe penalties than the framework decision. The recent reform (38/2006) provides measures against sexual exploitation of children and child pornography, including via the Internet, following the Council Framework Decision 2004/68/GAI of 22 December 2003 and the ratification of the Council Convention on Cybercrime of 8 November 2001. This reform has introduced the new offence of virtual pornography, raised the age of victims for some offences and hardened sanctions against the sexual exploitation of minors.[29] The following are punished:

- inducing, exploiting and even abetting the prostitution of persons under the age of 18 (article 600-*bis*, para. 1), without any other conditions (violence, threat, abuse of position of inferiority, etc.);
- the 'customer' of a prostitute younger than 18 years of age (article 600-*bis*, para. 2, as modified by law 38/2006, which raised the age limit from 16 to 18);[30]
- creating pornographic performances or producing pornographic material using persons less than 18 years of age; persuading a minor to participate in pornographic performances, as well as marketing, distributing, transfer or simply possessing pornographic material with minors (article 600-*ter* and -*quater*);
- virtual pornography, that is, pornographic material made of virtual images using minors under the age of 18 or parts of them (article 609-*quater* 1);[31]

---

29 See Cadoppi, *Commentario, supra* note 27, 35 ff; S. Aprile, 'I delitti contro la personalità individuale. Schiavitù e sfruttamento sessuale dei minori', in G. Marinucci and E. Dolcini (eds), *Trattato di diritto penale. Parte speciale*, Vol. VI, Padua, CEDAM 2006, 123 ff.

30 German legislation is not so consistent with the supranational guidelines: in the German criminal code no offence concerning 'child prostitution' exists. The conduct of induction, exploitation or solicitation can be punished on the grounds of the crime of Förderung sexueller Handlungen Minderjähriger (§ 180 StGB) or of Ausbeutung von Prostituirten (§ 180a StGB), which provides only a special aggravating circumstance in the case the victim is a minor of 18 years.

31 Also the Spanish legislators provided in the criminal code of 1995, in the framework of the crimes against sexual freedom, a chapter dedicated to delitos relativos a la prostituciòn y la corrupciòn de menores (articles 187, 188 and 189), which punish, on the one hand, the induction and the abetting of prostitution of minors, the exploitation of minors and also the constriction of minors to the exercise of prostitution, with violence, threat, authority's abuse, or superiority. On the other hand they punish the use of minors for creating exhibitions or pornographic shows and the production, sale, distribution and exhibition of pornographic material using minors, including virtual materials (the Ley organica of 30 April 1999, n. 11 modified these norms). See the commentary of F. Morales Pratts, R. Garcìa Albero in G. Quintero Olivares and F. Morales Pratts (eds), *Comentarios a la parte especial del codigo penal*, 5th edn, Thomson Aranzadi, Cizur Menor, 2005, 283 ff.

- organizing or advertising travel for the purpose of exploiting child prostitution (article 600-*quinquies*).

The measures taken by criminal law against pornography therefore spread across gradual levels, striking at child exploitation for creating pornographic performances or for producing pornographic material but also impeding the materials' circulation. The law also punishes acts facilitating this type of exploitation, from the sale of the material to merely possessing it. In addition to directly condemning child prostitution and pornography, the law also introduces measures punishing factors that influence the illegal market and the circulation of material, including via the Internet.[32] Even though in these cases the damage has already taken place (using a minor in the material in question was not prevented), nevertheless their criminalization strikes at acts increasing deviant behaviour; as a result the legal regulation examined here turns out to be more preventive. The legal system provides criminal measures protecting minors' sexual freedom early on, inhibiting behaviour that threatens free personal development by turning the child's body into merchandise and putting them on the paedophile market.[33]

In particular, the recent classification of virtual pornography as a criminal offence clearly illustrates the tendency to criminalize acts that do not directly damage the protected interest but that are indicative of moral inclinations deemed unacceptable and of individual perversion, with the risk of introducing unacceptable models of culpability centred on the author (*Täterschuld*). These types of measures rather aim to satisfy collective security needs and to stress the symbolic and exemplary content of criminal measures than to protecting minors. In this area, we can clearly see the typical features of legislation used as a weapon against the paedophile enemy,[34] to

---

32 In line with the Council Framework Decision 2004/68/GAI of 22 December 2003 on combating the sexual exploitation of children and child pornography.

33 So also the German legislation: see §§ 184 b, StGB (Verbreitung, Erwerb und Besitz kinderpornographischer Schriften) and 184 c StGB (Verbreitung pornographischer Darbietungen durch Rundfunk, Medien-und Teledienste), as modified by 'Gesetz zur Änderung der Vorschriften über die Straftaten gegen die sexuelle Selbstbestimmung (SexualdelÄndG)' of 27 December 2003. German legislation, admits only the possibility of prosecuting for pornographic material representing abuses committed on children or on minors less than 14 years old, providing penalties not as severe as the Italian criminal code.

34 On the concept of enemy criminal law, see Jakobs, 'Kriminalisierung im Vorfeld einer Rechstgutverletzung', Zeitschrift für die gesamte Strafrechtswissenschaft, 97, 1985, 751 ff; *idem*, 'Das Strafrecht zwischen Funktionalismus und alteuropäischem Prinzipiendenken', Zeitschrift für die gesamte Strafrechtswissenschaft, 107, 1995, 843 ff; idem, *Norm, Person, Gesellschaft. Vorüberlegungen zu einer Rechtsphilosophie*, Berlin, 1997 (2nd edn, 1999); *idem*, 'Das Selbsverständnis der Strafrechtswissenschaft vor der Herausforderung der Gegenwart', in A.Eser, W. Hassemer, B. Burkhardt (eds.), Die deutsche Strafrechtwissenschaft vor Jahrtausendwende: Rückbesinnung und Ausblick, Munchen, Beck, 2000, 47 ff. See also Cancio Melià in Jakobs, Cancio Meliá, *Derecho penal del enemigo*, 1st edn, Madrid, Civitas, 2003, 57–102; idem, 'Feindstrafrecht?', *Zeitschrift für die gesamte Strafrechtswissenschaft*, 117, 2005, 267–89; Muñoz Conde, 'De nuevo sobre el "derecho penal del enemigo"', *Revista Penal*, 16, 2005, 123–37; Vormbaum, '"Politisches" Strafrecht', *Zeitschrift für die gesamte Strafrechtswissenschaft*, 107, 1995, 734 ff; Prittwitz, 'Derecho penal del enemigo: ¿análisis

the disadvantage of a more rational approach based on precision, harm and *extrema ratio* principles.

The process of harmonizing penal measures regarding the sexual exploitation of minors demonstrates a strong inclination to using criminal instruments mainly as a repressive means in a 'zero tolerance' strategy. Unfortunately Italian legislation further reinforces this tendency when it goes beyond supranational and EU guidelines, notably extending criminal liability[35] and applying severe penalties, notwithstanding the EU's invitation to adopt effective and proportionate sanctions.

14.5.4 Slavery and trafficking in persons

The slavery crime reform with law 228 of 11 August 2003 completes the process of protecting the human person started by the laws on sexual assault, child prostitution and child pornography. This reform is also in line with the most recent international guidelines, in particular, the Palermo Convention, the Optional Protocol to the UN Convention on the rights of the child, on the sale of children, child prostitution and child pornography of 2000, and the Framework Decision of the EU of 2002.

Considering the law's multiple interests and its importance for protecting children from labour and sexual exploitation, we shall examine it more closely.

14.6 The legislation on 'reduction into slavery' and on human trafficking

In enacting the 1926 Geneva Convention, the 1930 Italian criminal code originally established three offences of slavery: the reduction into slavery (article 600), slave trafficking and trade (article 601), and the giving, selling and the purchasing of slaves (article 602). Faced with the radical transformation of the phenomenon of slavery, the norms provided by the code proved inadequate and insufficient. In fact, the entire normative framework concerning the protection of the human personality for a long time was not applied because it was constructed around the requirement of creating a legally recognized form of slavery.[36] In the Italian legal system crimes of slavery had an exclusively symbolic nature.

Starting in the 1980s, articles 600 ff have returned to the centre of attention and have found renewed application in increasingly wider contexts, especially regarding children kidnapped or bought to be used for begging and theft. Even before the law became enforceable, Italian court decisions (including the Court of Cassation,

---

crítico o programa del Derecho penal?', in S. Mir Puig, M. Corcoy Bidasolo and V. Gómez Martín (eds), *La política criminal en Europa*, 2004, 107 ff; M. Donini, M. Papa (eds), *Diritto penale del nemico*. Un dibattito internazionale, Milan, 2007.

35 Art. 3(2) of the Framework Decision of 2003, for example, contains some derogations regarding the obligation to criminalize child pornography. So States are free to make this decision.

36 See V. Manzini, *Trattato di diritto penale italiano*, 4th edn, 1964, at 630. Concerning the jurisprudence, see Cassazione, 26 May 1961 (Greco), Giustizia penale, 1962, II, 151 ff; and the famous decisions Cassazione, 30 September 1971 (Braibanti), Foro italiano, 1972, II, 1 ff; and Cassazione, 22 December 1983 (Barberio), Cassazione penale, 1985, 864 ff.

the highest court) connected the systematic use of children for begging, theft in apartments and pick-pocketing to criminal offences of reduction into slavery. These decisions recognized conditions similar to slavery in the act of buying or kidnapping minors who are then subject to their owner's total control and are forced to work or commit crimes, a condition similar to slavery according to the 1956 Supplementary Geneva Convention.[37] Afterwards, crimes of slavery began to be applied also to sexual exploitation of women, domestic servitude and forced labour. Despite this, there was an increasing need for a reform that could extend the field of application to acts exploiting children and female prostitution, mendicancy and every form of illegal labour exploitation. As increasingly complex forms of new slavery developed, it became more urgent to exactly establish what the punishable conduct consisted of.

The new law fights the new forms of slavery and trafficking in persons by means of modern instruments, placing Italy at the European forefront in the battle against this type of crime. It deals with substantive criminal law, rewriting the offences of reduction into slavery (article 600), of trafficking in persons (article 601), and of purchasing, selling or giving of slaves (article 602) and introducing aggravating circumstances when minors are involved. In addition, the law also includes aggravating circumstances for acts of criminal conspiracy (article 416, last paragraph) and administrative sanctions for legal entities.[38] Moreover, it gives a leading role to prevention and political cooperation between States, promotes international encounters and information campaigns, and has instituted the fund for anti-trafficking measures in order to support victims and finance integration programmes.[39]

The revision of the penalty, raised to between 8 and 20 years of imprisonment, underscores the extreme damages provoked and the high importance of the involved legal interests.[40]

---

37 See Corte di Assise Milano, 18 May 1988 (Salihi), Foro italiano, 1989, II, 121 ff; Cassazione, 7 December 1989 (Izet Elmaz), Foro italiano, 1990, II, 369; Cassazione, 9 February 1990 (Seyfula), Cassazione penale, 1992, 1203 ff; Cassazione, 24 October 1995 (Senka), Cassazione penale, 1997, 1017; Cassazione penale, 1992, 1203; Cassazione, 20 November 1996 (Ceric), Foro italiano, 1997, II, 313.

38 The necessity to introduce adequate penalties for juridical persons is strongly affirmed both at international and European level (see the Framework decisions of 2002 and of 2003 and Optional Protocol to the UN CRC rights of 2000).

39 For a commentary on this new legislation see Aprile, 'I delitti contro la personalità individuale', *supra* note 27, 3 K. Summerer, 'I delitti di schiavitù e tratta di persone', in A. Cadoppi, S. Canestrari and M. Papa (eds), *I reati contro la persona, vol. II, I reati contro l'onore e la libertà individuale*, Turin, Utet 2006, 193 ff.

40 The comparison with the regulation of slavery and human trafficking in other European legal orders stresses the differences concerning the range of the legislator's intervention. In particular the analysis of the German system reveals only a partial implementation (and consequently a partial adaptation) to the guidelines from European and international law. It implies the existence of some loopholes in the protection of the protected interest. In the Spanish criminal code, on the contrary, reduction into slavery of a person and its sexual exploitation are punished if they constitute delitos de lesa humanidad (art. 607-bis) and if they are part of a widespread or systematic attack against a civilian population or a part of this.

Reduction into slavery has been supplemented by servitude, defined as conduct that reduces the victim to a constant state of physical and psychological subjection in order to exploit his/her labour or sexual performances. In its new wording, the notion of slavery not only means a person having ownership of another, but it is also defined by using that ownership for exploitation, for forced or inhuman labour, forced sex work, forced begging, being forced to commit certain actions by physical or psychological violence.[41] The central element of the reform is to expressly identify and criminalize various forms of exploitation (sexual, economic, labour) that usually accompany the reduction into slavery and the trafficking in persons, in order to extend its application and to make criminal measures more precise. The legislation specifies, moreover, in what ways persons are forced into servitude: through violence, threats, deceit, abuse of authority, taking advantage of physical or mental inferiority or of a situation of necessity, and the promise or exchange of money or other benefits to a person that has authority over the victim.

In the new norm, exploitation is a defining characteristic of the state of continuous subjection in which the victim is kept and contributes to the permanent nature of the relationship of enslavement. The constant state of subjection presupposes that the exploitation is continuous and habitual since complete subjugation of the victim is not possible without repeatedly imposing the performance of acts of servitude. The objective of exploitation is what distinguishes the criminal offence of slavery from other forms of inhibiting personal freedom.[42]

Moreover, the third addition to the new article 600 provides three different aggravating circumstances: the penalty is increased by a third to a half if the crime jeopardizing a minor below 18 involved the exploitation of prostitution, or the removal of organs.

Naturally, the rewording of the criminal offence of slavery was accompanied by a change in the category of human trafficking. Faced with the substantial changes to the phenomenon, lawmakers tried to make up for the inadequacy of the previous measures regarding human trafficking. The new article 601 is the central part of a strategy that strikes directly at criminal activities of recruiting, illegally moving, and bringing persons for profit into a State's territory. The additional Protocol to the 2000 UN Convention on the trafficking in persons outlines the criteria for its criminalization as well as how to protect victims, the measures of prevention and the instruments of international cooperation.[43] On a European level, the Framework Decision of 19 July 2002 constitutes a significant point of reference, both for the legislator and for the interpreter as it establishes the standards that individual national legal frameworks need to adopt in order to create effective normative instruments against trafficking.[44]

The reform enlarges the law's content by describing in detail two types of conduct. First, it criminalizes trafficking persons in conditions of slavery or servitude

---

41 So, clearly, the Court of Cassation in the Judgment of 10 September, 2004, n. 39044, published in *Cassazione penale*, 2005, 2545 ff.

42 See the judgment of the Court of Cassation of 9 November 2005, n. 43868.

43 See *supra*, section 14.3.2.

44 See *supra*, section 14.3.3.

according to article 600. Second, it punishes the act of bringing persons in or out of the territory for slavery or servitude by deception, violence, threats, abuse of authority or taking advantage of a person's physical or mental inferiority or needs, or by promising or exchanging money or other benefits to a person with authority over the victim. It is worth noting that, with the reform, the crime of human trafficking can be committed even against a single person.

As for the case of a child victim, all penalties are increased when the victim is a minor. If the child trafficking in question has prostitution as its ultimate aim, also article 600-*bis* will be applied along with article 601. Although no express mention is made in the text, the law should be interpreted in accordance with the Palermo Protocol and the European Framework Decision's guidelines. This interpretation should reinforce the irrelevance of the use of violence or deception when the victim is a minor and of any consent obtained from a person who has authority over the minor.

14.7 Cumulative convictions

The interpreter must make a remarkable effort to coordinate and systematically reconstruct these overlapping norms on closely connected matters.

First of all, the criminal measures provided by law 977/1967 have the exclusive purpose of suppressing conduct that jeopardizes children's health, safety and education. Serious forms of child exploitation fall under different and more serious criminal offences as laid down by legislation on slavery, prostitution and child pornography.

Since protection regards the *status libertatis* of the individual, crimes of slavery can coincide with other offences: ill-treatment in the family (article 572), violence or threats in order to force an individual to commit a crime (article 611), sexual assault (article 609-*bis*), assault and battery (article 581 and 582). Others are substituted by article 600 of the criminal code: private violence (article 610), threats (article 612), abduction (article 605), extortion (article 629).

Considering the particularly high penalty envisaged and the particular harm the act produces, the need for restrictive interpretation should not be underestimated when it comes to norms on slavery. Aside from the elements of the offence, a *quid pluris* is therefore required as compared with simple violence (moral or physical) and threat or abuse of authority and power. In fact, the act is extremely grave because the victim's freedom and self-determination are completely annihilated. In other words, the conduct must put the victim in a state of continuous subjection that harms their capacity to express their individual personality and therefore implies total enslavement. If not, the judge will have to resort to other criminal provisions (for example, abduction, threats and private violence, sexual assault, ill-treatment in the family, exploitation of prostitution and pornography).

Moreover, the crime of reducing and keeping persons in a state of slavery or servitude for the purposes of prostitution can coincide with the criminal offence of prostitution and child pornography (article 600-*bis* and 600-*ter*). The crime of child prostitution does not require that the conduct is repeated and therefore can apply to a single act of exploitation. The criminal offences regarding child pornography and prostitution do not require conditions of total and constant subjugation. Therefore these norms do not have a relationship of speciality with norms on slavery; rather they are criminal situations that can potentially overlap. When the ultimate objective of a committed crime is the exploitation of prostitution, it constitutes an offence of specific intent. This leads to applying aggravating circumstances regardless of whether the exploitation actually took place. If a person actually makes a profit from a child's sex services, this determines complicity with the crime of child prostitution.

14.8 The rules of procedure and the protection of the child in the criminal trial

The supranational and European strategies for fighting human trafficking require instruments for judicial and investigative cooperation between States. The reason for this is the criminal activity's transnational nature.

Harmonizing procedural instruments as part of the fight against trafficking in persons and sexual exploitation of minors was introduced by the Palermo Convention on organized crime and the 2000 Additional Protocol on trafficking in persons. The Palermo Convention on organized crime requires States Parties to adopt measures for cooperating with extradition (article 16), transfer of sentenced persons (article 17), mutual legal assistance (article 18), joint investigations (article 19), special investigative techniques (article 20) and the transfer of criminal proceedings (article 21).[45]

As for judicial cooperation on criminal matters in the EU, several useful procedures have been developed for suppressing human trafficking. For instance, the procedures for exchanging information and collaboration between competent national authorities have been greatly reinforced by the Convention on Mutual Assistance in Criminal Matters between Member States, adopted by the Council on 29 May 2000. Cooperative institutions include Europol, the European Judicial Network and Eurojust.

In addition, there are more recent and innovative instruments such as joint investigative teams[46] and the European arrest warrant,[47] which were developed for dealing with areas where traditional means of judicial cooperation fell short (extradition and letters rogatory). With the latter the traditional system of extradition is substituted with the enforced transfer of a person from one member State to another.[48]

In terms of victim protection, the Palermo Convention provides measures for protecting witnesses (article 24) and assisting and protecting victims (article 25). Based on the Protocol, the State Parties are under a duty to develop comprehensive policies, programmes and other measures for the purpose of the protection of the victims. Articles 6, 7 and 8 of the Protocol contain safeguards for the protection

---

45 See also art. 6 of the Additional Protocol on sale of children.

46 Introduced by the Convention of 29 May 2000, entry into force 23 August 2005.

47 Created by the Framework Decision on the European Arrest warrant of 13 June 2002 (2002/584/GAI), implemented by Italy with the Law n. 69 of 22 April 2005.

48 J. Vervaele (ed.), *European Evidence Warrant*, Antwerp, Intersentia, 2006.

and rehabilitation of victims, in particular the protection of the victims' identity and safety, participation of victims in judicial proceedings, the possibility of obtaining compensation as well as the status and repatriation of victims.[49]

Also on a European level, there are provisions for victim assistance and protection: article 7 of the 2002 framework decision and article 9 of the 2003 framework decision specify that minors who are victims of human trafficking are considered particularly vulnerable victims also after the framework decision 220/2001 on the victim's position in the criminal proceeding.

In terms of Italian legislation, the 1998 law on child prostitution and pornography modified article 604 of the criminal code on the regulation of the acts committed abroad. It establishes the unconditional applicability of Italian measures regarding slavery and human trafficking, child prostitution and pornography, including sexual assault to acts committed abroad by an Italian citizen, to an Italian citizen, or by a foreign citizen in conspiracy with an Italian citizen (in this last case, the criminal liability is subject to a penalty of imprisonment of the maximum of five years and the request of the Minister of Justice). When the crime has been committed abroad by a foreigner alone or with other foreigners damaging another foreigner, the Italian law's applicability is determined by the presence of the general conditions mentioned in article 10 (2) of the criminal code.

Therefore, in this sector lawmakers depart from the territoriality principle and have notably extended national jurisdiction in comparison with the criteria for other crimes committed abroad (article 7 ff of the criminal code), giving the Italian law a universal quality. These special rules confirm the principles expressed in the Declaration and Agenda for Action of the World Congress against Commercial Sexual Exploitation of Children held in Stockholm in 1996, which ask Member States to formulate and strengthen criminal law *extra territorium* in the case of sexual tourism.[50]

---

49 The Optional Protocol to the CRC on the sale of children, child prostitution and pornography of 2000 establishes a list of measures in order to protect and to assist victims. In particular: 'Recognizing the vulnerability of child victims and adapting procedures to recognize their special needs, including their special needs as witnesses; Informing child victims of their rights, their role and the scope, timing and progress of the proceedings and of the disposition of their cases; Allowing the views, needs and concerns of child victims to be presented and considered in proceedings where their personal interests are affected, in a manner consistent with the procedural rules of national law; Providing appropriate support services to child victims throughout the legal process; Protecting, as appropriate, the privacy and identity of child victims and taking measures in accordance with national law to avoid the inappropriate dissemination of information that could lead to the identification of child victims; Providing, in appropriate cases, for the safety of child victims, as well as that of their families and witnesses on their behalf, from intimidation and retaliation; Avoiding unnecessary delay in the disposition of cases and the execution of orders or decrees granting compensation to child victims.'

50 See art. 8 of the Framework decision of 2003. See also article 6 of the Framework decision of 2002. The same regulation can be found in art. 4 of the Optional Protocol to the UN CRC on the sale of children, child prostitution and child pornography.

As regards implementing procedural instruments in order to more effectively suppress these crimes, the 2003 reform of slavery crimes assigned preliminary investigations to the District Public Prosecutor's Office and investigation coordination to the National Anti-Mafia Prosecutor's Office in order to facilitate coordinated investigation.

As for protecting victims who are minors during the criminal trial, reference should be made to the special proceeding created by the 1996 law on sexual assault and later extended to crimes of child prostitution and pornography (1998) and crimes of slavery and human trafficking (2003). Article 609-*decies* of the criminal code provides that in trials for these crimes against a minor the prosecutor must inform the juvenile court so that the minor is entrusted to a special court body with specialized judges and experts in the field of child abuse. During the proceedings, the child's psychological and emotional support is ensured with the presence of parents or other persons indicated by the child. Similarly, the child receives assistance from the juvenile services of the jurisdiction and local agencies. Lawmakers have also introduced the obligation that the trial proceedings take place behind closed doors when the victim of sexual assault, prostitution, pornography, slavery and human trafficking is a minor (article 472, co. 3-*bis* criminal procedure code).

In the event of investigations of the crimes under examination, the criminal procedure code provides that the judge can set the place, time and methods for proceeding with pre-trial special evidentiary hearings when necessary for protecting the minor. For this purpose the hearing may take place in a location other than the court and with the collaboration of special support bodies or at the minor's home (article 398-*bis* criminal procedure code). In examining the minor, reflective glass or an intercom system may be used (article 498, para. 4-*ter* criminal procedure code).[51]

Lastly, the 1996 law added a new crime to the criminal code (article 374-*bis*) that punishes the disclosure of information or of images of victims of sexual assault, prostitution and child pornography.

14.9 Conclusion: the role of criminal law in the fight against child labour

The protection of children from child labour and sexual exploitation is determined by the interplay of supranational – both international and European – legislation and national legislation in accordance with the harmonization process. An integral element of this process is the margin of autonomy States enjoy regarding supranational guidelines and, by the same token, the ability for international and European bodies to institute means for checking and monitoring their implementation.

See A. Di Martino, La frontiera e il diritto penale. Natura e contesto delle norme di diritto penale transnazionale, Giappichelli, Turin, 2006.

In the German system, the universal jurisdiction, Weltrechtsprinzip, exists for some offences. Reduction into slavery and human trafficking are located amongst them (§§ 232–233 StGB).

51 From a criminal procedure point of view, see G. Spangher, 'Le norme contro la pedofilia: b) le norme processuali', *Diritto penale e processo*, 1998, 1231 ff.

In this scenario and within the complex process of supranational integration, criminal law takes on a leading role. The supranational sources often indicate criminal law as *the* instrument for fighting these phenomena. Moreover, they specifically designate the form of the criminal offence and what conduct is to be punished by criminalizing complicity and providing penalties for attempts and incitement, establishing the liability of legal persons and defining the penalty's dimensions. Thus, we are witnessing the inception of a *ius criminale commune*.

The States, moreover, do not seem to resist this harmonizing process and implement the supranational guidelines in terms of law and criminal policy because the criminalization of child labour is strongly supported by public opinion. When the European criminalization process has the objective of creating a common identity and when it touches on interests already protected by national criminal law (as is the case for organized crime, human trafficking, trafficking in arms, etc.), it becomes a form of secondary *supracriminalization* in relation to national legislation that seeks to create a common European identity through a symbolic criminalization.[52] The lawmaker thus channels and adopts this social need with all the risks involved, especially the risk of adopting ineffective measures. In this sector, the norms seem to reflect symbolic criminal law in its most negative sense;[53] that is, when the criminal instrument is not really used as a means to safeguard a protected interest[54] but as a means for calming public opinion and soliciting approval of the fight against certain criminal phenomena.[55] Criminal law, in this case, is viewed as a symbol whose message is directed not at who commits the crimes but to their associates.[56]

We have to be wary of such tendencies: taking the short road by using criminal law weighed down by symbolism and the need to set examples can end up, as

---

52 In this sense, Sotis, *Il diritto*, *supra* note 6.

53 See M. Voß, *Symbolische Gesetzgebung*, Ebelsbach, Gremer, 1989; W. Hassemer, *Das Symbolische am symbolischen Strafrecht, Festschrift für Claus Roxin*, Berlin, New York: De Gruyter, 2001, at 1001; P. Noll, 'Symbolische Gesetzgebung', *Zeitschrift für Schweizerisches Strafrecht*, 1981, 347 ff; F. Bricola, 'Tecniche di tutela penale e tecniche alternative di tutela, Funzioni e limiti del diritto penale', in M. de Acutis and G. Palombarini (eds), *Funzioni e limiti del diritto penale: alternative di tutela*, Padua, CEDAM, 1984, 3 ff; C.E. Paliero, 'Il principio di effettività', in *Studi in memoria di Pietro Nuvolone*, Milan, Giuffrè, 1991, at 539–41 ff. On symbolic functions of criminal law in a positive sense, see M. Van De Kerchove, *Le droit sans peines. Aspects de la dépénalisation en Belgique et aux Etats-Unis, Publications des Fac*. Universitaire Saint Louis, 1987; K. Amelung, 'Strafrechtswissenschaft und Strafgesetzgebung', *Zeitschrift für die gesamte Strafrechtswissenschaft*, 1980, 54; M. Donini, *Teoria del reato. Una introduzione*, Milan, Giuffré, 1996, 145, n. 73.

54 On criminal law as means for protecting protected interests, see F. Bricola, 'Teoria generale del reato', in *Novissimo Digesto Italiano*, Turin, Utet, 1973, 82; G. Marinucci and E. Dolcini, *Corso di diritto penale*, Milan, Giuffré, 2001, 111.

55 On the idea that harmonization could encourage a conception of criminal law based on security, see M. Delmas Marty, Introduction, in M. Delmas Marty, M. Pieth, U. Sieber (dir.), *Harmonising Criminal Law*, *supra* note 2. Concerning the EU and on the risk of an over-criminalization see Sotis, *Il diritto*, *supra* note 6.

56 On the Täuschungsfunktion of the exemplar criminal law, see W. Hassemer, 'Symbolisches Strafrecht und Rechtsgüterschutz', *Neue Zeitschrift für Strafrecht*, 1989, 555 Paliero, 'Il principio di effettività', *supra* note 53, at 539–41.

we have seen, creating an ineffective paradigm. Keeping in line with the *extrema ratio* principle, criminal law in this specific situation falls within a much broader intervention framework and, therefore, it is neither the main instrument nor the only one.

Chapter 15

Trade, ILO Child Labour Standards and the Social Clause: Definitions, Doubts and (Some) Answers

Fabio Pantano and Riccardo Salomone[1]

15.1 Introduction

The purpose of this chapter is to clarify the sources of the debate on social clauses and their current outlines relating to child labour, and to outline some of the doubts or unanswerable questions presented. What follows is an attempt to clearly focus on the underlying issue and to offer some potential solutions. The purpose of this chapter is not to resolve the doubt as to whether or what limitations should be imposed on free trade in order to promote labour standards, nor to answer the perennial question as to whether or not the so-called social clause is an effective instrument for protecting children who work. In this chapter, we assume that the demand for trade will continue in the future and, above all, the global demand for free trade.[2] We also work on the assumption that there will be a continued determination that the liberalization of trade be qualified by the promotion of labour standards and – most of all – by the protection of the child worker's rights.[3]

This is not to say that we ignore the most difficult problem, namely the reconciliation of the demands for free trade, the interests of the workers and the well-being of the entire population in developing countries. We should not overlook the complexity of a large-scale phenomenon such as child labour. In fact, approaching child labour merely from the perspective of the social clauses could be of little or no importance.

---

1 This work is the fruit of a joint reflection by the two authors. However, sections 15.1-15.3 have been written by Riccardo Salomone, whereas Fabio Pantano is the author of sections 15.4-15.6. The conclusions have been written jointly.

2 See C. Summers, 'Free Trade v. Labor Rights/Human Rights: Doubts, Definitions, Difficulties', in R. Blanpain and M. Weiss, *Changing Industrial Relations and Modernisation of Labour Law, Liber Amicorum in Honour of Professor Marco Biagi*, The Hague/London/New York, Kluwer, 2003, 381 ff.

3 N. Valticos and G. von Potobsky, *International Labour Law*, Deventer/Boston, Kluwer, 1995, 17 ff and 216 ff. See also B. Creighton, 'Combating Child Labour: the Role of International Labour Standards', *Comparative Labour Law & Policy Journal*, Vol. 18, Spring 1997, 362 ff.

According to the latest ILO estimates, there is evidence of a decrease in abusive child labour throughout the world.[4] The reliability of these data is uncertain. We know that child labour remains an enormous problem and it still requires effective counteraction.[5] Poverty and limited access to schooling are among the most important factors affecting the number of child workers. Political indifference and cultural attitudes perpetuate the practice, both in developing and developed countries.[6] Economic analyses have been conducted on many aspects, with myriad subfields,[7] including the effect of ILO standards on child labour and school attendance; the interaction between technological innovations; investment in human capital and child labour; the connection between income distribution and child labour; the effect of minimum wage legislation on child labour and the relationship between child labour and fertility. What this suggests is that intervention for controlling child labour is both desirable and feasible. Nevertheless, empirical evidence and theoretical studies indicate that a firm solution to the problem of child labour involves a large-scale attack: holistic approaches should be avoided and partial measures are often misguided.[8]

Globalization has heightened concerns about the ineffectiveness of labour laws.[9] But, in recent years, the crisis of international labour regulation has probably taken a positive turn.[10] Several initiatives were launched with the strategy of having an overall and integrated view of the challenges in the labour and social field. In addition to the classic normative procedure of conventions and recommendations, there has been renewed interest in public and private *soft laws* (declarations, codes of conduct,

---

4 ILO, *The End of Child Labour: Within Reach – Global Report under the Follow-Up to the ILO Declaration on Fundamental Principles and Rights at Work*, Geneva, ILO, 2006, at 6.

5 ILO, *The End of Child Labour, supra* note 4, at IX.

6 See M. D'Avolio, 'Child Labour and Cultural Relativism: from 19th Century America to 21st Century Nepal', *Pace International Law Review*, Vol. 16, Spring, 2004, 109 ff. See also D.M. Smolin, 'Conflict and Ideology in the International Campaign against Child Labour', *Hofstra Labor & Employment Law Journal*, Vol. 16, Spring, 1999, 383 ff.

7 See K. Basu and Z. Tzannatos, 'The Global Child Labor Problem: What Do We Know and What Can We Do?', CAE Working Paper #03-06, June 2003, at 12.

8 Basu and Tzannatos, 'The Global Child Labor Problem', *supra* note 6, at 33. See also A. Ritualo, C. Castro and S. Gormly, 'Measuring Child Labor: Implications for Policy and Program Design', *Comparative Labor Law and Policy Journal*, 2003, 401 ff; A. Garg, 'A Child Labor Social Clause: Analysis and Proposal for Action', *New York University Journal International Law and Politics*, Vol. 31, 1999, 473 ff; V. Muntarbhorn, 'Child Rights and Social Clauses: Child Labour Elimination as a Social Cause', *International Journal of Children's Rights*, No. 6, 1998, at 305.

9 See F. Auvergnon, 'Some Lessons drawn from a Comparative Approach to the Issue of the Effectiveness of Labour Law', *Managerial Law*, Vol. 48, No. 3, 2006, 288 ff; M. Weiss, 'The Effectiveness of Labour Law – Reflections based on the German Experience', *Managerial Law*, Vol. 48, No. 3, 2006, 275 ff.

10 See B. Hepple, *Labour Laws and Global Trade*, Oxford and Portland OR, Hart, 2005, at 24. But see also B. Hepple, 'New Approaches to International Labour Regulation', *Industrial Law Journal*, Vol. 26, No. 4, 1997, 353 ff.

social labelling)[11] and the social clauses somehow are pieces of this patchwork.[12] Also the ILO is in the process of resolving the crisis that has threatened to reduce the organization to irrelevance[13] and it is likely that it will return to play a considerable role, giving the process of economic globalization the governance and social support it currently seems to lack.[14] Consequently, global labour laws have the potential of positively combining economic and moral dimensions in the near future.[15]

For all of these reasons, the question to be addressed in this chapter is not whether the so-called social clauses are efficient instruments for eradicating child labour, nor whether other measures would be more effective in tackling the problem of child labour around the world. Instead we ask whether, and how, social clauses may help to counterbalance one of the most negative effects of economic globalization in the field of child labour: the erosion of global democracy.[16]

15.2 Social clauses and labour standards: origins and practices

The debate on social clauses is not new, dating back to the origin of the influence of labour and social values on the global trading regime.[17] It is one of the most controversial issues in international (labour) law and a number of divergent theories and assumptions on this topic exist.

---

11 See H. Arthurs, 'Private Ordering and Workers' Rights in the Global Economy: Corporate Codes of Conduct as a Regime of Labour Market Regulation', in J. Conaghan, R.M. Fischl and K. Klare (eds), *Labour Law in an Era of Globalization*, New York, Oxford University Press, 2002, 471 ff. See also R. Blanpain and M. Colucci, *The Globalization of Labour Standards, The Soft Law Track, Bulletin of Comparative Labour Relations*, The Hague/London/Boston, Kluwer, 2004. R. Blanpain, *Multinational Enterprises and the Social Challenges of the XXIst Century, The ILO Declaration on Fundamental Principles at Work, Public and Private Corporate Codes of Conduct*, Bulletin of Comparative Labour Relations, The Hague/London/Boston, Kluwer, 2000.

12 See A. Perulli, *Diritto del lavoro e globalizzazione (clausole sociali, codici di condotta e commercio internazionale)*, Padua, CEDAM, 1999. In a strict sense, only codes of conduct and social labelling are soft law. The social clauses in fact, as we will see infra, have a different binding power.

13 See P. Alston, 'Facing Up to the Complexities of the ILO's Core Labour Standards Agenda', *European Journal of International Law*, Vol. 16, No. 3, 2005, 467 ff; F. Maupain, 'Revitalization not Retreat: the Real Potential of the 1998 ILO Declaration for the Universal Protection of Workers' Rights', *European Journal of International Law*, Vol. 16, No. 3, 2005, 439 ff.

14 On this point see B. Langille, 'Core Labour Rights – The True Story (Reply to Alston)', *European Journal of International Law*, Vol. 16, No. 3, 2005, at 423.

15 Hepple, *Labour Laws and Global Trade, supra* note 10, at 13, at 271.

16 K. Basu, 'Global Labor Standards and Local Freedoms', WIDER Annual Lecture 7, Helsinki, UN World Institute for Development Economics Research, 2003, at 3.

17 See J.M. Servais, 'The Social Clause in Trade Agreements: Wishful Thinking or an Instrument of Social Progress', *International Labour Review*, Vol. 128, No. 4, 1989, at 424. See also A. Perulli, 'La promozione dei diritti sociali fondamentali nell'era della globalizzazione', *Diritto delle relazioni industriali*, Vol. 21, No. 4, 2001, 155 ff.

In order to understand the term 'social clause', it should be noted that any social clause tries to connect trade with labour standards including, of course, child labour standards. The key argument in support of the mechanism is the aim of countering social dumping (or race to the bottom) through a binding clause in free trade agreements, not to use downward competition in labour regulations. Such an obligation is enforceable through trade sanctions.[18] If a country allows its workers to be employed under unacceptable conditions in violation of fundamental rights, it can export its products at lower prices and thus acquire an advantage over its competitors. According to many, this advantage is unfair. Social clauses maintain fair competition by ensuring that those who respect minimum labour standards are not penalized; producers and countries not observing these standards have to choose between the risk of increased trade barriers or labour reform.[19]

Discussing the protectionism of social clauses is another recurrent issue. One reason why social clauses have been strongly opposed is that the question of labour standards was often brought up without any reference to the broader problem of imbalances in the global free trade structure. Moreover, it has been asked why some countries strongly supporting the social clauses have not ratified many of the ILO Conventions. Those opposing the mechanism claim that it is nothing more than 'a protectionist wolf in social clothing', informed by the problem of unemployment in developed countries. Such measures, as well as trade sanctions in general, are viewed as ineffective or even counterproductive. In other words, any social clause is simply an attempt to raise the stakes for developing countries.[20]

In practice, there have been several efforts to include social clauses in free trade agreements, starting with article VII of the stillborn Havana Charter (1948).[21] US activism in calling for a multilateral global agreement on social clauses is also well-known. However, no specific provision relating to labour standards was made in the GATT (1947). The GATT (1994), updating the 1947 treaty, made no changes in this respect.[22] During the negotiations of the Uruguay Round, the inclusion of a social clause was hotly debated, but it was strongly opposed by many developing countries,

---

18 B. Langille, *What is International Labour Law For?*, Geneva, International Institute for Labour Studies, 2005, at 13.

19 M. Dessing, 'The Social Clause and Sustainable Development', ICTD Resource Paper, no. 1, 2001, at 10. See also Hepple, *Labour Laws and Global Trade*, *supra* note 9, at 129.

20 R. Pratap (this volume). See also K.D. Raju, 'Social Clause in WTO and Core ILO Labour Standards: Concerns of India and Other Developing Countries', in D. Sengupta, D. Chakraborty and P. Banerjee (eds), *Beyond the Transition Phase of WTO, An Indian Perspective on Emerging Issues*, Delhi, Academic Foundation, 2006, 313 ff: 'The underlying motive of the developed countries in linking the social clause with international trade, was yet another attempt to introduce unilateral and arbitrary non-tariff protectionist barriers to the multilateral free trade regime' (at 337). However, the ILO declaration on Fundamental Principles and Rights at Work (1998, at 5) stresses that labour standards should not be used for protectionist trade purposes, and that nothing in this Declaration and its follow-up shall be invoked or otherwise used for such purposes; in addition, the comparative advantage of any country should in no way be called into question by this Declaration and its follow-up.

21 See Dessing, 'The Social Clause and Sustainable Development', *supra* note 19, at 6.

22 Hepple, *Labour Laws and Global Trade*, *supra* note 10, at 130.

as the Singapore declaration of 1996 reveals. This declaration affirms that economic development fostered by increased trade liberalization will promote high labour standards. Labour standards should not be used for protectionist purposes and must 'in no way put into question' the relative advantage existing between countries.[23]

At present, there is little or no prospect for the formal inclusion of a general social clause within the GATT. Nevertheless, social clauses are more resilient than expected. On the one hand, judicial interpretations of the GATT have engendered an explicit consideration of a *social dimension* of the global trading regime.[24] On the other hand, there has been a steady development of social clause practices, and references to fundamental labour rights are increasingly being incorporated in regional and bilateral initiatives. In this respect, both the US and the EU have a unilaterally imposed generalized system of preferences (GSP), assisted by the GATT/WTO framework, whereby incentives or preferences might be given to a developing country in addition to those usually granted if it fulfils certain criteria related to labour rights, including child labour rights. The US and EU both adopt a 'carrot and stick' approach, even if the US system seems to be more aggressive, somehow undermining the rules of international law.[25]

Furthermore, the last two generations of bilateral trade agreements contain a remarkable variety of social clauses.[26] We will now survey, to this end, the last three generations of free trade agreements concluded by the US and the EU.

While the first generation of trade agreements contained no links to international labour laws having scarce implementation or enforcement machinery, the later ones do have a proper labour dimension in connection with ILO standards. These agreements also frequently provide for cooperative activities and a system for resolving conflicts, thanks to a parallel labour cooperation mechanism and financial penalties.

The US–Jordan free trade agreement (2000) was the first to include labour provisions in the main text instead of the side agreement, and these obligations are now subject to the same dispute settlement procedures as commercial obligations.[27] While the North American Agreement on Labor Cooperation (NAALC, 1993) simply

---

23 WT/MIN(96)/DEC/W, 13 December 1996, § 4. It was left to other institutions, particularly the ILO, to promote and develop social concerns relating to the global trading regime. On this point see R. Wai, 'Countering, Branding, Dealing, Using Economic and Social Rights in and around the International Trading Regime', *European Journal of International Law*, Vol. 14, No. 1, 2003, at 54. See also Alston, 'Facing Up', *supra* note 13, at 470.

24 See *infra* sections 15.5, 15.6.

25 See *infra* section 15.7. See also Hepple, *Labour Laws and Global Trade*, *supra* note 10, at 94.

26 Expanded now beyond privately purchased goods to services, intellectual property, investment and government procurement concerns. See M. Weiss, 'Architectural Digest for International Trade and Labor Law: Regional Free Trade Agreements and Minimum Criteria for Enforceable Social Clauses', University of Maryland School of Law, Legal Studies Research Paper, No. 2006 -2, at 4. See also Adinolfi (this volume).

27 See Hepple, *Labour Laws and Global Trade*, *supra* note 10, at 116. See also P. Alston, 'Core Labour Standards and the Transformation of the International Labour Rights Regime', *European Journal of International Law*, Vol. 15, No. 3, 2004, at 504.

provides for the enforcement of domestic labour law by each of the Parties without establishing any links to the international floor of labour rights, the US–Jordan agreement, like the subsequent generation of agreements, contains an express linkage between domestic standards and ILO standards.[28] First of all, the Parties recognize that it is inappropriate to encourage trade by relaxing domestic labour laws, and each Party shall '*strive to ensure*' that it does not waive or otherwise derogate from such laws as an encouragement for trade with the other Party. The Parties reaffirm their obligations as members of the ILO and their commitments under the ILO declaration on Fundamental Principles and Rights at Work (1998) and its follow-up, which is thus incorporated in the trade agreement as a benchmark (article 6). According to the same article 6(1), the Parties shall '*strive to ensure*' that such labour principles and the internationally recognized labour rights set forth in paragraph 6 are recognized and protected by domestic law. Paragraph 6 refers to many fundamental rights: the right of association, the right to organize and bargain collectively, prohibition of the use of any form of forced or compulsory labour, a minimum age for the employment of children and acceptable conditions of work with respect to a minimum wage, hours of work, and occupational safety and health.

However, like many others,[29] the US–Jordan agreement does not contain an enforceable commitment to respect core ILO labour standards. Instead, it contains only one enforceable labour commitment, namely to enforce domestic labour laws.[30] In this respect, it is argued that these initiatives have made 'loose use' of the ILO declaration on Fundamental Principles and Rights at Work, and have the effect of marginalizing international labour standards since, in the process, the specific standards themselves are ignored. Nevertheless, it is unclear what is meant by the 'major regression' which these commitments would reflect, if compared with the previous ones.[31] We should evaluate the instrument realistically. The analysis of the rights covered and the enforcement mechanisms defined suggests that their content and scope may depend on the specific context of each initiative.[32] What is significant in this situation is that standard-setting remains an important area for the social dimension of the free trade agreements and the ILO remains the point of reference as a standard-setting body. Thus, one of the most interesting features emerging from these agreements is that, through their inbuilt cooperation mechanisms and

---

28 Hepple, *Labour Laws and Global Trade*, *supra* note 10, at 114. See also M. Weiss, 'Two Steps Forward, One Step Back or Vice Versa: Labour Rights and Free Trade Agreements from NAFTA, Through Jordan via Chile to Latin America and Beyond', *University of San Francisco Law Review*, Vol. 37, 2003, 689 ff.

29 See also, US–Australia agreement (2004), US–Chile agreement (2003).

30 Weiss, 'Architectural Digest', *supra* note 26, at 9.

31 See Alston, 'Facing Up', *supra* note 13, at 471.

32 Alston, 'Core Labour Standards', *supra* note 27, at 520. See also P. Alston and J. Heenan, 'Shrinking the International Labor Code: an Unintended Consequence of the 1998 ILO Declaration on Fundamental Principles and Rights at Work', *New York University Journal of International Law and Politics*, Vol. 36, no. 2/3, Winter/Spring, 2004, at 114.

monitoring system, they may provide a 'window of opportunity' for strengthening the ILO's own supervisory work and related advisory services.[33]

Furthermore, the contemporary bilateral free trade agreements signed by the EU exhibit a quite similar approach. In the cooperation agreement between the European Community and Pakistan on partnership and development (1998), first of all, the Parties agree that human resources development constitutes an integral part of both economic and social development. In this respect, the Parties also recognize that education and skills development, as well as improving the living conditions of the poorer and disadvantaged sections of the population, with special emphasis on women and child welfare, will contribute to creating a favourable economic and social environment. Thus, the Parties clearly recall the importance of the observance of internationally recognized core labour standards set out in the relevant instruments of the ILO, 'which is the competent body to set and deal with these standards, as a major factor of social and economic progress'. Finally they 'commit their support to the promotion of these standards and to the discussion between the WTO and ILO Secretariats' (article 14). The EU–Chile agreement (1999) expressly refers to the promotion of the relevant conventions of the ILO covering such topics as the freedom of association, the right to collective bargaining and non-discrimination, the abolition of forced and child labour, and equal treatment between men and women (article 44). Lastly, in the partnership agreement between the EU and the members of the African, Caribbean and Pacific group of States (2000),[34] the Parties affirm their commitment to the internationally recognized core labour standards, as defined by the relevant ILO conventions, and in particular the freedom of association and the right to collective bargaining, the abolition of forced labour, the elimination of worst forms of child labour and non-discrimination in respect to employment.

Finally, all the more recent trade agreements concluded by the US reaffirm the ILO obligations and the commitments under the ILO declaration on Fundamental Principles and Rights at Work. They also contain an enforceable commitment to respect core ILO labour standards. The commitments to satisfy ILO obligations (and not to derogate from domestic labour laws to attract foreign trade or investment from other Parties) are no longer preceded by the term '*strive to ensure*'.

In the US–Korea agreement of 2007,[35] for example, article 19(2) stipulates that the Parties shall '*adopt and maintain*' the following rights in their statutes, regulations and practices as stated in the ILO declaration on Fundamental Principles and Rights at Work: freedom of association; the effective recognition of the right to collectively bargain; the elimination of all forms of compulsory or forced labour; the effective abolition of child labour and, for purposes of the agreement, a prohibition on the worst form of child labour; and the elimination of discrimination with respect of employment and occupation. In accordance with article 19(3) neither Party shall fail to '*effectively enforce its labour laws*', including those provisions it adopts or

---

33 See Maupain, 'Revitalization not Retreat', *supra* note 13, at 451–2. See also the ILO declaration on Fundamental Principles and Rights at Work (1998).

34 The so-called Cotonou agreement (2000).

35 See also US–Peru agreement (2006) and US–Colombia agreement (2006).

maintains in accordance with article 19(2), through a sustained or recurring course of action or inaction.

All the contemporary agreements aim to optimize their design in relation to the labour cooperation mechanism. The Parties, in fact, recognize that cooperation provides enhanced opportunities to improve labour standards and to further advance common commitments with respect to labour matters, not only concerning the ILO declaration on Fundamental Principles and Rights at Work, but also – even if unnecessary – ILO Convention 182 (1999) on the prohibition and immediate action for the elimination of the worst forms of child labour. The Parties may undertake cooperative activities through the labour cooperation mechanism, including advance understanding of, respect for, and effective implementation of the principles reflected in the ILO declaration and ILO Convention 182 (US–Korea agreement, annex 19-A). A Party may request cooperative labour consultation with another Party regarding any matter arising under the Labour Chapter (US–Peru agreement, article 17.7) and the consulting Party shall make every attempt to arrive at a mutually satisfactory resolution of the matter, taking into account opportunities for cooperation related to the matter, and may seek advice or assistance from any person or body they deem appropriate in order to fully examine the matter under discussion.

Of course there are many problems to be faced. Although some steps have been taken towards addressing the difficulties of enforcement, the results may be modest. In fact only a government can invoke the dispute settlement procedure against the other government for a labour violation under a bilateral free trade agreement and the violation must occur in a manner affecting trade or investment between the Parties. In other words, the lack of any 'prosecutorial authority' still remains to be tackled. Economic and social actors – be they foreign competitors, trade unions or child workers – injured by another government have little or no recourse, other than to induce their government to press their cause.[36]

15.3 Child labour and international law principles

As we have already seen, almost all of the last generation of bilateral and regional free trade agreements clearly consider the fight against child labour to be a priority issue. While the old agreements simply refer to a minimum age for the employment of children, the more recent ones consider the effective abolition of child labour, in line with the ILO declaration on Fundamental Principles and Rights at Work. Moreover, they often precisely refer to the prohibition of the worst forms of child labour and immediate action for their elimination according to ILO Convention 182.

However, the link between trade and child labour standards lies in the fact that free trade relationships reflect consistent practices. It is noteworthy that, since the beginning of the influence of labour standards on the global trading regime, child labour has been considered as a matter of peremptory norms and these prohibitions

---

36 Weiss, 'Architectural Digest', *supra* note 26, at 15. See also Hepple, *Labour Laws and Global Trade, supra* note 10, at 121.

involve banning most of the extreme forms of child labour.[37] There are, as is known, many identifiable standards regarding child labour. For example, many provisions of Convention 138 are embodied in other international rules delineating child labour standards, which have not been refused by most countries. In addition, the majority of these countries have accepted at least one international instrument outlining the rights of children as workers and their minimum age. Furthermore, the ILO declaration on Fundamental Principles and Rights at Work (1998) includes the effective abolition of child labour amongst the principles and fundamental rights which all members, even if they have not ratified the conventions in question, 'have an obligation ... to respect, to promote and to realize, in good faith and in accordance with the Constitution' of the ILO – an obligation arising from the very fact of membership in the Organization.[38]

Moreover, child labour standards are binding under agreements signed by most of the GATT contracting Parties. Thus, their respect, promotion and implementation bind all WTO *Member States*. These standards, therefore, should guide the interpretation and implementation of the global regulatory regimes system and prevail over conflicting regulations.[39] In the light of contemporary concerns of the community of nations, ILO child labour standards have to be taken into account within the continuous development of free trade initiatives, be they multilateral, bilateral or unilateral.

15.4 Article XX of GATT as a social clause

Besides the debate about the introduction of a social clause in the GATT, a very animated discussion has taken place on whether, at the present point, the current provisions contain rules that can be interpreted as social clauses; namely, whether the GATT provides for rules concerning the implementation of certain labour standards.

Article XX of the GATT admits exceptions to the Agreement's substantive provisions on the basis of requirements referring – directly or indirectly – to labour standards. It states, among other provisions, that 'nothing' in the GATT 'shall be construed to prevent the adoption or enforcement by any contracting Party of measures: (a) necessary to protect public morals; (b) necessary to protect human, animal or plant life or health; ... (e) relating to the products of prison labour'. However, according to article XX's head-note (or *chapeau*) such measures are not to

---

37 J.M. Diller and D.A. Levy, 'Child Labor, Trade and Investment: Toward the Harmonization of International Law', *American Journal of International Law*, Vol. 91, No. 4, 1997, 666 ff; M. Vasquez, 'Trade Sanctions and Human Rights – Past, Present, and Future', *Journal of International Economic Law*, Vol. 6, No. 4, 2003, at 811; B. Creighton, 'Combating Child Labour', *supra* note 3, at 362.

38 Alston, 'Facing Up', *supra* note 13, 467 ff. See also Maupain, 'Revitalization not Retreat', *supra* note 13, 439 ff.

39 Diller and Levy, 'Child Labor', *supra* note 37, 673 ff; see A. Blackett, 'Whither Social Clause? Human Rights, Trade Theory and Treaty Interpretation', *Columbia Human Rights Law Review*, Vol. 1, Fall, 1999, at 17.

be 'applied in a manner which would constitute a means of arbitrary or unjustifiable discrimination between countries where the same conditions prevail, or a disguised restriction on international trade'. Thus, waivers to the 'general most-favoured-nation treatment' principle and other substantive GATT rules are allowed in order to impose the implementation of the mentioned interests. If a legal basis exists for including labour standards amongst the justification for such waivers, then these provisions can be interpreted as social clauses, according to the definition proposed above.

Article XX(e) certainly refers to a labour standard, but it is a very specific provision and does not leave room for a more extensive interpretation.[40] For this reason, efforts to single out a more general social clause within GATT have been addressed toward other provisions of article XX.

Article XX(b) refers to values, such as 'human ... life and health' – linked to labour and working conditions. 'Public morals' in contrast, has a broader meaning, with a prominent reference to ethical standards. Therefore, the 'human ... life and health' requirement has a more substantial impact on the debate relating to social clause within the GATT, since, in this case, the link with social standards is a direct one, without any 'mediation' through ethical or excessively broad criteria.

The inclusion of specific labour rights or standards within the scope of the 'human ... life and health' waiver is supported by the most recent pronunciations of the WTO Appellate Body, which has appeared to be sensitive to claims for issues not strictly related to international trade liberalization, but which, however, are prominent in contemporary international law, such as environmental protection.[41] In fact, the General Agreement has been read consistently with social values protected by other

---

40 Nevertheless, on the basis of this provision it can be argued that art. XX is not alien to the labour rights' protection, and that waivers to substantive GATT rules on this ground can be consistent with the liberalization of the international market.

41 According to a traditional approach, any provision allowing waivers to substantive GATT rules is to be interpreted strictly, since it contrasts with the main objective of the General Agreement. Nevertheless, any legal provision can be read in an evolutionary manner, in accordance with the changes affecting social and economic phenomena (Blackett, 'Whither Social Clause?', *supra* note 39, at 15). The vagueness of GATT's definitions is often aimed to go along with the natural changes in the international community's ethical orientations. Issues that have not been the subject of negotiation during GATT bargaining nowadays can be included among the main concerns of international law. Social matters, like protection of labour and environmental standards, became prominent, because of the dramatic acceleration of technological development and globalization, which have created an urgent need to face the most abominable distortions of modern civilization on an international scale. These matters cannot be ignored when interpreting GATT in the light of modern trends of international law and political and cultural debates. In fact, 'obligations under the multilateral trade regime can be interpreted and implemented in light of either higher values, represented by peremptory norms of customary international law, or common commitments, where Parties to international trade obligations are also bound by international human rights and labour law'; Diller and Levy, 'Child Labor', *supra* note 37, at 664; U. Petersmann, 'The "Human Rights Approach" Advocated by the UN High Commissioner for Human Rights and by the International Labour Organization: Is it Relevant for WTO Law and Policy?', *Journal of International Economic Law*, Vol. 7, No. 3, 2004, at 608.

international rules of law, according to an 'evolutionary' perspective and 'in the light of contemporary concerns of the community of nations'.[42]

As we have seen, the ban on most of the extreme forms of child labour is included within international rules (child labour has been considered as a matter of peremptory norms and these prohibitions involve banning of most of the extreme forms of child labour) and child labour standards are binding under international instruments accepted by most of GATT contracting Parties. There are many arguments corroborating this perspective, such as the numerous references by the WTO Appellate Body to the Vienna Convention on the law of treaties as the source for GATT's interpretation rules. Article 31 of the Vienna Convention explicitly states that 'any relevant rules of international law applicable in the relationship between the Parties' has to be taken into account in interpreting international agreements.[43]

Nevertheless, the preamble of the WTO agreement establishes that the main purposes of GATT have to be achieved 'allowing for the optimal use of the world's resources in accordance with the objective of sustainable development, seeking both to protect and preserve the environment and to enhance the means for doing so in a manner consistent with the respective needs and concerns at different levels of economic development ...'. This statement directly affects the interpretation of article XX(b), because it is hard to maintain that the 'objective of sustainable development' is alien to the protection of children's interest not to be employed in exhausting jobs during their earliest youth, in order to preserve their physical and psychological well-being and their right to education.[44]

However, the inclusion of international child labour standards amongst the scope of the article XX(b) waiver does not demonstrate that this provision can actually be considered a social clause.[45] For this purpose, it has to be proved that a state is legitimated to waive GATT substantive rules in order to protect the health and life of working children, even when their working activities take place outside the territory of this state and they are not under its jurisdiction. In fact, it is beyond doubt that

---

42 Appellate Body Report, United States – Import prohibition of certain shrimp and shrimp products, WT/DS58/AB/R, adopted 22 October 2001, § 129; see Hepple, *Labour Laws and Global Trade, supra* note 10, at 141; Blackett, 'Whither Social Clause?', *supra* note 39, at 26.

43 Vienna Convention on the law of treaties, art. 31(3)(c). O. Chaudhary, 'The Propriety of Preference: an Evaluation of EC and U.S. GSP Schemes in the Wake of EC Preferences', *University of Manitoba Law School Review of International Business and Trade Law*, 2005, 13 ff; S. Charnovitz, 'The Moral Exception in Trade Policy', *Virginia Journal of International Law*, Vol. 38, Summer 1998, at 698.

44 The Appellate Body also refers to WTO agreement's preamble in Shrimps I, in order to justify its evolutionary interpretation of art. XX(g). Although this pronunciation refers to a provision 'relating to the conservation of exhaustible natural resources', nonetheless an interpretation of art. XX which allows waivers for the protection of maritime turtles as 'exhaustible natural resources' cannot deny the application of the same legal device to the protection of children's 'health' and 'life'. Such an approach would not be reasonable, and would be in contrast with a 'good faith' interpretation, imposed by art. 31(1), of the Vienna Convention.

45 Hepple, *Labour Laws and Global Trade, supra* note 10, at 142.

a state is allowed to limit the import of products dangerous for its citizens' life or health under article XX(b), but, on the other hand, it is often challenged that the same action is legitimate when the life or health of individuals outside of that state's jurisdiction is at stake.

In *Shrimps I*, concerning article XX(g), the WTO Appellate Body decided not to 'pass upon the question of whether there is an implied jurisdictional limitation' in article XX exceptions, 'and if so *the nature or extent of that limitation*' (emphasis added).[46] This statement does not resolve the problem at all, although confirming its prominent importance.

As noted above, the broadness of GATT's provisions as well as the variability of the social phenomena they regulate make the interpretation of article XX(b) very controversial, but the interpretation which better fits the claims of international social and economic backdrop and the principles of international law is to be preferred. Under this perspective, an 'outwardly directed' interpretation of article XX(b) of the GATT is not only possible but also convincing.

Referring to the 'public morals' exception, it has been argued that, 'given the long-time use of trade measures for moral and humanitarian purpose, the authors of article XX(a) could have understood it to be outwardly-directed in addition to being inwardly-directed'.[47] Besides, article 31(3)(c) of the Vienna Convention states that 'any relevant rules of international law applicable in the relations between Parties' is to 'be taken into account' when interpreting GATT provisions.[48]

Since many international rules, the ILO Declaration on fundamental principles and rights at work and various international instruments bind almost all WTO contracting Parties to comply with the ban on extreme forms of child labour and with most child labour standards, the protection of children's life and health from their exploitation by illegitimate forms of employment refers to a general interest, shared by the whole international community.[49] For this reason, it has to be held that under article XX(b), each WTO contracting Party is legitimated to waive substantial

---

46 On the ground of the fact that turtles naturally 'migrate to, or traverse, at one time or another, waters subject to United States jurisdiction', the Appellate Body held that 'in the specific circumstances of the case' there was 'a sufficient nexus between the migratory and endangered marine populations involved and the United States for purposes of article XX(g)'; Appellate Body Report, United States – Import prohibition of certain shrimp and shrimp products, WT/DS58/AB/R, adopted 12 October 1998, §133.

47 Charnovitz, 'The Moral Exception', *supra* note 43, at 698. This argument has been supported by an in-depth analysis of international agreements contemporary or precedent to the GATT, referring to supplementary means of interpretation provided for by art. 32 of the Vienna Convention, such as 'the preparatory work of treaty and the circumstances of its conclusion'.

48 Blackett, 'Whither Social Clause?', *supra* note 39, at 25.

49 Rather than assess whether 'labour standards in the targeted country have substantial effects in the importing state', the question to be answered appears to be 'whether these standards are common concerns of the community of nations' and whether, consequently, a state has a legitimate interest to target illegitimate child labour exploitation outside its territorial jurisdiction. Under this approach the answer to this question has to be a positive one. See Hepple, *Labour Laws and Global Trade*, *supra* note 10, at 142.

GATT provisions in order to pursue the protection of this internationally shared interest, even outside its own jurisdiction. Thus, an outwardly directed interpretation of article XX(b) appears as the one most consistent with the 'contemporary concerns of the community of nations', as referred to by the Appellate Body in *Shrimps I*.[50]

Moreover, under a systematic approach, an only inwardly directed interpretation of article XX(b) is not consistent with other provisions of the same article. For instance, article XX, letter (e), which permits waiving substantive GATT principles 'relating to products of prison labour', unanimously is considered an outwardly directed provision, since it targets the exploitation of prisoners' working activities within the State where the products originate.[51]

15.5 Article XX(b) and its 'reasonable' implementation

Article XX(b) posits the protection of 'human ... life and health' as an absolute value, irrespective of any territorial concerns, to be protected by legal devices endowed with outwardly directed effects.[52] Yet many developing countries affirm that, if interpreted in such perspective, article XX(b) can legitimate protectionist measures which impede their access to international trade. These arguments can be rejected on the basis of the recent jurisprudence of WTO. The proposed interpretation of article XX(b) GATT only refers to child labour standards' implementation, because of the particular status that relevant rules have in international law. So, the impact of such an interpretation would not be dramatic, even if important.

On the other hand, article XX(b) does not permit arbitrary protectionist measures. Article XX exceptions 'must be applied reasonably, with due regard both to the legal duties of the Party claiming the exception and the legal rights of the other Parties concerned'.[53] As established by article XX's *chapeau*, waivers cannot be applied 'in a manner which would constitute a means of arbitrary or unjustifiable discrimination between countries where the same conditions prevail, or a disguised restriction of international trade'. Nonetheless, article XX(b) subjects the legitimacy of waivers to a 'necessary test', in order to prevent measures proved to be not 'necessary' for the protection of 'human ... life or health'. On the basis of these provisions, possible protectionist abuses of article XX(b) are rather unlikely.[54] Moreover, the WTO shall 'provide due process for the defendant state'.[55]

---

50 Appellate Body Report, United States – Import prohibition of certain shrimp and shrimp products, § 129.

51 Charnovitz, 'The Moral Exception', *supra* note 43, at 699.

52 A contrary opinion in Vasquez, 'Trade Sanctions and Human Rights', *supra* note 37, at 816.

53 Appellate Body Report, United States – Standards for reformulated and conventional gasoline, adopted 29 April 1996, WT/DS2/AB/R, §§ 23 and 24.

54 Hepple, *Labour Laws and Global Trade*, *supra* note 9, at 143–4; S.H. Cleveland, 'Human Rights Sanctions and International Trade. A Theory of Compatibility', *Journal of International Economic Law*, Vol. 5 (1), 2002, 166; O. Chaudhary, 'The Propriety', *supra* note 43, at 189.

55 Hepple, *Labour Laws and Global Trade*, *supra* note 10, at 149.

According to the Appellate Body's jurisprudence, the legitimacy of a measure adopted by a contracting Party under article XX has to be scrutinized on the basis of its concrete effects, and of the specific circumstances within which it is implemented. In *US-Gasoline* it was specifically pointed out that it is the 'manner in which that measure is applied'[56] which determines the legitimacy of a waiver under article XX *chapeau* and not the nature of the measure itself. Briefly, every waiver measure is legitimate if not implemented in order to obtain a different aim from the one mentioned by the specific exception to article XX. In the contrary case, the proceeding state would abuse the prerogatives granted by article XX, by claiming its application in order to pursue an unlawful issue.

In *Shrimps I*, the Appellate Body has explicitly referred to the 'doctrine of *abus de droit*' as an 'expression of the principle of good faith', maintaining that 'while exceptions of Article XX may be invoked as a matter of legal right, they should not be so applied as to frustrate or defeat the legal obligations of the holder of the right under the substantive rules of the *General Agreement*'.[57] This statement has found application in *Shrimps II*, where the US's 'good faith efforts' in order to reach an agreed solution of the relevant controversy have been taken into account as evidence of a legitimate use of an XX(g) waiver. A strict link has been established between concrete circumstances that demonstrate the 'good faith' implementation of article XX(b) exceptions, and the proof of their legitimate and not 'abusive' use.[58]

Further restrictions on the implementation of 'human ... life and health' waivers are provided for by the same article XX(b), which requires waiver measures to be 'necessary' for obtaining the protected purpose. In order to stress the profound impact of this provision on the implementation of article XX(b), it has been pointed out that 'it is extremely difficult to demonstrate, in the context of human rights sanctions, that no less trade restrictive alternative is reasonably available to promote a legitimate human rights value'[59] than waivers to substantive GATT rules. Nonetheless, as for article XX *chapeau*, the fulfilment of necessity requirements has to be verified, not through an *a priori* analysis, but of a 'case-by-case' approach, on the basis of the concrete relevant circumstances. To this end, a specific 'necessity' test has been defined by the WTO Appellate Body. The criteria singled out by the Appellate Body are intended to evaluate whether the waiving state can 'reasonably' be required to adopt an alternative measure, not in contrast with GATT substantive rules. Both the 'necessity' and the article XX *chapeau* tests apply to article XX(b) waivers, not so as to evaluate whether the measures adopted are *a priori* compatible with the substantive aims of the GATT but, on the contrary, in order to ascertain if such measures are 'reasonable' according to the specific circumstances of the relevant case.

---

56 § 22.

57 Appellate Body Report, United States – Standards for reformulated and conventional gasoline, § 23.

58 Appellate Body Report, United States – Import prohibition of certain shrimp and shrimp products, §§ 122 ff; Cleveland, 'Human Rights Sanctions', *supra* note 54, at 176; Diller and Levy, 'Child Labor', *supra* note 37, at 685.

59 Cleveland, 'Human Rights Sanctions', *supra* note 54, at 164.

In the *Korea-Beef* case, it was stated that, in order to evaluate whether an alternative measure to article XX exceptions is reasonably available, the importance of interest at stake, the effectiveness of the measure, and the availability of alternatives have to be taken into account.[60] In the European Communities' 'Measures Affecting Asbestos and Asbestos-Containing Products'[61] it has been found that 'WTO Members have the right to determine the level of protection of health that they considered appropriate in a given situation'. Besides, 'the more vital or important' the interest at stake is, 'the easier it would be to accept as "necessary" a measure designed as an enforcement instrument'.[62] The concrete effect of the above statements is to impose a very heavy burden of proof on the state to which the relevant measure is addressed in order to disprove the legitimacy of the challenged waiver. To this end, it has to be demonstrated that an alternative measure (legitimate under GATT) exists. The more the interest at stake is important for the waiving contracting Party, the more the effectiveness of the alternative measure has to be certain. In fact, a state 'could not reasonably be expected to employ *any* alternative measure if that measure involve a continuation of the very risk' to be prevented.[63]

As interpreted by the WTO Appellate Body, GATT is not a single-purpose legal instrument, aiming to pursue the maximum level of trade liberalization without according any emphasis to other interests at stake. On the contrary, an 'evolutionary' interpretation has gradually gained ground. The importance of article XX(b) provisions has increased. In fact, due to its own structure and nature this provision is the suitable place where a balancing between interests concerned in GATT implementation can take place.

Debates on the effectiveness of this provision in pursuing the implementation of social standards are not to be taken into account in asking whether article XX(b) can actually be considered as a 'social clause' within GATT. To this end, at least from a legal point of view, it is to be ascertained whether WTO contracting Parties have included the respect of certain international social standards among the interests affecting the complex structure of reciprocally agreed relationships by means of

---

60 Appellate Body Report, Korea – Definitive safeguard measure on imports of certain dairy products, WT/DS98/AB/R, adopted 12 January 2000, §§ 166 and 163.

61 Appellate Body Report, European Communities – Measures affecting asbestos and asbestos-containing products, WT/DS135/AB/R, adopted 12 March 2001, § 168.

62 Appellate Body Report, Korea – Definitive safeguard measure on imports of certain dairy products, § 162.

63 Appellate Body Report, European Communities – Measures affecting asbestos and asbestos-containing products, § 172. Moreover, referring to art. XIV of GATS, the Appellate Body has expressly stated that a state which has issued a waiver measure has not to 'identify the universe of less trade-restrictive alternative measures and then show that none of those measures achieves the desired objective'. On the contrary, only 'if the complaining Party raises a WTO-consistent alternative measure that, in its view, the responding Party should have taken, the responding Party will be required to demonstrate why its challenged measure nevertheless remains "necessary" in the light of that alternative or, in other words, why the proposed alternative is not, in fact, "reasonably available"'. United States – Measures affecting the cross-border supply of gambling and betting services, WT/DS285/AB/R, adopted 7 April 2005, § 309.

GATT article XX(b). In this respect, the recent WTO Appellate Body's jurisprudence recognizes that 'bargains entail a broad range of policy considerations and include membership in a public international law community with interrelated legal principles': it seeks 'to identify a fluctuating "equilibrium line" between them where appropriate, and on a case-by-case basis by drawing on international principles'.[64]

The jurisprudence of the WTO Appellate Body has gradually incorporated 'human ... life or health' concerns amongst the main objectives of the General Agreement, finally stating that 'WTO objectives may well be pursued through measures taken under provisions characterized as exceptions'.[65] Besides, on the basis of reports recently issued by the UN High Commissioner for Human Rights, it has been argued that the 'trade liberalization' and 'human rights' approach do not necessarily contrast with each other. On the contrary, 'promotion and protection of human rights' should be treated 'as objectives of trade liberalization, not exceptions'.[66]

In the light of these arguments, the idea that article XX(b) can be considered a social clause is affirmative. This assessment does not necessarily mean that measures pursuing 'human ... life or health' concerns can be directly adopted under GATT. It merely allows every WTO contracting Party to waive substantive GATT obligations on the grounds of the curtailment of child labour. In fact, the respect of child labour standards is to be considered a shared interest among WTO States, and it directly affects the systematic interpretation of the GATT and the definition of a fair balancing amongst the interest concerned. The measures adopted have to be 'reasonable', on the grounds of article XX(b) and its *chapeau*, but they cannot be challenged only because they 'undermine the WTO multilateral trading system'[67] under an *a priori* analysis. The interest of 'security and predictability of trade relations'[68] does not automatically prevail over child labour rights claims. On the contrary, when these two interests are in conflict, they must be balanced on the basis of a 'reasonable' compromise, according to the criteria set by article XX itself.[69]

15.6 Enabling clauses and labour standards within the GSP system

Article XX GATT provides for exceptions to substantive GATT rules in order to protect social and environmental interests. The legal mechanism provided for by article XX(b) is based on a waiver system: States infringing social and environmental standards are deprived of substantive prerogatives which they commonly share with other contracting Parties.

---

64 Blackett, 'Whither Social Clause?', *supra* note 39, at 23.

65 Appellate Body Report, European Communities – Conditions for the granting of tariff preferences to developing countries, WT/DS46/AB/R, adopted 7 April 2004, § 94.

66 Petersmann, 'The "Human Rights Approach"', *supra* note 41, at 614.

67 Panel Report, United States – Import prohibition of certain shrimp and shrimp products, WT/DS58/R, adopted 15 May 1998, § 7.44.

68 Panel Report, United States – Import prohibition of certain shrimp and shrimp products, § 7.45.

69 Cleveland, 'Human Rights Sanctions', *supra* note 54, at 169.

Under a different approach, through Generalized System(s) of Preferences (GSP), developed countries have established a preferential custom tariffs system in order to foster developing countries' access to international trade. Under GSPs, special tariff treatments are granted to developing countries only if they fulfil precise social standards concerning labour, environment and 'transparency in governance' (corruption and laundering of black money).[70] A specific agreement has been annexed to the GATT in order to legitimate GSPs established by developed contracting Parties. The document on 'Differential and More Favourable Treatment Reciprocity and Fuller Participation of Developing Countries' or 'Enabling Clauses' establishes that 'notwithstanding the provisions of Article I of the General Agreement, contracting Parties may accord differential and more favourable treatments to developing Parties'. Article 2(a) mentions among the conditions that legitimate such an infringement of substantive GATT rules 'preferential tariff treatments accorded by developed contracting Parties to products originating in developing countries in accordance with the Generalized System of Preference'.[71] Article 3(b) affirms that most favourable treatments adopted under the Enabling Clause 'shall ... be designed and, if necessary, modified, to respond positively to the development, financial and trade needs of developing countries', in such a manner as to provide for a precise limit to the implementation of GSP measures.

The analysis of the Enabling Clause directly concerns the debate about social clauses and the weight of social issues within the GATT because of the prominent role attributed to labour standards. Article 2(a) of the Enabling Clause explicitly refers to the GSP, and thus legitimates legal devices set therein, including references to ILO labour standards, or labour standards or rights generally, as requirements for granting preference conditions. Moreover, whereas article XX(b) provides for a very general clause ('human ... life or health'), within which child labour standards are included by means of interpretation, GSP systems explicitly refer to ILO labour standards.

Unlike article XX(b), within the GSP the implementation of social standards gives room to preferential treatments and does not constitute the basis for economic sanctions. Under article 2(a) of the Enabling Clause, contracting Parties are allowed to adopt measures aiming to promote implementation of social standards by granting most-favourable treatments, waiving substantive GATT rules. However, a developing state not fulfilling the GSP social requirements cannot be deprived of rights generally granted under GATT's substantive rules to all contracting Parties.[72]

Nonetheless, article XX(b) waivers target only a limited range of international social standards, with child labour standards being included mainly on the basis of their particular legal status within international law. On the contrary, the GSP refers to a large range of social standards. In fact, the access to preferential treatments

---

70 On the GSP's legal mechanism, see L. Bartels, 'The WTO Enabling Clause and Positive Conditionality in the European Community's GSP Program', *Journal of International Economic Law*, Vol. 6, No. 2, 2003, 497 ff.

71 For some brief remarks on the Enabling Clause's History, see Bartels, 'The WTO Enabling Clause', *supra* note 70, at 511 ff.

72 Bartels, 'The WTO Enabling Clause', *supra* note 70, at 513.

is submitted to the implementation and subscription of international conventions, among which most of the ILO conventions on workers' rights are included.[73]

On the basis of these arguments, article 2(a) of the Enabling Clause can be interpreted as fostering the implementation of social standards, even more systematically than GATT article XX(b) and with a larger scope. Thus, arguments leading to include GATT article XX(b) among social clauses are even stronger when referring to article 2 of the Enabling Clause.

The Enabling Clause is not to be implemented in a restrictive way, since its purpose cannot be considered on a lower level than trade liberalization. On the contrary, 'the history and objective of Enabling Clause' demonstrate that 'members are *encouraged* to deviate from Article I in the pursuit of "differential and more favourable treatments for developing countries"'.[74] This scenario corroborates the idea that social clauses are already included among GATT provisions and that social issues directly affect the value system on which the GATT is based. In fact, by legitimating unilateral GSP measures, the Enabling Clause brings them into the WTO system, conferring upon them the status of measures directly related to the main objectives of the GATT.

GSP measures have to be 'generalized, non-reciprocal and non discriminatory'.[75] According to the Appellate Body, the differential treatment of objectively different situations is not 'discriminatory'.[76] In this perspective, the 'non-discrimination' requirement has been interpreted as strictly linked to article 3(c) of the Enabling Clause.[77] If GSP treatments have to 'respond positively to the development, financial and trade needs'[78] of the interested country, 'responding to the "needs of developing countries" may thus entail treating different developing-country beneficiaries differently', according to the different needs concerned.[79] So, GSP measures 'respond positively to the development, financial and trade needs' as far as 'a sufficient nexus ... exists between, on the one hand, the preferential treatment provided ... and, on the other hand, the likelihood of alleviating the relevant "development, financial (or) trade need"'.[80]

The requirement of a 'nexus' between the 'preferential treatment' and the 'relevant need' has to be interpreted, considering that 'the existence of a "development, financial

---

73 See Perulli, 'La promozione dei diritti sociali', *supra* note 17, at 166–7.

74 Appellate Body Report, European Communities – Conditions for the granting of tariff preferences to developing countries, § 111.

75 Enabling Clause, art. 2 (b). Bartels, 'The WTO Enabling Clause', *supra* note 70, 518 ff.

76 Bartels, 'The WTO Enabling Clause', *supra* note 70, at 524.

77 It has been expressly pointed out that the Appellate Body 'concurred with the EC's interpretation of "non-discriminatory" as permitting differentiation "between developing countries which have different developing needs"'; M. Mason, 'The Degeneralization of the Generalized System of Preferences (GSP): Questioning the Legitimacy of the U.S. GSP', *Duke Law Journal*, 54, November, 2004, 519.

78 Enabling Clause, art. 3 (c).

79 Appellate Body Report, European Communities – Conditions for the granting of tariff preferences to developing countries, § 164.

80 Chaudhary, 'The Propriety', *supra* note 43, at 176.

[or] trade need" must be assessed according to an *objective* standard', recognized among the ones 'set out in the *WTO Agreement* or in multilateral instruments adopted by international organizations'.[81] Moreover, the words 'development, financial and trade needs' have to be understood as distinguishing development, from financial and trade concerns. In fact, an understanding of development as a purely economic matter is not consistent with the weight unanimously attributed to environment and social issues by the community of nations. Under this approach, ILO labour standards constitute the natural criteria by which 'development needs' that legitimate the unilateral GSP measures can be determined.

Recently, the Appellate Body has denied the legitimacy of European GSP provisions precisely because they envisaged 'no mechanism under which additional beneficiaries may be added to the list of beneficiaries under the Drug Arrangements' and 'no criteria according to which a beneficiary could be *removed* specifically from the Drug Arrangements on the basis that it is no longer "similarly affected by the drug problem"'. According to the Appellate Body, the 'non-discrimination' principle requires for flexible mechanisms to adapt the GSP provisions to the concrete 'development ... needs' of the country concerned. GSP provisions thus cannot be conceived unalterable once adopted, since they have to provide for legal devices which allow the admission of other countries to preferential treatments, on the basis of their changed 'development, financial and trade needs'. At the same time, control mechanisms have to be provided for, in order to withdraw favourable treatments in case of insufficient implementation of relevant social standards.

Above all, according to article 3(c) of the Enabling Clause, access to GSP preferential treatments has to be based on the 'development, financial and trade needs' of the developing country concerned. Indefinite, overly broad or generic provisions are not legitimate and must be considered discriminatory. Provisions pursuing interests not related to the developing country concerned are unequivocally banned. For instance, many provisions of the US system, enacted with the 1974 Trade Act, should be considered discriminatory according to the Appellate Body's jurisprudence, especially those foreclosing the access to preferential treatments to 'communist' countries, or to countries failing to take 'steps to support the efforts of the United States to combat terrorism'. In general, measures that attribute a prominent role to geopolitical considerations in the definitions of beneficiary developing countries have to be considered inconsistent with the principles of the Enabling Clause, as it is the case in the United States' GSP, where, furthermore, a significant discretion is awarded to the President in adopting the measures concerned.[82]

Besides, in evaluating the discriminatory nature of a GSP measure, critical importance accrues to the binding effect under international law of the labour standard to be respected. In fact, if the receiving country is bound by the relevant standard on the basis of peremptory *norms*, or because it has accepted that standard through

---

81 Appellate Body Report, European Communities – Conditions for the granting of tariff preferences to developing countries, § 163.

82 Hepple, *Labour Laws and Global Trade*, *supra* note 10, at 148: See also Mason, 'The Degeneralization', *supra* note 77, at 522; Perulli, 'La promozione dei diritti sociali', *supra* note 17, at 166.

an international instrument, 'that country should be unable to argue that compliance with this condition is inconsistent with its "needs"'.[83] The impact of this statement is a particularly considerable one as regards child labour, since the almost unanimous ratification of ILO child labour covenants and the effective abolition of child labour established in the 1998 ILO declaration bind every WTO contracting Party. Thus, complaints against GSP measures targeting the infringement of such obligations cannot be admitted on the grounds of non-consistency with a 'development ... need' of the relevant country.

The principle established by enabling clauses demonstrates that, similarly and even more than article XX exceptions, GSP measures 'must be applied reasonably, with due regard both to the legal duties of the Party claiming the exception and the legal rights of the other Parties concerned'. The application of GSP measures is subjected to precise requirements that have been considered even 'more extensive than more typical defences such as those found in article XX' by the Appellate Body.[84] This statement protects developing countries from a distorted use of GSP measures, contrary to the very purpose on whose basis they are legitimated under the Enabling Clause. GSP measures pursuing protectionist aims are discriminatory, and the existence of a nexus with 'development, financial and trade needs' of the targeted country is to be demonstrated in order to prove their legitimacy. The jurisprudence of the Appellate Body on the Enabling Clause is aimed to prevent distortion of GSP measures and their illegitimate use by developed countries.

15.7 Conclusions

Given the complexity of the phenomenon, there is no doubt that approaching child labour merely from the perspective of the social clauses could be of little or no importance: a firm solution to the problem of child labour involves a large-scale attack. Nevertheless, in practice, there have been a number of efforts to establish social clauses in free trade agreements.

At present, there is little or no prospect for the formal inclusion of a general social clause in the GATT, but social clauses are more resilient than expected. In fact, there has been a steady development of social clause practices, and references to fundamental labour rights are increasingly being incorporated into regional and bilateral initiatives.

We argue that all of these instruments have to be evaluated realistically and that fears for protectionist abuses of these initiatives are the outcome of an anti-historical perspective. What is significant in the global context is that – in opposition to the erosion of global democracy – the last generation of free trade agreements contains an enforceable commitment to respect child labour standards and that the ILO remains the point of reference as a standard-setting body. It is noteworthy that child labour has been considered as a matter of peremptory norms and that child labour standards are binding under agreements accepted by most of the GATT contracting Parties.

83 Bartels, 'The WTO Enabling Clause', *supra* note 70, at 529.

84 Appellate Body Report, European Communities – Conditions for the granting of tariff preferences to developing countries, § 111.

In this respect, ILO child labour standards have to be taken into account within the process of development – that is formation, rationalization and interpretation – of all the free trade initiatives (unilateral, bilateral or multilateral).

Moreover, although GATT does not expressly provide for a general social clause, its provisions can be read in the light of contemporary concerns of the community of nations, and exceptions to substantives rules can be interpreted on the basis of an evolutionary approach. Article XX(b) allows waivers to substantive GATT rules in order to protect human health and life. According to the recent jurisprudence of Appellate Body, labour standards generally binding on all WTO contracting Parties can be included within the scope of these provision, either because they are the object of international agreements that the same WTO members have (almost) unanimously agreed to, or because they are considered peremptory rules. Under such an interpretation of article XX(b), trade sanctions can be adopted against contracting Parties not implementing child labour standards. Besides, by legitimating GSPs, the enabling clause permits exceptions to most-favoured-nation (MFN) principles to the benefit of developing countries that effectively implement ILO labour standards, granting them access to international trade. Both these provisions can be considered as social clauses providing for differentiated trade treatment in order to foster specific ILO labour standards, among which a prominent role is attributed to child labour-related issues binding on all WTO countries.

We also argue that fears of a protectionist abuse of these provisions as a consequence of such a broad interpretation are not justified. In fact, in cases related to other issues (mostly environmental ones) the Appellate Body has adopted a very 'fair' interpretation, based on a case-by-case approach and on a reasonable and non-discriminatory implementation of the exceptions and waivers to the substantive GATT rules. Both article XX and the Enabling Clause contain express limitations that prohibit measures addressing aims different from the ones that they specifically pursue. These limitations refer to the non-discrimination principle, and on their basis the Appellate Body has established a number of tests aimed to assess the existence of an abuse in the effective implementation of the relevant measures.

PART III
Case Studies

Chapter 16

The Implementation of ILO Child Labour Standards in Africa: Mali – an Assessment from a Socio-Legal Perspective

Amadou Keita

Although the phenomenon of child labour occurs in all regions of the world, it is a more worrying feature of developing countries. Among such countries, those of the African region seem to stand out and register the highest incidence of child labour. In the current international context, the issue of child labour has emerged as an important aspect of the debates on democratization and on the protection of human rights. Considering the indignation characterizing Western debates on the issue of child labour, the ratification of C182 by several African countries highlights their determination to gain respectability in the eyes of the international community.[1]

However, there is a long way between the ratification of the Convention and its effective application in the different national contexts. Difficulties and challenges emerge at all levels and often the Convention simply becomes a document for speculative debate between national and international experts, while children continue to lead their hard working lives.

After a short general overview of the characteristics of child labour in Africa, this chapter will focus on the specific situation in Mali, whose conditions are representative of the sub-Saharan part of the continent.

16.1 Child labour: a common issue to all African countries

According to ILO estimates, in 2000 there were 48 million economically active children in sub-Saharan Africa.[2] Confronted with the huge extent of the phenomenon

---

1 Between 1999 and 2005 C182 has been ratified by 49 African States; among the first were Malawi and the Seychelles, the last one was Djibouti. C138 has obtained 46 ratifications, including Libya (which was the first African country to ratify it in 1975), and Djibouti, Sao Tomé and Principe, and Chad, which ratified it in 2005.

2 ILO, Eliminating the Worst Forms of Child Labour under Time-Bound Programmes: Guidelines for Strengthening Legislation, Enforcement and Overall Legal Framework, at 9, available at <http://www.ilo.org/public/english/standards/ipec/themes/timebound/downloads/pp4_3en.pdf>.

and its continuous growth over the years, many States have put in place individual and collective policies aimed at eliminating child labour, with the assistance of the ILO.

16.1.1 Principal sectors of child employment

A common characteristic of African countries is their difficult economic situation, which has unavoidable consequences for the condition of children who get prematurely involved in activities that often exceed their physical and moral ability. This trend is reinforced by a special conception of child labour, typical of rural environments, according to which the work of children assumes also a socializing purpose. However, nowadays the work of children is often characterized by economic exploitation, which emerges in different forms and is more intense for certain activities.[3]

Child labour, especially in its worst forms, can be encountered in different sectors of the economy. Indeed, there are several activities, legal as well as illegal, in which children are systematically exploited. In general, the sectors that are most frequently cited in ILO documents are: agriculture, fishing and animal husbandry (cases are reported for Senegal, Kenya, Chad, Malawi), begging (Mali, Senegal, Mauritania), domestic child labour (Senegal, Mali, Kenya, Chad, Mauritania), trafficking and smuggling of children (Mali, Malawi, Mozambique, Burkina Faso, Chad, Côte d'Ivoire, Cameroun, South Africa, Mauritania), sexual abuse, sexual slavery, child prostitution, and sexual exploitation (Algeria, Sudan, Niger, South Africa, Madagascar, Malawi, Mozambique), street labour and children working in the informal sector (Central African Republic, Chad, Niger, Gabon, Zimbabwe, Angola, Madagascar, Morocco, Egypt, Malawi), child soldiers (Sudan, Chad, Angola), and mining, quarries and underground work (Kenya, Angola, Egypt). Obviously this list is far from exhaustive, especially if we consider that States avoid supplying detailed information in the reports they submit to the ILO.

The issue of the reservations formulated by some African States with regard to the traditional social utility of some types of child work represents another problematic aspect. At the ratification of C138, Senegal, for instance, decided to exclude from the scope of the Convention 'non-remunerated traditional types of farm or rural work in

---

3 The data reported here are taken from the individual direct requests of the CEACR addressed to 20 African States representing the different areas of the continent. Alphabetically, they are: CEACR, Individual Direct Request concerning Convention No. 182: Algeria 2007, Doc. No. 092007DZA182; Angola 2005, Doc. No. 092005AGO182; Cameroon 2006, Doc. No. 092006CMR182; Central African Republic 2004, Doc. No. 092004CAF182; Chad 2006, Doc. No. 092006TCD182; Egypt 2007, Doc. No. 092007EGY182; Gabon 2006, Doc. No. 092006GAB182; Kenya 2005, Doc. No. 092005KEN182; Madagascar 2006, Doc. No. 092006MDG182; Malawi 2007, Doc. No. 092007MWI182; Mali 2006, Doc. No. 092006MLI182; Morocco 2006 , Doc. No. 092006MAR182; Mauritania 2005, Doc. No. 092005MRT182; Mozambique 2006, Doc. No. 092006MOZ182; Niger 2005, Doc. No. 062005NER182; Nigeria 2006, Doc. No. 092006NGA182; Senegal 2004, Doc. No. 092004SEN182; South Africa 2006, Doc. No. 092006ZAF182; Sudan 2007, Doc. No. 092007SDN182; Zimbabwe 2006, Doc. No. 092006ZWE182.

the family context by children under 15 years of age, which are intended to improve their integration into their social environment and context'.[4]

In certain African countries, the phenomenon of child labour is embodied in traditional practices, such as the situation of *'enfants bouviers'* in Chad. These children are victims of a custom consisting of 'a contract for the hire of services, concluded between the child's parents or guardians and a cattle-owning pastoralist. The boy is paid in kind – one animal at the end of the year – but he is placed in semi-slavery where it is difficult to maintain his identity and personality.'[5]

16.1.2 The fight against child labour

Although the issue of child labour was generally covered by the legislation of the different African States, ratification of C182 meant that governments committed themselves to adopt and pursue much more energetic policies, at least formally, towards the elimination of the most unacceptable forms of child labour.

Through the support of the ILO, the fight against the worst forms of child labour in Africa broadly focuses on three mechanisms: the fight against poverty and illiteracy; the adoption of national policies against child labour, and bilateral or multilateral cooperation aimed at putting in place common programmes of action.

16.1.2.1 The fight against poverty and illiteracy In the reports submitted to the ILO, almost all African States highlight the link between child labour and poverty. Similarly, in the documents concerning strategies for action against poverty, States generally consider the issue of child labour. This aspect emerges clearly from the dialogue between the ILO and countries such as Angola, Madagascar, Chad or Kenya.[6] It can thus be assumed that these kinds of programmes will help break the vicious circle of poverty and will encourage the eradication of child labour in its worst forms.

The fight against illiteracy, especially among young girls, is equally considered an essential factor in the fight against child labour. Almost all African countries have committed themselves to an increase in the rate of school attendance among children and in particular among young girls.

16.1.2.2 The adoption of national policies against child labour National policies against child labour range from the establishment of agencies and programmes, to the adoption of legislative texts concerning the protection of children. In order to deal with these issues, the majority of African States have put in place public

---

4 CEACR, Individual Direct Request concerning Convention No. 182, Senegal 2004, *supra* note 3.

5 CEACR, Individual Direct Request concerning Convention No. 182: Chad 2006, *supra* note 3.

6 See the documents of the CEACR concerning these countries cited above.

services and have organized their functions in the form of directorates, councils or even ministries.[7]

From a legal perspective, certain States have adopted normative texts that directly tackle the issue of child labour and the prohibition of its worst forms.[8] The legislation of other States deals with the issue of child labour in general terms, relative to the protection of the rights of children.[9] These concerns have been translated into a common consensus among States to punish more severely, by means of penal sanctions, the most serious violations of the rights of children, such as child trafficking or their sexual exploitation. Accordingly, the criminal codes of several African countries have been revised in order to take account of such abuses.

16.1.2.3 Bilateral and multilateral cooperation In order to reinforce national policies for the eradication of child labour, the ILO encourages the adoption of cooperation agreements among States. In the context of the struggle against the trafficking and smuggling of children across borders, Mali has signed several bilateral agreements with the majority of its neighbour countries.

In several cases, multilateral agreements are concluded within certain regional contexts. For instance, under the sub-regional programme LUTRENA,[10] a multilateral cooperation agreement to combat the trafficking in children for labour exploitation in West Africa was concluded on 27 July 2005. The cooperation agreement was signed by nine countries: Benin, Burkina Faso, Côte d'Ivoire, Guinea, Liberia, Mali, Niger, Nigeria and Togo. The agreement provides for the adoption of measures to prevent the trafficking of children, the mobilization of resources to combat the phenomenon, the exchange of detailed information on the victims and the responsible agents, the criminalization and repression of actions facilitating the trafficking of children, the development of specific programmes of action and the establishment of national monitoring and coordination committees.[11]

With ILO/IPEC assistance other programmes have been launched in other African regions. Notably, in 2000, Kenya, Uganda, Tanzania, Malawi and Zambia were involved in the sub-regional, three-year project on the prevention, withdrawal

---

7 The National Council for Children's Services in Kenya, the National Child Welfare Council in Zimbabwe, the Office on the Rights of the Child in South Africa, the Ministry for the Advancement of Women, Children and the Family in Mali.

8 On 6 June 2003 Senegal adopted four orders: the Order respecting child labour, the Order determining and prohibiting the worst forms of child labour, the Order on the nature of the types of hazardous work prohibited for children and young persons, and the Order determining the categories of enterprises and types of work prohibited for children and young persons.

9 Reference is made to: the Kenyan Children's Act of 2001; the Malian Code on the Protection of the Child of 2002; the Nigerian Child Rights Act of 2003.

10 The programme against trafficking of children for labour exploitation in West and Central Africa (LUTRENA) was commenced in 2001 with the collaboration of ILO/IPEC and covers nine countries: Benin, Burkina Faso, Cameroon, Côte d'Ivoire, Gabon, Ghana, Mali, Nigeria and Togo.

11 CEACR, Individual Observation concerning Convention No. 182: Mali 2006, Doc. No. 062006MLI182.

and rehabilitation of children engaged in hazardous work in commercial agriculture in Eastern Africa (the COMAGRI project).[12] The project aimed to 'raise awareness on the hazards of child labour in commercial agriculture, to build national and sub-regional capacity to fight against this phenomenon, and to target as many as 3,000 children per country.'[13] Another cooperative effort that is worth mentioning is the programme of action entitled 'Building the foundations for eliminating the worst forms of child labour in Anglophone Africa', launched in September 2002. The core participating countries are Kenya, Ghana, Nigeria, Uganda and the United Republic of Tanzania.

As can be inferred from the examples cited here, under the auspices of the ILO/IPEC almost all African countries have undertaken national and multilateral efforts towards the eradication of the worst forms of child labour. Despite this, the practical difficulties encountered by these countries often do seriously jeopardize such policies. To understand this, one may start from the case of Mali, which in many respects is similar to other African countries.

Mali's adoption of several conventions in the area of child labour highlights the political determination of its authorities in the fight against this phenomenon. Nevertheless, the adoption of international instruments accompanied by specific national policies seem unable to gain control over a phenomenon whose magnitude – despite the elusiveness of official statistics to date – cannot be concealed. It was only on 11 April 2007 that the Council of Ministers could examine the document concerning the results of the national survey on child labour for the year 2005.[14] According to the national journal that published the communiqué of the Council of Ministers, almost two out of three children aged 5 to 17 years are economically active, and the phenomenon is more prevalent in agricultural (71 per cent) than urban areas (63 per cent). Moreover, 93 per cent of economically active children aged 5 to 14 years are employed in harmful occupations, while 40 per cent perform dangerous or hazardous work.[15]

In order to understand the difficulties with the application of C182 one has to start from an analysis of the Malian society itself. This type of approach is inspired by socio-juridical methods and leads us to inquire into the traditional customs and laws of the Malian culture in order to confront the issues of contemporary Malian society, whose law has gone through important changes determined by the political, social and economic development of the country. This chapter leaves aside the theoretical developments elaborated by different authors and focuses on the concrete situation of the country engaged in the difficult task of fulfilling the conventional obligations undertaken and the implementation of national legislation against the worst forms of child labour.

---

12 Tea, coffee, sugar and tobacco.

13 CEACR, Individual Direct Request concerning Convention No. 182: Kenya 2005, *supra* note 3.

14 L'Essor, No. 15931 of 12 April, 2007, at 4.

15 *Ibid.*

16.2 Child labour under the traditional and positive law of Mali

An analysis of the Malian juridical system reveals the existence of norms and institutions belonging both to the sphere of the State and to a customary system, which, due to the difficulties of the State and peoples' behaviour, tend to become a downright legal order. Each source entails a different concept of children and child labour.

16.2.1 The concept of 'child' under the traditional law: shaping a future adult

Although from a political point of view the different Malian ethnic groups have experienced different organizational systems,[16] a common aspect has been the similarity between social institutions. Such institutions, building upon a certain vision of the world, used to consider men as one of the elements of a harmonious whole made up of the living and the dead. In this perspective 'the law is characterised strongly by this interdependence that weighs upon man and by the feeling of overwhelming responsibility it generates, and from which no system of preestablished rules can really release him'.[17] Within strongly statutory traditional societies, the rights and obligations of individuals should be understood as functions of their statutes. The statute in its turn is inspired by the function that it is intended to accomplish for the group. There is therefore a primacy of this function which ultimately constrains individuals.[18]

In such a social system, children are primarily understood in terms of their present and future functions. The assignment of certain tasks to children and the expectation of a correct accomplishment of the duties therefrom deriving is legitimated by the aspiration for a scrupulous and conscientious growth of the child in view of their future role as adults. This concept of the role of children in society requires that the family and certain other community institutions – such as the 'age groups' and the 'initiation societies'– undertake and complete the process of 'socialization' of the child.

16.2.1.1 The child within his family In the first place the child belongs to a family, within which he/she occupies a certain status. The child may be a boy or a girl, and therefore be a brother or sister to the other children of the family. He/she may be the firstborn, the middle-born, or the youngest child, etc. His/her rights and obligations descend from this order. In any case the child is subject to the rules set by the head of the family. The child's participation in the economy of the family is determined by this figure or by another adult who has the right to decide for the child (the mother or the elder brother, for example). If the child does not fulfil their obligations to family,

---

16 For instance, the empire for the Mandingos, the kingdom for the Bambaras, or the village for the Miniankas.

17 'Le droit est fortement marqué par cette interdépendance qui pèse sur les hommes et par le sentiment de très grande responsabilité qui en découle et dont ne les décharge vraiment aucun système de règles préétablies.' M. Alliot, *Le Droit et le Service Public au Miroir de l'Anthropologie*, Paris, Karthala, 2003, at 314.

18 *Ibid.*, at 56.

he/she may be subject to punishment, whose nature and strength are left to the discretion of the person that has the authority to inflict penalties. It should be noted that the brother who has the right to punish his younger brothers may also undergo punishment inflicted by older members of the family. Within the domestic economy the role played by the child varies in conformity to its age and sex. Activities within the family context may range from work in the fields or the pasturing of small animals, to everyday housework. In the Mandingo families, the firstborn child, who is responsible for the work in the fields, every morning assigns the daily duties and tasks to his younger brothers. Even the younger children are part of this distribution of tasks depending on their age and health.

16.2.1.2 The age groups Although differently named by the diverse ethnic factions,[19] the 'age group' or *kari* may be defined as a community of children organized on the basis of common criteria, such as for instance the fact that the children were circumcised together. The age groups are horizontal social structures gathering children from different families and social conditions. They serve the purpose of socialization of children because it is within these contexts that the basic ideas and models permitting the reproduction and the continuity of the society are instilled.[20] For instance, among the Mandingos, the values of friendship and solidarity strongly link the members of the *kari*, beyond all difficulties in life. Each group has a chief who gives his name to the age group. Social organization through age groups is interesting for two practical reasons. On the one hand the *kari* establishes the rights and obligations of its members in their mutual relationships: for example ploughing the fields of a member who needs help, building the house of a member who is going to be married, reconciling a member in conflict with his wife, etc. On the other hand, the *kari* represents for the village a sort of 'working crew'. In special cases the chief of the village may engage the members of a *kari* for a job that entails a collective interest. All males of the village must necessarily belong to a *kari*.[21]

Age groups have generally an internal law that is accepted and applied without objections. As concerns the *waaldé*, Amadou Hampaté Bâ, who was a member of this age group writes that

> For the simpler infractions the penalties consisted in the payment of fines in terms of shellfish or cola nuts, in being thrown into the sea with all the clothes or in being showered using emptied cucumbers full of water. Sanctions could amount up to 10 strokes of the lash for the more serious offences, or even consist in the temporary or definitive exclusion from the community.[22]

---

19 *Kari* among the Mandingos, *sèrè* among the Bambaras and *waaldé* among the Peuls.

20 A. Keita, 'Au Détour des Pratiques Foncières à Bancoumana. Quelques Observations sur le Droit Malien', in G. Hesseling, M. Djiré and B. Oomen (eds), *Le Droit en Afrique. Expériences Locales et Droit Etatique au Mali*, Paris, Karthala, 2005, at 84.

21 *Ibid.*

22 A. Hampâté Bâ, *Amkoulel l'enfant peul: Mémoires*, Paris, Editions J'ai lu, 1996, at 206–7.

16.2.1.3 The initiation societies Almost all ethnic groups in Mali (that is, the Mandingos, the Bambaras, the Sénoufos, the Bobos, the Dogons, the Peuls, the Sonrhaïs, the Kakolos) have known so-called 'initiation societies' or 'religious brotherhoods' or 'secret societies'.[23] Despite their different roles and functions, all of these societies have been particularly relevant from a social, religious, and political perspective.

From a social point of view, the *N'tomo* and the *Korè* had the function to organize ritual ceremonies celebrating the passage of young boys from childhood to adulthood. Among the Mandingos, the Miniankas, the Bambaras of Beledougou and the Peuls of Birgo, the *N'tomo* pursued the aim of teaching the virtue of silence by persuading children to control their speech. After the initiation to *N'tomo*, the education of children proceeded through the *Korè*, whose objective was to build up the identity of young men. After that, the child had to be 'killed at the Korè'[24] in order to become an adult. The initiation to the *Korè* used to take place in classes organized on the basis of age difference (up to seven years) and lessons were held in the savannah. The initiation required the overcoming of different humiliation and oppression tests that were meant to reveal the cleverness and courage of the young men involved. Contemporaneously, initiation rites provided lessons in the field of medicine (knowledge of plants), on sexuality, on the cycle of life, or on the obligations towards the elderly and the ancestors.

It can be deduced that the underlying characteristic of the age groups and the initiation societies is their coercive nature. Such organizational forms subject their members to a series of situations that can be considered as violations of their rights as human beings and, more importantly, of their rights as children. Indeed, traditional law considers childhood in function of the formation of the personality of the adult and of the role that the latter will play in society. What positive law considers as a violation of rights is perceived by traditional law as a test aimed at shaping and strengthening the character of the child. Under the perspective of traditional law, far from being a 'subject' of law, the child is merely an 'object' of law.

Born on the ashes of decolonization, the Malian State chose to adopt the juridical model of its colonizer, which postulates a different legal status for the child.

16.2.2 The child in the Malian positive law: a subject of law with the right to be protected

As highlighted by F. Dekeuweur-Défossez,

> [T]he adult can live on his own and the law treats him as an individual. The child cannot live unless he is surrounded by adults. In principle his family is the most favourable

---

23 There are many of these societies: *N'tomo*, *Korè*, *Nama* or *Ciwara*, *Kono*, *Komo*, *Jo*, *Nya*, *Manya*, *Poro*, *Holley-horey*, etc.

24 The expression is taken from the text 'Rites de passage, rites d'initiation et associations' commenting on the rites of initiating societies and their masks, presented at the permanent exhibition 'Masterpieces of Ritual Art' at the Malian National Museum.

environment for his growth ... However, it may happen that his family does not play its role: the State must therefore control and, if necessary, replace the family...[25]

This statement summarizes very well the conception of 'child' that emerged from the Malian national legislation on minors. This conception has, however, undergone an important evolution due to the influence of international legal instruments, which have transformed children into authentic subjects of law.

16.2.2.1 The concept of the rights of the child after independence This concept is grounded on the rights of the child. The child is perceived as a vulnerable individual, requiring the protection of the family and under particular circumstances also of the State. This concept summarizes the legal status of the child after independence, which can be drawn from different legal texts of the period, notably: the Code of Marriage and Tutorship, the Code of Malian Nationality, the Family Code, the Law on the Civil Status, the Labour Code, etc.

These texts regulate the tutorship of minors in case of the death of their parents, the rights and duties descending from Malian nationality by origin, the modes of acquisition of Malian citizenship, the rules of affiliation and the parental authority (that is, *patria potestas*). An analysis of these norms highlights that children are granted certain rights which aim to protect their life and development. This is the case, for instance, of the provisions concerning the consolidation of the relationship between the child and his/her parents, the exercise of parental rights, and the general legal provisions on the protection of the child in his/her labour relations.

The consolidation of the relationship between the child and the parents. The child needs to grow and develop his/her personality within a family. For that reason, the child needs his/her parents with respect to whom he/she enters a juridical relationship. Order No. 73-036 of 31 July 1973, containing the Family Code, establishes in article 28 that *'l'enfant légitime porte le nom de son père'*.[26] Other norms regulate the situation of children born out of wedlock. Affiliation not only generates the creation of reciprocal rights and obligations between children and their parents (article 80 of the Family Code) but also gives rise to a certain status that can be vindicated towards the State. Accordingly, Law No. 62-18 of 3 February 1962, containing the Code of Malian Nationality, modified by Order No. 95-70 of 25 August 1995, lists in article 8 the grounds for the acquisition of Malian nationality. It establishes that, independently from the place of birth the following persons acquire the Malian citizenship:

1) l'enfant légitime né d'un père malien; 2) l'enfant légitime né d'une mère malienne et d'un père apatride ou de nationalité inconnue; 3) l'enfant naturel lorsque celui de ses parents à l'égard duquel la filiation a d'abord été établie est malien; 4) l'enfant naturel

---

25 'L'adulte peut vivre seul et le droit le traite comme une personne isolée. L'enfant ne peut survivre s'il n'est pas entouré d'adultes. En principe, c'est le milieu familial qui est le plus favorable pour son épanouissement ... Néanmoins, il peut se produire que la famille ne remplisse pas son rôle: l'Etat va donc contrôler et, le cas échéant, suppléer la famille...'. F. Dekeuweur-Défossez, *Les droits de l'enfant*, 7th edn, Paris, PUF, 2006, at 4.

26 'The legitimate child bears his father's name.'

lorsque celui de ses parents à l'égard duquel la filiation a été établie en second est malien, si l'autre parent est apatride ou de nationalité inconnue; 5) l'enfant de mère malienne et de père étranger sauf à lui de répudier la nationalité malienne par les formes de droit dans les six mois avant sa majorité.[27]

By virtue of article 21, Malian nationality may also be acquired by the child who has been legally adopted, as well as by certain categories of minors such as the legitimate or the legitimized child whose father or whose mother as a widow has obtained Malian citizenship. As concerns Law No. 62-17 of 3 February 1962 containing the Code of Marriage and completed by Order No. 26 of 10 March 1975, it is established that when a marriage is dissolved because of the death of one of the parents, the tutorship for the minor and non-emancipated children is assigned to the surviving consort (article 103). In the case of the death of both parents, the head of the administrative district, upon a proposal of the 'family council', appoints a tutor for the minor (article 106). The family council names also a 'vice-tutor' whose function is to '*surveiller la gestion tutélaire et à représenter le mineur lorsque ses intérêts seront en opposition avec ceux du tuteur*'[28] (article 114 Ord.).

All this should guarantee the creation of a physical and psychological environment favourable to the child's development and growth. However, parental authority has other effects in terms of rights that the parents exercise over their children.

The exercise of parental rights. The Malian Family Code treats contextually rights and obligations within parental rights. It is established that '*les droits des parents se résument dans la puissance paternelle, leurs obligations dans l'entretien et l'éducation des enfants*'[29] (article 81).

Parental authority, exercised under the form of rights and obligations, may affect either the child or his/her goods. Concerning the first aspect, parents exercise their authority by protecting, guiding, watching over and mending the character of their child. Parents have the right to choose the place of living, to decide over the child's education, to control his/her relationships and his/her correspondence, and even to decide to send particularly difficult children to appropriate corrective centres. On the other hand, the exercise of parental powers over the goods owned by the child involves the right to use and administer these goods.

General legal provisions on the protection of the child in his/her labour relations. The norms on the protection of the child in his/her labour relations are part of Law

---

27 '1) the legitimate child of a Malian father; 2) the legitimate child of a Malian mother and of a stateless father or whose citizenship is unknown; 3) the natural child when the parent towards whom affiliation is primarily established is Malian; 4) the natural child when the parent towards whom affiliation is secondarily established is Malian upon condition that the other parent is stateless or of unknown citizenship; 5) the child of a Malian mother and of an alien father, save the possibility for the child to renounce the Malian nationality in the six months preceding his majority, under the forms established by law.'

28 '… to supervise the tutorship and to represent the interest of the child in case a conflict of interests occurs.'

29 'The rights of the parents consist of the parental authority (*patria potestas*) and the duties of education and entertainment of their children.'

No. 92-020 of 23 September 1992, which contains the Labour Code and its Executive Decree No. 96-178 of 16 June 1996.

The work of children has always been a common phenomenon in Malian society. Whether employed in the family fields or involved in economic activities in the urban environment, the child is broadly considered an economic agent of immediate availability. In the rural areas, the activities performed by children (such as baby-sitting, looking after oxen, bringing water to the workers, chasing away birds that harm the crops or helping with the housework) are deemed to be compatible with their age and their role within the social and economic organization of the community. In the urban areas, the work performed by children for their parents, such as small commercial activities, giving a helping hand as a mechanic, tailor or carpenter, etc., is considered as training and the efforts made at that age will be rewarded when the child has become an adult and working for himself.

A large part of these activities is performed in the informal sector and is often ignored by labour legislation. Nonetheless, the legislation contains some safeguards for the protection of children. The establishment of a minimum age for work and the prohibition of certain types of work for children below 18 years represent two examples in this regard.

As concerns the minimum age for the admission of children to work, the Labour Code establishes that '*les enfants ne peuvent être employés dans aucune entreprise, même comme apprentis, avant l'âge de quatorze ans, sauf dérogation écrite édictée par arrêté du Ministre chargé du travail, compte tenu des circonstances locales et des tâches qui peuvent leur être demandées*'[30] (article 187). If the labour inspector suspects, or is informed by the child, that the work being performed exceeds his/her strength, he can ask for a medical examination of the conditions of the child, and it will not be permitted to keep the latter in such a position (article 188). The stringent prohibition established in the first part of article 187 seems to be moderated by the notions of 'local circumstances' and 'types of activities to be performed'. In this provision the legislator clearly acknowledges the difficulties in the application of a stricter law. It should be noted that the Minimum Age Convention No. 138 of 1973, ratified by Mali in 2001,[31] provides in article 7 that Member States may, through national laws or regulations, authorize the employment of children of 13 to 15 years of age in light work. Those persons will be allowed to perform such employment, on the one hand, upon the condition that it is not harmful to the health or development of children and, on the other, that it does not prejudice their school attendance nor impede their participation in vocational orientation or training programmes. The executive decree of the Malian Labour Code, on its part, introduces a derogation for children who are 12 years of age and above, allowing them to perform domestic work or light seasonal work. However, at the moment of the ratification of C138, Mali had

---

30 The Labour Code establishes a general ban on the employment of children below the age of 14, not even as apprentices, save for the written authorization of the Minister responsible for labour allowing for a partial derogation once the local circumstances and the types of activities to be performed have been taken into account.

31 Law No. 01-061, of 3 July 2001 ratifying Minimum Age Convention No. 138 of 1973.

specified a minimum age for admission to employment in conformity with article 2 of the Convention.[32] This age was set at 15 years. It follows that the provisions of the Malian Labour Code and its executive decree are in contrast with C138. On this point the CEACR has requested the Malian government 'to take the necessary steps to bring the relevant provisions of the Labour Code and of Decree No. 96-178/P-RM of 13 June 1996 into line with the Convention and to prohibit work by children under the age of 15 years'.[33] As has been pointed out above, the derogation under article 7 of C138 concerns the age of 13 years, but in these cases the government should indicate the activities for which the employment of children between 13 and 15 years is authorized.[34]

The annex to Decree No. 96-178 of 16 June 1996, containing the Labour Code, encloses a list of the types of work prohibited to children and of the establishments in which they can be employed upon certain conditions. The Decree identifies 84 types of work that are prohibited for children under the age of 18 years[35] and 120 establishments in which the employment of children under 18 is authorized upon the fulfilment of certain conditions. One might then wonder what kind of effective supervision is carried out for monitoring these two aspects. For instance, children can be employed in public and private abattoirs, but those under the age of 17 should not be directly involved with animal slaughtering. However, when one knows that many firms are invaded by meal-seekers who enter into informal relationships with official agents and help them for payment in kind, one might wonder how effective control mechanisms are. Legal texts intending to provide a more protective discipline regulate also other aspects of child labour, such as the prohibition of night work (between 9 pm and 5 am) in all industrial establishments for children under 18 years, the prohibition of employment of children under 16 years in artistic performances presented in public halls, etc.

From the analysis of the different legal texts mentioned, it follows that the legal status of the child is strongly influenced by the concept of the child as an object of law. Nevertheless, the former concept has undergone an important evolution during the last ten years in the sense of a stronger emphasis on the protection of the rights of the child.

16.2.2.2 The rights of the child under the influence of international instruments and of the national democratization process Two major events that have undeniably influenced the perception of the rights of the child in Mali: the ratification of several

---

32 Art. 2 reads: 'Each Member which ratifies this Convention shall specify, in a declaration appended to its ratification, a minimum age for admission to employment or work within its territory and on means of transport registered in its territory; subject to Articles 4 to 8 of this Convention, no one under that age shall be admitted to employment or work in any occupation.'

33 CEACR, Individual Direct Request concerning Convention No. 138: Mali 2006, Doc. No. 092006MLI138.

34 *Ibid.*

35 For instance, the lead fusion and the manipulation of lead oxides in the fabrication and reparation of electric accumulators, the production of calcium chloride and of bleaching substances, the dry cleaning of glass and crystal, the production of methyl nitrate, etc.

international instruments and the prevailing political environment after the events of March 1991.[36] As regards this last aspect, the demand for democratization required the new government to try and undertake measures that would have satisfied all social classes. In addition, the claims formulated by the Western donors,[37] who were concerned about the situation of the most vulnerable segments of society (namely women and children), should by no means be overlooked.

Although Mali had already ratified the UN Convention on the Rights of the Child (in 1990), from 1992 onwards the newly elected Malian authorities have shown more incisiveness and enthusiasm on the issue of the protection of the rights of children. It should be recalled that when Mali ratified the CRC, the government in charge presented a reservation on article 16 of the Convention, concerning the right of the child not to 'be subjected to arbitrary or unlawful interference with his or her privacy, family, home or correspondence, nor to unlawful attacks on his or her honour and reputation'. It was argued that the provision presented serious difficulties of enforcement in Malian society insofar as children were subject to the authority of their parents. The Malian authorities made another reservation on article 32 of the CRC which deals with the economic exploitation of children. Once again the argument put forward was the consideration of the social and economic situation of the country. For both cases the influence of the traditional concept of children and of the work by performed them is apparent. These reservations were reconfirmed in the initial report submitted by Mali in 1996.[38]

Since the end of the 1990s Mali has undertaken a more vigorous political approach which has been translated into the adoption of legislation and the creation of specific administrative facilities. Among the most important laws are: Law No. 99-046 of 28 December 1999 on education, Law No. 00-039 of 7 July 2000 concerning orphans, Decree No. 01-534/P-RM of 1 November 2001 concerning facilitated mechanisms for the expatriation of children up to 18 years, and Order No. 02-062 of 5 June 2002 containing the Code of the Protection of the Child. Being inspired by the CRC, this last text can be considered as highly innovative. Other legal instruments have been revisited in the light of these developments, notably the Law on Juvenile Justice and the Code of Criminal Procedure. As regards the latter the Malian government has established several specialized detention centres; centres for the re-education and the reintegration of young boys and girls; a specific jurisdiction for juveniles; the National Tutorial Council, etc.

---

36 Following a popular rebellion in 1999, the single-party regime was overthrown.

37 That is the group of Western countries and international organizations (such as the International Monetary Fund or the World Bank) that provide development finance for poor countries.

38 Periodical Report of Mali concerning the Application of the Convention on the Rights of the Child for the Period 1999–2004, Bamako, March 2005, at 7.

16.3 The application of C182: the contrast between political will and the practical weakness of governmental authorities

The formal adoption of C182 on 14 July 2000[39] highlighted the determination of Malian authorities to ensure a more effective protection of children by combating the phenomenon of child labour and especially its worst forms. Nevertheless, this political determination collides with an inflexible social and economic situation. This aspect emerges clearly in the process of the national implementation of policies against child labour.

16.3.1 National policies in the fight against the worst forms of child labour

Within the Malian social context, the adoption of C182 and the issue of its application and implementation has revealed the existence of two paradigms. The first one, referring to the idea of child work as an element of socialization, assumes that the different national context should be taken into consideration and that the work of children presents not only an economic utility but is equally important from a social and cultural point of view. Evidently, those who hold this opinion must be driven by some 'unmentioned benefit' considering that, without denying the socio-cultural importance of the work of children in traditional societies, child labour constitutes an important additional income for the rest of the family, parents included. This aspect subjects children, their childhood and their growth to many dangers and deprives them of their childhood. The second paradigm builds exactly on these concerns and is focused on the protection of children. However, the fact that it is backed by the government as well as by NGOs casts some doubts on this paradigm, often being labelled an element of the Western 'conspiracy' against African societies.

If, on the one hand, the political choices of African States are certainly influenced by the *donor organizations*, on the other hand it is also true that, with the ratification of international standards, States commit themselves towards the international community. As regards the specific case of Mali, its Constitution of 25 February 1992 asserts in article 116 that 'As of the date of issuing, duly ratified or approved treaties and agreements assume an authority that is superior to laws, conditionally upon the application of the treaty or the agreement by the other party'.[40] The application of C182 requires the adoption of national measures aimed at the elimination of the worst forms of child labour. This becomes even more mandatory considering the existence of a real economic exploitation of children forced to obtain revenues for their parents or other persons.

The policies against the worst forms of child labour in Mali have been undertaken by the general mechanism for the fight against child labour. With a view to better understand them we shall examine both the legislative measures and those that have brought about the creation of administrative facilities or action programmes.

---

39 ILO Convention 182 was adopted through Order No. 00-006/P-RM, 9 February 2000.

40 Translation by the editors.

16.3.1.1 Legislative measures In the first place it should be noted that the Malian legislation does not contain a specific definition of the worst forms of child labour like the one contained in article 3 of C182. However, some of the categories listed in article 3 were already present in the existing laws, while others necessitated a reinterpretation of the existing regulation in some cases accompanied by the adoption of new texts.

As regards slavery and practices similar to slavery and forced labour (as defined in article 3(a), C182), article 6 of the Labour Code of 1992 establishes that 'forced or compulsory labour is absolutely prohibited. The term "forced or compulsory labour" includes all work or service performed under the threat of any penalties or which is not performed voluntarily by the individual'. Clauses (b) and (c) of article 3, C182 (concerning child prostitution and illicit activities), are echoed in article 50 of the Code on the Protection of the Child of June 2002, which considers the sexual exploitation of children and their involvement with organized crime as harmful to their health, development, physical and moral integrity. Finally, as to article 3(d) of C182 on hazardous child labour, section D 189-31 of the Labour Code contains an updated list of the tasks which are deemed to be dangerous and which may not be performed by children. Moreover, with regard to article 4 of C182 concerning the consultations with employers' and workers' organizations, the Malian authorities report that the different texts (the Labour Code and related norms) were adopted after consultations with the High Labour Council, consisting of 12 members, equally representing workers and employers.

Several other legislative texts have been revisited in the light of new practices developed in recent years. This is the case of the Criminal Code that tackles specifically the issue of child trafficking, defining it as 'all processes of the transfer of children within and outside a country in conditions which make them a marketable asset for at least one of the persons involved, whatever the purpose of the transfer'.[41] Child trafficking is punished as a penal offence, with sanctions ranging from five to twenty years of imprisonment. The same sanction, accompanied by the payment of a fine from 20,000 to one million francs is envisaged for the crime of paedophilia which comprises 'all acts of sexual penetration or contact of whatever kind perpetrated on minors under 13 years, as well as exposition and exploitation for commercial or tourist ends of pornographic pictures, films or drawings depicting one or more minors under the age of 13 years'[42] (article 228).

16.3.1.2 Administrative facilities and programmes of action In addition to the adoption of legal norms tackling the different aspects of the fight against child labour, the Malian authorities have put in place several administrative mechanisms and national programmes of action. These efforts are supported by the participation in different multilateral programmes.

Along these lines the most relevant facility is the Ministry for the Advancement of Women, Children and the Family created in 1997. The Ministry comprises a

---

41 Article 224 of Law No. 01-079, 20 August 2001 containing the Criminal Code of the Republic of Mali. Translation by the editors.

42 Translation by the editors.

National Directory for the Advancement of Children and the Family which includes among its goals the protection of children. Thus, the Ministry has contributed in rendering more visible the specific problems of children and in the inclusion of these issues into governmental policies. In this direction the Ministry and its partners have undertaken several sensitizing campaigns. For instance, during the World Day against Child Labour, several child workers are invited to talk about their condition. Furthermore, taking advantage of the organization of the African Cup in Mali in 2002, the government launched a campaign named 'Red Card to Child Labour'.

The implementation of C182 is mainly realized under the framework of the National Programme on the Fight against Child Labour.[43] It is through this programme that Mali participates in the IPEC Programme of the ILO.[44] Under this framework, several action programmes have been undertaken for the eradication of child labour, with a specific focus on four groups: child workers in rural areas (agriculture, animal breeding, fishing and forestry); child workers on gold-panning sites; child apprentices in dangerous professions in the informal economy (car mechanic, welding and smelting of metals, woodworking and leather manufacture, construction, transport and waste disposal); and girls working in urban areas (domestic service, street trades, entertainment industry, night clubs, bars, hotels and restaurants).[45]

The cooperation between the Malian authorities and the ILO under the IPEC framework has stimulated the starting-up of several other programmes in cooperation with national and international NGOs. These programmes are often financed by other States. With the contribution of the US, and of non-governmental organizations such as World Vision and Care International, a programme was launched in 2003 against the economic exploitation of children and their trafficking in the administrative regions of Ségou and Mopti, and in the District of Bamako. Similar activities are performed by 'WINROCK International' in the regions of Sikasso and Ségou.

Child trafficking is one of the problems attracting a large part of the economic resources deployed by the Malian government in the fights against child labour. The trafficking of children constitutes a highly lucrative activity for certain persons in Mali and neighbouring countries. The situation is so worrying that the Malian authorities had to adopt an emergency national plan of action in the fight against cross-border trafficking of children for the period 2000–01. This effort was followed by a similar plan for the period 2002–06. In the context of these action plans several research activities and sensitization campaigns have been carried out in partnership with different organisms such as UNICEF or the Canadian 'Aide à l'Enfance'.

Besides the issue of trans-border trafficking of children, street begging represents another delicate issue, given its links with religious circles. The sight of children engaged in begging has now become a constant part of the décor of the city of

---

43 Under the programme a national directive committee has been appointed which includes 12 ministries, 9 associations, different NGOs and UN agencies. See Periodical Report of Mali, March 2005, *supra* note 38, at 132.

44 The agreement protocol for this participation was signed in 1998 and renewed in 2001.

45 CEACR, Individual Direct Request concerning Convention No. 138: Mali 2006, *supra* note 33.

Bamako and of other cities in Mali. However, a distinction should be made between children who beg in order to help their indigent parents[46] and the Koranic students who are often exploited by their masters. As to this, a survey carried out by the NGO 'Mali Enjeu' in 1999 reported 1,404 cases of children under the age of 18 years, being forced to beg for the duration of their Koranic education.[47] Despite the different campaigns for the education of students as well as their masters, the phenomenon persists or even expands.

16.3.2 The limits of State action

Despite the efforts undertaken by the Malian political authorities in the fight against child labour, especially in its worst forms, the situation in Mali remains worrying and these difficulties risk compromising the success of governmental policies. Indeed, there is still a long way to go from the political declaration of intents to institutional reforms and the elimination of child labour.

In addition to underlining the positive outcomes of the Malian national policies in the field of child labour, it will also be useful to highlight the limits of these efforts so that government members may revise their strategies and methods of intervention.

16.3.2.1 Some positive outcomes The first positive outcome that needs to be mentioned is the ratification by Mali of numerous international legal instruments which have become part of the national legal system in virtue of article 116 of the Constitution of 25 February 1992.[48] In other words the protection accorded by these international instruments can be invoked before Malian judges. Their relevance, therefore, is not purely symbolic but also juridical, even if citizens have little knowledge of this circumstance or are unwilling to seize this opportunity.

Another positive outcome of the Malian political efforts in the fight against child labour are the actions taken against trans-border trafficking of children. After the adoption of an emergency plan of action on the elimination of child trafficking, Mali has signed cooperation agreements with Côte d'Ivoire (September 2000), Burkina Faso (June 2004), Senegal (July 2004) and Guinea (June 2005). These agreements

---

46 It should be noted that certain practices were strongly linked to traditional beliefs which can be considered as perverted in our days. For instance, after the birth of a child the tradition was to take him for a walk in order to pick up some coins. The scope of the behaviour was not to gain money, but was driven by the belief that this ritual would have protected the child from bad luck. In our days children are often exploited by their parents living in poor conditions. It may also happen that children are hired to other beggars in exchange for remuneration at the end of the day.

47 Periodical Report of Mali, March 2005, *supra* note 38, at 139.

48 In addition to C182 and C13 this is also the case of the African Charter on the Rights and Welfare of the Child of 1998, ratified through Order No. 98-008/P-RM of 3 April 1998; the Hague Convention on the Protection of Children and Cooperation in Respect of Intercountry Adoption of 2001 ratified through Order No. 01-033/P-RM of 7 April 2001; the United Nations Convention against Transnational Organized Crime and its Protocol to Prevent, Suppress and Punish Trafficking in Persons, especially Women and Children, ratified through Orders No. 02-09/P-RM and No. 02-10/P-RM, of 16 January 2002.

have led to the organization of different campaigns of control and repatriation of children who have fallen victim to trafficking. Different NGOs have participated in the creation of welcome centres for the victims of trafficking in the regions of Sikasso, Ségou and Mopti. Moreover, within smaller communities several sensitization campaigns have been organized and social networks have been established with the aim to 'identify the children and the traffickers, inform the security services in case of suspect persons, and inform the parents and the children about the ways of travelling outside the country'.[49]

Thanks to these efforts, 700 children were sent back to their families in 2005. However, the phenomenon persists, as can be inferred from the frequent announcements of Malian authorities concerning the dismantling of trafficking networks operating between Mali and the Ivory Coast. Of course, the number of groups that manage to escape detection remains unknown.

The CEACR notes that, according to a study carried out in Mali by the ILO/IPEC programme, 'since the launching of the IPEC programme (adopted following the signature of the Memorandum of Understanding in 2001), some 2,807 children (2,407 boys and 400 girls) have been removed from exploitative work'. According to the same report, between January 2001 and June 2005, 'some 1,307 children were removed from the worst forms of child labour in the agricultural and mining sectors and the informal economy. Over the same period, some 3,050 families and children benefited from vocational training measures and 1,500 children benefited from improved legal protection.'[50]

Finally, the instigation of forums for debate on the issue of child labour should be again highlighted as a positive outcome. Under this perspective, the National Programme on the Fight against Child Labour, in cooperation with different NGOs, has organized several discussion and training seminars on the topic of the eradication of child labour. Moreover, the sessions of the 'Children's Parliament' have become an important forum for a strong denunciation of practices of exploitation of children.

16.3.2.2 The limitations of governmental policies Despite the different positive results, governmental policies in Mali have suffered serious insufficiencies. Statistics measuring the nature, extent and evolution of the phenomenon of child labour are mostly unreliable.[51] The lack of data has rendered the adoption of effective measures in the fight against child labour rather problematic. Two main shortcomings may be identified in the policies of Malian government: an uncompleted process of normative production and unrealistic political choices.

The uncompleted process of normative production. This incompleteness is not a new phenomenon in the Malian legal history. Indeed, in several cases, norms adopted in different domains remain ineffective because of the lack of enforcement

---

49 Periodical Report of Mali, March 2005, *supra* note 38, at 135–6. Translation by the editors.

50 CEACR, Individual Direct Request concerning Convention No. 182: Mali 2006, *supra* note 3.

51 Republic of Mali, Ministère de l'Emploi et de la Formation Professionnelle, First Report, n.d., at 3.

regulation. The Malian Constitution defines the concepts of 'law' and 'regulation' and assumes that there are two types of regulations: enforcement regulations which permit the application of laws, and autonomous regulations. Quite often, laws make explicit reference to enforcement regulations, therefore their non-adoption is tantamount to an incomplete process of normative production. The 2005 Malian Report concerning the application of the UN Convention on the Rights of the Child clearly highlights that:

> Despite legal and regulatory efforts, certain measures remain to be taken in terms of harmonisation and application, thus hampering the effective implementation of the CRC. For instance, several executive decrees of the Code on the Protection of the Child have not been issued, the decree concerning the regulation of school attendance, the decrees of application of the law prohibiting children from engaging in begging.[52]

Moreover, no steps have been taken towards the enforcement of article 66 of the Code on the Protection of the Child, which provides for the nomination of a delegate among the State representatives at the eight administrative regions and at the District of Bamako, whose function is to protect the interests of children. According to article 67 of the Code on the Protection of the Child, the delegate may intervene each time the child's health or physical and moral integrity is harmed or risks being harmed because of his/her life conditions, the activities performed, or the ill treatment to which he/she is subjugated.

The situation created by this form of 'disability' of the law seems to relieve certain categories of Malian citizens who despise or at best ignore the legislation concerning child labour. In their eyes this is another example of the State's incapacity to enforce enacted regulation.

The application of C182 is also compromised by the fact that the Malian authorities, except for the labour inspectors,[53] have not created any other appropriate surveillance mechanism. This constitutes a lack of conformity with article 5 of the Convention. The point has been raised by the CEACR in the individual direct requests submitted to Mali. Referring to the comments made to Mali under the Labour Inspection Convention, 1947 (No. 81) the Committee noted that the efficiency of labour inspection in Mali is impaired by the derisory remuneration of labour inspectors, and by the inadequacy of the resources made available to the staff of the inspection services. Among the difficulties of a practical nature in the application of the Convention were also mentioned the shortcomings of the public transportation system, the absence of any transport facilities for the professional travel of labour inspectors, and the derisory level of fines for violations of the labour legislation.[54]

---

52 Periodical Report of Mali, March 2005, *supra* note 38, at 9. Translation by the editors.

53 Concerning C182, inspection visits may be carried out either by surprise or upon a complaint. Employers may be asked to keep a list of employed children or young workers to be exhibited to labour inspectors. During inspection visits, the working conditions of children are checked as well as the record of their hours of work, holidays and wages.

54 CEACR, Individual Direct Request concerning Convention No. 182: Mali 2004, *supra* note 3.

One may think that the concerns of the Committee remain well-grounded despite the indications of the Malian authorities concerning the establishment of focal points in each regional labour inspectorate and their provision 'through the ILO/IPEC programme, with transport facilities so that they can inspect establishments likely to employ children'.[55]

Within the context of internationally supported programmes, on several occasions the Malian government has embarked upon pre-packaged reform policies without taking into consideration the social and economic situation of the country.

Unrealistic political choices: the issue of the 'aides-familiales'. In Mali, the phenomenon of the employment of young girls between 12 and 20 years as housemaids in families in urban areas is called *'aides-familiales'*. It constitutes a widespread practice involving almost every family in the urban area of Bamako. However, the phenomenon raises several problematic issues concerning both domestic servants and their employers. As to the *aides-familiales* and the regime of protection of their rights, the most frequent problems emerge in terms of premature employment, lack of precision of contractual duties that are often agreed upon orally, ill-treatment and abuse, non-payment of wages, etc. This situation calls for a more effective protection of the rights of this category of child workers, especially if the problem is considered within the framework of C182, article 3(d) concerning 'work which, by its nature or the circumstances in which it is carried out, is likely to harm the health, safety or morals of children'. Along this line of reasoning the CEACR has communicated to the Malian authorities its concern over 'the situation of girl migrants, who leave rural areas to work in domestic service in urban areas and who, according to some sources, work a 16-hour day on average for very low or non-existent wages, are often subjected to rape, ill treatment and even prostitution'.[56]

Considering the urgent need to put in place a protective regime for children employed as domestic workers, the steps taken by the Malian government do not seem to be realistic. Although the definition of domestic workers provided in Decree No. 96-178/P-RM of 16 June 1996 is applicable also to the *aides-familiales*, the provisions concerning general conditions of employment and remuneration are not compatible with the social and economic situation in Mali. According to article D.86-1 of the decree, 'domestic workers are the persons employed at the private residence of their employer in order to perform part of, or all the domestic tasks'. The *aides-familiales* are included in this category of workers. In addition the Decree categorizes domestic workers according to their monthly wages, which range from 21.936 francs CFA for the first category to 35.049 francs CFA for the seventh category. Considering that the minimum wage paid by the State for this type of work is fixed at 28.460 francs CFA and that the majority of the *aides-familiales* are employed in middle- to low-income families, some concerns may arise over the lack of realism of the amounts established in the Decree. These considerations have generated a lot of confusion among inspectors and other agents dealing with

---

55 CEACR, Individual Direct Request concerning Convention No. 182: Mali 2006, *supra* note 3.

56 CEACR, Individual Direct Request concerning Convention No. 182: Mali 2004, *supra* note 3.

the issue of child labour on whether the *aides-familiales* are actually covered by the Decree. Moreover, Decree No. 96-178/P-RM requires the issuing of a hiring letter, the deposit of a copy of the employment contract at the labour inspectorate, the grant of a long-service bonus, the establishment of the length of working hours, etc. Considering these requirements, it can be held that almost all employers of *aides-familiales* in Mali behave contrary to the law.

Even NGOs, considered as the most assiduous supporters of the rights of the *aides-familiales*, believe that the Decree 'is inadequate and cannot be objectively applied to the real situation of the aides-familiales and to the economic conditions of their employers'.[57]

The issue of the *aides-familiales* has become a delicate social problem in Mali and therefore should be treated as such. Consequently, the debate on this issue that currently involves almost exclusively the administrative services and the NGOs should be tackled on a larger basis by involving also the employers' category. This may be a good opportunity for the elaboration of a legal framework for the *aides-familiales*, one that is more adequate to their real situation.

However, there are some delicate aspects that need to be emphasized. In the first place, despite governmental efforts to stimulate development and employment in Mali, families in the urban areas constitute at the moment the only suppliers of employment opportunities for thousands of young girls moving to the city in search of better wages and living perspectives. For the time being Mali lacks a formal market that would permit the absorption of this workforce. In the second place, notwithstanding the constitutional and conventional commitments to the protection of the rights of women and children, social relations in Mali are still governed, to a great extent by the traditional statutes – although with some transformations in the urban areas. Once entering the family of their employer, the *aides-familiales* are integrated in this system which makes them 'part of the family'. However, the 'integration' within the employer's family is often limited to an ambiguous status which is not always favourable to the *aides-familiales*. Therefore, in the case of the *aides-familiales* the employment relationship between the parties is governed by a social contract presenting imprecisions and shaded areas that each party tries to drag to its own advantage: the *aide-familiale* may be asked to perform all kinds of tasks and, in exchange, in addition to a salary, he/she may also benefit from different forms of aid and protection. A similar type of relationship is established between the *srougas* (manual workers) and the families in which they are employed in the rural areas. Often the relationship between the *srougas* and their employers is of a tutorial nature.

The challenge is not to give way to the temptation of overregulation while trying to guarantee that the *aides-familiales* be no more exploited by the employers. Policies inspired by both social imprint and rules of modern law are clearly conceivable.

---

57 K. Sangaré and M. Danté, Recueil de Textes Juridiques Applicables aux Aides-Familiales, Bamako, APAF MUSO-DANBE, July 2002, at 12. Translation by the editors.

16.4 Concluding remarks

After the publication of the above-mentioned survey on child labour in Mali in the communiqué of 11 April 2007, the Council of Ministers made several recommendations concerning the intensification of campaigns aimed at awakening public opinion on the child labour issue; strengthened measures towards the prevention and the repression of violations of the labour Code provisions; the integration of the elimination of child labour within the strategic framework of the fight against poverty; and increased efforts towards the education of children.[58] These proposals reveal all the above-mentioned difficulties encountered by the State in the accomplishment of its obligations in the fight against child labour. This point is confirmed by the fact that the government became acquainted with the report almost two years after it had been carried out. However, the communiqué of the Council of Ministers makes it clear that 'a distinction should be made between the socialization of children by making them work in the family context, which forms part of our customs and social habits, and the employment of children for merely commercial ends and without any educational purpose'.[59] Once again one can discern the unease of governmental policies trapped between international conventional obligations and the pressures of powerful Western donors on the one hand, and the persisting attachment of the population to the traditional customs on the other, at the cost of the violation of existing laws on the protection of children. Unfortunately this is a common characteristic of all African States.

Nevertheless, the cooperative approach favoured by the ILO instead of the sanction approach not only raises the problem of the effectiveness of international judicial instruments, but at the same time sheds light on the difficulties encountered by African States in facing problems emerging within their societies.

The elimination of child labour, especially in its worst forms, is undoubtedly linked to the improvement of the living conditions of families so that they can meet the needs of their children and guarantee their education. In order to ensure their effective application, ILO Convention 182 and the national legislation on child labour should therefore be framed in the general social dynamics with all other components. Indeed, law is not an isolated phenomenon, but a social product, which is nonetheless capable to guide the society according to the chosen model.

---

58 L'Essor, no. 15931, 12 April 2007, at 4.
59 *Ibid*. Translation by the editors.

Chapter 17

The Implementation of ILO Child Labour Standards in Asia: Overview and Selected Issues

Ravindra Pratap[1]

17.1 Introduction

The implementation of ILO child labour standards in Asia has takes various forms with varying degrees of effectiveness: Asia is a region of various cultures, customs and identities. Bonded children are delivered in repayment of a loan or other favours granted, real or imaginary, usually to the parents or the guardians of the child. Having a help in the household of middle- and upper-class families is a historically embedded practice in almost all Asian countries. The sight of children pushing carts, carrying garbage bags or toiling on top of smoking dumps is unfortunately one of the most common sights in Asia. Armed conflicts increase the number of orphans and sometimes involve children directly as combatants. Traffickers of children feed largely on the desire of poor families for economic and personal advancement through migration for work.

This paper covers two aspects of the implementation of ILO child labour standards in Asia. It first gives an overview of the implementation and then discusses common implementation issues. While it is not possible to discuss the implementation of ILO child labour standards in each Asian country, an attempt has been made to cover all Asian regions in discussing the implementation of ILO child labour standards.

17.2 Overview of the implementation of the ILO child labour standards in Asia

17.2.1 The effectuation of ILO standards into municipal law

17.2.1.1 Afghanistan While the political situation in Afghanistan continues to unfold, the principle of the effective abolition of child labour is recognized in its Constitution, legislation, judicial decisions and collective agreements. Ratification

---

1 The author is grateful to Rahmatullah Khan for his reference to this project and to Marco Pertile for his invaluable documentary assistance. Mistakes are the author's only.

of the Minimum Age Convention, 1973 (No. 138),[2] and the Worst Forms of Child Labour, 1999 (No. 182), is currently in process. The new Constitution (2004) provides that education for all shall be free and compulsory. The Labour Code of Afghanistan prohibits the worst forms of child labour. The types of work covered are: operating big/heavy machinery, working in coalmines and chemical laboratories and drug trafficking. In practice children are involved in street begging, the army and agriculture.[3] With regard to the worst forms of child labour, sale and/or trafficking, debt bondage, serfdom, forced or compulsory labour, forced recruitment for armed conflict, prostitution, illicit activities, in particular production and trafficking of drugs and the sale of body organs all exist in Afghanistan for both boys and girls. However, child pornography does not exist.[4]

17.2.1.2 Bangladesh In 2001 Bangladesh ratified the Worst Forms of Child Labour Convention, 1999 (No. 182), and some references are made to its application.[5] The main challenges in promoting this principle and right are as follows: harmonization and interpretation of existing labour laws with regard to the minimum age for admission into employment; implementation and enforcement of the laws, particularly in the informal sector where child labour mainly occurs; the magnitude of child labour, particularly hazardous child labour (currently estimated to be around 1.3 million); and the multi-sectoral and complex nature of the child labour problem such as difficulties of cooperation among the large number of agencies, departments and actors, and the high incidence of poverty leading to child labour.

In Bangladesh, the principle of the effective abolition of child labour is recognized in the Constitution and legislation. There is no national policy/plan aimed at the effective abolition of child labour. National legislation does not establish a general minimum age for admission to employment, nor does it cover the following: work performed in a family-owned or operated enterprise; work performed in enterprises below a certain size; home work; domestic service; self-employed work; commercial agriculture; family and small-scale agriculture; or light work. However, work performed in export processing zones is covered and no child under 14 years of age is allowed to work. Hazardous work is defined in section 87 of the Factories Act, 1965, which makes a reference to dangerous operations. The minimum age for engaging in this type of work is 18 years for both boys and girls. The age for compulsory schooling is 10 years for both boys and girls, with a general requirement of five years of instruction.[6] Specific measures have been implemented or are envisaged to bring

---

2 See B. Boockmann, 'The Effect of ILO Minimum Age Conventions on Child Labour and School Attendance', Centre for European Economic Research, Discussion Paper No. 4-52.

3 *Review of Annual Reports under the Follow-Up to the ILO Declaration on Fundamental Principles and Rights at Work, Part II*, ILO, 2005, 208.

4 *Ibid.* Further, see Afghanistan Independent Human Rights Commission, An Overview on Situation of Child Labourers in Afghanistan, available at <http://www.aihrc.org.af/rep_child_labour_2006.pdf>.

5 *Review of Annual Reports under the Follow-Up to the ILO Declaration on Fundamental Principles and Rights at Work, Part II*, ILO, 2006, 214.

6 *Review of Annual Reports*, 2005, *supra* note 3, 229.

about the effective abolition of child labour: these measures are in the areas of legal reform, inspection/monitoring mechanisms, penal sanctions, civil or administrative sanctions, special institutional machinery, free compulsory education, employment creation/income generation, social assistance, child rehabilitation following removal from work, vocational and skills training for young workers, awareness raising/ advocacy, international cooperation programmes or projects, and other measures. Special attention is given to the 5–14 age group in sectors like manufacture of *bidi* (local cigarettes), construction, domestic work and leather/tanneries. Employers' and workers' organizations are involved in the implementation of action programmes. They are also active members of different committees such as the Tripartite Consultative Council, the National Steering Committee, Subcommittee and Monitoring Committee. Apart from the ILO, the government is working with the US Agency for International Development (USAID) towards the eradication of hazardous child labour. In relation to the abolition of child labour, the government records information on the number of children withdrawn from child labour as well as information regarding the number of ex-child labourers pursuing formal or non-formal education. However, there are no sanctions applied to users of child labour. The government also undertakes surveys that provide statistical information on the extent and/or nature of child work. The last survey was undertaken in 2003 and the results are presented separately on the basis of age group; from 5 to 14 years. During the last census carried out in 2001, the lowest age of persons for which questions were asked about economic activity was five.[7]

Child labour exists in Bangladesh. More than 76 per cent of the Bangladeshi population lives in rural areas and half of them live below the poverty line. Extreme forms of poverty play a crucial role in driving children to work for a living. Total child workers of ages 5–14 are estimated at about 6.3 million, of which about 3.8 million are boys and 2.5 million are girls. Only 6 per cent are employed in the formal sector and the rest, 94 per cent, in the informal sector. Of all the working children, 83 per cent are found in the rural areas and the remaining 17 per cent in urban areas. The government has been trying to eliminate child labour through the IPEC programme since 1995.[8] The government will formulate a national child labour policy and has already drafted a new Labour Code, which is now under consideration for approval from the appropriate authority. The Eradication of Hazardous Child Labour project, supported by USAID, will provide training and assistance to 10,000 working children and microcredit to 5,000 parents of child labourers in the Dhaka and Chittagong Metropolitan areas, in particular in the field of shops, factories, bangle-making, rickshaw/van-pulling, fisheries, book binding, welding and automobile workshops.[9] The main obstacles encountered in Bangladesh with respect to the effective abolition of child labour are: lack of adequate awareness and education (skill development); poverty; lack of adequate effective rehabilitation programmes; and lack of adequate institutional and logistic support. There is a need for ILO technical cooperation to

---

7 *Ibid.*, 230–31.
8 *Ibid.*, 230.
9 *Ibid.*, 231.

facilitate the effective abolition of child labour,[10] particularly in employment creation, skills training and income generation, also special programmes for the elimination of the worst forms of child labour and social protection systems.

17.2.1.3 China China ratified Convention 138 in 1999 and Convention 182 in 2002. New regulations ban the employment of children under the age of 16, imposing fines for violations and requiring employers to check workers' identification cards. There are other indications that China is increasingly willing to address the issue of child labour. There is recognition that there are children in need of special protection measures, including street children, children of migrants and those vulnerable to trafficking. China still faces a number of challenges in child protection due to disparities between urban and rural areas and a culture that favours boys over girls. Moreover, the problem of child labour may spread with the rapid growth of labour-intensive industries. IPEC has been working in China since 2000 to combat trafficking in children and women and in 2004 launched a new project to prevent trafficking in girls and young women for labour exploitation. China was also represented at the first ILO regional capacity-building training course on child labour data collection, together with the inter-agency research project 'Understanding Children's Work' (UCW), held in Bangkok in 2004. This reflects a growing willingness by China to learn from experiences in other countries.[11]

China has 350 million children, accounting for 20 per cent of the world's total. However, in the past 25 years, China has taken more people out of poverty and enrolled more children in school than any other country. There is thus a strong inference that this has also had a dramatic impact on child labour in China.[12] Much of the world's progress in alleviating extreme poverty has occurred in China, which dramatically reduced large-scale poverty through specific government reforms and rapid economic growth. China's reforms began in agriculture. Since poverty in China was mainly a rural phenomenon, growth in the rural sector has been key to reducing poverty levels. When rural economic growth slowed down in the second half of the 1980s and the late 1990s, China saw slower progress in poverty reduction, accompanied by widening inequalities.[13]

17.2.1.4 India India has ratified neither the Minimum Age Convention, 1973 (No. 138), nor the Worst Forms of Child Labour Convention, 1999 (No. 182).[14] The practice of bonded child labour violates ILO Convention 29 concerning Forced or Compulsory Labour, ILO Convention 105 concerning the Abolition of Forced Labour and the International Covenant on Civil and Political Rights, to all of which India is a party. The adoption of ILO Convention 182 on Worst Forms of Child Labour has tremendously raised the social and governmental awareness and commitment to this

---

10 *Review of Annual Reports* 2006, *supra* note 5, 214.

11 *Ibid.*, 13.

12 Global Report under the Follow-Up to the ILO Declaration on Fundamental Principles and Rights at Work, 95th Session 2006, § 48.

13 *Ibid.*, para. 49.

14 *Review of Annual Reports* 2006, *supra* note 5, 247.

issue. Although India is not a party to the Convention, the government has passed an order restraining government officers from employing children as domestic workers. In addition, under the Indian Penal Code, rape, extortion, causing grievous hurt, assault, kidnapping, abduction, wrongful confinement, buying or disposing of people as slaves, and unlawful compulsory labour are criminal offences, punishable by up to ten years' imprisonment and fines.

In India, the principle of the effective abolition of child labour is recognized in the Constitution,[15] in legislation and in judicial decisions. However, this principle is not found in collective agreements. The government has a national policy on child labour, enunciated in 1987, which contains an action plan for tackling the problem of child labour. Indian legislation does not establish a general minimum age for admission to employment. Laws/regulations do exist with the aim of eliminating all of the worst forms of child labour. The following worst forms of child labour are believed to exist or are suspected to exist in India for both boys and girls: sale and/or trafficking; debt bondage; serfdom; forced or compulsory labour; prostitution and pornography. However, forced recruitment for armed conflict and illicit activities, in particular production and trafficking of drugs, do not exist in India. Under the Juvenile Justice Act 1986, cruelty to juveniles and withholding the earnings of a juvenile are criminal offences, punishable with up to three years' imprisonment and fines. Debt bondage violates the Bonded Labour System (Abolition) Act 1976, and the Children (Pledging of Labour) Act 1933. This is true even in those rare instances where no advantage has been taken of the child; the Bonded Labour System (Abolition) Act 1976 includes within its ambit work for 'nominal wages', defined by the Supreme Court as wages less than the minimum wage.[16] Since the Indian Supreme Court's decision of December 1996 in *M.C. Mehta* v. *State of Tamil Nadu & Others*,[17] States have been obliged to identify children employed in worst forms of child labour. Other child labour prohibition laws include the Child Labour (Prohibition & Regulation) Act 1986, which prohibits the employment of children below the age of 14 in 13 occupations and 57 processes, including cloth printing, dyeing and weaving and, as of 1999, sericulture processing and the making of *zari* (gold thread). The law does not apply to children working for their immediate families (parents or siblings) or in schools that the government has established, financed or recognized. In addition, the Factories Act 1948, forbids the employment of children below the age of 14 in

---

15 The Indian Constitution was amended by the Constitution (86th) Amendment Act, 2002, to make education for children in the age group of 6–14 years a fundamental right and reads as follows: 'Insertion of new article 21A. The State shall provide free and compulsory education to all children of the age of six to fourteen years in such manner as the State may, by law, determine; Substitution of new article for article 45. The State shall endeavour to provide early childhood care and education for all children until they complete the age of six years; New clause to article 51A after the clause (j) i.e. clause (k) imposes on a parent or guardian to provide opportunities for education to his child or, as the case may be, ward between the age of six and fourteen years.'

16 Government of Tamil Nadu, District-wise Integrated Statement of Bonded Labour Identification, Release, Prosecution, Rehabilitation and Expenditure Incurred Report for the Month of February 2002, 6.

17 Supreme Court Cases, Vol. 6, 1996, 756.

all factories, and allows 14- and 15-year-olds to work only with a medical certificate of fitness. Otherwise, children aged 14 and older are not protected, although, like all workers, they are covered by the Bonded Labour System (Abolition) Act 1976.

Specific measures or programmes of action have been implemented in India to bring about the effective abolition of child labour, namely: legal reform; inspection/ monitoring mechanisms; penal sanctions; civil or administrative sanctions; free compulsory education; employment creation/income generation; social assistance; child rehabilitation following removal from work; vocational and skills training for young workers; awareness raising/advocacy and international cooperation programmes or projects. The government works with multilateral agencies other than the ILO, bilateral donors and/or other organizations to combat child labour. The government records the following information in relation to the abolition of child labour: the number of children withdrawn from child labour; the number of ex-child labourers pursuing formal or non-formal education; and sanctions applied to users of child labour.[18] The provisions of the Child Labour (Prohibition and Regulation) Act 1986 are enforced by the governments of the States and the union territories. In 1993, the government set up an autonomous human rights body, the National Human Rights Commission (NHRC).[19] The government has undertaken special measures for the abolition of child labour and, to give some examples, the national child labour projects, grant-in-aid projects and projects under IPEC have yielded encouraging results. Civil society organizations have also played an important role. Provisions of midday meals and stipends have been important motivational factors for parents to send their children to the special schools. The Parliament of India has amended the Constitution to make free and compulsory education a fundamental right to all children (both girls and boys) for the age group of 6 years in 2002. Poverty, unemployment and illiteracy are the main obstacles in realizing the principles of effective abolition of child labour. The government does not see a need for new or continued cooperation with the ILO to assist in the effective abolition of child labour. The ILO/IPEC Programme is approved until 31 December 2006.[20] The government has proposed to expand the National Child Labour Project to all endemic districts during the 11th Plan period.[21]

---

18 *Review of Annual Reports 2006*, *supra* note 5, 247.

19 While the NHRC can encourage law enforcement, with limited powers and resources, it cannot replace it. And, unlike a civil court's ruling, its recommendations are not binding, although the Commission has been able to pressure the government into complying with its recommendations on many occasions. In addition, the NHRC has the powers of a civil, not criminal, court. The NHRC's role in child labour rehabilitation is important, but it is no substitute for regular law enforcement.

20 According to the Representative of India: 'The new instruments should not address the problem of the worst forms of child labour purely in a political and civil rights context. The Convention should combine in a balanced manner elements relating to the eradication of poverty, unemployment and illiteracy.' ILO Convention 182 – (ILC) Travaux préparatoires, para. 25.

21 The Scheme is operational in 250 districts in 20 States, where 7,328 special schools are functioning for children withdrawn from work. *The Hindu* (Delhi), 12 June 2007, 12.

17.2.1.5 Indonesia Indonesia ratified Convention 182 in 2000.[22] The CEACR acknowledges ICFTU's indication that the trafficking of persons, including for the purpose of prostitution, is widespread. The ICFTU also states that as many as 20 per cent of the 5 million migrant workers who leave Indonesia to work in other countries are victims of trafficking. The ICFTU further indicates that there are reports of the sale of children in exchange for promises of work and money. The government has indicated that a draft Bill on trafficking is under preparation.[23] A five-year National Action Plan for Abolishing Woman and Child Trafficking was endorsed through Presidential Decree No. 88/2002 dated 30 December 2002. The Plan's objectives are to reduce by half the number of child victims of trafficking by 2013. The National Action Plan aims at: (a) ensuring the existence of legal norms and actions against traffickers of women and children; (b) guaranteeing the social rehabilitation and reintegration of victims of trafficking; (c) preventing all forms of trafficking; and (d) developing cooperation and coordination between institutions at the national and international level that deal with the trafficking of women and children.[24]

The IPEC programme in Indonesia has been working closely together with the ILO Jakarta office and other technical cooperation projects in Indonesia. Early in 2006, IPEC and ILO offices collaborated on a youth employment project to implement a major survey on the relation of early school dropout and child labour with future performance in the labour market. The results of the survey provided valuable information that has been utilized by ILO Jakarta in developing programme concepts related to child labour and youth employment. This is only one example of a global cooperation pattern that includes IPEC, the ILO's Youth Employment Network, the ILO's Youth Employment Team and other parts of the Employment Sector.[25] While access to education in Indonesia has been improving, poverty and other factors still result in many children dropping out of school to join the labour force. The ILO is running a number of projects with partners in the country and it was believed that a better understanding of parents' attitudes would improve the efficiency of communication and awareness-raising.[26]

17.2.1.6 Nepal Nepal ratified the Worst Forms of Child Labour Convention in 2002.[27] The CEACR notes that, by virtue of sections 2(a) and 16(4) of the Children's Act, it is prohibited to involve a child under 16 in the sale, distribution or trafficking of alcohol, narcotics or other drugs. The Committee also reminds the government that, by virtue of article 3(c) of the Convention, the use, procuring or offering of a child under 18 for illicit activities, in particular the production and trafficking of drugs, is considered to be one of the worst forms of child labour. It therefore requests

---

22 CEACR: Individual Observation concerning Convention No. 182: Indonesia 2005, Doc. No. (ilolex): 062005IDN182. CEACR, General Observations, Individual Observations, Individual Direct Requests on Convention 182, 38.

23 *Ibid.*, 38.

24 *Ibid.*, 39.

25 ILO-IPEC, *IPEC Action Against Child Labour*, Highlights 2006, 15.

26 *Ibid.*, 19.

27 CEACR, Individual Direct Request concerning Convention No. 182: Morocco 2006, 1034.

the government to indicate the measures taken or envisaged to ensure that the use, procuring or offering of a child under 18 for the production and trafficking of drugs is prohibited under national legislation. The Committee notes that, by virtue of section 3 of the Begging (Prohibition) Act 1962 it is an offence to ask or encourage a child under 16 to beg in a street, junction or any other places. The Committee has encouraged the government to raise the age to 18 years. The Committee also observes that article 20(2) of the Constitution provides that a minor shall not be employed in any factory or mine, or in any other hazardous work, and that sections 2(a) and 3 of the Child Labour (Prohibition and Regulation) Act prohibit the employment of children under 16 years of age in hazardous work or enterprises listed in the schedule which includes hotels, casinos, restaurants, *bidi* manufacturing, the carpet weaving industry, construction industry, drawing rickshaws or pushcarts, or the undertaking of underground or underwater work. Section 43(1) and (2) of the Labour Rules of 1993 also provides for a detailed list of hazardous machines, and operations that shall not be performed by child workers under 16 years of age. Section 39 of the Labour Rules provides that males below 19 shall not lift, carry or move any load of more than 25 kg (20 kg for females under 18). The Committee has further noted that the government indicates that it is fully aware that national legislation is not in line with the Convention.[28]

17.2.1.7 The Philippines Republic Acts Nos 7610 and 7658 are considered to be landmark child protection laws. The Republic Act No. 9231 of the Philippines provides for the elimination of the worst forms of child labour and affords stronger protection for the working child. According to section 12-D (prohibition against the worst forms of child labour), no child shall be engaged in the worst forms of child labour, which refer to all forms of slavery as defined under the 'Anti-trafficking in Persons Act 2003', or to practices similar to slavery such as sale and trafficking of children, debt bondage, serfdom and forced or compulsory labour, including recruitment of children for use in armed conflict.[29]

17.2.1.8 Sri Lanka Sri Lanka ratified the Convention 182 in 2001.[30] Section 360A of the Penal Code, as amended by Act No. 22 of 1995 and Act No. 29 of 1998, provides that whoever:

> … (2) procures or attempts to procure any person under 16 years of age to leave Sri Lanka (whether with or without the consent of such persons) with a view to illicit sexual intercourse with any person outside Sri Lanka, or removes or attempts to remove from Sri Lanka any such person (whether with or without the consent of such person) for the said purpose; (3) procures or attempts to procure any person of whatever age to leave

---

28 CEACR, Individual Direct Request concerning Convention No. 182: Nepal 2006, Doc. No. (ilolex): 092006NPL182.

29 *Review of Annual Reports* 2005, *supra* note 3, 187. See also Concepcion Sardaña, 'Combating Child Labour in Philippines', available at <http://www.adb.org/Doc.s/Events/2002/SocialProtection/sardana_paper.pdf>.

30 CEACR, Individual Observation concerning Convention No. 182: Sri Lanka 2005, Doc. No. (ilolex): 062005LKA182.

Sri Lanka (with or without the consent of such person) with intent that such person may become the inmate of, or frequent, a brothel elsewhere, or removes or attempts to remove from Sri Lanka any such person for the said purpose; (4) brings or attempts to bring into Sri Lanka any person under 16 years of age with a view to illicit sexual intercourse with any other person in Sri Lanka or outside Sri Lanka, commits the offence of procuration and shall, on conviction, be punished with imprisonment for a term of not less than two years and not exceeding ten years and may also be punished with a fine.

Section 360B of the Penal Code provides penalties for the sexual exploitation of children below 18 years (imprisonment for a term not less than five years and not exceeding 20 years and possibly a fine too). Furthermore, section 288A of the Penal Code (Amendment) Act No. 29 of 1998 makes provision to penalize any person who knowingly hires, employs, persuades, uses, induces or coerces a child to procure any person for illicit sexual intercourse (imprisonment for a term not less than five years and not exceeding seven years and possible liability to a fine as well).[31] The Committee observes that, while the Sri Lankan legislation appears to be in line with the Convention, the commercial sexual exploitation of children under 18 is a problem in Sri Lanka.[32]

17.2.1.9 Thailand In Thailand, the principle of the effective abolition of child labour is recognized in the Constitution, legislation and judicial decisions. In 2001, Thailand ratified the Worst Forms of Child Labour Convention.[33] There is a national policy/plan aimed at ensuring the effective abolition of child labour. National legislation establishes a general minimum age for admission to employment of 15 years for boys and girls, which covers light work, work performed in export processing zones and work performed in enterprises below a certain size. The minimum age for admission to employment in the fisheries sector (at sea) is 16 years, while for dock work it is 18 years. However, national legislation does not cover work performed in enterprises below a certain size, homework, domestic service, self-employed work, commercial agriculture, or family and small-scale agriculture. Hazardous work is not defined in national legislation, but the minimum age for engaging in this type of work is 18 years for both boys and girls. In view of bringing about the effective abolition of child labour, the following measures have been implemented to enforce minimum age(s) for employment: legal reform, inspection/monitoring mechanisms, penal sanctions, civil or administrative sanctions, free compulsory education, social assistance (such as stipends, subsidies, vouchers), child rehabilitation following removal from work, vocational and skills training for young workers, awareness raising/advocacy, and international cooperation programmes/projects.[34]

17.2.1.10 Conclusion Thus, with the exception of India, one of the major child labour countries, ILO child labour standards, mainly Conventions 138 and 182, have been implemented in national laws. The implementation has taken various forms

---

31 *Ibid.*
32 *Ibid.*
33 ILO, *The Effective Abolition of Child Labour*, Geneva, ILO, 2004, 130.
34 *Ibid.*, 131.

depending upon differences in the national legal systems, constitutional guarantees and judicial systems, resulting in varying degrees of effectiveness of ILO child labour standards in eradicating child labour. For instance, in Thailand legislation excludes work performed in enterprises below a certain size, homework; domestic service, self-employed work, commercial agriculture, and family and small-scale agriculture, and hazardous work remains undefined. And the national law of Nepal is not in conformity with Convention 182. Practical difficulties also plague the implementation of Convention 182 in Sri Lanka. The case of China, however, is noteworthy, and its linking of education to eligibility for employment sets an example for other Asian countries.

Among the several remedies discussed and employed for the more effective implementation of ILO child labour standards is the use of trade sanctions. Besides being of dubious legality generally[35] and under WTO law, such measures have been found to be ineffective or even counterproductive. The demand for eliminating child labour and enforcing labour standards through trade is 'an attempt to raise the stakes for developing countries'.[36] It cannot be denied, however, that there is a need to strengthen the enforcement and monitoring mechanism of the ILO by universal ratification of its core conventions, particularly the Minimum Age Convention (No. 138) and the Worst Forms of Child Labour Convention (No. 182). While the need for more intensive ILO technical cooperation is generally recognized, it is unlikely to produce optimal results in the absence of a complementary participation of other agents, such as international organizations and NGOs, to which we now turn.

17.2.2 The role of international organizations and NGOs in the national implementation of ILO standards

17.2.2.1 Bangladesh Given the relative governmental ineffectiveness and weak enforcement mechanisms to combat the menace of child labour, NGOs have started playing an increasing role in stimulating public concern about child labour. The Bangladesh Garment Manufacturers' and Exporters' Association (BGMEA) signed a Memorandum of Understanding with the ILO and UNICEF in 1995. The BGMEA

---

35 R. Pratap, 'Sovereign Economic Freedom and Interests of Other States', in Patel (ed.), *India and International Law*, Leiden: Martinus Nijhoff, 2005, 127.

36 'Child Labour in South Asia: Are Trade Sanctions the Answer?', Briefing Paper, Centre for International Trade, Economics & Environment, 2003, No. 3, 1. See also K. Bagwell, P.C. Mavroidis and R.W. Staiger, 'Symposium: The Boundaries of the WTO: It's a Question of Market Access', *American Journal of International Law*, Vol. 96, 2002, 56. On India's experience with trade sanctions and their impact on the rural shrimp-farming community, see R. Pratap, *India at the WTO Dispute Settlement System*, New Delhi: Manak, 2004, chapter IV.8. 'The only way in which the issue of social and labour rights can be once more given precedence in an increasingly socially disembedded world economy is through political engagement with the forces of globalization: the World Bank, the International Monetary Fund, and the World Trade Organization.' S. Toor, 'Child Labour in Pakistan: Coming of Age in the New World Order', *Annals of the American Academy of Political and Social Science*, Vol. 575, 2001, 194; S. Chaulia, 'Social Clause in WTO', *Economic and Political Weekly*, Vol. 37, 2002, 613.

successfully identified an estimated 10,546 child labourers from garment factories. These children have been withdrawn and rehabilitated to schooling programmes. After withdrawing the children below the age of 14 years, UNICEF, ILO and BGMEA have jointly provided non-formal education, skills training, part-time employment in light work and a subsistence stipend to compensate for their income loss. Following the tremendous success of the first phase of this programme, in 2000 BGMEA signed a second Memorandum of Understanding with the same partners. Under this component, BGMEA has given job training to 900 students through local NGOs, ILO and UNICEF. They are also providing skills training on tailoring, embroidery, garment-machine maintenance and wool-knitting to 200 students.[37] With the support of BGMEA, the ILO Dhaka Office has undertaken two projects for the former child labour students. Under the projects, in 2004, over 1,400 students were given skills training and 100 of their older family members were provided microcredit, ranging from Tk2,000 to Tk10,000 (about US$34 to US$170), for income generation. Moreover, the Underprivileged Children Education Programme (UCEP) and SUIROVI, two NGOs, along with Singer Bangladesh (a national company) have provided skills training to the students. As of July 2000, a total of 1,149 have received skills training and 56 families have received microcredit.[38] However, the Bangladesh Mukto Sramic Federation notes that despite the fact that the government, trade unions, NGOs and other social organizations are trying to eliminate child labour, the problem is acute and requires many initiatives. While the labour law does not allow children to be employed in dangerous work/jobs, etc., in reality a large number of children are still engaged in hazardous jobs.[39]

17.2.2.2 India As awareness on the issue of child labour was generated, largely by actions of activists against bonded child labour in carpet industries[40] and sports goods manufacturing from the late 1980s, there is an observable decrease in the incidence of child labour in these industries in the regions targeted by the campaigns, but it is possible that child labour is still practised in new places where subcontractors have moved. The government maintains that opening transitional schools for working children and distributing anti-child labour propaganda is preferable to enforcing the law, which would remove and rehabilitate children and punish employers. While the former tactics are clearly useful, they presume that children are free to leave their work. For bonded children, who are not free, they provide little remedy. NGOs that run transitional schools and conduct public awareness campaigns, and the students who attend their schools, report that employers use threats and intimidation to keep bonded children working. Transitional schools need local and state governments to

---

37 *Review of Annual Reports* 2005, *supra* note 3, 231.

38 *Ibid.*

39 *Ibid.*, 236.

40 On the role of Rugmark in the carpet industry, see G. Chawdhary and M. Beeman, 'Challenging Child Labor: Transnational Activism and India's Carpet Industry', *Annals of the American Academy of Political and Social Science*, Vol. 575, 2001, 158; A. Ravi, 'Combating Child Labour with Labels', *Economic and Political Weekly*, Vol. 36, 2001, 1141; A.N. Sharma, 'Impact of Social Labelling on Child Labour in the Carpet Industry', *Economic and Political Weekly*, Vol. 37, 2002, 5196.

enforce the bonded and child labour laws so that they can reach bonded children. Where NGOs have managed to free bonded children, employers might continue to threaten the children and their parents, and insist that the parents repay the loans or pass down the advance to another child. In some instances, parents are forced to send another child to the employer in exchange. In some cases, children are sent back to work. NGO staff connected with schools also report that silk unit owners threatened their employees with violence for removing bonded children from silk units. Employers locked them up and beat them. Thus, the failure to enforce the law makes the work of NGOs and other internationally funded organizations who are trying to withdraw children from work and keep them in school difficult and, in some cases, impossible. It also handicaps the government's own education programmes, which, in any event, cover only a tiny fraction of working children. There is a need to look more closely into industries that serve primarily domestic consumers, for example child domestic work, and the brick kilns industry.[41]

17.2.2.3 Nepal Approximately 42 per cent of Nepalese children between the ages of 5 and 14 work, even though the Labour Act of 1992 and the Children's Act of 1992 have declared that the employment of children under the age of 14 is illegal.[42] The Nepalese law does not provide for compulsory education. Again, the main cause of child labour is poverty.[43] UNICEF is working to increase parents' awareness of the harmful effects of child labour through a Parenting Education initiative, and to give children between the ages of three and five a safe, encouraging place to learn and play in community-based child development centres. In 1999, 50,000 parents and caregivers participated in the initiative.[44] The Child Workers in Nepal Concerned Centre notes that the authorities have 'neither effectively implemented the law nor formulated any effective plans of action for the welfare and rehabilitation of the victims of child labour exploitation'.[45] In addition to demanding effective law enforcement by the government, NGOs in Nepal call for the need to mobilize people against child labour, and for coordinating their efforts with the government.

17.2.2.4 Sri Lanka The ongoing conflict in Sri Lanka has discouraged the required non-governmental participation for a successful implementation of ILO child labour standards. A Programme for the Rehabilitation and Reintegration of Former Child

---

41 See U. Jayachandran, 'Taking Schools to Children', *Economic and Political Weekly*, Vol. 36, 2001, 3347.

42 ILO/IPEC Country Profile: Nepal, 2001, 1.

43 See M. D'Avolio, 'Child Labor and Cultural Relativism: From 19th Century America to 21st Century Nepal', *Pace International Law Review*, Vol. 16, 2004, 19.

44 UNICEF, Factsheet: Child Labour, 3, available at <http://www.unicef.org/protection/files/child_labour.pdf>. See also the relevant article of the Convention on the Rights of the Child: art. 32(1): 'States Parties recognize the right of the child to be protected from economic exploitation and from performing any work that is likely to be hazardous or to interfere with the child's education, or to be harmful to the child's health or physical, mental, spiritual, moral or social development.'

45 G. Pradan, 'Challenging Child Labour', available at <http://www.cwin.org.np/resources/issues/child_labour.htm>.

Soldiers is run by OXFAM/CAA. This programme considers the special needs of the former child soldiers, their families and their communities. There is also a Project for Rehabilitation through Education and Training run by the World University Service Canada, which focuses on former child soldiers but also includes the broader community in improving employment-oriented skills.[46] The Canadian International Development Agency has undertaken a child rights project in Sri Lanka that aims to support institutions and organizations in their work to promote and protect the rights of vulnerable children. In addition, the Child Protection Research Fund is supporting a number of research initiatives that address the needs of exploited and abused children, including child soldiers.[47] The Committee on the Rights of the Child has recommended that Sri Lanka develop, in collaboration with international organizations and NGOs, a comprehensive system of psychosocial support and assistance for children affected by the conflict, in particular child combatants, unaccompanied internally displaced persons and refugees, returnees and landmine survivors, which also ensures their privacy. [48]

17.2.2.5 Thailand As a result of the advocacy of the social welfare sector and NGOs in Thailand, the government has recognized its responsibility to provide protection not only for Thai children but also for trafficked child workers from other countries. Trafficked migrant children are no longer detained in the immigration detention centre when the police find them. Instead, they are housed in a social welfare centre where they learn various skills while their return to their families is being worked on by social workers from the Thai government and the countries of origin, with support from international NGOs. This success though is quite limited, given that repatriation alone is not the answer to the issue of trafficking and child labour migration. The Development and Education Programme for Daughters and Communities applies prevention as the pathway, and education, protection and development as the preventive tools to combat child labour and trafficking.[49]

17.2.2.6 Conclusion International organizations and NGOs have complemented the role of governments in the implementation of ILO child labour standards. Again, for various reasons their role has had varying degrees of effectiveness and, consequently, has been less than optimal. While the relative unfamiliarity of external agencies with the domestic situation has been a negative factor, governments' views and perceptions have also been a determining factor in the implementation of ILO child labour standards. For instance, failure to enforce the law in India has made the work of NGOs and other internationally funded organizations difficult and, in some cases, impossible. Other factors that have typically impinged on the effectiveness of these agencies include the relative differences in levels of development, varying

---

46 *Review of Annual Reports 2005, supra* note 3, 224.

47 *Ibid.*, 240.

48 CEACR, Individual Observation concerning Convention No. 182: Sri Lanka 2005, Doc. No. (ilolex): 062005LKA182.

49 Information on the Development and Education Programme for Daughters and Communities is available at <http://www.depdc.org/eng/aboutus/strategy.html>.

incidence and causes of poverty, armed conflicts, cultural constraints, the lack of rule of law, caste bias, corruption, political will, education, and the ineffectiveness of rehabilitation mechanism. These will be discussed in the next section.

17.3 Selected issues in the implementation of ILO child labour standards in Asia

17.3.1 Poverty constraints

Despite laws prohibiting bondage, people can still be found living in conditions of bondage. While it is accepted that poverty is not the only reason for child labour, it remains a major push factor for the decisions of many parents to allow their children to work, even in exploitative and hazardous conditions. '[I]n societies like those in India, child labour is not only (or always even dominantly) about poverty: it is about social exclusion, inequality and discrimination, which allow the relative poverty of some to be exploited in this manner.'[50] When the programmes are over and funds run out, the generation of children who could benefit from the programmes will still be pushed back to work if poverty is not properly addressed. Child labour and poverty are therefore both a cause and effect. The child's entry into the labour force is triggered by poverty but also perpetuates their families' poverty.[51] Thus, helping the children break away from child labour means breaking the cycle of poverty, which in turn helps children break away from child labour. If we are really serious about addressing the child labour problem, our initiatives must contribute to the core issues related to poverty alleviation, such as good governance, environment, agricultural development and land reform, social equity, and development of basic social service systems.[52]

17.3.2 Cultural constraints

It is difficult to establish regulations concerning domestic workers because every family has its own way of dealing with them. Cultural values that need to be examined for the impact they have on child labour include views with respect to education, gender, ethnicity and social class, along with cultural perceptions of the proper role of the child in society and in the family.[53] '[S]ocieties must be prepared to address the powerlessness that often results from class, caste or gender discrimination against a social group. One way to reduce this powerlessness and equalize all people is by

---

50 J. Ghosh, 'Stolen Childhood', *Frontline* (Chennai), 17 November, 7.

51 G.K. Lieten, 'Child Labour and Food Security', *Economic and Political Weekly*, Vol. 38, 2003, 3467; Centre for Policy Dialogue, Child Labour Policy of Bangladesh: What are We Looking For?, Report No. 61, available at <http://www.cpd-bangladesh.org/publications/dr/DR-61.pdf>.

52 G.S. Vijay Kumar, 'No More Kidding on Child Labour', *Economic Times* (New Delhi), 18 November 2006, 12.

53 S. Chand Aggarwal, 'Child Labour and Household Characteristics in Selected States', *Economic and Political Weekly*, Vol. 39, 2004, 173; A. Hamid, 'Domestic Workers: Harsh, Everyday Realities', *Economic and Political Weekly*, Vol. 41, 2006, 1235.

mandating compulsory, free, accessible primary education for all children irrespective of gender, ethnicity, or social class.'[54] Education, therefore, has a key role to play in neutralizing cultural constraints on the elimination of child labour. Education is 'an excellent investment for governments because they gain an educated labour force and electorate'.[55]

17.3.3 Armed-conflict constraints

Not only does war induce the increasing involvement of children, it also breaks up families, separates children from their parents, and creates more orphans. Sri Lanka has been the scene of an armed conflict between the government and the Liberation Tigers of Tamil Eelam since 1983, but there is no specific law to deal with the forced or compulsory recruitment of children for use in armed conflict.[56] Among the root causes are the availability of light, inexpensive small firearms (like assault rifles), economic and social reasons and the lack of schooling.[57] While these facts are accepted, addressing the issue of peace and war is tough for many child labour organizations.

17.3.4 Lack or ineffectiveness of rehabilitation mechanisms

The increased awareness of the corporate and industrial sectors on child labour standards, coupled with the vigilant campaigns against child labour in workplaces is a two-edged sword. While they may be consistent with ILO standards, they may also push children to worse conditions when they leave the workplace. What is called for is a participatory approach. A child worker is not a unthinking passive victim of fate but an individual, responding to what life offers. Child workers often are persons with a sense of responsibility and human quality. Given the opportunity, they could teach us a lot on how to better plan, implement, and monitor our programmes that aim to help them. Organized groups of child workers are the strongest advocates and most effective partners of NGOs and governments in addressing child labour problems. If we can tap their power, there will be much hope in the coming years, not only for the present generation but also for a greater number of children in Asia.

---

54 D'Avolio, 'Child Labour', *supra* note 43, at 126.

55 K. Tomaševski, 'Has the Right to Education a Future within the United Nations? A Behind-the-Scenes Account by the Special Rapporteur on the Right to Education 1998–2004', *Human Rights Law Review*, Vol. 5, 2005, 225. See also W.E. Myers, 'The Right Rights? Child Labour in a Globalized World', *Annals of the American Academy of Political and Social Science*, Vol. 575, 2001, 38.

56 CEACR, Individual Observation concerning Convention No. 182: Sri Lanka 2005, Doc. No. (ilolex): 062005LKA182.

57 S. Valentine, 'SYMPOSIUM: "GLOBAL HUMAN RIGHTS: Panel Remarks: Trafficking of Child Soldiers: Expanding the United Nations Convention on the Rights of the Child and its Optional Protocol on the Involvement of Children in Armed Conflict', *New England Journal of International and Comparative Law*, Vol. 9, 2003, 24.

17.3.5 Education

In the particular context of India, the government's primary strategy against child labour has been to run schools designed to lure children out of hazardous labour and prepare them for formal schools or for a vocation. Operating special schools for former working children who lag far behind children their age in regular schools and who may not be acclimatized to a school environment is theoretically a good idea. However, such schools serve very few children compared to the number still working, and channel even fewer into a vocation or into formal schools. These schools also face problems in their basic operations, including achieving their primary goal of either mainstreaming students into formal schools or providing them with a vocation. Rehabilitating child workers is critical to preventing them from returning to work. It is generally conceived of as providing education to the child and employment or sources of credit to parents. Rehabilitation of child labourers became legally required in 1996, when the Supreme Court found that the continued use of child labour was prohibited under the Child Labour (Prohibition & Regulation) Act of 1986; state labour inspectors are ordered to identify children employed illegally and to fine employers about US$415 per child. The money received from fines is to be deposited in a 'Child Labour Rehabilitation-cum-Welfare Fund', the income of which must be used only for the child concerned.[58]

Education is a fundamental right under Indian law. Education certainly has an important role to play, but bonded child labourers are not free to benefit from the educational opportunities that may exist. When schools are not available, are of poor quality, charge prohibitive fees, or discriminate against children of lower class, children instead go to work. The compulsory age for schooling of children in India is 6–14 years of age for boys and girls. To complete compulsory education, eight years of instruction are required. The Indian government has taken some steps to improve access to education, but children still lack access to schools. The government 'does not recognize the fact that the majority of the working children are not working out of choice; they are deprived of education and childhood'.[59] The myth that only children not attending schools are working children has been challenged.[60] Gender parity in enrolment is another serous issue that has not yet attracted adequate governmental attention.[61] Thus, rehabilitation of children under state-sponsored schemes is almost non-existent.

---

58 Supreme Court Cases, *supra* note 16, § 29. Further, see R.K. Agarwal, 'The Barefoot Lawyers: Prosecuting Child Labour in the Supreme Court of India', *Arizona Journal of International and Comparative Law*, Vol. 21, 2004, 663.

59 T.K. Rajlakshmi, 'Primary Lessons', *Frontline* (Chennai), 17 November 2006, 10. On the experiment of mobile schools in India, see Jayachandran, 'Taking Schools to Children', *supra* note 41. Further, see R. Ray, 'Simultaneous Analysis of Child Labour and Child Schooling', *Economic and Political Weekly*, Vol. 37, 2002, 5215.

60 G.K. Lieten, 'Child Labour in India: Disentangling Essence and Solutions', *Economic and Political Weekly*, Vol. 37, 2002, 5190; and 'Child Labour', *Economic and Political Weekly*, Vol. 41, 2006, 108.

61 See P. Sengupta and J. Guha, 'Enrolment, Dropout and Grade Completion of Girl Children in West Bengal', *Economic and Political Weekly*, Vol. 37, 2002, 1621.

Unlike India and many other Asian countries, China experienced a major educational expansion, managing to achieve nearly universal primary education despite having the largest number of children to enrol. China enacted the Law of Compulsory Education in 1986. The new law extended basic education to include three additional years of junior secondary school, decentralized the education financing and administrative systems, diversified senior secondary education, and started to introduce market elements to the management of the system. As a result, the aim of achieving at least five years of primary education for virtually all children by 2000 has been largely attained.[62] China, at the same time, is well on the way to implementing its nine-year compulsory education policy, although problems persist. One important element of China's strategy has been the prohibition of the employment of children who have not had nine years of schooling. This is probably a unique requirement among developing countries.[63] China has achieved universal education at a lower cost than most other countries due to slower population growth and market reforms. Educational reforms in China have been part of much wider socio-economic reforms. These have had a dramatic impact in terms of poverty reduction, universal education and child labour.[64]

17.3.6 Deficiencies and loopholes in the law

Even in the uncommon case in which an official tries to enforce the Indian Child Labour (Prohibition & Regulation) Act of 1986, deficiencies and loopholes make its enforcement very difficult. Compared with the bonded labour law, the child labour law has broad loopholes for family-based labour and the minimum age, and carries light penalties. It is also more difficult for officials to initiate cases. First, the Act excludes any work done in the family or in government-run or recognized schools, even if the act prohibits children from doing that work in any other context.[65] This exception creates an incentive for factory owners to contract with or bond adults for work to be done in their homes. The adults then use their own children or bond other children to help with the work, claiming, if inspected, that the bonded children are their own. Second, unlike the Bonded Labour System (Abolition) Act of 1976, and the Scheduled Castes and Scheduled Tribes (Prevention of Atrocities) Act of 1989, the Child Labour (Prohibition & Regulation) Act of 1986 is not cognizable, meaning that a police officer may not arrest without a warrant. Instead, it is incumbent on labour inspectors to bring cases against employers. Because the act is not cognizable, it is more difficult for inspectors to collect evidence. Third, the Act, which only covers children up to age 14, places the burden on the inspector, not the employer, to prove with a doctor's certificate that a child is under age.[66] Prosecutions under the

---

62 Global Report, *supra* note 12, § 51.

63 *Ibid.*, § 52.

64 *Ibid.*, § 53.

65 Section 3 of the Act explicitly exempts 'any workshop wherein any process is carried on by the occupier with the aid of his family or to any school established by, or receiving assistance or recognition from, Government'.

66 Art. 10 of the Child Labour (Prohibition and Regulation) Rules (1988).

Act for employing children in occupations deemed hazardous have been rare and convictions rarer still. After the 1996 *M.C. Mehta* Supreme Court decision,[67] there was good work on child labour. However, one defeating effect has been to push the work from factories into private homes, where children working for their parents are not covered by the Child Labour Act and where compliance is harder to monitor.

17.3.7 Caste bias

The caste bias stands in the way of eliminating child labour in many an Asian country. In India, caste bias also impedes law enforcement. Upper castes dominate local political bodies, the police and the judiciary, bonded labour vigilance committees and the child labour committees that are supposed to enforce the law on bonded and child labour, whereas most bonded labourers are *Dalit* (the lowest caste). 'Untouchability' is illegal under Indian law. Compelling or enticing a member of a scheduled caste or scheduled tribe into forced or bonded labour is specifically outlawed under the Scheduled Castes and Scheduled Tribes (Prevention of Atrocities) Act of 1989. Unfortunately, these protections have not been implemented with the required vigour. For instance, the implementation of the 1989 Act is hampered by police unwillingness to duly register offences, or their ignorance of the terms of the Act itself. The police often take on the role of the judiciary and determine the merits of the case even before pursuing investigations. Even when cases are registered, the absence of special courts to try them can delay conviction for up to three or four years. All Act cases go to regular sessions courts, which are already overburdened with original and appellate jurisdiction over district-level civil and criminal cases. In India, the NHRC has been able to put pressure on district governments against these. But, as noted above, the NHRC's scope and resources are limited.

17.3.8 Lack of the rule of law

The lack of the rule of law and due process in a country like Myanmar is clearly a serious obstacle to the implementation of ILO child labour standards. Despite the frequent reference in the Child Law to 'every child', children are discriminated against in the law and in practice, on the grounds of citizenship, ethnicity and religious beliefs. There is therefore a need to harmonize the Child Law, the Constitution and the Citizenship Act of 1982, in order to protect all children in Myanmar against *de jure* discrimination. Current legislation and practice contravene not only ILO standards but also the 1961 Convention on the Abolition of Statelessness. In practice, the government itself is the worst violator of its own laws, by directly and indirectly forcing thousands of children to work as porters or as day labourers for no pay. As has been noted in Chapter 1 of this volume, the use of forced labour in Myanmar led to an investigation by the ILO under article 37. The Child Law is also inadequate with regard to the trafficking of children into sexual or other slavery in foreign countries. Implementation of the Convention on the Right of the Child, and the State Law and

---

67 Supreme Court Cases, *supra* note 17.

Order Restoration Council's own Child Law, is severely handicapped by the lack of accountability and access to justice in Myanmar.[68]

17.3.9 Lack of political will

Eradicating child labour requires not only the adoption of legal instruments but also the political will to implement them. One problem in countries like India is that government officials are frequently transferred, especially with a change in government in particular States.[69] There is little supervision or review from higher levels of government. There is also the problem of coordination. 'The action plans of state government need help from Departments other than the Labour Department ... the most important Department for the rehabilitation of working children and those in the hazardous sector is Education.'[70] There are few incentives for law enforcement. The lack of political will is also evidenced by the fact that each year more money is allocated than actually spent for child labour rehabilitation.

17.3.10 Corruption

Corruption also prevents effective law enforcement. Inspectors may be bribed, and raids typically fail because employers have been forewarned and hide or send away the children. Many district magistrates and law enforcement officials in India and Bangladesh are openly sympathetic to employers, who in turn pressure them to turn a blind eye to the problem of child labour. While there is a need to enact anti-corruption provisions into domestic law where they are not already enacted, their implementation would depend on the same governmental machinery that prevents effective implementation of ILO child labour standards.

It emerges from the above that child labour and poverty form a vicious circle. Discrimination in law and the lack of accountability and access to justice in countries such as Myanmar are serious obstacles to the implementation of ILO child labour standards. Cultural constraints continue to hamper the implementation of these standards and therefore the effective elimination of child labour. The role of parents is equally important.[71] Except for China, schools set up to rehabilitate child labour face basic operational problems. China has indeed set an example for other Asian countries. While the importance of education is continued to be recognized, as a rehabilitation strategy it has yet to make its impact. The child labour law has broad loopholes for family-based labour and determining age, and carries light penalties. The scourge of caste has cast its shadow on the proper implementation of the ILO child labour standards. The lack of political will is manifest in many ways, such as the lack of coordination among governmental departments and of supervision and

---

68 *Review of Annual Reports* 2006, *supra* note 5, 100.

69 The government is still mulling over giving a fixed tenure of at least two years to District Magistrates.

70 S. Meezan, *Frontline* (Chennai), 17 November 2006, 12–13.

71 See, for instance, CEACR, Individual Observation concerning Convention No. 182: Niger 2005, Doc. No. (ilolex): 062005NER182.

review of programme implementation. Corruption in many ways prevents effective law enforcement.

17.4 Conclusions

Differences in Asian legal systems, constitutional guarantees and judicial systems have resulted in differences in implementation of ILO child labour standards. Out of 29 countries in Asia, 14 have ratified Conventions 138 and 182. In Bangladesh, for instance, there is no national policy/plan aimed at ensuring the effective abolition of child labour, and in Thailand, legislation excludes work performed in enterprises below a certain size, homework, domestic service, self-employed work, commercial agriculture, and family and small-scale agriculture, while hazardous work remains undefined. The fact that neither Convention has been ratified by India, which has the world's biggest child population, raises the global percentage of child labour not covered by the fundamental Conventions. The case of China, however, is noteworthy, and its linking of education to eligibility for employment sets an example for other Asian countries. While non-party countries need to be further sensitized to eradicating child labour and persuaded to sign the two Conventions, we do not believe that trade sanctions can best serve to eliminate child labour.

National priorities, the degree of participation of the governmental machinery and administrative structures, along with infrastructures required for the effective implementation of child labour standards, have conditioned the role of international organizations and NGOs in the implementation of ILO child labour standards. For instance, the Indian government's failure to enforce the law has made the work of NGOs and other internationally funded organizations difficult and, in some cases, impossible. However, while there are evidently problems and complacency at governmental levels, there have also been stark problems, reinforced by natural calamities. Strategies such as capacity-building for social partners and IPEC-implementing agencies, advocacy for adherence and implementation of ILO Conventions, awareness-raising of the public and target groups and focused direct assistance have slowly but surely made inroads into the child labour problem. Agreed ILO priorities for national action include combating all forms of child labour, promoting education for all, and promoting decent work opportunities through facilitating the school-to-work transition. While a lack of familiarity of external agencies with the domestic situation has no doubt been a constraining feature, the governments' views and perceptions of the extent of their desirability have also been a determining factor in the success of these agencies. ILO's efforts are beyond doubt, but there is a need for further independent research into a more fruitful approach to eradicate child labour in Asia.

The Asian experience of the implementation of ILO child labour standards underscores a vicious circle created by child labour and poverty. The Chinese example underlines the message that poverty reduction and mass education are important prerequisites for moving countries to the transition point in child labour elimination. Legal discrimination and the lack of accountability and access to justice in countries such as Myanmar are serious obstacles to the implementation of ILO child labour standards. Cultural constraints continue to hamper the child labour elimination. Except for China, schools established to rehabilitate child workers face basic operational problems. China has clearly set an example for other Asian countries. The lack of political will is manifest in many ways, such as lack of coordination among governmental departments and of supervision and review of programme implementation. While the importance of education is continuously recognized, education as a rehabilitation strategy has yet to make an optimal impact. The child labour law has broad loopholes for family-based labour and determining age, and carries light penalties. The scourge of caste casts its shadow on the proper implementation of ILO child labour standards. And corruption in many ways seriously hampers effective law enforcement.

Chapter 18

The Implementation of the ILO's Standards Regarding Child Labour in South America: A General Overview and the Most Meaningful Achievements

Wilfredo Sanguineti Raymond[1]

18.1 Latin America, the main testing ground of the ILO's strategy for the elimination of child labour

The data disseminated by the ILO in May 2006 through its second global report on child labour, entitled *The End of Child Labour: Within Reach*,[2] show with total clarity that Latin America is the global leader in the fight against this social evil.

In order to realize the extent to which this holds true, it is enough to consider that the reported 11 per cent decrease in the number of working children, which occurred worldwide between 2000 and 2004, finds its main explanation in the spectacular decline in the rate of child work in South America. During this period the number of working children decreased from 17.4 million in 2000 to 5.7 million four years later, causing a decline in the activity rate from 16.1 to a mere 5.1 per cent. Compared to this, the progress in other regions was not sufficient to explain the global trend. For example, mentioning only the regions where this problem has a major impact, in Asia and in the Pacific, the activity rate during this period went from 19.4 to 18.8 per cent, corresponding to a decrease in the number of active children from 127.3 to 122.3 million; in sub-Saharan Africa the rate fell from 28.8 to 26.4 per cent, with the number of working children falling from 28.8 to 26.4 million.[3]

---

1 The author wants to express his gratitude to Manuela Goñi Arbide, Chief Technical Advisor of the Project for the Elimination of Child Labour in South America, and to Alfredo Villavicencio Ríos, Professor of Labour Law at the Pontifical Catholic University of Peru, for their invaluable collaboration during this research.

2 ILO, *The End of Child Labour: Within Reach – Global Report under the Follow-Up to the ILO Declaration on Fundamental Principles and Rights at Work*, Geneva, ILO, 2006.

3 However, it must be kept in mind that these data, on pages 5 to 10 of the report, are estimates of the number of working children in the world, based on an extrapolation of the available information in a limited number of countries. As such they are susceptible to specification and clarification when compared with more precise information or estimates, obtained in the field, as will be shown below. The complete results of this study, as well as the

This allows us to understand that the statement by the Director-General of the ILO, according to which the Organization's strategy for combating child labour based on 'standard setting, backed by a promotional approach' and 'advocacy and technical assistance', 'has been proven to be effective', is supported, almost exclusively, by the results obtained in Latin America. The same holds true for the goal of 'eliminating the worst forms of child labour in the next ten years' considered by the Director-General as 'ambitious but achievable'.[4] Without the progress in Latin America the ILO would have had no options but to repeat in its second report the less optimistic observations contained in the first report on this issue, entitled more cautiously *A Future Without Child Labour*, which characterized child labour as 'a stubborn phenomenon', whose complete elimination had not yet been accomplished in any economic sector or in any region of the world.[5]

Hence, the knowledge of the experience of Latin American countries in the fight against child labour, and the evaluation of the promotion and technical assistance provided by the ILO's IPEC programme, is not only a fascinating task, but also a necessary one, if one wants to fully comprehend the effectiveness of ILO standards regarding this subject, and the ability of its strategy to promote their effective enforcement by the States.

This study aims to reach this objective by focusing on the experience of South American countries. To this end, the regional situation at the beginning of IPEC's activities, the strategy IPEC designed, and the main achievements will be presented. In the light of this information, as well as that of the available evidence on the persistence of the phenomenon, it will be possible to clearly see the huge challenges that still confront the elimination of child labour on the American continent.

18.2 IPEC, driving force of the action of the governments of the region against child labour

The fight against labour exploitation of children through the adoption of specific measures by the States is not a goal which was introduced in 1999 by Convention 182.[6] As has been seen elsewhere in this book, in addition to being part of the ILO's mission since its foundation, this aim has been explicitly stated in international labour standards at least since 1973, when Convention 138 concerning the minimum age for admission to employment[7] provided in article 1 that

> Each Member for which this convention is in force undertakes to pursue a national policy designed to ensure the effective abolition of child labour and to raise progressively the

---

methodology used, can be found in F. Hagerman, Y. Diallo, A. Etienne and F. Mehran, *Global Child Labour Trends 2000–2004*, Geneva, ILO, 2006.

4 Both statements in ILO, *The End of Child Labour*, *supra* note 2, ix.

5 ILO, *A Future Without Child Labour – Global Report under the Follow-Up to the ILO Declaration on Fundamental Principles and Rights at Work*, Geneva, ILO, 2002, 21.

6 See Pertile (this volume); Trebilcock, Raimondi (this volume).

7 See Borzaga (this volume).

minimum age for admission to employment or work to a level consistent with the fullest physical and mental development of young persons.

Nevertheless, until very recently South American societies have not perceived child labour as a problem to be eliminated. In fact, in comparison to the critical evaluation of this phenomenon by the ILO since the beginning of its activity, on the continent a tolerant and even favourable view of it has traditionally prevailed, because child labour was seen 'as a solution to the precarious economic situation of thousands of families as well as providing children with the education and the opportunity to acquire values'.[8]

This culture, which is tolerant of, and to a certain extent even justifies, child labour and which has been shared historically by governmental bodies, workers' and employers' organizations and society as a whole, can surely explain that as late as 1996, when IPEC started its activities in most of the region, Convention 138 had obtained the ridiculously low number of two ratifications in Latin America.[9] It is evident that the indifference to the incorporation of this legal tool into national legal systems, despite the fact that it contains several mechanisms which allow for its conditional and progressive implementation by economically less-developed countries,[10] can only be considered an expression of the absence of the abolition of child labour as a priority issue on the legislative agendas of these countries, in accordance with the dominant social conscience regarding this issue.

The natural consequence of such an understanding of this phenomenon, which has at its roots both economic and ideological factors, has been the chronic shortage – and in some cases absence – of information, both qualitative and quantitative, regarding its characteristics and its dimensions, as well as the non-existence of governmental programmes and policies which, in line with what was recommended by Convention.

---

8 Programa IPEC América Latina y el Caribe, *La acción del IPEC contra el trabajo infantil en América Latina y el Caribe 1996–2004*, Lima, Publicaciones de la Oficina Regional para América Latina y el Caribe de la Organización Internacional del Trabajo, 2004, 13, translation by the editors. The report evaluates the situation of child labour in the region at the beginning of IPEC's activities. There is a lot of evidence of this tendency to attribute a positive value to child labour in Latin American societies. Examples of this are the following observations, contained in the Brazilian Plan Nacional de Prevención y Erradicación del Trabajo Infantil: 'throughout its history, child labour in Brazil was never portrayed as a negative phenomenon in the mentality of the Brazilian society' (translation by the editors). On the contrary, until the 1980s there was a consensus on considering it as 'a positive factor as concerns children that, because of their social and economic situation, lived in conditions of poverty, exclusion, and social risk'. Even more, 'both the elite and the poorer class fully shared' this way of looking at the problem. See Ministerio de Trabajo y Empleo del Brasil, *Plan Nacional de Prevención y Erradicación del Trabajo Infantil y Protección del Trabajo Adolescente*, Brasilia, Secretaría de Inspección del Trabajo, 2004, 20. Available at <http://www.oit.org.pe/ipec/pagina.php?se ccion=238pagina=102>.

9 The ones by Uruguay, completed on 2 June 1977, and by Venezuela, which took place on 15 July 1987.

10 See, in particular, art. 2(4), according to which every Member State 'whose economy and educational facilities are insufficiently developed may', after consultation, 'initially specify a minimum age of 14 years'.

138, tried to confront it by means of concrete measures. As mentioned, the subject of child labour simply 'was not on the agenda of the governments' of the region.[11] In addition, it was not even a demand by workers' organizations, nor by the citizenship as a whole, in which 'a certain approval' or even 'accustomedness to child labour' was predominant.[12]

If one adds to this the structural problems characterizing the region and the negative effects of the economic crisis that hit the region from the 1980s, it is easy to conclude that South America was a particularly fertile territory not only for the existence, but also for the proliferation of child labour. Initially the ILO was not in a condition to do much because its modus operandi is based on the voluntary adoption by States of international standards establishing minimum levels of protection; a decision which, at least with reference to Convention 138, the States did not seem particularly willing to embrace.

And this is in fact what happened during the 1980s and the better part of the 1990s, when the condemnation of the increase in child labour, in many cases in conditions of serious exploitation, became more and more frequent in all countries, often making a big impact in the media.[13] The result was a slow but constant process of putting into question the existing perception of child labour, at first by international bodies, but subsequently by larger and larger sections of civil society in the affected countries. The extent and the aggravation of the problem generated, in this way, the conditions for the emergence of a critical view, which replaced the hitherto dominant one.

In addition to the crisis of the traditional paradigm of child labour, another fact contributed in a decisive manner to the translation of the existing discontent into concrete measures for combating this burning problem. In this case, the change originated from the ILO. In 1992, the Organization, surely being aware of the ineffectiveness of the system for the implementation and the monitoring of the enforcement of the international labour standards concerning child labour, especially when States lack the means and experience or have doubts about the convenience of such a step, chose to create the IPEC programme of technical cooperation, directed at assessing and supporting action by States, workers' and employers'

---

11 Programa IPEC América Latina y el Caribe, *La acción del IPEC*, *supra* note 8, p. 74. Translation by the editors.

12 As is pointed out by the Peruvian 'Plan Nacional de Prevención y Erradicación del Trabajo Infantil'. See also Comité Directivo Nacional para la Prevención y Erradicación del Trabajo Infantil, *Plan Nacional de Prevención y Erradicación del Trabajo Infantil*, Lima, Ministerio de Trabajo y Promoción del Empleo del Perú, 2005, 5. Available at <http://www. oit.org.pe/ipec/pagina.php?seccion=238pagina=102>.

13 As is reported for the case of Brazil in the *Plan Nacional de Prevención y Erradicación del Trabajo Infantil*, *supra* note 8, 23, back then 'the international protests which indicated Brazil as one of the countries with the highest indicators of economic inequality and social injustice came to the surface. The "country of the future" of the 1970s was substituted by the "country without future" of the end of the century, the postcard of which was the face of the street-children in Copacabana or in the Avenida Paulista, the poverty of children working in sugar-cane plantations, the sorrow of children in the mines, the shortage in informal urban work, inadmissible sexual exploitation, the poverty of teenagers in shantytowns and jails'.

organizations and civil society, aimed at abolishing child labour. This programme began its activities in the region in the year of its creation, through the signing of a Memorandum of Understanding with the Brazilian government. However, four years later the activities were enlarged to involve all South American countries, with the aim of favouring a common response to the problem.

The changes this region has been undergoing during the last decade, as shown above, have resulted from the combination of new perceptions regarding the problem of child labour, and the support and technical assistance developed by IPEC since then.

IPEC's goal evidently is not to eliminate child labour by means of its implementation, but to contribute to the elimination of child labour through the stimulation of action by States and civil society. Thus, its strategy is based on the strengthening of national capacities by means of technical and financial cooperation. This means that a necessary condition for IPEC's implementation is the existence of political will and commitment on the part of the States to address the problem of the labour exploitation of minors.[14] Such a commitment, while not being evident earlier, started to emerge in the region during the 1990s, thus making it possible to develop plans and concrete programmes in all countries.

Starting from this basis, IPEC's strategy to strengthen national capacities has been organized around two fundamental instruments. The first of them is represented by the shaping of stable national structures which make it possible to design and implement national policies for the elimination of child labour in a sustained way. To this end IPEC has supported the formation of national committees for the fight against child labour, usually presided over by the ministers of labour and composed of representatives of the other governmental bodies with responsibilities in the field plus different sections of civil society, as for example workers' and employers' organizations and relevant NGOs. The main goal of these committees is to design, with IPEC's support, national plans for the prevention and elimination of child labour. The plans will put into practice the legislative, administrative and promotional means to be undertaken and will establish the necessary mechanisms for their implementation, monitoring and evaluation. The outcome will be the design and execution of an authentic national strategy for the elimination of child labour, in line with the commitments States have to undertake under Conventions 138 and 182.

However, to this first instrument, in which IPEC as a means of technical cooperation is predominant, a second and decisive tool of a very different character has been added. It is the implementation of programmes giving direct attention to working children and to their families. In this case, it is about developing concrete experiences of child labour prevention in sectors at risk, and effective withdrawal of

---

14 According to what is reported in Programa IPEC América Latina y el Caribe, *La acción del IPEC, supra* note 8, 37. It must be kept in mind that the commitment to eliminate child labour is incumbent upon the Member States which signed the international conventions on this subject and not upon the ILO, which is, rather, competent to check their effective enforcement and, in any case, to support with concrete measures the actions which the States decide to take.

minors who are subject to labour exploitation, with special attention for those affected by the worst forms of child labour as defined by Convention 182. The purpose of these programmes, which are generally executed by specialized institutions counting on IPEC's technical and financial assistance, is twofold. First, to remove from labour exploitation groups of children who are affected by it or are at risk of becoming so. Second, to implement procedures and methods of intervention that may effectively be used in the fight against this pernicious phenomenon. From this perspective, the usefulness of these programmes cannot be measured only – and maybe not even mainly – in terms of the number of children 'prevented' or 'withdrawn', but in terms of their demonstrative effect, showing both that the effective elimination of child labour can be achieved even in the most difficult settings, and demonstrating how to reach this goal in specific situations.[15]

The extent to which this two-pronged strategy can be considered correct will be known once the actions undertaken in this framework and the results obtained become known. The next section deals with these issues.

18.3 The implementation of a policy aimed at the elimination of child labour: main progress at the regional level

The general obligation for States to 'pursue a national policy designed to ensure the effective abolition of child labour' through the provision of 'all necessary measures' for the achievement of this objective, to which Convention 138 refers in articles 1 and 9, has been subsequently influenced by Convention 182, which specifies and clarifies, with reference to the particular forms of labour exploitation of children it refers to, what the scope and the main instruments of such policy should be.[16]

Given its distinctive purpose, this convention is rather more severe than the previous one with respect to the commitment required of States, in the sense that starting from article 1 it requires state interventions in order to ensure 'the prohibition and elimination of the worst forms of child labour', to be 'immediate and effective' and to be adopted 'as a matter of urgency'. This convention also deals with a more precise indication of what such measures shall consist of. A schematization of these measures allows us to distinguish among three different levels of realization, strictly linked to one another. The first is the adoption of normative decisions directed towards the realization of a triple objective: (a) the prohibition of what are considered the worst forms of child labour (article 1); (b) the determination of the hazardous types of work, regarded as particularly reprehensible forms of child labour, characterized by capacity to harm 'the health, safety or morals of children' (article 4); and (c) the provision of sanctions, including penal ones, aimed to ensure the enforcement of such legislation (article 7). To this is added, as a second level of intervention, the creation of 'appropriate mechanisms to monitor the implementation' of the provisions adopted to give effect to the Convention (article 5). It is possible to give a double meaning to this obligation: (a) the designing of instruments which make

---

15 On IPEC's strategy in the region, see: Programa IPEC América Latina y el Caribe, *La acción del IPEC, supra* note 8, especially 9–10, 19–20, 37 and 88–9.

16 On the scope of Convention 182, see Rishikesh (this volume).

it possible for 'detailed information and statistical data on the nature and extent of child labour' to 'be compiled and kept up to date',[17] and (b) the establishment of effective monitoring and control systems. The scheme is finally completed by the launch of 'programmes of action' for the elimination of child labour and of its worst forms (article 6). These programmes, according to article 7 of the convention, will have to include in any case 'effective and time-bound measures' to: (a) 'prevent the engagement of children' in the said activities (prevention); (b) 'provide the necessary and appropriate direct assistance for the removal of children' from those activities (withdrawal); and (c) guarantee the rehabilitation and reintegration of minors freed from exploitation, ensuring them 'access to free basic education' and 'vocational training' (rehabilitation).

Given that the 'effective abolition of child labour' represents one of the principles enshrined in the ILO Declaration on Fundamental Principles and Rights at Work,[18] all of its Member States 'have an obligation arising from the very fact of membership in the Organization to respect, to promote and to realize' this objective, 'even if they have not ratified' the relevant international conventions. It means that the scheme of intervention described above can, in principle, also be required of those States which have not incorporated the provisions of the conventions concerned into their own legal systems. Even so, it is evident that the ratification of such conventions is a first and fundamental step towards the realization of their objectives. In other words, ratification is a precondition without which it is evidently extremely difficult for the State in question to proceed in this direction.

The remainder of this section is devoted to the examination of the way in which the States of South America, with IPEC's assistance and support, have complied with these requirements, from the ratification of the corresponding conventions to the adoption of measures on the three levels of intervention illustrated above. This will allow us to appreciate the progress achieved so far in the region, as well as the existing shortcomings.

18.3.1 Legislative adaptation: the ratification of the international conventions regarding child labour and the adoption of a legislation adjusted to their requirements

Even if not sufficient in itself for solving the problem, the adoption of adequate legislation is a fundamental instrument for effectively combating child labour.[19]

Counting on IPEC's support and advice, in the last few years South American countries have made an effort to adapt their legislation to the requirements deriving from the fight against the labour exploitation of minors. Inevitably, the starting point of such adaptation has been the ratification of the fundamental conventions on this subject. As has been shown, it took a long time for the States in the region to take this

---

17 As is stated in art. 5(1) of Recommendation 190 concerning the prohibition and immediate action for the elimination of the worst forms of child labour.

18 See Swepston (this volume).

19 M. Rodríguez-Piñero, 'Trabajo infantil', *Relaciones Laborales*, no. 22, 1997, 7.

step. Yet, at present, all of them, without exception, have ratified both Conventions 138 and 182.[20]

This unanimity evidently shows that the elimination of child labour, and in particular of its worst forms, is an objective shared by all South American countries. This consensus did not emerge spontaneously, but was the result of a process of progressive acknowledgement by the States of the problem, as well as of the convenience of adopting measures to tackle it. A fundamental role in the development of this consensus has been played by various bodies of intergovernmental cooperation, both at the regional level and at higher levels, which have made it possible for a common point of view to emerge. Following this it has been possible to put the issue more quickly on the countries' socio-economic agendas. This process has been given expression through a set of institutional declarations, adopted by different bodies, meetings of people responsible for youth policy and of Ministers of Labour or Chiefs of State, all of which have agreed on the condemnation of child labour and the need to firmly act against it. The culmination of all these declarations can be found in the commitment made by the Presidents in November 2005, in the so-called Summit of the Americas, to achieve the elimination of the worst forms of child labour by 2020.[21] As has been affirmed by IPEC, the high level of ratification of Conventions 138 and 182 would have been unthinkable without the existence of political agreements binding on the States, reached at different meetings and regional forums.[22]

Of course, equally or even more important than the ratification of conventions or the adoption of international commitments is the approval of rules which incorporate these provisions into the countries' legal systems.

The ratification of Conventions 138 and 192 has had, from this point of view, the virtue of unleashing a reform of the national rules regulating child labour, which gradually eliminated the provisions not in accordance with international standards.

---

20 It has to be stressed that all these ratifications, with the exception of the two cases mentioned previously, have occurred since 1996, when IPEC's action spread out to all the countries of the region, and especially since 1998, when the ILO approved its Declaration on Fundamental Principles and Rights at Work. The last States to ratify Convention 138 were Peru (2002) and Paraguay (2004). Regarding Convention 182, ratifications started in 2000 with Brazil and Ecuador and ended in 2005 with the accession of Colombia and Venezuela.

21 The list of these declarations is available at <http://www.oit.org.pe/ipec/pagina.php? seccion=16&pagina=159>. The text of the Declaration of Mar del Plata is available at <http:// www.summit-americas.org/defaults-htm>.

22 Programa IPEC América Latina y el Caribe, *La acción del IPEC*, *supra* note 8, 20. Translation by the editors. This document emphasized as meetings which have 'marked important milestones' in this process: the First Latin American Tripartite Meeting at the Ministerial Level on the Elimination of Child Labour, convened in the city of Carthagena of Indies, Republic of Colombia, in May 1997, where agreement was reached on the creation of national committees for the gradual elimination of child labour, and the X Ibero-American Summit of Presidents and Heads of States, convened in Panama in November 2000, which included among the agreements reached the one on making efforts to achieve by 2015 the universal access to free primary education for children, and where States which had not ratified Conventions 138 and 182 were urged to do so.

This is the case, first of all, for the rules regulating the minimum age for admission to employment. After having overcome previous deficiencies, all countries in the region now provide for minimum ages in compliance with the requirements of Convention 138. Even so, it must be said that the countries which have chosen to make use of the exception provided for in paragraph 4 of article 2 and have established a minimum age of 14 years[23] outnumber those who have raised the minimum age to 15 years.[24] Only Brazil, which is especially meaningful for its high rate of child population, has chosen to set it at 16.[25] Therefore, the objective of a gradual rise of the minimum age for admission to employment, affirmed in article 1 of Convention 138, does not appear, at least at present, on the agenda of most of the countries of the region, which are more inclined to set the lowest age possible in order to stimulate the development of their economy and educational systems.

Furthermore, the adaptation of domestic legislation is not even complete, since it is evident from the recent CEACR Reports that there are States whose legislation does not comply with the requirements of Convention 138 with all the necessary rigour. This is so in the case of Argentina, which the Committee has repeatedly recommended to ensure the implementation of the provisions of Convention 138 regarding children who exercise activities on their own account and to authorize only persons of 12 to 14 years of age to carry out light works.[26] In the case of Bolivia, the CEACR has repeatedly requested the adoption of measures to prohibit the work in undertakings of persons under the age of 14 years as part of an apprenticeship.[27] In the case of Venezuela, the government has been urged to take the necessary decisions in order to avoid that people under 18 years of age are authorized, beyond the exceptions provided for by the Convention, to carry out hazardous works.[28]

However, the complete normative adaptation to the international standards regarding child labour requires quite a lot more than raising of the minimum age for admission to employment. In addition to this, it demands reform of the national legislation with the aim of turning it into an instrument for the repression of child labour, especially its worst forms. This process evidently requires a quite stronger adaptation effort, which implies the revision not only of labour standards, but also

---

23 This is the case in Argentina, Bolivia, Ecuador, Paraguay, Peru and Venezuela.

24 Specifically, Chile, Colombia and Uruguay.

25 In 1999, Constitutional Amendment No. 20, of 8 December 1998, entered into force, prohibiting all children under 16 years of age from carrying out any works, with the only exception of those connected to an apprentice position, which can be carried out from the age of 14.

26 ILO, *Report of the Committee of Experts on the Application of Conventions and Recommendations.* International Labour Conference, 93rd Session, 2005, Geneva, ILO, 2005, 199–200. The second observation is restated in ILO, *Report of the Committee of Experts on the Application of Conventions and Recommendations.* International Labour Conference, 96th Session, 2007, Geneva, ILO, 2007, 214.

27 Both observations are contained in the reports cited *supra* note 26, at 204 and 216, respectively.

28 ILO, *Report of the Committee of Experts on the Application of Conventions and Recommendations.* International Labour Conference, 95th Session, 2006, Geneva, ILO, 2006, 234.

of civil, criminal, administrative and even educational and sanitary legislation, with the aim of achieving a coherent treatment of the phenomenon in all the spheres of the legal system.

This is an area that the States of the region have started covering, but which cannot be regarded as finished yet. In the last few years, several countries have surely complied with the identification, in accordance with paragraph 1, article 4 of Convention 182, of the hazardous works prohibited to minors. It is enough to cite as the most recent examples the cases of Brazil,[29] Colombia,[30] Paraguay[31] or Peru.[32] It is incomprehensible that there are legal systems in the region that permit, or do not intervene against, the unconditional worst forms of child labour, as defined in article 1 of Convention 182. The steps taken to achieve their repression through specific laws are almost exclusively linked to the sexual exploitation of minors, in relation to which criminal laws have been approved in the last few years in Bolivia,[33] Brazil,[34] Chile,[35] Ecuador[36] and Uruguay.[37] The same has not occurred in the area of child forced labour, nor child recruitment for the carrying out of illicit activities, as for example drug production or trafficking, even though such activities, as is well-known, are not at all foreign to the region. Here, however, one can cite the case of Peru, which has recently approved a norm specifically directed to the criminal repression of human trafficking, with special attention to cases involving minors.[38] In this point at least, the situation corresponds to the one which has been denounced with special concern by the ILO in general terms.[39]

---

29 Ordinance MTE/SIT No. 6 draws up a list of the premises and services forbidden for children younger than 18 years of age because considered hazardous or unhealthy. This standard, as well as the ones mentioned in the following note, are available at <http://www.ilo.org/dyn/natlex>.

30 Resolution No. 4448 of 2 December 2005 draws up a list of the activities which no child or adolescent will be allowed to carry out and establishes labour conditions forbidden to them because of the harm to their health and security which they may cause.

31 Decree No. 4951, which regulates Law No. 1657/2001 and approves the list of hazardous child work.

32 Supreme Decree No. 007-2006-MIMDES, which approves the list of works and activities hazardous or harmful to the physical or moral health of adolescents.

33 Law No. 2033, of 29 October 1999, for the protection of victims of crimes against sexual freedom.

34 Law No. 10764, of 12 November 2003, amending Law No. 8069, of 13 July 1990, which established the children's and adolescents' statute. This law regulates the sanctions applicable to those who exploit children or adolescents for the production of pornographic scenes.

35 Law No. 19927, of 5 January 2005, which modifies the regulation by the Penal Code of the crimes in the field of child pornography.

36 Law No. 2005-2, of 15 June 2005, which categorizes in the Penal Code the crimes of sexual exploitation of minors.

37 Law No. 17815, of 9 June, on commercial or non-commercial sexual violence committed against children, adolescents or incapable people.

38 Law 28950, of 5 January 2007, against human trafficking and illicit migrant trafficking.

39 See ILO, *The End of Child Labour, supra* note 2, 18.

18.3.2 The designing of effective information, monitoring and supervision mechanisms: SIMPOC's role and labour inspection

Although indispensable, the adaptation of national legislation to the international requirements is just a first step towards the elimination of the labour exploitation of children. Of equal importance is the designing of instruments for the effective implementation of such legislation. Without any doubts, this is a particularly difficult task, given the characteristics of the problem at hand. Child labour, as has been pointed out, is a hidden, invisible phenomenon[40] or, in any case, scarcely transparent,[41] insofar as it is generally carried out in the informal economy, in private homes, family enterprises, or in illegal and clandestine activities.

This is why any policy directed at its elimination has to add to the approval of repressive rules two additional measures of special importance: (a) the designing of instruments which make it possible to generate serious and reliable quantitative and qualitative information regarding the extent and characteristics of the problem which has to be tackled and (b) the putting into operation of effective systems for the surveillance and control of the enforcement of such rules. As will be shown below, the progress reported in South America is related more to the first than to the second of these aspects.

One of the shortcomings which has impeded, in an extremely evident way, the development of effective national policies against child labour is the lack of precise and verifiable data on its dimensions and characteristics. In spite of this, in the last few years significant progress has been made concerning the knowledge about child labour in South America. This progress can largely be attributed to the ILO's Statistical Information and Monitoring Programme on Child Labour (SIMPOC). In several countries of the region SIMPOC has stimulated the development of surveys on child labour, either with an independent character or through the inclusion of specific modules in national household surveys. SIMPOC is based on agreements with the Ministries of Labour and National Institutes of Statistics of various countries, aimed at the implementation of systems for the measurement of child labour. It has put at our disposal updated and verifiable data on the extent of labour exploitation of children in Argentina, Brazil, Colombia, Chile and Ecuador. On the other hand, this result has not yet been achieved by Paraguay, Uruguay, Bolivia and Peru, where the process of statistical adaptation is still in the designing or executing phase.[42]

These improvements in the acknowledgement of the general extent of the problem, incomplete but undoubtedly meaningful, contrast with the almost total absence of reliable data regarding the extent of the worst forms of child labour. This is mainly due to the nature of these activities, whose hidden and clandestine character prevent them from being reflected in the household surveys. Even so, the shortage of information regarding the matter is sensational, and is clearly reflected in the different

---

40 See J. Neves Mujica, 'El trabajo infantil en las acciones de interés público', *Ius et Veritas*, No. 23, 2001, 229.

41 Rodríguez-Piñero, 'Trabajo infantil', *supra* note 19, 7.

42 For a list of the surveys and additional statistical information developed in the region, see <http://www.oit.org.pe/ipec/pagina.php?seccion=44>.

national plans for the elimination of child labour, in which it is extremely difficult to find even indirect estimates regarding the probable extent of these abominable forms of exploitation. For example, the National Plan for the Prevention and Elimination of Child Labour of an important country such as Brazil, in its analysis of the situation does not include any mention of the matter.[43] Other plans, like the Peruvian one, only point out that the worst forms of child labour represent 'a relevant problem', which 'manifests itself' in different manners, although 'no statistical data exist' regarding its extent.[44] However, the exception is the Colombian Third National Plan for the Elimination of Child Labour which, based on different sources, offers concrete numbers in support of its statement that 'the incidence of child labour is very high' in that country.[45]

This disregard for the worst forms of child labour turns out to be particularly worrying if one considers that their complete elimination in the coming years is an objective shared by the ILO and the governments in the region, through the raising of qualitative information. Therefore, on IPEC's initiative, in the last few years an extremely important number of national studies, baseline studies and rapid assessments has been carried out; starting from those studies one can gain information, based on the examination of specific cases, regarding the main characteristics of the worst forms of child labour, their geographical distribution and the activities which they affect within each country. To mention some examples, in Bolivia, these studies cover such activities as sexual exploitation, work in small-scale mining or in the sugarcane harvest; in Brazil, sexual exploitation and child pornography on the Internet, agricultural work, domestic service, informal activities and drug trafficking; in Colombia, human trafficking, sexual exploitation, participation in armed conflicts, domestic service and work in small-scale gold, clay, emerald and coal mining; in Ecuador, sexual exploitation, work in banana plantations, in small-scale gold mining or in floriculture; and finally, in Peru, child trafficking, commercial sexual

---

43 See Ministerio de Trabajo y Empleo del Brasil, *Plan Nacional, supra* note 8, 10–14. This insufficiency has not gone unnoticed by the CEACR, which in its 2005 report notes that the Brazilian Government 'does not give an overview of the extent of the worst forms of child labour in the country', at the same time expressing 'its serious concern about the actual number of children in Brazil who are sexually exploited for commercial purposes'. Both observations are in ILO, *Report of the Committee of Experts*, 2005, *supra* note 26, 208 and 207 respectively.

44 Comité Directivo Nacional para la Prevención y Erradicación del Trabajo Infantil, *Plan Nacional de Prevención, supra* note 12, 7. Translation by the editors.

45 Comité Interinstitucional para la Erradicación del Trabajo Infantil y la Protección del Joven Trabajador, *III Plan Nacional para la Erradicación del Trabajo Infantil y la Protección del Trabajo Juvenil 2003–2006*, Bogotá, Publicaciones del Ministerio de la Protección Social de Colombia, 2003, 47–8, available at <http://www.oit.org.pe/ipec/pagina.php?seccion=238 pagina=102>. Translation by the editors. The figures about children involved in these practices are: armed conflicts, between 6,000 and 11,000; sexual exploitation, 25,000; domestic service, 32,000; mining, between 200,000 and 400,000; construction, 33,428; industry, 195,892; illicit cultivations, 200,000; and trade, especially street trade, 187,744.

exploitation, domestic service, work in coca areas, in small-scale gold mining, on rubbish dumps or in wholesale markets.[46]

Although it needs to be developed further, the information gathered through these two channels represents a tool of the highest usefulness, both for the designing of strategies for surveying and controlling child labour and for the planning of public policies for its elimination. For this purpose, IPEC simultaneously created the Regional Information System on Child Labour (SIRTI) as a management unit in charge of the organization, analysis, systematization and dissemination of data available at national and regional level. Its action guarantees a quick dissemination, by prevalently digital and electronic means, of the progress achieved in the knowledge of the phenomenon by the aforementioned statistics and studies.[47]

Concerning the establishment of effective monitoring mechanisms, the first thing to note is that all countries in the region currently have labour inspection systems within their Ministries of Labour, whose tasks include monitoring the enforcement of laws regarding child labour. However, the typical features of this phenomenon, essentially located in the informal sector of the economy and characterized by a hidden and clandestine character, make effective action rather difficult. This is even more so if one adds, as an aggravating factor, the limitations to which this class of administrative bodies is subject in developing countries. The result is a clear inability of national inspection systems to tackle the phenomenon of labour exploitation of minors.

Given this disquieting reality, however surprising this may appear, no meaningful efforts can be detected, either at the level of the ILO or at the level of the States, to reverse the situation by providing the labour inspections with the means and capacities for an adequate fulfilment of their tasks in this field.

As far as IPEC is concerned, its attention has been focused on supporting the creation of inspection units specializing in child labour by the Ministries of Labour of some countries, and the implementation of specialized monitoring models for child labour in strategic export sectors.[48] Despite the good quality of both initiatives, no data exist which allow verification that these experiences are producing tangible results. On the contrary, the impression given by their own managers is that in this field 'one has advanced at a lower pace' than in statistical adaptation.[49]

Shifting the focus to the action by the States, the results are no different. Here it is possible to refer only to some specific interventions, from which one cannot deduce the existence of a general trend towards the strengthening of labour inspections as supervisory body of child labour. This is the case, for example, of Venezuela and

---

46 For a list of the national studies, baseline studies and rapid assessments carried out in the region, see <http://www.oit.org.pe/ipec/pagina.php?seccion=13>.

47 Access to all the information gathered by SIRTI can be obtained from <http://www.oit.org.pe/ipec>.

48 Specifically, IPEC has offered support to specialized inspection units in Ecuador, Chile and in the MERCOSUR countries. Strategic export sectors to which inspection models have been applied are coal mining and flower export in Colombia, the textile sector in Peru and tinned food export in Chile. See Programa IPEC América Latina y el Caribe, *La acción del IPEC*, *supra* note 8, 48.

49 Programa IPEC América Latina y el Caribe, *La acción del IPEC*, *supra* note 8, 24.

Argentina, of whose progress regarding the extension of the sphere of intervention of the inspection to child labour in the informal sector the CEACR Experts takes note in its 2006 and 2007 reports.[50] Similarly the CEACR notes with interest in its 2007 report another type of isolated action in the field of criminal repression of the worst forms of child labour, namely the creation in Ecuador of a national police unit specializing in the protection of minors, whose action led 'to the arrest and conviction of persons involved in the crime of sexual exploitation'.[51]

However, two experiences deserve to be emphasized for their innovative character. The first is the development of a 'Guide for the implementation of a system of inspection and monitoring of child labour in the MERCOSUR countries and Chile' by the experts of the respective Ministries of Labour. In addition to representing a previously unknown example of horizontal cooperation, this document is relevant for the effort it makes to adapt the traditional structure and forms of intervention of labour inspection to the particular reality and problem of child labour.[52] The second experience is the launch in Peru of the National Information, Monitoring and Verification System of Child Labour in Small-Scale Mining.[53] As has been emphasized, this is a pioneering initiative at the global level, through which a permanent instrument for the institutional monitoring of child labour in this highly risky activity is created, and whose implementation is accompanied by commitments by the State to assist minors and their families in order to make withdrawal and rehabilitation possible.[54]

18.3.3 The progress in institutional development and the designing of public policies: the proliferation of committees and national plans for the elimination of child labour

As argued, the fundamental aim of IPEC's strategy in the region is to strengthen the States' ability to tackle the problem of child labour. The main tool for this is the promotion of national committees for the war against the labour exploitation of minors, aimed at coordinating the action of the various governmental bodies with responsibilities in the field and channelling civil society engagement. The national plans designed by these committees should systematize the measures to be adopted by the different areas of social policy for the prevention and elimination of child labour. The originality of the design evidently lies in its capacity to favour a wide commitment, both public and private, to the goal of restraining child exploitation, and to integrate policy measures into the general framework of social policies. Thus it implements the recommendation to adopt 'an integrated approach to children's

---

50 See, ILO, *Report of the Committee of Experts*, 2006, *supra* note 28, p. 234; and ILO, *Report of the Committee of Experts*, 2007, *supra* note 26, 213–214.

51 ILO, *Report of the Committee of Experts*, 2007, *supra* note 26, 238.

52 Guía para la Implementación de un Sistema de Inspección y Monitoreo del Trabajo Infantil en los países del MERCOSUR y Chile, available at <http://www.oit.org.pe/ipec/doc/documentos/guía_inspeccion.pdf>.

53 Sistema Nacional de Información, Monitoreo y Verificación del Trabajo Infantil en la Minería Artesanal.

54 See Programa IPEC América Latina y el Caribe, *La acción del IPEC*, *supra* note 8, 47.

issues', linking the decisions adopted in the specific sector of labour with measures of a wider scope, especially in the field of education and access to social services.[55]

This strategy has demonstrated its effectiveness in practice. At present there are committees for the fight against child labour with a wide and participative composition in all of the countries of the region, all of which have designed the corresponding national prevention and elimination plans.[56] Moreover, this approach has been recently extended to the international sphere, through the approval by the MERCOSUR of a specific regional plan regarding this subject,[57] and the adoption by the Andean Community of an agreement to implement a plan with similar features.[58]

The existence of these committees and plans is an extremely important institutional achievement by the ILO and IPEC, insofar as it demonstrates that the fight against child labour enjoys priority on the agendas of all of the countries of the area and within the existing agreements on regional integration. At present, their elaboration expresses an important effort at coordination, both within the state apparatus and between the State and civil society, counting on the engagement of the different governmental bodies linked to child protection, as well as on representatives of workers, employers, civil society organizations and even of the children involved in these practices. This is without doubt a particularly valuable element for the ability of the policies to reflect the different aspects of the problem and to tackle them in an integrated way.

---

55 ILO, *A Future Without Child Labour, supra* note 5, 81. It implies, as this document states on p. 81, that 'at the same time as maintaining a specific policy on child labour, each government must mainstream the issue within overall policy frameworks in, for example, employment, poverty reduction, education and vocational training, labour and social protection'.

56 For a complete list of these plans, see <http://www.oit.org.pe/ipec/pagina.php?seccio n=238pagina=102>.

57 The 'Plan Regional para Prevención y Erradicación del Trabajo Infantil en el MERCOSUR' was approved on 18 July 2006. Its fundamental goal is to develop a regional policy on the subject. For this purpose it aims at three specific objectives: (a) harmonize the 'Declaración Sociolaboral del MERCOSUR' with international standards regulating child labour, developing mechanisms for the supervision, control and monitoring of its implementation; (b) get a reliable knowledge of the extent, reach and diversity of the problem of child labour in the region; and (c) strengthen the institutional mechanisms of horizontal cooperation among States, aimed at the enforcement of the national and regional rules for the elimination of child labour.

58 This agreement was adopted on 27 August 2004 by the 'XII Reunión de Viceministros de Trabajo de la Comunidad Andina de Naciones'. The 'Plan Subregional de Prevención y Erradicación Progresiva del Trabajo Infantil', whose designing was planned at this meeting, is based on the establishment of common policies and mechanisms of horizontal cooperation regarding the following issues: integration of child labour into public policies, information systems, child labour inspection, advocacy and transformation of cultural models, adaptation and implementation of the legislation and strengthening of the social actors. Its text is available at <http://www.comunidadandina.org/documentos/actas/de27-8-04.htm>.

However, the heterogeneity of these plans, due to the different features and dimensions of the child labour phenomenon in each country and to specific policy choices, makes the global evaluation of their contents very difficult.[59]

Among their most positive characteristics is, without any doubt, the effort, which can be found in the majority of them, to establish links with other sectional or general plans dealing with subjects related to the fight against child labour (mainly child protection plans, plans for the promotion of education and for the fight against poverty). Thus, the integration of action and policy is at the very heart of these plans. However, it is important to note that this integration emphasizes the development of general lines of action, which would seem undoubtedly adequate, given the structural character of child labour in the region. Nevertheless, the design may turn out to be insufficient if it is not accompanied by specific instruments to prevent the engagement of children in prohibited activities, and to withdraw and rehabilitate those who are affected by it in accordance with article 7 of Convention 182. In spite of that, there are only a few plans which include practical programmes for the prevention or elimination of child labour in specific regions or which contribute in an indirect manner, as, for example, through the promotion of universal access to compulsory education. Yet in this type of actions there are some important and commendable exceptions, almost totally in the hands of the cooperation activity developed by the ILO through IPEC, as will be described next.

18.3.4 Prevention, withdrawal, rehabilitation and social assistance action: the effects of direct action programmes, time-bound programmes and conditional cash transfer programmes

As pointed out, in accordance with Convention 182, States are obliged to take 'effective and time-bound measures' to prevent the engagement of children in the worst forms of child labour, to withdraw them from those forms of labour and to ensure their reintegration into society.

From the beginning of its activity in South America, IPEC has tried to encourage this type of intervention through the stimulation of direct action programmes with a demonstrative character, aiming to show that there are methods to achieve the removal of children from these particularly reprehensible forms of labour exploitation. Being designed not to significantly reduce the number of child workers but to introduce governmental bodies and social actors to strategies proven to be effective, these programmes obviously have a limited scope.

Nevertheless, IPEC's support to direct action programmes in the region has been relevant in the last few years not only qualitatively but also quantitatively. Being focused on certain priority sectors at risk like commercial sexual exploitation, artisanal mining, domestic work, urban work or agricultural work, these programmes now number far in excess of 100, with the number of minors already

---

59 For a description and comparative analysis of these plans, see Programa Internacional para la Erradicación del Trabajo Infantil-IPEC, *Reflexiones para el cambio. Análisis de los planes nacionales de prevención y erradicación del trabajo infantil en América Latina y el Caribe*, Lima, Publicaciones de Oficina Internacional del Trabajo, 2006.

directly benefiting estimated at 60,000 in 2004.[60] The fundamental feature of such programmes is the combination, in their design and implementation, of elements which go beyond the purely repressive sphere, so as to give a complete response to the problem, as for example the emphasis put on child educational retention and enrolment, the promotion of family and community commitment to the elimination actions and the search for economically productive solutions which would favour an improvement of family income, thus freeing the minors from the pressure that urges them to work.[61]

With such features, the experience of these programmes can only be evaluated very positively. Even so, it must be kept in mind that their ultimate objective is to promote the development of similar actions at the national level by the States. This does not depend on IPEC exclusively, but on States' political will, and here difficulties arise. The approach to the national plans for the prevention and elimination of child labour has been useful for showing the limited ability of the different national administrations to replicate this kind of experiences through the designing of national programmes aimed at the prevention, withdrawal and rehabilitation of children affected by the labour practices prohibited by Convention 182.

The causes of this weakness are surely several, with organizational, technical and, most of all, financial difficulties playing in all likelihood a predominant role. IPEC has tried to alleviate these shortcomings through another instrument: time-bound programmes. Unlike direct action programmes, TBPs consist of an integrated set of measures aimed at the prevention and elimination of the worst forms of child labour, designed and launched directly by the States, but relying on IPEC's technical assistance and financial support for a predefined period of time. This type of programme is designed as a sort of 'intermediate step' between those with a purely demonstrative character, and independently implemented State programmes. Their main problem is their high cost, despite the fact that IPEC acts as a co-financing entity, which restricts their implementation to a limited number of countries. In South America, two programmes of this type have been launched. The first one, in Brazil, is mainly aimed at supporting the goals of the national plan for the elimination of child labour and to strengthen the work of its national committee. But it also envisages the development of programmes for combating the worst forms of child labour focused on limited geographical areas and specific activities, such as commercial labour exploitation, domestic labour, work in the informal sector or agricultural work. The second one, in Ecuador, focuses on the withdrawal and prevention of child labour in specific sectors, such as flower production, banana cultivation, the construction industry or commercial sexual exploitation.[62] Both programmes expired at the end of 2006.

---

60 According to data provided by Programa IPEC América Latina y el Caribe, *La acción del IPEC*, *supra* note 8, 80.

61 For a review of the direct action programmes launched by IPEC in South America, see <http://www.oit.org.pe/ipec/pagina.php?seccion=42>.

62 For more details about these programmes and their implementation, see <http://www.oit.org.pe/ipec>.

Beyond these programmes, States' interventions directly aimed at the prevention, rescue and rehabilitation of children involved in the worst forms of child labour are rare in the region. This is particularly worrying if one considers that the fight against this kind of practice requires not only general political decisions, but also specific actions in support of those who suffer from them. This deficiency puts at risk the objective of achieving their elimination within the periods planned by the ILO and the national governments.

However, the experience of the countries of the region, and especially of Brazil, demonstrates that there is an instrument located halfway between political measures of indirect intervention and direct assistance interventions, able to make a relevant contribution to the reduction of the rates of child labour. It is the so-called conditional cash transfer (CCT) programmes. These are social assistance programmes through which a certain amount of money is periodically given to families with scarce resources and with minors to support, on condition that they will fulfil certain obligations aimed at favouring the children's human development, such as school attendance, participation in sanitary programmes or others.[63]

In the last few years various South American countries have launched programmes of this type, even if with extremely different achievements and goals. Beside small and medium-size ones, there are also some gigantic programmes, like the *Programa Bolsa Familia* (previously *Bolsa Escuela*) in Brazil, from which no less than 6.5 million families currently benefit.[64] The objectives of these programmes and their experiences are extremely different, as they range from the improvement of the living conditions of the needy population, through the increase in social services' coverage, to more specific objectives, such as the promotion of children's school attendance or their removal from work.

Being designed in this way, CCT programmes cannot be regarded as a general tool to combat child labour. Even so, their implementation may have positive effects also in this field, insofar as it contributes to the alleviation of some of the structural problems which stand at its base, such as chronic poverty, vulnerability to economic

---

63 For an evaluation of these programmes and of their impact on child labour, see especially H. Tabatabai, *Eliminating Child Labour: The Promise of Conditional Cash Transfers, Geneva*, ILO, 2006. H. Tabatabai, *Erradicación del trabajo infantil: la promesa de los programas de transferencias en efectivo condicionadas*, Geneva, ILO, 2006. Available at <http://www.oit.org/alc/documentos/doc_tec_ipec_06.pdf>. As pointed out by this author on page 3 of this study, these programmes represent 'a way to use financial incentives in order to motivate the participants or citizens to adopt behaviour which may not be in their immediate personal interest, but which is important for society'. Translation by the editors. The following mainly draws on the information provided by this author.

64 Source: Tabatabai, *Erradicación del trabajo infantil, supra* note 63, 29. Regarding these programmes and their antecedents, see also G. di Giovanni, *Aspectos cualitativos do trabalho infantil no Brasil*, Brasilia, Publicaciones de la Oficina Internacional del Trabajo, 2004, 39–47, available at <http://www.oit.org.pe/ipec/documentos/ti_cuali_br.pdf>. Other examples of programmes of this kind in the region are: Familias en Acción (Colombia) and Chile Solidario y Bono de Desarrollo Humano (Ecuador).

crises, the lack of access to educational services or the limited attractiveness of schooling as an alternative to work.[65]

However, these positive effects may significantly increase if these programmes adopt the reduction of child labour as one of their explicit objectives and develop the appropriate instruments. This was demonstrated by the Programme for the Elimination of Child Labour (PETI), launched in Brazil in 1996 with the aim of contributing to the elimination of its worst forms, especially in rural areas and in hazardous activities.[66]

Similar to most programmes of its type, PETI gives cash incentives to families with scarce resources and with working children between 7 and 15 years of age. In exchange they have to support the children or send them to school. However, there is a difference between this programme and the others: in order for the families to have access to the economic support, children also have to take part in a programme of after-school activities called *Jornada Ampliada*, composed of activities of student support, recreation, arts education, sport and food supplementation.[67] The idea on which this programme is based could not be simpler: to contribute to the reduction of child labour by shortening time which children can devote to it through the doubling of their stay at school.[68] In this way, the risk that children will devote themselves to studies and work at the same time considerably decreases, with the transfers having a clearer and more perceptible effect on the children's work.

Available studies on the impact of PETI support this statement. In this sense, the doubts about the positive repercussions on child labour by transfer programmes with a general scope, especially aroused by the ability to reconcile work with school attendance, become watered down in the case of this programme, as it has been possible to demonstrate that not only has it achieved an increase in the school day and an improvement in the academic success of children benefiting from it, but it has also allowed for a reduction of their participation in the economically active population and a decrease in the hazardous labour index.[69]

---

65 Tabatabai, *Erradicación del trabajo infantil, supra* note 63, 7.

66 At present this programme has been integrated into the *Programa Bolsa Escuela*. In this sense, see ILO, International Programme on the Elimination of Child Labour, *IPEC Action Against Child Labour: Highlights 2006*, Geneva, ILO, 2007, 60–61.

67 Di Giovanni, *Aspectos cualitativos, supra* note 64, 40.

68 Tabatabai, *Erradicación del trabajo infantil, supra* note 63, 8, 10–11, according to whom 'the programme of extra-curricular activities is the most important element to combat child labour' introduced by PETI. (Translation by the editors.) This observation is based on the view that even if in principle 'school and work may be combined', there is nevertheless 'a natural limit to this option', whenever 'the longer time spent at school necessarily limits the time available for child labour beyond a certain point'.

69 The empirical evidence is summarized by Tabatabai, Erradicación del trabajo infantil, *supra* note 63, 10. According to the evidence, the probability of working among the children taking part in the programme decreased by 30 per cent to 75 per cent, depending on the region. Regarding its quantitative impact, it is estimated that PETI has reached over one million children. See ILO, *The End of Child Labour, supra* note 2, 14. In its 2005 report, the CEACR noted the existence of this programme and made an assessment of its activity. See ILO, *Report of the Committee of Experts*, 2005, *supra* note 26, 205.

The experience of PETI demonstrates that CCT programmes can be a powerful instrument in the fight against child labour, and particularly its worst forms, especially if they are specifically aimed in this direction; if their implementation is focused on sections of the population particularly affected by these practices, and if complementary elements are added that make it more difficult to combine them with work.

Here the main difficulty lies in the high level of financial resources required for the implementation of these programmes, which are not always within the reach of South American States. To this must be added the need to dispose of educational services in a sufficient quantity and of an adequate quality, in order to form an effective alternative to work. This condition is not necessarily satisfied in the region, and even less in the particularly run-down areas where the worst forms of child labour proliferate. However, recent ILO-sponsored studies demonstrate that the costs of widespread interventions of this kind, together with specific withdrawal actions if needed, are lower than the economic benefits to them, their families and the whole society, generated in the long term by an improvement in the education and health of the children involved in child labour.[70]

18.4 The huge challenge posed by a stubborn problem

In the light of what has been said in the previous section, it does not seem possible to question the huge institutional effort made by the ILO through IPEC with the goal of promoting the development by the States of South America of policies aimed at the elimination of child labour. That this effort has not been in vain is demonstrated by the fact that the fight against this social evil appears at present as a priority issue on the public agendas of all the countries of the region, with a widespread consensus among them concerning the need to take significant steps towards its abolition. Furthermore, this commitment has been accompanied by an important effort at States' internal adaptation to the international standards regarding the subject, in which an especially important role has been played by the different instruments designed by IPEC, as well as by its activity of cooperation and technical assistance.

Clear examples of this are the recorded unanimity regarding the ratification of the fundamental conventions on the subject; the concern shown by the States when it was time to adapt their domestic legislation to the provisions of these conventions; the progress made in the implementation of tools to measure the extent of the phenomenon and gain a better knowledge of its causes and characteristics; the widespread creation of national committees for the fight against child labour; and the

---

70 See, P. Sauma, *Construir futuro, invertir en la infancia. Estudio económico de los costos y beneficios de erradicar el trabajo infantil en Iberoamérica*, San José de Costa Rica. ILO, 2005. Specifically, by the same author, *Construir futuro, invertir en la infancia. Estudio económico de los costos y beneficios de erradicar el trabajo infantil en los Países Andinos*, Lima, ILO, 2006; and *Construir futuro, invertir en la infancia. Estudio económico de los costos y beneficios de erradicar el trabajo infantil en los Países del Cono Sur*, Lima, ILO, 2006.

adoption of national plans for the prevention and elimination of child labour based on the integration of action and policy in various fields.

However, these developments should not lead us to overlook the limitations which characterize the regional approach to the problem. Let us remember, just to cite the most relevant deficiencies, the abandoning by a majority of States of the goal of keeping a policy which favours a gradual rise of the minimum age for admission to employment; the States' poor diligence when it was time to approve specific rules aimed to repress some of the unconditionally worst forms of child labour, such as illicit labour and forced labour; the lack of ability to develop reliable assessment systems for this class of particularly reprehensible practices or to launch effective systems for the surveillance and control of the enforcement of the legislation; or, finally, the difficulties in launching plans and programmes aimed at the prevention, withdrawal and rehabilitation of children at risk of being involved in, or affected by prohibited activities.

Furthermore, if one compares the aspects in which progress has been significant with those in which the stalemate is evident, it is not difficult to discern a general scenario in which the formal acceptance of the international requirements regarding child labour and ILO's proposals coexists with an evident lack of the instruments which may lead to their real and effective implementation. This is, to a greater or lesser extent, common to all the countries of the region. The only exception deserving to be mentioned is represented by Brazil, where normative and institutional adaptation has been accompanied by a real concern about the development of tools able to yield positive results. And the results indeed are evident: in this country the child labour participation rate among the 5–14 age group decreased over the years from 1992 to 2002 from 12.1 to 6.1 per cent, with a total of 2 million children leaving labour activities.[71] This result undoubtedly explains to a great extent the good comprehensive performance of child labour indicators of the region as a whole, given the significant demographic weight of Brazil.

Naturally, as long as this dualism persists it will be difficult to take firm steps in the whole of South America to achieve, if not its total elimination, at least the elimination of the worst forms of labour prohibited to minors. One should not lose sight of the fact that, even if global ILO estimates report a significant decrease in the children's activity rate in South America and the Caribbeans over the period 2000–04, the extent of child labour to be eliminated continues to record truly alarming proportions in the southern part of the continent.

In accordance with Convention 138 children between the ages of 5 and 14 should not be allowed to carry out any activity, except for light work. In addition, Convention 182 mandates the urgent withdrawal of 5–14-year-olds who carry out hazardous work or are entangled in the unconditional worst forms of child exploitation. According to estimates contained in recent ILO-sponsored reports, both groups add up to the astronomical figure of 7,904,315 South American minors who need to be withdrawn

---

71 Specifically, the number of working children in this age group decreased from 4.1 million to 2.1 million. Source: Ministerio de Trabajo y Empleo del Brasil, *Plan Nacional*, *supra* note 8, 11.

from child labour.[72] Thus, we find ourselves confronted with a phenomenon which, notwithstanding the recorded progress, remains of an enormous magnitude.

It must be added, as the ILO itself has pointed out in its first global report on the matter, that child labour is a stubborn problem. Even if one may be under the impression that it has been overcome in specific places or sectors, it may re-appear or turn up elsewhere with unexpected intensity and frequency.[73] Thus, the progress recorded at a given moment may easily diminish in a short time, especially if the effort is not firmly kept up. A good example of this is the Brazilian case, where the labour activity rate of 5–14-year-olds, after a period of uninterrupted decrease over more than ten years, has experienced a 10.3 per cent increase between 2004 and 2005, from 11.8 to 12.2 per cent.[74] The situation is rather worse, of course, in those countries where, in spite of the institutional effort made, the number of working children has not stopped growing over the last few years. This is the case, for example, in Argentina where the number of working children grew sixfold from 1998 to 2005, increasing to 1,500,000 from the initial 250,000;[75] in Paraguay, where 56,500 children joined the active population in the years from 2002 to 2005;[76] and in Peru, whose child labour participation rate increased fourfold between 1993 and 2005, from 7.9 to 31.8 per cent.[77]

Consequently, even if the progress achieved is not at all insignificant, all the more so if one takes into account the unfavourable starting point, it does not appear able to guarantee the achievement of the goals set by Conventions 138 and 182. Therefore, it is necessary not only to support, but to significantly increase this effort, extending it to all the areas where deficiencies are currently recorded. This includes, evidently, the development of short-term programmes of assistance to children affected by child labour, but also medium- and long-term social policy measures aimed at ensuring universal access to social services, quality education for all children and a decent job for adults. Only through a coherent combination of immediate actions and longer-

---

72 This number is the sum of the subtotals of child labour to be eliminated in the Andean sub-regions and in the sub-regions of the southern cone of the continent. The figures are contained in the previously mentioned studies on the costs and benefits of this option. For the complete data, see Sauma, *Construir futuro ... en los Países Andinos, supra* note 70, 13–21; and Sauma, *Construir futuro ... en los países del Cono Sur, supra* note 70, 13–21. It is important to note that the difference between this amount and the one recorded at the global level by the ILO can be explained to a great extent by the estimate made in these studies of the number of children between 15 and 17 years of age who carry out prohibited works.

73 ILO, *A Future Without Child Labour, supra* note 5, 21 and 57.

74 Source: Instituto Brasileiro de Geografía e Estadísticas, Pesquisa nacional por amostra de domicilios (PNAD). Sintese de Indicadores 2005. Available at <http://www.ibge.gov.br>.

75 The figure was taken from a joint investigation carried out by UNICEF and the National Committee for the Elimination of Child Labour in Argentina. See <http://www.rel-uita.org/laboral/argentina-trabajo-infantil.htm>.

76 Source: UNICEF. For further information, see <http://www.abc.com.py/articulos.php?fec=2006-05-11&pid=251535&sec=3>.

77 See J.C. Cortés Carcelén, *La aplicación de los principios y derechos fundamentales en el trabajo en el Perú en el contexto de la integración regional*, Lima, ILO, 2005, 31.

term policies will it be possible to offer satisfactory and sustainable results for a problem with such an intensity and persistence as child labour.[78]

The instruments for carrying out this two-pronged strategy exist and they have been validated, both by the experience of the IPEC and by the practice of the countries which have employed them. What is now missing is for the States to use them effectively.

The problem is that doing so in most of the cases requires something more than political will. It must be kept in mind that child labour, even when it stems exclusively from poverty, is not only the reflection of poverty, but also of the absence or ineffectiveness of the instruments used to tackle it, in particular of educational systems, social protection systems and the systems for guaranteeing decent work. It means that child labour is also a sign of the absence of the State or of its ineffectiveness. The great challenge posed by the elimination of child labour in the region is not, therefore, just one of finding a way to convince States to adopt concrete measures, but also one of achieving a transformation of their structures, which would place before other goals the attention to the social needs of the majority of their population: health, education, access to an employment with rights, etc. This is the great challenge South American countries will have to face in the coming years, and on this depends their future as democratic societies. Under this perspective, the fight against child labour is nothing else but a part of the general fight for the construction of fairer and more evenly balanced societies in the region.

---

78 Quote from W. Alarcón Glasinovich, '¿Por qué erradicar el trabajo infantil?', available at <http://gin.org.pe/alarcon-trabajoinf.htm>. For the rest of the people, this is an approach widely adopted by the ILO. An expression of this is the statement in the second global report on the situation of child labour: 'A comprehensive and coherent approach to child labour must … aim at poverty reduction, provision of quality education, and social protection measures including protection of workers' rights, to respond to the multidimensional reality of child labour'. ILO, *The End of Child Labour: Within Reach, supra* note 2, 24.

PART IV
An Epilogue?

Chapter 19

Is the Eradication of Child Labour 'Within Reach'? Achievements and Challenges Ahead

Bob Hepple

19.1 Transforming the fight against child labour

Should we be pessimistic or optimistic about the prospect of eliminating exploitative child labour? In its first global report on the subject in 2002, the ILO reported that child labour 'is a stubborn phenomenon, whose complete elimination has not yet been accomplished in any economic sector or in any region of the world'.[1] The second global report, in 2006, significantly titled *The End of Child Labour: Within Reach*, reported an 11 per cent decrease in the number of working children worldwide between 2000 and 2004.[2] This led the Director-General to claim that the goal of 'eliminating the worst forms of child labour within the next ten years' was 'ambitious but achievable'.[3]

There are many reasons to be sceptical about the ILO's optimism. The scale of the problem remains uncertain. Child labour tends to be hidden in the informal economy and in illegal and clandestine activities. There are doubts about the reliability of statistical estimates based on extrapolation of available information in a limited number of countries.[4] Moreover, as Sanguineti Raymond points out, 'even if one may be under the impression that it has been overcome in specific places or sectors, it may reappear or turn up elsewhere with unexpected intensity and frequency'.[5] This phenomenon is richly illustrated in the case studies in Part III of this volume.

This scepticism should not, however, lead us into facile pessimism. There have been real achievements in the fight against exploitative child labour since 1992 when the International Programme for the Elimination of Child Labour (IPEC) was launched. The conception of child labour has been transformed into a fundamental

---

1 ILO, *A Future Without Child Labour – Global Report under the Follow-Up to the ILO Declaration on Fundamental Principles and Rights at Work*, Geneva, ILO, 2002, 21.

2 ILO, *The End of Child Labour: Within Reach – Global Report under the Follow-Up to the ILO Declaration on Fundamental Rights and Principles at Work*, Geneva, ILO, 2006.

3 *Ibid.*, ix.

4 The details are to be found in F. Hagerman, Y. Diallo, A. Etienne and F. Mehran, *Global Labour Trends 2000–2004*, Geneva, ILO, 2006; see Sanguineti Raymond (this volume).

5 Sanguineti Raymond (this volume); ILO, *A Future Without Child Labour*, *supra* note 1, 21 and 57.

human right of children against exploitative labour and this is now (arguably) enshrined in customary international law. Positive duties to protect the rights of children have been developed. The elimination of exploitative child labour has been brought from the margins into the mainstream of socio-economic development policies.

Yet these achievements are not guaranteed, and serious challenges remain. There are undoubtedly still millions of child labourers, whatever the precise numbers. Countries are reluctant to introduce a minimum age for access to employment. There is defective application of international standards and a lack of effective enforcement. Children in many countries are still not getting to school and some are even conscripted into armed conflicts. Above all, poverty remains a root cause of child labour in developing countries, and the rights of the child have not yet been embedded into the world trade systems. So the elimination of exploitative child labour – characterized by the Director-General of the ILO in 1983 as an affront to the conscience of the international community[6] – remains an urgent project.

I have been asked, as someone who was not involved in the extensive research on which this study is based, to provide some reflections on the achievements of the campaign, and of the main challenges that lie ahead. I shall not attempt to summarize the detail of the findings or to restate the conclusions of the various authors. What follows are simply some personal reflections after reading this impressively researched volume.

19.2 Achievements

19.2.1 Freedom from child labour as a fundamental human right

The most conspicuous achievement has been the transformation of concerns about child labour into a fundamental human right of children.

The earliest laws on the employment of children were essentially public health measures. When the first industrial revolution started in cotton manufacturing in 18th-century Britain, children were regarded as the best operatives because of their small size and the delicacy of their touch. They were a cheap source of labour, often 'apprenticed' to factory owners by local communities who had the responsibility to support pauper children. When epidemics of fever broke out in 1784 and 1796 in Manchester, agitation led to the Health and Morals of Apprentices Act in 1802, aimed at preventing abuses which endangered not only children but also the health of the community.

Humanitarian concerns of entrepreneurs like Robert Owen led to the British Act of 1819 limiting the hours of work of children in factories – 'the real beginnings of industrial legislation'.[7] The Swiss banker Jacques Necker and the Alsatian manufacturer Daniel Legrand were the first to argue that international regulation of labour, in particular that of children, was the only way to overcome the dilemma

---

6 ILO, *Report of the Director-General*, Geneva, ILO, 1983, 6.

7 J.W. Follow, *Antecedents of the ILO*, Oxford, Oxford University Press, 1951, 2.

faced by industrializing countries that might expose themselves to destructive foreign competition if they adopted humanitarian measures to protect their own workers.[8] Their ambition of international labour legislation was never achieved, but in 1919, article 427 of the Treaty of Versailles declared that one of the 'methods and principles' of 'special and urgent importance' for the new ILO would be 'the abolition of child labour and the imposition of such limitations on the labour of young persons as shall permit the continuance of their education and ensure their proper physical development'. True to the spirit of article 427, the ILO gave a high priority to setting standards, from 1919 onwards, on the minimum age for access to employment, night work of young persons and medical examinations of young persons.[9]

The conceptual basis of these standards reflected both humanitarian and health considerations. One might also argue that the rather limited scope of these standards, concentrating on the minimum age for employment, reflected the reluctance of States to become involved in the essentially private sphere of the family. It is normal in pre-industrial societies for children to be involved in domestic and agricultural employment within the family. It is only when children leave the sphere of the family to go into factories, mills and mines that the state is likely to regulate their labour. However, the state has to remain sensitive to the way in which parents choose to bring up their children, and to avoid undermining parental authority or reducing family income. This helps to explain the reluctance to treat children as having autonomous 'rights'.

The 1998 Declaration on Fundamental Principles and Rights at Work symbolized the transformation of humanitarian concerns into human rights. Convention 182 and Recommendation 190 gave concrete expression to those rights in the context of the worst forms of exploitation. Children were no longer simply 'victims' but were turned into rights-holders.[10] This was not a sudden or unexpected development. Since the 1960s the children's rights movement has campaigned for the recognition of children as rights-holders. This rests on a developmental model of childhood: every child has the right to be prepared to have an individual life in society and to be brought up in the spirit of the ideals proclaimed in the Charter of the UN. This rights-based approach finds its expression in the crucially important UN Convention on the Rights of the Child (1989) (CRC). This sets out a number of rights of the child including 'the right of children to be protected from economic exploitation and from performing any work that is likely to be hazardous or to interfere with the child's education or be harmful to the child's health or physical, mental, spiritual, moral or social development' (article 32).

The CRC and C182 together constitute a striking rejection of the notion that children are too young, immature or incompetent to claim rights. However, a problem

---

8 V. Ghebali, *The ILO: A Case Study on the Evolution of United Nations Specialised Agencies*, Boston MA/The Hague, Nijhoff, 1989, 3.

9 Trebilcock and Raimondi (this volume).

10 Cf. Sanna (this volume) who points out that C182 bans the worst forms of child labour because children are the 'victims' of those activities. While this is correct, I would add the important rider that C182 also turns those 'victims' into rights-holders, and this is the most important feature of C182.

with this rights-based approach is that children are often dependent on those who may be acting in breach of their rights. Moreover, the mere fact that international treaties and conventions assert children's rights does not mean that children have enforceable rights in practice. Indeed, some argue that by declaring children's 'rights' in formal terms, States are able to cloak their inactivity behind a smokescreen of rhetoric.[11] In domestic contexts, many assertions of children's rights are simply aspirations and not reality. The rhetoric of rights is no more than a hollow promise unless matched by effective international supervision and domestic enforcement of these rights by the state, trade unions, NGOs and other agencies (see below).

A question which arises is how we should classify children's rights as they appear in the various international instruments. Hammerberg[12] suggests a classification based on the four Ps: participation, protection against discrimination, protection against harm, and provision for assistance with basic needs. Participation is recognized in respect of the rights of the child to freedom of association (CRC, article 15), and children are clearly 'workers' protected in their rights to freedom of association and collective bargaining under ILO Conventions 87 and 98. Protection against discrimination is specifically recognized in article 2(1) of the CRC, and children as workers are covered by the ILO conventions on discrimination. Protection against harm is recognized in both the CRC and in C182's provisions on hazardous work. Provision for assistance with basic needs is to be found mainly in the CRC. This shows the importance of the links between these international instruments in creating children's rights.

19.2.2 Rights against exploitative child labour are being transformed into customary international law

The unique character of the 1998 Declaration is that the obligations to provide minimum ages for employment and to eliminate the worst forms of child labour are placed on all ILO member States not by reason of their ratification of named conventions but 'from the very fact of membership'.[13] This is a constitutional obligation and not one which rests upon voluntary acceptance.

It might be argued that those few countries that have failed to ratify C182 are bound by the principles of the relevant conventions by virtue of their membership of the ILO. Such an argument is unlikely to make any practical difference, however, because the Declaration is purely promotional.

The more interesting question, from a legal perspective, is whether the rights embodied in C182 have become a part of customary international law. This is not directly considered by the authors of the present study, but it is of significance. If exploitative child labour is to be treated as universally contrary to international law, in the same way as piracy, slavery and forced labour, it would need to be shown

---

11 For a general discussion see M. Freeman, *The Rights and Wrongs of Children*, London/ Dover, Frances Pinter, 1983, Chap. 2.

12 T. Hammerberg, 'The UN Convention on the Rights of the Child and How to Make it Work', *Human Rights Quarterly*, Vol. 12, 1990, 97.

13 Swepston (this volume).

that standards on child labour form part of 'habitual state practice' and that States appreciate that this practice is required by international law. The state practices must be 'broadly consistent'.[14] These criteria clearly cannot be met in respect of the minimum age for employment. Despite the significant increase since 1998 in the number of ratifications of C138, only 150 out of 181 ILO member States had done so by 2007. Some of these ratifications may simply have been formalities in order to benefit from technical assistance, and the high number of CEACR observations addressed to developing countries highlights the compliance problems. There is neither habitual nor consistent state practice.

However, by 2007 there had been 165 ratifications of C182, which became the most rapidly and widely ratified of all ILO conventions. The conclusions by Rishikesh in Chapter 5 of this volume are that C182 has had demonstrable positive effects in bringing down the extent of exploited child labour – particularly in regard to trafficking and commercial sexual exploitation and hazardous work – and that there is a major political consensus regarding this convention. The majority of States have moved a long way towards habitual and consistent practices to eliminate the worst forms of child labour. This supports the case for arguing that the elimination of the worst forms of child labour (as identified in C182) can now be recognized, or may soon be recognized, as part of customary international law.

19.2.3 Positive duties have been imposed on States to protect and promote children's rights in respect of work

As Marco Pertile points out in his introduction to this volume, international legal obligations are generally framed as duties on States to 'recognize' or to 'protect' certain rights, in this case those of children. The special feature of C182, as he indicates, is that States are obliged to 'design and implement programmes of action to eliminate as a priority the worst forms of child labour'. This marks a shift of international legal obligations from a negative to a positive duty.

Theoretically, the notion of positive duties may be said to embody Amaryta Sen's 'capabilities' theory.[15] This sees freedom not as absence of coercion by the state, but as agency or the ability of being able to do what one values. The things people may want to do he calls 'functionings'; the functionings that are feasible for a person to achieve are 'capabilities'. What people can achieve is influenced by economic opportunities and political liberties as well as factors such as good health and basic education. The achievement of freedom therefore entails the removal of major obstacles such as poverty, tyranny, social deprivation and lack of education. The logical conclusion is that in order to acquire capabilities people need positive action to be taken.[16] Nussbaum has developed the conceptual basis of capability to argue that there is a threshold level of capability below which human functioning is

---

14 *Nicaragua v United States* [1986] ICJ 14 at 98; B. Hepple, *Labour Laws and Global Trade*, Oxford and Portland OR, Hart, 2005, 60.

15 A. Sen, *Development as Freedom*, Oxford, Oxford University Press, 1999, Chap. 5.

16 See S. Fredman, *Human Rights Transformed*, Oxford, Oxford University Press, 2008, 12.

not possible. The social goal is to get human beings above this minimum capability threshold. This gives rise to a positive duty on the state to ensure that people have the threshold level of functioning.[17]

When applied to children's rights, these theories imply that the capabilities of children and their families to function in society depend on state measures for basic education, the relief of poverty and so on. Without such state action the rights of the child to be free from economic or sexual exploitation cannot be achieved. The positive duties can be seen as a means of achieving equality of opportunity; that is, for children to have a fair chance to achieve a decent life. The examples given in Chapter 18 of this volume by Saguineti Raymond of over 100 direct action programmes in South America show how these programmes – mandated by C182 – can improve the capabilities of children. The programmes include education, the support of families and communities, and the search for alternative economic production solutions to improve family income in order to free children from exploitative labour.

The new emphasis on positive duties also demolishes the old artificial distinction between civil and political rights, on the one hand, and socio-economic rights, on the other.[18] All human rights are based on the values of freedom, equality, democracy and solidarity. Solidarity, in the context of children's rights, means that adults and the state have legal duties, as well as moral ones, to ensure the freedom of children from exploitative labour. Democracy, in this context, means that children should be able to participate in decisions that affect their lives. Article 2 of Recommendation 190 recommends that 'the programme of action [referred to in article 6 of C182] should be designed and implemented ... taking into account the views of the children directly affected by the worst forms of child labour'. This empowerment of children, as Pertile points out in the Introduction, is one of the remarkable features of C182. Moreover, article 6 of C182 requires consultation with relevant government institutions and employers' and workers' organizations.

19.2.4 The elimination of child labour as a development goal

The campaign against child labour has, in the past, suffered from a Western-centric approach. This was a legacy of the early history of industrial legislation which started in Europe, and was reflected in ILO conventions on child labour from 1919. Attempts to extend the Western levels of minimum ages for access to employment to developing countries, emerging from colonialism, were seen as 'social imperialism', an attempt by developed countries to seek to exclude competition by imposing standards that they themselves ignored in the process of industrialization.[19] It is no surprise, therefore, that there were relatively few ratifications of C138 before the adoption of the ILO Declaration in 1998, and of C182 in 1999. In my view, this was not an issue of cultural relativism but rather one of economic underdevelopment. The inflexible application of C138 (which I noticed when acting as an ILO expert

---

17 M. Nussbaum, *Women and Human Development*, New York, Cambridge University Press, 2000, 5–6.

18 Fredman, *Human Rights Transformed*, *supra* note 16, 240.

19 See Hepple, *Labour Laws and Global Trade*, *supra* note 14, 2.

drafting a labour code for newly independent Namibia in 1990) failed to take account of the absence of adequate schooling for children below the age of 14 or 15, family poverty, and the traditional ways in which children had been educated within the family or community as shepherds and domestic workers.

Until the mid-1990s the World Bank and other institutions concerned with development had largely ignored the issue of child labour.[20] Under well-targeted pressure from the ILO and NGOs, the World Bank was persuaded to pioneer a developmental approach to child labour. The significance of this is that economic considerations – the 'business case' – were used to justify the enforcement of prohibitions on child labour in developing countries and to mainstream the issue in the Bank's work. The approach was pragmatic, triggered by the ILO's adoption of C182. The case studies in Part III of this volume emphasize the close links between child labour and poverty. Breaking the cycle of deprivation by cutting its weakest link – exploitative child labour – is proving to be an effective development strategy.

This does not, however, free developing countries from the fundamental dilemma posed by the phenomenal expansion of global trade. They face in an acute form the problem first posed in the 18th century by Necker and Legrand (see above): how can countries secure a competitive advantage if they are undercut by others that exploit low-cost child labour? One solution is the application by countries in a similar situation of the international standards on child labour. Another is by pursuing domestic policies which enhance labour productivity. Markets tend to generate differentials in wages and conditions that bear no relation to the value added by individual workers. Under-valued labour leads to productive inefficiency, hampers innovation and results in destructive competition. Only regulation – including the enforcement of child labour standards – can correct this market failure.

Moreover, domestic regulation can be justified on redistributive grounds. Those who oppose or seek to minimize the regulation of child labour see wealth maximization (or allocative efficiency) as the primary goal and the competitive market model as the just distribution. Those who regard the elimination of child labour as a fundamental human right regard this right as a means to achieve distributive justice. Of course, regulation should be avoided if it will harm those whom it is designed to help – putting a child on the street without education or family support is a cure worse than the disease. Only if the elimination of child labour forms part of a broader strategy of education, training and the relief of family poverty will it truly benefit those who are the right-holders.

19.3 Challenges

19.3.1 Defining the goal more precisely

It is to the case studies in Part III of this volume that one must mainly turn in order to highlight the significant obstacles to the achievement of the goal of eliminating exploitative child labour by 2016. One is immediately struck by the confusion

---

20 Schlemmer-Schulte (this volume).

between 'work' by children and exploitative 'labour'. This is illustrated by the case study of Mali.[21] The need of the child to grow and develop his or her personality within a family is fundamental. In rural societies the activities performed by children, under parental control, such as looking after the oxen, chasing birds away from the crops and doing housework, are deemed to be compatible with their age and their status in the family. Generally, this kind of traditional activity, although it involves 'work', falls outside the sphere of labour legislation. It is when children go outside this environment of the farm or home, under the control of others, that 'labour' in the sense of employment begins. Even within the sphere of 'labour' C182 recognizes that it is only the 'worst' forms of exploitation that should be the subject of priority action.

Unfortunately, these distinctions are not always maintained in practice. As Keita points out in Chapter 16 of this volume, governments in developing countries are caught between their international obligations and the pressure of Western donors to eliminate child labour on the one hand, and the persisting attachment of the population to traditional ways of socializing children within the family on the other hand. They can escape these conflicting pressures only by framing development strategies to improve the living conditions of the poorest families so that these families can meet the educational needs of their children. Rather than speak loosely of eliminating child labour in general, it would be better to make it clear that, at the present stage, the target is the 'worst forms' of exploitative child labour identified in C182.

19.3.2 Achievement of a minimum age for access to employment

One of the most effective ways of eliminating abuses of child labour would be the adoption and enforcement of minimum ages for admission to employment.[22] However, the history of C138 shows that it is too prescriptive and inflexible to take account of the circumstances of both developed and developing countries, and it lacks priorities for national policy.[23] C182 has proved to be more effective because it emphasizes the shared values of all countries in eliminating the worst forms of child labour. The new convention concentrates on the most intolerable forms of child labour and it provides for progressive implementation of its norms. However, the International Labour Conference decided not to abandon or revise C138, but instead to list it alongside C182, as a core convention for purposes of the Declaration of Fundamental Principles and Rights at Work in 1998. This has led to an extraordinary increase in ratifications of C138, but there are few signs that this has resulted in widespread elimination of child labour.

A new approach is needed. This would involve a revision of C182, going beyond the worst forms of child labour set out in C182 into a statement of more positive and longer-term objectives for the elimination of all forms of child labour. This integrated approach would indicate clearly the circumstances in which child labour is permitted

---

21 Keita (this volume).

22 B. Creighton, 'Combating Child Labour: the Role of International Labour Standards', *Comparative Labor Law Journal*, Vol. 18, 1997, 362 ff, at 395.

23 Borzaga (this volume).

(for example within the family), it would avoid an unduly prescriptive approach, it would impose positive duties on ratifying States to avoid exposing children to harm (physical, sexual and moral) and to provide real educational opportunities. Within this context, minimum ages for admission to employment could be set as targets. This would render C138 obsolete.

19.3.3 Defective application and inadequate enforcement

The case studies in this volume identify a number of defects in the application and enforcement of standards on child labour. These include lack of resources for enforcement,[24] corruption,[25] and the symbolic use of inappropriate and ineffective legal methods such as the criminal law.[26] Some of these problems cannot be resolved outside the general framework of democratic economic and social development. Others, such as the choice of the most effective legal instruments, can be dealt with provided that there is a combination of political will and technical expertise. Effective and properly resourced inspection systems, involving workers' representatives as well as state inspectors, should be the cornerstone of domestic strategies.

19.3.4 Getting children to school

China is the leading example of a country which has succeeded in dramatically reducing child labour by taking people out of poverty and enrolling children in school.[27] Universal primary education for five years has been achieved, and China is well on the way to implementing its nine-year compulsory education policy. A lesson from China is that by prohibiting the employment of children who have not had nine years' schooling, there can be a dramatic impact on poverty reduction, and the achievement of universal education.

India has tried to tackle the problem of rehabilitation of child labourers. Pratap reports that this became a legal requirement in 1996, when the Supreme Court ordered state inspectors to identify children employed illegally and to use the fines collected from their employers for the rehabilitation of the child concerned. However, he found that state-sponsored schemes for rehabilitation are almost non-existent, and that lower-class and female children suffer from discrimination and lack access to schools.[28]

The experience of some South American countries, in particular Brazil, shows that rates of child labour can be reduced by the so-called conditional cash transfer systems (CCT). These are social assistance programmes through which money is given to families with scarce resources and children to support on condition that they fulfil certain obligations, including ensuring school attendance.[29]

---

24 Keita (this volume); Sanguineti Raymond (this volume).
25 Pratap (this volume).
26 Fronza and Summerer (this volume).
27 Pratap (this volume).
28 *Ibid.*
29 Sanguineti Raymond (this volume).

19.3.5 Trade conditionality as a way out of poverty and child labour

Chapters 13 and 15 of this volume make it clear that there is little immediate prospect of using existing trade rules or a new social clause to bring about change in respect of the use of child labour. I have examined this complex topic in detail elsewhere, and will not attempt to restate my views here.[30] Put simply, I do not believe that it is feasible to relocate international labour standards, including those on child labour, into international economic law. The aim of securing compliance with specified labour standards by imposing trade and financial sanctions against countries that do not observe them will not work in practice, nor will it spread the benefits of global trade and investment to the poorest. Moreover, the WTO is not a suitable body to enforce international labour standards. There may be some room, however, for using trade preferences (such as the EU's Generalized System of Preferences) as incentives for the observance of these standards, but this is relatively marginal.

19.3.6 Alternative strategies[31]

Instead, I propose that the efforts of those who are committed to ending exploitative child labour would be better directed to strengthening many of the strands that are emerging in the new global labour law.

The first important new strand is the social and employment dimensions of regional economic treaties. Chapter 12 in this volume shows how effective the EC directives and other measures have been in eliminating child labour, and how regional policies have also promoted fundamental rights of children in the foreign relations of the EU.

A second strand is the culture of corporate social responsibility developing in transnational corporations (TNCs), mainly in the forms of voluntary codes of conduct and collective agreements. Most of these contain prohibitions on exploitative child labour either expressly or by incorporation of ILO standards. These codes and agreements have the potential to harness processes within the market activities of TNCs that favour the raising of labour standards, that is a 'race to the top'. The essential point is that the internal labour markets of TNCs usually provide better labour standards than domestic firms. The enforcement of these codes needs to be strengthened, and national laws should place States under legal obligations to observe their own codes. There needs to be effective national and international complaints mechanisms.

A third strand is the empowerment of local actors. Unions and new social movements – including the children's rights movement – need to build alliances with groups in developing countries. Social labelling and other campaigns have already raised public awareness of abuses of child labour. It is in this context that selective trade boycotts by consumers and disinvestment in companies abusing child labour become relevant and important.

---

30 Hepple, *Labour Laws and Global Trade*, *supra* note 14, Chapters 4, 5 and 6.
31 This section draws heavily on Hepple, *Labour Laws and Global Trade*, *supra* note 14, 271–6.

A fourth strand is to improve the application of international labour standards on child labour. I have already suggested (above) the revision of C182 so as to integrate C138. The rights-based approach to child labour which, in my view, has been the most important achievement of the past 15 years, has not yet been matched by changes in the ILO's supervisory structure. The biggest gap in supervision is the absence of express linkage between the follow-up mechanisms under the Declaration and the regular supervisory machinery of the ILO. A more satisfactory follow-up of the core conventions on child labour would be to create a Governing Body committee, similar to the Committee on Freedom of Association, to consider complaints of breaches of the core standards. This committee would report to the Governing Body which could then consider further action against defaulting States. Moreover the ILO should adopt methods of coordination of national policies similar to those of the EU's open method of coordination. This would require the targeting of specific groups of countries at a similar stage of development so as to maximize peer pressure, with an effective monitoring system, as an essential part of expanded ILO technical assistance.

As I have said elsewhere:

None of these new strategies will be easy. They will face resistance and distortion. The revolution in global trade opens enormous opportunities for economic growth and world-wide prosperity. The urgent task of labour and social law at the local, national and international levels, is to provide the essential framework within which these benefits can be enjoyed by the poor, the weak [including children] and the dispossessed, as well as by those who live in relative affluence.[32]

---

32 *Ibid.*, 275.

Appendix

Convention concerning the Prohibition and Immediate Action for the Elimination of the Worst Forms of Child Labour

(C182 Worst Forms of Child Labour Convention, 1999)
Date of adoption: 17 June 1999; Date of entry into force: 19 November 2000, Geneva; Ratifications at 27 August 2007: 165.

The General Conference of the International Labour Organization,
Having been convened at Geneva by the Governing Body of the International Labour Office, and having met in its 87th Session on 1 June 1999, and
Considering the need to adopt new instruments for the prohibition and elimination of the worst forms of child labour, as the main priority for national and international action, including international cooperation and assistance, to complement the Convention and the Recommendation concerning Minimum Age for Admission to Employment, 1973, which remain fundamental instruments on child labour, and
Considering that the effective elimination of the worst forms of child labour requires immediate and comprehensive action, taking into account the importance of free basic education and the need to remove the children concerned from all such work and to provide for their rehabilitation and social integration while addressing the needs of their families, and
Recalling the resolution concerning the elimination of child labour adopted by the International Labour Conference at its 83rd Session in 1996, and
Recognizing that child labour is to a great extent caused by poverty and that the long-term solution lies in sustained economic growth leading to social progress, in particular poverty alleviation and universal education, and
Recalling the Convention on the Rights of the Child adopted by the United Nations General Assembly on 20 November 1989, and
Recalling the ILO Declaration on Fundamental Principles and Rights at Work and its Follow-up, adopted by the International Labour Conference at its 86th Session in 1998, and
Recalling that some of the worst forms of child labour are covered by other international instruments, in particular the Forced Labour Convention, 1930, and the United Nations Supplementary Convention on the Abolition of Slavery, the Slave Trade, and Institutions and Practices Similar to Slavery, 1956, and
Having decided upon the adoption of certain proposals with regard to child labour, which is the fourth item on the agenda of the session, and
Having determined that these proposals shall take the form of an international Convention;

adopts this seventeenth day of June of the year one thousand nine hundred and ninety-nine the following Convention, which may be cited as the Worst Forms of Child Labour Convention, 1999.

Article 1
Each Member which ratifies this Convention shall take immediate and effective measures to secure the prohibition and elimination of the worst forms of child labour as a matter of urgency.

Article 2
For the purposes of this Convention, the term *child* shall apply to all persons under the age of 18.

Article 3
For the purposes of this Convention, the term *the worst forms of child labour* comprises:
(a) all forms of slavery or practices similar to slavery, such as the sale and trafficking of children, debt bondage and serfdom and forced or compulsory labour, including forced or compulsory recruitment of children for use in armed conflict;
(b) the use, procuring or offering of a child for prostitution, for the production of pornography or for pornographic performances;
(c) the use, procuring or offering of a child for illicit activities, in particular for the production and trafficking of drugs as defined in the relevant international treaties;
(d) work which, by its nature or the circumstances in which it is carried out, is likely to harm the health, safety or morals of children.

Article 4
1. The types of work referred to under Article 3(d) shall be determined by national laws or regulations or by the competent authority, after consultation with the organizations of employers and workers concerned, taking into consideration relevant international standards, in particular Paragraphs 3 and 4 of the Worst Forms of Child Labour Recommendation, 1999.
2. The competent authority, after consultation with the organizations of employers and workers concerned, shall identify where the types of work so determined exist.
3. The list of the types of work determined under paragraph 1 of this Article shall be periodically examined and revised as necessary, in consultation with the organizations of employers and workers concerned.

Article 5
Each Member shall, after consultation with employers' and workers' organizations, establish or designate appropriate mechanisms to monitor the implementation of the provisions giving effect to this Convention.

Article 6
1. Each Member shall design and implement programmes of action to eliminate as a priority the worst forms of child labour.

2. Such programmes of action shall be designed and implemented in consultation with relevant government institutions and employers' and workers' organizations, taking into consideration the views of other concerned groups as appropriate.

Article 7

1. Each Member shall take all necessary measures to ensure the effective implementation and enforcement of the provisions giving effect to this Convention including the provision and application of penal sanctions or, as appropriate, other sanctions.

2. Each Member shall, taking into account the importance of education in eliminating child labour, take effective and time-bound measures to:

(a) prevent the engagement of children in the worst forms of child labour;

(b) provide the necessary and appropriate direct assistance for the removal of children from the worst forms of child labour and for their rehabilitation and social integration;

(c) ensure access to free basic education, and, wherever possible and appropriate, vocational training, for all children removed from the worst forms of child labour;

(d) identify and reach out to children at special risk; and

(e) take account of the special situation of girls.

3. Each Member shall designate the competent authority responsible for the implementation of the provisions giving effect to this Convention.

Article 8

Members shall take appropriate steps to assist one another in giving effect to the provisions of this Convention through enhanced international cooperation and/ or assistance including support for social and economic development, poverty eradication programmes and universal education.

Article 9

The formal ratifications of this Convention shall be communicated to the Director-General of the International Labour Office for registration.

Article 10

1. This Convention shall be binding only upon those Members of the International Labour Organization whose ratifications have been registered with the Director-General of the International Labour Office.

2. It shall come into force 12 months after the date on which the ratifications of two Members have been registered with the Director-General.

3. Thereafter, this Convention shall come into force for any Member 12 months after the date on which its ratification has been registered.

Article 11

1. A Member which has ratified this Convention may denounce it after the expiration of ten years from the date on which the Convention first comes into force, by an act communicated to the Director-General of the International Labour Office for

registration. Such denunciation shall not take effect until one year after the date on which it is registered.

2. Each Member which has ratified this Convention and which does not, within the year following the expiration of the period of ten years mentioned in the preceding paragraph, exercise the right of denunciation provided for in this Article, will be bound for another period of ten years and, thereafter, may denounce this Convention at the expiration of each period of ten years under the terms provided for in this Article.

Article 12

1. The Director-General of the International Labour Office shall notify all Members of the International Labour Organization of the registration of all ratifications and acts of denunciation communicated by the Members of the Organization.

2. When notifying the Members of the Organization of the registration of the second ratification, the Director-General shall draw the attention of the Members of the Organization to the date upon which the Convention shall come into force.

Article 13

The Director-General of the International Labour Office shall communicate to the Secretary-General of the United Nations, for registration in accordance with article 102 of the Charter of the United Nations, full particulars of all ratifications and acts of denunciation registered by the Director-General in accordance with the provisions of the preceding Articles.

Article 14

At such times as it may consider necessary, the Governing Body of the International Labour Office shall present to the General Conference a report on the working of this Convention and shall examine the desirability of placing on the agenda of the Conference the question of its revision in whole or in part.

Article 15

1. Should the Conference adopt a new Convention revising this Convention in whole or in part, then, unless the new Convention otherwise provides

(a) the ratification by a Member of the new revising Convention shall ipso jure involve the immediate denunciation of this Convention, notwithstanding the provisions of Article 11 above, if and when the new revising Convention shall have come into force;

(b) as from the date when the new revising Convention comes into force, this Convention shall cease to be open to ratification by the Members.

2. This Convention shall in any case remain in force in its actual form and content for those Members which have ratified it but have not ratified the revising Convention.

Article 16

The English and French versions of the text of this Convention are equally authoritative.

Ratifications as of 27 August 2007
(source ILOLEX, at www.ilo.org/ilolex)

Albania, 2 August 2001; *Algeria*, 9 February 2001; *Angola*, 13 June 2001; *Antigua and Barbuda*, 16 September 2002; *Argentina*, 5 February 2001; *Armenia*, 2 January 2006; *Australia*, 19 December 2006; *Austria*, 4 December 2001; *Azerbaijan*, 30 March 2004; *Bahamas*, 14 June 2001; *Bahrain*, 23 March 2001, *Bangladesh*, 12 March 2001; *Barbados*, 23 October 2000; *Belarus*, 31 October 2000; *Belgium*, 8 May 2002; *Belize*, 6 March 2000; *Benin*, 6 November 2001; *Bolivia*, 6 June 2003; *Bosnia and Herzegovina*, 5 October 2001; *Botswana*, 3 January 2000; *Brazil*, 2 February 2000; *Bulgaria*, 28 July 2000; *Burkina Faso*, 25 July 2001; *Burundi*, 11 June 2002; *Cambodia*, 14 March 2006; *Cameroon*, 5 June 2002; *Canada*, 6 June 2000; *Cape Verde*, 23 October 2001; *Central African Republic*, 28 June 2000; *Chad*, 6 November 2000; *Chile*, 17 July 2000; *China*, 8 August 2002; *Colombia*, 28 January 2005; *Comoros*, 17 March 2004; *Congo*, 23 August 2002; *Democratic Republic of the Congo*, 20 June 2001; *Costa Rica*, 10 September 2001; *Côte d'Ivoire*, 7 February 2003; *Croatia*, 17 July 2001; *Cyprus*, 27 November 2000; *Czech Republic*, 19 June 2001; *Denmark*, 14 August 2000; *Djibouti*, 28 February 2005; *Dominica*, 4 January 2001; *Dominican Republic*, 15 November 2000; *Ecuador*, 19 September 2000; *Egypt*, 6 May 2002; *El Salvador*, 12 October 2000; *Equatorial Guinea*, 13 August 2001; *Estonia*, 24 September 2001; *Ethiopia*, 2 September 2003; *Fiji*, 17 April 2002; *Finland*, 17 January 2000; *France*, 11 September 2001; *Gabon*, 28 March 2001; *Gambia*, 3 July 2001; *Georgia*, 24 July 2002; *Germany*, 18 April 2002; *Ghana*, 13 June 2000; *Greece*, 6 November 2001; *Grenada*, 14 May 2003; *Guatemala*, 11 October 2001; *Guinea*, 6 June 2003; *Guyana*, 15 January 2001; *Haiti*, 19 July 2007; *Honduras*, 25 October 2001; *Hungary*, 20 April 2000; *Iceland*, 29 May 2000; *Indonesia*, 28 March 2000; *the Islamic Republic of Iran*, 8 May 2002; *Iraq*, 9 July 2001; *Ireland*, 20 December 1999; *Israel*, 15 March 2005; *Italy*, 7 June 2000; *Jamaica*, 13 October 2003; *Japan*, 18 June 2001; *Jordan*, 20 April 2000; *Kazakhstan*, 26 February 2003; *Kenya*, 7 May 2001; *Republic of Korea*, 29 March 2001; *Kuwait*, 15 August 2000; *Kyrgyzstan*, 11 May 2004; *Lao People's Democratic Republic*, 13 June 2005; *Latvia*, 2 June 2006; *Lebanon*, 11 September 2001; *Lesotho*, 14 June 2001; *Liberia*, 2 June 2003; *Libyan Arab Jamahiriya*, 4 October 2000; *Lithuania*, 29 September 2003; *Luxembourg*, 21 March 2001; *The former Yugoslav Republic of Macedonia*, 30 May 2002; *Madagascar*, 4 October 2001; *Malawi*, 19 November 1999; *Malaysia*, 10 November 2000; *Mali*, 14 July 2000; *Malta*, 15 June 2001; *Mauritania*, 3 December 2001; *Mauritius*, 8 June 2000; *Mexico*, 30 June 2000; *Republic of Moldova*, 14 June 2002; *Mongolia*, 26 February 2001; *Montenegro*, 3 June 2006; *Morocco*, 26 January 2001; *Mozambique*, 16 June 2003; *Namibia*, 15 November 2000; *Nepal*, 3 January 2002; *Netherlands*, 14 February 2002; *New Zealand*, 14 June 2001; *Nicaragua*, 6 November 2000; *Niger*, 23 October 2000; *Nigeria*, 2 October 2002; *Norway*, 21 December 2000; *Oman*, 11 June 2001; *Pakistan*, 11 October 2001; *Panama*, 31 October 2000; *Papua New Guinea*, 2 June 2000; *Paraguay*, 7 March 2001; *Peru*, 10 January 2002; *Philippines*, 28 November 2000; *Poland*, 9 August 2002; *Portugal*, 15 June 2000; *Qatar*, 30 May 2000; *Romania*, 13 December 2000; *Russian Federation*, 25 March 2003; *Rwanda*, 23 May 2000; *Saint Kitts and Nevis*, 12 October 2000; *Saint Lucia*, 6 December

2000; *Saint Vincent and the Grenadines*, 4 December 2001; *San Marino*, 15 March 2000; *Sao Tome and Principe*, 4 May 2005; *Saudi Arabia*, 8 October 2001; *Senegal*, 1 June 2000; *Serbia*, 10 July 2003; *Seychelles*, 28 September 1999; *Singapore*, 14 June 2001; *Slovakia*, 20 December 1999; *Slovenia*, 8 May 2001; *South Africa*, 7 June 2000; *Spain*, 2 April 2001; *Sri Lanka*, 1 March 2001; *Sudan*, 7 March 2003; *Suriname*, 12 April 2006; *Swaziland*, 23 October 2002; *Sweden*, 13 June 2001; *Switzerland*, 28 June 2000; *Syrian Arab Republic*, 22 May 2003; *Tajikistan*, 8 June 2005; *Tanzania (United Republic of)*, 12 September 2001; *Thailand*, 16 February 2001; *Togo*, 19 September 2000; *Trinidad and Tobago*, 23 April 2003; *Tunisia*, 28 February 2000; *Turkey*, 2 August 2001; *Uganda*, 21 June 2001; *Ukraine*, 14 December 2000; *United Arab Emirates*, 28 June 2001; *United Kingdom*, 22 March 2000; *United States*, 2 December 1999; *Uruguay*, 3 August 2001; *Vanuatu*, 28 August 2006; *Bolivarian Republic of Venezuela*, 26 October 2005; *Viet Nam*, 19 December 2000; *Yemen*, 15 June 2000; *Zambia*, 10 December 2001, *Zimbabwe*, 11 December 2000.

Convention concerning Minimum Age for Admission to Employment
(C138 Minimum Age Convention, 1973)
Date of entry into force: 19 June 1976; Date of adoption: 26 June 1973, Geneva; Ratifications at 27 August 2007: 150.

The General Conference of the International Labour Organisation,
Having been convened at Geneva by the Governing Body of the International Labour Office, and having met in its Fifty-eighth Session on 6 June 1973, and
Having decided upon the adoption of certain proposals with regard to minimum age for admission to employment, which is the fourth item on the agenda of the session, and
Noting the terms of the Minimum Age (Industry) Convention, 1919, the Minimum Age (Sea) Convention, 1920, the Minimum Age (Agriculture) Convention, 1921, the Minimum Age (Trimmers and Stokers) Convention, 1921, the Minimum Age (Non-Industrial Employment) Convention, 1932, the Minimum Age (Sea) Convention (Revised), 1936, the Minimum Age (Industry) Convention (Revised), 1937, the Minimum Age (Non-Industrial Employment) Convention (Revised), 1937, the Minimum Age (Fishermen) Convention, 1959, and the Minimum Age (Underground Work) Convention, 1965, and
Considering that the time has come to establish a general instrument on the subject, which would gradually replace the existing ones applicable to limited economic sectors, with a view to achieving the total abolition of child labour, and
Having determined that these proposals shall take the form of an international Convention,
adopts this twenty-sixth day of June of the year one thousand nine hundred and seventy-three the following Convention, which may be cited as the Minimum Age Convention, 1973:

Article 1
Each Member for which this Convention is in force undertakes to pursue a national policy designed to ensure the effective abolition of child labour and to raise

progressively the minimum age for admission to employment or work to a level consistent with the fullest physical and mental development of young persons.

Article 2

1. Each Member which ratifies this Convention shall specify, in a declaration appended to its ratification, a minimum age for admission to employment or work within its territory and on means of transport registered in its territory; subject to Articles 4 to 8 of this Convention, no one under that age shall be admitted to employment or work in any occupation.

2. Each Member which has ratified this Convention may subsequently notify the Director-General of the International Labour Office, by further declarations, that it specifies a minimum age higher than that previously specified.

3. The minimum age specified in pursuance of paragraph 1 of this Article shall not be less than the age of completion of compulsory schooling and, in any case, shall not be less than 15 years.

4. Notwithstanding the provisions of paragraph 3 of this Article, a Member whose economy and educational facilities are insufficiently developed may, after consultation with the organisations of employers and workers concerned, where such exist, initially specify a minimum age of 14 years.

5. Each Member which has specified a minimum age of 14 years in pursuance of the provisions of the preceding paragraph shall include in its reports on the application of this Convention submitted under article 22 of the Constitution of the International Labour Organisation a statement

(a) that its reason for doing so subsists; or

(b) that it renounces its right to avail itself of the provisions in question as from a stated date.

Article 3

1. The minimum age for admission to any type of employment or work which by its nature or the circumstances in which it is carried out is likely to jeopardise the health, safety or morals of young persons shall not be less than 18 years.

2. The types of employment or work to which paragraph 1 of this Article applies shall be determined by national laws or regulations or by the competent authority, after consultation with the organisations of employers and workers concerned, where such exist.

3. Notwithstanding the provisions of paragraph 1 of this Article, national laws or regulations or the competent authority may, after consultation with the organisations of employers and workers concerned, where such exist, authorise employment or work as from the age of 16 years on condition that the health, safety and morals of the young persons concerned are fully protected and that the young persons have received adequate specific instruction or vocational training in the relevant branch of activity.

Article 4

1. In so far as necessary, the competent authority, after consultation with the organisations of employers and workers concerned, where such exist, may exclude

from the application of this Convention limited categories of employment or work in respect of which special and substantial problems of application arise.

2. Each Member which ratifies this Convention shall list in its first report on the application of the Convention submitted under article 22 of the Constitution of the International Labour Organisation any categories which may have been excluded in pursuance of paragraph 1 of this Article, giving the reasons for such exclusion, and shall state in subsequent reports the position of its law and practice in respect of the categories excluded and the extent to which effect has been given or is proposed to be given to the Convention in respect of such categories.

3. Employment or work covered by Article 3 of this Convention shall not be excluded from the application of the Convention in pursuance of this Article.

Article 5

1. A Member whose economy and administrative facilities are insufficiently developed may, after consultation with the organisations of employers and workers concerned, where such exist, initially limit the scope of application of this Convention.

2. Each Member which avails itself of the provisions of paragraph 1 of this Article shall specify, in a declaration appended to its ratification, the branches of economic activity or types of undertakings to which it will apply the provisions of the Convention.

3. The provisions of the Convention shall be applicable as a minimum to the following: mining and quarrying; manufacturing; construction; electricity, gas and water; sanitary services; transport, storage and communication; and plantations and other agricultural undertakings mainly producing for commercial purposes, but excluding family and small-scale holdings producing for local consumption and not regularly employing hired workers.

4. Any Member which has limited the scope of application of this Convention in pursuance of this Article

(a) shall indicate in its reports under Article 22 of the Constitution of the International Labour Organisation the general position as regards the employment or work of young persons and children in the branches of activity which are excluded from the scope of application of this Convention and any progress which may have been made towards wider application of the provisions of the Convention;

(b) may at any time formally extend the scope of application by a declaration addressed to the Director-General of the International Labour Office.

Article 6

This Convention does not apply to work done by children and young persons in schools for general, vocational or technical education or in other training institutions, or to work done by persons at least 14 years of age in undertakings, where such work is carried out in accordance with conditions prescribed by the competent authority, after consultation with the organisations of employers and workers concerned, where such exist, and is an integral part of

(a) a course of education or training for which a school or training institution is primarily responsible;

(b) a programme of training mainly or entirely in an undertaking, which programme has been approved by the competent authority; or

(c) a programme of guidance or orientation designed to facilitate the choice of an occupation or of a line of training.

Article 7

1. National laws or regulations may permit the employment or work of persons 13 to 15 years of age on light work which is

(a) not likely to be harmful to their health or development; and

(b) not such as to prejudice their attendance at school, their participation in vocational orientation or training programmes approved by the competent authority or their capacity to benefit from the instruction received.

2. National laws or regulations may also permit the employment or work of persons who are at least 15 years of age but have not yet completed their compulsory schooling on work which meets the requirements set forth in sub-paragraphs (a) and (b) of paragraph 1 of this Article.

3. The competent authority shall determine the activities in which employment or work may be permitted under paragraphs 1 and 2 of this Article and shall prescribe the number of hours during which and the conditions in which such employment or work may be undertaken.

4. Notwithstanding the provisions of paragraphs 1 and 2 of this Article, a Member which has availed itself of the provisions of paragraph 4 of Article 2 may, for as long as it continues to do so, substitute the ages 12 and 14 for the ages 13 and 15 in paragraph 1 and the age 14 for the age 15 in paragraph 2 of this Article.

Article 8

1. After consultation with the organisations of employers and workers concerned, where such exist, the competent authority may, by permits granted in individual cases, allow exceptions to the prohibition of employment or work provided for in Article 2 of this Convention, for such purposes as participation in artistic performances.

2. Permits so granted shall limit the number of hours during which and prescribe the conditions in which employment or work is allowed.

Article 9

1. All necessary measures, including the provision of appropriate penalties, shall be taken by the competent authority to ensure the effective enforcement of the provisions of this Convention.

2. National laws or regulations or the competent authority shall define the persons responsible for compliance with the provisions giving effect to the Convention.

3. National laws or regulations or the competent authority shall prescribe the registers or other documents which shall be kept and made available by the employer; such registers or documents shall contain the names and ages or dates of birth, duly certified wherever possible, of persons whom he employs or who work for him and who are less than 18 years of age.

Article 10

1. This Convention revises, on the terms set forth in this Article, the Minimum Age (Industry) Convention, 1919, the Minimum Age (Sea) Convention, 1920, the Minimum Age (Agriculture) Convention, 1921, the Minimum Age (Trimmers and Stokers) Convention, 1921, the Minimum Age (Non-Industrial Employment) Convention, 1932, the Minimum Age (Sea) Convention (Revised), 1936, the Minimum Age (Industry) Convention (Revised), 1937, the Minimum Age (Non-Industrial Employment) Convention (Revised), 1937, the Minimum Age (Fishermen) Convention, 1959, and the Minimum Age (Underground Work) Convention, 1965.

2. The coming into force of this Convention shall not close the Minimum Age (Sea) Convention (Revised), 1936, the Minimum Age (Industry) Convention (Revised), 1937, the Minimum Age (Non-Industrial Employment) Convention (Revised), 1937, the Minimum Age (Fishermen) Convention, 1959, or the Minimum Age (Underground Work) Convention, 1965, to further ratification.

3. The Minimum Age (Industry) Convention, 1919, the Minimum Age (Sea) Convention, 1920, the Minimum Age (Agriculture) Convention, 1921, and the Minimum Age (Trimmers and Stokers) Convention, 1921, shall be closed to further ratification when all the parties thereto have consented to such closing by ratification of this Convention or by a declaration communicated to the Director-General of the International Labour Office.

4. When the obligations of this Convention are accepted

(a) by a Member which is a party to the Minimum Age (Industry) Convention (Revised), 1937, and a minimum age of not less than 15 years is specified in pursuance of Article 2 of this Convention, this shall ipso jure involve the immediate denunciation of that Convention,

(b) in respect of non-industrial employment as defined in the Minimum Age (Non-Industrial Employment) Convention, 1932, by a Member which is a party to that Convention, this shall ipso jure involve the immediate denunciation of that Convention,

(c) in respect of non-industrial employment as defined in the Minimum Age (Non-Industrial Employment) Convention (Revised), 1937, by a Member which is a party to that Convention, and a minimum age of not less than 15 years is specified in pursuance of Article 2 of this Convention, this shall ipso jure involve the immediate denunciation of that Convention,

(d) in respect of maritime employment, by a Member which is a party to the Minimum Age (Sea) Convention (Revised), 1936, and a minimum age of not less than 15 years is specified in pursuance of Article 2 of this Convention or the Member specifies that Article 3 of this Convention applies to maritime employment, this shall ipso jure involve the immediate denunciation of that Convention,

(e) in respect of employment in maritime fishing, by a Member which is a party to the Minimum Age (Fishermen) Convention, 1959, and a minimum age of not less than 15 years is specified in pursuance of Article 2 of this Convention or the Member specifies that Article 3 of this Convention applies to employment in maritime fishing, this shall ipso jure involve the immediate denunciation of that Convention,

(f) by a Member which is a party to the Minimum Age (Underground Work) Convention, 1965, and a minimum age of not less than the age specified in pursuance of that Convention is specified in pursuance of Article 2 of this Convention or the Member specifies that such an age applies to employment underground in mines in virtue of Article 3 of this Convention, this shall ipso jure involve the immediate denunciation of that Convention,

if and when this Convention shall have come into force.

5. Acceptance of the obligations of this Convention

(a) shall involve the denunciation of the Minimum Age (Industry) Convention, 1919, in accordance with Article 12 thereof,

(b) in respect of agriculture shall involve the denunciation of the Minimum Age (Agriculture) Convention, 1921, in accordance with Article 9 thereof,

(c) in respect of maritime employment shall involve the denunciation of the Minimum Age (Sea) Convention, 1920, in accordance with Article 10 thereof, and of the Minimum Age (Trimmers and Stokers) Convention, 1921, in accordance with Article 12 thereof,

if and when this Convention shall have come into force.

Article 11

The formal ratifications of this Convention shall be communicated to the Director-General of the International Labour Office for registration.

Article 12

1. This Convention shall be binding only upon those Members of the International Labour Organisation whose ratifications have been registered with the Director-General.

2. It shall come into force twelve months after the date on which the ratifications of two Members have been registered with the Director-General.

3. Thereafter, this Convention shall come into force for any Member twelve months after the date on which its ratifications has been registered.

Article 13

1. A Member which has ratified this Convention may denounce it after the expiration of ten years from the date on which the Convention first comes into force, by an act communicated to the Director-General of the International Labour Office for registration. Such denunciation shall not take effect until one year after the date on which it is registered.

2. Each Member which has ratified this Convention and which does not, within the year following the expiration of the period of ten years mentioned in the preceding paragraph, exercise the right of denunciation provided for in this Article, will be bound for another period of ten years and, thereafter, may denounce this Convention at the expiration of each period of ten years under the terms provided for in this Article.

Article 14

1. The Director-General of the International Labour Office shall notify all Members of the International Labour Organisation of the registration of all ratifications and denunciations communicated to him by the Members of the Organisation.

2. When notifying the Members of the Organisation of the registration of the second ratification communicated to him, the Director-General shall draw the attention of the Members of the Organisation to the date upon which the Convention will come into force.

Article 15

The Director-General of the International Labour Office shall communicate to the Secretary-General of the United Nations for registration in accordance with Article 102 of the Charter of the United Nations full particulars of all ratifications and acts of denunciation registered by him in accordance with the provisions of the preceding Articles.

Article 16

At such times as it may consider necessary the Governing Body of the International Labour Office shall present to the General Conference a report on the working of this Convention and shall examine the desirability of placing on the agenda of the Conference the question of its revision in whole or in part.

Article 17

1. Should the Conference adopt a new Convention revising this Convention in whole or in part, then, unless the new Convention otherwise provides:

a) the ratification by a Member of the new revising Convention shall ipso jure involve the immediate denunciation of this Convention, notwithstanding the provisions of Article 13 above, if and when the new revising Convention shall have come into force;

b) as from the date when the new revising Convention comes into force this Convention shall cease to be open to ratification by the Members.

2. This Convention shall in any case remain in force in its actual form and content for those Members which have ratified it but have not ratified the revising Convention.

Article 18

The English and French versions of the text of this Convention are equally authoritative.

Ratifications as of 27 August 2007
(source ILOLEX, at www.ilo.org/ilolex)

Albania, 16 February 1998; *Algeria*, 30 April 1984; *Angola*, 13 June 2001; *Antigua and Barbuda*, 17 March 1983; *Argentina*, 11 November 1996; *Armenia*, 27 January 2006; *Austria*, 18 September 2000; *Azerbaijan*, 19 May 1992; *Bahamas*, 31 October 2001; *Barbados*, 4 January 2000; *Belarus*, 3 May 1979; *Belgium*, 19 April 1988; *Belize*, 6 March 2000; *Benin*, 11 June 2001; *Bolivia*, 11 June 1997; *Bosnia and Herzegovina*, 2 March 1993; *Botswana*, 5 June 1997; *Brazil*, 28 June 2001; *Bulgaria*, 23 April 1980; *Burkina Faso*, 11 February 1999; *Burundi*, 19 July 2000; *Cambodia*, 23 August 1999; *Cameroon*, 13 August 2001; *Central African Republic*, 28 June 2000; *Chad*, 21 March 2005; *Chile*, 1 February 1999; *China*, 28 April

1999; *Colombia*, 2 February 2001; *Comoros*, 17 March 2004; *Congo*, 26 November 1999; *Democratic Republic of the Congo*, 20 June 2001; *Costa Rica*, 11 June 1976; *Côte d'Ivoire*, 7 February 2003; *Croatia*, 8 October 1991; *Cuba*, 7 March 1975; *Cyprus*, 2 October 1997; *Czech Republic*, 26 April 2007; *Denmark*, 13 November 1997; *Djibouti*, 14 June 2005; *Dominica*, 27 September 1983; *Dominican Republic*, 15 June 1999; *Ecuador*, 19 September 2000; *Egypt*, 9 June 1999; *El Salvador*, 23 January 1996; *Equatorial Guinea*, 12 June 1985; *Eritrea*, 22 February 2000; *Estonia*, 15 March 2007; *Ethiopia*, 27 May 1999; *Fiji*, 3 January 2003; *Finland*, 13 January 1976; *France*, 13 July 1990; *Gambia*, 4 September 2000; *Georgia*, 23 September 1996; *Germany*, 8 April 1976; *Greece*, 14 March 1986; *Grenada*, 14 May 2003; *Guatemala*, 27 April 1990; *Guinea*, 6 June 2003; *Guyana*, 15 April 1998; *Honduras*, 9 June 1980; *Hungary*, 28 May 1998; *Iceland*, 6 December 1999; *Indonesia*, 7 June 1999; *Iraq*, 13 February 1985; *Ireland*, 22 June 1978; *Israel*, 21 June 1979; *Italy*, 28 July 1981; *Jamaica*, 13 October 2003; *Japan*, 5 June 2000; *Jordan*, 23 March 1998; *Kazakhstan*, 18 May 2001; *Kenya*, 9 April 1979; *Republic of Korea*, 28 January 1999; *Kuwait*, 15 November 1999; *Kyrgyzstan*, 31 March 1992; *Lao People's Democratic Republic*, 13 June 2005; *Latvia*, 2 June 2006; *Lebanon*, 10 June 2003; *Lesotho*, 14 June 2001; *Libyan Arab Jamahiriya*, 19 June 1975; *Lithuania*, 22 June 1998; *Luxembourg*, 24 March 1977; *The former Yugoslav Republic of Macedonia*, 17 November 1991; *Madagascar*, 31 May 2000; *Malawi*, 19 November 1999; *Malaysia*, 9 September 1997; *Mali*, 11 March 2002; *Malta*, 9 June 1988; *Mauritania*, 3 December 2001; *Mauritius*, 30 July 1990; *Republic of Moldova*, 21 September 1999; *Mongolia*, 16 December 2002; *Montenegro*, 3 June 2006; *Morocco*, 6 January 2000; *Mozambique*, 16 June 2003; *Namibia*, 15 November 2000; *Nepal*, 30 May 1997; *Netherlands*, 14 September 1976; *Nicaragua*, 2 November 1981; *Niger*, 4 December 1978; *Nigeria*, 2 October 2002; *Norway*, 8 July 1980; *Oman*, 21 July 2005; *Pakistan*, 6 July 2006; *Panama*, 31 October 2000; *Papua New Guinea*, 2 June 2000; *Paraguay*, 3 March 2004; *Peru*, 13 November 2002; *Philippines*, 4 June 1998; *Poland*, 22 March 1978; *Portugal*, 20 May 1998; *Qatar*, 3 January 2006; *Romania*, 19 November 1975; *Russian Federation*, 3 May 1979; *Rwanda*, 15 April 1981; *Saint Kitts and Nevis*, 3 June 2005; *Saint Vincent and the Grenadines*, 25 July 2006; *San Marino*, 1 February 1995; *Sao Tome and Principe*, 4 May 2005; *Senegal*, 15 December 1999; *Serbia*, 24 November 2000; *Seychelles*, 7 March 2000; *Singapore*, 7 November 2005; *Slovakia*, 29 September 1997; *Slovenia*, 29 May 1992; *South Africa*, 30 March 2000; *Spain*, 16 May 1977; *Sri Lanka*, 11 February 2000; *Sudan*, 7 March 2002; *Swaziland*, 23 October 2002; *Sweden*, 23 April 1990; *Switzerland*, 17 August 1999; *Syrian Arab Republic*, 18 September 2001; *Tajikistan*, 26 November 1993; *Tanzania (United Republic of)*, 16 December 1998; *Thailand*, 11 May 2004; *Togo*, 16 March 1984; *Trinidad and Tobago*, 3 September 2004; *Tunisia*, 19 October 1995 ; *Turkey*, 30 October 1998; *Uganda*, 25 March 2003; *Ukraine*, 3 May 1979; *United Arab Emirates*, 2 October 1998; *United Kingdom*, 7 June 2000; *Uruguay*, 2 June 1977; *Bolivarian Republic of Venezuela*, 15 July 1987; *Viet Nam*, 24 June 2003; *Yemen*, 15 June 2000; *Zambia*, 9 February 1976; *Zimbabwe*, 6 June 2000.

Bibliography

Articles and papers

Agarwal, R.K. (2004), 'The Barefoot Lawyers: Prosecuting Child Labour in the Supreme Court of India', 21 *Arizona Journal of International and Comparative Law* 663.

Aggarwal, S.C. (2004), 'Child Labour and Household Characteristics in Selected States', 39 *Economic and Political Weekly* 173.

Allain, J. (2007), 'The Definition of "Slavery" in General International Law and the Crime of Enslavement within the Rome Statute', ICC, Guest Lecture Series of the Office of the Prosecutor, available at: <www.icc-cpi.int/otp/otp_guest_lectures. html>.

Alston, P. (2005), 'Facing up to the Complexity of the ILO's Core Labour Standards Agenda', 16 *European Journal of International Law* 467.

———— (2004), '"Core Labour Standards" and the Transformation of the International Labour Rights Regime', 15 *European Journal of International Law* 457.

———— (1994), 'A Guide to Some Legal Aspects Connected to the Ratification and Implementation of the Convention on the Rights of the Child', 20 *Commonwealth Law Bulletin* 1110.

Anker, R. (2000), 'The Economics of Child Labour: A Framework for Measurement', 139 *International Labour Review* 257.

Arreeba, H. (2006), 'Domestic Workers: Harsh, Everyday Realities', 41 *Economic and Political Weekly* 1235.

Arts, K. 'ACP-EU Relations in a New Era: the Cotonou Agreement', 40 *Common Market Law Review* 95.

Bagwell, K., Mavroidis, P.C., and Staiger, R.W. (2002), 'Symposium: The Boundaries of the WTO: It's a Question of Market Access', 96 *American Journal of International Law* 56.

Basu, K. (2005), 'Child Labor and the Law: Notes on Possible Pathologies', 87 *Economics Letters* 169.

———— (2001), 'Compacts, Conventions and Codes: Initiatives for Higher International Labor Standards', 34 *Cornell International Law Journal* 487.

———— (2000), 'On the Intriguing Relation between Adult Minimum Wage and Child Labor', 110 *Economic Journal* 462.

———— (1999), 'Child Labor: Cause, Consequence and Cure, with Remarks on International Labor Standards', 37 *Journal of Economic Literature* 1083.

———— (1999), 'International Labor Standards and Child Labor', 42 *Challenge* 80.

Basu, K. and Tzannatos, Z. (2003), 'The Global Child Labor Problem: What Do We Know and What Can We Do?', 17 *World Bank Economic Review* 147.

Basu, K. and Pham Hoang Van (1999), 'The Economics of Child Labor: Reply', 89 *American Economic Review* 1386.

—— (1998), 'The Economics of Child Labor', 88 *American Economic Review* 412.

Bhala, R. (1998), 'Clarifying the Trade–Labor Link', 37 *Columbia Journal of Transnational Law* 11.

Boivin, I. and Odero, A. (2006), 'The Committee of Experts on the Application of Conventions and Recommendations: Progress Achieved in National Labour Legislation', 45 *International Labour Review* 207.

Boockmann, B. (2004), 'The Effect of ILO Minimum Age Conventions on Child Labour and School Attendance', Centre for European Economic Research, Discussion Paper No. 4–52.

Borzaga, M. (2006), 'Accommodating Differences: Discrimination and Equality at Work in International Labor Law', 30 *Vermont Law Review* 749.

Brandtner, B. and Rosas, A. (1998), 'Human Rights and the External Relations of the European Community: An Analysis of Doctrine and Practice', 9 *European Journal of International Law* 468.

Bullard, M.G. (2001), 'Child Labor Prohibitions Are Universal, Binding, and Obligatory Law: The Evolving State of Customary International Law Concerning the Unempowered Child Laborer', 24 *Houston Journal of International Law* 139.

Canagarajah, S. (2001), 'Child Labor in Africa: A Comparative Study', 575 *Annals of the American Academy of Political and Social Science* 71.

Celek, B.M. (2004), 'The International Response to Child Labor in the Developing World: Why Are We Ineffective', 11 *Georgetown Journal on Poverty Law & Policy* 88.

Charnovitz, S. (2004), 'The Labor Dimension of the Emerging Free Trade Area of the Americas', GWU Legal Studies Research Paper No. 140.

—— (1998), 'The Moral Exception in Trade Policy', 38 *Virginia Journal of International Law* 689.

—— (1987), 'The Influence of International Labour Standards on the World Trading Regime', 126 *International Labour Review* 565.

Chaulia, S. (2002), 'Social Clause in WTO', 37 *Economic and Political Weekly* 613.

Chawdhary, G. and Beeman, M. (2001), 'Challenging Child Labor: Transnational Activism and India's Carpet Industry', 575 *Annals of the American Academy of Political and Social Science* 158.

Cho, (2007), 'The Bush Administration and Democrats Reach a Bipartisan Deal on Trade Policy', 12 *American Society of International Law Insight*, available at <http://www.asil.org/insights.htm>.

Cleveland, S. (2002), 'Human Rights Sanctions and International Trade: A Theory of Compatibility', 5 *Journal of International Economic Law* 133.

—— (2001), 'Norm Internalization and US Economic Sanctions', 26 *Yale Journal of International Law* 1.

Cole, A.N. (2003), 'Labor Standards and the Generalized System of Preferences: The European Labor Incentives', 25 *Michigan Journal of International Law* 179.

Cox, K. (1999), 'The Inevitability of Nimble Fingers? Law, Development, and Child Labor', 32 *Vanderbilt Journal of Transnational Law* 115.

Cox, L. (1999), 'The International Labour Organisation and Fundamental Rights at Work', 4 *European Human Rights Law Review* 451.

Creighton, B. (1997), 'Combating Child Labour: The Role of International Labour Standards', 18 *Comparative Labour Law & Policy Journal* 362.

—— (1996), 'ILO Convention No. 138 and Australian Law and Practice Relating to Child Labour', 2 *Australian Journal of Human Rights* 293.

Cullen, H. (2006), '*Siliadin* v *France*: Positive Obligations under Article 4 of the European Convention on Human Rights', 6 *Human Rights Law Review* 585.

Cutillo, M. (1999), 'La Convenzione OIL n. 182 relativa alla proibizione delle forme peggiori di lavoro minorile ed all'azione immediata per la loro eliminazione: un passo importante contro lo sfruttamento del lavoro dei minori', XII *Rivista internazionale dei diritti dell'uomo* 721.

CUTS Centre for International Trade Economics and Environment (2003), 'Child Labour in South Asia: Are Trade Sanctions the Answer?', Briefing Paper No. 3/2003.

Davidson, M.G. (2001), 'The International Labour Organisation's Latest Campaign to End Child Labor: Will it Succeed Where Others Have Failed?', 11 *Transnational Law & Contemporary Problems* 203.

D'Avolio, M. (2004), 'Child Labor and Cultural Relativism: From 19th Century America to 21st Century Nepal', 16 *Pace International Law Review* 109.

Daza, J.L. (2005), *Informal Economy, Undeclared Work and Labour Administration*, DIALOGUE Working Paper No. 9.

Dennis, M.J. (1999), 'The ILO Convention on the Worst Forms of Child Labour', 93 *American Journal of International Law* 943.

Diller, J. (1999), 'A Social Conscience in the Global Marketplace? Labour Dimensions of Codes of Conduct, Social Labelling and Investor Initiatives', 138 *International Labour Review* 99.

Diller, J. and Levy, D. (1997), 'Child Labor, Trade and Investment: Toward the Harmonization of International Law', 91 *American Journal of International Law* 663.

Di Turi, C. (2000), 'Globalizzazione dell'economia e diritti fondamentali in materia di lavoro', 1 *Rivista di diritto internazionale* 113.

Doek, J.E. (2003) 'The UN Convention on the Rights of the Child: Some Observations on the Monitoring and the Social Context of its Implementation', 14 *Journal of Law and Public Policy* 125.

—— (2003), 'The Protection of Children's Rights and the United Nations Convention on the Rights of the Child: Achievements and Challenges', 22 *St Louis University Public Law Review* 235.

Feddersen, C.T. (1998), 'Focusing on Substantive Law in International Economic Relations: The Public Morals of GATT's Article XX(a) and "Conventional" Rules of Interpretation', 7 *Minnesota Journal of Global Trade* 75.

Garcia, F.J. and Jun, S. (2005), 'Trade-Based Strategies for Combating Child Labor', Boston College Law School Research Paper No. 59.

Garg, A. (1999), 'A Child Labor Social Clause: Analysis and Proposal for Action', 21 *NYU Journal of International Law and Policy* 473.

Garrard, V. (2006), 'Sad Stories: Trafficking in Children – Unique Situations Requiring New Solutions', 35 *Georgia Journal of International & Comparative Law* 145.

Glut, T.A. (1995), 'Changing the Approach to Ending Child Labor: An International Solution to an International Problem', 28 *Vanderbilt Journal of Transnational Law* 1203.

Green, L.A. (2001), 'The Global Fight for the Elimination of Child Labor in Pakistan', 20 *Wisconsin International Law Journal* 176.

Grynberg, R. and Qalo, V. (2006), 'Labour Standards in US and EU Preferential Trading Agreements', 40 *Journal of World Trade* 619.

Hanson, K. and Vandaele, A. (2003), 'Working Children and International Labour Law: A Critical Analysis', 11 *International Journal of Children's Rights* 73.

Harris-Short, S. (2003), 'International Human Rights Law: Imperialist, Inept and Ineffective?', 25 *Human Rights Quarterly* 130.

Hayter, S. (2004), *The Social Dimension of Global Production Systems: A Review of the Issues*, ILO Policy Integration Department, Working Paper No. 25.

Helfer, L.R. (2006), 'Understanding Change in International Organisations: Globalisation and Innovation at the ILO', 59 *Vanderbilt Law Review* 651.

Hepple, B.A. (1997), 'New Approaches to International Labour Regulation', 26 *Industrial Law Journal* 353.

Hiatt, J.P. and Greenfield, D. (2004), 'The Importance of Core Labor Rights in World Development', 26 *Michigan Journal of International Law* 39.

Hilowitz, J. (1997), 'Social Labelling to Combat Child Labour: Some Considerations', 136 *International Labour Review* 215.

Jayachandran, U. (2001), 'Taking Schools to Children', 36 *Economic and Political Weekly* 3347.

Jenks, C.W. (1934), 'Les origines de l'Organisation Internationale du Travail', 30 *Revue internationale du travail* 575.

Kaime, T. (2005), 'The Convention on the Rights of the Child and the Cultural Legitimacy of Children's Rights in Africa: Some Reflections', 5 *African Human Rights Law Journal* 221.

Kellerson, H. (1999), 'La Déclaration de 1998 de l'OIT sur les principes et les droits fondamentaux: Un défi pour l'avenir?', 137 *Revue internationale du travail* 244.

——— (1998), 'The ILO Declaration of 1998 on Fundamental Principles and Rights: A Challenge for the Future', 137 *International Labour Review* 223.

Kilkelly, U. (2001), 'The Best of Both Worlds for Children's Rights? Interpreting the European Convention on Human Rights in the Light of the UN Convention on the Rights of the Child', 23 *Human Rights Quarterly* 308.

Langille, B.A. (2005), 'Core Labour Rights – The True Story (Reply to Alston)', 16 *European Journal of International Law* 409.

——— (2005), 'What Is International Labour Law For?', ILO Governing Body public lecture, available at <http://www.ilo.org/public/english/bureau/inst/download/langille.pdf>.

——— (2003), 'Re-reading the 1919 ILO Constitution in Light of Recent Evidence on Foreign Direct Investment and Workers Rights', 42 *Columbia Journal of Transnational Law* 101.

Lenzerini, F. (2001), 'La definizione internazionale di schiavitù secondo il Tribunale per la *ex*-Iugoslavia: un caso di osmosi tra consuetudine e norme convenzionali', LXXXIV *Rivista di Diritto internazionale* 1026.

——— (2000), 'L'evoluzione contemporanea del concetto di schiavitù nel diritto internazionale consuetudinario', 3 *Studi Senesi* 470.

——— (2000), 'La tutela del minore nei conflitti armati', XIII *Rivista internazionale dei diritti dell'uomo* 781.

——— (1999), 'Sfruttamento sessuale dei minori e norme internazionali sulla schiavitù', LIV *La Comunità internazionale* 474.

Lieten, G.K. (2002), 'Child Labour in India: Disentangling Essence and Solutions', 37 *Economic and Political Weekly* 5190.

——— (2003), 'Child Labour and Food Security', 38 *Economic and Political Weekly* 3467.

McCrudden, C. (1999), 'International Economic Law and the Pursuit of Human Rights: A Framework for Discussion of the Legality of "Selective Purchasing" Laws under the WTO Government Procurement Agreement', 2 *Journal of International Economic Law* 3.

McElduff, T.P. and Veiga, J. (1996), 'The Child Labor Deterrence Act of 1995: A Choice Between Hegemony and Hypocrisy', 11 *St John's Journal of Legal Commentary* 581.

McMahon, J.F. (1965/66), 'The Legislative Techniques of the International Labour Organization', 41 *British Yearbook of International Law* 1.

Manley, T.J. and Lauredo, L. (2004), 'International Labor Standards in the Free Trade Agreements of the Americas', 18 *Emory International Law Review* 85.

Marceau, G. (2002), 'WTO Dispute Settlement and Human Rights', 13 *European Journal of International Law* 753.

Maupain, F. (2005), 'Revitalisation Not Retreat: The Real Potential of the 1998 ILO Declaration for the Universal Protection of Workers' Rights', 16 *European Journal of International Law* 439.

——— (1999), 'L'OIT, la justice sociale et la mondialisation', 278 *Recueil des Cours de l'Académie de Droit international de la Haye* 201.

Mitro, M.T. (2002), 'Outlawing the Trade in Child Labor Products: Why the GATT Article XX Health Exception Authorizes Unilateral Sanctions', 51 *American University Law Review* 1223.

Myers, W.E. (2001), 'The Right Rights? Child Labour in a Globalizing World', 575 *Annals of the American Academy of Political and Social Science* 38.

Neves Mujica, J. (2001), 'El trabajo infantil en las acciones de interés público', 23 *Ius et Veritas* 229.

Noguchi, Y. (2002), 'ILO Convention No. 182 on the Worst Forms of Child Labour and the Convention on the Rights of the Child', 10 *International Journal of Children's Rights* 355.

Nunin, R. (1999), 'Il lavoro minorile nell'era della globalizzazione: riflessioni a margine di una recente convenzione dell'Organizzazione Internazionale del Lavoro'. Available at <www.labourlawjournal.it>.

Pandiaraj, S. (2006), 'Elimination of Child Labour in India: Towards a Glorious Illusion?', 46 *Indian Journal of International Law* 84.

Pauwelyn, J. (2001), 'The Role of Public International Law in the WTO: How Far Can We Go?', 95 *American Journal of International Law* 535.

Petersmann, E.U. (2003), 'Human Rights and the Law of the WTO', 37 *Journal of World Trade* 241.

Potter, E.E. (2005), 'The Growing Significance of International Labor Standards on the Global Economy', 28 *Suffolk Transnational Law Review* 243.

Pouyat, A.J. (1982), 'Les normes et les procédures de l'O.I.T. en matière de liberté syndicale. Un bilan', 121 *Revue internationale du travail* 309.

Quéguiner, J-F. (2003), 'Direct Participation in Hostilities under International Humanitarian Law', Working Paper, available at <www.ihlresearch.org/ihl/pdfs/briefing3297.pdf>.

Quirk, J. (2006), 'The Anti-Slavery Project: Linking the Historical and Contemporary', 28 *Human Rights Quarterly* 565.

Rassam, A.Y. (1999), 'Contemporary Forms of Slavery and the Evolution of the Prohibition of Slavery and the Slave Trade Under Customary International Law', 39 *Virginia Journal of International Law* 303.

Ravi, A. (2001), 'Combating Child Labour with Labels', 36 *Economic and Political Weekly* 1141.

Ray, R. (2002), 'Simultaneous Analysis of Child Labour and Child Schooling', 37 *Economic and Political Weekly* 5215.

Ritualo, A.R., Castro, C.L. and Gormly, S. (2003), 'Measuring Child Labour: Implications for Policy and Program Design', 24 *Comparative Labor Law & Policy Journal* 401.

Rodríguez-Piñero, M. (2000), 'Trabajo Infantil', 22 *Relaciones Laborales* 7.

Salazar-Xirinachs, J.M. (2000), 'The Trade–Labor Nexus: Developing Countries' Perspectives', 3 *Journal of International Economic Law* 377.

Scarpa, S. (2006), 'Child Trafficking: International Instruments to Protect the Most Vulnerable Victims', 44 *Family Court Review* 429.

Sengupta, P. and Guha, J. (2002), 'Enrolment, Dropout and Grade Completion of Girl Children in West Bengal', 37 *Economic and Political Weekly* 1621.

Sharma, A.N. (2002), 'Impact of Social Labelling on Child Labour in the Carpet Industry', 37 *Economic and Political Weekly* 5196.

Smolin, D.M. (2000), 'Strategic Choices in the International Campaign Against Child Labor', 22 *Human Rights Quarterly* 942.

——— (1999), 'Conflict and Ideology in the International Campaign against Child Labour', 16 *Hofstra Labor & Employment Law Journal* 383.

Stevenson, B.J. (2002), 'Pursuing an End to Foreign Child Labour through US Trade Law: WTO Challenges and Doctrinal Solution', 7 *UCLA Journal of International Law and Foreign Affairs* 129.

Swepston, L. (1993), 'The Convention on the Rights of the Child and the ILO', 61 *Nordic Journal of International Law* 7.

Todres, J. (1998), 'Emerging Limitations on the Rights of the Child: The UN Convention on the Rights of the Child and its Early Case Law', 30 *Columbia Human Rights Law Review* 159.

Tomaševski, K. (2005), 'Has the Right to Education a Future within the United Nations? A Behind-the-Scenes Account by the Special Rapporteur on the Right to Education 1998–2004', 5 *Human Rights Law Review* 225.

Toor, S. (2001), 'Child Labour in Pakistan: Coming of Age in the New World Order', 575 *Annals of the American Academy of Political and Social Science* 194.

Trebilcock, M.J. and Howse, R. (2005), 'Trade Policy and Labor Standards', 14 *Minnesota Journal of Global Trade* 261.

Tucker, L. (1997), 'Child Slaves in Modern India: The Bonded Labor Problem', 19 *Human Rights Quarterly* 572.

Valticos, N. (1968), 'Un système de contrôle international: La mise en oeuvre des conventions internationales du travail', 123 *Recueil des Cours de l'Académie de Droit international de la Haye* 311.

White, B. (1994), 'Children, Work and Child Labour: Changing Responses to the Employment of Children', 25 *Development and Change* 849.

Wissenkirchen, A. (2005), 'The Standard-Setting and Monitoring Activity of the ILO: Legal Questions and Practical Experience', 144 *International Labour Review* 253.

Books

Adam, R. (1993), *Attività normative e di controllo dell'O.I.L. evoluzione della comunità internazionale* (Milan: Giuffrè).

Alcock, A.E. (1971), *History of the International Labour Organisation* (London/ Basingstoke: Octagon Books).

Alliot, M. (2003), *Le Droit et le Service Public au Miroir de l'Anthropologie* (Paris: Karthala).

Alston, P. (ed.) (2005), *Labour Rights as Human Rights* (Oxford: Oxford University Press).

——— (ed.) (1994), *The Best Interests of the Child: Reconciling Culture and Human Rights* (Oxford: Clarendon Press).

Alston, P., Parker, S. and Seymour, J. (eds) (1993), *Children, Rights, and the Law* (Oxford: Clarendon Press).

Alston, P., Tobin, J. and Darrow, M. (2005), *Laying the Foundations for Children's Rights: An Independent Study of some Key Legal and Institutional Aspects of the Impact of the Convention on the Rights of the Child* (Florence: UNICEF).

Amarasinghe, S.W. (2002), *Sri Lanka: The Commercial Sexual Exploitation of Children: A Rapid Assessment* No. 18 (Geneva: ILO-IPEC).

Archard, D. (1993), *Children: Rights and Childhood* (London and New York: Routledge & Kegan Paul).

Arnal, E., Robin, S., Torres, R. and Wickramanayake, H. (eds) (2003), *Combating Child Labour: A Review of Policies* (Paris: OECD Press).

Bales, K. (2004), *Disposable People: New Slavery in the Global Economy* (Berkeley CA: University of California Press).

——— (2005), *Understanding Global Slavery: A Reader* (Berkeley CA: University of California Press).

Bal Kumar, K.C., Subedi, G., Gurung, Y.B. and Adhikari, K.P. (2001), *Nepal: Trafficking in Girls with Special Reference to Prostitution: A Rapid Assessment* No. 2 (Geneva: ILO-IPEC).

Barnard, C., Deakin S. and Morris, G.S. (eds) (2004) *The Future of Labour Law: Liber Amicorum Bob Hepple QC* (Oxford and Portland OR: Hart).

Bartels, L. (2005), *Human Rights Conditionality in the EU's International Agreements* (Oxford: Oxford University Press).

Bartolomei de la Cruz, H.G. and Euzéby, A. (1997), *L'Organisation Internationale du Travail* (Paris: Presses Universitaires de France).

Bartolomei de La Cruz, H.G., von Potobsky, G. and Swepston, L. (eds) (1996), *The International Labor Organization: The International Standards System and Basic Human Rights* (Boulder, Co.: Westview Press).

Basu, K., Horn, H., Roman, L. and Shapiro, J. (eds) (2003), *International Labor Standards* (Malden MA: Blackwell).

Bequele, A. and Myers, W. (1995), *First Things First in Child Labour: Eliminating Work Detrimental to Children* (Geneva: Publications of the International Labour Office).

Bhargava, P.H. (2003), *The Elimination of Child Labour: Whose Responsibility? A Practical Workbook* (New Delhi: Sage).

Blanpain, R. and Colucci, M. (eds) (2007), *L'Organizzazione internazionale del lavoro: diritti fondamentali dei lavoratori e politiche sociali* (Naples: Jovene).

Blengino, C. (2003), *Il lavoro infantile e la disciplina del commercio internazionale* (Milan: Giuffrè).

Charnovitz, S. (2002), *Trade Law and Global Governance* (London: Cameron and May).

Cortés Carcelén, J.C. (2005), *La aplicación de los principios y derechos fundamentales en el trabajo en el Perú en el contexto de la integración regional* (Lima: Publicaciones de la Oficina Internacional del Trabajo).

Cunningham, H. (1995), *Children and Childhood in Western Society since 1500* (London: Longman).

——— (1991), *The Children of the Poor: Representations of Childhood Since the Seventeenth Century* (Oxford: Blackwell).

Cunningham, H. and Viazzo, P.P. (eds) (1996), *Child Labour in Historical Perspective: 1800–1985. Case Studies from Europe, Japan and Colombia* (Florence: UNICEF).

Dekeuweur-Défossez, F. (2006), *Les droits de l'enfant*, 7th edn (Paris: PUF).

Detrick, S. (ed.) (1992), *The United Nations Convention on the Rights of the Child: A Guide to the 'Travaux Préparatoires'* (Dordrecht: Martinus Nijhoff).

Dinstein, Y. (2004), *The Conduct of Hostilities under the Law of International Armed Conflict* (Cambridge: Cambridge University Press).

Di Turi, C. (2007), *Globalizzazione dell'economia e diritti umani fondamentali in materia di lavoro: il ruolo dell'OIL e dell'OMC* (Milan: Giuffrè).

Dowdney, L. (2003), *Children of the Drug Trade – A Case Study of Children in Organised Armed Violence in Rio de Janeiro* (Rio de Janeiro: 7letras).

Dröge, C. (2003), *Positive Verpflichtungen der Staaten in der Europäischen Menschenrechtskonvention* (Heidelberg, Berlin: Springer).

Dunn, L. (forthcoming), *Investigating the Unconditional Worst Forms of Child Labour: A Synthesis Report on Selected Rapid Assessments*, National and Institutional Reports (Geneva: Publications of the International Labour Office).

Duong, L.B. (2002), *Viet Nam Children in Prostitution in Hanoi, Hai Phong, Ho Chi Minh City and Can Tho: A Rapid Assessment* No. 16 (Geneva: ILO-IPEC).

Ewing, K.D., Gearty, C.A. and Hepple, B.A. (eds) (1994), *Human Rights and Labour Law: Essays for Paul O'Higgins* (London and New York: Mansell).

Forastieri, V. (2002), *Children at Work: Health and Safety Risks*, 2nd edn (Geneva: Publications of the International Labour Office).

Fottrell, D. (ed.) (2000), *Revisiting Children's Rights: 10 Years of the UN Convention on the Rights of the Child* (The Hague: Kluwer Law International).

Freeman, M. (ed.) (1996), *Children's Rights: A Comparative Perspective* (Aldershot: Ashgate).

Ghebali, V.Y. (1989), *The International Labour Organisation. A Case Study on the Evolution of United Nations Specialised Agencies* (Boston MA: Martinus Nijhoff).

Gioffredi, G. (2006), *La condizione internazionale del minore nei conflitti armati* (Milan: Giuffrè).

González de Innocenti, Z. and Innocenti, C. (2002), *El Salvador: la explotación sexual comercial infantil y adolescente: una evaluacion rapida* No. 30 (Geneva: ILO-IPEC).

Haas, E. (1964), *Beyond the Nation State. Functionalism and International Organisation* (Stanford CA: Stanford University Press).

Hagerman, F., Diallo, Y., Etienne, A. and Mehran, F. (2006), *Global Child Labour Trends 2000–2004* (Geneva: Publications of the International Labour Office).

Hampâté Bâ, A. (1996), *Amkoulel l'enfant peul. Mémoires* (Paris: Editions J'ai lu).

Henckaerts, J.M. and Doswald Beck, L. (eds) (2005), *Customary International Humanitarian Law*, Vol. 1 (Cambridge: Cambridge University Press).

Hepple, B.A. (2005), *Labour Laws and Global Trade* (Oxford and Portland OR: Hart).

———— (ed.) (2002), *Social and Labour Rights in a Global Context: International and Comparative Perspectives* (Cambridge: Cambridge University Press).

Himes, J.R. (ed.) (1995), *Implementing the Convention on the Rights of the Child: Resource Mobilization in Low-Income Countries* (The Hague: Martinus Nijhoff).

ILO (forthcoming), *A Shared Responsibility: Workers Organizations in the Fight Against the Commercial Sexual Exploitation of Children* (Geneva: Publications of the International Labour Office).

———— (2006), *The End of Child Labour: Within Reach – Global Report under the Follow-Up to the ILO Declaration on Fundamental Principles and Rights at Work* (Geneva: Publications of the International Labour Office).

———— (2005), *Rules of the Game: A Brief Introduction to International Labour Standards* (Geneva: Publications of the International Labour Office).

———— (2005), *Decent Work and the Millennium Development Goals: An Information Folder* (Geneva: Publications of the International Labour Office).

—————— (2004), *Gender Equality and Child Labour: A Tool for Facilitators* (Geneva: Publications of the International Labour Office).

—————— (2004), *Child Labour: A Text Book for University Students* (Geneva: Publications of the International Labour Office).

—————— (2002), *Every Child Counts – New Global Estimates on Child Labour* (Geneva: Publications of the International Labour Office).

—————— (2002), *Eliminating the Worst Forms of Child Labour: A Practical Guide to ILO Convention No. 182. Handbook for Parliamentarians* (Geneva: Publications of the International Labour Office).

—————— (2002), *A Future Without Child Labour. Global Report under the Follow-Up to the ILO Declaration on Fundamental Principles and Rights at Work* (Geneva: Publications of the International Labour Office).

—————— (1996), *Child Labour – Targeting the Intolerable* (Geneva: Publications of the International Labour Office).

—————— (1996), *Child Labour: What Is to Be Done?* (Geneva: Publications of the International Labour Office).

ILO-IPEC (2007), *IPEC Action Against Child Labour, Highlights 2006* (Geneva: Publications of the International Labour Office).

—————— (2006), *IPEC Action Against Child Labour 2004–2005: Progress and Future Priorities* (Geneva: Publications of the International Labour Office).

—————— (2005), *Resources and Processes for Implementing the Hazardous Child Labour Provisions of ILO Conventions Nos. 138 and No. 182*, Report of the ILO Asian Regional Tripartite Workshop held in Phuket, Thailand, 11–13 July.

—————— (2005), *Investigating the WFCL: A Synthesis Report of Selected Rapid Assessment and National Reports* (Geneva: Publications of the International Labour Office).

—————— (2003), *Rapid Assessment of Trafficking in Children for Labour and Sexual Exploitation in Ukraine* (Geneva: Publications of the International Labour Office), available at <http://www.ilo.org/iloroot/docstore/ipec/prod/eng/2004_traff_cee_ukraine_ra_en.pdf>.

—————— (2003), *Ethical Considerations When Conducting Research on Children in the Worst Forms of Child Labour* (Geneva: Publications of the International Labour Office).

—————— (1999), *IPEC Action Against Child Labour Achievements, Lessons Learned and Indications for the Future 1998–1999* (Geneva: Publications of the International Labour Office).

ILO-UNICEF (2005), *Manual on Child Labour Rapid Assessment Methodology* (Geneva: Publications of the International Labour Office), available at <http://www.ilo.org/iloroot/docstore/ipec/prod/eng/2005_ra_manual_en.pdf>.

Imber, M. (1989), *The USA, ILO, UNESCO and IAEA* (New York: Palgrave Macmillan).

International Labour Conference (2006), *The End of Child Labour: Within Reach – Global Report Under the Follow-Up to the ILO Declaration on Fundamental Principles and Rights at Work* (Geneva: Publications of the International Labour Office).

IPEC-SIMPOC (2002), *Every Child Counts – New Global Estimate on Child Labour* (Geneva: Publications of the International Labour Office).

Jenks, C.W. (1970), *Social Justice and the Law of Nations* (London and New York: Oxford University Press).

———— (1960), *Human Rights and International Labour Standards* (New York: Praeger).

Johnston, G.A. (1970), *The International Labour Organisation. Its Work for Social and Economic Progress* (London: Europa).

Kabeer, N., Nambisan, G.B. and Subrahmanian R. (eds) (2003), *Child Labor and the Right to Education: Needs versus Rights?* (New Delhi: Sage).

Kamala, E., Lusinde, E., Millinga, J., Mwaitula, J., Gonza, M.J., Juma, M.G. and Khamis, H.A. (2001), *Tanzania: Children in Prostitution: A Rapid Assessment* No. 12 (Geneva: ILO-IPEC).

Kilkelly, U. (1999), *The Child and the European Convention on Human Rights* (Aldershot: Ashgate).

Landy, E.A. (1966), *The Effectiveness of International Supervision – Thirty Years of I.L.O. Experience* (London and New York: Stevens & Sons).

Moeliono, L. and Sunarno, N. (2005), *Guidelines for Participatory Action-Oriented Research in Assessing the Situation of Children in the Production, Sales and Trafficking of Drugs* (Geneva: Publications of the International Labour Office).

Morse, D.A. (1969), *The Origin and Evolution of the ILO and Its Role in the World Community* (Ithaca NY: Cornell University Press).

Mower, A.G. (Jr) (1997), *Convention on the Rights of the Child: International Law Support for Children* (London and Westport CT: Greenwood).

Nowak, M. (2005), *UN Covenant on Civil and Political Rights – CCPR Commentary* (Arlington VA: N.P. Engel).

Picone, P. and Ligustro, A. (2002), *Diritto dell'Organizzazione mondiale del commercio* (Padua: CEDAM).

Politakis, G. (ed.) (2007), *Protecting Labour Rights as Human Rights: Presence and Future of International Supervision*, Proceedings of International Colloquy of the 80th Anniversary of the ILO Committee of Experts on the Application of Conventions and Recommendations (Geneva: Publications of the International Labour Office).

Pratap, R. (2004), *India at the WTO Dispute Settlement System* (New Delhi: Manak).

Ravaozanany, N., Razafindrabe, L.N. and Rakotoniarivo, L. (2002), *Madagascar: Les enfants victimes de l'exploitation sexuelle à Antsirana, Toliary et Antananarivo: une evaluation rapide* No. 25 (Geneva: ILO-IPEC).

Raynauld, A. and Vidal, J.-P. (1998), *Labour Standards and International Competitiveness* (Cheltenham: Edward Elgar).

Rodgers, G. and Standing, G. (eds) (1981), *Child Work, Poverty and Underdevelopment* (Geneva: Publications of the International Labour Office).

Rubin, N., Kalula, E. and Hepple, B. (eds) (2005), *Code of International Labour Law: Law, Practice and Jurisprudence*, Vol. 1 (Cambridge: Cambridge University Press).

Sanna, S. (2002), *Diritti dei lavoratori e disciplina del commercio nel diritto internazionale* (Milan: Giuffrè).

Sauma, P. (2006), *Construir futuro, invertir en la infancia. Estudio económico de los costos y beneficios de erradicar el trabajo infantil en los Países del Cono Sur* (Lima: Publicaciones de la Oficina Internacional del Trabajo).

———— (2006), *Construir futuro, invertir en la infancia. Estudio económico de los costos y beneficios de erradicar el trabajo infantil en los Países Andinos* (Lima: Publicaciones de la Oficina Internacional del Trabajo).

———— (2005), *Construir futuro, invertir en la infancia. Estudio económico de los costos y beneficios de erradicar el trabajo infantil en Iberoamérica* (San José de Costa Rica: Publicaciones de la Oficina Internacional del Trabajo).

Scelle, G. (1930), *L'Organisation Internationale du Travail et le BIT* (Paris: Rivière).

Schlemmer, B. (ed.) (2000), *The Exploited Child* (London and New York: Zed Books).

Sengenberger, W. and Campbell, D. (1994), *International Labour Standards and Economic Interdependence* (Geneva: Publications of the International Labour Office).

Tabatabai, H. (2006), *Erradicación del trabajo infantil: la promesa de los programas de transferencias en efectivo condicionadas* (Geneva: Publications of the International Labour Office).

Tajgman, D. (2007), *Modern Policy and Legislative Responses to Child Labour* (Geneva: Publications of the International Labour Office).

Valticos, N. (1983), *Droit international du travail* (Paris: Dalloz).

Valticos, N. and von Potobsky, G. (1995), *International Labour Law* (Deventer and Boston MA: Kluwer).

Weston, B.H. (ed.) (2005), *Child Labor and Human Rights: Making Children Matter* (Boulder CO and London: Lynne Rienner).

Chapters in edited books

Adam, R. (1993), 'ILO (International Labour Organization)', in *Digesto delle discipline pubblicistiche*, Vol. VIII (Turin: UTET).

Armstrong, L.H. (2006), 'The Child's Right to Play, Rest, Recreation, and Cultural Activities', in J. Todres, *The U. N. Convention on the Rights of the Child: An Analysis of Treaty Provisions and Implications of US Ratification* (New York: Ardsley Transnational).

Basu, K. (2003), 'Global Labor Standards and Local Freedoms', in UNU-WIDER (ed.), *WIDER Perspectives on Global Development* (Helsinki: UNU World Institute for Development Economics Research).

Boschiero, N. (2001), 'Art. 4 – Proibizione della schiavitù e del lavoro forzato', in S. Bartole, B. Conforti, and G. Raimondi (eds), *Commentario alla Convenzione europea per la tutela dei diritti dell'uomo e delle libertà fondamentali* (Padua: CEDAM).

Creighton, B. (2004), 'The Future of Labour Law: Is There a Role for International Labour Standards?', in C. Barnard, S. Deakin and G.S. Morris (eds), *The Future of Labour Law. Liber Amicorum Sir Bob Hepple QC* (Oxford and Portland OR: Hart).

Francioni, F. (2001), 'Environment, Human Rights and the Limits of Free Trade', in F. Francioni (ed.), *Environment, Human Rights and International Trade* (Portland OR: Hart).

Gaja, G. (1981), 'Organizzazione Internazionale del Lavoro', in *Enciclopedia del Diritto*, Vol. XXXI (Milan: Giuffrè).

Hagemann, F. (2001), 'Action against Child Labour: An International Perspective', in R. Blanpain and C. Engels (eds), *The ILO and the Social Challenges of the 21st Century: The Geneva Lectures* (The Hague: Kluwer Law International).

Hammarberg, T. (2001), 'Children', in A. Eide, C. Krause and A. Rosas (eds), *Economic, Social and Cultural Rights* (The Hague: Kluwer International Law).

Hernandez-Pulido, R. and Caron, T. (2003), 'Protection of Children and Young Persons', in International Labour Office, *Fundamental Rights at Work and International Labour Standards* (Geneva: Publications of the International Labour Office).

Hoffman, S. and Maaßen, H. J. (1994), 'Der Kampf gegen die Kinderarbeit – Eine entwicklungspolitische Aufgabe der Internationalen Arbeitsorganisation', in Bundesministerium für Arbeit und Sozialordnung, Bundesvereinigung der Deutschen Arbeitgeberverbände und Deutscher Gewerkschaftsbund (eds), *Weltfriede durch soziale Gerechtigkeit. 75 Jahre Internationale Arbeitsorganisation* (Baden-Baden: Nomos Verlagsgesellschaft).

Jacobs, A. (2006), 'Prohibition of Child Labor and Protection of Young People at Work (Article 32)', in B. Bercusson, *European Labour Law and the EU Charter of Fundamental Rights* (Baden-Baden: Nomos).

Keita, A. (2005), 'Au Détour des Pratiques Foncières à Bancoumana. Quelques Observations sur le Droit Malien', in G. Hesseling, M. Djiré and B. Oomen (eds), *Le Droit en Afrique. Expériences locales et Droit etatique au Mali* (Paris: Karthala).

Krebber, S. (2002), 'Art. 137', in C. Calliess and M. Ruffert (eds), *Kommentar zu EU und EG Vertrag* (Neuwied: Luchterhand).

Lenzerini, F. (2001), 'International Trade and Child Labour Standards', in F. Francioni (ed.), *Environment, Human Rights and International Trade* (Portland OR: Hart).

McCrudden, C. and Davies, A. (2001), 'A Perspective on Trade and Labour Rights', in F. Francioni (ed.), *Environment, Human Rights and International Trade* (Portland OR: Hart).

Pratap, R. (2005), 'Sovereign Economic Freedom and Interests of Other States', in B.N. Patel (ed.), *India and International Law* (Leiden: Martinus Nijhoff).

Raimondi, G. (2006), 'ILO (International Labour Organization)', in S. Cassese (ed.), *Dizionario di diritto pubblico*, Vol. IV (Milan: Giuffrè).

Röselaers, F. (2005), 'The Challenge of Child Labour', in R. Blanpain (ed.), *Confronting Globalization: The Quest for a Social Agenda* (The Hague: Kluwer Law International).

Saini, D.S. (2006), 'Child Labour in India and the International Human Rights Discourse', in L. Williams (ed.), *International Poverty Law: An Emerging Discourse* (London: Zed Books).

Trebilcock, A. (2006), 'Using Development Approaches to Address the Challenge of the Informal Economy for Labour Law', in G. Davidov and B. Langille (eds), *Boundaries and Frontiers of Labour Law* (Oxford: Hart Publishing and IILS).

——— (2001), 'The ILO Declaration on Fundamental Principles and Rights at Work: A New Tool', in R. Blanpain and C. Engels (eds), *The ILO and the Social Challenges of the 21st Century* (The Hague: Kluwer Law International).

Valticos, N. and Wolf, F. (1974), 'L'O.I.T. et les pays en voie de développement: techniques et mise en oeuvre des normes universelles', in Société française de droit international, *Pays en voie de développement et transformation du droit international* (Paris: A. Pedone).

Index